The Assault on Priesthood

The Assault on Priesthood

A Biblical and Theological Rejoinder

Lawrence B. Porter

WIPF & STOCK · Eugene, Oregon

THE ASSAULT ON PRIESTHOOD
A Biblical and Theological Rejoinder

Wipf & Stock
An Imprint of Wipf and Stock Publishers
199 W. 8th Ave., Suite 3
Eugene, OR 97401
www.wipfandstock.com

ISBN 13: 978-1-661097-292-5
Manufactured in the U.S.A.

Unless otherwise noted, all Scripture texts in this work are taken from the *New American Bible, revised edition* © 1986 Confraternity of Christian Doctrine, Washington D.C. and are used by permission of the copyright owner.

Nihil Obstat: Rev. Msgr. Charles W. Gusmer, S.T.D., *Censor Librorum.*
Imprimatur: +Most Rev. John J. Myers, D.D., J.C.D., Archbishop of Newark, New Jersey, March 15, 2012.
The *Nihil Obstat* and *Imprimatur* are official declarations that a book or pamphlet is free of doctrinal or moral error. No implication is contained therein that those who have granted the *Nihil Obstat* and *Imprimatur* agree with the contents, opinions or statements expressed.

For those priests who have labored long and hard
Often in difficult circumstances and with little thanks or recognition
And especially those who remained faithful when
The august profession was attacked from every side,
May you continue to trust in the promise of the Lord:
I will lavish choice portions on the priests. (Jer 31:14)

Contents

Acknowledgments

I THANK SEVERAL OF my colleagues on the faculty and in the administration of Seton Hall University for the encouragement and assistance they have provided me during the writing of this book: Father Lawrence Frizzell, D. Phil., associate professor and program director of Jewish Christian Studies has been especially helpful in guiding me with rabbinic sources; Father Pablo Gadenz, S.S.L., S.T.D., assistant professor of Biblical Studies in the Seminary School of Theology has offered expert counsel regarding scriptural questions; Monsignor Anthony Ziccardi, S.S.L., S.T.D., the university's vice-president for mission and member of the Seminary School of Theology's Biblical Studies department, read and commented on parts of the text; Father Thomas Guarino, S.T.D., Professor of Systematic Theology in the Seminary School of Theology has been an endless source of encouragement and sage advice. And thus any errors in this book should be attributed to me alone.

Introduction

The History of the Assault and the Rationale of This Rejoinder

It could well be argued that priesthood, along with kingship and prophecy, is one of the great and enduring archetypes of human experience. By this I mean not only did priesthood, prophecy, and kingship appear early in human history but to this day we have significant examples of each in our midst. No doubt, certain and serious qualifications have to be made with regard to the contemporary character of these ancient, perhaps eternal, archetypes. For example, while there are still some kings among us, today most kings reign but do not rule. As for prophecy, false prophets have always been a problem. And today when prophetic voices abound, the very abundance of these voices often creates more confusion than understanding because today prophetic voices can be found on every side of every issue. As for the institution of priesthood, though it still has several important expressions—the Brahmans of Hinduism, the lamas of Tibetan Buddhism, the *kennushi* of Shinto, and the principal clergy of Orthodox and Catholic Christianity—today there are significant challenges to both the concept and institution of priesthood. In Tibet the challenge comes externally from political oppression. But in Catholic Christianity both the idea and the institution of priesthood have been challenged, and in Catholic Christianity the challenges have come not only from outside but also from within. To understand this latest assault on priesthood, we need to see it within the broad context of the history of priesthood in general and more specifically within the Christian tradition. And so here, after some initial observations regarding the phenomenon of priesthood in the history of religions, we look at the origin and development of priesthood in the biblical traditions of both Old and New Testaments and then the evolution of the concept of priesthood in Christian thought both ancient and modern. After that survey we describe the origin and character of the current assault and propose a strategic response to it.

Priesthood in the History of Religions

In terms of comparative religion, a priest can be defined as that individual who not only discerns and communicates the will of God but can effectively mediate between the divine and humankind. This is because, as a priest, he knows how to present a sacrificial offering so that it becomes the most eloquent expression of grateful praise to a gracious god, or the most effective means of expressing sorrow and contrition before offended deity. This idea has found significant expression in the general history of religions, both in the ancient past and even to this day.

The academic discipline of history of religions demonstrates how the ancient world was full of priestly cults. No doubt atheism has always been an option. The Bible itself witnesses to this truth. See Ps 53:1, "The fool says in his heart, 'There is no God.'" In classical Greece, the philosopher Epicurus (341–270 BC), who espoused a philosophy of atomic materialism, gave atheism a certain intellectual character. Nevertheless, all evidence suggests earliest human beings were not only markedly religious but, from early on, primitive human beings were quick to intuit the special importance of sacrificial offerings. Moreover, cultural historians have also made it clear to us that it is not just among primitive societies that priesthood and sacrifice are observable. Indeed, there is considerable evidence to illustrate the fact that in the most sophisticated societies of the ancient world, Greece and Rome, priesthood and sacrifice were not just a prominent aspect of public life but also the object of the highest philosophical inquiry.

For example, Athens of the fifth century before Christ is now regarded as one of the most remarkable periods in the history of human development, a time when science, medicine, politics, and theater were all being invented. But at that same time, Pericles (495–429 BC), the great military commander and statesman, ordered the construction of a great temple at Athens, the Parthenon, at the pinnacle of the city. Although the outline of this temple towers over Athens to this day, it is in London's British Museum that one can view a relief sculpture from the south frieze of the Parthenon that depicts the sacrificial rite of cattle being led to slaughter. Consider also how Plato (427–347 BC) dedicated an entire dialogue to a consideration of priesthood and sacrifice. Plato's dialogue *Euthyphro* presents us with yet another archetype of human experience: the religious zealot. The title character is a young Athenian whose religious enthusiasm leads him to assume the role of the priest, for as he himself says, "I speak in the assembly on religious matters and predict the future for them."[1] The assembly he refers to is the Athenian political assembly and his predicting the future is a reference to his performing the priestly rite of divination. His religious enthusiasm is such that he is intent on offering his father as an expiatory sacrifice. But his interlocutor in this dialogue, Socrates, challenges the young man regarding the nature of true piety and the role of sacrifice therein.

And so it was for Roman civilization. Not only did Julius Caesar, in his *Commentaries on the Gallic War*, describe the work of Druid priests, but he himself

---

1. Plato, *Defense of Socrates, Euthyphro, Crito,* p. 4.

served for a time as *Pontifex Maximus*, chief priest of Roman religion.[2] And when Caesar's nephew Octavian put an end to the thirty years of civil war that followed upon his uncle's assassination, a grateful Roman senate ordered the construction of an altar to peace at which Octavian, now Caesar Augustus, was the first to offer sacrifice (a scene observable to this day on a sculptured relief on that very same altar, now preserved in its own museum on the banks of the Tiber at Rome). But it is also important to consider how at Rome too priesthood and cult were not just observed but subjected to serious philosophical scrutiny. In that regard, consider Cicero's dialogue *On the Nature of the Gods*. There, unlike in Plato's *Euthyphro*, the principal interlocutor is not a young and zealous priest but an old and skeptical one, the Roman pontiff Gaius Aurelius Cotta. The dialogue consists of a conversation among three characters, Veilleius, Balbus and Cotta. Cicero is for the most part a silent auditor. During the dialogue it becomes clear that Cotta's philosophical learning leads him not only to criticize any naive anthropomorphism of the gods and express considerable skepticism regarding divine providence and the effectiveness of religious rites, but he also expresses his doubt regarding the very existence of the gods. But Cicero in his concluding words makes it clear he does not share the old priest's impiety.[3] While the priesthoods of the ancient Greeks and Romans have all disappeared, there are yet numerous priesthoods that function in the world today, for example, I have already noted the priesthoods of Hinduism, Shinto, and Tibetan Buddhism. But one could well argue it is within Christianity that the doctrines of priesthood and sacrifice have undergone their most serious intellectual and moral probing. That is, while the phenomena of priesthood and sacrifice are basic to comparative religion, though they can be found almost everywhere and always, even to this day, the concepts of priesthood and sacrifice have experienced a very significant and, arguably, a unique development in the Judeo-Christian tradition. Indeed, here I hope to demonstrate how this development in Christianity poses a challenge to all these other priesthoods and all other forms of sacrifice.

2. The Druids and their rites are described in Caesar's *The Gallic War*, Bk. 6, 13-19, which is pp. 335-344.

3. Cicero, *De Natura Deorum*. Cf. p. 61 where Cotta says, "I, who am a high priest, and who hold it to be a duty most solemnly to maintain the rights and doctrines of the established religion, should be glad to be convinced of this fundamental tenet of the divine existence, not as an article of faith merely but as an ascertained fact. For many disturbing reflections occur to my mind, which sometimes make me think there are no gods at all," with Cicero's much later but concluding remark on p. 383: "Here the conversation ended, and we parted, Velleius is thinking Cotta's discourse to be the truer, while I felt that of Balbus approximated more nearly to a semblance of the truth." Balbus represented the convictions of Stoic theology that taught both divine existence and providential government of the world.

Priesthood in the Bible

The Bible, in its portrayal of the religious character of the primitive human being, is at one with the evidence of cultural anthropology. That is, the Bible itself portrays earliest man, Cain and Abel (Gen 4:3–4), and the ancient Hebrew patriarchs Noah (Gen 8:20) and Abraham (Gen 22:13), all offering sacrifice long before the appearance of a formal priesthood in Israel. But the Bible also witnesses to the establishment of a priestly caste and cult at the very command of God himself to Moses on Sinai (Gen 29) and to the growth of this professional priesthood and sacrificial cult into one of the major religious institutions of ancient Israel. But the biblical story of priesthood does not end with the Old Testament, for the New Testament witnesses to the paramount importance of the concepts of priesthood and sacrifice for the Christian tradition. This is to say, not only was the institution of temple priesthood one of the most prominent expressions of Old Testament religion but the concepts of priesthood and sacrifice were appropriated and applied early in the Christian movement as essential tools for understanding the death of Jesus, the life of his followers, and the work of certain Christian ministers.

One of the earliest literary works of the Christian movement, Paul's First Letter to the Church at Corinth, written about the year 56, describes Jesus as employing cultic language at his last supper with his disciples. And one should not underestimate the importance of that choice of words: Jesus' option for cultic language. Indeed, one could argue that when Jesus of Nazareth, at his last meal with his disciples, took the cup and said "this is the New Covenant in my blood" (1 Cor 11:25), he initiated the central rite of the Christian faith. For, while baptism is of fundamental importance, it is nevertheless a once-and-for-all event; whereas the Eucharist, according to 1 Cor 11:24, is to be celebrated repeatedly in memory of him. Moreover, Jesus' words over the bread and cup at his last supper contain an implicit challenge to all other priesthoods and sacrifices. More precisely, his words there strongly suggest that the only sacrifice that really works is one's self; thus the sacrifice of Christ became a challenge not just to the sacrificial cult of the Jerusalem temple but to all other sacrificial rites in the history of religion, wherein everything but oneself had been offered—sheep and cattle, incense, oil and wine, even one's child, enemy or neighbor. This theme of the priesthood of Christ comes in for extended treatment in the Epistle to the Hebrews when, in Heb 5:6, the line from messianic Psalm 110 (verse 4), which describes the Davidic Messiah as a priest as well as a king, is applied to Jesus: "you are a priest forever according to the order of Melchizedek." Twentieth-century scholar Avery Cardinal Dulles, SJ, in his work on *The Priestly Office*, insists the priesthood of Christ is not just a theme in the Epistle to the Hebrews, rather "the idea of priesthood is pervasive in the New Testament descriptions of Jesus as the one who bore the sins of many and allowed his body to be broken and his blood poured forth on behalf of others."[4] We must also consider the fact that in the first fifty years after the death of Christ, the one supreme sacrifice of Christ had been extended to become a moral lesson for all Christians. More precisely, in the New Testament we can see the beginning of not only the doctrine of the priesthood of Christ but of all his followers, as in Rom 12:1, "I urge you . . . to offer your bodies as a living sacrifice," or in 1 Pet 2:5 "let yourselves be built into a spiritual house to be a holy priesthood to offer spiritual sacrifices acceptable to God." We can also observe in the New Testament the beginning of yet another extension and development of this priestly theme in Paul's use of cultic language to describe his own ministry. In Rom 15:16 Paul describes himself as "a minister of Christ Jesus to the Gentiles in performing the priestly service of the gospel." But the most explicit and direct application of priestly imagery to Christian ministers and ministry came slightly later than Paul.

Priesthood in the Early Church

Despite Paul's use of sacral or cultic language to describe his apostolic ministry, the New Testament language for early Christian ministers is not the language of cultic worship but of contemporary public and domestic service. Numerous commentators are quick to point out how the New Testament terms *episkopos*, *presbyteros*, *diaconos* (bishop, presbyter, deacon), used to describe certain ministries in the early Christian community, were loanwords from the Greek secular or domestic workplaces. An *episkopos* (literally "overseer") was the secular Greek term for a municipal inspector. The word *presbyter* literally means "elder" and was used to refer to both the male head of a family and to those male heads of families who presided over community decisions. The word *diakonos* literally meant "server" and was used to refer to domestic servants who waited at table. Far fewer commentators note that the terms "overseer" and "elder" did have some religious usage. The word *episkopos* was used at times to designate the overseer of a temple. The term *presbyter* was used to refer to the lay board that oversaw the running of Jewish synagogues, and it also served as the designation for the heads of Jewish families who in the past had handed down sacred Jewish traditions (as in the expression "the traditions of the elders"). Nevertheless, it was in the work called The First Letter of Clement to the Church at Corinth, usually dated circa AD 95—that is, coterminous with the last works of the New Testament (the Johannine literature) at the end of the first generation of Christians and within twenty years of the deaths of Peter and Paul at Rome—that we

4. Dulles, *Priestly Office*, p. 6.

see for the first time the general cultic language, which Paul used metaphorically to describe his own ministry, applied with much greater precision to refer to a range of Christian ministries.

Many scholars regard the author of the so-called First Letter of Clement as having been the overseer (*episkopos*) of the Christian community at Rome, its principal presiding elder. And because of his eminent position at Rome, he writes to the Christian community at Corinth to give them some authoritative advice regarding church disorder, advice that they sorely needed because of a problem that had arisen among them. It seems that in the Christian community at Corinth rivalries in ministry had led to the ouster of some duly appointed elders. And so in chapter 40, Clement lectures the Christians at Corinth regarding the authority and sacred character of such duly appointed elders. Clement not only insists this is an order given by the Lord but also compares the organization of Christian ministries according to the ranks of bishop, presbyter, and deacon to the hierarchy of the sacred ministries of high priest, priest, and Levite given to Moses by God (in Num 3:5–10):

> We are bound to do in an orderly fashion all that the Master has bidden us to do at the proper times he set. He ordered sacrifices and services to be performed; and required this to be done, not in a careless and disorderly way, but at times and seasons he fixed. Where he wants them performed, and by whom, he himself fixed by his supreme will, so that everything should be done in a holy way and with his approval, and should be acceptable to his will. Those therefore, who make their offerings at the time set win his approval and blessing. For they follow the master's orders and do no wrong. The high priest is given his particular duties; the priests are assigned their special place, while on the Levites particular tasks are imposed. The layman is bound by the layman's code.[5]

Even more significantly, later on in this same First Letter of Clement to the Church at Corinth, Clement insists his is not just a descriptive analogy or poetic metaphor. Clement makes it clear there is a very real sense in which certain of these Christian ministers do indeed function as priests. He does this in First Clement 44.4 when he warns: "For we shall be guilty of no slight sin if we eject from the episcopate men who have offered the sacrifices with innocence and holiness."[6]

Moreover, there is evidence that the title "priest," applied to the bishop as the principal presiding elder of the local Christian community, was becoming a tradition not just at Rome but elsewhere. For example, there is Hippolytus's *The Apostolic Tradition.*[7] While there is some debate as to the authorship and character of this

---

5. Clement of Rome, "First Letter," p.62.

6. Ibid., p. 64.

7. The best critical edition is that of G. Dix, as edited by H. Chadwick. However, at times I prefer

work, the majority of scholars support the claim that it was written at Rome in the early third century, that is, around the year 215, but it witnesses to liturgical practices at Rome that had become standard several decades earlier, that is, by the mid-second century, around the year 150. The man to whom the work is ascribed, Hippolytus (ca. 170–ca. 236), was a conservative presbyter of the Church at Rome who objected to what he felt was some doctrinal and disciplinary laxity on the part of his contemporary Pope Zephyrinus. Hippolytus, eager to make clear what, indeed, was "*the apostolic tradition*" to be handed down, wrote a work bearing that very title. And in that work Hippolytus describes the ordination ritual "traditionally" used at Rome. There, in the ordination prayer for bishops, we hear the words, "Father who knowest the heart, grant to this thy servant, whom Thou hast chosen for bishopric, to feed thy flock; and to exercise high priesthood (*primatum sacerdotii*) for thee."[8] The term priest, as applied to Christian ministers, is also found in two early church orders, the *Didache* 13.3, a work that some scholars date as early as the late first century, and the *Didascalia apostolorum* 2.26.4, that is, "The Teaching of the Twelve Apostles," a work appearing about 230. Indeed, "priest" is found so often in the works of second- and third-century North African church fathers that many scholars believe "priest" was, from early on, the common designation for bishops in North Africa.

For example, "priest" as a Christian ministerial title is found numerous times in the works of Tertullian (ca. 160–ca.225): in his treatises *De baptismo* 17.1, *De exhortatione castitatis* (On exhortation to chastity) 11.1–2, *De monogamia* (On marrying only once) 12, *De pudicitia* (On modesty) 20.10; 21.17. Moreover, Tertullian's use of the term "priest" is particularly telling because, while he insists we must recognize in certain Christian ministers "the ministry of a priest ordained to his sacred office" (*Exhortation to Chastity* 11.1–2),[9] Tertullian is also keenly aware of the New Testament doctrine of the common priesthood of all the baptized. In fact, Tertullian is so strong on the common priesthood of all the baptized that when he applies the term "priest" to designate a bishop, he uses not the simple *sacerdos* but rather the more distinguished, *summus sacerdos*, "high priest." We see this in his *On Baptism* 17.1, "it remains to put you in mind also of the due observance of giving and receiving baptism. Of giving it, the chief priest who is the bishop has the right, in the next place the presbyters and deacons."[10] But in his *On Monogamy* (ch.12), Tertullian also warns the laity against unduly exalting their claim to a common priesthood as "when

---

the translation of Hippolytus's ordination prayers in H. B. Porter's *Ordination Prayers of the Ancient Western Churches*.

    8. Porter, *Ordination Prayers*, p. 7.

    9. Tertullian, *Exhortation to Chastity*, p. 56.

    10. Tertullian, *On Baptism*, p. 677.

we are extolling and inflating ourselves in opposition to the clergy, by invoking such biblical passages as 'we are all one,' and 'we are all priests, because he has made us priests to (His) God and Father.'"[11] Tertullian is quoting from Gal 3:28 and Rev 1:6.

Yet another North African who employs the term "priest" to describe the principal Christian clergy is Origen of Alexandria. Take for example, his *Homilies on Leviticus* (there is common agreement that these homilies were delivered in a three year cycle sometime between 238 and 244). In those homilies, Origen continually draws comparisons between the Aaronid or Levitical priesthood and what he calls "the priests of the Church" (homily 6, pt. 6, para. 2)[12] or the "priests of the Lord" (homily 5.8.3).[13]

In the literary works of Cyprian of Carthage (d. 258), we see the term "priest" used regularly as a reference to bishops. In his *Epistle 10*, 1, he refers to the bishop as "God's Priest."[14] In *Epistle 11*, 2, he speaks of "reserving to the bishop the honor of his priesthood"[15] In *Epistle 13*, 1 he speaks of "obeying the priests of God."[16] There are numerous other such references, as in *Epistle 34*; *39*, 4–5; *41*, 1 and 2, to cite but a few. No doubt in most of these works the term "priest" is applied to bishops. The term "priest" as applied to presbyters would not become common for some time yet. This was because, at that time, Christianity was mostly an urban phenomenon and the Christian community would gather as one at a liturgy presided over by its bishop. We can see this in the letters of Ignatius of Antioch (ca. 35–ca. 107), which are all addressed to Christian communities in urban centers such as Rome, Ephesus, Smyrna, Philadelphia, Tralles, etcetera. Even so, one of those letters, the epistle to the Church at Smyrna 8.1, witnesses to the fact that even then there were liturgies presided over by delegates of the bishop: "Let that be considered a valid Eucharist which is celebrated by the bishop, or by one whom he appoints."[17] Nevertheless, as Christianity grew to be a rural as well as an urban phenomenon, and presidency at the Eucharist began to be delegated regularly to presbyters, the cultic language of priest quickly came to be applied to presbyters.

Indeed, in the succeeding centuries Clement's daring analogy between Christian ministry and Old Testament priesthood was probed, ratified, and extended. The foremost examples of this are three treatises on priesthood, one each by Gregory of

---

11. Tertullian, *On Monogamy*, p. 69.

12. Origen, *Homilies on Leviticus*, p. 127

13. Ibid., p. 105.

14. Cyprian, "Epistles," p. 291.

15. Ibid., p. 292.

16. Ibid., p. 293.

17. Ignatius of Antioch, "Epistles," p. 261.

Nazianzen (329–389), John Chrysostom (ca. 347–407), and Cyril of Alexandria (d. 444). All three of these theological treatises on the priesthood have an intellectually combative character. One was written in apologetic form and the two others were written in dialogue form, that is, like both Plato's and Cicero's works on priesthood, probing intellectual dialogues wherein various opinions, indeed, often clashing perspectives, are allowed to encounter each other. But most importantly, all three continue to expand and explore the analogy between the Christian ministries of bishop, presbyter, deacon, and Jewish temple hierarchy of high priest, priests, and Levites.

The earliest theological presentation of the priesthood is Gregory of Nazianzen's work called "In Defense of his Flight to Pontos."[18] Gregory was born in the year 329 in Nazianzus in Cappadocia (modern day southern Turkey), where his father was the bishop. Young Gregory went off to Athens for his education, but upon his return to Cappadocia he retired in the hill country to become a monk. His father put great pressure on him to come out of monastic seclusion and help him with pastoral duties. Indeed, under pressure and against his will, Gregory was ordained a priest by his father in the year 361. Soon after however, he fled back to his monastic seclusion at Pontos. But by Easter of 362 he had returned to Nazianzus and delivered the apologetic oration called "An Apology for his Flight to Pontos," an attempt to explain that the reason he had resisted ordination, and indeed fled so quickly after ordination, was not for any despising of the office but because he feared its numerous and awesome responsibilities. Indeed, one of the most revealing passages in the oration are the sections now numbered 93–96, wherein he compares his plight with that of the sons of two famous Old Testament priests, Aaron and Eli. The sons of Aaron and Eli proved themselves inadequate for priestly ministry.

The last of these three works is Cyril of Alexandria's *On Worship in Spirit and in Truth*,[19] written about the year 420, in the form of a dialogue between Cyril and a questioner Palladius. This work deals precisely with appropriateness of employing Old Testament cultic terminology such as high priest, priest, and Levite to Christian ministers. Palladius is troubled as to how one might reconcile two sayings of Jesus: Matt 7:17–18, "I have come not to abolish the law and the prophets but to fulfill them" and John 4:23, "true worshippers will worship the Father in spirit and in truth." It seems to Palladius that the second implies the abolition rather than the completion of Jewish worship. In reply, Cyril gives an exegesis of a selection of passages from the Pentateuch in order to show how the law given to Moses, including

18. Gregory of Nazianzen's "In Defense of His Flight," in NPNF (Second Series), Vol. VIII , pages 204-227,

19. There is yet no English translation. The Greek with Latin translation on the opposite page is available in J. P. Migne's *Patrologia Graeca*, Vol. 68 (Paris, 1858), pages 113–1125.

all the cultic ceremonies and even the color of the threads in the priestly vestments, find their fulfillment in Christian beliefs and observances.

But the most influential of these three works is John Chrysostom's *Peri hiero-sunis* or *On the Priesthood*, written sometime between AD 381 and 386. The work was written in the form of a probing dialogue between Chrysostom and his friend Basil. The precise identity of this Basil is a much disputed point. Nevertheless, in this dialogue Chrysostom tries to explain to his friend, who is a bishop, why Chrysostom himself always preferred the ascetic life and withdrawal from the crowds, despite pressures put upon him to assume the pastoral charge of a Christian minister. In one passage (bk. 3, art. 4), Chrysostom is trying to convey his temerity before what he regarded to be the awesome responsibility of the office. In this passage he draws a comparison between the spectacle of the Jewish high priest, entering the holy of holies with the blood of a sacrificial lamb on the great feast of the atonement, with the image of the presider at a Christian Eucharist, who has just distributed the host and the chalice. Some details in Chrysostom's description of the high priest's vestments need explanation, for example, his reference to the bells and the pomegranates, small ornaments sewn into the hem of the high priest's robe (see Exod 39:24–25). The bells had a practical purpose. If they ceased to sound, it was the signal that the high priest, who entered in the inner sanctum alone, had either been struck dead or fainted:

> The things, indeed, which preceded the law of grace were fearful and awe-inspiring: the bells, the pomegranates, the precious stones on the breast and on the shoulders, the girdle, the mitre, the garment reaching down to the feet, the plate of gold, the Holy of Holies and the solemn stillness within. But if you examine the things of the law of grace, you will find that those awful and awe-inspiring things are small in comparison, and that what was said of the law is true also here. "For that which was glorious in this part was not glorified by reason of the glory that excelleth" [2 Cor 3:10] For when you behold the Lord immolated and lying on the altar, and the priest standing over the sacrifice and praying, and all the people purpled by that precious blood, do you imagine that you are still on earth amongst men, and not rather rapt up to heaven; and casting away all worldly thought from your mind, do you not contemplate with a clean heart and pure mind the things of heaven? O miracle! O goodness of God! He that sitteth above with the Father is at that moment in the hands of all![20]

The passage quoted is of great theological and historical importance, and for several reasons. In its description of communion in the hand and congregational reception from the chalice, it is an important historical witness to early Christian worship practices. In its visually stunning image of Christians smeared with the

---

20. Chrysostom, *On the Priesthood*, pp. 40–41.

blood of Christ, which purples their lips in the communion rite, it is an important witness to the development in the patristic era of the biblical doctrine of sacramental realism (John 6). But its image of "the Lord immolated and lying on the altar, and the priest standing over the sacrifice and praying" may have had even more influence. The rhetorical power of this entire passage helps us understand why later generations were quick to bestow on its author the epithet "the golden mouthed." But it is more difficult to calculate the effect that this powerful visual image had on the later church, specifically, the church's understanding of the Eucharist, or Memorial, of the Lord's Supper as a sacrifice; and the identity of the presider at the Eucharist as a priest. As a witness to its early influence and prestige, we can point to the fact that it was *On the Priesthood* that gained Chrysostom an entry (ch. 129) among Jerome's short notices on 135 Christian writers in his *On Illustrious Men* (written in AD 392).[21] But Johannes Quasten witnesses to the much more extended influence of Chrysostom's *On the Priesthood* when he says in his *Patrology*, vol. 3: "No work of Chrysostom is better known and none has been more frequently translated and printed . . . it has ever been regarded as a classic on the priesthood and one of the finest treasures of Patristic literature."[22] Moreover, we should call to mind the fact that, as late as the 1950s, seminarians in both Europe and America were often required to read Chrysostom's *On the Priesthood* during the retreat on the eve of their priestly ordination.

Priesthood in the Middle Ages

Whatever the precise influence of Chrysostom's *On the Priesthood*, the fact is that in the century after his and these other writings on priesthood appeared, we begin to see the title of priest applied not just to bishops but also to presbyters. For example, the earliest witness to liturgical practice at Rome after Hippolytus's *Apostolic Tradition* is a work called the Leonine Sacramentary. Though named for Pope Leo I who died in 451, it was not composed by Leo or anyone under his patronage. Nevertheless it is a witness to Roman liturgical practice around his time or, at most, in the century after. In the Leonine Sacramentary, we find sacerdotal language employed in the ordination prayer for presbyters: "Hear us, O God of our salvation, and pour forth the benediction of the Holy Spirit and the power of priestly grace (*sacerdotalis effunde virtutem*) upon these your servants."[23] In a work that can be dated with much more precision, *The Eccesliastical Hierarchy* ascribed to "Dionysius the

---

21. Jerome, *On Illustrious Men*, p. 162.

22. Quasten, *Patrology*, Vol. 3, p. 459.

23. Porter, *Ordination Prayers*, pp. 24–25.

Pseudo-Aeropagite" and cited by Severus the Patriarch of Antioch in the year 513, the bishop is called "the hierarch," while to the presbyter is given the title "priest." An example of this is the reference to the baptism of adults (ch. 2, art. 7), "the god-like hierarch begins the sacred anointing but it is the priests who actually perform the sacrament."[24] See also chapter 5, article 5 where it is said of the presbyter, "He would not even be a priest if the hierarch had not called him to this."[25] A century later, Isidore of Seville (b. 560, d. 636), Archbishop of Seville from 600 and one of the most learned men of his time, composed a work entitled *Ecclesiastical Offices*. It is a comprehensive survey of ministries in the church. In book 2, Isidore treats of clerics and their classification. And in part 5 of that book, he speaks of the bishop as "high priest" and presbyters as "priests," indeed, claiming "presbyters in the church have been constituted to be just like bishops."[26] And then there is Hugh of St. Victor (ca. 1078-1141) who, in the section of his *On the Sacraments of the Christian Faith* which is entitled "On Presbyters" (bk. 2, pt. 3, art. 11), says: "Whether they are priests of the lower or the higher order, that is, whether presbyters or bishops, they perform the duty of the highest pontiff when they call delinquent peoples to repentance and heal with the remedy of their sermons."[27]

From this point on the title "priest" is given more commonly to those of the presbyteral rank, while other exalted titles are given to bishops. For example, William Durand (1230–1296), bishop of Mende from 1285, was one of the principal medieval canonists. A legal official of the Roman Curia, in 1274 he attended Pope Gregory X at the Second Council of Lyons, the decrees of which Durand himself drafted. However, his best known work is his *Rationale divinorum officiorum*, a compendium of liturgical knowledge with mystical interpretation. Therein those of presbyteral rank are referred to as "priests,"[28] a bishop is referred to either as a prelate[29] or a pontiff,[30] and the title "high priest" is reserved for Christ alone.[31]

And so it was with Thomas Aquinas (ca.1225–1274). While acknowledging the common priesthood of the faithful and the prelatial authority of bishops, Aquinas, nevertheless, is emphatic about the priestly dignity of the presbyter. For example, in his *Summa Theologica* 2a2ae (questions 85 and 86), Aquinas undertakes an extensive

---

24 Pseudo-Dionysius, *Complete Works*, p. 207.

25. Ibid., p. 237.

26. Isidore of Seville, *Ecclesiastical Offices*, p. 78.

27. Hugh, *On the Sacraments*, p. 267.

28. William Durand, *Rationale*, p.47.

29. Ibid., p. 50.

30. Ibid., p. 83.

31. Ibid., p. 82.

treatment of the concept of sacrifice and its various forms, material and spiritual, in human history and the Old Testament. So too, in the 3a Pars of the *Summa Theologica* questions 73 to 83, form the equivalent of a lengthy treatise on the Eucharist. There, in question 82, "Of the Minister of this Sacrament," Aquinas constantly calls the presbyter a priest and identifies him with the apostles. I am referring to article 1, which treats of the question "Whether the consecration of this sacrament belongs to a priest alone?" There Aquinas not only answers affirmatively, insisting "the power of consecrating this sacrament on Christ's behalf is bestowed upon the priest at his ordination," but he adds, "thereby he is put on a level with them to whom the Lord said (Luke 22:19): *Do this for a commemoration of me.*"[32] Aquinas also acknowledges the common priesthood of the faithful, for in his reply to Objection 2, he says:

> A devout layman is united with Christ by spiritual union through faith and charity, but not by sacramental power: consequently has a spiritual priesthood for offering spiritual sacrifices, of which it is said (Ps 1:19): *A sacrifice to God is an afflicted spirit;* and (Rom 12:1): *Present your bodies a living sacrifice.* Hence, too, it is written (1 Pet 2:5): *A holy priesthood, to offer up spiritual sacrifices.*[33]

And, while Aquinas acknowledges the superior authority of bishops, he argues even that can be shared with priests, for in reply to Objection 4 he says: "The bishop receives power to act on Christ's behalf upon His mystical body, that is, upon the Church; but the priest receives no such power in his consecration, although he may have it by commission from the bishop."[34] And, finally, in that same reply to Objection 4, Aquinas goes on to make clear the role of the bishop is not just to rule over, teach and direct, preside and govern the people of God but *to serve* both laity and priests: "it belongs to the bishop to deliver, not only to the people, but likewise to priests, such things as serve them in the fulfillment of their respective duties [*Ad episcopum vero pertinet trader non solum populo, set etiam sacerdotibus ea ex quibus possunt propriis officiis uti*]."[35]

Arguably, it is Bonaventure who gives the most eloquent expression to the idea that the presbyteral office is the fullness of the priesthood. He does this in his work called the *Breviloquium.* There in chapter 12, he says: "There are seven Orders gradually rising to culminate in the priesthood, in which is the fulfillment of all Orders: for it is the priest who consecrates the sacrament of the body of Christ, in which is the fullness of all graces. Thus the other six degrees are attendants upon this one, and

---

32. Aquinas, *Summa Theologica*, Vol. 2, p. 2504.

33. Ibid.

34. Ibid.

35. Ibid.

resemble the steps leading to the throne of Solomon."[36] That last line is a reference to the description of the throne of Solomon in 1 Kgs 10 which records the visit of the Queen of Sheba to the court of Solomon. There in 1 Kgs 10: 18–19: "The king also had a large ivory throne made, and overlaid it with refined gold. The throne had six steps." The "seven orders" that Bonaventure refers to here are, in ascending order: porter, lector, exorcist, acolyte, subdeacon, deacon, and priest. This pattern of formally recognized ministries developed over a long period of time, the gradation according to proximity to the Eucharistic table. Each is referred to in early patristic literature, but references to the office of subdeacon appear for the first time in the letters of Cyprian of Carthage, who died in 258.[37] The Council of Trent (in its session 23, ch. 2), taught that "From the very beginning of the church the names and proper functions of each of the following orders are known to have been in use (though not of equal rank), namely: subdeacon, acolyte, exorcist, reader, and doorkeeper. For the subdiaconate is included among major orders by fathers and holy councils, and we often read in them of the other lower orders."[38] But changes were soon to come. First came the challenge of the Protestant Reformation and, later still, reorganization of ministries at the Second Vatican Council and after by Pope Paul VI.[39]

Challenges to the Catholic Notion of Priesthood

After having said all this about the importance of the concept of priesthood in both ancient and modern times, in Christianity as well as in world religions, and after having traced something of the development of the notion of priesthood in Christianity in its first twelve centuries, one must also note that the concept of priesthood in the Christian tradition has become a very disputed point in modern times. More precisely, in modern times the concept of ministerial priesthood has been seriously delimited in Christianity, both Protestant and Catholic. This began when the Protestant reformers chose to limit the notion of priesthood to Jesus and the baptized and deny its application to pastoral ministers.

The theme of the common priesthood of the faithful, or of all the baptized, is found throughout Luther's so-called "Reformation pamphlets" of 1520. According to Luther, this common priesthood is the source of all ministries. For example, in his "The Babylonian Captivity of the Church," he says, "let everyone, therefore, who

---

36. Bonaventure, *Breviloquium*, pp. 266–67.

37. Cyprian, *"Epistles,"* 23, p. 301 and 27, p. 306.

38. Tanner, *Decrees*, Vol. 2, p. 742.

39. Paul VI, in his apostolic letter *Ministeria quaedam* of August 15, 1972, suppressed the subdiaconate.

knows himself to be a Christian, be assured of this, that we are all equally priests, that is to say, we have the same power in respect to the Word and the Sacraments."[40] In Luther's "To the Christian Nobility of the German Nation. . . ," sometimes called "An Appeal to the Ruling Class," he says "We are all consecrated priests through baptism . . . Therefore when a bishop consecrates it is nothing else than that in the place and stead of the whole community, all of whom have like power, he takes a person and charges him to exercise this power on behalf of the others."[41]

In Calvin, the assault on priesthood took two forms, Christological and ecclesiological. In his *Institutes of the Christian Religion*, Calvin replaced the *duplex munus Christi* of the Epistle to the Hebrews, the idea that Christ was both priest and king, with the concept of the *munus triplex Christi*, the idea that Jesus' ministry besides having a priestly and kingly dimension also had a prophetic one. But while adding the prophetic note to Jesus' ministry, Calvin totally removed any priestly sense from Christian ministry, namely the ministry of Jesus' disciples. That is, when we look at Calvin's ecclesiology, we find that priests disappear entirely. Calvin in his *Institutes of the Christian Religion* (bk. 4, ch. 3, art. 8), defines presbyters as elders chosen from among the people to exercise discipline in the Church.[42] And in his *Draft Ecclesiastical Ordinances* of September and October 1541 for the organization of the Church at Geneva, he replaces the traditional triad of ordained ministries, bishop-priest-deacon, with four orders of office: pastors, doctors, presbyters, and deacons.[43]

The second great modern challenge to priesthood came with the Second Vatican Council. Between 1962 and 1965 all the bishops of the Catholic Church met in Rome for a deliberative assembly that we know as the Second Vatican Council. That assembly produced significant statements about the nature of the church (the Dogmatic Constitution on the Church called *Lumen gentium*) and church order (both the Decree on Bishops, *Christus dominus*, and the Decree on the Ministry and Life of Presbyters, *Presbyterorum ordinis*). In those statements there is a discernibly similar attitude toward priestly language that was exhibited by the Protestant reformers. Indeed, in 1966, shortly after the conclusion of the Second Vatican Council, Joseph Ratzinger, who had served through all four sessions of the council as theological consultant to Cardinal Frings of Cologne, compared the approach of the Second Vatican Council regarding the language of priesthood to Luther's stance: "Luther's protest against the Catholic notion of priesthood was really based on the fact that in the Catholic view the priesthood was almost exclusively a sacrificial priesthood.

40. Luther, "Babylonian Captivity of the Church," p. 116.
41. Luther, "To the Christian Nobility," pp. 127–28.
42. Calvin, *Institutes*, Vol. 1, pp. 1060–61. Cf. book 2, chapter 15, article 6.
43. Calvin, *Theological Treatises*, pp. 58–72.

In fact, even in patristic theology and especially in medieval theology, the old association between *sacerdos* and *sacrificium*, between priest and sacrifice, had been emphasized again in contradiction to the view of the New Testament."[44]

One of the practical effects of the Council's reaction against the older theology's emphasis upon the cultic aspect of ordained ministry was to opt for noncultic language. Indeed, the Second Vatican Council, while employing the language of priesthood in reference to Christ and the baptized, very much limited its use of such language when referring to Church ministers, preferring instead to go back to the New Testament language of bishop, presbyter, and deacon. These are noncultic, emphatically pastoral terms of leadership and service. Avery Dulles, in his *The Priestly Office*, makes much of the theological importance of this shift in language: "The council showed considerable restraint in applying priestly language to bishops and presbyters. It spoke of them as exercising a three-fold office—prophetic, priestly, and royal. Priestly ministry, therefore, was only one dimension of an office that involved the ministry of the word (the prophetic) and the ministry of the shepherd (the pastoral). In only a few texts did Vatican II designate bishops and presbyters by the title 'priest' (Latin *sacerdotes*, corresponding to the Greek *hiereus*)."[45]

Lest we underestimate the momentous character of that change in terminology, Dulles pronounces upon it, describing it as an "abrupt departure from a tradition of many centuries."[46] Unfortunately, this momentous decision on the part of the Second Vatican Council is not always immediately recognizable to us today. By that I mean there is more than one theological commentator on the council documents who has lamented the fact that the available English translations of these documents obscure this important theological point by constantly refusing to use the literal equivalent of presbyter, and instead consistently translate the council's use of the word presbyter as "priest." For example, consider what Patrick Dunn in his book, *Priesthood: A Re-Examination of the Roman Catholic Theology of the Presbyterate*, says: "Unfortunately, the English translation of the Council Documents has effectively concealed the theological precision for which the Fathers were striving. As a general rule the conciliar texts try to follow the Scriptures and to restrict the word 'priest' (*sacerdos*) to Jesus himself and to the 'common priesthood' of the baptized; and when talking about the ordained, they use the word '*presbyteros*.' But the English translation uncritically translates both '*sacerdos*' and '*presbyteros*' as 'priest.'"[47]

---

44. Ratzinger, *Theological Highlights*, pp. 175–76.

45. Dulles, *Priestly Office*, p. 2.

46. Ibid.

47. Dunn, *Priesthood*, p. 110.

A few years later, Daniel Donovan in his *What Are They saying about the Ministerial Priesthood?* registered a similar complaint: "The issue of terminology is not insignificant. It points to deeper realities reflecting fundamentally different theological approaches. For this reason our treatment of Latin documents will use 'priest' as a translation of *sacerdos* and the somewhat awkward 'presbyter' for its Latin equivalent. This is all the more important as the available English translation of the conciliar documents use 'priests' for both Latin words, thus making it all but impossible to understand the nuances of the council's teaching."[48]

More precisely, this kind of obfuscation is found in all the authoritative translations: in *The Sixteen Documents of Vatican II,* a translation by the National Catholic Welfare Conference (Boston: the Daughters of St. Paul , 1966); in the translation of *The Documents of Vatican II,* edited by Jesuit Walter M. Abbott (New York: Herder and Herder, 1966); in Irish Dominican Austin Flannery's *Vatican II: the Conciliar and Post Conciliar Documents* (Northport, NY: Costello Publishing, 1975); and in Jesuit Norman Tanner's two-volume *Decrees of the Ecumenical Councils* (Washington, DC: Georgetown University Press, 1990). All four of these editions, in their translation of the Decree on the Ministry and Life of Presbyters, consistently translate *presbyteros* as "priest." Tanner's edition at least provides something of a corrective in that it has, on the facing page, the original Greek or Latin text. Paul McPartlan, professor of theology at Catholic University in Washington DC, in his essay "Presbyteral Ministry in the Roman Catholic Church" says of his own use of Flannery's translation: "Our translations of the Vatican II documents can themselves mislead by lapsing almost instinctively into a pre-conciliar vocabulary and mindset and not heeding the nuances of the Council's actual words. It is striking how frequently, as here, the Council actually says 'presbyters' rather than 'priests.'"[49] And for that reason McPartlan, when he quotes from Flannery's translation, amends that translation so as to reflect the more precise term used in the original Latin text, indeed, inserting the original Latin term in brackets within his citation (see footnote 17 in his essay). I have made the decision to quote herein from Abbott's edition of the council documents because its American English will be more familiar to my readers than Tanner's or Flannery's British English.[50] Occasionally, and for reasons of comparison, I will quote from Tanner's translation or one of the other English translations. Nevertheless, whether quoting from Abbott's edition or from one of the others, I will follow McPartlan's example and correct the translation in Abbott whenever it renders

48. Donovan, *What Are They Saying?*, p. 5.

49. McPartlan, "Presbyteral Ministry," p. 13.

50. The translations in Abbott's edition are for the most part the work of Joseph Gallagher with the assistance of some few others. See his "Preface to the Translation," pp. 9–12.

presbyteros as priest; and I too will always be careful to insert after my emendation of the English translation the original Latin or Greek of the conciliar text. With regard to this problem of translation, it is worth noting: In October of 2005, in an address at the opening of the academic year at Rome's Athenaeum of Saint Anselm, William Cardinal Levada, prefect of the Vatican's Congregation for the Doctrine of the Faith, criticized the present translations of the documents of Vatican II as "imprecise." He also expressed his hope that the Council's fiftieth anniversary in 2015 will bring with it a more careful, official translation.

But what happened to ministerial priesthood at the Second Vatican Council was hardly limited to simply an adjustment in terminology. Most commentaries on the council agree that the principal concern of the council fathers at Vatican II was to speak authoritatively on the role of bishops and laity in the church. Ever since the First Vatican Council's pronouncements on papal primacy and infallibility in 1870, there had been concern that some things needed to be said about the role of the diocesan bishop in relation to the supreme authority of the pope. And, even earlier, a theological movement had begun to reconsider the role of the laity in the church. John Henry Newman's 1859 essay, "On Consulting the Faithful in Matters of Doctrine," might be considered one of the earliest products of this movement. And Yves Congar's *Jalons pour un théologie du laicat* (Paris: Les Editions du Cerf, 1951; trans. by D. Attwater: *Lay People in the Church* [London: G. Chapman, 1957]) could well be considered one of its finest achievements. Congar became one of the principal theological consultors at the Second Vatican Council.

It is the opinion of more than one commentator on Vatican II that the council's preoccupation with those two important themes, the bishops and the laity, resulted in the simple priest or presbyter having gotten lost in the shuffle. For example, no sooner had the council ended when Sulpician Father Frank B. Norris, ecclesiologist at St. Patrick's Seminary, Menlo Park, California, published a commentary on Vatican II's Decree on the Ministry and Life of Priests. There Norris said of the overall work of the council: "From the moment of preparation for Vatican Council II began, it was clear that the roles of bishops and of laymen would receive major attention on the conciliar agenda . . . The simple priest, or 'presbyter' . . . turns out to be something of a forgotten man in this picture."[51] Some few years later, University of Chicago Divinity School Professor Martin Marty, a historian of Christianity in America, extended Norris's judgment to include consecrated religious as well as priests. Noting the already precipitous decline in vocations to both the priesthood and religious life in the Catholic Church in America, Marty, in an article entitled "What Went Wrong?" (which he published in the magazine of Catholic culture, *The*

51. Norris, *Commentary on the Decree*, pp. 69–70.

Critic 34, fall 1975, pages 49–53), expressed the opinion that there were winners and losers at the Second Vatican Council. He saw the winners as the bishops and the laity, the losers as the priests and religious. Using sociological language he analyzed the situation in these terms:

> The service ranks of the Church are in trouble; their rationale was cut into by Vatican II. Vatican II knew pretty much about what it was to be a bishop, and gave the episcopacy new morale. The Council knew very much more than Catholicism earlier had known about what it was to be a lay person: How only the laity could go most places where the Church would go. But no fresh rationales for being a priest or a religious emerged, while the old ones were effectively undercut by the advances in understanding of bishop and lay person.[52]

When the council documents are scrutinized, this judgment about the treatment of priests at Vatican II, a judgment shared by a Catholic and a Protestant commentator, is not difficult to understand. Take for example the Second Vatican Council's Dogmatic Constitution on the Church, called *Lumen gentium*, from its opening words, it is a document that many regard as the major doctrinal achievement of that council. While there are entire chapters on the episcopacy (ch. 3, "The Hierarchical Character of the Church and in Particular the Episcopate") and the laity (ch. 2, "The People of God," ch. 4, "The Laity," ch. 5, "The Universal Call to Holiness"), on the religious life of consecrated men and women (ch. 6, "Religious"), even on the Blessed Virgin Mary and the church in heaven (ch. 7, "The Eschatological Character of the Pilgrim Church"), there is no chapter on those who were once called priests but now called presbyters. Instead the role of presbyters in the church is treated in one short article (28) of chapter 3, "The Hierarchical Structure of the Church with Special Reference to the Episcopate," and the spirituality appropriate to a presbyter is treated in one short paragraph of yet another article (41) of chapter 5, a chapter entitled "The Call of the Whole Church to Holiness."

Priesthood in the Documents of Vatican II

If we look closely at the contents of *Lumen gentium*, it is readily observable how the empowerment of bishops and laity are not only its principal themes; there is also an attendant diminishment of the once priestly, now presbyteral office. As for the empowerment of bishops, in article 22 the council speaks of "the supreme and full power" (*supremae ac plenae potestatis*) of bishops. In article 27, the council fathers go on to define the power of bishops more precisely, that is, in relation to Christ and the pope. While they were obviously somewhat self-conscious about their numerous

52. Marty, "What Went Wrong?," p. 53.

references to power (they use the word six times in two paragraphs), they do try to soften their insistence upon the power that is rightfully theirs by adding biblical references to humility. Nevertheless, article 27 of *Lumen gentium* is so emphatic in its assertion of episcopal power that it reads like a lecture to the pope on how even he must respect this, for it is the will of God. And though it is a lengthy passage, it is worth quoting in its entirety so as to appreciate its cumulative effect:

> Bishops govern the particular churches entrusted to them as vicars and ambassadors of Christ. This they do by their counsel, exhortations, and example, as well, indeed as by their authority and sacred *power*. This *power* they use only for the edification of their flock in truth and holiness, remembering that he who is greater should become as the lesser and he who is more distinguished, as the servant (cr. Luke 22:26–27). This *power*, which they personally exercise in Christ's name, is proper, ordinary, and immediate, although its exercise ultimately regulated by the supreme authority of the Church, and can be circumscribed by certain limits, for the advantage of the Church or of the faithful. In virtue of this *power*, bishops have the sacred right and the duty before the Lord to make laws for their subjects, to pass judgment on them, and to moderate everything pertaining to the ordering of worship and the apostolate.
>
> The pastoral office or the habitual and daily care of their sheep is entrusted to them completely. Nor are they to be regarded as vicars of the Roman Pontiff, for they exercise an authority which is proper to them, and are quite correctly called "prelates," heads of the people whom they govern. Their *power*, therefore, is not destroyed by the supreme and universal *power*. On the contrary, it is affirmed, strengthened, and vindicated thereby, since the Holy Spirit unfailingly preserves the form of government established by Christ the Lord in His Church.[53]

As for the role of the laity, a major theme of *Lumen gentium* is their priestly character. This is boldly and eloquently set forth in the first paragraph of article 10 of *Lumen gentium*:

> Christ the Lord, High Priest taken from among men (cf. Heb 5:1–5), "made a kingdom and priests to God his Father" (Apoc. 1:6; cf. 5:9–10) out of this new people. The baptized, by regeneration and the anointing of the Holy Spirit, are consecrated into a spiritual house and a holy priesthood. Thus through all those works befitting Christian men they can offer spiritual sacrifices and proclaim the power of Him who has called them out of darkness into His marvelous light (cf. 1 Pet 2:4–10). Therefore all the disciples of Christ, persevering in prayer and praising God (cf. Acts 2:42–47), should present themselves as living sacrifice, holy and pleasing to God (cf. Rom 12:1). Everywhere on earth

---

53. Abbott, *Documents of Vatican II*, pp. 51–50.

they must bear witness to Christ and give an answer to those who seek an account of that hope of eternal life which is in them (cf. 1 Pet 3:15).[54]

The role of the laity is expanded upon in article 33 of *Lumen gentium,* where it is made clear that, just as the bishop's authority and power are not by delegation of the church but derive immediately from Christ, so too lay participation in the "apostolate," the universal mission assigned by Christ to the apostles, is not a privilege extended by church authorities but a commission which comes from Christ himself: "The lay apostolate, however, is a participation in the saving mission of the Church itself. Through their baptism and confirmation, all are commissioned to that apostolate by the Lord Himself. Moreover, through the sacraments, especially the Holy Eucharist, there is communicated and nourished that charity toward God and man which is the soul of the entire apostolate."[55]

In article 36 of *Lumen gentium,* the council fathers employ legal language to secure the role of the laity in both church and world: "Because the very plan of salvation requires it, the faithful should learn how to distinguish carefully between those rights and duties which are theirs as members of the church, and those which they have as members of human society."[56] And in article 37 the rights of the laity in relation to their pastors are specified: "The laity have the right, as do all Christians, to receive in abundance from their sacred pastors the spiritual goods of the Church, especially the assistance of the Word of God and the sacraments."[57]

More than once this theme of the rights of the laity within the church is carried over in the Council's Decree on the Laity. For example, article 3 of the council's Decree on the Laity says, "The laity derive the right and duty with respect to the apostolate from their union with Christ their Head."[58] In article 25 of the Decree on the Laity, the clergy are warned: "Bishops, pastors of parishes, and other priests of both branches of the clergy should keep in mind that the right and duty to exercise the apostolate is common to all the faithful."[59]

As for simple priests, now called presbyters, when we look at the one article of *Lumen gentium,* article 28, in which the council fathers address their role in the church, there is little talk of power and none of rights. Whatever power they might be able to exercise is totally derived from the bishop. Indeed, the opening words of *Lumen gentium* 28 make it clear it is bishops who have received consecration and

---

54. Ibid., pp. 26–27.
55. Ibid., p. 59.
56. Ibid., p. 63.
57. Ibid., p. 64.
58. Ibid., p. 492.
59. Ibid., p. 514.

mission from the Lord, and that whatever power presbyters may have is delegated to them by their bishop: "Christ, whom the Father sanctified and sent into this world (John 10:36) has, through His apostles, made their successors, the bishops, partakers of His consecration and His mission. These in their turn have legitimately handed on to different individuals in the church various degrees of participation in this ministry. Thus the divinely established ecclesiastical ministry is exercised on different levels by those who from antiquity have been called bishops, presbyters and deacons."[60] When in the third paragraph of *Lumen gentium* 28 the mission of presbyters is spelled out, there is no mention of any innate dignity, much less any power they might have. Instead, an elaborate vocabulary of service (*inserviendum*) is employed by which we hear of not only the presbyter's duties (*officiis*), cares (*cura*), concerns (*sollicitudinem*), and obligations (*munera*), but it is made clear that those duties cares, concerns and obligations are not the presbyter's own but rather in each instance the presbyter is the prudent cooperator, instrument, and help of the bishop. Indeed, we are told presbyters take upon themselves their bishop's duties and concerns and discharge them to such an extent that it may be said in all these actions they make their bishop present to the congregation: "Presbyters [*presbyteri*], prudent cooperators with the episcopal order as well as its aids and instruments, are called to serve the People of God. They constitute one presbyterium although that presbyterium is comprised of different functions. Associated with their bishop in a spirit of trust and generosity, presbyters make him present in a certain sense in the individual local congregations of the faithful, and take upon themselves, as far as they are able, his duties and concerns."[61] And, as if this were not enough, one could also point to the distinct note of paternalism in the next paragraph of *Lumen gentium* 28: "On account of this sharing in his [the bishop's] priesthood and mission, let priests sincerely look upon the bishop as their father, and reverently obey him."

However, we have yet to consider the fact that the Council in its deliberations did eventually dedicate an entire decree to a consideration of "The Ministry and Life of Presbyters." However, it is important that to note the fact that when the council did directly address at length what used to be the office of priest, now presbyter, what they wrote was late and poorly formulated. Numerous commentators have noted this fact, though often in a cautious and cursory fashion. For example, the earliest commentators on the council documents all express some disappointment. Frank Norris in his commentary published by Paulist Press in 1966, says of the decree: "The cautiousness and lack of clarity it exhibits in certain sections leaves one a bit unsatisfied; so too the rather long list of moral exhortations tend to pall the modern

60. Ibid., pp. 52–53.
61. Ibid., p. 54.

reader."[62] Hervé Legrand, in his entry, "Presbyter/Priest," for the *Encyclopedia of Christian Theology*, describes *Presbyterorum ordinis* as "a decree focused more on spirituality than on dogma, and that juxtaposed without critical analysis some rather heterogeneous theological elements."[63] Tubingen theologian Peter Hünermann expressed his opinion of *Presbyterorum ordinis* with the judgment: "The Decree on the Ministry and Life of Priests was one of the Council's stepchildren."[64] And then he goes on to more specific:

> During the third period, in October 1964, the schema that had been prepared was rejected by 1,199 negative votes against 930 positive ones. When the new text was finally discussed during the final period, in October 1965, it drew numerous and far-reaching criticisms. Over 10,000 suggestions for changes were submitted. It is a minor miracle that a revision was done at all, and it is not surprising that the result was fragmentary from a theological point of view. The 2,390 yes votes, against 4 no votes, at the solemn final vote should not blind us to the unresolved problems in the text.[65]

Whereas Legrand simply referred to "heterogeneous theological elements," Hünermann is more specific: "How tangled up the different approaches seem to be—medieval, Counter-Reformational, patristic, and at the same time, modern!"[66]

Observers of the council, such as the Americans Douglas Horton and Xavier Rynne, provide more candid witness and corroborative evidence. Douglas Horton (1891–1968) had long been a leader in ecumenism. Originally a Congregationalist minister, he helped to cofound the United Church of Christ and, while dean of Harvard Divinity School, established a chair in Roman Catholic theology. He was present at the council for all four sessions and at the end of each published a volume setting forth his observations. For our interests, his notation on Tuesday, October 26, 1965, the day the final draft of the decree on the ministry and life of priests was presented to the Council fathers, is particularly informative:

> If the morning for the most part was not devoted to the killing of time, it was at least designed to exhaust it, for after the amended schema on priestly life and ministry was introduced, the first half of it was read, word for word. Here Rome did what we Protestants always do when the church lawyers get hold of our assemblies—as if printing had not been invented and reading was an art still known only to the few. The secretaries took turns reading the text aloud, during which the fathers variously dozed, chatted, read their mail, sipped

---

62. Norris, *Commentary on the Decree*, p. 70.
63. Legrand, "Presbyter/Priest," p. 1278.
64. Hünermann, "The Final Weeks," p. 457.
65. Ibid.
66. Ibid., p. 460.

coffee in the bar, sat and read their breviaries, or simply sat. (*Vatican Diary 1965* [Boston: United Church Press, 1966], p. 145)

Xavier Rynne's description of the council session some six weeks later on the day of the final vote on the decree is even more dramatic. "Xavier Rynne" was the pen name of an American Redemptorist priest, Francis Xavier Murphy, who lived in Rome and taught at both the Pontifical Lateran University and the Accademia Alfonsiana from 1959 to 1971, and thus was able to observe many of the council sessions first hand. His accounts of the public sessions in Saint Peter's Basilica were initially serialized in what was then the high-toned American cultural journal, the *New Yorker*. Later his accounts were republished in book form as four volumes, corresponding to each of the four sessions of the council. In the fourth volume, *The Fourth Session: The Debates and Decrees of Vatican Council II, Sept. 14 to Dec. 8, 1965*, Xavier Rynne describes the final presentation of the decree on the ministry and life of presbyters. His narrative suggests that the bishops were well aware of their shabby treatment of priests and that is the reason why so many speakers wanted to say something on the last day of debate on *Presbyterorum ordinis*, the second to last day of the council itself: "Many of the speakers, obviously, were airing their views for the benefit of the record, because this was the final debate, or in order to impress the clergy back home because of a certain feeling that the Council had tended to concentrate its attention too much on bishops to the exclusion of mere priests," or what *Presbyterorum ordinis* 2.2 more dispassionately describes as "those to whom the ministry of service has been delegated in a subordinate capacity."[67]

Moreover, the judgments of Horton and Rynne are supported by the historical witness of at least one important participant in the council's work. The French Dominican friar and conciliar *peritus*, Yves Congar, had a major role in the composition and final editing of the decree on the ministry and life of presbyters. In his personal diary of his work at the council, Congar describes the difficulties he encountered when working on the composition of the text. His entry for November 9th, 1964, toward the end of the council's third session is particularly revealing:

At 4:30 PM, at the Commission *De disciplina cleri* for the *De presbyteris* . . . A big room, a big long table around which the periti were interspersed with bishops. No microphone, so that sometimes, around the long table, three or four separate conversation were going on. No one chaired it. The "debates" were not directed. Or they were a little by the secretaries, del Portillo and Lécuyer . . . The bishops did not say anything of note, or only some comments on details. It could not be said that any work was being done. Soon, tea or fruit juice was served to us where we sat. This had nothing in common with the

67. Rynne, *The Fourth Session*, pp. 151–52.

Theological Commission, which, nevertheless, does have another way of conducting itself, and which does work . . . There was no one here of the stature of Rahner or even Parente. Lécuyer, del Portill, Herranz, did more or less what they liked. They rearranged and somewhat shortened the texts; I found that they had ruined mine, on the evangelical form of life, deleting some vigorous statements and adding works of piety. With fairly extensive collaboration, this will be to some degree Lécuyer's schema . . . I am afraid it will be more pious and verbose, not sufficiently theological or ontological.[68]

Ten years after the council, Congar delivered his summary judgment of Vatican II's statement on priests. Even though he worked hard at trying to revise the first draft of Presbyterorum ordinis, Congar was not happy with the results:

For the most part I was much engaged in the preparation of the major conciliar texts: *Lumen gentium*, above all the twelfth chapter; *Gaudium et spes*; *Dei Verbum*, the text on revelation; ecumenism; religious freedom; the declaration on relations with non-Christians; the missions. I worked a great deal also with the commission of clergy who produced the text *Presbyterorum Ordinis*. The [Council] Fathers seemed to have forgotten priests. There was certainly a text, very mediocre, a clumsy message, drawn up in haste in the final period of the council. I protested: priests do not need a lecture, only for someone to tell them who they are, what is their mission in the world of today. It was then that Monseigneur Marty [Francois Cardinal Marty, archbishop of Paris] invited me to work on the elaboration of a new text. I must admit this text does not correspond exactly to the expectations of priests. I have had to explain it many times.[69]

As for an analysis of the contents of *Presbyterorum ordinis*, we do well to begin by noting its concurrence with central themes of *Lumen gentium*, the dogmatic constitution on the church. For example, the very title of the council's decree on the ministry and life of presbyters, and the history of the changes that title underwent, is clear evidence that this decree shares with that dogmatic constitution the same avoidance of cultic language and a steadfast focus upon pastoral service. The first

---

68. Congar, *My Journal*, p. 664.

69. From Jean Puyo's book *Jean Puyo interroge le Père Congar* (Paris: Le Centurion, 1975), p. 149: *J'ai été très engagé dans la préparation de la plupart des grands textes conciliaires: Lumen gentium, surtout le chapitre deuxième; Gaudium et spes; Dei Verbum, le text sur la Révélation; l'oecuménisme; la liberté religieuse; la Déclaration sur les relations non chrétiennes; les Missions. J'ai beaucoup travaillé également avec la commission du clergé qui a donné le texte Presbyterorum Ordinis. Les Pères semblaient avoir oublié les prêtres. On avait bien un texte, assez médiocre, espèce de message, rédigé à la hâte dans la dernière période du Concile J'ai protesté: les prêtres n'ont pas besoin d'une exhortation, mais qu'on leur dise qui ils sont, quelle est leur mission dans le monde d'aujourd'hui. C'est alors que Mgr. Marty m'a invité à travailler a l'élabortion d'un nouveau texte. Je suis bien obligé de reconnaître que ce texte ne correspond pas partfaitement à l'attente des prêtres; j'ai pu le vérifier plusieurs fois.*

draft, or schema, of what became the decree on the ministry and life of presbyters bore the title *de clericis* (concerning clerics). This was later changed to *de sacerdotibus* (concerning priests) because the term "clerics" was regarded as too general since bishops and deacons are also clerics. Next, the title became *de vita et ministerio sacerdotali* (concerning priestly life and ministry). Finally it was changed to *de presbyterorum ministerio et vita* (on the ministry and life of presbyters) so as to stress the more pastoral rather than cultic aspect of this ministry and to insist on the priority of work over life in this ministry.

Yet another theme carried over from *Lumen gentium* is the emphatic note of subordinationism and limitation of presbyteral ministry. First set forth in *Lumen gentium*, the subordination of presbyters to bishops now becomes a repeated, insistent theme. And, lest we miss this subtle maneuver, in Abbott's translation of *Presbyterorum ordinis* this theme is made emphatically clear in the essay that introduces the decree. In Abbott's translation of the council documents, each document is prefaced by an introductory essay written by what Lawrence Cardinal Sheehan of Baltimore, in his general introduction to the volume) describes as "especially competent and knowledgeable experts."[70] The Decree on the Ministry and Life of Presbyters is introduced by Guilford Clyde Young, then archbishop of Hobart, Tasmania (Australia), who had been in attendance at all four sessions of the council. At one point in his introduction, Archbishop Young lectures us on the presbyter as assistant and representative of the bishop:

> The Decree teaches unequivocally that the bishop fully possesses (in the sacramental order) the priesthood of Christ, while the priest participates in that priesthood in a derived and dependent manner. The bishop alone is the direct and immediate sign of Christ to his flock, while the priest is a sign, not directly of Christ the Priest, but of the bishop. In some way it is the bishop whom the priest immediately makes present to the community over which he presides. The bishop, limited by time and space, cannot be everywhere at once, and this is why he has a body of coworkers, extensions of himself, the priests who teach, sanctify and rule in his name. Hence the duty of loyalty and obedience that priests have to the bishop.[71]

And, sure enough, when we read the Decree itself we find article 2, paragraph 3:

> So it was that Christ sent the apostles just as He Himself had been sent by the Father. Through these same apostles He made their successors, the bishops, sharers in his consecration and mission. Their ministerial role has been handed down to presbyters [*presbyteris*] in a limited degree. Thus established

70. Abbott, *Documents*, p. 17.
71. Ibid.,p. 527–28.

in the order of the presbyters [*ordine presbyteratus*], they are co-workers of the episcopal order in the proper fulfillment of the apostolic mission entrusted to the latter order by Christ.[72]

This theme is repeated several times throughout the Decree. For example, in article 5, paragraph 1, we are reminded "presbyters [*presbyteri*] by various titles are bound together hierarchically to the bishop. Thus in a certain way they make him present in every gathering of the faithful."[73] In 6.1, "To the degree of their authority and in the name of their bishop, presbyters [*presbyteri*] exercise the office of Christ the Head and the Shepherd."[74] In article 7, paragraph 5: "Keeping in mind the fullness of the sacrament of orders which the bishop enjoys, presbyters [*presbyteri*] must respect in him the authority of Christ, the chief Shepherd."[75] In article 9, paragraph 5, "Presbyters [*presbyteri*] are defenders of the common good, with which they are charged in the name of the bishop."[76]

What *Lumen gentium* implied in its use of a variety of languages of service, duty, obligations, cares, and concern are now spelled out in what Frank Norris refers to as "the rather long list of moral exhortations." Indeed, these exhortations make up the huge majority, the central content, of this decree, a work of three chapters, of which chapter 2, entitled "The Ministry of Presbyters," and chapter 3, entitled "The Life of Presbyters," are in fact long lists of responsibilities toward God, the church, the bishop, the people, the world, and the presbyter's own personal spiritual life. Indeed, while *Lumen gentium* insisted on the duties, concerns, and daily cares of a priest/presbyter, *Presbyterorum ordinis* more than once reminds us that when it comes to obligations, priests/presbyters "owe it to all" (article 4, *Omnibus ergo debitores sunt presbyteri*). Indeed, later we are told that the presbyter "has obligations toward all men" (article 6: *vero omnibus debitores sunt*). Article 4, paragraph 1 states, "presbyters [presbyteri] as co-workers with their bishops, have as their primary duty the proclamation of the gospel of God to all." And the "all" here refers to both the church and the world. Then in 4.2, when the council fathers assert "the ministry of the word is discharged in a variety of ways," they go on to point out the presbyter has a duty to preach not just at Mass but in the celebration of all the sacraments. And in article 6.1, it is made clear that the ministry of the word also includes instruction and correction (*docentes et . . . monentes*). But in article 6.4, presbyters are also instructed that preaching and teaching and celebrating sacraments are not enough, for "care of

72. Ibid., p. 534.
73. Ibid., p. 541.
74. Ibid., p. 543.
75. Ibid., p. 549.
76. Ibid., p. 553.

the faithful as individuals . . . also properly extends to the formation of real Christian community." In article 7, we are reminded once again that presbyters must be obedient to their bishop (all of art. 7) and, in article 8, that they must be supportive of other priests, especially the elderly, and solicitous of the needs of young priests. Article 9 treats of the presbyter's relation to the laity: "Presbyters [*presbyteri*] must sincerely acknowledge and promote the dignity of the laity and the role which is proper role to them in the mission of the Church."

Chapter 3 of *Presbyterorum ordinis*, "The Life of Presbyters," begins with an exhortation to holiness. Indeed, the council fathers, quoting Jesus' words in Matt 5:48, "You must be perfect as your heavenly father is perfect," insist "priests are specially bound to attain that perfection." And then they proceed to specify how a priest might do this: "daily read and listen to God's word," "strongly urged to celebrate" Mass daily, "at any moment to hear confessions," "recite the divine office daily," "exercise obedience to the bishop." In article 16 priests are told they must observe perfect and perpetual continence, (art. 16 is all about celibacy). In article 17, "they are invited to embrace voluntary poverty." In article 18, they are urged to personal prayer, that is, "daily conversation with Christ." Article 19 urges them to study the fathers: "be thoroughly familiar with documents of the magisterium, and attend courses and conferences on methods of evangelization and apostolic work." Hünermann says of chapter 3, "One wonders how the bishop could harbor such an abstract and spiritualistic picture of the life of priests."[77] This, my brief summary, does not convey the sometimes patronizing quality, what some call the overly moralizing character, of this section. For example, note article 5, paragraph 3, where, in Tanner's translation, priests/presbyters are admonished in the strongest terms: "The house of prayer in which the most holy eucharist is celebrated . . . should be spotlessly clean."[78]

Further Challenges to Priesthood After the Council

After the council, things only got worse. For what began as outright banishment or carefully calculated demotion (banishment by the Protestant Reformers, careful demotion by the Second Vatican Council), became an even more aggressive effort. After the council, numerous scholars, following the lead of the council's preference for the sociological language of presbyters and the canonical language of the rights of the laity, proceeded to further obscure the distinctive sacramental character of the priesthood of pastors and curates so as to emphasize their sociological role as office holders and servants of the community. This effort began as early as David N.

77. Hünermann, "Final Weeks," p. 458.
78. Tanner, *Decrees*, Vol. II, p. 1048.

Power's 1969 work, *Ministers of Christ and His Church: The Theology of Priesthood*. Indeed, in the conclusion of that work, Power makes a statement, the logic of which, if followed upon, would deny even the bishop his priestly character:

> We have already in this study remarked on the use of the term "priest." It is not applied to the ordained pastors in the New Testament or in the early writings of the Fathers. Christ is the unique priest, and the people saved through him is a priestly people. The term "priestly" belongs to the church as such rather than to any particular section of its members. We also noted that the association of the New Testament ministry with the Aaronic priesthood of the Old is a relatively late development and one which served to lay undue stress on one particular function of the ministry. It also belongs to a clericalizing trend in the church which served to set the clergy as a body apart from the faithful.[79]

Swiss theologian and conciliar peritus, Hans Kung, was also quick to offer his assistance in implementing the council's teachings with regards to ministry. He did this in his *Wozu Priester? Ein Hilfe* (Zurich: Benzier, 1971). The title means quite literally, "Whither the Priest? A Help." But when the work was translated into English by John Cumming (London: Collins, 1972), the title was rendered as simply *Why Priests?* In the foreword to his book, Kung made clear the compassionate concern that motivated his writing: "I was concerned about the dire situation of priests in the Catholic Church and in the other Christian Churches, as something that I have been faced with constantly and in a variety of ways. The loss rate and, above all, the decline in vocations not only in North and South America, but in Europe are clear evidence that the crisis is approaching disaster point."[80] But on that same page of his foreword he also prepares us for the fact that the "help" he is about to offer to priests is somewhat radical: "my answer . . . ruthlessly discards some now untenable traditional ideas."[81] The reader might have been prepared for Kung's radical solution when, later on, Kung reminds us how "Jesus (himself a layman) introduces the figure of the priest once in all his parables, and then only to reject the particular example chosen (Luke 10:31)."[82] Kung then goes on to argue there is no way the word "priest" or even the concept of priest can be applied to any Christian minister. Thus no one should have been surprised when, in his final chapter, Kung proposes to replace the language and concept of priest with that of "community leader." It is thus understandable why Kung's English translator omitted the subtitle, "a help," lest it be taken as sarcasm.

79. Powers, *Ministers of Christ*, p. 169.
80. Kung, *Why Priests?*, p. 9.
81. Ibid.
82. Ibid., p. 28.

The Flemish Dominican Edward Schillebeeckx took to heart the council's emphasis upon the church as community and church ministry as office or service. He produced three emphatically sociological works, *Ministry: Leadership in the Community of Christ* (1981), *The Church with a Human Face* (1985), and *Church: The Human Story of God* (1990), the last work with its part 4 on the church as a democratic community and its leadership as "ministers." Moreover, Schillebeeckx, in his *Ministry: Leadership in the Community of Jesus Christ* (New York: Crossroad, 1981), uses the council's (and the new code of canon law's) language of the rights of the laity to sacramental ministry as the justification for their electing and ordaining their own presbyter/priests. More than once, indeed it becomes like a mantra in Schillebeeckx's work, he tells us, "the community knows that it has the right by grace to leaders,"[83] "throughout the pre-Nicene church it was held . . . that a community . . . had the right to a priest,"[84] "the apostolic right of the community to have leaders."[85]

While Schillebeeckx obsessed about the community's right to a priest, there were others who were finding creative ways to make do without a priest. In June of 1988, the Vatican's Congregation for Divine Worship published a "Directory for Sunday Celebration in the Absence of a Priest." In 1994, the United States Conference of Catholic Bishops published a ritual for "Sunday Celebration in Absence of a Priest." At about that same time, or soon after, there began to appear books in which the narrative or content could be described as products of enthusiastic opportunism in the absence of priests, indeed, near celebrations at the reduction of priests to roles of visiting sacramental supply agents for a local parish now ministered to and presided over by deacons or laity. For example, there are the two books by Ruth A. Wallace, *They Call Her Pastor: A New Role for Catholic Women* (Albany: State University of New York, 1992) and *They Call Him Pastor: Married Men in Charge of Catholic Parishes* (Mahwah, NJ: Paulist, 2003), and Virginia Stillwell's *Priestless Parishes: The Baptized Leading the Baptized* (Allen, TX: Thomas More, 2002). Finally, it should be noted: there is a tremendous irony in all of this. By that I mean, while the Second Vatican Council preferred to call parish priests presbyters precisely so as to avoid the identification of their ministry as mainly cultic—the title presbyter made clear their wider pastoral responsibilities—the growing phenomenon of priestless parishes or lone pastors given responsibility for multiple parishes has resulted in the fact that many post-Vatican II presbyters are more than ever taken up with cultic ministry, though now of an emphatically itinerant sort.

83. Schillebeeckx, *Ministry*, p. 40.
84. Ibid., p.72.
85. Ibid., p. 78.

While all this was going on, other voices were raised that expressed sincere concern and genuine alarm about what was happening to priestly ministry after the council. One example is Gisbert Greshake's 1982 work *Priestersein*, published in English translation in 1989 as *The Meaning of Christian Priesthood*. The English title obscures the fact made clear by the original German title that this is a study of ministerial priesthood and not the general concept of Christian priesthood. The first chapter of Greshake's book is entitled "Priesthood in Crisis," and it is prefaced by a quotation from Ernst Troeltsch, "Everything is tottering." In that chapter Greshake expresses his conviction:

> All this indicates that today's crisis of the priestly office is basically a crisis of identity. Not a few priests, and very many lay people, have no clear idea of the essential and central nature of priesthood, of the specific mission and task proper to the priest. The priest himself and anyone who is considering becoming a priest have been to a great extent left to work out their own answer to this question. In fact, as far as the understanding of the nature of ecclesiastical office is concerned, theology and the Church have in recent years resembled, and still resemble, a building which is in a state of reconstruction and one can say without too much exaggeration that everyone is concentrating on those parts of the building which interest him most.[86]

Nor has the situation significantly improved since Greshake wrote those words. Take, for example, German theologian Paul Josef Cordes. In 1972 he published a comprehensive study of *Presbyterorum ordinis*, surveying carefully its literary history and analyzing its theological content. Cordes's work bears the title *Sendung zum Dienst*, "Called to Serve" (published at Frankfurt am Main: Josef Knecht). Thirty-seven years later, the now Cardinal Cordes has published yet another book on priesthood. The very title of this new book, *Warum priester?* (Augsburg, Germany: Sankt Ulrich Verlag, 2009), is clear indication the author is convinced there remains a pressing need to try to answer the question, "Why priests?", which is the title of the English translation (by P. Spring and A. Figueiredo, New York: Scepter, 2010).

What are we to think of all this? Some theologians have made some very harsh judgments about what happened to ministerial priesthood at Vatican II. Take, for example, the opinion of the French Oratorian, former Lutheran pastor, Louis Bouyer in his *L'Eglise de Dieu* (Paris: Les Editions du Cerf, 1970). Bouyer, respectful of council teaching yet identifies currents in its work that soon proved very problematic not just for presbyters but even for the papacy. Indeed, as regards the presbyter/bishop relationship, Bouyer describes it as a ruthless, even abusive, power grab on the part of the bishops:

---

86. Greshake, *Meaning of Christian Priesthood*, p. 17.

Vatican II, without destroying or minimizing the doctrinal work of Vatican I—quite on the contrary, confirming it—proclaimed its desirable complements. But during the course of this council, and even more in what followed, it became apparent to what extent misunderstanding of the real sense of Christian authority was eviscerated in the consciousness of its possessors. Even though the doctrinal texts had formally acknowledged that conflict between primacy and collegiality can arise only in an ecclesiology of power, not in one of service, the episcopate again, intending to its regeneration, too often thought of itself in terms of ecclesiological power. Even after the council, under the false cover of a restoration of collegiality, there were attempts to resurrect Gallicanism. In the council itself, it was shown to what extent the restoration of the power of a number of bishops signified capacity to act with regard to their subordinates exactly as they had reproached the "curia" for doing in the past. Neglect of the presbyterate and the priests of second rank in the conciliar deliberations and, even worse (when one thinks of it), the almost exclusive concern to bully them (though with honeyed words) constituted scandal for anyone who, desirous of reform, was exasperated by the long latent crisis in the Church.[87]

When Bouyer speaks of "Gallicanism," he is using a term commonly employed to refer to a historic theological current that seeks to minimize papal authority in favor of national churches. It is called Gallicanism because it first arose among French medieval theologians (Gerson and d'Ailly) and found repeated expression in France until the nineteenth century when writers such as de Maistre and Lammenais championed papal authority over national churches in an intellectual movement called ultramontanism. Vatican II's Decree on Bishops, paragraph 38, mentioned national episcopal synods as a legitimate expression of episcopal collegiality, or corporate guidance of the church. And, indeed, after Vatican II, national episcopal conferences, territorial associations of bishops such as the United States Conference of Catholic Bishops, appeared everywhere. However, in the late 1980s considerable debate arose over the authority of these conferences, not simply as a potential challenge to papal authority but also as a challenge to the autonomy and freedom of diocesan bishops. Yet another problem became evident when in the early 1980s two episcopal conferences, the French and the American, issued statements on the morality of nuclear deterrence that are not easily reconciled with each other. Indeed, many read the French Bishops' pastoral on nuclear warfare as a pointed counterstatement to the American pastoral letter. No wonder Pope John Paul II in his encyclical letter *Apostolos suos*, a *motu proprio*, dated May 21, 1998, insisted on the limited doctrinal authority of such conferences.

87. Bouyer, *Church of God*, pp. 505–6.

But for our concern, it is Bouyer's criticism of episcopal authority, not as a challenge to papal authority but as a drastic diminishment of priestly or presbyteral authority, that is even more telling. He gives this history of the Second Vatican Council's treatment of priestly ministry in the second rank, that is, the rank of presbyters, a disdainfully negative interpretation. I am referring to the fact that in the passage quoted above, Bouyer is so bold as to label Vatican II's treatment of priests a "scandal."

In contrast with Bouyer's angry protest, Franciscan theologian Bonaventure Kloppenburg, in his 1974 book *The Ecclesiology of Vatican II*, simply registers amazement. In that book, Kloppenburg, who served as a peritus at the council, shows himself to be a staunch defender of Vatican II and especially *Lumen gentium*. Yet he describes well the problematic situation left us by that document. But unlike Bouyer, Kloppenburg sees the source of the problem as having been not so much an episcopal power grab but an exceedingly generous recognition of the laity:

> The theology of the laity seems to have put a question mark behind the theology of the priesthood. From Vatican II's abundant instruction on the laity we learn that all the baptized "share a true equality with regard to the dignity and to the activity common to all the faithful for the building up of the Body of Christ" (LG 32c/58); that all share "in the mission of the whole Christian people with respect to the Church and to the world" (LG 31a/57); that all "have an active part to play in the life and activity of the Church" (AA 10a/500); that laymen are now "brothers" to their pastors (LG 32e/59);37a/64); that all without exception are called upon by the Lord "to expend all their energy for the growth of the Church and its continuous sanctification" (LG 33a/59; cf. AA 2a/491); that "all are commissioned to that apostolate by the Lord Himself" (LG 33b/59); that "upon all the laity . . . rests the noble duty of working to extend the divine plan of salvation ever increasingly to all men of each epoch and in every land" (LG 33d/60); that all the baptized are "made sharers in the priestly, prophetic, and kingly functions of Christ" (LG 31a/57; cf. AA 2b/491; 10a/500); that "the supreme and eternal Priest, Christ Jesus, wills to continue His witness and serve through the laity too" (LG 34a/60), and "gives them a share in His priestly function" (LG 34b/60); that "the great Prophet . . . fulfills His prophetic office . . . not only through the hierarchy who teach in His name and with His authority, but also through the laity (LG 35a/61) and "for that very purpose He made them His witnesses and gave them understanding of the faith and the grace of speech" (*ibid.*); that the laity too should take an active part in the Eucharistic action and should learn to offer themselves, and this "not only through the hands of the priest (SC 48/154).
>
> A generous doctrine indeed on the nature of the laity and its place and role in the Church! But it causes many to ask why there are or should continue to be priests (presbyters) in the Church and in what precise way they differ from those who possess the common or universal priesthood.[88]

---

88. Kloppenburg, *Ecclesiology of Vatican II*, pp. 263–64.

Yet other theologians have made more precise criticisms of key formulas that the council employed to express the relationship between priests and people, the hierarchy and the laity.

In the literature after Vatican II, several theologians have called attention to the problematic character of the teaching in *Lumen gentium* 10 regarding the essential difference between the common and the ministerial priesthoods. I have already quoted previously the first paragraph of *Lumen gentium* 10, wherein the council stated in clear and cogent terms the common priesthood of the laity. Now I quote the second paragraph of *Lumen gentium* 10, which seeks to clarify the relationship between the two:

> Though they differ from one another in essence and not only in degree, the common priesthood of the faithful and the ministerial or hierarchical priesthood are nonetheless interrelated. Each of them in its own special way is a participation in the one priesthood of Christ. The ministerial priest, by the sacred power he enjoys, molds and rules the priestly people. Acting in the person of Christ, he brings about the Eucharistic Sacrifice, and offers it to God in the name of all the people. For their part, the faithful join in the offering of the Eucharist by virtue of their royal priesthood. They likewise exercise that priesthood by receiving the sacraments, by prayer and thanksgiving, by the witness of a holy life, and by self-denial and active charity.

Several theologians have called attention to the fact that while the council fathers in this second paragraph insist upon the essential difference between the common and ministerial priesthoods, it is a bald assertion for which they give no demonstration. This is the judgment of American Franciscan Kenan Osborne. In his *Priesthood: A History of Ordained Ministry in the Roman Catholic Church* (1989), Osborne says of this assertion in *Lumen gentium* 10: "Nowhere do the documents attempt to give a theological description or definition of this essential difference."[89] German theologian Gisbert Greshake in his *The Meaning of Christian Priesthood*, translated by P. MacSeumais (Westminster, MD: Christian Classics, 1989), German original *Priestersein* (Freiburg: Herder and Herder, 1982), is a little more generous in his judgment regarding *Lumen gentium* 10: "The Council did in fact try to answer this difficulty as well [regarding the relationship between the common and ministerial priesthoods] (cf. *Lumen gentium*, no. 10) but it did not give a sufficiently clear solution for the problem thus posed."[90] I tend to agree with Greshake because the examples that the council gives of differences between the common and ministerial priesthoods are significant differences but not essential differences. I am refer-

89. Osborne, p. 324.
90. Greshake, p. 22.

ring to the fact that, when the council insists that the ministerial priesthood "molds and rules" (*efformat ac regit*) the priestly people (Tanner translates it as "forms and governs"), it is hardly an exclusive or distinguishing role. One can point to the fact that, in a very real sense, Catholic parents in their home, the catechist in a church, or the average Catholic high school teacher in his or her classroom also mold and rule a portion of the people of God. And there is a further problem to consider, namely, the prospect that without a more precise explanation such a claim that there is an essential difference between the common and ministerial priesthoods cannot help but result in polarization in the church, polarization between those who piously accept the church's bald assertion here and those who more boldly demand a clearer explanation. André Feuillet, in his *The Priesthood of Christ and His Ministers*, long ago complained of a sizeable amount of such skepticism: "The traditional doctrine asserts the existence of a ministerial priesthood that 'differs . . . in essence and not only in degree' from the priesthood shared by all the baptized. Today, however, many Christians doubt the validity of this distinction. The result is that priests themselves find it difficult to determine exactly where they belong in the people of God. They even ask what is the use of their being priests."[91]

English Dominican friar, Aidan Nichols, in his *Holy Order: The Apostolic Ministry from the New Testament to the Second Vatican Council* (1990), shows that his concern is more the way the council sets forth the relationship between bishops and presbyters. In his book, Nichols exhibits both knowledge and respect for the Second Vatican Council's Dogmatic Constitution on the Church. Nevertheless, he does not hesitate to express a salient critique of one particular teaching of the council, to which I have already referred:

> The conciliar texts, by stressing that the presbyter receives his sacramentality by receiving a share in that of the bishop, and acts not only as the bishop's assistant, but also as his vicar, surrogate and extension, can give the impression that the only reason for having a presbyterate in the Church is that the bishops cannot do everything themselves. But as we have seen from investigating the New Testament and early patristic evidence, the presbyterate is by no means so thoroughly derivative from the episcopate, and parasitic upon it, as this might suggest. The presbyterate is the original ordained ministry of the local church. Although the significance of the presbyterate was naturally affected when chief presbyters with *episkopé* inherited the universal, rather than local, ministry of the apostles, the emergence of the episcopate as the apostolic ministry *par excellence* cannot overthrow the fact that the presbyterate is itself an apostolic creation.[92]

91. Feuillet, *Priesthood of Christ*, p.13.
92. Nichols, *Holy Order*, pp. 135–36.

In fact Nichols' criticism was also made several years before by Louis Bouyer in his 1970 work, *L'Egliese de Dieu*. There Bouyer says: "We have shown that the presbyterate, in one sense, is older than the episcopate, for before there were bishops there were apostles. And one of the first things the apostles did when they founded a church was to install 'presbyters.'"[93] The historical-biblical evidence to which both Nichols and Bouyer refer are such New Testament passage as Acts 14:23, which says of the work of Paul and Barnabas in founding churches at Lystra and Iconium during what has come to be called Paul's first missionary journey: "They appointed presbyters for them in each church." See also the statement in the Letter to Titus 1:5: "For this reason I left you in Crete so that you might set right what remains to be done and appoint presbyters in every town."

I share Aidan Nichols' concern that presbyteral ministry is being made all too subservient to episcopal ministry, especially when in LG 28 we hear it stated that the presbyter makes his bishop present. This is a daring incursion upon the older doctrine that says that the principal dignity of the priest-presbyter resided in the idea that he made Christ present to the congregation in word and sacrament. For example, we have already seen how Aquinas, in his *Summa Theologica* (pt. 3, ques. 82, art. 1),[94] describes the priest as operating "in the person of Christ" (*in persona Christi*) and as "a minister of Christ" (*ministrum Christi*). That is, Aquinas has quite a different conception of the relationship between a priest and his bishop. For, when Aquinas speaks of bishops, he speaks not of their power but about their obligations to both the priests and the people: "It belongs to the bishop to deliver, not only to the people, but likewise to priests, such things as serve them in the fulfillment of their respective duties" (in *Summa Theologica* 3, 82, 1, reply to part 4).[95] And when Aquinas does speak of priestly power, it is to note that, when ordaining a priest, "the bishop gives the priestly power of order, not as though coming from himself, but instrumentally, as God's minister, and its effect cannot be taken away by man" (3, 82, 8, reply to part 2).[96] In pointing out such things I do not mean to deny that there are times in his ministry when the priest-presbyter makes the bishop present to the local congregation, for example when reading to the congregation a pastoral letter from the bishop or making known to them a decision of the bishop. But we also know that making the bishop present is hardly a distinguishing characteristic of the parish priest or pastor. Indeed, any diocesan official or modestly paid lay person can make the bishop present, that is, represent the bishop (see canon 231 of the Code of Canon

93. Bouyer, *Church of God*, p. 390.

94. Aquinas, *Summa Theologica* (ST), Vol. 2, p. 2504.

95. Ibid.

96. Ibid., p. 2509.

Law for proper remuneration of lay church workers; and note that increasingly in the United States diocesan officials are lay employees). No doubt one could qualify the statement that the priest-presbyter makes the bishop present by pointing out that it says "in a certain sense," and specify that that sense is secondary or accommodated. But the council fathers did not choose to make such qualifications.

One cannot overestimate the dramatic change effected by this only vaguely qualified assertion. It undercuts, even undermines the presbyter's immediate relationship to his congregation. Left as it is without careful theological qualification, it cannot help but suggest a momentous demotion in dignity of office of the priest/presbyter has taken place in this the Second Vatican Council's Dogmatic Constitution on the Church. Finally, before we leave this topic, it is important to note that Aquinas's insistence upon the obligations of bishops (rather than their power) is hardly original with him, much less a peculiarly medieval theme. In this regard, compare Origen of Alexandria's statement in his *On Prayer* 28.4. Origen is commenting on the Matthean version of the Lord's Prayer (Matt 6:9–13), which unlike the Lucan version (Luke 11:2–4) asks for the forgiveness of our "debts" (*opheilemata*) rather than our "sins" (*hamartia*). Of this Origen says: "There is a certain 'debt' due from a widow for whom the Church provides, and another due from a deacon, and another from a presbyter, but the 'debt' due from a bishop is the heaviest, since it is demanded of him by the Savior of the whole Church, and retribution follows if it be not paid."[97] But as we have seen, when bishops insist on their power (and the laity on their rights), then all debts are transferred to the presbyters who as *Presbyterorum oridinis* article 4 says, "owe everyone" (*omnibus ergo debitores sunt presbyteri*).

On the other hand, it is important that the reader be made aware of the fact that there are many theologians who have no problems whatsoever with the subservient role of the presbyter regarding both bishops and laity, as set forth at Vatican II. Take, for example, the essay entitled "Presbyteral Ministry in the Roman Catholic Church," published in 2005 in the journal *Ecclesiology*. The essay is written by Paul McPartlan, a professor at Catholic University in Washington, DC. He begins by noting: "A friend of mine who is a priest and a liturgist summed up the paradox of presbyteral ministry in the modern Roman Catholic Church very well when he once said, 'I preside at Mass in place of the bishop; I proclaim the Gospel in place of the deacon—I'm not at all sure what I actually do in my own right!'"[98] McPartlan then goes on to make a spirited defense of all that was said at Vatican II and even what happened after. In fact, he cheers the appearance of priestless parishes as only

97. Origen, *On Prayer*, p. 306.
98. McPartlan, "Presbyteral Ministry," p. 11.

furthering what he calls Vatican II's "reappropriation of patristic perspectives,"[99] a return to Ignatius of Antioch's model of monarchical episcopacy, wherein presbyters are "as closely tied to the bishop as the strings to a harp" (Ignatius to the Ephesians 4.1).[100] In response to his friend's complaint, McPartlan says: "When considered individually, in their parish ministry, there is very little that presbyters do on their own behalf. The Council repeatedly stresses that presbyters act in the name of the bishop, sharing with him in a lesser degree that ministerial priesthood which itself serves the royal priesthood of the People of God."[101] As for parishes without resident pastors he concludes:

> Parishes were an eventual arrival on the scene, a convenient solution to a prac-tical problem as numbers of Christians hugely increased, particularly in the fourth century, but not by any means essential; a device, we might even say. It would be wrong historically to think of them as fundamental and needing to be sustained at all costs. The full implementation of Vatican II must involve a review and critique of Church structures, and the division of dioceses into parishes is a prime example. Catholics have tenaciously and in many ways understandably clung to the parish system, but that system is becoming in-creasing unsustainable because of falling numbers of priests. If the familiar network of parishes is now, in some places at least, effectively being taken from us, I suggest both historically and theologically that we do not need to cling on, we *can* let it go.[102]

But besides McPartlan's point of view, surely there will be others eager to defend the council's teaching by quoting a rare passage or two wherein the council does indeed seem to insist upon the dignity of the presbyteral office. For example, they might well point to *Lumen gentium* 28, where, with careful qualification, it says, "Although priests do not possess the highest degree of the priesthood, and although they are dependent on the bishops in the exercise of their power, they are neverthe-less united with the bishops in sacerdotal dignity."[103] Such a passage hardly answers the criticisms made by Dulles, Bouyer, Nichols, Kloppenburg, Osborne, Norris, and Greshake. Instead, such a quotation can be used as evidence for the problem that Peter Hünerman has already pointed out to us: in the council documents at times there are "juxtaposed without critical analysis some rather heterogeneous theologi-cal elements," that is, various theologies of the priesthood, patristic, scholastic, and

---

99. Ibid., p. 12.

100. Ignatius, *The Epistles*, p. 177.

101. Ibid., p. 23.

102. Ibid., p. 24.

103. Abbott, *Documents of Vatican II*, p. 53.

modern are juxtaposed without any real attempt at synthesis. It is for that reason, among others, that I have chosen a different path here.

The Need for a Carefully Considered Response

I, for my part, take the point of view outlined by John Henry Newman and Josef Ratzinger. While I understand and agree with Vatican II's desire to give the episcopate a certain dignity and a new vision to lay spirituality, I yet feel that the teaching of Vatican II in these matters needs careful commentary and qualification because, as we have seen, all too often the council spoke not just of the service of a presbyter to bishop and people but in words that suggest the presbyter's subservience to both.

Faced with this situation, it is worth recalling some comments of Newman, the great student of the development of Christian doctrine. For example, Newman's observation to a Mr. Daunt, in a letter dated August 7, 1870: "There has seldom been a council without great confusion after it."[104] We should also consider Newman's "Letter addressed to His Grace the Duke of Norfolk," in which he makes an observation regarding the Church's proclamation of solemn teaching: "Hardly has she spoken out magisterially some great general principle, when she sets her theologians to work to explain her meaning in the concrete, by strict interpretation of its wording, by the illustration of its circumstances, and by the recognition of exceptions, in order to make it as tolerable as possible, and the least of a temptation, to self willed, independent, or wrongly educated minds."[105] This, Newman's judgment about ecumenical councils, is supported by certain observations made by Joseph Ratzinger, one of the principal theological consultants at the Second Vatican Council. In 1982, Ratzinger published a collection of his essays called *Theologische Prinzipenlehre* (Munich: Erich Wewel Verlag), which was translated into English and published by Ignatius Press in 1987 as *Principles of Catholic Theology*. An epilogue of that book is an essay entitled "Review of the Postconciliar Era—Failures, Task, Hopes." In that essay, Ratzinger quotes Gregory of Nazianzen who had attended the Council of Constantinople in 381 and soon after was invited to attend yet another synodal assembly. Ratzinger quotes Nazianzen's response to this second invitation: "To tell the truth, I am convinced that every assembly of bishops is to be avoided, for I have never experienced a happy ending to any council; not even the abolition of abuses . . . but only ambition or wrangling about what was taking place."[106] Later, Ratzinger gives as an example, "The Council of Nicea, which formulated the definitive statement of the divine Sonship of

104. Newman, *Letters and Diaries*, Vol. 25, p. 174.

105. Newman, *Certain Difficulties*, p. 321.

106. Ratzinger, *Principles*, p. 368. J. H. Newman quotes those very same words of Nazianzen in his *The Arians of the Fourth Century*, p. 451.

Jesus, was followed by a crushing dispute that brought about the first great heresy in the Church, that of Arianism, and, for a decade, rent the Church to her very core."[107] Then he says: "From time to time, councils are a necessity, but they always point to an extraordinary situation in the Church and are not to be regarded as a model for her life in general or even as the ideal content of her existence. They are medicine, not nourishment. Medicine must be assimilated and its immunizing effect must be retained by the body, but, in general, it achieves its effect precisely by becoming superfluous, by continuing to be an extraordinary measure."[108] And of Vatican II in particular, Ratzinger says, "While the Council formulated its pronouncements with the fullness of power that resides in it, its historical significance will be determined by the process of clarification and elimination that takes place subsequently in the life of the Church. In this way, the whole Church participates in the Council; it does not come to an end in the assembly of bishops."[109] Moreover, there is considerable evidence that that kind of dialogue has already begun.

There is also evidence that the church is well aware of the confusion regarding the role and character of the presbyter-once-called-priest, and that it is working hard to do something about it. For example, after the council, popes addressed the problem in encyclicals and national episcopal synods addressed it in pastoral letters. To some degree, the very titles of these statements reflect that the authors were concerned more with the sacral or pastoral aspect of presbyteral ministry. For example, note the titles of the United States Catholic Conference of Bishops' pastoral letter *De sacerdotio ministeriali* (December 9, 1971) and John Paul II's encyclical letter *Pastores dabo vobis* (March 25, 1992). After the council there have appeared significant historical and theological studies meant to help us understand, once again, ministerial priesthood. An example of this is Albert Vanhoye's 1980 work entitled *Pretre Nouveau, selon le Nouveau Testament* (translated in 1986 as *Old Testament Priests and the New Priest: According to the New Testament*). I have already quoted from German theologian Gisbert Greshake's 1982 work, *The Meaning of Christian Priesthood*, which focuses precisely on defining ministerial priesthood. One should also consider Belgian Jesuit Jean Galot's *Teologia del Sacerdozio* (translated in 1984 as *Theology of the Priesthood*, San Francisco: Ignatius Press), which is a fine work. There have even been very practical things undertaken to restore and promote the image of the priest in the community of faith, take for example the Vatican's recent sponsorship of "The Year of the Priest." Nonetheless, I have some doubts as to the effectiveness of all these efforts. For example, the works of Vanhoye, Greshake, and

---

107. Ratzinger, *Principles*, p. 369.

108. Ibid., p. 374.

109. Ibid., pp. 374–75.

Galot have been read mostly by scholars who at times take issue with what the authors have said. As for the effectiveness of these magisterial statements endorsing priesthood, the current number of vocations to the priesthood has remained low, such that one might easily conclude these statements of the magisterium will have the same effectiveness as John XXIII's apostolic letter on the promotion of the study of Latin, *Veterum sapientia* (February 22, 1962). As for this "Year of the Priest," one cannot help but wonder if continual appeal to the image of the Curé of Ars is going to be truly helpful. Though this simple, nineteenth-century rural French parish priest (with a congregation numbering less than 250), was undoubtedly an assiduous pastor, one cannot help but question whether the already humbled institution of ministerial priesthood needs yet another object lesson in humility and servitude.

It is for reasons such as these that I feel there is still much to be done. No doubt, the pervasive secularism and hedonism of contemporary Western culture does work against priestly vocations. Nevertheless, we should not be satisfied to simply blame the world for our problems, especially when there is evidence that suggests we ourselves are the source of much of this crisis in the priesthood. That is why it is important that we take seriously the critiques of the council's treatment of priest/presbyters made by Dulles, Legrand, Osborne, Norris, Bouyer, Nichols, Greshake, and Kloppenburg. They all bring up problems that need to be addressed. By contrast, in this book I try to respond to this crisis of priestly identity in an appreciably different way, a way that might be helpful not just to theologians and canonists but to presbyters in pastoral ministry, pastors, and associate pastors, as a means for them to ponder their own self-identity. I am convinced we need to reconsider the question: did Clement of Rome and John Chrysostom lead us astray when they compared certain Christian ministries with those of the Old Testament Levitical priesthood? Moreover, I believe the means to answer that question are ready to hand.

The Rationale for this Rejoinder

Just as the theologians and bishops at Vatican II undertook a *ressourcement*, and went back to the fundamental sources of the Christian faith, Scripture, and Tradition and rediscovered there the value of a return to the terminology of presbyters, as that term is used in the New Testament and by Ignatius of Antioch, so herein I want to want to undertake a *ressourcement* and go back to the Bible so as to recapture something of the biblical theology of priesthood, not just in the New Testament but also in the Old Testament. The Bible confronts us with several detailed and vivid portraits of priestly figures in action, relating to God and his people, the world and its problem. None of these portraits is a mere historical reminiscence; rather each narrative is theologically informed. We can to this day still learn from them some important things about ministry to God's people. For example, scattered throughout the books of Exodus, Leviticus, Numbers, and Deuteronomy there are several detailed portraits of Aaron, the brother of Moses and Miriam, and the first high priest of Israel. It does not require great imagination to recognize that in these narratives of Aaron-in-action we see Aaron in a cooperative pastoral ministry much like a Catholic pastor today. That is, just as Aaron is shown working alongside his brother, Moses, the great prophet, and his sister Miriam, a gifted charismatic, so too parish priests today must work alongside and with a lay staff of talented professionals. But we should also note the way that Aaron bears the brunt of the burden of working, not just alongside prophets and charismatics but with and for God's people who are angry and impatient. Indeed, we shall see how Aaron, while his brother Moses communed with God in mystic encounter on the heights of Sinai, was left below to deal with the impatient and demanding people of God and the challenges they provided. Similarly, in the story of Eli and his sons, tending the shrine at Shiloh, as recounted in the first book of Samuel, we have an amazing parallel to recent scandals wherein our chief priests, like Eli, have not exercised sufficient vigilance over their priestly sons. Or, consider Mattathias of Modein whose story is told in the first book of Maccabees. He was a simple priest living at a distance from Jerusalem, but nevertheless was caught between religious zealots on the one hand, murderous secularists on the other, and a Jerusalem temple hierarchy that itself was compromised in various ways. And thus his plight was not at all unlike Christian pastors today who are caught between an aggressively secular society and extreme forms of pietism that seek simply to reject the world, all the while receiving direction from religious superiors who themselves do not seem to have a grasp of the situation.

However, most people are not much acquainted with these biblical portraits of priests. For example, these portraits of priests are rarely featured in the lectionary readings at Mass or in the readings of the Divine Office, and thus Catholic laity remain ignorant of them. As for Catholic theologians, many continue to work out of an all-too-simplistic caricature of Levitical priests as totally cultic, exclusively focused upon ritual observances, with no social or doctrinal consciousness or duty. As for Protestants, their doctrinal dismissal of any notion of ministerial priesthood may well have had the effect that those who may have encountered these portraits in their consecutive and systematic personal reading of the Bible may have quickly passed over them as nothing but ancient and obscure relics, long superseded by more distinctly Christian notions of priesthood and ministry. It is precisely for such reasons that I urge the reader to consider the portraits of Old Testament priests, which I present herein.

And so what I attempt to do in this book is to reacquaint Christians with ten powerful images of Levitical priesthood as a lead up to and preparation for my focus, in the final two chapters, upon the identifiably priestly character of the ministries of both Jesus and Paul. I begin each chapter with several quotations of the biblical narrative that describes the ministry of these priests. I then go on to give an historical-critical analysis of that biblical narrative. Next I make theological assessment of the relevance of that biblical narrative for ministry today. All along I make comparisons of these biblical portraits to historic examples of priestly service in the history of the church up to our own day.

No doubt there will be some who will object to what I do here, and these will not be just Protestants with strong convictions about the disparity between law and gospel. For example, the Jesuit theologian, Jean Galot, in his opening chapter of *Theology of the Priesthood*, entitled "Inadequate Criteria," (listing "The Old Testament" as well as "The History of Religions") warns us against using Old Testament models of priesthood or comparisons with priesthood in the history of religions. Daniel Donovan has explained Galot's position: "For Galot, the Christian use of the language of sacrifice as well as of priesthood comes less from the world of Jewish cult than from the nature of Jesus' mission as the shepherd. Laying down his life for his sheep, he offers the sacrifice that buys forgiveness constitutes authentic worship."[110] As for the other objectors, I would ask that they consider several things. First, I ask those readers to consider Jesus' own words in Matt 5:17, "Do not think that I have come to abolish the law or the prophets. I have come not to abolish but to fulfill." Also please consider Saint Paul's description in Col 2:17, of the Law of Moses as "shadows of things to come." This kind of biblical exegesis is called typology, of which St. Paul gives us two examples. Adam is called a type of Christ in Rom 5:14; and in 1 Cor 10:6, the Israelites of the Exodus are called types, or examples, for Christians making the journey to baptism. This is certainly the method followed by early church fathers such as Augustine of Hippo, who, in his *The City of God*, (bk. 17, ch. 6) says: "The very priesthood after the order of Aaron was appointed as the shadow of a future eternal priesthood."[111] So too Bede the Venerable (d. 735) said specifically of the biblical accounts of Old Testament priesthood, "We are not to believe that anything was done or said which did not represent the grace of the gospel, if they are properly understood."[112]

As for those readers who are less than edified, indeed, maybe even shocked by my references to pagan priests, Greek and Roman, in the very opening pages of this introduction, I suggest they consider the fact that Moses learned much from a Midianite

---

110. Donovan, *What Are They Saying,* p. 79.

111. Augustine, *City of God*, p. 345.

112. Bede, *Homilies on the Gospels*, book 2, p. 207.

priest, his father-in-law, Jethro (Exod 18). Indeed the Bible strongly suggests Aaron too learned much about what it meant to be a priest when it says in Exod 18:12: "Aaron learned much when he came with all the elders of Israel to participate with Moses' father-in-law in the meal before God." Moreover, we should realize the NT designation of Jesus as a priest "according to the order of Melchizedech" relates the ministry of Christ not to a Levitical priest but to that of a Canaanite priest (Gen 14).

I am well aware of the salutary warning in Heb 10:1: "the law was only a shadow of the good things to come, and not the very image of them." And yet there must be some analogies, or how could anyone, as I have done, make the claim that priesthood has had a unique development in the biblical tradition. When I insist upon this analogy I am following the lead of Thomas Aquinas in his treatment of the priesthood of Christ in his *Summa Theologica*, the third part, question 22. There he readily admits that in one sense Old Testament priesthood is a very inadequate tool for comparison with or understanding of Christ's own priesthood. In part three, question 22, article 6, the section called *Sed contra*, he says: "The priesthood of the Law was a figure of the priesthood of Christ, not as adequately representing the reality, but as falling far short thereof; both because the priesthood of the Law did not wash away sins, and because it was not eternal, as the priesthood of Christ."[113] And yet Aquinas goes on to insist there is yet a sense in which Old Testament Hebrew priesthood was actually a more precise foreshadowing of the priesthood of Christ than was that of Melchizedech. In part 3, question 22, article 6, reply to objection 2, he says: "As to the actual offering, the priesthood of Christ was more distinctly foreshadowed by the priesthood of the Law, by reason of the shedding of blood, than by the priesthood of Melchizedek in which there was no blood-shedding."[114] For the importance of a blood offering, see Hebrews 9. Moreover, Aquinas (in his *Summa Theologica*, 1a 2ae, ques. 101, art. 4, reply to objection 1) employs the patristic doctrine of typologies to teach that the ceremonies of the Old Law are a foreshadowing of Christ: "Just as their sacrifices signified Christ the victim, so too their sacraments and sacred things foreshadowed the sacraments and sacred things of the New Law."[115]

Finally, there are modern theologians, even important *periti* at the Second Vatican Council, who would endorse this method. For example, note the comment of Gisbert Greshake in his book on *The Meaning of Christian Priesthood*: "His is a priesthood of a new and unique kind, in which all other human priesthood is taken away, and yet elevated and preserved."[116] Long before the Council, in his 1957 work

---

113. Aquinas, *Summa Theologica*, Vol. 2, p. 2145.

114. Ibid.

115. Aquinas, *Summa Theologica*, Vol. 1, p. 1054.

116. Greshake, p. 44.

Lay People in the Church, The French Dominican Yves Congar, a major *peritus* at the Second Vatican Council, expressed a positive attitude not only toward Old Testament models of priesthood but also priesthood as seen in the general history of religions: "Jesus Christ, the Word of God made flesh, is the only true wisdom—yet there was wisdom in the world before him. Jesus Christ is the only true priest—yet there was already a natural priesthood, drawing all its worth from him, referred to him and subsisting in him (*Omnia in ipso constant*: Col 1:17)."[117]

Yet another important theological expert at that Council, Joseph Ratzinger, was later promoted to the office of prefect of the Vatican's Congregation for the Doctrine of the Faith, and in that capacity addressed the World Synod of Bishops on October 1, 1990. His words that day were later published as an essay entitled "Biblical Foundations of Priesthood." In that address he urged the bishops to consider "in what sense this ministry of the succession of the apostles is something truly new and in what sense this Christian newness received into itself anticipatory figures of the Old Testament (p.625)."[118] Indeed, he went so far as to say, "The new priesthood of the apostles of Jesus Christ and of their successors bears in itself all that was contained prophetically in the Old Testament."[119]

Finally, the reader should be alerted to the fact that I have included portraits of impious priests as well as pious priest. I do this out of the conviction that if we can learn from biblical portraits of drunken patriarchs (Noah in Gen 9:18–28) and adulterous kings (David in 2 Sam 11), and false prophets (Hananiah in Jer 28), surely there is something to be learned from scriptural accounts of a wandering Levite (Jonathan from Bethlehem), two greedy clerics (Eli's sons, Hophni and Phineas), and a ruthless hierarch (Caiaphas).

Also the reader should note that I have decided that, lest I inadvertently feed into the Second Vatican Council's preoccupation with high priesthood, I have taken care to feature portraits of lowly or simple priests (Jonathan the wandering Levite from Bethlehem, Ezra the priest-scribe; Mattathias, the rural priest in the village of Modine; and Zechariah, the father of John the Baptist) and to give these equal dignity alongside portraits of chief priests (Eli at Shiloh and Ahimelech at Nob) and high priests (Aaron, Zadok, Simon the Just, Caiaphas).

No doubt there will be some who will see in this modest effort at retrieving some value in the concept of ministerial priesthood the specter of a renewed or returning clericalism or the return to an older, sacral concept of priesthood. Rather this book should be seen as a small contribution to what Avery Dulles described as

117. Congar, *Lay People in the Church*, p. 112.

118. Ratzinger, "Biblical Foundations," p. 625.

119. Ibid.

a legitimate concern and a much needed effort. In the very first edition of his *Models of the Church* (1974), he said: "In Roman Catholicism today we are witnessing a full-scale revolt against the excesses of the sacral concept of ministry. Rejection of this stereotype is one of the sources of the present crisis in the Church. Still there are valid elements in this controverted view . . . [and] Catholicism has perhaps a special responsibility to keep alive this sacral dimension."[120]

120. Dulles, *Models of the Church*, pp. 158–59.

1

Imperfections in a Priest

The Example of Aaron, the Brother of Moses

Post-Tridentine language about priests exhibits, at times, an extreme ideal-ization of ministerial priesthood. Take for example *The Catechism of the Council of Trent* of 1566. Part 2, chapter 7 treats of the sacrament of orders. There we read "that no dignity on earth excels the Order of the priesthood."[1] Moreover, there we find Scripture, cited as evidence, that priests "are rightfully called not only angels [Mal 2:7] but even gods [Ps 82:6] because they represent among us the power and majesty of the immortal God."[2] Such exalted claims and hyperbolic language are perhaps understandable as an exaggerated response to the Reformation polemics against ministerial priesthood or as motivational tools intended to encourage a striving for moral perfection that would work to remedy the moral decadence among Catholic clergy that was one of the causes of the Protestant Reformation. Nevertheless, while such Counter-Reformation insistence upon the sacredness of the priestly office and the requisite moral perfection of its members might have served to motivate and inspire to high sanctity some aspirants to the Catholic priesthood, those same meth-ods might also have worked to set up others for the serious disappointments, indeed grave disillusionments, that occurred a few years ago when, yet again, the serious moral failures among priests were revealed. These moral failures are clear evidence that many priests are not "angels" and that their behavior at times is far from godlike. I believe a more balanced and realistic understanding of both the dignity and fragil-ity of priests can be gained from the story of the very first priest whom we consider here.

---

1. *Catechism According to the Decree*, p. 275.
2. Ibid.

1

Aaron's Less than Perfect Ministry

Aaron was the brother of Moses and the very first among the Hebrew people to be publically designated and formally installed as a priest. Aaron's life was less than perfect, both before his ordination as a priest and afterward. Before his ordination, Aaron served as an assistant to his brother Moses. For the most part, Aaron's service to God and Moses at that time was exemplary, but there was at least one glaring failure, an episode called the Worship of the Golden Calf. More precisely, while Moses communed with God on the summit of Mount Sinai, Aaron was at the base of the mountain leading the people into idolatry. Even after Aaron was chastened for that mistake and ordained, his life was full of problems, some of his own creation. His priestly sons proved liturgically inept, for example. There was jealousy in the ministry, his own and that of others, and, yet again, the people of God proved to be not just a major challenge to Aaron but a source of failure. Nevertheless, we will also see that, despite all his failures in life and ministry, Aaron came to be revered in both Jewish and Christian tradition as a great figure in the history of faith. Aaron's story asks us to consider and question what place "perfection" has in the life of God's people and their ministers. I think we shall see something of an answer when we very carefully trace the life and ministry of Aaron.

The major events of Aaron's life are related in several discreet, often only loosely connected, narratives spread across four books that form part of the very first division among the books of the Bible, indeed the very first part of every Bible, the part that is called the Pentateuch, the Torah, or sometimes simply the five books of Moses: Genesis, Exodus, Leviticus, Numbers, and Deuteronomy. The reason for the disconnectedness of the account of Aaron's life in the last four books of the Pentateuch (Exodus, Leviticus, Numbers, and Deuteronomy) is that Aaron is but one figure in the larger narrative, which is the story of the Hebrew people's deliverance from bondage in Egypt. Moreover, Aaron is not the central figure in that drama; rather, it is his brother Moses. Nevertheless, here we ferret out and focus upon those parts of Exodus, Leviticus, Numbers, and Deuteronomy that feature or even just mention Aaron (only three mentions in Deuteronomy). When we treat these references or narratives in chronological order, we are able to get an idea of the history of Aaron, the course of his life, and, most importantly for our interests here, the shape and character of his ministry as a priest.

Aaron's Vocational Call

It seems that Aaron was born in Egypt around about the middle of the fourteenth century before Christ, that is, around the year 1350 BC, when the Hebrew people dwelt and worked as slave labor in Egypt. The meaning of Aaron's name is uncertain, and scholars conjecture its origin is Egyptian rather than Hebrew. He was the second of three children born to the man Amram and his wife Jochebed, a married couple from the Hebrew tribe or clan called Levi (a detailed genealogy is given in Exod 6:14–24). Amram and Jochebed's first and thus oldest child was a girl whom they named Miriam. Aaron was their second child. Moses was their youngest, that is, their third and final child, who was born three years after Aaron. Aaron's infancy and youth and even middle age seem to have been normal and uneventful. Of those years we are simply told (in Exod 6:23) that he married Elisheba and she bore him four sons: Nadab, Abihu, Eleazar, and Ithamar. It seems that as a mature man Aaron developed a reputation of being "an eloquent speaker" (Exod 4.14) and perhaps developed some measure of stature among his people (for when in Exod 4:29–30 he addresses the elders, they listen). But late in life everything changed dramatically for Aaron when he was reunited with his long estranged brother Moses.

Moses' life had always been much more eventful than Aaron's. Indeed, Moses' birth and infancy were high drama. Exodus 2 tells us how Moses was conceived and born at a time of tension between the Egyptians and their servant class, the Hebrews; such tension that Moses' mother, in order to save the life of her child, had to devise a clever way to get him adopted into the royal family of Egypt, the family of the Pharoah. But the drama does not stop there. For when Moses was a young man, he murdered an Egyptian in a fit of rage and then left Egypt seeking refuge in the land of Midian. There Moses met and married a Midianite woman and worked for his wife's father, Jethro, who was a shepherd. Indeed, it was while tending Jethro's flock that Moses had an intense religious experience that would change not only his own life and that of Aaron's but also that of the Hebrew people.

Exodus 3 and 4 contain the narrative of the call of Moses by God to lead the Hebrew people out of bondage in Egypt. Chapter 3 tells us of Moses' encounter with God on Mount Sinai, where God speaks at length to Moses, detailing precisely for him the mission for which God has called him. Aaron enters into this drama when, in chapter 4, we are told of Moses' less than enthusiastic response to God's call. In fact, Moses points out what he feels is his serious inadequacy for the task God has designated him. This is where Aaron enters, and here is how the incident is described in Exod 4:10–17:

> Moses, however, said to the LORD, "If you please, LORD, I have never been eloquent, neither in the past, nor recently, nor now that you have spoken to your servant; but I am slow of speech and tongue." The LORD said to him, "Who gives one man speech and makes another deaf and dumb? Or who gives sight to one and makes another blind? Is it not I, the LORD? Go, then! It is I who will

assist you in speaking and will teach you what you are to say." Yet he insisted, "If you please, LORD, send someone else!" Then the LORD became angry with Moses and said, "Have you not your brother, Aaron the Levite? I know that he is an eloquent speaker. Besides, he is now on his way to meet you. When he sees you, his heart will be glad. You are to speak to him, then, and put the words in his mouth. I will assist both you and him in speaking and will teach the two of you what you are to do. He shall speak to the people for you: he shall be spokesman, and you shall be as God to him. Take this staff in your hand; with it you are to perform the signs."

And, sure enough, in Exod 4:27–31, we read of the meeting between Moses and Aaron:

The LORD said to Aaron, "Go into the desert to meet Moses." So he went and when they met at the mountain of God Aaron kissed him. Moses informed him of all the LORD had said in sending him, and of the various signs he had enjoined upon him. Then Moses and Aaron went and assembled all the elders of the Israelites. Aaron told them everything the LORD had said to Moses, and he performed the signs before the people. The people believed, and when they heard that the LORD was concerned about them and had seen their affliction, they bowed down in worship.

From now on the two brothers work together so intimately that, in Exodus 5, immediately after the call of Aaron, we begin to see the use of what will become an almost formulaic phrase that yokes them closely together: the words "Moses and Aaron." For example, in Exod 5:1 we are told, "After that, Moses and Aaron went to Pharoah and said, 'Thus says the LORD, the God of Israel: "Let my people go."'" And in verse 4, we are told, "The king of Egypt answered them, 'What do you mean, Moses and Aaron, by taking the people away from their work?'" And then in Exod 5:19–21, we are told how, when the Hebrew people get in trouble with Pharoah, they complain to both Moses and Aaron: "The Israelite foremen knew they were in a sorry plight, having been told not to reduce the daily amount of bricks. When therefore, they left Pharoah and came upon Moses and Aaron, who were waiting to meet them they said to them, 'The LORD look upon you and judge! You have brought us into bad odor with Pharoah and his servants and have put a sword in their hands to slay us.'" This formula "Moses and Aaron" is repeated again and again (Exod 7:6; 8:1, 4, 8, 21; 9:8, 27; 10:3,16, 24; 12:1, 31, 43, 50 and many more).

Aaron's Ministerial Authority

Without doubt, in all this narrative Moses is the most important figure, for it is Moses who speaks with God and later relates it to Aaron. Nevertheless, there are some passages in the Exodus narrative where we see Aaron portrayed not simply as Moses' assistant. He is given some power in his own right. One example is that both Moses and Aaron are given pastoral staffs. In Exod 4:1–5, the shepherd's staff, which Moses had been carrying when tending the flock of his father-in-law, Jethro, on Sinai, is endowed by God with miraculous power as a confirmation of Moses' authority now to lead not sheep but God's people:

> "But," objected Moses, "suppose they will not believe me, nor listen to my plea? For they may say, 'The LORD did not appear to you.'" The LORD therefore asked him, "What is that in your hand?" "A staff," he answered. The LORD then said, "Throw it on the ground." When he threw it on the ground it was changed into a serpent, and Moses shied away from it. Now, put out your hand," the LORD said to him, "and take hold of its tail." So he put out his hand and laid hold of it, and it became a staff in his hand. This will take place so that they may believe," he continued, "that the LORD, the God of their fathers, the God of Abraham, the God of Isaac, the God of Jacob, did appear to you."

In Exodus 7:8–12, we hear how Aaron too is given by God a pastoral staff that is equally miraculous:

> The LORD told Moses and Aaron, "If Pharaoh demands that you work a sign or wonder, you shall say to Aaron: Take your staff and throw it down before Pharaoh, and it will be changed into a snake." Then Moses and Aaron went to Pharaoh and did as the LORD had commanded. Aaron threw his staff down before Pharaoh and his servants, and it was changed into a snake. Pharaoh, in turn, summoned wise men and sorcerers, and they also, the magicians of Egypt, did likewise by their magic arts. Each one threw down his staff, and it was changed into a snake. But Aaron's staff swallowed their staffs.

And it is indeed Aaron's staff, not Moses' staff, that is used in Exod 8:1–8 to bring down the plague of frogs on Egypt and in Exod 8:12–13 the plague of gnats. Aaron's role in the infliction of the ten plagues is recorded in Exodus, chapters 7, 8, and 9. By stretching out his rod at the behest of Moses, Aaron brought on the first three plagues (blood, frogs, and lice). Together they were involved in producing the sixth plague (boils) and the eighth one (locusts). Only Moses is mentioned in connection with the other five.

But we must also be aware of the fact that there are other passages that portray Moses working quite independently of Aaron. For example, it is Moses alone who parts the Red Sea so that Israel might pass through. Indeed, there is no mention at all of Aaron in Exodus, chapters 13, 14, 15, and 16, and only two small mentions of Aaron in the events after the crossing. In Exod 17:8–13, we are told how, after the dramatic crossing, the Israelites were attacked in the desert by the fierce Amalekite nomads. Here Aaron is shown once again in a purely ancillary but important role when he and Hur stand on either side of Moses and hold up his hands until the attackers are repulsed:

> At Rephidim, Amalek came and waged war against Israel. Moses, therefore, said to Joshua, "Pick out certain men, and tomorrow go out and engage Amalek in battle. I will be standing on top of the hill with the staff of God in my hand." So Joshua did as Moses told him: he engaged Amalek in battle after Moses had climbed to the top of the hill with Aaron and Hur. As long as Moses kept his hands raised up, Israel had the better of the fight, but when he let his hands rest, Amalek had the better of the fight. Moses' hands, however, grew tired; so they put a rock in place for him to sit on. Meanwhile, Aaron and Hur supported his hands, one on one side and one on the other, so that his hands remained steady till sunset. And Joshua mowed down Amalek and his people with the edge of the sword.

In Exodus 19, the Israelites arrive at Mount Sinai. And in chapters 20 through 23, we hear of God's revelation of the moral code by which the Israelites must relate to each other and to God himself. Here are precise instructions regarding such topics as the treatment of slaves (21:1–11), capital crimes (21:12–17), burglary and theft (22:1–4), the seduction of a young woman (22:16–17). In chapter 23, Moses is given some religious laws. In all of this Moses is alone. It is only in chapter 24, the ratification of the covenant, that mention is made again of Aaron. It is here that Aaron and seventy elders are allowed to ascend the mountain with Moses. In Exod 24:1–2: "Moses himself was told, 'Come up to the LORD, you and Aaron, with Nadab, Abihu, and seventy of the elders of Israel. You shall all worship at some distance, but Moses alone is to come close to the LORD; the others shall not come too near, and the people shall not come up at all with Moses.'"

Then after Aaron and the elders climb back down the mountain, Moses spends forty days and forty nights there, after which he is given precise instructions by God as to the organization of the Hebrew cult. In Exodus, chapters 25–31, God gives Moses precise instructions as to building the Ark of the Covenant (25:10–25), a lampstand (25:31–40), the altar of holocausts (27:1–8), priestly vestments (ch. 28), ceremonies for the consecration of priests (29:1–9), and making of incense (30:34–38).

Aaron's Great Mistake

Ironically, however, while Moses was getting all these instructions for setting up an Israelite cult, Aaron was at the base of Mount Sinai leading the Hebrew people into an idolatrous cult to another god, in an episode recounted in Exodus 32. This episode is known as the Worship of the Golden Calf. More specifically, while Moses was up on the mountain receiving the instructions about the organization of the Hebrew cult, down below Aaron was gathering gold to make a golden calf. Exod 32:1–6 relates the events:

> When the people became aware of Moses' delay in coming down from the mountain, they gathered around Aaron and said to him, "Come, make us a god who will be our leader; as for the man Moses who brought us out of the land of Egypt, we do not know what has happened to him." Aaron replied, "Have your wives and sons and daughters take off the golden earring they are wearing, and bring them to me." So all the people took off their earrings and brought them to Aaron, who accepted their offering, and fashioning this gold with a graving tool, made a molten calf. Then they cried out, "This is your God, O Israel, who brought you out of the land of Egypt." On seeing this, Aaron built an altar before the calf and proclaimed, "Tomorrow is a feast of the LORD." Early the next day the people offered holocausts and brought peace offerings. Then they sat down to eat and drink, and rose up to revel.

In anger Moses descends the mountain and confronts his brother, punishes with death the idolaters among the people, and then goes back up Mount Sinai to intercede for God's mercy upon Aaron and the people for their grave sin. When Moses comes back down the mountain he ordains Aaron and his sons. Lev 8:1–15 provides us with a precise account of the event:

> The LORD said to Moses, "Take Aaron and his sons, together with the vestments, the anointing oil, the bullock for a sin offering, the two rams, and the basket of unleavened food. Then assemble the whole community at the entrance of the meeting tent." And Moses did as the LORD had commanded. When the community had assembled at the entrance of the meeting tent, Moses told them what the LORD had ordered to be done. Bringing forward Aaron and his sons, he first washed them with water. Then he put the tunic on Aaron, girded him with the sash, clothed him with the robe, placed the ephod on him and girded him with the embroidered belt of the ephod, fastening it around him. He then set the breastpiece on him, with the Urim and Thummim in it, and put the miter on his head, attaching the gold plate, the sacred diadem, over the front of the miter, at his forehead, as the LORD had commanded him to do.
>
> Taking the anointing oil, Moses anointed and consecrated the Dwelling, with all that was in it. Then he sprinkled some of this oil seven times on the altar, and anointed the altar, with all its appurtenances, and the laver, with its base, thus consecrating them. He also poured some of the anointing oil on Aaron's head, thus consecrating him. Moses likewise brought forward Aaron's sons, clothed them with tunics, girded them with sashes, and put turbans on them, as the LORD had commanded him to do.
>
> When he had brought forward the bullock for a sin offering, Aaron and his sons laid their hands on its head. Then Moses slaughtered it.

After the ordination ceremony, Aaron offered a sacrifice and blessed the people (Lev 9). But the early practice of the Hebrew cult also provides high drama. Indeed, tragedy befalls Aaron and his family. When Aaron's eldest sons, Nadab and Abihu, ignore the precise rubrics laid down by God for incense offerings, they are punished by God in a most violent manner. In Lev 10:1–2, we are told: "During this time Aaron's sons Nadab and Abihu took their censers and, strewing incense on the fire they had put in them, they offered up before the LORD profane fire, such as he had not authorized. Fire therefore came forth from the LORD's presence and consumed them, so that they died in his presence."

Nor is this the only dramatic incident suffered by the new priesthood of the Hebrew people. Aaron's two surviving sons also made liturgical mistakes, failing to follow all of the meticulous instructions given by God for certain offerings. However, this time, through the intercession of Aaron, punishment is allayed. In Lev 10:16–20, we read that:

> When Moses inquired about the goat of the sin offering, he discovered that it had all been burned. So he was angry with the surviving sons of Aaron, Eleazar and Ithamar, and said, "Why did you not eat the sin offering in the sacred place, since it is most sacred? It has been given to you that you might bear the guilt of the community and make atonement for them before the LORD. If its blood was not brought into the inmost part of the sanctuary, you should certainly have eaten the offering in the sanctuary, in keeping with the command I had received." Aaron answered Moses, "Even though they presented their sin offering and holocaust before the LORD today yet this misfortune has befallen me. Had I then eaten of the sin offering today, would it have been pleasing to the LORD?" On hearing this, Moses was satisfied.

Next, in Num 3:5–10, we hear of how God appointed the sons of Levi to serve as liturgical assistants to Aaron and his sons:

> Now the LORD said to Moses: "Summon the tribe of Levi and present them to Aaron the priest, as his assistants. They shall discharge his obligations and those of the whole community before the meeting tent by serving at the Dwelling. They shall have custody of all the furnishings of the meeting tent and discharge the duties of the Israelites in the service of the Dwelling. You shall give the Levites to Aaron and his sons; they have been set aside from among the Israelites as dedicated to me. But only Aaron and his descendants shall you appoint to have charge of the priestly functions. Any layman who comes near shall be put to death.

At about this same time God reveals to Moses the famous priestly blessing (Num 6:22–27): "The LORD said to Moses: 'Speak to Aaron and his sons and tell them: This is how you shall bless the Israelites. Say to them: / The LORD bless you and keep you! / The LORD let his face shine upon you, and be gracious to you! / The LORD look upon you kindly and give you peace! / So shall they invoke my name upon the Israelites, and I will bless them.'"

Jealousy and Rivalry in Ministry

The next important event in the life of Aaron was an incident called "the Jealousy of Aaron and Miriam" (Num 12). Aaron's new role as the chief priest of Israel, however, may have undermined his willingness to accept the leadership of his younger brother. Aaron and his sister, Miriam, who both had been designated as prophets of the LORD, challenged Moses' right to act as God's unique spokesman. We are told in Num 12:1–14:

> While they were in Hazeroth, Miriam and Aaron spoke against Moses on the pretext of the marriage he had contracted with a Cushite woman. They complained, "Is it through Moses alone that the LORD speaks? Does he not speak through us also?" And the LORD heard this. Now, Moses himself was by far the meekest man on the face of the earth. So at once the LORD said to Moses and Aaron and Miriam, "Come out, you three, to the meeting tent." And the three of them went. Then the LORD came down in the column of cloud, and standing at the entrance of the tent called Aaron and Miriam. When both came forward, he said, "Now listen to the words of the LORD: / Should there be a prophet among you, / in visions will I reveal myself to him, / in dreams will I speak to him; Not so with my servant Moses! / Throughout my house he bears my trust: / face to face I speak to him, / plainly and not in riddles. / The presence of the LORD he beholds. / Why, then, did you not fear to speak against my servant Moses?"
>
> So angry was the LORD against them that when he departed, and the cloud withdrew from the tent, there was Miriam, a snow-white leper! When Aaron turned and saw her a leper, "Ah, my lord!" he said to Moses, "please do not charge us with the sin that we have foolishly committed! Let her not thus be like the stillborn babe that comes forth from its mother's womb with its flesh half consumed." Then Moses cried to the LORD, "Please, not this! Pray, heal her!" But the LORD answered Moses, "Suppose her father had spit in her face, would she not hide in shame for seven days? Let her be confined outside the camp for seven days; only then may she be brought back." So Miriam was confined outside the camp for seven days, and the people did not start out again until she was brought back.

How did this event come about? That is, what was the motivation or the source of Aaron and Miriam's challenge to Moses' authority? Some have conjectured that Aaron's newfound dignity as chief priest of Israel might have undermined his willingness to continue to accept or defer to Moses' role of principal leadership. Other biblical scholars have argued that the severe punishment visited upon Miriam suggests that she was the principal instigator of this rebellion; that is, Miriam proposed and indeed convinced her brother Aaron that the two of them were the equal of Moses. Moreover, there was yet another challenge to religious authority among the

Hebrews, and this time it was a challenge not just to Moses' authority but to that of Aaron and his sons, the anointed priests of Israel.

A Challenge from the Laity

In Num 16:1–3, we are told of a rebellion originating when three tribal chieftains stir up discontent among the elders of Israel: "Korah, son of Ishar, son of Kohath, son of Levi and Dathan and Abiran, sons of Eliab, son of Pallu, son of Reuben, took two hundred and fifty Israelites who were leaders in the community, members of the council and men of note. They stood before Moses, and held an assembly against Moses and Aaron, to whom they said, 'Enough from you! The whole community, all of them, are holy; the LORD is in their midst. Why then should you set yourselves over the LORD's congregation?'"

Once again, it is Moses who takes control of the situation and responds decisively. Indeed, Moses not only accuses these rebels of seeking the priesthood (Num 16:10, "you now seek the priesthood too") but he challenges them to try and offer incense to the Lord. When they do this, the results are disastrous. Here is the account in Num 16:31–33: "The ground beneath them split open, and the earth opened its mouth and swallowed them and their families [and all of Korah's men] and all their possessions. They went down alive to the nether world with all belonging to them; the earth closed over them, and they perished from the community. And all the Israelites near them fled at their shrieks, saying, 'The earth might swallow us too!'"

And then, we read in Num 17:16–26, that God, so as to drive home the lesson even more effectively, instructs Moses to enact a highly symbolic prophetic lesson for all of the Israelites to see:

> The LORD now said to Moses, "Speak to the Israelites and get one staff from each ancestral house, twelve staffs in all, one from each of their tribal princes. Mark each man's name on his staff; and mark Aaron's name on Levi's staff, for the head of Levi's ancestral house shall also have a staff. Then lay them down in the meeting tent, in front of the commandments, where I meet you. There the staff of the man of my choice shall sprout. Thus will I suppress from my present the Israelites' grumbling against you."
>
> So Moses spoke to the Israelites, and their princes gave him staffs, twelve in all, one from each tribal prince; and Aaron's staff was with them. Then Moses laid the staffs down before the LORD in the tent of the commandments. The next day, when Moses entered the tent, Aaron's staff, representing the house of Levi, had sprouted and put forth not only shoots, but blossoms as well, and even bore ripe almonds! Moses thereupon brought out all the staffs from the LORD's presence to the Israelites. After each prince identified his own staff and too it, the LORD said to Moses, "Put back Aaron's staff in front of the commandments, to be kept there as a warning to the rebellious, so that their grumbling may cease before me; if it does not, they will die." And Moses did as the LORD had commanded him.

In Num 18:8, we hear God tell Aaron of the financial provisions for priests: "The LORD said to Aaron, 'I myself have given you charge of the contributions made to me in the various sacred offerings of the Israelites; by perpetual ordinance I have assigned them to you and to your sons as your priestly share. You shall have the right to share in the oblations that are the most sacred.'"

Next, we must examine the incident related in Num 20:1–13, wherein God blames Moses and Aaron for the petulance of the whole Israelite community:

> The whole Israelite community arrived in the desert of Zin in the first month, and the people settled at Kadesh. It was here that Miriam died, and here that she was buried.
>
> As the community had no water, they held a council against Moses and Aaron. The people contended with Moses, exclaiming, "Would that we too had perished with our kinsmen in the LORD's presence. Why have you brought the LORD's community into this desert where we and our livestock are dying? Why did you lead us out of Egypt, only to bring us to this wretched place which has neither grain nor figs nor vines nor pomegranates? Here there is not even water to drink!" But Moses and Aaron went away from the assembly to the entrance of the meeting tent, where they fell prostrate.
>
> Then the glory of the LORD appeared to them, and the LORD said to Moses, "Take the staff and assemble the community, you and your brother Aaron, and in their presence order the rock to yield its waters. From the rock you shall bring forth water for the community and their livestock to drink." So Moses took the staff from its place before the LORD, as we was ordered. He and Aaron assembled the community in front of the rock, where he said to them, "Listen to me, you rebels! Are we to bring water for you out of this rock?" Then, raising his hand, Moses struck the rock twice with his staff, and water gushed out in abundance for the community and their livestock to drink. But the LORD said to Moses and Aaron, "Because you were not faithful to me in showing my sanctity before the Israelites, you shall not lead this community into the land I will give them."
>
> These are the waters of Meribah, where the Israelites contended against the LORD, and where he revealed his sanctity among them.

Indeed, God's resentment is so strong that we are told God decided they would never see the promised land, and that they would die before the Hebrews entered in. And thus we read in Num 20:22–29:

> Setting out from Kadesh, the whole Israelite community came to Mount Hor. There at Mount Hor, on the border of the land of Edom, the LORD said to Moses and Aaron, "Aaron is about to be taken to his people; he shall not enter the land I am giving to the Israelites, because you both rebelled against my commandment at the waters of Merebah. Take Aaron and his son Eleazar and bring them up on Mount Hor. Then strip Aaron of his garments and put them on his son Eleazar; for there Aaron shall be taken in death."
>
> Moses did as the LORD commanded. When they had climbed Mount Hor in view of the whole community, Moses stripped Aaron of his garments and put them on his son Eleazar. Then Aaron died there on top of the mountain. When Moses and Eleazar came down from the mountain, all the community under-

stood that Aaron had passed away; and for thirty days the whole house of Israel mourned him" [the same amount of time they will mourn the death of Moses].

The Historical Accuracy of Aaron's Ministry

Regarding the biblical narrative of the life and ministry of Aaron, modern biblical scholarship has called into question the historical accuracy of his portrayal. This criticism rests upon the fact that the Pentateuch, the first five books of the Bible, is a composite work. The Pentateuch is derived from the weaving together of four earlier sources or literary traditions, the Jahwist, the Elohist, the Deuteronomist, and the Priestly, usually abbreviated JEDP, I present them here in chronological order: the Jahwist is the oldest and the Priestly the most recent. These critics claim to discern evidence among J, E, D, P that Aaron is portrayed differently in those four traditions. More specifically, he is either ignored or portrayed negatively in the earlier traditions, and more prominently and positively in the priestly tradition. Also, we must consider the fact that most biblical scholars agree that about 90 percent of the narratives concerning Aaron appear in the Priestly source. More precisely, scholars are generally of the opinion that in the earlier traditions about the Exodus, as reflected in the J and E documents, Aaron has only a minor role, and in fact those two literary sources make no reference to Aaron's priestly functions at all. Instead, the special role of the priesthood and the details of temple worship were elaborated in P, the Priestly document, composed in the post-exilic period in about the fourth-century BC. One blatant example of an effort to make Aaron important appears in Num 18:1–4. In this passage, God appoints the Levites to be liturgical assistants to Aaron and his sons. This passage seems to be a doublet of Num 3:5–10, that is, a second version; but in Numbers 3, God gives the instruction to Moses who passes it on to Aaron while in Numbers 18, God speaks directly to Aaron. Other attempts to inflate the importance of Aaron and his sons can be found in the episodes that reveal obsession with the precise performance of cultic actions. Examples can be found in the narratives that describe Aaron's eldest sons who are punished with death because of their failure to observe all the requirements of the cult. No doubt, that incident was meant to be an object lesson for and warning to later readers about the absolute importance of following liturgical rubrics. Also, the descriptions of the vestments for Aaron and his sons probably reflect much later historical developments in the Jerusalem cult.

In response to such criticism, I want to make three points. First, even though the Priestly source is the latest of the four sources, nonetheless one would be wrong to underestimate the antiquity of its narrative of Aaron's priestly ministry. While certain elements in the Priestly narrative, such as the elaborate description of priestly vestments, might indeed be more a reflection of later Jerusalem temple practice, not everything here is so anachronistic. The fact is that Israel certainly had a priesthood with customs and traditions that went back far beyond the time of the monarchy and the Jerusalem temple, indeed back to the very beginning of the Hebrew religious tradition. One very clear example of this is the antiquity of the priestly blessing in Num 6:22–27: "The Lord bless you and keep you! The Lord let his face shine upon you, and be gracious to you! The Lord look upon you kindly and give you peace!" All biblical scholars concede its great antiquity and recognize in it one of the oldest relics of the Hebrew religious tradition. Its highly polished poetic style, with its techniques of parallelism and expansion, strongly suggests it is a piece of oral tradition pre-exilic in origin, indeed, possibly one of the oldest portions of the Hebrew Bible. (There is even archeological witness to the antiquity of this blessing: two silver cylinders with this blessing written upon them were found in burial caves dating from 600 BC, that is, from the first temple period in Jerusalem. They are the earliest known fragments of any biblical texts, antedating the Dead Sea Scrolls by 400 years.)

Second, even though we might concede that much in the Priestly narrative of Aaron's life and ministry is shaped by theological interests peculiar to priests, there is also considerable evidence that suggests the Priestly authors did not ride roughshod over history, but instead exercised a certain measure of reverence and respect for historical accuracy despite their profoundly religious motives and intentions. Regarding Aaron's life, for example, it seems apparent that the Priestly editors were very respectful of the humble or less than flattering, indeed embarrassing, elements in Aaron's life story. We have already seen how the biblical narrative leaves totally unchanged the fact that while Aaron was some help to Moses in challenging Pharoah, it was Moses alone who led the people out of Egypt into the promised land. Nor were the Priestly editors ashamed to portray Aaron in such an ancillary role as working alongside Hur to hold up Moses' arms during the battle against the Amalekites. Nor did the Priestly editors try to cover up Aaron's role in the golden calf episode. Indeed, the latter can be taken as clear indication of the genuine historicity of that event, for it is seriously doubtful that the clan of Aaron would have allowed the propagation of stories about the moral failings of Aaron if such stories had no foundation in history.

Third, while we must concede there is a certain stylization or theological intention discernible in the Priestly source's presentation of Aaron, we must recognize that these features are far from being a limitation in the narrative. Instead these features help us discern more precisely what the Priestly authors are trying to make of the historical evidence they had, and in so doing reveal more clearly their theological values and thus the meaning of Scripture. In other words, it would be naive to think that the narrative in Exodus, Leviticus, Numbers, and Deuteronomy ever presumes to be nothing but objective historical narrative. In all four of these books, the authors were men of faith who selected and interpreted certain historical events so as to bring out what they were convinced was the religious significance of those events. But from our perspective of seeking a theological meaning in this narrative, this is far from a liability. For our own interests, it is far from an embarrassment that Aaron's role in the Pentateuch has been enhanced and embellished. Rather, we should rejoice in the fact that the Pentateuchal narrative of Aaron's life and ministry is much more than a simple historical account but is in some measure, to some degree, intentionally shaped by theological interests. That is, we should be happy to acknowledge that the portrayal of Aaron in the Pentateuch is in part an intentional idealization of him as the archetypal priest, the Levite par excellence, the paradigm for all later priests, the preeminent model for what it meant to be a priest of the Old Covenant.

Now we are prepared to ask the question: what relevance does all this have for you and me today? Are there any enduring lessons in the life and ministry of Aaron that might speak to Christian ministry today and indeed to the ministry of those who in Catholic Christianity claim to exercise a self-consciously priestly ministry?

The Importance of Cooperative Ministry

One of the enduring lessons that can be drawn from this, our study of the priestly ministry of Aaron in the Pentateuch, is the concept of cooperative pastoral ministry. The portraits of Aaron we have surveyed make it clear Aaron never worked alone. As a priest Aaron always worked alongside a great prophet, Moses, and a great charismatic, Miriam.

Aaron's relationship with his brother, Moses, is particularly important as an example of cooperation between priesthood and prophecy. Moses and Aaron were effective because they worked together: Moses was a man of action not words, but prophetic actions need the accompaniment of clarifying words. Thus priesthood and prophecy not only can, but should, work together. And the priest should at times take a secondary role and simply support a right-minded prophet, as Aaron and Hur did when they held up the arms of Moses.

But Aaron's relationship with Miriam is equally important. The second important lesson is that cooperative ministry must also include working alongside women. It is not insignificant that Miriam, the sister of Moses and Aaron, is the first woman in the Bible to be given the title prophetess. In Exod 15:20–21 we read: "The prophetess Miriam, Aaron's sister, took a tambourine in her hand, while all the women went out after her with tambourines, dancing; and she led them in the refrain: / 'Sing to the LORD, for he is gloriously triumphant; / horse and chariot he has cast into the sea.'"

Miriam leads the ecstatic victory dance of the Israelite women to celebrate the salvation of Israel from the Egyptians and the drowning of Pharoah's charioteers in the Sea of Reeds. While the priestly blessing in Numbers 7 is a genuine relic of very early Hebrew piety, so too the famous words of the Song of Miriam are among the oldest poetic couplets in the Scriptures: "Sing to the LORD, for he has triumphed gloriously; / horse and chariot he has cast into the sea" (Exod 15:21).

Moreover, Miriam is not alone. She is but the first in a long line of charismatic women in the Bible. Another famous Old Testament prophetess is Deborah in Judg 4:4–7:

> At this time the prophetess Deborah, wife of Lappidoth, was judging Israel. She used to sit under Deborah's palm tree, situated between Ramah and Bethel in the mountain region of Ephraim, and there the Israelites came up to her for judgment. She sent and summoned Barak, son of Abinoam, from Kedsh of Naphtali. "This is what the LORD, the God of Israel, commands," she said to him; "go, march on Mount Tabor, and take with you ten thousand Naptalites and Zebulunites. I will lead Sisera, the general of Jabin's army, out to you at the Wadi Kishon, together with his chariots and troops, and will deliver him into your power."

Note also Huldah, the wife of King Josiah's wardrobe keeper, the only prophetess mentioned in the monarchical period. She was of such high repute that the king sought her advice when the book of the law was found in the temple. Huldah foretold that the LORDwould "bring [evil] upon this place and upon its inhabitants . . . because they have forsaken me and have burned incense to other gods" (2 Kgs 22:16–17), but that the king would die peacefully. Josiah in fact died in battle; but the rest of Huldah's wrathful prophecy came true: in little more than two decades following the king's death, Jerusalem fell to the Babylonians.

There are also NT references to prophetesses, as in Luke 2:36: "There was also a prophetess, Anna, the daughter of Phanuel." And Acts 21:8–9, "On the next day we resumed the trip and came to Caesarea, where we went to the house of Philip the evangelist, who was one of the Seven, and stayed with him. He had four virgin daughters gifted with prophecy." Moreover, both Jesus and Paul had their female assistants. So too today in the one-priest parish there is often a large administrative staff often comprised entirely of women who function as director of religious education, director of liturgy, catechists, in the ministries of mourning, marriage preparation, et cetera. However, this brings up the question of ministry within the congregation and ministry in the world. The Second Vatican Council in *Lumen gentium* 30 taught that: "A secular quality is proper and special to laymen . . . the laity, by their very vocation, seek the kingdom of God by engaging in temporal affairs and by ordering them according to the plan of God. They live in the world, that is, in each and in all of the secular professions and occupations. They live in the ordinary circumstances of family and social life, from which the very web of their existence is woven."[3] Ironically, the great boom in lay ministry occurring since Vatican II has produced much involvement within the church and not so much outside, in the world. However, there are at least two outstanding examples of prophetic and charismatic ministries carried out by laity who have concentrated upon a Catholic Christian presence in the world. Witness the work today of the layman William Donahue who heads up the Catholic League for Religious and Civil Rights. That organization, which seeks to respond to discrimination against and defamation of Catholics and Catholicism, was originally founded by a priest, the Jesuit Virgil Blum of Marquette University. But under Donahue's leadership, the organization has become far more prominent and vocal. This is due in part to the fact that Donahue, precisely because he is not a cleric, a priest, or bishop, is able to pursue a much more intensely-focused and prophetic witness than priests or bishops. The latter would be open to the accusation of defending clericalism, the church, and its faith solely from self-interest. Witness also the work of Mother Mary Angelica of the Annunciation (born Rita Rizzo in Canton, Ohio), a member of the Poor Claires of Perpetual Adoration (a Franciscan order for women). In 1981, Mother Angelica founded the Eternal Word Television Network, and in so doing proved that she could not only envision but organize a Catholic television network perhaps more readily and effectively than a whole conference of Catholic bishops.

Challenging the People

However, we must still address the more disturbing elements in the life and ministry of Aaron. Indeed, the title of this chapter describes him as a less than perfect priest. Here I want to focus upon a sin of Aaron, a moral failure that happened before he was ordained a priest, but one that did not augur well for one who would become a priest. I am referring to the scandalous interlude of the worship of the golden calf. Apostasy is a serious sin. But it is only one serious sin to which priests are liable. Indeed, in succeeding chapters of this book we shall detail the principal sins of priests as portrayed in the Bible, namely, sex, money, and ambition. But it is important that

3. Abbott, *Documents of Vatican II*, p. 57.

we look carefully at Aaron's sin of apostasy to discern more precisely what it can teach us.

Before we begin, let me note that we could make excuses for Aaron. This apostasy is an incident that occurs before the fuller revelation to Moses on Sinai made clear: the LORD your God is LORD Alone, there can be no other gods (Exod 20:2–3). And indeed, some have interpreted this episode as not so much apostasy but as idolatry, that is, as an offense against graven objects, portrayals of Yahweh. However, I think it is better not to make excuses for Aaron. Instead it is important to see this episode as an object lesson in how a future priest must learn early on that while he is, in a sense, sent to serve the people of God, in the more primary sense he is sent to serve the will of God and to make it clear to the people. Thus he must not so pander to the will of the people such that he allows them to obscure or even deny the will of God. Indeed, the major theme in the Exodus narrative of the apostasy at Sinai is not so much that Aaron was remiss in all this but that God's people is a rebellious people. In Exod 32:9 we hear God say to Moses, "I see how stiff-necked this people is." And in Exod 32:21–22, Aaron says to Moses, "Let not my LORD be angry, you know well enough how prone the people are to evil." Moreover, it is important to recall the fact that the obdurate rebelliousness of the people before the demands of God is not a priestly theme but a major prophetic theme observable in the writings of all the prophets. See Isa 57:4, where they are called "children of rebellion," or Ezek 2:3 where we hear it said: "Son of Man, I am sending you to the sons of Israel, to a rebellious people." Compare also Jer 14:7, "our rebellions are many."

Thus, one might well argue: the most important lesson in the episode of the apostasy of Aaron is the way in which it can serve as a warning against the priestly temptation to so serve the needs of the people as to forget the even more important task of serving the Word of God. Aaron was so acutely sensitive to the needs and demands of the Hebrew people that he let their inappropriate demands obscure his original duties. And so it is to this day. The people of God still clamor and complain. No doubt some of their demands and some of their complaints are legitimate. But there are other demands and complaints that need to be challenged, need to be corrected rather than given into. There is the danger of pandering to discordant voices. No doubt while there are some voices among the people of God today that clamor for change, there are other voices that clamor as loudly for a return to tradition. But these are only "some voices"; that is, no one group should claim to be "the voice of the faithful." And even if there were such a thing as "one voice of the faithful," it is the Word of God and not the voice of the people that must prevail if a priest is to be a true servant of both God and the people. The Second Vatican Council does not make this easy for pastors when, in its dogmatic constitution on the church, *Lumen gentium*, it teaches that not only is the pope infallible but so too the bishops (LG 25); and even in a sense are all the people of God (LG 12). If this then leaves the impression that only priests are fallible, that is perhaps not a bad thing. Nonetheless, we would do well to call to mind the words of Yves Congar, the great theologian of the laity: "Too much must not be attributed to the *sensus fidelium*, not only in view of the hierarchy's prerogatives but in itself. History tells us of widespread failures of faith in the Christian people: in the East in the Seventh century in face of Islam, in England and in the Scandinavian countries in face of the Protestant Reformation, in unhealthy enthusiasms here and superstitious devotions there, and so on."[4]

Two related incidents in the life and ministry of Aaron give further illustration to the theme of the formidable challenge that is ministry to God's rebellious people. One is the rebellion of the sons of Korah. The other is the liturgical mayhem committed by Aaron's sons.

The rebellion of the sons of Korah teaches us there will always be some among the people of God who will be convinced that they can do your job better than you can, "armchair quarterbacks" as it were. Indeed, the episode of the rebellion of the sons of Korah and the laymen Dathan and Abiram makes it clear that the insistence "we are all priests" was not new with the Protestant Reformation. Indeed, we should not have been surprised to have seen it arise among Catholics after the Second Vatican Council.

Among John Henry Newman's *Parochial and Plain Sermons* there is one that is entitled "The Gainsaying of Korah."[5] To "gainsay" is to deny or contradict, to speak against or oppose. Newman in that sermon compares the rebellion of Korah to the "opposition made to God's Church in these days [which] is professedly based upon reason"[6] He identifies the complaint of Korah and his followers as "they accused Moses and Aaron of what is now called *priestcraft*."[7] And he concludes: "A very few words will suffice to suggest the lesson to be derived from this awful history; it is this . . . how great must be the sin of resisting the ministers of Christ, or of intruding into their office! How great the sin of presuming to administer the rites of the Church; to baptize, to celebrate the Holy Communion, or to ordain, or to bless, without a commission!"[8] Newman provides a description of those conservatives, Lefebrists, who ordained without commission after Vatican II and those liberals who performed clandestine ordinations of women. Neither had such a commission. Both

---

4. Congar, *Lay People*, p. 275.

5. Newman, *Parochial*, pp. 896–905.

6. Ibid., p. 899.

7. Ibid.

8. Ibid., p. 904

proceeded with contempt for ecclesiastical authority (in both cases Rome) and on the presumption they had the right to do so.

Next, in the story of Aaron's sons and their punishment for not following liturgical rubrics, there is a timely and important lesson for us today. The English word "rubrics" is a word meaning an authoritative rule, especially rules for conducting a liturgical service. Our English word rubric is derived from the classical Latin word *rubrica* meaning red (in the Middle Ages in the west, the tradition developed of using red lettering in a liturgical manuscript to distinguish the liturgical directives from the black lettering reserved for the liturgical text). No doubt the Pentateuchal narratives, which we have read of the death of two of Aaron's sons and the jeopardy of his remaining two sons because of liturgical errors, will impress some as being rather humorous and evidence of a liturgical obsessiveness that is all too characteristic of the clergy.

In the gospels, Jesus himself is critical of rubrical obsessiveness among the priests: surely everyone recalls the Parable of the Good Samaritan in Luke 10:29–37, wherein both a Jerusalem temple priest and a Levite from the temple neglect the needs of a severely beaten and wounded man because of their fear that if they were to help him, they just might incur cultic impurity. But note carefully: in the gospels it is not just the priests and Levites who are obsessive about the letter of the law, the laity in the form of the strictly observant Pharisees are just as obsessive. The Pharisees were a lay group who stood in opposition to the Sadducees, the sacerdotal party. In Mark's gospel they are constantly critical of Jesus for not observing the letter of the law (Mark 2:18—28; 3:1–6; 7:1–23). In response, Jesus more than once severely criticizes the Pharisees. In Matt 15:1–20, he sees them as hypocritical. See also Jesus' invective discourses against them in Matthew 23 and Luke 11:37–52. And so it is to this day, those who obsess about rubrics are not just clergy and professional liturgists. Indeed, I doubt that it will be a fellow priest or professional liturgist who will be the first to delete someone to the bishop if they find any liturgical irregularity incidental or intentional in a liturgical celebration. Instead it will probably be a self-appointed, that is, lay guardian of orthodoxy.

The Moral Character of Priests

We have yet to consider the problem posed by Aaron's moral character. As a priest, Aaron was jealous of his younger brother, Moses. In this regard there is some important teaching from a Roman Catholic archbishop of Canterbury.

The English ecclesiastic Baldwin of Canterbury should be better known to us. He was born at Exeter, in Devon, England, around the year 1125, and educated at the cathedral school at Exeter. When Baldwin was about twenty-five years of age, that is, about the year 1150, he went to Bologna to study canon law and theology. In 1155, he returned to England and joined the staff of the bishop of Exeter. In about the year 1161, he was appointed Archdeacon of Totnes. In medieval England, the office of archdeacon was a diocesan administrative position comparable to that of vicar general today. Baldwin, however, had a contemplative bent, and so in about the year 1169, he entered the Cistercian Abbey of Ford in Devonshire, a daughter house of Waverley, the first Cistercian abbey in England. And in 1175, he was elected abbot of Ford. But on August 10, 1180, he was consecrated bishop of Worcester. In December of 1184, he became archbishop of Canterbury. In the 1980s, Cistercian Studies of Kalamazoo, Michigan, sponsored a translation of some of Baldwin's works. Among those works is "An Exhortation to Priests," an address that apparently Baldwin gave as the primate of England before a large assembly of priests and bishops. At the very beginning of his exhortation, he read to them the words, which according to the Acts of the Apostles, chapter 20, Saint Paul had addressed to the assembled presbyters of Miletus: "Keep watch over yourselves and over the whole flock of which the Holy Spirit has appointed you overseers" (Acts 20:28). Then Baldwin went on to comment on Paul's words: "Priests of the Lord and ministers of our God, it is to you that these words of the Apostle are addressed. You are told to consider yourselves and the whole flock: firstly, yourselves; and then the flock. Those who are involved with the business of the salvation of others should have a care for their own salvation. Those who are entrusted with watching over moral discipline ought to live their own lives correctly. Those who must first account for themselves should begin with themselves and not neglect themselves."[9]

However, Baldwin was not naive about perfection among priests. Two paragraphs later Baldwin invokes the very same biblical texts (Mal 2:7 and Ps 82:7), which in the opening of this chapter we saw used by the Catechism of the Council of Trent in order to urge his clergy on to moral idealism. However, Baldwin, while recalling to his audience the noble mission and high dignity which is theirs as priests, is also very realistic and thus warns them: "If, however, the priests of the Lord can be likened to angels because of the similarity of their office and can also be called angels, then just as they should always seek the fellowship of the good angels, so they should always avoid any similarity to wicked angels. Wicked priests are certainly not grouped with good angels, but are more appropriately compared to wicked angels, those who fell from heaven and did not stand in the truth, who lost the honor of their angelic dignity."[10] It might well be that Baldwin's moral realism here is based on his own life situation. By that I mean his modern biographer says that Baldwin was "probably the son of Hugh d'Eu, archdeacon of Totnes, and a woman of unknown name."[11] But we must also consider the fact that Baldwin was involved in ecclesiastical and political

9. Baldwin, *Spiritual Tractates*, Vol. 2, p. 118.

10. Ibid., 120.

11. Holdsworth, "Baldwin of Forde," pp. 442–43.

struggles of his time, and some of his enemies did indeed perpetrate slanders and calumnies about him. And this might be one of them. But this matter of calumnies also leads to our next consideration.

The People of God expect a high level of morality from their clergy. But moral failures in the clergy have even more negative effects than the sins of the laity. We are warned of this in John Chrysostom's *On the Priesthood*, book 3:

> The sins of ordinary people, as though committed in secret, injure only those who commit them, but the sins of one who holds a position of eminence and is known to many are detrimental to all, for they render the fallen more remiss in striving to do good, and they excite the diligent to pride. Moreover, the faults of ordinary persons, even though public, do no great injury. But they who occupy the pinnacle of this dignity are conspicuous to all, and besides, even though the things in which they fail be small, those small things seem great to others. For all measure the gravity of sin, not by the gravity of the act, but by the dignity of him who commits it. A priest, therefore, should put on, as it were, armor of adamant, by means of constant care and unceasing vigilance over himself, watching on every side that no one may be able to discover an unprotected or neglected part, and inflict on him a deadly wound. For all surround him ready to strike and cast him down.[12]

Moreover, Chrysostom alerts us to the fact that all the people exercise a great deal of scrutiny in this regard and will be merciless when failures are found:

> As long as the life of a priest is well ordered he is exposed to no such attack. But if he be negligent in the smallest thing, as may easily happen, since he is but a man, and voyages on the tempestuous sea of this life, his past good works are powerless to protect him from the tongues of accusers. That one small fault casts a shadow on all the rest of his actions, for all wish to judge of a priest, not as of a man clothed in the flesh and subject to human infirmity, but as of an angel exempt from every weakness.[13]

And this is where the importance of the biblical doctrine of perfection enters in.

Priesthood and Moral Idealism

In the matter of "perfection," we must urge seminarians and clergy to take seriously the biblical doctrine of perfection. To do so, we must represent accurately the biblical doctrine of perfection.

In Lev 11:44, God said to Moses and Aaron to tell all the people, regarding cultic purity, "you shall make and keep yourselves holy, because I am holy." See also

---

12. Chrysostom, *On the Priesthood*, p. 58.

13. Ibid., p. 59.

by comparison, Lev 19:2, "Be holy, for I the Lord, your God, am holy." In Matt 5:48, Jesus extends this to moral purity, "Be perfect [*teleioi*] as your heavenly Father is perfect." So too Saint Paul says in 2 Cor 7:1, "Since we have these promises, beloved, let us cleanse ourselves from every defilement of flesh and spirit, making holiness perfect in the fear of God." In Col 4:12, Paul describes his coworker Epaphras as "always striving for you in his prayers so that you may be perfect [*teleioi*]." And in Phil 2:15, Paul himself prays "that you may be blameless and innocent, children of God without blemish." But we must also stress that such holiness comes not from within oneself but from reliance on the Lord. In these same works Paul makes clear the source of such perfection when he prays in Eph 3:16, that you may be "strengthened with His power through His Spirit in the inner self." In Eph 6:10, "draw your strength from the Lord and from His mighty power." Also, Phil 4:13, "I have the strength for everything through Him who empowers me." Nor is perfect holiness simply a Pauline doctrine. Compare Jas 1:4, "let perseverance be perfect [*teleion*], so that you may be perfect and complete." Consider also 1 Pet 1:15–16, which quotes the teaching of Lev 19:2. Even so, we must also admit that perfection is rare; witness the number of canonized saints.

Here, indeed, it is important to recall the observation of American Benedictine, Aelred Cody: "Priests in Israel were religious men, but like all men of religion they were also very human."[14] No doubt, in the New Testament holiness is postulated as a moral imperative of the highest order. Nevertheless, even there absolute holiness is attributed only to God. I am referring to Jesus' words in Luke 18:19, "no one is good, but God alone." Compare Matt 19:17, "Why do you call me good, there is only One who is good."

Consider also John Henry Newman's essay "Men, Not Angels, The Priests of the Gospel." It is the third discourse in Newman's first published work written as a Catholic, the volume entitled *Discourses Addressed to Mixed Congregations*. Therein, Newman says of Catholic priests, comparing them to St. Paul who complained of being chronically buffeted by "an angel of Satan:"

> Such are your Ministers, your Preachers, your Priests, O my brethren; not Angels, not Saints, not sinless, but those who would have lived and died in sin except for God's grace, and who, though through God's mercy they be in training for the fellowship of Saints hereafter, yet at present are in the midst of infirmity and temptation, and have no hope, except from the unmerited grace of God, or persevering to the end.
>
> What a strange, what a striking anomaly is this! All is perfect, all is heavenly, all is glorious, in the Dispensation which Christ has vouchsafed us, except the persons of His Ministers . . . those very Priests, so set apart, so consecrated, they with their girdle of celibacy and their maniple of sorrow, are sons of

14. Cody, *History of Old Testament Priesthood*, p. 3.

Adam, sons of sinners, of a fallen nature, which they have not put off, though it be renewed through grace, so that it is almost the definition of a Priest that he has sins of his own to offer for.[15]

Consider also article 1550 in the *Catechism of the Catholic Church* (1994):

This presence of Christ in the minister is not to be understood as if the latter were preserved from all human weaknesses, the spirit of domination, error, even sin. The power of the Holy Spirit does not guarantee all acts of ministers in the same way. While this guarantee extends to the sacraments, so that even the minister's sin cannot impede the fruit of grace, in many other acts the minister leaves human traces that are not always signs of fidelity to the Gospel and consequently can harm the apostolic fruitfulness of the Church.[16]

In this matter of judging priests according to their imperfections, there might be something to be learned from the later history of Aaron, that is, the manner in which Jewish and Christian tradition came to regard and judge him long after his death.

The Dignity of Aaron

It is important to note that even if Moses' role in the original drama of Israel's liberation was of paramount importance, we cannot afford to ignore the phenomenon by which Aaron's role came to be heightened and honored not just early on in the priestly narratives of the Pentateuch but also later, not just in priestly, but in scribal and rabbinic tradition. Indeed, it is important for us to recognize that it is not just the priestly source in the Pentateuch that exalts Aaron's importance. Perhaps we should not be much surprised to find Aaron idolized in the psalms of the Jerusalem temple, for example, as in Ps 133:1–2: "Behold how good it is, and how pleasant where brethren dwell at one! It is as when the precious ointment upon the head runs down over the beard, the beard of Aaron, till it runs down upon the collar of his robe." But, surely, there is some reason to be surprised when we find that, in a late work of the Old Testament, the book of Sirach, written by a Jerusalem scribe, in the great catalogue of the worthies of Israel, the celebration of Israel's great ancestors, which culminates that work (chapters 44–50), Aaron is praised in more lofty terms than Moses. While Moses receives five verses of praise, Aaron receives seventeen. And in rabbinic literature such as the *haggadah* (rabbinic literature is divided into two parts: the *halakah*, legal discussions, and the *haggadah*, history, legends, folklore, philosophy, and theology) praise is heaped upon Aaron. Indeed, there Aaron is often presented as a figure to be revered as much and in some cases even more so

15. Newman, *Discourses Addressed*, pp. 43–61.
16. *Catechism of the Catholic Church*, p. 387.

than Moses. For example, the rabbis often contrast the volatile personality of Moses, who is prone to quick acts of violent rage (his murdering the officer of Pharoah in Exod 2:12; his smashing the tablets of the Law in Exod 32:19; and his anger at Aaron's surviving sons in Lev 10:16–18 who, after the mortal punishment of Nadab and Abihu, commit yet another rubrical blunder) with Aaron who pursues reconciliation and avoids disputes and constantly intercedes with Moses so as to mitigate the punishment given to Miriam or threatened upon Eleazar and Ithamar (Lev 10:19–20). An example of this is the saying of the famous first-century rabbi Hillel, "Be of the disciples of Aaron, loving peace and pursuing peace, loving one's fellow man and bringing them nigh to the Torah," in the tractate of the *Mishnah* called the *Pirke Aboth* or "Teaching of the Fathers," 1:12—a tractate that sets forth maxims regarding right conduct.[17] Aaron also figures significantly in the Dead Sea Scrolls, that is, the literature of Qumran, the Jewish sect that flourished in the era just before and contemporary with the birth of Christianity. For example, in *The Manual of Discipline*, two messiahs were expected, one of Aaron, the priestly one, and one of Israel.

Nor is this adulation of Aaron purely gratuitous. While there can be no doubt about the primary importance of Moses in the history of Israel, nevertheless we need to recognize the enormous importance also of Aaron, an importance that at times not only compares with but even overshadows that of Moses. More precisely, while later generations would look back to Moses as a unique figure without any real successor, Aaron began a priestly dynasty that, despite many vagaries, continued more than a thousand years, until the Romans put an end to temple worship when they captured and destroyed Jerusalem in AD 70. In this regard, note the reference to Aaron in Luke 1:5, where we are told, "In the days of Herod, King of Judea, there was a priest named Zechariah of the priestly division of Abijah; his wife was from the daughters of Aaron, and her name was Elizabeth." This noble title of "a daughter of Aaron" is also an historic witness to the monumental longevity of the Aaronid priesthood.

Indeed, we would be remiss if we failed to note the fact that Aaron receives more than one honorable mention in the New Testament. In the seventh chapter of the Acts of the Apostles, we are provided with a description of the preaching of an early member of the first Christian community in Jerusalem, Stephen the deacon. Stephen identifies himself with the moral situation of Aaron in the golden calf episode of Exodus 32. More precisely, when Stephen experiences resistance to conversion from the Jews at Jerusalem, he dips into Israel's ancient history and employs as an object lesson the golden calf episode as an example of how the Jews have always been resistant to God's commands. In the Epistle to the Hebrews, Aaron is referred to no less than three times, sometimes with strong theological implications. No doubt,

17. *The Mishnah* , p. 447.

Heb 7:11 cautions Christians about the limitations of the Aaronid or Levitical priesthood: "If, then, perfection came through the Levitical priesthood, on the basis of which the people received the law, what need would there still have been for another priest to arise according to the order of Melchizedek, and not reckoned according to the order of Aaron." But the other two citations of Aaron in the Epistle to the Hebrews employs his example to make important moral and doctrinal points, such as the idea that priesthood is as much a vocation, a divine calling, as is prophecy, and that pastoral authority as symbolized by Aaron's staff is as much a divine gift as the law. I am referring to Heb 5:4, where we are told: "No one takes this honor upon himself; he must be called by God, just as Aaron was." Yes, priesthood became hereditary after Aaron, but mere birth did not automatically qualify one for priestly ministry. In this regard see the long list of irregularities in Lev 21:16–23, which would disqualify a descendent of Aaron from ever functioning as a priest. And in Heb 9:3–4, we are reminded that it was not just the stone tablets of the covenant that were housed in the ark of the covenant but also a token of Aaron's ministry: "Behind the second veil was the tabernacle called the Holy of Holies, in which were the gold altar of incense and the ark of the covenant entirely covered with gold. In it were the gold jar containing the manna, the staff of Aaron that had sprouted, and the tablets of the covenant." This juxtaposition of the tablets of the law alongside Aaron's staff served as a graphic reminder that pastoral authority was as much a gift from God as was the law.

Some biblical exegetes have been very hard on Aaron. Indeed, some indulge in what almost amounts to a sort of priest bashing when they interpret the death of Aaron in the worst terms, that is, as a defrocking. In this regard note how the New American Bible translates Num 20:28: "Moses *stripped* Aaron of his garments"; while the New International Version says "Moses *removed* Aaron's garments." The Hebrew verb used here, *p-sh-t*, and its Septuagint Greek equivalent *ekduo*, do indeed have the sense of someone actively, purposefully undressing another, divesting another. And this can have the sense of degradation or punishment, as in Gen 37:23 when Joseph is stripped by his brothers; or when in Mark 15:20, Jesus is stripped by the soldiers. However, there is other literary evidence that makes it clear these same verbs can be used in a way that conveys a much more positive connotation. An example of this is 1 Macc 10:62. There the king orders his servants to divest Jonathan of his clothing. But they do this only to dress him in even finer robes. Moreover, H. Schmoldt, in his analysis of the various uses of the Hebrew verb *pasat*, says, "Within the cultic sphere, the verb *p-sh-t* occurs in connection with the transfer of office," and then offers as an example precisely the same text we are considering, the description in Numbers 20 of Moses taking the high priestly vestments from Aaron and putting them on Eleazer.[18] So too, Baruch Levine, in his commentary on the book of Numbers, interprets this verse as a transfer of office saying, "Moses divested Aaron of his garments and clothed his son Eleazar with them."[19] Indeed, in this matter of how to understand the death of Aaron, I suggest much can be learned by comparing it with the narrative of the death of Moses in Deuteronomy 34. Therein, we are told how, though Moses was not allowed to enter the promised land, God did concede him the blessing of seeing it from a distance (Deut 34:4). Surely there is a parallelism here with the fact that, though Aaron does not see the promised land, he is allowed to see his son Eleazar vested as high priest after him. There is also a significant parallelism in the fact that the period of national mourning at Aarons' death is the same as that for Moses (Num 20:29, cf. Deut 34:8). And it is probably equally important to note that in the rabbinic writings Aaron's death is considered a noble death. For example, the death of Aaron is related in the rabbinic commentary called *Midrash Petirat Aharon,* and described in the *Sefer Ha-Aggadah,* as a death of wonderful tranquility (see *Leviticus Rabbah* 10 and *Midrash Tannaim* 133,1).[20] And thus it is hardly gratuitous to think that Aaron's chest must have heaved with pride when he saw his son Eleazar vested as the new high priest or that the Hebrew people must have rejoiced when they beheld Eleazar descending from the mountain vested as the new high priest. True, the Bible does not record the people's reaction when Moses and Eleazar come down the mountain after Aaron's death. If there is no thunderous, joyful response, I believe it was only because their sense of loss at the death of Aaron was still with them. All the evidence suggests that, though Aaron was indeed flawed and far from perfect, he was nevertheless a great and good man. I suspect the same could be said of many a Catholic priest whose pastoral ministry was in no small measure a genuine blessing for his flock despite the fact that his "perfection" never even approached that of the angels. Am I wrong to suggest that with such priests, their reward, though it might not be *great* in heaven, will be *real,* nonetheless?

---

18. Schmoldt, "*pasat,*" p. 130.

19. Levine, "Book of Numbers," p. 486.

20. See "Aaron's Death" in *The Book of Legends: Sefer Ha-Aggadah,* pp. 94–95.

2

The Importance of Permanent Pastors

Jonathan, the Wandering Levite

"The National Fatherhood Initiative" is a nonprofit, nonpartisan organization. Its mission is to promote responsible fatherhood. It was founded in the United States in 1994 out of the conviction that fatherlessness has serious and damaging social consequences for children. To remedy or at least diminish those consequences, the organization sponsors several programs aimed at promoting involved, responsible, committed fathers. This program is designed to teach men what good fatherhood is and encourage them to become a good father. The Bible too contains lessons about fatherhood. And one of those bible lessons has particular relevance for our understanding of that aspect of priestly ministry which is spiritual fatherhood. The lesson I refer to is the story of Jonathan, the wandering Levite from Bethlehem, which is told in chapters 17 and 18 of the book of Judges. The story of Jonathan the Levite can help us to understand the enduring value of spiritual fatherhood and how threatened that value is in the contemporary Catholic Church, especially regarding the ministry of priests.

The most famous Jonathan in the Bible, the man most associated with that name, was the son of King Saul and the great friend of David. This Jonathan was an Israelite prince and valiant warrior, and his story is told in chapters 14, verses 18–20 of the first book of Samuel. However, that is not the Jonathan with whom we are here concerned. The Jonathan named in the title of this chapter of this book was not a warrior but a Levite. Moreover, this Jonathan traveled alone. The story of Jonathan the wandering Levite appears in two chapters of the book of Judges, chapters 17 and 18. He is described as the grandson of Moses, and thus lived a generation or two after Moses and Aaron, but long before the establishment of the Jerusalem temple with its centralization of Hebrew cultic worship. And this is why our Jonathan wanders. He wanders in search of employment as a priest at one of the numerous domestic sanctuaries that existed at that time. For example, the Bible mentions shrines at Nob, Mizpah, Gibeah, Shiloh, Bethel, Gilgal, Shechem, Manasseh, Dan, and Napthali.

One other thing the reader should know is that this Jonathan remains obscure, and intentionally so. As for his obscurity, the two chapters of the Bible in which Jonathan, the wandering Levite, appears, Judges 17 and 18, have no place in the lectionary of readings used in the Roman Catholic Church for Sunday and weekday Masses. Nor are those chapters found among the biblical selections that go into making up the Office of Readings in the practice of prayer that is called the Divine Office or Liturgy of the Hours. Nor have I been able to find any significant mention of Jonathan, the wandering Levite, in the writings of the early church fathers. The only references to Judges 17 and 18 among the patristics are brief explanatory references to such technical terms as *teraphim* (household god) in Judg 17:5. In Jerome's Letter 29, written to Marcella at Rome in the year 384, he explains the *teraphim* in Judg 17:5. So does Basil of Caesarea, in his work called Prologue to the Judges of God (before the monarchy, Israel was governed by figures called the judges). Then, there is a reference to Judg 18:2 in Gregory of Nyssa's *De oratione dominica* (On the Lord's Prayer). The reason for the neglect and obscurity of Jonathan, the wandering Levite, is most probably the moral ambiguity of his story. These many ambiguities make his story less than edifying, at least at first glance. Indeed, most modern exegetes admit its peculiar difficulties. For example, Jason Bray, in his study of religious traditions and cultic practices in the book of Judges, describes the Jonathan narrative as "one of the most unusual pericopes in the Hebrew Bible" and "there is no scholarly agreement as to what the story is about."[1] I, however, despite this consensus of ancient and modern exegetical dismay, hope to show the reader that the story is understandable. Moreover, working out of the principal that "all scripture is inspired of God and is useful for teaching" (2 Tim 3:16; cf. Rom15:4), and with a concern to treat not just high priests but lowly, simple priests, I hope to demonstrate to the reader that there is an important spiritual lesson and an important practical, pastoral lesson to be learned from an examination of this Jonathan's life and ministry.

A Priest Looking for Work

As I have said, our Jonathan's story is told in two narratives, or tales, from the book of Judges. One tale is told in chapter 17 and the other in chapter 18. Those two chapters form a sort of "diptych." Diptych, from the Greek *diptychos* meaning "folded in two," is an art term used to describe two panel paintings held together by hinges so that they can be viewed side by side. Let us consider the first story, the first panel of this biblical diptych. This first story begins with Jonathan leaving his home at Bethlehem and setting out looking for work. It tells us about how Jonathan came to

1. Bray, *Sacred Dan*, page 4.

serve as a priest at the home, the domestic shrine, of a man named Micah who lived in the mountain region of Ephraim. Indeed, this chapter focuses initially not upon Jonathan but upon Micah and his need for a priest. In Judg 17:1–12 we read:

> There was a man in the mountain region of Ephraim whose name was Micah. He said to his mother, "The eleven hundred shekels of silver over which you pronounced a curse in my hearing when they were taken from you, are in my possession. It was I who took them; so now I will restore them to you." When he restored the eleven hundred shekels of silver to his mother, she took two hundred of them and gave them to a silversmith, who made of them a carved idol overlaid with silver. Then the mother said, "May the LORD bless my son! I have consecrated the silver to the LORD as my gift in favor of my son, by making a carved idol overlaid with silver." It remained in the house of Micah. Thus the layman Micah had a sanctuary. He also made an ephod and household idols, and consecrated one of his sons, who became his priest. In those days there was no king in Israel; everyone did what he thought best.
>
> There was a young Levite who had resided within the tribe of Judah at Bethlehem of Judah. From that city he set out to find another place of residence. On his journey he came to the house of Micah in the mountain region of Ephraim. Micah said to him, "Where do you come from?" He answered him, "I am a Levite from Bethlehem in Judah, and am on my way to find some other place of residence." "Stay with me," Micah said to him. "Be father and priest to me, and I will give you ten silver shekels a year, a set of garments, and your food." So the young Levite decided to stay with the man, to whom he became as one of his own sons. Micah consecrated the young Levite, who became his priest, remaining in his house. Therefore Micah said, "Now I know that the LORD will prosper me, since the Levite has become my priest."

As for the meaning of this narrative, we must first consider its monarchist and temple bias. That is, this narrative aims at showing the miserable state of the Israelite nation before the advent of the monarchy, the social and religious chaos that prevailed during the time of the judges.[2] This intent is most clear from the statement in Judg 17:6: "In those days there was no king in Israel; everyone did what he thought best" and is a signal that we are reading a story that, in large measure, is meant to show the benefits of the monarchy. That is, Israelite society and its religious observances are portrayed as primitive and poorly organized. Micah and his mother are presented as devout Yahwists (the idol she has the silversmith make is one of Yahweh), but they are also presented as having little or no understanding of their religion. That his mother would have a statue made of Yahweh is not only a direct affront to the first

---

2. The domestic social setting is well treated in P. J. King and L. E. Stager's *Life in Biblical Israel* (Louisville: Westminster John Knox Press, 2001), pages 9–19, a section entitled "Micah and the Levite, A Day in Micah's Household."

commandment that bans all figurative representations of God (Exod 20:4), but it is also patent evidence that she is totally ignorant of that commandment. Moreover, Micah himself appears if not ignorant then totally uncomprehending of such basic Mosaic commandments as "you shall not steal" (Exod 20:15) and "honor your father and your mother" (Exod 20:13). It is also scandalous that Micah would keep small statues of "household gods," the *teraphim* that Saint Jerome had to explain to Marcella. This violates the first part of the first commandment (Exod 20:3) about having other gods besides Yahweh. And on top of all this, Micah is into do-it-yourself religion, previously appointing his own son to be a priest for him. But by the end of this story in Judges 17, hope arrives for both Micah and his mother in the person of Jonathan, the wandering Levite from Bethlehem. Here at last is a professional priest who knows how to do things right. Not only is there a sort of emotional crescendo in this story when Micah pleads with Jonathan saying, "Stay with me . . . be father and priest to me," but there is a sense of finality and peace in the final line wherein Micah says, "Now I know that the Lord will prosper me, since the Levite has become my priest." But in fact that line is only setting us up for the tragedy in the second story about Jonathan, the wandering Levite from Bethlehem.

A Priest under Pressure

This second tale about Jonathan the Levite is told in chapter 18 of the book of Judges. Like the first tale, this story begins by focusing not upon Jonathan but upon other characters who find themselves in need of priestly ministry. Here I quote that chapter in its entirety:

> At that time there was no king in Israel. Moreover, the tribe of Danites were in search of a district to dwell in, for up to that time they had received no heritage among the tribes of Israel.
>
> So the Danites sent from their clan a detail of five valiant men of Zorah and Eshtaol, to reconnoiter the land and scout it. With their instructions to go and scout the land, they traveled as far as the house of Micah in the mountain region of Ephraim, where they passed the night. Near the house of Micah, they recognized the voice of the young Levite and turned in that direction. "Who brought you here and what are you doing here?" they asked him. "What is your interest here?" "This is how Micah treats me," he replied to them. "He pays me a salary and I am his priest." They said to him, consult God, that we may know whether the undertaking we are engaged in will succeed." The priest said to them, "Go and prosper: the LORD is favorable to the undertaking you are engaged in."
>
> So the five men went on and came to Laish. They saw that the people dwelling there lived securely after the manner of the Sidonians, quiet and trusting,

with no lack of natural resources. They were distant from the Sidonians and had no contact with other people. When the five returned to their kinsmen in Zorah and Eshtaol and were asked for a report, they replied, "Come, let us attack them, for we have seen the land and it is very good. Are you going to hesitate? Do not be slothful about beginning your expedition to possess the land. Those against whom you go are a trusting people, and the land is ample. God has indeed given it into your power: a place where no natural resource is lacking."

So six hundred men of the clan of the Danites, fully armed with weapons of war, set out from where they were in Zorah and Eshtaol, and camped in Judah, up near Kiriath-jearim; hence to this day the place, which lies west of Kiriath-jearim, is called Mahaneh-dan.

From there they went on to the mountain region of Ephraim and came to the house of Micah. The five men who had gone to reconnoiter the land of Laish said to their kinsmen, "Do you know that in one of these houses there are an ephod, household idols, and a carved idol overlaid with silver? Now decide what you must do!" So turning in that direction they went to the house of the young Levite at the home of Micah and greeted him. The six hundred men girt with weapons of war, who were Danites, stood by the entrance of the gate, and the priest stood there also. Meanwhile the five men who had gone to reconnoiter the land went up and entered the house of Micah. When they had gone in and taken the ephod, the household idols, and the carved idol overlaid with silver, the priest said to them, "What are you doing?" They said to him, "Be still: put your hand over your mouth. Come with us and be our father and priest. Is it better for you to be priest for the family of one man or to be priest for a tribe and a clan of Israel?" The priest, agreeing, took the ephod, household idols, and carved idol and went off in the midst of the band. As they turned to depart, they placed their little ones, their livestock, and their goods at the head of the column.

The Danites had already gone some distance, when those in the houses near that of Micah took up arms and overtook them. They called to the Danites, who turned about and said to Micah, "What do you want, that you have taken up arms?" "You have taken my god, which I made, and have gone off with my priest as well," he answered. "What is left for me? How, then, can you ask me what I want?" The Danites said to him, "Let us hear no further sound from you, lest fierce men fall upon you and you and your family lose your lives." The Danites then went on their way, and Micah, seeing that they were stronger than he, returned home.

Having taken what Micah had made, and the priest he had had, they attacked Laish, a quiet and trusting people; they put them to the sword and destroyed their city by fire. No one came to their aid, since the city was far from Sidon and they had no contact with other people. The Danites then rebuilt the city, which was in the valley that belongs to Beth-rehob, and lived there. They name it Dan after their ancestor Dan, son of Israel. However, the name of the city was formerly Laish. The Danites set up the carved idol for themselves, and Jonathan, son of Gershom, son of Moses, and his descendants were priests for the tribe of the Danites until the time of the captivity of the land. They maintained the carved idol Micah had made as long as the house of God was in Shiloh.

The Priest as Mediator

If we are going to understand the meaning of this second tale about Jonathan, we must consider two things. First, in this story we are once again reminded of the chaotic haphazard character of life in Israel before the monarchy: individual priests wandering about looking for work and whole clans looking for a place to live. Let us also not forget the gross injustices that could be committed by such wandering bands. And, as in the previous story, the principal protagonist of the second story is not Jonathan but the Danites, one of the twelve tribes of Israel, noted from the beginning for their fighting qualities (see Gen 49:16–17. The Danites are indeed portrayed here as particularly ruthless, attacking and destroying "a quiet and trusting people." Their ruthlessness seems also to exonerate in some measure Jonathan's desertion of Micah, for when confronted by 600 Danite warriors he has little or no choice in the matter. The second thing that we must consider is a more decidedly antique element: the discernment of the will of God by the casting of lots, or what is technically called "sortition."

In the first story, we are introduced to the fact that Micah, in addition to the statues of Yahweh and the household gods, also keeps an ephod in his home shrine. The ephod is first encountered in the story of Aaron, where it is a priestly vestment, a vest worn over the high priest's linen robe. It features pockets that contain the *Urim* and *Thummim*, divining stones, that is, stones used to discern the will of God. While Exod 28:29–30 describes the ephod as a vestment worn by the high priest and used by him alone, later biblical narrative suggests that it was employed by more than just the high priest, indeed by other priests. Moreover, this last narrative suggests that later it was not just a vestment but an earthenware or metalware receptacle in which the sacred lots were stored. The latter is probably what is being referred to as kept by Micah at his domestic shrine.

As bizarre and primitive as it may seem to us moderns, the fact is that in the ancient world, and not just ancient Israel, the casting of lots served several religious, civic, and moral purposes. It was employed to solve practical problems, to insure justice, and to determine the will of God. In the Old Testament (OT), for example, the casting of lots was the method employed to determine the division of land among the Hebrew clans when they entered the land of Canaan (Num 26:55–56; Josh 18:6). It was the method used by Saul, in 1 Sam 14:40–41, for determining tactics and strategy for military engagement on the way into Canaan. It was the method used by the temple priests for the assignment of tasks therein (1 Chr 25:8) and for the selection of the scapegoat on the Day of Atonement (Lev 16:8). The casting of lots was still in use in the temple in NT times for the assignment of priestly duties (Luke 1:9, "when he was serving as priest in his division's turn before God, according to the practice of the priestly service, he was chosen by lot to enter the sanctuary of the Lord to burn incense."), and it was the method employed by the disciples of Jesus to determine which among them would take Judas's place in the apostolic college after his suicide (Acts 1:15–26).[3]

As for the theological relevance of the rite of sortition in this second tale of Jonathan, we should note that the story of Jonathan serves to make clear to us that biblical priests were never simply ministers of the cult, that is practitioners of rituals such as the offering of incense and sacrifices at an altar. Instead, and from earliest times, one of the principal responsibilities of Israelite priests was to serve as mediators of God's will. More precisely, the religious tradition of Israel as revealed at Sinai was that one must do more than teach people right worship; one must also help them discern the will of God in their individual lives. How this was done in earliest Israel is well-described by Aelred Cody in his "Excursus on Priesthood in Israel," which is an appendix to his commentary on the book of Ezekiel. After noting how priests were the ones who offered sacrifice at a shrine, Cody says:

> A function of priests which was more significant in this early period was their oracular consultation of God. If someone had a question to put to God, he did so by resorting to a priest. That God should be consulted through a priest, and should respond through a priest, is consonant with the role of a priest as a holy person. Since a holy person was, by definition, a person set apart for close contact with God and for the direct service of God, he could approach God to serve as a mediator between God and secular persons. Just as ordinary persons would present questions to an earthly ruler through his household

---

3. Israel was not unique in employing the casting of lots for moral purposes. Aristotle in his *The Athenian Constitution*, written in the year 350 BC, describes a number of ways in which sortition was used in the government of Athens. For example, in book 8, part 62, he describes how certain magistrates were chosen by the casting of lots, the logic being that this method functioned as a practical restraint on personal ambition and the power of wealthy patricians to buy votes. In book 8, parts 63–64, he describes how juries for the law courts at Athens were chosen by lottery. Indeed, its value as a moral option has not been lost in modern times. For there is the occasional war story of selecting a man for a dangerous mission by drawing straws of various lengths from a hat, the dangerous mission falling to the man who draws the short straw.

attendants or courtiers, or through his aide-de-camp when he was leading the army on an expedition, and receive answers from him, through the mediation of those who ministered to God as his priestly attendants, either at his residence, the sanctuary (Judg 18:5–7; 1 Sam 22:10, 13, 15), or in the field with a military company fighting for the cause of Israel, which was also Yahweh's cause (1 Sam 14:18–19, 36–42; 23:.9–12; 30:7–8)[4]

Note also Gisbert Greshake's comment in his *The Meaning of Christian Priesthood*: "In the Old Testament (above all in the earliest layers), priesthood is placed in a context wider than that of cult and sacrifice: the priest is above all the 'man of God,' who is specially near to God and is called and empowered by him to give others access to God in many different ways."[5]

Priesthood and Spiritual Fatherhood

After having thus explored the two peculiar historical elements in the story of Jonathan, the wandering Levite, we must now address two other aspects of his ministry that have much more immediate relevance for us today. First is the theme of spiritual fatherhood. More than once in Judges 17–18 we heard the title "father" applied to Jonathan. In Judg 17:10, Micah said to Jonathan, "Be father and priest to me." Later, in Judg 18:19, the Danite warriors say to Micah, "Be father and priest to us." Here it is important that we know something about the use of the term "father" in both Old and New Testaments.

No doubt, most often the title "father" in the Old Testament (OT) is used to refer to biological parenthood or historic ancestry. Indeed, in the OT the appellatives "my father" and "our father" are common designations for one's biological parent. In Gen 22:7, we are told, "As the two walked on together, Isaac spoke to his father Abraham. 'Father!' he said. 'Yes, son.' He replied." In Gen 27:18, we read, "Bringing them to his father, Jacob said, "Father!" "Yes?" replied Isaac." But in the OT the title "father" is also used to refer to historic, founding fatherhood, that is, the relationship of the Israelite tribes to their historic patriarchal chieftains, as in Gen 19:36–39 where Moab is called father of the Moabites and Ammon father of the Ammonites, or in Gen 17:4–5 where God says he will make Abraham "the father of many nations." In Psalms and in the Major Prophets, however, we see the title applied to God himself. For example, in Ps 68:5, "The father of orphans and the defender of widows is God in his holy dwelling." In Ps 89:7, we hear the prayer, "You are my father, my God, the rock, my savior." In the book of the Prophet Jeremiah, verse 31:9, God himself

4. Cody, *Ezekiel*, p. 257.

5. Greshake, *Meaning of Christian Priesthood* , p. 43.

says, "I am a father to Israel." And in Jer 3:4, we hear God reprimanding Israel for not acknowledging that relationship, "Even now you do not call me, 'My father.'" Similarly in Jer 3:19, with regret and disappointment God says, "I had thought: How I should like to treat you as my sons, and give you a pleasant land . . . you would call me, 'My Father,' I thought."

It is also important to note that in the OT the title "father," while most often applied to a biological parent, a dead patriarch, or God in heaven, was also occasionally used to indicate spiritual fatherhood. In 2 Kgs 2:12, we hear Elisha the disciple of the prophet Elijah, address his master saying, "My father, my father!" Later, after the assumption of Elijah and Elisha's having assumed the mantle of his great mentor, we hear the title "father " now applied to Elisha himself, and this time not by a humble disciple but by powerful kings. The title is implicit in the narrative of 2 Kgs 8:9, where we are told the messenger of the king of Aram, "Hazael stood before the prophet and said, 'Your son, Ben-hadad, King of Aram has sent me.'" And in 2 Kgs 13:14, we read, "When Elisha was suffering from the sickness of when he was to die, King Joash of Israel went down to visit him. 'My father, my father, he exclaimed.'"

Similarly, in the New Testament (NT) we find the title "father" often applied to Abraham, as in Matt 3:9, "we have Abraham as our father," or in Luke 1:73 and 3:8 and John 8:53, "our Father Abraham." So too Jesus uses the title "father" to refer to God himself as in Matt 5:45, "that you may be sons of your Father in Heaven" or in Matt 6:14, 6:26, and 6:32, as "father in heaven." But the doctrine of spiritual fatherhood is also strong in the NT, especially in the Pauline writings. Saint Paul employs the title numerous times; moreover, he not only approved of it but insisted upon the appropriateness of its used in reference to himself, indeed, as an apt description of his ministry so as to indicate his spiritual fatherhood, his relationship to those whom he nurtured in the faith. In this regard, see 1 Thess 2:11, "For you know we dealt with each of you as a father deals with his own children." In 1 Cor 4:15, we hear Paul say, "Even if you should have countless guides to Christ, yet you do not have many fathers, for I became your father in Christ Jesus through the gospel." In 1 Cor 4:14, he says "For this reason, I am sending you Timothy, who is my beloved and faithful son in the Lord." In Phil 2:22, Paul, when announcing his intention to send Timothy to them, once again refers to his relationship with Timothy by using the father-son metaphor, "But you know his worth, how as a child with a father he served along with me in the cause of the gospel." And in the Letter to Philemon, verse 10, Paul says, "I urge you on behalf of my child Onesimus, whose father I have become in my imprisonment." And in the opening paragraph of the Epistle to Titus we hear Paul refer to "Titus, my true son in our common faith" (1:4).No wonder then that, to this day, the most common title of respect for a priest in both Catholic and Orthodox Christianity is "father."

Clerical Titles

"Father" is the most common title of respect for priests, whether Catholic or Orthodox, in the United States, Canada, England, Ireland, France, South America, Africa, Russia, Greece, and Eastern Europe. For example, Russian Orthodox priests are titled *otets* (father), whether monks or pastors. While Greek Orthodox priests may have further titles of honor, such as archpriest or protopresbyter, they are still addressed as *papas* (father). It is interesting to note how the pope, though he bears several impressive titles, such as bishop of Roman, Supreme Pontiff, sovereign of the Vatican State, is nevertheless often addressed by the simple term, "Holy Father." Not only does the very word "pope" have the same etymology as "father," such that in Romance languages the word for pope, as in the Italian "papa," is identical to the affection term, "father." However, there are some variations. For example, in Italy and Spain, the honorific "father" or "padre" is used to refer to religious order priests, while the title "Don" or "Sir" is used to address a diocesan priest. In Germany, priests are addressed as "Herr" plus their title, as in *Herr Pastor, Herr Vikar,* or *Herr Doktor*. Only religious order priests are called *Herr Pater* (*pater*, Latin for father). Also, we should take into account the fact that the use of other titles of honor, often derived from secular honorifics, not only reflect the older aristocratic heritage of those European countries but tend to obscure the identity of spiritual fatherhood. For example, the honorific "Monsignor" ("my lord"), which *The Catholic Encyclopedia* (1912) tells us that "until the seventeenth century French nobles demanded of their subjects and dependents,"[6] is often bestowed upon priests either in conjunction with an ecclesiastical office of curial or diocesan responsibility (in the United States the title of monsignor used to be given quite regularly to senior pastors or pastors of major churches). Orthodox bishops are styled biblically as "your beatitude," that is "your blessedness," but the title of "excellency," used for Roman Catholic bishops in the United States, is originally a secular honorific given to the chief officer of the executive branch of state government. In England, archbishops often carry the ducal honorific of "your grace." And, of course, cardinals are addressed as "your eminence," which is a historical style of reference for high nobility but used of a cardinal to indicate his status as a "prince of the church." That bishops and archbishops, patriarchs and pope should indeed have such exalted titles can be understood as consonant with the hierarchical authority that they exercise in the church. But that

6. "Monsignor" by P. M. Baumgarten in *The Catholic Enycyclopedia*, Vol. 10, p. 510.

the term "father" is still the most appropriate title for a simple priest, the pastor of a parish, can be seen from the words of Yves Congar: "The parish priest has very great powers in the sphere of the interior personal life, "private life," we might say, if the term were not so ambiguous. But from the strictly social point of view, he has only a private, not a public power and authority. He is father far more than he is head. The hierarchical head of the parish is the bishop, not the parish priest. The parish priest, like the father of the family, can administer his community, give precepts, not laws: he can rebuke and correct paternally, but cannot coerce or punish."[7]

However, we must also contend with the fact that, since the Protestant Reformation, the title of "father" has come in for considerable criticism. This usually results from two criticisms. First, from those who reject any and all honorifics for Christian clergy by insisting we are all brothers (and sisters) in the faith. Secondly, by biblical literalists who object to any honorifics. As for the first complaint, the example of Augustine of Hippo is helpful. For example, when Augustine the presbyter wrote to Bishop Maximin, he saw no problem in addressing that bishop in both reverential and egalitarian terms, calling that bishop both "Lord" and "brother." Indeed, he begins the letter with the salutation, "To Maximin, my well-beloved Lord and Brother" and then goes on to explain to the bishop why there is no problem in his calling Bishop Maximin both "lord" and "brother."[8] So too bishops and pastors today have no problem addressing their congregation as "brothers and sisters." But a more formidable challenge to the use of reverential honorifics when addressing clergy comes from biblical literalists who will point to Jesus' words in Matt 23:8–10 where he warns against using any honorifics and in particular the title "father": "Call no one on earth your father; you have but one Father in heaven" (Matt 23:9). Such biblical literalism however only reveals a striking insensitivity to a form of speech very distinctive of Jesus—his use of hyperbole or prophetic exaggeration. In this regard, see especially Jesus' words in Mark 9:43–48 (with parallels in Matt 5:29–30 and 18:8–9):

> If your hand causes you to sin, cut it off. It is better for you to enter into life maimed than with two hands to go into Gehenna, into that unquenchable fire. And if your foot causes you to sin, cut it off. It is better for you to enter into life crippled than with two feet to be thrown into Gehenna. And if your eye causes you to sin, pluck it out. Better for you to enter the kingdom of God with one eye than with two eyes to be thrown into Gehenna, where "their worm does not die, and the fire is not quenched."

---

7. Congar, *A Gospel Priesthood*, p.158.

8. Augustine, *Letters*, p. 242.

If this passage was taken as literally as some insist Matt 23:9 should be taken, then we would, no doubt, expect to find many maimed among biblical literalists. But most people realize that when Jesus uses such dramatic terms he does not want to be taken literally. Rather, he wants to be taken seriously. And as for titles for Christian clergy, it is amazing that not even biblical literalists take seriously Jesus' saying in Mark 10:44, "Whoever wants to be first must be slave of all." Paul took Jesus literally in that regard. Witness the opening salutation of his Epistle to the Romans where he refers to himself as "a slave of Christ."

Irenaeus of Lyons (ca. 130–ca. 200) certainly saw no contradiction in calling both one's spiritual teacher and the Almighty God "father." I am referring to Irenaeus's treatise *Against Heresies* (bk. 4, ch. 41, para. 2), where he makes telling distinctions between natural and spiritual fatherhood. "For when any person has been taught from the mouth of another, he is termed the son of him who instructs him, and the latter [is called] his father. According to nature, then—that is, according to creation, so to speak—we are all sons of God, because we have all been created by God. But with respect to obedience and doctrine we are not all sons of God."[9] In this regard also, we might do well to consider Origen of Alexandria's deference to both bishop and priests in his *Homilies on Luke*. In homily 20, on Luke 2:49–51, "And he said to them, 'Why were you looking for me? Did you not know that I must be in my Father's house?' but they did not understand what he said to them. He went down with them and came to Nazareth, and was obedient to them; and his mother kept all the things in her heart. And Jesus advanced in wisdom and age and favor before God and man." Origen preached these homilies in Caesarea, perhaps around AD 234 or 240, to a congregation of catechumens and faithful. He says:

> Children, we should learn to be subject to our parents. The greater is subject
> to the lesser. Jesus understood that Joseph was greater than he in age, and
> therefore he gave him the honor due a parent. He gave an example to every
> son. Sons should be subject to their fathers; and, if they have no fathers, they
> should be subject to those who serve as fathers. But why am I speaking about
> parents and children? If Jesus, the Son of God, is subject to Joseph and Mary,
> shall I not be subject to the bishop? God appointed him a father to me. Shall
> I not be subject to the presbyter, whom the Lord's choice set over me? I think
> Joseph understood that Jesus, who was subject to him, was greater than he. He
> knew that the one subject to him was greater than he and, out of reverence,
> restrained his authority. So each one should realize that often a lesser man is
> put in charge of better men. Sometimes it happens that he who is subject is
> better than he who appears to be in authority. Once someone who enjoys a
> higher position understands this, he will not be lifted up in pride by the fact

9. Irenaeus, *Against Heresies*, p. 524.

that he is greater. He will know that a better one is subject to himself, just as Jesus was subject to Joseph.[10]

The translator has a note at this point: "Origen may have had his own relationship to the bishop of Alexandria in mind when he speaks about a lesser man put in charge of a greater, and, more generally, about the place of scholars and the learned in the Church with respect to bishops and presbyters."[11]

The Biblical Doctrine of Spiritual Fatherhood

Before we leave the question of proper titles for priests and Christian clergy in general, we do well to say something about the biblical doctrine of spiritual fatherhood. Biological and social paternity in ancient Israel was in large measure about authority and power, which were often used absolutely and arbitrarily. For example, the father in a Hebrew family, as undisputed head of that family, possessed the power of life and death over his children. Such is implied in the story of Abraham's sacrifice of Isaac (Gen 22) and is witnessed to by Jephthah's sacrifice of his daughter in Judges 11 (cf. Gen 38:24 and 2 Kgs 16:3). The law of Exod 21:7 supports the right of a father to sell his daughter into slavery. A father also had the right to arrange the marriage of his sons and daughters. Isaac sent Jacob to marry one of his cousins (Gen 28:1–2); Caleb decided on his daughter's marriage (Josh 15:16). In 1 Sam 18:17, King Saul offers his daughter Merob to David as his wife, even though it was in fact Saul's daughter Michal who was in love with David. However, those passages need to be tempered by others that show a more gentle, consultative aspect to the father as head of the family. Moreover, spiritual paternity in Israel as seen, for example, in the title of Yahweh as father of Israel, implied not power and authority but care and forgiveness. That is, the spiritual father assumes the role of teacher and provider. In this regard, see God's care for Israel in Exod 4:22; Deut 1:31 and 85; Isa 43:6. As for God's paternal compassion and forgiveness, see Ps 103:13; Jer 3:19 and 31:9, as well as Hos 2:1. One should also consider Jesus' parable about the merciful father, all too often called the parable of the prodigal son. Also one should consider the Letter of Paul to the Colossians 3:20–21, "Children, obey your parents in everything, for this is pleasing to the Lord. Fathers, do not provoke your children, so they may not become discouraged."[12]

---

10. Origen, *Homilies on Luke,* p. 86.

11. Ibid., footnote #14.

12. Cf. Pieter Arie Hendrik de Boer's *Fatherhood and Motherhood in Israelite and Judean Piety* (Leiden: Brill, 1974).

Another biblical concern about spiritual fatherhood, which is prominent in the tale of Jonathan, the wandering Levite, is that in the divine economy, human values are sometimes surprisingly reversed. That is, a spiritual father might be considerably younger than his spiritual son. In Judges 17 and 18, almost every reference of Jonathan also mentions his youth. For example, when he is first introduced in Judg 17:7, we are told, "There was a young Levite who had resided within the tribe of Judah at Bethlehem of Judah." When Micah asks Jonathan to be father and priest to him, we are told in Judg 17:10, "so the young Levite decided to stay with the man." And in the next verse, "Micah consecrated the young Levite, who became his priest." And in Judg 18:3, we are told that the Danite scouts, as they approached "near the house of Micah, they recognized the voice of the young Levite." Here it is important to observe the comment of Aelred Cody in his *History of Old Testament Priesthood*, "The supposed contradiction involved in Micah's asking a young man to be "a father and priest" to him is no contradiction at all: 'father" here is clearly an epithet not of age but of functional office, and perhaps even a title given regularly to priests."[13] It is interesting how this continues to be a pastoral problem. Look at 1 Tim 4:12, where Paul says, "Let no one have contempt for your youth." Also one would do well to note Ignatius of Antioch's Letter to the Magnesians, 3.1: "Now it becomes you not to presume on the youth of the bishop, but to render him all respect according to the power of God the Father, as I have heard even the holy presbyters have not taken advantage of his outwardly youthful appearance, but yield to him in their godly prudence."[14] Isidore, archbishop of Seville, who lived from 560 to 636, makes clear in his *De Ecclesiasticis Officiis* (bk. 2, ch. 7), "Presbyters are named such, however, by merit and wisdom, not by age."[15] Hugh of St. Victor (1078–1141), in his *On the Sacraments of the Christian Faith* (bk. 2, pt. 3, art. 11), "On Presbyters," says: "Presbyters should be the elders among the people of God, not so much in age of body as in prudence of character and in maturity of good conversation, as it is written 'Venerable old age is not that of long time, nor counted by the number of years, but the understanding of a man is grey hairs. And a spotless life is old age'" (Wisdom, 4, 8, and 9).[16]

But we have yet one more important lesson to be learned from the tale of Jonathan, the wandering Levite. And this lesson is about the importance of stability in the pastoral office.

13. Cody, *History of Old Testament Priesthood* , p. 53.

14. *The Apostolic Fathers* with an English translation by Kirsopp Lake (Cambridge, MA: Harvard, 1912), p. 199.

15. Isidore, *On Ecclesiastical Offices*, p. 78.

16. Hugh of St. Victor, *On the Sacraments*, p. 267.

Itinerant Preachers and Stable Pastors

There is no doubt that during the public ministry of Jesus, preachers of the gospel were all mobile, that is, itinerants or peripatetics, indeed, constantly on the move. For example, according to the gospels, Jesus did not just call the Twelve to follow him (Mark 1:16–20), but he also sent them forth on mission (Mark 3:13–14) and then, according to Luke 10:1, "the Lord appointed seventy-two others whom he sent ahead of him." Moreover, there is considerable evidence in such works as the Acts of the Apostles and the New Testament Epistles that after the death of Jesus the early church continued to send forth preachers and prophets. Indeed, the first missionary journey of Saint Paul begins with the account in Acts 13:1–3:

> "Now there were in the church at Antioch prophets and teachers: Barnabas, Symeon who was called Niger, Lucius of Cyrene, Manaen who was a close friend of Herod the tetrarch, and Saul. While they were worshiping the Lord and fasting, the holy Spirit said, 'Set apart for me Barnabas and Saul for the work to which I have called them.' Then completing their fasting and prayer, they laid hands on them and sent them off."

The eighth chapter of the Acts of the Apostles describes the itinerant ministry of Philip the evangelist who left Jerusalem to preach the gospel in Samaria, north of Jerusalem, and then on the Gaza Strip, south of Jerusalem, and eventually ended up in the shore town of Caesarea Maritima, situated far northwest of Jerusalem. The Acts of the Apostles also tells us of the wandering charismatic Agabus. In Acts 11:27, we are told, "At that time some prophets came down from Jerusalem to Antioch, and one of them [was] named Agabus." Later in Acts 21:10, we are told that while Paul and Luke were staying in the house of Philip the Evangelist in Caesarea, "a prophet named Agabus came down from Judea." However, the Acts of the Apostles and the New Testament epistles also witness to the fact that some of these same wandering apostles began to appoint local church authorities who did not roam but whose job was to direct or even preside over the local church. For example, in Acts 14:23 it is said of Paul and Barnabas that during their missionary efforts in Lystra and Iconium, "they appointed presbyters for them in each church." In the Epistle to Titus 1:5, we hear Paul say, "For this reason I left you in Crete so that you might set right what remains to be done and appoint presbyters in every town." When Luke in Acts 21:18 says, "The next day, Paul accompanied us on a visit to James, and all the presbyters were present," some exegetes have suggested this is an indirect witness: that while Paul and Barnabas and Philip the Evangelist went forth to preach the gospel, others meanwhile stayed in Jerusalem to preside over the local church there. As the early church continued to grow and become a prominent urban phenomenon, we hear less and less of such itinerant ministries as those of apostles, evangelists, and prophets; and we hear more of such domestic clergy as bishops, presbyters, and deacons. However, there is also evidence that these stable or settled domestic ministries began to have problems precisely with their stability. For example, the Letter of Clement to the Church at Corinth, a work written about the year AD 94 was sent precisely to address what the writer calls an "abominable and unholy sedition, alien and foreign to the elect of God" (1.1)[17]. It seems that there was a strong movement in the Church at Corinth to oust some of their presiding elders. And thus Clement admonishes the Corinthians in 44.4–5: "For our sin is not small, if we eject from the episcopate those who have blamelessly and holily offered its sacrifices. Blessed are those Presbyters who finished their course before now, and have obtained a fruitful and perfect release in the ripeness of completed work, for they have now no fear that any shall move them from the place appointed to them."[18] Other early church documents not only warn against the eviction of bishops and presbyters but also give witness of how some of these supposedly settled ministers began to wander. I am referring to canon 15 of the Council of Nicea, which was held in AD 321. Canon 15 was set forth precisely to address such situations:

> "On account of the great disturbance and the factions which are caused, it is decreed that the custom, if it is found to exist in some parts contrary to the canon, shall be totally suppressed, so that neither bishop nor presbyters nor deacons shall transfer from city to city. If after this decision of this holy great synod anyone shall attempt such a thing, or shall lend himself to such a proceeding, the arrangement shall be totally annulled, and he shall be restored to the church of which he was ordained bishop, or presbyter or deacon."[19]

The Council of Chalcedon in 451, in its canon 5, reaffirmed the stricture first set forth by Nicea, saying, "In the matter of bishops or clerics who move from city to city, it has been decided that the canons issued by the holy fathers [at Nicea] concerning them should retain their proper force." But the Council of Chalcedon went even further and insisted that there is no such thing as a "freelance" priest, indeed, it is essential to ecclesiastical order that clerics are ordained for a specific pastoral charge, and that pastoral charge should not be tampered with. Moreover, it should be noted that while canon 15 of Nicea sought to censure and control bishops, presbyters, and deacons who wander at their own will, the Council of Chalcedon found a way to put pressure on bishops by insisting that they should not ordain anyone without giving them a specific pastoral charge, a specific pastoral appointment. Thus

17. *The Apostolic Fathers*, p. 9.
18. Ibid., p. 85.
19. Tanner, *Decrees*, Vol. 1, p. 13.

canon 6 of Chalcedon reads: "No one, whether presbyter or deacon or anyone at all who belongs to the ecclesiastical order, is to be ordained without title, unless the one ordained is specially assigned to a city or village church or to a martyr's shrine or a monastery. The sacred synod has decreed that the ordination of those ordained without title is null, and that they cannot operate anywhere, because of the presumption of the one who ordained them."[20]

The History of the Stability of Pastors

During the Middle Ages, yet other problems arose regarding the stability of pastors. In the Middle Ages, peripatetic ministries continued—there were always missionary priests and bishops, and the Middle Ages would see the rise of a new phenomenon, the appearance of itinerant friars like the Dominicans and the Franciscans. Among the domestic or settled clergy there began to develop the phenomenon of absentee bishops and pastors. This was especially a problem with ambitious pastors or bishops who wanted to spend more time in the centers of power (the lordly manor, the king's court, or the archbishop's palace), than in their country parish or rural diocese. Thus reform-minded popes and councils took measures to counteract this trend. For example, the Fourth Lateran Council (1215) and the pope who summoned it, Innocent III, insisted on the permanent residence of parish priests. The Fourth Lateran was a reforming council and the most important of the councils held at the Lateran basilica. The Lateran basilica, Constantine's gift to the bishop of Rome, was the cathedral church of Rome and the official residence of the popes till 1308. Under the personal supervision of the pope who convoked it, Innocent III, himself a canon lawyer, the Fourth Lateran, besides defining the Eucharist and insisting on annual confession, is the council that in its Constitution 32, gave juridical strength to the idea of permanent pastors when it insisted on "a suitable and permanent vicar canonically instituted in the parish church."[21] Yet another problem affecting the stability of domestic clergy in the Middle Ages was the fact that powerful laity, kings, and nobles began to exercise authority over the local clergy with regard to both vesture and divesture. That is, not only did bishops and popes have to legislate against lay investiture of the clergy, but they also had to make strong provisions that pastors should not be removed except by church authority and even then only after church authorities followed precise and involved canonical procedures, namely a canonical trial. Here, the work of Pope Boniface VIII provided the decisive factor. Born Benedetto Gaetani in 1235 at Anagni, he became pope in 1294. He, like Innocent III,

20. Ibid., p. 90.
21. Ibid., p. 250.

was also a canon lawyer by profession. And indeed the third volume of the *Corpus Juris Canonici*, which was promulgated in 1298, is regarded by historians of canon law as a monumental achievement. In that third volume (in the section cap. "Unic. De capelli. Mon." in 6, 3, 18), he sought to protect pastors from removal by nobles. He did so by insisting that rectors who have the cure of souls should be irremovable.

The Council of Trent, arguably the greatest reforming council, no less than three times addressed the issue of resident, significantly present, indeed permanent pastors. Thus the reforming council of Trent in its sixth session issued its Decree on the Residence of Bishops and Others of Lower Rank. In session 7, the seventh article of the Second Decree on Reform, it insisted that local ordinaries "are to insure that there is careful provision that the care of souls is carried out in a praiseworthy manner by means of 'competent vicars, even perpetual' (*idoneos vicarious, etiam perpetuos*)."[22] But the Council of Trent also went on to decree (session 24, Decree on Reform, canon 13) that diocese should, wherever it is possible be divided into canonical parishes, be governed by *irremovable* parish-priests: "The holy council bids bishops, for the good spiritual state of the souls entrusted to them, to divide the people into separate and clear parishes and to assign to each their own proper and permanent who will be able to know them."[23] Implicit in the last words of that line is a reference to John 10:14, "I am the good shepherd, and I know mine and mine know me." The reason Trent gives for the requirement of permanency should not be passed over: a lifetime pastor will not only know his flock well, but his flock will know him because as far back as most in the parish could remember, it was the same pastor who had been there every Sunday and at many times in between. That is, it was he who baptized them, married them, buried them, and was at their side during domestic crises such as stillbirths or prolonged illnesses. Maybe he even assisted them outside their sacramental life, for example, during tough financial times. And if he had done these things well, he might even have become something of a patriarchal figure. For some young men in the parish, that pastor might have become even an iconic figure, a role model, with whom those young men might have begun to identify and whose ministry they might want to imitate.

Before going on to note what became of "permanent pastors" at and after the Second Vatican Council, it is perhaps worthwhile noting that the Protestant Reformer John Calvin, while he radically reconfigured the naming and ordering of Christian ministries, yet retained the importance of stability in the pastoral office. See his *The Institutes of the Christian Religion* (bk. 4, ch. 2, art. 7), which is entitled "The Pastor is Bound to his Church."

22. Tanner, *Decrees*, Vol. 2, p. 688.
23. Ibid., p. 768.

Let us proceed to see what happened to "permanent pastors" in the modern period. The residence of pastors, their stability, whereby they often spent their whole lives in one parish, was a common thing up until Vatican II. Indeed, as late as 1947 the French Dominican Yves Congar, in his book-length work on the relation between priest and people, *Sacerdoce et laïcat dans l'église*, spoke eloquently and knowingly as he wrote:

> The parish priests have the concrete charge of a people: they are not purely and simply apostles: they are also heads of a people, heads of Christendom. They have to reckon with a mass of concrete situations, habits, relations and influences. Moreover, they are bound, there in the midst of their people, to *stay*. They are not there just for today, they will be there tomorrow too, and for several years more.[24]

However, there were already changes afoot (and had been for some time), currents that sought to challenge the principal of pastoral stability, currents that would surface at the Second Vatican Council and after its conclusion. These would prevail. For example, although the Council of Trent had decreed that each parish was to have its own perpetual pastor, a class of removable pastors was introduced as a result of the Concordat with Napoleon in 1801. Two species of parishes were in fact constituted, even though the designations "parish" and "chapels of ease" were used in the Organic Articles of April 8, 1802, implementing the Concordat (articles 31, 61, and 63). A "chapel of ease" is a church building other than the main church of a parish. It is another building erected for the convenience of some parishioners, that is, so as to be more accessible to some parishioners than the main church. The rector of a "chapel of ease" was called a *deservant* and could be removed by the bishop at any time. But what must be seen is that the Holy See not only tolerated the practice of appointing movable pastors, but actually allowed it to spread. The Vatican was impressed that movable pastors seemed to facilitate the administration of a diocese, especially in troubled times (in the wake of the French Revolution or during the Kulturkamp in Germany), or in mission areas such as the United States where the church was just getting organized, or places like England where the church was just emerging from a period of prolonged persecution.

Another example is what happened with the restoration of the hierarchy in England. On September 11, 1853, the Oratorian Catholic priest, John Henry Newman, wrote a letter to his friend Ambrose St. John. Newman said, "I fear a good deal unpleasant has gone on between the cardinal and others."[25] The cardinal he was referring to was Nicholas Wiseman. The "others" to whom Newman was referring

24. Congar, *A Gospel Priesthood*, p.189.
25. Newman, *Letters and Diaries*, vol. 15, p. 423.

were the priests of Wiseman's archdiocese of Westminster. The bone of contention was the stability of parish priests. Indeed, the editors of Newman's letters, Dessain and Blehl, have a footnote attached to Newman's above quotation: "Many of the old Catholic priests were discontented that with the restoration of the hierarchy had not also come that check on Episcopal absolutism, irremovable parish priests."[26] On September 29, 1850, in the bull *Universalis Ecclesiae*, Pope Pius IX restored the Catholic hierarchy in England, which had been extinct since the death of the last Catholic bishop during the reign of Mary Tudor. For three hundred years Catholics in England had been ministered to first by archpriests and then by vicars apostolic. However, Nicholas Wiseman had prevailed upon the pope to omit any provision for lifetime pastorates because Wiseman wanted a totally free hand in his reorganization of the Catholic Church in England. The priests in England were so upset over this change that they agitated forcefully against Wiseman such that, when the First Provincial Council of Westminster met in 1852, one of its first decisions was to order for England the institution of irremovable rectors (pastors with the right of perpetuity of tenure). A similar thing had happened in the United States. In the initial organization of the church here, no pastors were given stability in office. Instead, it was felt that in such a young church, mobility of pastors was absolutely necessary. Even so, when the Third Plenary Council of Baltimore met in 1886, they legislated perpetuity of tenure for pastors in the Unites States.

Yet another incursion against the principle of stability occurred in August of 1910 when, during the pontificate of Pope Pius X, the Vatican's Consistorial Congregation issued the decree *Maxima cura*, which defined the causes and procedures for the removal of "irremovable pastors." Moreover, the new Code of Canon Law promulgated in 1917, while maintaining that a pastor had firm tenure, recognized degrees of stability (C454, §1). That is, those who enjoyed greater stability were called "irremovable" pastors; those with lesser degree were designated as "movable." The difference derived from the status of the parish, not from that of the individual person. Both classes of pastors could be removed for any cause that rendered their ministry harmful or inefficacious. In both situations a canonical process was required, but in the case of irremovable pastors the process was more complicated.

The Instability of Pastors Today

Episcopal impatience with the principal of pastoral stability reached a high point at Vatican II. For example, while the Second Vatican Council's Decree on the Pastoral Office of Bishops in the Church (*Decretum de pastorali episcoporum munere*

---

26. Ibid., , footnote #3.

in ecclesia), in chapter 2, article 31, does contain an endorsement of the principal of "stability" for pastors when it recommends terminating the distinction between "movable" and "unmovable" pastors, it opened up the possibility of considerable changes: "Each parish priest in his own parish should enjoy that stability of tenure in office which the good of souls requires. Accordingly the distinction between movable and unmovable parish priests should be re-examined and simplified. This should enable the bishop, while observing the just requirements of natural and canon law, to make better provision for the good of souls."[27] No doubt, the council invokes here no less than three motives for stability—in addition to the good of souls, also nature and canon law. However, after the Council, when the implementation of such directives were considered for practical application and the revision of the Code of Canon Law was undertaken, even further incursions against stability were legislated. For not only was the distinction between movable and irremovable pastors done away with, but the new code of canon law opened up limited, even short term, pastoral appointments.

This new attitude can be seen in the Apostolic Letter, *Ecclesiae sanctae* of Pope Paul VI, dated August 6, 1966. The form of this letter was that of a *motu proprio*, which means literally "on his own initiative," and is used to designate an administrative directive from the pope. This one carried the subtitle, "On the Implementation of the Decrees *Christus Dominus*, *Presbyterorum Ordinis* and *Perfectae Caritatis*." Section 20 gave three directives for implementation of *Christus Dominus*, number 31 regarding the "removal, transfer, and resignation of parish priests." I quote here only the sections pertaining to the removal and transfer of pastors:

1. The bishop may, without prejudice to the existing law concerning religious, lawfully remove any parish priest from his parish whenever his ministry, even without grave fault on his part, suffers injury or is rendered ineffective by reason of any of the causes recognized in law or for some other similar reason in the judgment of the bishop, provided that the form of procedure laid down for irremovable parish priests (canons 2157–2161) is followed, until the revision of the Code of Canon Law and without interference with the right of the Eastern Churches.

2. Should the good of souls or the need or advantage of the Church require it, the bishop may transfer a parish priest from his parish, in which he renders useful service, to another parish or to any other ecclesiastical office whatsoever.

It is interesting how Klaus Mörsdorf, in volume 2 of Vorgrimller's *Commentary on the Documents of Vatican II* expresses concern about this:

27. Tanner, *Decrees*, Vol 2, p. 934.

The reform desired by Vatican II aims at a further loosening of the law of procedure, so that a parish priest may be removed as soon as possible. The final solution of this difficult problem can be expected only in the course of the reform of canon law; it is to be hoped that the pastoral requirement of the stability of the parish priest will be harmonized with that of removing him when desirable. But in order to eliminate any arbitrary decisions it is indispensable to institute a legal enquiry which will give the parish priest concerned an adequate opportunity for defense.[28]

Promulgated in January of 1983, the new code went considerably beyond the Second Vatican Council in its allowing for the possibility of pastors being appointed not *in perpetuam* but for a term of office. Canon 522 of the current code of canon law, promulgated in January of 1983, reads: "The pastor ought to possess stability in office and therefore he is to be named for an indefinite period of time; the diocesan bishop can name him for a certain period of time only if a decree of the conference of bishops has permitted this."[29] In November of 1983, within months of the promulgation of the new code, the U.S. National Council of Catholic Bishops (NCCB) in their first conference meeting since the publication of the new code, approved a decree that diocesan bishops may appoint pastors for a limited period of time, with both the precise length of tenure and its possible renewability left to the bishop's determination. This decree was reviewed by the Vatican's Congregation for bishops on May 16, 1984. And on September 4, 1984, Archbishop Pio Laghi, the apostolic Pro-Nuncio for the United States, sent to the U.S. Bishops the following decree as amended and approved by Rome; the emendation being principally the specification of a six year term of office: "In accord with canon 522, the National Conference of Catholic Bishops decrees that diocesan bishops may appoint pastors to a six-year term of office. The possibility of renewing this term is left to the discretion of the diocesan bishop."[30] This decree was promulgated by the president of the NCCB on September 24, 1984.

It is interesting to read the opinions expressed regarding this dramatic change in the church's attitude toward the stability of pastors. In 1982, a year before the promulgation of the new code, Paulist Father John E. Lynch, a faculty member of the Department of Canon Law at the Catholic University of America, published an essay entitled "The Parochial Ministry in the New Code of Canon Law," which appeared in a canon law journal called *The Jurist*. *The Jurist* was at that time a twice-yearly review

---

28. Mörsdorf, "Decree," pp. 262–63.

29. *Code of Canon Law* p. 199.

30. See the "complimentary legislation for canon 522" which is on the website of the United States Conference of Catholic Bishops at www.usccb.org under the heading "Canon 522-Stability of the Office of Pastor."

edited by the Department of Canon Law at Catholic University. In his essay, Lynch makes clear the reason he can comment on the new code even before it was formally promulgated: as a member of a pontifical canon law, faculty was in on the drafting of the new code from the beginning. Lynch gives an evaluation, pro and con, of the new legislation:

> The limited rather than lifelong tenure is seen by some as a valuable way to assure pastoral evaluation and accountability. Their arguments in favor of a rotation of pastors generally hold: (1) it promotes the introduction of new and creative ideas in a parish; (2) it spreads different pastoral experiences and charisms over a large area; (3) it permits priests to become pastors at an earlier age. Opponents of a limited term point to the difficulties a pastor experiences in becoming acquainted with an entirely different scene and his frustrations at leaving programs uncompleted. They also think it prevents a pastor from knowing his people well and forces parishioners to adjust themselves to different pastoral orientations. An effective parish council, however, could ensure a large measure of continuity in parish projects.[31]

In 1985, just two years after the promulgation of the new code, the Canon Law Society of America published (Paulist Press of New York) a large one volume work entitled *The Code of Canon Law: A Text and Commentary*. It was edited by James A. Coriden, Thomas J. Green, and Donald F. Heintschel. In the 1985 commentary, part 2 of the code, "The People of God," and its subsection, chapter 6, "Parishes, Pastors, and Parochial Vicars," were the works of Joseph A. Janicki, JCL, the vicar for priest personnel of the Archdiocese of Milwaukee. After quoting in its entirety canon 522 to the effect that "the pastor ought to possess stability in office," Janicki emphasizes the novelty of this move: "Limitations on the term of an ecclesiastical office are not entirely new to church law. Certain offices, e.g., diocesan consultors, have always had a limited term. However, the term of office for pastors has never been limited before by the general law of the Church. Stability in the pastoral office has always been the norm so that the pastor could exercise the parochial office, get to know his people well, and receive adequate sustenance."[32] Regarding the policy change opted for by the U.S. Bishops' Conference, Janicki is very balanced, pointing out both the advantages and disadvantages of this policy:

> Limited terms of office for pastors make sense for various reasons. From the standpoint of the parish, it prevents the deleterious effects of long-term appointments, gives relative stability to parishes, and provides new leadership. For the priest the limited term of office can lessen the burdens of the pastorate,

---

31 Lynch, "Parochial Ministry," p. 397.

32 *The Code of Canon Law: A Text and Commentary (1985)*, p. 422.

permit a graceful exit at times from a difficult situation, prevent personal stagnation, and provide stimulation and job satisfaction. However, there are definite risks to a limited term of office. Moving is always difficult and can lead to an emotional crisis in a priest's life and unwillingness to undertake needed programs and decisions; furthermore, it may prevent the pastor from knowing the people well.[33]

In the year 2000, the Canon Law Society of America published yet a second effort at explaining the new code. Once again Paulist Press produced another large volume, this one entitled *The New Commentary on the Code of Canon Law*. It was again edited by Coriden, Green, and this time not Donald Heintschel but John P. Beal. In the *New Commentary* of 2000, the section of the code that treats of "Parishes, Pastors and Parochial Vicars" is written by John A. Renken, STD, JCD, vicar general and moderator of the curia, judicial vicar, and a pastor in the Diocese of Springfield, Illinois. Father Renken, in his remarks on the principal of stability, clarifies even further the change that has taken place and makes clear how much farther beyond the intention of the Fathers at Vatican II the revisers of the code have gone:

> The 1917 code had legislated that pastors should have stability, but they could be removed according to the norm of law. Not all pastors enjoyed the same stability. Some were designated as *irremovable* (enjoying greater stability) and others as *removable* (with less stability). Since pastors of either category could be removed, there was technically no such things as a true "irremovable pastor," but the process to remove an unwilling irremovable pastor (CIC 2147–2156) was more involved than that to remove an unwilling removable pastor (CIC 2157–2161). *Christus Dominus* 31 called for the elimination of the distinction between irremovable and removable pastors, and a simplification of the procedure to remover or transfer pastors for the good of souls. The conciliar decree, however, did not envision appointment of pastors for specific periods, which is new legislation for the church in the current code.[34]

As for the pros and cons of this momentous decision, Renken issues no opinion or response of his own but instead quotes at length the opinion of Paulist Father John Lynch, which we have already seen.

Yet another opinion is that of Antonio Sánchez-Gil. His commentary on canon 522 regarding the stability of pastors appears in *Exegetical Commentary on the Code of Canon Law*, which is a work of the Faculty of Canon Law of the University of Navarre, Spain:

> All in all, an opportune balance should be reached, with canonical equity and for the good of souls, between the freedom of the bishop and the stability

---

33. Ibid, p. 423.

34. *The New Commentary on the Code of Canon Law*, p. 693.

of the parish priest, whose legitimate interest in not being transferred too frequently and without being burnished a reason, must be protected against arbitrary decisions, which would be contrary to the judgment of the Church.

Consequently, it is necessary to overcome, on the one hand, a vision that too much favors the non-removability of an appointment for an indefinite time, as if the greater stability which it certainly produces is a personal right of the parish priest, forgetting his function of fostering continuity in pastoral work for the good of souls. On the other hand, it is also important to avoid an appointment for a determinate time be considered in practice as a mere juridical recourse to foster periodic removal of parish priest, at the exclusive service of a greater freedom for the bishop, forgetting the unquestionable usefulness that this kind of appoint has in case of a lack of priests. All in all, an opportune balance should be reached, with canonical equity and for the good of souls, between the freedom of the bishop and the stability of the parish priest, whose legitimate interest in not being transferred too frequently and without being furnished a reason, must be protected against arbitrary decisions, which would be contrary to the judgment of the church.[35]

Meanwhile, some pastors had registered their opinion. As early as 1986, for example, the Reverend Brian Byron, DD, a parish priest of Gladesville, New South Wales, Australia, had written a criticism of canon 522's treatment of the stability of pastors. It was published in the very first issue of the magazine, *The Priest*, Vol. 1, no. 1 (Autumn 1986). Ten years later he returned to that same theme publishing in the theological journal *The Australasian Catholic Record* 23 (1996) 304–22 an essay entitled "The Stability Necessary for a Parish Priest."

A much more recent assessment of this situation by an American priest is provided us by Father Mark A. Pilon, a priest of the Diocese of Arlington (Virginia) and, for a time, professor in the Systematic Theology Department at Mount St. Mary's Seminary in Emmitsburg, Maryland. Pilon wrote of this issue in his article "Pastors and Stability in Office," which appeared in *Homiletic and Pastoral Review* 106 (April 2006, 8–17). In this article, Pilon decries the degrading effect that terms of office have had on both bishops and priests, precisely in terms of its damaging effect on the notion of spiritual fatherhood: "The bishop becomes more like a CEO than a father in relation to his diocese, and the pastor is reduced to a manager of parishes. Moreover, and this has significant ecclesiological implications, the principle of continuity in parish life now necessarily and easily shifts to the lay employees, much as the continuity of the State Department resides in the career officers more than in a current Administration's political appointees."[36] Pilon then adds: "A theological shift, perhaps not yet fully articulated on the conscious level, has taken place in the

35. *Exegetical Commentary on the Code of Canon Law*, pp. 1300–1301.

36. Pilon, "Pastors," p. 13.

way bishops view the pastor in relation to his parish. In reality, he is no longer really understood to be a father or a spiritual shepherd as much as an administrator of ecclesial goods. Pastors are now like lower-echelon military officers who are moved every few years 'to keep them sharp.'"[37]

But the theological shift that has taken place is not just in terms of what Pilon calls "the way bishops view the pastor in relation to his parish." There has also been a very significant shift in the way the parish views its pastor. And this shift is perhaps even more ominous. More precisely, it can be doubted whether a Catholic pastor can ever achieve that spiritual paternity; instead he is reduced to little more than a temporary provider of religious services. And then there are such ironies as the fact that while in some parishes pastors come and go, lay assistants such as directors of religious education, budget keepers, and permanent deacons may stay on for years! No doubt, the older system did have its potential abuses. A permanent pastor might become authoritarian. But it also had its advantages, for in not a few cases the pastor became a revered patriarchal figure. One should not doubt the power of that sign. A revered pastor, respected by the parish, is an attractive role model for a young man considering a priestly vocation. An overworked itinerant pastor of three parishes, or an ambitious assistant to the bishop trying to impress the bishop with his endless energy in rushing around to three parishes, is comparatively unattractive. It is an old Thomistic axiom that "grace builds upon nature." And Jesus, a wise promoter of vocations, capitalized on that motive. The gospels relate that while Jesus told all his disciples, "Whoever wishes to come after me must deny himself, take up his cross, and follow me" (Mark 8:34; Matt 10:38; 16:24; Luke 9:23; 14:27), for the Twelve he added a significant incentive, "You will sit on thrones" (Matt 19:28; Luke 22:30).

Micah was part of a community, the family of his mother and son. So too the Danites had a strong sense of community in their clan identity. But there were problems in both those communities of family and clan that needed to be addressed by values from on high, by someone who could bring a strong sense of the transcendent, and that is why both Micah and the Danites appealed to Jonathan to be father and priest to them. And that is also why in neither case was Jonathan merely hired for a term, six years and renewable for six years more if everyone was satisfied. However, we do not know how long Jonathan lived. He might have lived to a great old age, as did some other biblical figures. But if he did indeed live to a great old age, another problem might have arisen, a problem which we treat next.

37. Ibid.

Knowing When to Retire

To be fair to both sides on the issue of permanent pastors, we have a historical account that can give us a deeper perspective, because it helps us understand the importance of provisions for retirement. It is an article that appeared in the August 21, 1914, issue of the *New York Times*. The article was entitled "Bomb on Cardinal's Train: Vannutelli Delayed on Journey to Rome." This article relates problems that arose following the death of Pope Pius X, and the preparations for an electoral conclave to decide on his successor. This article makes reference to three cardinals who were important in the process of the looming papal conclave. Two of these cardinals were very advanced in age and the other was not so old but suffered from infirmities of the mind. More precisely, the problems detailed in this article make it clear why it is important, at times, to have provisions for the retirement of clergy:

> Rome, August 10. Contrary to custom, the Cardinals up to noon had not received an invitation to go to the Vatican for the first meeting after the death of the Pope. The delay was due to the absence from Rome of Cardinal Serafino Vannutelli, Dean of the Sacred College, by whom such invitations must be issued.
>
> Cardinal Vannutelli was in Naples when he received the message from Cardinal Merry del Val announcing the grave condition of the Pope. He took the night train for Rome, but shortly after leaving Naples a dynamite bomb was exploded in the train, wounding ten of the passengers. The cardinal was not injured, but was obliged to wait for the next train.
>
> Cardinal Vannutelli is almost blind, is stone deaf, and is so weakened by nervous prostration, from which he has suffered for years, that it is possible he may not be able to perform the functions of his office, in which case Cardinal Agliardi, Sub-Deacon of the Sacred College, will take his place.
>
> Cardinal Martinelli, Prefect of the Congregation of Rites, is ill at Geneva. He is suffering from a mental affliction, and it is doubtful whether it would be possible for him to attend the Conclave, or, if he does so, whether he will be allowed to vote. The constitution governing the Conclave makes provision for incapacity on the part of a Cardinal through illness. In such case a deputation is sent to take the Cardinal's vote. The constitution, however, does not provide for mental incapacity.

It helps to know that Cardinal Vannutelli was eighty years old at the time, Antonio Cardinal Agliardi was eighty-two, and Sebastiano Cardinal Martinelli was sixty-four.

Of course, there are endless ironies: in July of 2009 the archdiocese of Boston raised the mandatory retirement age of priests from 70 to 75.

3

Money, Sex, and Ministry

Eli and His Sons at Shiloh

In September of 1999, while sitting in the reception area of my physician's office awaiting my annual physical, I was able to fill my waiting time by looking through the several magazine subscriptions that were on a table in front of me. When I picked up the September 13th issue of *Sports Illustrated*, the most popular sports magazine in America, I came across an article by William Nack and Don Yaeger entitled "Every Parent's Nightmare." It treated what it called "sporting culture's dirty little secret," namely, the surprising number of aggressive pedophiles among athletic coaches of adolescents. This did little to prepare me for the shock of reading the numerous reports of similar crimes perpetrated by priests, news of which surfaced in the press a few years later. But the Bible, in its narrative of the ministry of Eli and his sons at the Israelite shrine at Shiloh as recounted in the first book of Samuel, makes it clear to us that not just illicit sex but also financial greed were problems that plagued priestly ministry from its beginning. In this chapter we look carefully at this very early biblical narrative about these "sins of the clergy." In doing so, I believe the reader will see that this ancient narrative about the moral indiscretions of early Israelite priests has more than one lesson to teach Christian ministers today and Catholic priests in particular.

But before we proceed with Eli's story, I want to warn the reader: if you have been reading the chapters of this book consecutively, then brace yourself. For while our first two chapters introduced us to flawed but good priests, these stories of Eli and his sons reveal few redeeming virtues in these men. In fact, Eli and his sons represent a sort of moral nadir in our survey of Old Testament priests.

The sorry tale of Eli and his sons, priests at Shiloh, is related in the first four chapters of The First Book of Samuel. For the sake of brevity, I have selected four episodes from those first four chapters. I have given a title to each episode, which I believe brings out the essential drama in each. I have entitled the first episode "Eli's Sorry Judgment." This title refers to the narrative in 1 Sam 1:1–19 that recounts Eli's mistaken judgment of Hannah, a woman on pilgrimage to Shiloh. The second episode in the story of Eli and his sons at Shiloh has to do with the financial and sexual misdeeds of Eli's sons. These are set forth in two passages from The First Book of Samuel, chapter 2:12–17 and chapter 2:22–25. The second drama from these two passages is entitled "Eli's Sorry Sons." The third episode of Eli's life has to do with not just a wrong but a fatal judgment he made. I have entitled the episode "Eli's Sorry Response to a National Crisis." I have given the fourth and final episode a self-explanatory title: "Eli's Sorry Death: Aged, Blind, and Fat." This episode is set forth in 1 Sam 4:12–21.

Eli's Sorry Misjudgment

The first episode to consider is related in 1 Sam 1:1–19:

> There was a certain man from Ramathaim, Elkanah by name, a Zuphite from the hill country of Ephraim. He was the son of Jeroham, son of Elihu, son of Tohu, son of Zuph, an Ephraimete. He had two wives, one named Hannah, the other Peninnah; Peninnah had children, but Hannah was childless. This man regularly went on pilgrimage from his city to worship the LORD of hosts and to sacrifice to him at Shiloh, where the two sons of Eli, Hophni and Phinehas, were ministering as priests of the LORD. When the day came for Elkanah to offer sacrifice, he used to give a portion each to his wife Peninnah and to all her sons and daughters, but a double portion to Hannah because he loved her, though the LORD had made her barren. Her rival, to upset her, turned it into a constant reproach to her that the LORD had left her barren. This went on year after year; each time they made their pilgrimage to the sanctuary of the LORD, Peninnah would approach her, and Hannah would weep and refuse to eat. Her husband used to ask her: "Hannah, why do you weep, and why do you refuse to eat? Why do you grieve? Am I not more to you than ten sons?"
>
> Hannah rose after one such meal at Shiloh, and presented herself before the LORD; at the time, Eli the priest was sitting on a chair near the doorpost of the LORD's temple. In her bitterness she prayed to the LORD, weeping copiously, and she made a vow, promising: "O LORD of hosts, if you look with pity on the misery of your handmaid, if you remember me and do not forget me, if you give your handmaid a male child, I will give him to the LORD for as long as he lives; neither wine nor liquor shall he drink, and no razor shall ever touch his head." As she remained long at prayer before the LORD, Eli watched her mouth, for Hannah was praying silently; though her lips were moving, her voice could not be heard. Eli, thinking her drunk, said to her, "How long will you make a drunken show of yourself? Sober up from you wine!" "It isn't that, my lord," Hannah answered. "I am an unhappy woman. I have had neither wine nor liquor; I was only pouring out my troubles to the LORD. Do not think your handmaid a ne'er-do-well; my prayer has been prompted by my deep sorrow

and misery." Eli said, "Go in peace, and may the God of Israel grant you what you have asked of him." She replied, "Think kindly of your servant," and left. She went to her quarters, ate and drank with her husband, and no longer appeared downcast. Early the next morning they worshiped before the LORD, and then returned to their home in Ramah.

In order that this biblical episode might be understandable to the modern reader, we must first say something about monogamy and polygamy in Israel of Eli's day. From the opening lines of this narrative, it is obvious that one of the figures in this story, Elkanah, has two wives. While there is considerable evidence that suggests polygamy was allowed in Israel before the Babylonian exile, there is also much evidence that suggests it was allowed only as a moral expediency, that is, as an indulgence for a wealthy man or as a provision for the husband of a barren wife. As for its indulgence by a wealthy man, we have evidence that the kings of Israel had more than one wife. For example, in 2 Sam 2:2, we are told that when David went up to Hebron to be anointed king, "David went up there accompanied by his two wives." And a few chapters later, in 2 Sam 5:13, we are told "David took more concubines and wives in Jerusalem after he had come from Hebron." And in 1 Kgs 11:3, we are told of King Solomon, David's son, "He had seven hundred wives of princely rank." However, most biblical commentators agree that "seven hundred" is hyperbole, a gross exaggeration, meant to suggest Solomon's enormous wealth and paramount social importance. Moreover, there are numerous passages in the OT that make it clear monogamy was the moral ideal from the beginning. For example, Gen 2:18–25, the account of God's creation of Eve as "a suitable partner of Adam," is meant to teach that God originally intended marriage to be monogamous. And the narrative in Genesis 4, wherein Cain's sons begin to take more than one wife, is meant to suggest that polygamy is evidence of the deterioration of humankind from that original ideal. Consider also the fact that most commentators see Deut 17:17 as a protest against the idea that a king should have many wives: "Neither shall he [the king over you] have a great number of wives, lest his heart be estranged." And throughout the Wisdom literature of the Old Testament monogamy is again and again proposed as the ideal state. Indeed, it is a recurrent theme in the book of Proverbs. Prov 12:4 tells us "a worthy wife is the crown of her husband." Prov 19:14 proclaims "a prudent wife is [a blessing] from the LORD." The book of Proverbs ends in an extended, poetic celebration of the ideal wife, Prov 31:10–31. But most important for our concerns, namely the narrative of Eli's sorry misjudgment in 1 Sam 1:1–19, it is apparent that the reason Elkanah has two wives is precisely because Hannah was barren and thus could not provide him with children.

The modern reader must next understand the significance of the shrine at Shiloh. As we have already noted in the introduction to chapter 2 herein, in early Israelite history before the construction of the temple at Jerusalem, there were several religious shrines in Israel. For example, there were shrines not just at Shiloh but also at Nob, Mispah, Gibeah, Bethel, Gilgal, just to name a few. Eli was the chief priest at the sanctuary of Shiloh some time during the period of "The Judges." Though neither Eli's ancestry nor progeny is clearly outlined in the Bible, it appears that Eli was descended from Aaron's fourth son, Ithamar. Indeed, the time period of the ministry of Eli and his sons is indicated by the fact that his sons, Hophni and Phinehas, have Egyptian names. Hophni is Egyptian for "tadpole" and Phinehas means "the Nubian." Nubia is the region in the south of Egypt that extends along the Nile into Northern Sudan. But among the various shrines in Israel during the time of Eli and his sons, Shiloh, a small village about ten miles north of Jerusalem, had a certain measure of prestige because it housed the most important relic of the exodus, the ark of the covenant. Thus, Shiloh was considered the central shrine for the Israelite confederacy of twelve tribes.

Also, it is important that the modern reader understand the significance of the phrase, "Eli the priest was sitting on a chair near the doorpost of the Lord's temple." It was a priest's duty to guard the entrance to the shrine, to make sure that none should enter who were ritually unclean. Indeed, many important things took place at the entrance to holy places, such as the tent of meeting. For example, Lev 16:7 and Lev 19:15 describe how sacrifices are brought there to be given to the priest, and Num 6:10 and 18 describe how the Nazirite fulfilled his vow before the priest at the entrance to the tent of meeting. Ps 14:1 begins with a poetic evocation of a pious Israelite's entrance into the holy place: "O Lord, who shall sojourn in your tent? . . . He who walks blamelessly and does justice." And in 1 Chronicle 26, we read how Solomon assigned an entire class of Levitical gatekeepers to guard the entrance of his new temple at Jerusalem. Also, it could be argued that it is a sad judgment against Eli that he is sitting rather than standing at the doorpost, relaxing rather than vigilant (cf. Abraham in Gen 181, sitting in the shade at the entrance of the tent that was *his home*). But there is yet another line that is far more damning of Eli's ministry, namely his response when he sees Hannah praying, "Eli, thinking her drunk." This is the sorry misjudgment that I refer to in the title of this section. And the gravity of this misjudgment should not be underestimated, for moral judgment was an important work of every priest.

Eli lived in "the period of 'the Judges.'" The descriptive title "the Judges" is used to indicate one of the principal functions of the various tribal chieftains, charismatic or heroic figures, who provided leadership among the Hebrew people during the time from their first settlement in the land of Canaan to the establishment of a monarchy in Israel, a period of time stretching from approximately 1280 to 1045 BC. That Eli was both a priest and one of the judges of Israel is not surprising, for there is provision for this in Deut 17:8–9 where we read: "If in your own community there is a case at issue which proves too complicated for you to decide, in a matter of blood-shed or of civil rights or of personal injury, you shall then go up to the place which the LORD, your God, chooses, to the levitical priests or to the judge who is in office at that time. They shall study the case and then hand down to you their decision."

Eli's Sorry Sons

Now we can proceed to consider the second episode in the story of Eli and his sons at Shiloh. This second episode contains not one but two moral infractions on the part of Eli's sons. The first moral infraction is related in 1 Sam 2:12–17:

> Now the sons of Eli were wicked; they had respect neither for the LORD nor for the priests' duties toward the people. When someone offered a sacrifice, the priest's servant would come with a three-pronged fork, while the meat was still boiling, and would thrust it into the basin, kettle, caldron, or pot. What-ever the fork brought up, the priest would keep. That is how all the Israelites were treated who came to the sanctuary at Shiloh. In fact, even before the fat was burned, the priest's servant would come and say to the man offering the sacrifice, "Give me some meat to roast for the priest. He will not accept boiled meat from you, only raw meat." And if the man protested to him, "Let the fat be burned first as is the custom, then take whatever you wish," he would reply, "No, give it to me now, or else I will take it by force." Thus the young men sinned grievously in the presence of the LORD; they treated the offerings to the LORD with disdain.

In order to understand this passage we need to know something about clergy com-pensation in early Israel. When the Hebrews entered Canaan, the promised land, portions of that land were allotted to each tribe except for the priestly tribe, that is, the tribe of Levi. And thus provision was made that the tribe of Levi, instead of living off the land, would live off of a portion of each sacrificial offering. This is put eloquently in Deut 18:1–2: "The whole priestly tribe of Levi shall have no share in the heritage with Israel; they shall live on the oblations of the LORD and the portions due to him. Levi shall have no heritage among his brothers; the LORD himself is his heritage, as he has told him." The precise allotment of portions is set forth in detail in Deut 18:3–8 and Lev 7:28–36. For example, in Deut 18:3 we read: "from those who are offering a sacrifice, whether the victim is from the herd or from the flock, the priest shall receive the shoulder, the jowls and the stomach." And, in Exod 30:11–16 (cf. Nah 10:33) we find that there was also a poll tax that every Israelite twenty years and older was required to contribute, not for the direct support of the priests but for the support of what was called "the meeting tent" or "tabernacle in the wilderness," and later the temple at Jerusalem (indeed, in Jesus' time this tax was known as "the temple tax," see Matt 17:24–25). This revenue was used to purchase oil for the lamps that burned in "the meeting tent' (and later, the temple), as well as for the oil used for anointing priests and for purchase of incense and other liturgical appurtenances such as priestly vestments.

But there is yet a second part of the tale of "Eli's Sorry Sons," and this second part is told in 1Sam 2:22–25:

> When Eli was very old, he heard repeatedly how his sons were treating all Israel [and that they were having relations with the women serving at the entry of the meeting tent]. So he said to them: "Why are you doing such things? No, my sons, you must not do these things! It is not a good report that I hear the people of the LORD spreading about you. If a man sins against another man, one can intercede for him with the LORD; but if a man sins against the LORD, who can intercede for him?" But they disregarded their father's warning, since the LORD had decided on their death.

Of this narrative it is important that we note the significance of the bracketed portion in the very first sentence that says, "When Eli was very old, he heard repeatedly how his sons were treating all Israel [and that they were having relations with the women serving at the entry of the meeting tent]." The editors of the New American Bible have set a portion of that sentence in brackets because while it is found in Hebrew manuscripts, it is missing in the most important Greek translation of the Hebrew Scriptures, the Septuagint, made between 285 and 246 BC. Thus, some exegetes regard this sentence as a later interpolation into the Hebrew text. If it is indeed part of the original Hebrew text, then it is most probably a reference to women who performed menial duties in the premonarchical (pre-temple) Israelite sanctuaries. Those who argue for this interpretation often cite Exod 38:8, where Moses' instructions to the Hebrew people regarding the tabernacle in the desert include a reference to "the women who serve at the entrance of the meeting tent." Some other scholars, however, argue its meaning is even more offensive than casual promiscuity. That is, some scholars argue it might even be a reference to Hophni's and Phinehas's having allowed temple prostitution. There is reference to such in 2 Kgs 23:7, where it describes part of the religious reform undertaken by Josiah, king of Judah 640–609 BC, as "He tore down the apartments of the cult prostitutes which were in the temple of the LORD." However, Josiah's reform occurred several centuries after Hophni and Phinehas, and thus some scholars use this as evidence that it is indeed a later interpolation meant to further vilify Hophni and Phinehas. If that is true, then it is an example of "piling on." "Piling on" is a term from American football referring to an illegal play where several players jump on the player with the ball after he's been tackled. The offending team is penalized for such conduct. Later in this chapter, when we consider the relevance of this narrative for us today, we shall return to this theme of false accusations. But now we continue with the tale of Eli and his sons.

Eli's Sorry Response to a National Crisis

The third episode in the tale of Eli and his sons at Shiloh deals with Eli's response to a national crisis. During the time that Eli was chief priest at Shiloh, Israel entered into in a desperate struggle with their neighbors, the Philistines. This struggle came to a crisis point when the Israelite army encamped at a place called Ebenezer while a Philistine force encamped nearby at a place called Aphek. What happened next is related in 1 Sam 4.1–11:

> At that time, the Philistines gathered for an attack on Israel. Israel went out to engage them in battle and camped at Ebenezer, while the Philistines camped at Aphek. The Philistines then drew up in battle formation against Israel. After a fierce struggle Israel was defeated by the Philistines, who slew about four thousand men on the battlefield. When the troops retired to the camp, the elders of Israel said, "Why has the Lord permitted us to be defeated today by the Philistines? Let us fetch the ark of the Lord from Shiloh that it may go into battle among us and save us from the grasp of our enemies.
>
> So the people sent to Shiloh and brought from there the ark of the Lord of hosts, who is enthroned upon the cherubim. The two sons of Eli, Hophni and Phinehas, were with the ark of God. When the ark of the Lord arrived in the camp, all Israel shouted so loudly that the earth resounded. The Philistines, hearing the noise of shouting, asked, "What can this loud shouting in the camp of the Hebrews mean?" On learning that the ark of the Lord had come into the camp, the Philistines were frightened. They said, "Gods have come to their camp." They said also, "Woe to us! This has never happened before. Woe to us! Who can deliver us from the power of these mighty gods? These are the gods that struck the Egyptians with various plagues and with pestilence. Take courage and be manly Philistines; otherwise you will become slaves to the Hebrews, as they were your slaves. So fight manfully!" The Philistines fought and Israel was defeated; everyman fled to his own tent. It was a disastrous defeat, in which Israel lost 30,000 foot soldiers. The ark of God was captured, and Eli's two sons, Hophni and Phinehas, were among the dead.

Not only did Eli's sons, Hophni and Phinehas, escort the ark to the battlefield for the second assault on the Philistines, which became a disastrous rout of the Isaraelites, but the sons of Eli were counted among the dead. Even worse, the Philistines captured the ark and brought it to the temple of Dagon in Ashdod.

There can be little doubt that in all three of these episodes the central figure is Eli. Moreover, the central message is that Eli was a profound failure both as a priest and as a judge. Indeed, concern for the cult is not enough; a good priest must also exercise moral insight and moral judgment and act upon those. A priest cannot be concerned only with the proprieties of the cult, with getting right ritual observances, but must also be concerned to observe and discern people and their lives. But the problem with Eli is that he misjudged grossly. He showed no aptitude for discernment or moral vision. He misjudged Hannah's weeping as drunkenness; he did not exercise good oversight of his sons; indeed, he *overlooked* rather than oversaw their conduct; later still he foolishly conceded to the request to take the ark into battle. And the loss of the ark of the covenant is the culminating lesson, for its loss makes clear to us how moral weakness in the priesthood can lead to disaster for God's people. And that is why Eli's death is presented in so ignominious a fashion.

Eli's Sorry Death: Aged, Blind, and Fat

In 1Sam 4:12–21, we are told of what happened when Eli was informed of the death of his sons and the capture of the ark of God:

> A Benjaminite fled from the battlefield and reached Shiloh that same day, with his clothes torn and his head covered with dirt. When he arrived, Eli was sitting in his chair beside the gate, watching the road, for he was troubled at heart about the ark of God. The man, however, went into the city to divulge his news, which put the whole city in an uproar. Hearing the outcry of the men standing near him, Eli inquired, "What does this commotion mean?" (Eli was ninety-eight years old, and his eyes would not focus, so that he could not see.) The man quickly came up to Eli and said, "It is I who have come from the battlefield; I fled from there today." He asked, "What happened, my son?" and the messenger answered: "Israel fled from the Philistines; in fact, the troops suffered heavy losses. Your two sons, Hophni and Phinehas, are among the dead, and the ark of God has been captured." At this mention of the ark of God, Eli fell backward from his chair into the gateway; since he was an old man and heavy, he died of a broken neck. He had judged Israel for forty years. His daughter-in-law, the wife of Phinehas, was with child and at the point of giving birth.

That is, when news of the disaster reached Eli, the ninety-eight-year-old stout, blind priest—sitting by the road in dread anticipation—fell over backward and broke his neck. Because Eli's sons, Hophni and Phinehas, both died in the battle at Aphek,

Eli's line survived only in a grandson, Ichabod, who was born to Phinehas's wife shortly after the battle. Though other descendants are mentioned, namely, Ahijah, Ahimelech, and Abiathar, and the priesthood of Shiloh continued as custodians of the shrine of the ark of the covenant, even when it was moved to Jerusalem, nevertheless, Eli's progeny came to an end when Abiathar was deposed from the priesthood by Solomon (1Kgs 2:27).

At the end of this chapter we shall return to this theme of the moral blindness of Eli and his failure to exercise careful oversight of his priestly sons. However, at this time I want to focus instead upon the lessons to be learned from not just from the failures of Eli but also from the failures of his sons, their sins regarding money and sex. I believe these narratives of Eli and his sons have important lessons to teach us regarding money, sex, and clerical oversight. But before we draw any conclusions, it is important that we see how these issues have been addressed in Christian history.

Clergy Compensation in the Time of Jesus

Earlier in this chapter we noted the provisions that the Mosaic law made for the financial support of Israel's priests, the stipendiary part of the sacrificial offerings and the tax for the support of the meeting tent and later the temple. In Jesus' time, there had developed a considerable variation and contrast in the "economy" of worship in Israel, that is, between financial support for the high priest, the chief priests, the simple priests, and the rabbis. Jesus' words in John 2:16, "stop making my Father's house a market place" are a critique of the fact that the high priests and the chief priests who lived in or near Jerusalem had turned the selling of sacrificial animals into a lucrative industry (we see this in detail in my chapter on Caiaphas). Meanwhile, the simple priests who lived at a distance and only served two weeks in the year at the temple found they had to become resourceful and find occupations for themselves. Deut 14:22–27 not only detailed precisely what that should be, but it ended in verse 27 with the admonition, "Do not neglect the Levite who belongs to your community, for he has no share in the heritage with you." Nevertheless, hundreds of years later Sirach (Sir 7:31) felt a need to repeat the admonition: "Honor god and respect the priest; give him his portion as you have been commanded." We have several witnesses that attest to the fact that this obligation was, at times, ignored. For example, Philo of Alexandria, sometimes called Philo Judaeus, in his *The Special Laws* (bk. 1, chs. 153–55), says that many people neglected to pay the traditional tithe due to priests.[1] Flavius Josephus, in his *Antiquities of the Jews* (bk.

---

1. Philo, *The Works*, pp. 546-549, especially p. 548: "But the neglect of some persons (for it is not right to blame everyone) is the cuase of poverty to those who have been dedicated to God."

20, ch. 9, sec. 2), actually claims that some priests died from hunger because the clerical tithes were neglected.[2] Because Josephus himself was of priestly descent, this could be an example of exaggerated clerical bitterness rather than precise historical remembrance. As for the rabbis in Jesus' time, they were all self-supporting lay preachers. In *The Mishnah*'s tractate *Aboth* 4:5, Rabbi Zadok (about AD 50) is quoted as having warned, "Make not the words of the Law a spade wherewith to dig."[3] And J. D. Eisenstein, employing references from tractates in the Jerusalem Talmud, gives us a precise account of how rabbis in ancient times supported themselves:

> The rabbis invariably had their private occupations. The elder Hillel earned a half-denarius a day as a wood-chopper . . . Shammai was a builder (Shab. 31a), Rabbi Joshua, a blacksmith (Ber. 281), Rabbi Jose, a tanner (Shab. 49a), Abba Hoshaiah of Turya, a laundryman . . . Rabbi Hanina and Rabbi Oshaya, shoemakers; Karna, a wine-taster . . . Zemina, a tailor, and Hisda and Pappa were brewers of mead . . . The rabbis were indirectly assisted by the preference given to them in their trades and business enterprises. Thus when Rabbi Dimi of Nehardea imported a vessel-load of dried figs, the president of the community gave order to "hold the market" for Rabbi Dimi to allow him to dispose of his goods first. (B.B. 22A)[4]

It is possible to argue that the Christian tradition of clergy compensation began with Jesus himself and, moreover, that it was a radical departure from all that we have seen. That is, we can cite evidence that Jesus intended those of his disciples who would work as preachers and teachers should be supported not by ancillary professional occupations but rather by free-will offerings from their hearers. For example, according to the Synoptic Gospels, Jesus, when he first sent out the Twelve on mission, instructed them to travel light, that is, to take no money, no change of clothing, not even any food provisions. Instead they were to live on whatever hospitality was given them by their hearers. For example, in Mark 6:7–12 we read:

> He summoned the Twelve and began to send them out two by two and gave them authority over unclean spirits. He instructed them to take nothing for the journey but a walking stick—no food, no sack, no money in their belts. They were, however, to wear sandals but not a second tunic. He said to them, "Wherever you enter a house, stay there until you leave from there. Whatever place does not welcome you or listen to you, leave there and shake the dust off your feet in testimony against them." So they went off and preached repentance.

2. Joseph, *Complete Works*, p. 424: "Some of the priests, that of old were want to be supported with those tithes, died for want of food."

3. *Mishnah*, p. 453.

4. *Jewish Encyclopedia*, Vol. 10, pp. 294–95.

It is interesting to speculate about the rationale behind these precise instructions regarding religious mission. For example, that Jesus sends his disciples out "two by two" might be simply for safety's sake. There is, after all, strength in numbers. But it could also be for companionship; time on the road passes more quickly when one has a companion. But it also could be for the sake of honesty: one can correct the other if the other is not properly representing the gospel as Jesus first presented it to the Twelve. For our interests, the instruction "to take nothing for the journey" is more pertinent. Jesus expects his disciples to be hosted by their audience. It is also interesting that Jesus does not want them to make a spectacle of their "poverty" by walking barefoot and thus arriving with bleeding feet. Indeed, some have argued that the instructions to "take no sack" and "wear sandals" is an indirect reference to itinerant Cynic philosophers who went about barefoot and carried a bag in which they put the donations they received. Also, Jesus warns against moving from house to house. Is this an admonition against searching for better, maybe luxurious, accommodations? But the Matthean and Lukan versions speak even more directly to the issue of ministerial compensation. In Matt 10:5–10 we read:

> Jesus sent out these twelve after instructing them thus, "Do not go into pagan territory or enter a Samaritan town. Go rather to the lost sheep of the house of Israel. As you go, make this proclamation: 'The kingdom of heaven is at hand.' Cure the sick, raise the dead, cleanse lepers, drive out demons. Without cost you have received; without cost you are to give. Do not take gold or silver or copper for your belts; no sack for the journey, or a second tunic, or sandals, or walking stick. The laborer deserves his keep. Whatever town or village you enter, look for a worthy person in it, and stay there until you leave. As you enter a house, wish it peace. If the house is worthy let your peace come upon it; if not, let your peace return to you. Whoever will not receive you or listen to your words—go outside that house or town and shake the dust from your feet. Amen, I say to you, it will be more tolerable for the land of Sodom and Gomorrah on the day of judgment than for that town."

With regard to this biblical passage, scholars have expressed considerable interest in Jesus' use of a proverb-like expression "the laborer deserves his keep." Some scholars have argued that in using those words Jesus was employing a moral aphorism, the origin of which was in the labor and management controversies of his day. And, no doubt, there is another passage in Matthew's gospel that shows Jesus' acute sensitivity to the issue of just compensation for laborers. Matt 20:1–16, the parable of the laborers in the vineyard, shows Jesus' acute awareness of the labor conditions of his day and the moral obligation that was just wages. Regardless of whether or not Jesus was quoting a moral proverb of his own time, there is considerable biblical evidence that whoever coined the phrase was hardly original or creative, but rather was very traditional. There is, after all, a whole string of Old Testament statements on the importance of paying laborers their hard-earned wages. See Lev 19:13, "You shall not withhold over night the wages of your day laborer." And Deut 24:14–15: "You shall not defraud and poor and needy hired servant, whether he be one of your own countrymen or one of the aliens who live in your communities. You shall pay him each day's wages before sundown on the day itself, since he is poor and looks forward to them." And Mal 3:5 warns against "those who defraud the hired man of his wages."

It is also important to note the variations in the NT quotation of Jesus' instruction regarding ministerial compensation. For example, Matthew's quotation of this saying does not use the word "wages." I have quoted here the New American Bible (NAB) translation that says "the laborer deserves his keep." The Revised Standard Version (RSV) translates Matt 10:10 as "the laborer deserves his food." The RSV translation is more literal, for the word in Matthew's Greek is *trophe* which means literally "food." However, Luke's translation actually uses the word "money," which in Greek is *misthos*. The RSV translates Luke 10:7 as "the laborer deserves his payment." The NAB translated Luke 10:7 as "the laborer deserves his wages." When this saying is quoted in 1 Tim 5:18 (with reference to Christian clergy compensation), it is the Lucan version with its precise reference to pay, *misthos*, that is quoted.

No doubt when Saint Paul quotes this saying, his wording is identical with that of Matthew's gospel. Nevertheless, there can be little doubt that Paul is referring to material compensation and not charity. I quote at length from 1 Cor 9:7–11, 13–14:

> Who ever serves as a soldier at his own expense? Who plants a vineyard without eating its produce? Or who shepherds a flock without using some of the milk from the flock? Am I saying this on human authority, or does not the law also speak of these things? It is written in the law of Moses, "You shall not muzzle an ox while it is treading out the grain." Is God concerned about oxen, or is he not really speaking for our sake? It was written for our sake, because the plowman should plow in hope, and the thresher in hope of receiving a share. If we have sown spiritual seed for you, is it a great thing that we reap a material harvest from you? . . .
>
> Do you not know that those who perform the temple services eat [what] belongs to the temple, and those who minister at the altar share in the sacrificial offerings? In the same way, the Lord ordered that those who preach the gospel should live by the gospel.

However, there is clear evidence from the NT writings that, from early on, some disciples of Christ began abusing his directive regarding clergy compensation. The earliest surviving work of the Christian movement, Paul's First Letter to the Church at Thessalonika, gives witness to the fact that early on there were some preachers of the gospel who were financially exploiting their congregations. I am referring to 1 Thess 2:5: "Nor, indeed, did we ever appear with flattering speech, as you know, or with a pretext for greed." Moreover, in another letter of Paul, Second Corinthians, he suggests these were not small and limited incidents. Second Cor 2:17: "For we are not like the many who trade on the word of God." Indeed, 1 Cor 16:1–4 witnesses to just how scrupulous or careful Paul became with regard to handling church funds. In this passage, Paul makes it clear that not only does he want the Corinthians to take up their collection for the assistance of Christians in Jerusalem before he gets to Corinth but when it has been taken up, he prefers that others deliver it to Jerusalem: "Now in regard to the collection for the holy ones, you also should do as I ordered the churches of Galatia. On the first day of the week each of you should set aside and save whatever one can afford, so that collections will not be going on when I come. And when I arrive, I shall send those whom you have approved with letters of recommendation to take your gracious gift to Jerusalem. If it seems fitting that I should go also, they will go with me."

And precisely because of this corrupt practice by which some preachers of the gospel were making excessive money off their flocks, Paul refused to accept any clergy compensation for himself. Instead, he reverted to supporting himself through the craft of leather work which no doubt he had originally learned so as to be able to support himself as a rabbi. See in this regard Acts 18:1–3: "After this he left Athens and went to Corinth. There he met a Jew named Aquila, a native of Pontus, who had recently come from Italy with his wife Priscilla because Claudius had ordered all the Jews to leave Rome. He went to visit them and, because he practiced the same trade, stayed with them and worked, for they were tentmakers by trade."

However, it is also important to note that, while Paul became self-supporting in his ministry, and often made a point of pride out of this, he also never failed to remind his audience that ministerial compensation was nevertheless a right and not an option. I am referring to passages such as 1 Cor 9:16–18: "If I preach the gospel, this is no reason for me to boast, for an obligation has been imposed on me, and woe to me if I do not preach it! If I do so willingly, I have a recompense, but if unwillingly, then I have been entrusted with a stewardship. What then is my recompense? That, when I preach, I offer the gospel free of charge so as not to make full use of my right in the gospel." A similar sentiment is found in 2 Thess 3:7–9: "We did not act in a disorderly way among you, nor did we eat food received free from anyone. On the contrary, in toil and drudgery, night and day we worked, so as not to burden any of you. Not that we do not have the right."

Clergy Compensation in the Early Church

The earliest witness to the problematic character of clergy compensation in the early church can be found in the *Didache*, a short, early Christian manual of morals and church practice. Its dating is greatly disputed; some date it as early as AD 60, others as late as the mid-second century, that is, circa AD 150. But it is interesting how in its instructions regarding the proper compensation of Christian ministers, it describes itinerant apostles, prophets, and teachers in a way that suggests more the ethos of the first century rather than second century church. For example, in the *Didache* 11:3–6, we read:

> Now concerning the apostles and prophets, deal with them as follows in accordance with the rule of the gospel. Let every apostle who comes to you be welcomed as if he were the Lord. But he is not to stay for more than one day, unless there is need, in which case he may stay another. But if he stays three days, he is a false prophet. And when the apostle leaves, he is to take nothing except bread until he finds his next night's lodging. But if he asks for money, he is a false prophet.[5]

Then in verse 12 of that same chapter, when the author addresses the phenomenon of early Christian prophecy, he says, "if anyone should say in the spirit, "Give me money" or anything else, do not listen to him."[6] Thus it is probably no accident that when the *Didache* in 13:1–2 quotes the maxim, "the laborer deserves his keep or food," it is the Matthean version with its *trophes*, "food" rather than the Lucan "wages," that is used: "But every genuine prophet who wishes to settle among you is worthy of his food. Likewise, every genuine teacher is, like the worker, worthy of his food."[7] Witness also the problems caused by Augustine of Hippo.

Beginning with Augustine of Hippo (the once moral profligate now becomes moral rigorist and ascetic even), there was an attempt to impose upon the diocesan clergy a monastic spirituality. That is, Augustine wanted his diocesan clergy not just recite the Psalter, to observe the monastic liturgical hours, but he even wanted his diocesan clergy to practice a monastic style poverty and thus reject any ownership of material goods. I am referring to the fact that Augustine had been living the monastic life in community at the time he became bishop of Hippo. After he became bishop, he did not want to give it up. And so he turned his episcopal residence into the equivalent of a monastery by requiring that the clergy who lived there with him ascribe to a common life and observe evangelical poverty, that is, forego all ownership

5. *Didache*, p. 363.

6. Ibid.

7. Ibid., p. 365.

of money and goods. He did not stop there, however. Instead he decided that this style of life, which combined the practices of the monastic life with the duties of the clerical office, should become the ideal for all his diocesan clergy. He did this by turning his episcopal house not only into a monastery but also into the seminary for his diocese by requiring all candidates for the priesthood to live in community with him and the other priests in the bishop's residence, the *episcopium* (from the Greek *episkopeion*), and according to his ascetic/monastic rule of life. This caused problems. Not all candidates for the clergy wanted to do this. In his Sermon 355, given shortly before the feast of the Epiphany in January of 426 before an assembly of clergy and laity in the cathedral at Hippo, Augustine concedes he had probably been too overbearing in making this an obligation on all, and that he would provide for those candidates for ordination who do not want to live as monks:

> I'm the one, as you know, who determined to ordain no one a cleric unless he were willing to stay with me; on such terms that if he chose to turn away from his purpose, I would have the right to deprive him of his clerical status, because he was throwing over his membership in a sacred association, which he had promised and begun.
>
> Well here and now, in the presence of God and of yourselves, I am changing my policy: those who wish to keep some private property, for whom God and the Church are not enough, may stay where they like and where they can; I will not deprive them of their clerical status. I don't want to have any hypocrites.[8]

From time to time there have also been sensitive, intelligent bishops who, while themselves ascetics, have made more judicious provisions for their clergy. An outstanding example of this is Pope Gregory the Great who lived circa 540 to 604. He was born and raised in Rome amid aristocratic comfort. The son of a senator, Gregory himself embarked upon a political career, becoming prefect of the city in 573. However, his devout Christian convictions led him to abandon his political career, sell off his vast property holdings and devote the proceeds to the relief of the poor. After a few years of a very austere monastic life, however, the pope compelled Gregory to leave the cloister and become one of the seven deacons of the church at Rome. Eventually, Gregory himself became pope. His papacy was characterized by that same solicitude for the poor that characterized his conversion. More precisely, Pope Gregory's papacy was characterized in part by his careful administration of the vast estates of the church, such that priority was given to assisting the poor. There is some evidence to suggest Gregory also had an eye for the needs of the clergy. This may be observed in a letter written by Gregory in July–August 592. It is addressed to a top church administrator, one "Peter, subdeacon of Sicily." It is now numbered

---

8. Augustine, *Sermons*, Vol. 3/10, p. 169.

Gregory's *Epistle 32* and it deals with the proper administration of large estates of church property in Sicily. Therein, Pope Gregory shows himself especially solicitous of the tenant farmers on those church properties, for he says "Arrange that the farmers, through their possessions, can produce something useful from their cultivation of the earth."[9] But Pope Gregory is also concerned for the needs of the priest, one Cyriacus, who had brought the original report from Sicily to which Gregory was responding. Part of the report brought by Cyriacus detailed that priest's handling of an attempted bribery of the clergy (himself?). Pope Gregory was so impressed with Cyriacus's handling of the affair that he says, "I brought in the account book in the presence of the clergy, increased his stipend and placed him in a higher rank."[10] Gregory, more precisely, literally increased this priest's *presbyterium*, a term which at that time referred to the pecuniary allowance for clergy. The stipend increase that Gregory gave to Cyriacus might be considered a reward for honesty, but it might also be considered Gregory's way of increasing the odds that priests like Cyriacus would not be sorely tested by such bribes, and thus stave off that all too common vice among poorly paid clergy, "occult compensation," slyly making up for the deficient compensation provided them by their bishop or the diocesan rules for clergy compensation.

Yet another sensitive and balanced approach to clergy compensation is given by Saint Chrodegang. Chrodegang was bishop of Metz from 742 till his death in 766. He is considered one of the principal ecclesiastical reformers of his time. An example of his reform is the rule for his clergy, which he published in 755. It is called the *Regula Canonicorum*, later known as the Rule of Chrodegang, wherein, while retaining the rule for the observance of the divine office, he innovated a provision that allowed his clergy to hold private property.[11]

Our survey of the history of clergy compensation would not be complete without taking note of the historic discrepancy between the compensation of lower clergy and upper clergy, which has been a near constant issue throughout church history. While Jesus' sayings in the first letter to Tim 5:17–18 applies to presbyters, "the worker deserves his wages" and advises that "presbyters who do well at preaching and teaching deserve double compensation," he also warns that the presbyter must not be "a lover of money" (1 Tim 3:3). So too the work called *The Apostolic Constitutions*, composed between 375 and 400 in Syria. It is a work that Bruno Steimer describes as "a voluminous compilation of earlier church orders" and marks

9. Gregory, *Letters*, p. 229.

10. Ibid., p. 230.

11. This is treated in Jerome Bertram's *The Chrodegang Rules*, published by Ashgate in 2005, and in M. A. Claussen's *The Reform of the Frankish Church: Chrodegang of Metz*, published by Cambridge Univ. Press in 2004).

its significance as "the most comprehensive and best preserved church order, and the most important for research into the discipline, ethics, liturgy, theology of office, and constitution of the early church."[12] There we find in book 7 (article 29) an admonition to the laity of their obligation to support their clergy. This admonition employs distinctly OT terminology: "Give to the priest those things that are due to him—the first-fruits of your threshing floor and of your wine-press, along with sin offerings. For he is a mediator between God and those who stand in need of purgation and forgiveness."[13] In book 2, section 4 (preface to article 25), it admonishes bishops regarding their own lifestyle: "Let the bishop view such food and clothing sufficient as meets necessity and decency. Let him not make use of the Lord's goods as another's. Rather, let him use them moderately, 'for the laborer is worthy of his reward.' Let him not be luxurious in diet or fond of idle furniture."[14] This last sentence is my quotation from the only English translation available, a translation done in 1870 and which some might judge to be more poetic than precise. Nevertheless, it makes dramatically clear the author's original concern that a bishop be "neither lavish nor vainglorious" (*me statalos mede perperos*) in his use of church funds. Indeed, the translator's use of the phrase "idle furniture" makes for a powerful image suggesting such vain luxuries as couches for reclining at banquets in post-Constantinian episcopal palaces, an implicit contrast to "service furniture" such as the liturgical appurtenances of a chancel or sanctuary: altar and presidential chair, bench for presbyters, stools for acolytes and readers, credence table.

Yet another example of hierarchical self-indulgence or episcopal greed is the phenomenon called "spoliation." The word literally means "plundering goods by force," but its more technical, canonical meaning, is a bishop's using his authority to commandeer and seize parochial funds or property. Some conjecture that it was precisely a historic act of spoliation or episcopal greed that gave birth to the now proverbial expression "robbing Peter to pay Paul." That is, it has been argued that this proverbial expression began as an a complaint or cry of indignation when the bishop of London in 1550 arrogantly appropriated funds from the Benedictine monks at Westminster Abbey (the Collegiate Church of St. Peter) so as to pay for the repair of "Old St. Paul's," the bishop's cathedral church in London, the building which in 1708 was replaced by today's St. Paul's, the magnificent edifice designed by Christopher Wren.

---

12. Dopp and Geerling, *Dictionary of Early Christian Literature*, p. 44.
13. *Constitutions of the Apostles*, p. 471.
14. Ibid., p. 408.

Clergy Compensation in Modern Times

Despite the clarity of the New Testament teaching on clergy compensation, the church even in modern times has never done very well in this regard. Witness how modern scholars are able to dispute the true meaning of Paul's teaching in 1 Tim 5:17. There Paul says that presbyters who labor in preaching and teaching do well deserve *duplēs timēs*. The phrase has been translated as referring to either financial reward or social honor. The Greek word *timēs* refers to something rendered to someone on the basis of the recipient's worth or value. It can mean "honor," "esteem," or "dignity;" but it can also mean "payment" or "wages." This dual option is reflected in two modern translations of the Bible, and, ironically, each option was made in the first and second editions. I refer to the first edition of the New American Bible translation (1970) wherein 1 Tim 5:17 renders: "Presbyters who do well deserve to be *paid double*, especially those who work in preaching and teaching." But in the second edition of the New American Bible (1986), 1 Tim 5:17 has been changed to read: "Presbyters who preside well deserve *double honor*, especially those who toil in preaching and teaching." The Jerusalem Bible Translation of 1966 renders it as "The elders who do their work well while they are in charge are to be given *double consideration*, especially those who are assiduous in preaching and teaching." But the New Jerusalem Bible Translation renders it as "Elders who do their work well while they are in charge earn *double reward*, especially those who work hard at preaching and teaching." The proper translation and interpretation of this phrase *duplēs timēs* is a hotly disputed point, and eminent biblical authorities can be found to support either side. For example, Martin Dibelius and Hans Conzelmann, in their commentary on 1 Tim 5:17 insist "A financial compensation is certainly intended here . . . The next verse makes the connection with material reimbursement unmistakably clear."[15] This is also the opinion of I. Howard Marshall in his commentary on the Pastoral Epistles (published by T and T Clark of Edinburgh in 1999, p. 613). Some of the alternative readings border on the ingenious if not ludicrous. For example, Jesuit Benjamin Fiore, in his commentary on the Pastoral Epistles for the Sacra Pagina series says, "A double salary might not be what the phrase means. It might well refer to a double portion at the *agapē* meal."[16]

In the United States today, clergy compensation takes many different forms. While most Protestant ministers make modest salaries, and indeed some with very small congregations must support themselves with secular jobs, there are also Protestant pastors of large urban congregations who receive immense salaries along with

---

15. Dibelius and Conzelmann, *Commentary*, p. 78.
16. Fiore, *Pastoral Epistles*, p. 111.

perquisites, such as a parsonage and travel allowance. The justification for this is that large wealthy congregations must be willing to pay competitive salaries in order to secure a renowned preacher or a pastor with a distinguished record of pastoral service and social awareness. Among Catholics priests there is a considerable discrepancy or variance among the dioceses regarding the salaries and retirement benefits of diocesan priests. The Catholic clergy association, which is called the National Federation of Priests' Councils, used to publish triennially (now only once every five years) a profile of priests' compensation statistics, including salary and retirement benefits. This publication bears the title *The Laborer is Worthy of His Hire*. It witnesses to considerable differences in the compensation of priests in the various dioceses, differences that are not always readily explainable. For example, a few years ago there was one large and wealthy northeast archdiocese where the salary allotted to a simple priest was one half that provided for the same by a small Midwest diocese, and this was despite the fact that the cost of living was much higher in that northeast diocese.

It is also important to note the teaching and reception of the Second Vatican Council regarding ministerial compensation. The Second Vatican Council treated ministerial compensation in sections 20 and 21 of its Decree on the Ministry and Life of Priests. And its teaching has come in for comment by scholars such as Sulpician Father Frank B. Norris, SS, a one-time professor of ecclesiology at Saint Patrick's Seminary in Menlo Park, California. Father Norris published in 1966 a *Commentary on the Second Vatican Council's Decree on The Ministry and Life of Priests*. There he says of the decree's sections 20 and 21, the sections that treat of the remuneration of priests:

> Both the letter and spirit of the Decree suggest a radical rethinking of our present system of clerical remuneration, at least in many countries. As it is now, most diocesan priests receive an inadequate basic salary. They necessarily depend upon Mass stipends and other "stole fees" (the very title has an odious sound) to augment their income. Furthermore, the differences in the "net gain" from parish to parish within a diocese (and also from diocese to diocese within the same country or region) are sometimes shocking. In light of what the Council has said in this Decree and elsewhere about the collegial nature of the priestly collaborators of the bishop, such inequities should cease.[17]

Other commentators on Vatican II have not been so positive about Vatican II's treatment of clergy compensation. For example, more than one writer has remarked on the great difference between the perforce wealth of prelates who do not simply administer but in fact own the resources of their diocese, and the very modest

---

17. Norris, *Commentary on the Second Vatican Council's Decree*, p.97.

salaries of pastors and curates who have little or no temporal possessions of their own. In most dioceses of the United States the ordinary is what is legally termed "corporation-sole," that is, all the assets of the diocese "belong" to the bishop of the diocese for he not only administrates them, but they are all in fact "in his name." On the other hand there are also some dioceses in the United States in which each parish and diocesan institution is incorporated with the bishop, vicar general, and two other trustees. Regardless of the model used, "The Temporal Goods of the Church," which is the title of book 5 (canons 1254–1310) of the current code of canon law, in such canons as 1263, 1276, 1301, makes clear the bishop's right to these temporal goods. This contrast between the wealth of prelates and the modest (even at times penurious) circumstances of simple priests has come in for comment in recent times. For example, it is interesting to read the opinion of a cloistered monk with a vow of poverty. I am referring to Cistercian Father M. Basil Pennington's comment on the section of Vatican II's Decree on the Ministry and Life of Presbyters (article 17) that invites priest/presbyters to "embrace voluntary poverty": "When the fathers tell priests to be grateful for everything they receive to live a decent life and go on to invite them to embrace voluntary poverty, one racks one's brain for something similar in the decree the bishops wrote for themselves. When one hears the priest told he should have the kind of dwelling that no one will fear to visit, even the humblest one cannot help but think of cardinalatial mansions and episcopal palaces that even priests are afraid to approach."[18]

That Pennington's comments are not just capricious or gratuitously malicious can be seen from the following comments made decades earlier by Henri Fesquet, a journalist correspondent sent by the Paris newspaper *Le Monde* to report on the Second Vatican Council. Fesquet wrote in October of 1963 regarding the draft of the Second Vatican Council's Pastoral Constitution on the Church in the Modern World:

> The great material misery of the French clergy, for example, borders on the scandalous. We can recall very bitter comments by priests that bishops who live in comfort, and in certain countries in luxury, are in no position to speak of the "Church of the poor" while their own priests are their most immediate poor, whom they give no thought to. "Would to God," one of them wrote me recently, "that we received the salary of a simple subway worker or even a day laborer so we would not be forced to live by our wits." This is a serious problem that has not yet been resolved.[19]

18. Pennington, *Vatican II*, p.72.
19. Fesquet, *Drama of Vatican II*, p. 154.

That it is not to be resolved anytime soon can be inferred from a comment made by a Brooklyn diocesan official in the *New York Times* of Thursday, October 21, 2010. That issue of the *Times* carried an article entitled "Despite Speculation, Dolan is Not Named a Cardinal," and in it the author of the article, newspaper reporter Paul Vitello, interviewed a number of church historians and church officials about Archbishop Timothy Dolan of New York City being passed over, as seen from the recent announcement of a consistory to create new cardinals. Vitello concludes his article with some general remarks about the office and honor of cardinal, among which is his estimate: "Aside from the hat, the tangible benefits are apparently few." And in support of that judgment he quotes a spokesman for the neighboring Diocese of Brooklyn: "There's no pay raise, I can tell you that. In most cases, bishops and cardinals are paid what a priest is paid." The newspaper reporter's conclusion and the remarks of the spokesman for the diocesan of Brooklyn, in their omission of any reference to the numerous perquisites and access to discretionary funds that go with the office of bishop or cardinal, must be taken as disingenuous. It is yet another example of the church's unwillingness to take seriously the problem of clergy compensation for simple priests.

A clear witness to a certain imbalance in clergy compensation is the guidelines for post-retirement benefits for priests and bishops as issued by the United States Conference of Catholic Bishops (USCCB) in 2002.[20] The section on post-retirement benefits for priests consists of three pages of broad principles that are often phrased in technical language, such as the following:

> The regular, systematic practice of providing certain benefits to retired priests (such as monthly pension payments, payment of premiums for Medicare supplemental insurance policies, payment of medical and dental bills, housing subsidies, etc.) is evidence of a post-retirement benefit plan, whether or not a written plan document exists. The benefits may be in the form of a reimbursement to the retiree or direct payment to a provider. Under these circumstances, benefits are viewed as deferred compensation arrangements whereby the diocese agrees to future benefits in exchange for current services. Therefore, the expected cost of providing pension and other post-retirement benefits to priests is to be recognized over their years of active service in the diocese. The obligation of the diocese for pension and other post-retirement benefits is to be fully accrued by the date that full eligibility for benefits is attained.

In dramatic contrast, the section on bishops' retirement benefits is but one page of clear and precisely defined items such as:

---

20 The guidelines appear in a document entitled "Diocesan Financial Issues." I know of no hard copy publication of this document. But there is an electronic copy available for consultation at the website of the U.S. Conference of Catholic Bishops: http://old.usccb.org/bishops/dfi/pension.htm.

Appropriate housing and board. Health and welfare benefits, including major medical and the full cost of all medical and hospital care" [no co-pays for bishops]. An office with secretarial assistance . . . Transportation including an automobile for personal use . . . Travel expenses (i.e., transportation, lodging, food, etc.) to allow the retired bishops to attend: a. provincial meetings and workshops; b. regional meetings, workshops and retreats; c. meetings of the USCCB; d. *ad limina* visits to the Holy See . . . Suitable funeral and burial.

To end our survey of biblical principles and historic practices regarding ministerial compensation, we do well to consider the following quotation from Father Raymond Brown's study, *Priest and Bishop: Biblical Reflections*. It is an especially apt quotation for this book because it too attempts to relate the ministerial priesthood in Catholic Christianity to the Old Testament ideal of priesthood. Moreover, in view of the statements we have just considered, Brown's moral realism is refreshing. On page 9, he says:

> With a certain amusement we may report that the OT ideal of the priesthood was not entirely idealistic. If a man was born into the priestly tribe, he still had to be installed in the priestly office. Over the centuries this was done in several ways, but the oldest seems to have involved "the filling of his hands" (Exod 32:29). Presumably this referred to putting into his hands some of the revenues that he had a right to, as an installment at the beginning of his ministry (Judg 17:10; 18:4). (While we heartily praise reforms within Catholicism about stipends in order to erase once and for all the image of a priest as a man with his hand out, it may be of some comfort to reflect on the antiquity of the image.) And so if Israelite theology demanded of priests a holiness of separation, it was eminently practical about the priests' need for support. It is curious that our times, which are so insistent on plunging the priest into the secular, seem to be becoming less practical about the needs of religion for money.[21]

And there is yet another lesson to be learned from the story of Eli and his sons at Shiloh, and this is with regard not to the temptations of money but those of sex. That is, we must also note that the biblical text seems to indicate that the greed of Eli's sons Hophni and Phinehas was not their only sin. And, whether or not Hophni and Phinehas were involved in sexual offenses as well as greed, or were merely the victims of moral "piling on," the fact is that sex has been problematic for Christian ministers from the beginning. And this despite the fact that the entire biblical tradition, Old Testament and New Testament, sets forth severe strictures regarding this most powerful of human drives, sexual desire, which unless restrained by a heightened sense of human morality can all too easily lead to moral exploitation of one's self, neighbor, neighbor's spouse, or child.

21. Brown, *Priest and Bishop*, p. 9.

Sexual Morality in the Bible

Listed among the Ten Commandments that Moses received on Sinai are certain brief strictures regarding sex, such as Exod 20:14, "you shall not commit adultery" and Exod 2:17 "you shall not covet your neighbor's wife." These simple apodictic statements are treated at greater length in Leviticus 18, which is an entire chapter given over to sexual morality. It is there we find further strictures, such as "None of you shall approach a close relative to have sexual intercourse with her" (Lev 18:6), "You shall not lie with a male as with a woman, such a thing is an abomination," (Lev 18:22), "You shall not have carnal relations with an animal" (v. 23).

These OT sexual laws are not only validated in the NT but are sometimes made even more stringent. Consider Jesus' teaching in Matt 5:27–28, "You have heard it said, 'You shall not commit adultery.' But I say to you, everyone who looks at a woman with lust has already committed adultery with her in his heart." So too Paul warns about adultery and coveting one's neighbor's wife in 1 Thess 4:3–7: "This is the will of God, your holiness: that you refrain from immorality, that each of you know how to acquire a wife for himself in holiness and honor, not in lustful passion as do the Gentiles who do not know God; not to take advantage of or exploit a brother in this matter, for the Lord is an avenger in all these things, as we told you before and solemnly affirmed. For God did not call us to impurity but to holiness." Consider also St. Paul's warnings against homosexuality in Rom 1:26–27, "Therefore, God handed them over to degrading passion. Their females exchanged natural relations for unnatural, and the males likewise gave up natural relations with females and burned with lust for one another. Males did shameful things with males and thus receive in their own persons the due penalty for their perversity." It should also be noted that when Jesus (in the eunuch logion of Matt 19:10–12) and Paul (in 1 Cor 7:1–8) recommend lifelong celibacy, they are not working out of a vacuum. The Old Testament presents us with not only rules regarding periodic sexual abstinence, the strictures in Exod 19:15 and Lev 15:18 that required all Israelites to abstain from sex before offering a sacrifice and the witness in 1 Sam 21:5–6 to the sexual abstinence required of dedicated soldiers, but also examples of lifelong celibacy. The celibacy of Jeremiah is made quite clear in Jer 16:1, "This message came to me from the Lord: do not marry any woman." And a similar abstinence, though not so clearly stated, is implied in the accounts of the ministries of the prophets Elijah, Elisha, and Daniel.

Nevertheless, despite the moral strictures regarding sexuality in the Old Testament and the moral idealism proposed by Jesus and Paul, there is evidence that some in the earliest Christian communities nonetheless felt justified in taking a much more liberal stance toward sexuality. Indeed, there is evidence in the NT that an attitude of sexual libertarianism was to be found among some new Christians. Paul's letter to the Galatians was probably written around AD 54 or 55. In Gal 5:13, Paul says, "You were called for freedom, brothers. But do not use this freedom as an opportunity for the flesh." And in Gal 5:19, he warns them against "impurity and licentiousness." In the First Letter to the Corinthians, written about the year 51, Paul has several warnings: in 1 Cor 6:12, he warns against an attitude of sexual libertarianism; in 1 Cor:15–20, he warns against indulgence in prostitution; and in 1 Cor 5:1, he feels a need to warn against incest: "it is widely reported that there is immorality among you, and immorality of a kind not found even among the pagans." And thus we can conclude all those were real problems in the Christian community at Corinth.

Sex and Ministry in Church History

Early Christian literature in the subapostolic era is not so clear about sexual indiscretions among the clergy. We have already seen that there is considerable and clear witness to financial sins on the part of the clergy. But there is no such clear witness regarding their sexual mores. However, there are passages in early Christian literature that can lend themselves to such interpretation and that might even be circumspect, indirect witness to such. Take for example Polycarp of Smyrna's Letter to the Philippians, chapter 11:1 where he says "I am deeply grieved for Valens, who once was a presbyter among you, because he so fails to understand the office which was entrusted to him. I warn you, therefore: avoid love of money; and be pure and truthful."[22] That he warns not only against avarice but also issues an admonition to be pure (*sitis casti*) in the sense of chaste, but also later (11:4) remarks, "I am deeply grieved for him *and for his wife*," we might understand that Valens' problems, as with Hophni and Phinehas, were sexual as well as financial. Then there is also the letter of Ignatius of Antioch to the Ephesians (7:1). In this instance, the problem seems to be more than just heretical teaching, but malfeasance: "For there are some who make a practice of carrying about the Name with wicked guile and do *certain things unworthy of God*."[23] In its very indirectness, that final phrase leaves open many prurient possibilities.

The strictures produced by ecumenical councils are more explicit. The First Council of Nicea (325) is famous for its dogma of the incarnation or the divinity of Christ. However, that same council also passed practical measures, such as its canon 3: "This great synod absolutely forbids a bishop, presbyter, deacon or any of the clergy to keep a woman who has been brought in to live with him, with the exception

22. Polycarp, "Letter to the Philippians," p. 293.
23. Ignatius, "Epistles," p. 181.

of course of his mother or sister or aunt, or of any person who is above suspicion."[24] Even so, there is clear evidence that eight hundred years later concubinage was still a major problem with the clergy. The First Lateran Council (1123) says in its canon 7: "We absolutely forbid priests, deacons, or subdeacons to live with concubines, and to cohabit with other women, except those whom the Council of Nicea permitted to dwell with them solely on account of necessity, namely a mother, sister, paternal or maternal aunt, or other such persons, about whom no suspicion could justly arise."[25]

Yet another intriguing reference is Jerome's Letter to Eustochium, written about the year AD 384. It is lengthy and replete with vivid images of Roman society of the time, one of which is Jerome's description of the younger clergy: "There are others— I speak of those of my own order—who seek the presbyterate and the diaconate simply that they may be able to see women with less restraint. Such men think of nothing but their dress; they use perfumes freely, and see that there are no creases in their leather shoes. Their curling hair shows traces of the tongs; their fingers glisten with rings; they walk on tiptoe across a damp road, not to splash their feet. When you see them acting in this way, think of them rather as bridegrooms than as clergymen."[26] Of course, rather than a depiction of clerical philandering this might be nothing much more than Jerome, the self-styled celibate and ascetic, satirizing the younger clergy in pursuit of a wife in a time when that was still an option.

Medieval church history provides us with much more scurrilous references to the sins of the clergy. Take for example "The Book of Gomorrah" written by the zealous reformer Peter Damian (1007-72). There he indicts the clergy of his day not just for concubinage but also for bestiality, homosexual acts, and the sexual abuse of children. Here I have chosen to begin with historically verifiable incidents and only later do I treat of scandalous allegations. What follows, then, are a few narratives that cover a broad range of church history from patristic times to modern times, namely from Chrysostom to Newman and feature more examples from the ranks of simple priests than from the hierarchy. I have chosen these stories not just for scandalous revelation but for the moral lesson that each embodies. Indeed, while Chrysostom (ca. 347–407) and Evagrius Ponticus, (345–399) were contemporaries, I begin with Evagrius precisely because Chrysostom's story has a moral lesson that is best treated later.

Evagrius Ponticus, one of the great spiritual writers of the patristic era, indeed, a central figure in the history of Christian spirituality, was on the fast track to a high ecclesiastical career when he was ambushed by sexual temptations. The son of an

---

24. Tanner, *Decrees*, Vol. 1, p. 7.

25. Ibid., p. 191.

26. Jerome, *Letters*, p. 34.

important ecclesiastic (his father was a *chorepiscopos*, that is, a rural bishop), Evagrius early on became associated with several saintly and brilliant ecclesiastics. Ordained a lector by Basil of Caesarea, then a deacon by Gregory of Nazianzus, at that time Patriarch of Constantinople, Evagrius rapidly became a renowned preacher in the great capital city and was a theological influence at the Second Ecumenical Council held at Constantinople in 381. When Gregory resigned as patriarch in July 381, the new patriarch, Nectarius, made Evagrius his archdeacon, or principal assistant, in the administration of that archdiocese (equivalent to today's vicar general). But within a year Evagrius made the decision to leave Constantinople and ecclesiastical administration forever. He had fallen in love with a married women, the wife of a high official at the imperial court at Constantinople, and the relationship was getting out of hand. We know this from Evagrius's contemporary and disciple, Palladius, who devotes an entire chapter to Evagrius in his *Lausiac History*, a collection of saints lives dedicated to one Lausus, a devout layman and high official at the imperial court who had commissioned that work. In chapter 38, which sets forth Evagrius's life, Palladius is quite candid in conveying Evagrius's passionate relationship with the woman:

> Now it so happened that he, honored as he was by the entire city, was ensnared in the contemplation of desire for a woman, as he later told us when he was freed of the thought. This woman also loved him in return. She was of the highest social class. So Evagrius, with a fear of God and a respect for his own conscience, perceived plainly the magnitude of the disgrace and the delight which heretics would take in his transgression, and he prayed humbly to God to put some impediment in his path. He wished to break off with the woman, who by now was eager and frantic, but he could not do so, so caught up was he in the bonds of concupiscence.[27]

Evagrius soon made the decision to leave that woman and the capital city forever. Instead of becoming the next Patriarch of Constantinople, Evagrius joined the large colony of Christian hermits living in the Nitrian desert, the region in Libya lying west of the Nile river. There he lived out his life writing treatises on prayer and the ascetical life that gained him his modern reputation as one of the greatest and most influential spiritual writers of the early church. One of his treatises is entitled "On the Eight Evil Thoughts."

Medieval theologian and philosopher, cleric, and canon Peter Abelard (1079–1142) suffered a similar fate when his academic career as brilliant lecturer, debater, and author at Paris was cut short by his affair with Héloïse, or Eloise, ward and niece of Fulbert, a canon of Notre Dame Cathedral. Fulbert had hired Abelard to tutor

---

27. Palladius, *Lausiac History*, p. 111.

his niece. She was a brilliant student, but Abelard taught her more than just Greek and Latin, philosophy, and theology. Abelard got Eloise pregnant and when the child arrived they capriciously named him Astrolabe after the ancient but popular astronomical instrument (this is comparable to someone today naming their child "iPod"). Fulbert was so outraged that he hired hooligans to waylay Abelard in the streets of Paris and cut off the offending member. Eloise and the maimed Abelard both left Paris to take refuge in separate monasteries, one for men and one for women. Soon enough, several of Abelard's intellectual rivals took this as an opportunity to call into question the theological soundness of his teachings and his writings. Had so brilliant a cleric as Abelard behaved more properly with Eloise he might have attained high ecclesiastical office as did his mentor, scholastic philosopher William of Champeaux, who eventually became bishop of Chalons sur Marne.[28]

Finally, of the Renaissance pope, Julius III, sovereign pontiff from 1550 to 1555, we can be satisfied to quote the observation of J. N. D. Kelly, in his *The Oxford Dictionary of Popes* (1986). Kelly says of Julius as bishop of Rome, "Essentially weak, he created scandal by his infatuation with a fifteen-year-old youth, Innocenzo, picked up in the streets of Parma, whom he made his brother adopt while Julius himself named cardinal" [29]

A sensitive scholar and historian like J. N. D. Kelly is able to discern even further variations on this theme of sex and ministry. I am referring to Kelly's biography of John Chrysostom. This work contains a particularly insightful analysis of the relationship between the great Patriarch of Constantinople and the deaconess, Olympias:

> As the leading deaconess attached to his cathedral, John must have made the acquaintance of Olympias almost immediately after his arrival in the capital. From the start there seems to have developed between them a deep and, as events were to show, lasting friendship founded on an affinity which was both spiritual and intellectual . . . Her convent was separated from his palace by a single wall, and he was the only outsider, man or woman, who had leave to cross the threshold. Indeed, he took over the spiritual direction of her community; his inspired talks, her unknown biographer records, by means of the divine charity with which they overflowed, set ablaze the love of God in its inmates. In return Olympias made herself responsible for taking care of his clothes and for preparing his simple meals, which she sent across each day to the *episkopeion*. There was no one in Constantinople with whom he was to have a deeper or more sympathetic understanding, no one with whom he was

---

28. In Abelard's autobiographical account, "Letter of Consolation to a Friend: A Story of Calamity," (p. 28), he describes Eloise at the time of the affair reminding him that he was "a cleric and a canon."

29. Kelly, *Oxford Dictionary of Popes*, p. 263.

to feel more at ease or to whom he was to pour out his heart more unreservedly, than this independent, strong-willed but also intensely emotional woman.

Modern students, influenced by the post-Freudian atmosphere in which they have been brought up, are bound to discern a sexual element in this close and strong relationship. They are entirely correct in so doing. It would be a mistake, however, to suppose that John and Olympias were unaware of this factor. The temptations to which relations between the sexes can give rise were never far from the thoughts of committed Christians of that epoch, least of all from John's. But while acutely alive to the sexual dimension, they viewed it with a profound repugnance which modern people usually find it hard to understand. Hence they employed a well-organized self-discipline (including, for example, the elaborate formal courtesy by which they distanced themselves from one another) to keep it at arm's length. What their heroic efforts cost them we can only surmise.[30]

Scholars less appreciative of the effectiveness of Christian asceticism and perhaps more influenced by Freudian psychology are able to see sex everywhere. For example, Brian Patrick McGuire's article, "Love, Friendship and Sex in the 11th Century: the Experience of Anselm,"[31] is a study of the correspondence between the great medieval theologian and one of his finest pupils, the young monk, Maurice. When Anselm was abbot of Bec, he sent Maurice to Canterbury for further studies. During that time Anselm wrote ten letters to Maurice. McGuire finds them inappropriately affectionate.[32] Yale history professor Frank M. Turner holds similar suspicions regarding Newman. In his book-length study, *John Henry Newman: The Challenge to Evangelical Religion* (New Haven: Yale, 2002), Turner sets forth his totally unsympathetic portrayal of the young Newman at Oxford as manipulative, duplicitous, morose, narcissistic, and driven by deeply psychological (homosexual) needs.

The Historical Problem of False Accusations

These prurient interpretations of Anselm's letters and Newman's life can serve as an introduction to the historic problem of malicious rumors and false accusations regarding sex and ministry. Here the New Testament is particularly helpful.

30. Kelly, *Golden Mouth*, pp. 113–14

31. In *Studia Theologica* 28 (1974) 111–152.

32. But compare chapter 7, "The Nature and Importance of Friendship," in R. Southern's *St. Anselm: a Portrait in Landscape* (Cambridge Univ. Press, 1992), pp. 138–65., also the comment, "Anselm later embraced with emotional intensity the new "romantic" ideal of friendship in his letters which might encompass persons he did not know well, indeed some of whom he had never met," in M. McLaughlin's edition of *The Letters of Eloise and Abelard*, p. 329.

Indeed, in this regard 1 Timothy 5 is once again very helpful. We have already quoted 1 Tim 5:17, "Presbyters who do well deserve to be paid double". But 1 Tim5:19 is equally suggestive and important: "Do not accept an accusation against a presbyter unless it is supported by two or three witnesses." It is not entirely clear what was the precise nature of the accusation to which Paul refers. Was it sexual or financial? It could be either or both. But the principal is of utmost importance. Of this passage, Raymond F. Collins in his *Commentary on the Pastoral Epistles* says:

> In 5:17 the Pastor turns his attention to elders, especially those who labor in word and teaching. Elders who are engaged in the ministry of prophecy and teaching must be taken care of by the community. The Pastor cites a passage from Scripture and an appropriate adage to remind the community of this responsibility. Elder engaged in prophecy and teaching have a right to be supported; they also have a right to their good name. The Pastor evokes biblical jurisprudence to remind Timothy that a charge should not be brought against an elder except if there are at least two witnesses ready to testify against him. With its halakhic or regulatory use of Scripture, this pericope (5:17–19) is unlike any other passage in 1 Timothy. Concerned with elders' rights to a just wage and "judicial" equity, the pericope contains a kind of elder's bill of rights.[33]

When Collins claims that the author of First Timothy "evokes biblical jurisprudence," he is referring to Deut 19:15, which says, "One witness alone shall not take the stand against a man in regard to any crime or any offense of which he may be guilty; a judicial fact shall be established only on the testimony of two or three witnesses." But Risto Saarinen, in his commentary on this passage in First Timothy, makes a further point: "The apostle here thinks of Deut. 19:15 and maybe Matt. 18:16 [where Jesus quotes Deut. 19:15], but he is actually stricter than the Mosaic law. In Deut. 19:15 a person can be convicted on the basis of two or three witnesses, whereas in 1 Tim. 5:19 they suffice only for the serious hearing of the accusation. This reflects the apostle's intention to safeguard the position of elders in a congregation."[34]

Ambrose of Milan (339–397), raised in a family of Roman civil servants and himself trained as a Roman lawyer and having practiced in the Roman law courts, shows himself particularly sensitive to matters of justice in his *De Officiis*, "On the Duties of the Clergy." Modeled after the famous *De Officiis* of Cicero, which Cicero had written for his son Marcus as a guide to ethical conduct for an aspiring political leader, Ambrose addressed his treatise on duty to his spiritual "sons," the clergy of Milan. There in book 2, chapter 24, he says: "Never protect a wicked man, nor allow

---

33. Collins, *Commentary on the Pastoral Epistles*, p. 143.
34. Saarinen, *The Pastoral Epistles*, p. 93.

the sacred things to be given over to an unworthy one, on the other hand, do not harass and press hard on a man whose fault is not clearly proved."[35]

Augustine of Hippo's Letter 65, written in AD 402 to Xantippus, another bishop, is a fine example of episcopal care and moderation in the censure of a priest for sexual misconduct. It begins:

> Saluting your Excellency with the respect due to your worth, and earnestly seeking an interest in your prayers, I beg to submit to the consideration of your wisdom the case of a certain Abundantius, ordained a presbyter in the domain of Strabonia, belonging to my diocese. He had begun to be unfavorably reported of, through his not walking in the way which becomes the servants of God; and I being on this account alarmed, though not believing the rumors without examination, was made more watchful of his conduct, and devoted some pains to obtain, if possible, indisputable evidences of the evil courses with which he was charged.[36]

Later in that same letter, Augustine says that *prima facie* evidence was eventually found against the presbyter Abundantius. But Augustine also discloses the well-articulated process by which Abundantius, if he wanted to, could appeal Augustine's judgment against him:

> Upon a day of fasting which was observed as such also in the place in which he was, [the presbyter Abundantius] having taken leave of his colleague in the ministry in that place, and being unattended by any ecclesiastic, ventured to tarry in the house of a woman of ill fame, and to dine and sup and spend the night there, it seemed to me, whatever others might think, that he behoved to be deposed from his office, as I durst not commit to his charge a Church of God. If it should happen that a different opinion be held by the ecclesiastical judges to whom he may appeal, seeing that it has been decreed by the Council [of Carthage in AD 318, canon 11], that the decision of the six bishops be final in the case of a presbyter, let him who will commit a church to him in his jurisdiction, I confess, for my own part, that I fear to entrust any congregation whatever to persons like him.[37]

Augustine might have been particularly careful in his handling of prurient or scurrilous rumors against Abundantius because Augustine himself had once been the victim of a malicious rumor. Shortly after Augustine's nomination to the see of Hippo, but before his episcopal ordination, a report began to circulate that during Augustine's time as a priest he had given a potion to a married woman that allowed him to seduce her. When this report reached the ears of Megalius of Calama, the

35. This is the translation of Ambrose's *De Officiis* in *Select Works and Letters*, p. 62.

36. Augustine, *Letters* p. 322.

37. Ibid., p. 323.

senior bishop and primate of Numidia, Megalius, who it seems resented Augustine's episcopal nomination, quickly wrote an angry letter to the synod of bishops announcing that he had decided not to go ahead with the ordination of Augustine to the episcopate. The synod however decided the matter deserved further careful investigation and thus set up a committee to investigate this accusation. When the committee announced that their investigation led them to conclude the accusation was nothing but a slander, Megalius apologized and went ahead with Augustine's episcopal ordination. It is interesting how Augustine of Hippo's contemporary and biographer Possidius (ca. 370–ca. 440), a pagan convert who lived in Augustine's monastery at Hippo until 397, omitted this episode from his short but valuable sketch of Augustine's life, the *Vita Augustini*. Nevertheless, we know the details well from the several references to the slander made in Augustine's own, anti-Donatist, writings (see his *Against Petilian*, bk. 3, chs. 16–19 and his *Against Cresconius* bk. 3, chs. 80 and 92; bk. 4, chs. 64, 78, 79). The Donatists, too, made much of this slander, which seems to have had its origin in a gift of blessed bread, a *eulogion*, which Augustine (when he was a priest) had sent to a woman who was having serious problems in her marriage.

Augustine's contemporary Jerome was not so fortunate. In the year 382, Jerome went to Rome to become secretary to Pope Damasus. Jerome quickly made both friends and enemies. As for friends, the scholar quickly formed close relationships with a number of aristocratic Christian women, such as the wealthy widow Paula to whose daughter, Eustochium, Jerome became spiritual director. But at that same time Jerome annoyed many among the Roman clergy with his satirical attacks on their manners, their social deportment. An example of this is Jerome's *Epistle 22* to Eustochium. So long as Jerome enjoyed the patronage of the pope, little could be done about this. But when Damasus died and was succeeded by Pope Siricius in December of 384, Jerome's clerical enemies lobbied for an investigation into his behavior with women. In 385, following an official enquiry, he was condemned and effectively banished from Rome by a clerical body whom he labeled a "senate of the Pharisees" (Did. Spir. Sanct. Praef; also see *Epistles 33,5* and *127,9*).

A modern example of the problem of false accusation is made known from the final years of ministry in the life of Joseph Bernardin (1928–1996). Bernardin was first ordained a priest for the diocese of Charleston, South Carolina, but later he went on to become, successively, an auxiliary bishop of Atlanta, archbishop of Cincinnati (1972–1982), and archbishop of Chicago in 1982; and in 1983 he was made a cardinal. In November of 1993, one Stephen Cook, a former seminarian of the Archdiocese of Cincinnati, filed an 810 million dollar lawsuit against the Archdiocese of Cincinnati claiming that in the 1970s he had been molested by Bernardin and a priest of that archdiocese. On February 28, 1994, Cook dropped Bernardin from the lawsuit claiming he was no longer certain that his memories, which had emerged while he was under hypnosis, were truthful.

The Current Situation

No wonder then that in our day the heinous sin of pedophilia by clergy has prompted concern for balance in the treatment of both victim and accused. From June 13–15 of 2002, bishops met at the USCCB in Dallas, Texas. One of the principal concerns at that meeting was to address the phenomenon of priests who sexually abused minors. This problem, which the media had exposed, was in urgent need of attention. Indeed, at the Dallas meeting the very first thing the bishops did was to promulgate by unanimous vote a "Charter for the Protection of Children and Young People."[38] The charter not only set up several important measures for screening church personnel who work with children, but it also promulgated "essential norms for . . . dealing with allegations of sexual abuse of minors by priests or deacons." While the provisions for the protection of children received general approval, voices of concern were quickly raised regarding the bishops norms for the treatment of accused offenders. These grave concerns centered upon the bishops' measures for barring any priest from ministry after even one credible accusation of abuse. For example, the president of the canon law society of America, Kevin E. McKenna, expressed his concern in an article entitled "The Dallas Charter and Due Process," which was published in the magazine *America* September 16, 2002. Msgr. Thomas Green of the canon law faculty of the Catholic University of America published his strong critique of the "Dallas Charter" in the September 19, 2002 issue of *The National Catholic Reporter*. But it was not just canon lawyers who expressed concern. On October 14, 2002, Cardinal Giovanni Battista Re, the prefect for Rome's Congregation for Bishops, wrote to Bishop Wilton Gregory, the president of the USCCB, a letter wherein he expressed praise for the U.S. bishops' effort in drafting their Charter for the Protection of Children and Young People. As well, he expressed concern that "the 'Norms' and 'Charter' contain provisions which in some aspects are difficult to reconcile with the universal law of the church."[39] Cardinal Re did not specify precisely what he was referring to, but the fact is the Vatican quickly set up a mixed-commission of four U.S. bishops and four Vatican officials to review the June Dallas charter. The U.S. bishops were Cardinal Francis George of Chicago, who led the delegation, Archbishop William Levada of San Francisco, Bishop Thomas Doran of Rockford, Illinois, and Bishop William Lori of

38. USCCB, *Charter for the Protection*. Washington, DC: The Conference, 2002.
39. Re, "Letter to Bishop Gregory," *Origins* (Oct. 31, 2002), p. 344.

Bridgeport, Connecticut. The Vatican representatives were Cardinal Dario Castrillon Hoyos, prefect of the Congregation for Clergy; Archbishop Julio Harranz, president of the Pontifical Councilf for Legislative Texts; Archbishop Tarcisio Bertone, secretary of the Congregation for the Doctrine of the Faith; and Archbishop Francesco Monterisi, secretary for the Congregation for Bishops. The essential norms were indeed revised by the USCCB at its November 11–14, 2002, meeting. Even this revision however did not escape criticism. On May 27, 2004, Cardinal Avery Dulles delivered an address to the Thomas More Society in Fort Lauderdale, Florida. The Thomas More Society is an association of Catholic civil lawyers. His address to those lawyers was later published in the June 21, 2004, issue of *America* magazine as an article entitled "Rights of Accused Priests." There Dulles said:

> The church must protect the community from harm, but it must also protect the rights of each individual who may face an accusation. The supposed good of the totality must not override the rights of individual persons. Some of the measures adopted went far beyond the protection of children from abuse. The bishops adopted the very principles that they themselves had condemned in their critique of the secular judicial system. In so doing they undermined the morale of their priests and inflicted a serious blow to the credibility of the church as a mirror of justice.
>
> Although the charter was modified as a result of consultation with Vatican officials, the revised norms are still subject to criticism. Groups of priests still protest that they are not accorded the basic requirements of due process.[40]

The Charter and its Norms were yet again revised by the USCCB's Ad Hoc Committee on Sexual Abuse and approved by the full body of U.S. Catholic bishops in June 2005.[41]

In this final revision, no doubt, Avery Dulles's concerns were indeed addressed. The Norms now define quite clearly and completely the procedures for investigation of accusations and for the punishment of those convicted. Moreover, "due process" is explicitly mentioned and its components enumerated. As for the procedure to be followed in investigating accusations, in Norm #4 the bishops mandated the creation of "a review board" in each diocese, and then detailed its responsibilities: "To assist the diocesan/eparchial bishops, each diocese/eparchy will also have a review board which will function as a confidential consultative body to the bishop/eparch

---

40. Avery Dulles's "Rights of Accused Priests," p. 20. Though Dulles never refers to it, Christian tradition is also greatly concerned about calumny. See Aquinas in *Summa Theologica* 2a2ae, questions 63–79, his tract on injustice. Question 72 treats of defamation and question 73 of detraction. The 1994 *Catechism of the Catholic Church*, in its articles 2475–87, treats of "Offenses Against Truth," and in 2479, specifically detraction and calumny.

41. The Dallas Charter and norms for implementation are all available at the website of the United States Conference of Catholic Bishops: http://www.usccb.org/issues-and-action/child-and-youth-protection.

in discharging his responsibilities. The functions of this board may include: a. advising the diocesan bishop/eparch in his assessment of allegations of sexual abuse of minors and in his determination of suitability for ministry; b. reviewing diocesan/eparchial policies for dealing with sexual abuse of minors; and c. offering advice on all aspects of these cases, whether retrospectively or prospectively." In Norm #5 the composition of the board is stated:

> The review board, established by the diocesan/eparchial bishop, will be composed of at least five persons of outstanding integrity and good judgment in full communion with the Church. The majority of the review board members will be lay persons who are not in the employ of the diocese/eparchy; but at least one member should be a priest who is an experienced and respected pastor of the diocese/eparchy in question, and at least one member should have particular expertise in the treatment of the sexual abuse of minors. The members will be appointed for a term of five years, which can be renewed. It is desirable that the Promoter of Justice participate in the meetings of the review board.

Norm #6 describes the preliminary investigation that follows upon any formal accusation. This involves the temporary suspension of priestly powers: "When there is sufficient evidence that sexual abuse of a minor has occurred, the Congregation of the Doctrine of the Faith shall be notified. The bishop/eparch shall then apply the precautionary measures mentioned in CIC, canon 1722, or CCEO, canon 1473—that is, withdraw the accused from exercising sacred ministry or any ecclesiastical office or function, impose or prohibit residence in a given place or territory, and prohibit public participation in the Most Holy Eucharist pending the outcome of the process." Norm #8 spells out the punishment resulting from a determination that there indeed has been an act of sexual abuse: "When even a single act of sexual abuse by a priest or deacon is admitted or is established after an appropriate process in accord with canon law, the offending priest or deacon will be removed permanently from ecclesiastical ministry, not excluding dismissal from the clerical state, if the case so warrants." Of this latter provision we do well to consider the following opinion of Father Richard John Neuhaus.

While canon lawyers and Cardinal Dulles were most concerned about "due process," Father Richard John Neuhaus was more concerned about what he called the "no mercy route," which the bishops had taken at Dallas. In an essay entitled "Scandal Time III," which appeared in the August–September 2002 issue of *First Things*, Neuhaus voiced his concern that the bishops "by caving to demands for 'one strike' and 'zero tolerance' policies' . . . will remove from ministry faithful priests who did one bad thing thirty years ago and have since had an impeccable record and are clearly no threat to anybody." Indeed, he goes on to say, "the bishops have succeeded in scandalizing the faithful anew by adopting a thoroughly unbiblical, untraditional, and an un-Catholic approach to sin and grace."

One last point: after the revelation of priest pedophilia, numerous revelations came to light regarding high school teachers taking sexual advantage of their students. The news media have also since then carried stories of scout masters, rabbis, and ministers who have done as much. In this regard there are two very important points made in the 150-page report of the USCCB's National Review Board on sexual abuse, which was released in Washington, DC, on February 27, 2004.[42] One is the warning that we must not take refuge in the claim that sexual abuse of minors should not be identified as exclusively the sin of priests. No doubt pedophilia can be found everywhere, especially among professions who work with youth, nevertheless this cannot be allowed to hide the fact that pedophilia committed by priests is worse: "It is clear that the abuse of minors is not unique to the Church. However, given the moral stature of the Church, the role of priests and bishops in providing moral leadership within the Church, and the obligations of priests and bishops to foster the spiritual and moral development of children and young people, when sexual abuse of minors occurs in the Church it is particularly abhorrent. Thus Catholics take no solace from the fact that the sexual abuse of minors occurs outside the Church as well" (as quoted by Neuhaus on p. 49). Later that same report says: "Sexual abuse is inherently traumatic; when committed by a priest, it is especially traumatic. Because a priest is quite literally a 'father figure,' abuse by a priest is likely to cause more harm to a child than abuse by any other individual outside the family. Moreover, a unique consequence of abuse by a member of the clergy is the damage to the victim's faith."

Indeed, others have held the same position long before. Take, for example, Désiré Joseph Mercier (1851–1926), a diocesan priest of the archdiocese of Malines, Belgium. Mercier had been a professor of philosophy at both the seminary at Malines and at Louvain University, and an ardent promoter of the Thomist revival. But in 1906, he was made archbishop of Malines and in 1907 a cardinal. He proved himself to be as fine a pastor as a pedagogue. One of the first things he did when he became archbishop was to preach a retreat to his clergy. In the seventh discourse, "on the mission of a priest," he says. "The noise our enemies are wont to make when they see any weakness or failing in the ranks of Christ's army, is usually on their part a deliberate and premeditated exhibition of Pharisaic indignation; but considered from our own standpoint, their complaints are justified. For we profess to follow a higher ideal than mankind in general; and God gives us the graces we need for

---

42. USCCB, *Report on the Implementation of the Charter*, Washington.DC: The Conference, 2004.

fidelity to this idea: *noblesse oblige*; the higher the elevation, the more ignominious the fall: the more deliberate the sin, the greater the enormity."[43]

In conclusion, whether or not they know well the story of Eli and his sons, it is apparent the bishops of the United States are working hard to make sure they will not repeat again the moral blindness of Eli regarding his priestly sons. Thus seminarians or priests who recognize in themselves any degree of inordinate attraction to minors of either sex would do well to seek professional counseling immediately. And if that does not help, then they should consider resigning from their pursuit or practice of priestly ministry. As for the rest of us, all simple priests would do well to imitate the historic examples of Saint Paul and Saint Augustine with regard to sex, and that other lesson from Eli and his son with regard to money.

We have already noted in our section on clergy compensation in the early church how St. Paul, in reaction to the phenomenon of greedy preachers, became extremely circumspect with regards to church finances. I am referring to 1 Cor 16:1–4: "Now in regard to the collection for the holy ones, you also should do as I ordered the churches of Galatia. On the first day of the week each of you should set aside and save whatever one can afford, so that collections will not be going on when I come. And when I arrive, I shall send those whom you have approved with letters of recommendation to take your gracious gift to Jerusalem. If it seems fitting that I should go also, they will go with me." Saint Paul will not allow himself to be entrusted alone with church funds.

But not only would clergy do well to imitate Saint Paul's circumspection regarding the handling of money, and let others count the collection and deposit it, but they would also do well to imitate the careful provisions that Augustine undertook to forestall sexual allegations against himself. For, if Possidius's biography of Augustine can be trusted, Augustine adopted extreme circumspection with regards to women. Chapter 26 of Possidius's *Vita Augustini* describes the protocols regarding women that he adopted when he became bishop of Hippo:

> No woman ever lived or stayed within Augustine's household, not even his own widowed sister, although she had long served God and lived as superior of His handmaids until the day of her death. He also refused his brother's daughters who were also serving God, although they were considered exception to this law by the councils of bishops. However, Augustine used to say that, even if no evil suspicion could arise from the fact that his sister and nieces lived with him, they could not exist without other servants and women being with them, and that still others would enter from outside to visit them. From these, in turn, a stumbling block or scandal might arise from the weak. He added that those men who happened to be staying with the bishop might

43. Mercier, *Retreat to his Priests*, pp. 219–20.

perish by human temptation, resulting from all those women living together or coming there, or at least be most disgracefully maligned by the evil suspicions of men. For this reason, then, Augustine stated that women should never live in the same house with God's servants, even the most chaste, lest by such example (as we read) some scandal or stumbling block be placed before the weak. Moreover, if some women asked to see or greet him, they never came to him except with some of the clerics as witnesses, and he never spoke to them alone, even if it was a matter of secrecy.[44]

Simple priests today would do well to adopt a similar extreme circumspection with regard to their relationship with minors. More precisely, simple priests today should make sure that no encounter between a priest and a minor, and even numbers of minors as in a youth group, is ever undertaken alone. An adult lay person or, better, more than one adult layperson should be present as a witness. As for hearing the confessions of minors, this should be done through a grill or in a place allowing transparent observation even if only from a discrete distance, as is possible when a confessional wall or door is made of transparent glass. The post-Vatican II closed-box confessional, which provides for the option of a direct, face-to-face encounter between priest and penitent puts the priest in jeopardy when the penitent is a minor. In this regard it is worth recalling the fact that the closed confessional box is a modern invention, exiting only from the sixteenth century. In the early church, penance was a public act performed before the bishop with the entire congregation in attendance. Even in the medieval church confessions were most often heard by a priest sitting in the chancel of the church, the area of the church immediately around the altar, now called the sanctuary, and thus if not in full view of the congregation certainly in view of whoever might venture into the church outside set times of worship. If this might seem extreme caution, then one should consider how one accusation, whether proven or not, can bring ruin upon a simple priest's entire life.

44. Possidius, "Life of St. Augustine," p. 105.

4

Anticlericalism and Violence Against Priests:

Ahimelech at Nob

PRIEST BASHING OR VERBAL violence against priests is a prominent feature of modern society. But the often witty slanders against priests spoken in the past by savants such as Voltaire ("God created sex; priests created marriage") and nihilists like Nietzsche ("Priests make everything more dangerous") pale in malevolence when compared to the ridicule and vicious satires committed by the stand-up comedians of today. Even so, when considering anticlericalism we need to consider not just verbal abuse aimed at priests but also physical violence committed against priests. Physical violence against priests, while conspicuous in modern times, goes far back in history. During the period of 1933–1945, the Dachau concentration camp had a special "priest block" where 2,579 Catholic priests were held and where more than 800 of them died. During the civil war of 1936–1939 in Spain, not only were thousands of churches destroyed and monasteries burned or sacked, but close to 7,000 priests were executed or assassinated. Following the Mexican revolution of 1910, a number of laws were enacted that outlawed monastic orders, closed Catholic schools, and denied clergy basic political rights. The effects of these actions were very real: between 1926 and 1934 the number of priests in Mexico declined from 4,500 to 334. In that deep decline "only" 40 were killed; the rest were eliminated by either voluntary emigration or expulsion. During the French Revolution, not only was the church outlawed and all monasteries destroyed, but 30,000 priests were exiled and hundreds sent to the guillotine. While the assassination of Thomas Becket, the archbishop of Canterbury in 1170 is well documented (and has been celebrated in music, on the stage, and at the cinema), less well known is the fate of more than 200 priests who, during the Protestant Reformation in England, were beheaded or drawn and quartered. Among them was Thomas More's pastor, Father John Larke.[1]

1 *The Lives of Thomas Becket* translated and edited by M. Staunton (New York: Manchester University Press, 2001) includes no less than three eye-witness accounts of Becket's death.

And, of course, during the time of the Roman persecutions, the acts of the Christian martyrs bear witness to their great heroism. Not only were famous bishops, such as Polycarp of Smyrna and Cyprian of Carthage, put to death for their faith but so were obscure but noteworthy priests, such as Pionius of Smyrna[2] and Victor and Lucian at Carthage.[3]

But it is the Bible that preserves for us what is probably the oldest literary account of violence against priests. I am referring to the episode in chapter 22 of the first book of Samuel, a narrative called "the slaughter of the priests at Nob." This account details the shocking destruction of the entire company of priests, 85 in all, at a major Hebrew holy site or shrine. This literary tale is so shocking that it has occasioned a modern cinematic representation in the 1985 film "King David," by Australian director Bruce Beresford.

I believe the biblical account of the slaughter of the priests at Nob holds lessons for contemporary Catholic priests that go beyond merely those of anticlericalism and violence. This story also holds lessons for today's readers about the priest's role in guarding the integrity of the sacraments (determining who should or should not have access to them), reserving the Eucharist and making it available for reverence outside communion (the pious tradition of what is called "adoration of the Blessed Sacrament"), and the enduring value of such priestly observances as celibacy and solidarity. So that we can appreciate those lessons, I shall first present the biblical narrative with attendant commentary in order to help explain both the historical and religious meaning of the narrative. Then, together, we shall look at the interpretations that Christian writers, pastors, and theologians have given to the narrative in 1 Samuel 22.

The story of Ahimelech and the other priests with him at Nob is told in the first book of Samuel in chapters 21 and 22. It is comprised of three narrative episodes, which I have entitled "Ahimelech's Care for the Holy Bread" (1 Sam 21:2–8); "Ahimelech and the Votive Offering of the Sword of Goliath" (1 Sam 21:9–10); and

---

T. S. Eliot's verse drama *Murder in the Cathedral* was first performed in 1935; Ildebrando Pizzetti's opera, *Assassinio nella Cattedrale* ,was premiered in 1958; Jean Anouilh's play *Becket, or L'Honneur de Dieu*, premiered in 1959; and director Peter Glenville's movie *Becket* in 1964.

2. "The Martyrdom of Pionius" in *The Acts of the Christian Martyrs*, pp. 136–67, written around the year 300, during the Decian persecution, is particularly valuable for its witness to the homiletic style of the day, for it includes several examples of Pionius's preaching and his prison homilies.

3. "The Acts of Montanus and Lucius" in *The Acts of the Christian Martyrs*, pp. 214–39, was written toward the end of the year 258. It is a description of the imprisonment and execution of Christians of Carthage under the second edict of the Emperor Valerian. It includes cameo depictions of the prison ministry of the presbyters Victor and Lucian. For example, [on p. 221] Lucian is described as "our dearest brother Lucian, who pierced the most stubborn obstacle of our imprisonment, and ministered to all of us that food that does not fail."

"Ahimelech and the Slaughter of the Priests at Nob." (1 Sam 22:6–23). We shall look at all three episodes and then try to understand them in an effort to disclose their potential meaning for us today.

Ahimelech's Care for the Holy Bread

The first incident, which I have titled "Ahimelech's Care for the Holy Bread," is related in 1 Sam 21:2–8:

> David went to Ahimelech, the priest of Nob, who came trembling to meet him and asked, "Why are you alone? Is there no one with you?" David answered the priest: "The king gave me a commission and told me to let no one know anything about the business on which he sent me or the commission he gave me. For that reason I have arranged a meeting place with my men. Now what have you on hand? Give me five loaves, or whatever you can find." But the priest replied to David, "I have no ordinary bread on hand, only holy bread; if the men have abstained from women, you may eat some of that." David answered the priest: "We have indeed been segregated from women as on previous occasions. Whenever I go on a journey, all the young men are consecrated—even for a secular journey. All the more so today, when they are consecrated at arms!" So the priest gave him holy bread, for no other bread was on hand except the showbread which had been removed from the LORD's presence and replaced by fresh bread when it was taken away. One of Saul's servants was there that day, detained before the LORD; his name was Doeg the Edomite, and he was Saul's chief henchman.

To understand the context of this passage, one must know a little of the social and religious history of Israel. Ahimelech, whose name means "brother of the king," lived in the eleventh century before Christ. He was a priest at Nob, which was an Israelite shrine or holy place. Exegetes debate as to Nob's precise geographical location but most argue that it was not far from Jerusalem, indeed the nearest town to Jerusalem on the north, so close to Jerusalem that it lay within sight of the city. As for the necessary historical background: there is a reason why Ahimelech, the priest of Nob, "came trembling" to meet David. The political situation at the time is what made Ahimelech tremble. Saul was Israel's first king and an insecure one at that. More precisely, up until Saul's time Israel was a very loose tribal confederation held together more by common religious traditions than by any firm legal ties. Indeed, that period in Israel's history was called the time of the judges because the only leadership was supplied by charismatic figures like Samuel. But this loose association made Israel militarily weak and vulnerable. And so Israel's elders came to Samuel and asked him to appoint a king for them (see 1 Sam 8:5). Saul was a humble, unambitious man. In fact, the only thing that made him stand out from other Israelite men was his tall height. But when he led the defense of the Israelite town of Jabesh-Gilead from Ammonite aggression, the elders of Israel were impressed. And so Saul became king. But Saul was always plagued by self doubts, and these came to the fore with the appearance of David. King Saul grew envious and fearful of the young David who, after slaying Goliath, became a popular hero. Indeed, Saul became paranoid by the thought of David unseating him. 1 Sam 18:6–9 witnesses to this development:

> At the approach of Saul and David (on David's return after slaying the Philistine), women came out from each of the cities of Israel to meet King Saul, singing and dancing, with tambourines, joyful songs, and sistrums. The women played and sang: / "Saul has slain his thousands, / and David his ten thousands." / Saul was very angry and resentful of the song, for he thought: "They give David ten thousands, but only thousands to me. All that remains for him is the kingship." [And from that day on Saul was jealous of David.]

Indeed, relations between Saul and David quickly deteriorated to the point that David felt he must leave Saul's presence. However, Saul decided to have David followed and if possible slain. In fact, Saul employed an Edomite named Doeg to spy on David. David took refuge at the village of Nob because it had a sanctuary which he felt Saul would not dare violate.

History of the Holy Bread

To understand the drama of 1 Sam 21:2–8, one must also know something about "the holy bread" that Ahimelech keeps. As we have already seen in chapters 2 and 3 of this book, in earliest Israelite history, the time before the monarchy, there was not yet a great and central religious shrine. That would come later, the temple in Jerusalem. Instead, at this early point in Israel's history, there were several religious shrines in Israel. Each of these shrines, besides serving as a place of prayer and sacrifice, also hosted a particular object of devotion. In the last chapter, we studied Eli and his sons, the priests who tended the Israel shrine at Shiloh. Shiloh was the central shrine of the Israelite tribal confederacy because it housed the principal relic of the Exodus, the ark of the covenant. Nevertheless, the shrine at Nob had not one but two great relics. One was a relic of the Exodus, and that was "the showbread" or "the bread of the presence." The other was a relic called "The Sword of Goliath." We shall discuss the showbread first.

While everyone probably knows something about the ark of the covenant (indeed, director Steven Spielberg's 1981 movie "Raiders of the Lost Ark," in which archeologist and adventurer Indiana Jones is hired by the US government to find the ark of the covenant before the Nazis do, made the ark of the covenant familiar even to nonreligious people), few people, even readers of the Bible who have come across references to the showbread, know much about it.

We first hear of the showbread in the book of Leviticus (24:5–9). "Leviticus" means "priestly things," and it is the name that the Septuagint Greek translators of the Bible bestowed upon the third book of Moses, the third book of the Torah, because that book primarily contains sacrificial and other ritual laws prescribed for the priests of the tribe of Levi. Leviticus begins with the words, "The LORD called Moses and from the meeting tent gave him this message." Throughout Leviticus we hear the phrase repeated again and again, "The LORD said to Moses," as in Lev 4:1; 5:20; 6:1, 12, 17; 7:22, 28; 8:1, et cetera. So too chapter 24 of Leviticus begins with the words, "The LORD said to Moses"; and then in verses 5–9 it says:

> You shall take fine flour and bake it into twelve cakes, using two tenths of an ephah of flour for each cake. These you shall place in two piles, six in each pile, on the pure gold table before the LORD. On each pile put some pure frankincense, which shall serve as an oblation to the LORD, a token offering for the bread. Regularly on each sabbath day this bread shall be set out afresh before the LORD, offered on the part of the Israelites as an everlasting agreement. It shall belong to Aaron and his sons, who must eat it in a sacred place, since as something most sacred among the various oblations to the LORD, it is his by perpetual right.

What in Leviticus 24 is called "twelve cakes" and in 1 Samuel 21 is called "holy bread," is called in the Bible by several other names. For example, in Exod 25:30; 35:14; 39:36; Num 4:7; and 1 Kgs 7:48, it is called "the bread of the presence." Although what is translated as the bread of the presence is quite literally in Hebrew "bread of the face" (*lekhem happanim*). In 1 Chr 9:32, it is called "the bread of the arrangement" or "the bread of the setting forth" (*lekhem hamma 'arakheth*). In 2 Chr 13:11, it is called "the bread of the row" or the "bread set forth in rows." In Num 4:7, it is called the regular or established bread (*lekhem hattamidh*). In the King James translation of the Bible, it is called the "showbread." The strangest translation is that of the Douay Old Testament, wherein the twelve loaves are called the "loaves of proposition." This came about because the Greek *artoi tes protheseos*, literally "bread to be set forth," which was translated in the Latin Vulgate quite literally as *panes propositionis*. The New American Bible translation, which we employ herein, uses the terminology of "the showbread" as in its translation of Exod 25:30, "On the table you shall always keep showbread set before me."

The twelve loaves of bread were placed in the meeting tent, just outside the holy of holies, which is the tabernacle where God dwelt with the Israelites. The loaves were placed there on a table construed for the purpose. In Exod 25:23–30, this table was made of acacia wood and plated in gold. But the language of 1 Kgs 7:48 and 2 Chr 4:19 suggests that in the temple of Solomon this table was made of pure gold. The twelve loaves stood for the twelve tribes of Israel, presented and shown later, in the temple of Jerusalem in the presence of God. The loaves were a symbolic acknowledgement that God was the resource for Israel's life and nourishment, and they also served as Israel's act of thanksgiving to God. The arrangement of the bread on a table in two rows of six (Lev 24) was an important aspect of the presentation. Some verses in the Bible literally speak of "the rows of the bread," as in the Revised Standard Version's quite literal translation of the Hebrew of Neh 10:33. The table, which stood at the west end of the "holy place" of the temple, next to the holy of holies, was also important.

The Jewish historian Flavius Josephus treats of the showbread in his *Antiquities of the Jews* 3.10, 7.[4] He claims the loaves were provided out of the common charge; they were without leaven, and contained twenty-four tenths of a "deal" of flour. Two heaps were baked the day before the Sabbath, and on the morning of the Sabbath the loaves were brought into the holy place where they were set upon the holy table, six in a heap, one loaf leaning against another. On the top of each heap two golden cups of frankincense were placed, where they remained until the next Sabbath when fresh loaves were brought and the old loaves were given to the priests for consumption. The frankincense was then burned in the sacred fire, and a new supply was placed upon the fresh loaves.

If you go to Rome today, you can observe yet another witness to the tradition of the showbread or bread of the presence. Take time to go to the ruins of the ancient Roman Forum. Once you are there, search out the Arch of Titus, the Roman general who conquered and destroyed Jerusalem. On that triumphal monument honoring Titus's achievements as a general, there is a carved panel depicting Titus's soldiers marching with the spoils of war taken from the Jerusalem temple. The most obvious spoil is the great menorah or seven-tiered lampstand (sometimes erroneously called a seven-tiered "candelabra"). Also readily noticeable are the silver trumpets that the Jewish temple priests used to alert the people in the temple precincts to important moments in the liturgy. Not so readily observable on that same panel of the Arch of Titus, though art historians tell us it is depicted there, is another relic of the Jerusalem temple, another holy object of the rituals. And that is the golden table of "the bread of the presence."

But what was the meaning of all this? In Lev 24:8, something of its meaning was indicated when it is declared, "Regularly on each Sabbath day this bread shall be set out afresh before the Lord, offered on the part of the Israelites as an everlasting agreement." This clearly suggests it was a votive offering, a way of showing homage

4. Josephus' *The Complete Works*, p. 80.

to God. But why it should be bread is not entirely clear. Twelve loaves of bread could no doubt serve as a symbolic acknowledgement of how in a generous and general sense God was the resource for Israel's life and nourishment. But it might also have been a reminder of a very precise moment in history when God had provided for Israel's nourishment and sustenance. In Exodus 16, God exhibits his miraculous mercy toward the Hebrew people during their flight from Egypt. We are told in that chapter of Israel's complaint about their hunger and deprivation on the journey through the desert. And we hear the Lord's response when we read in Exod 16:4, "the Lord said to Moses, 'I will now rain down bread from heaven for you.'" It is perhaps also helpful to recall that Exodus 16 ends with the story of how God expressed that the lesson of his merciful care for the Israelites in flight from Egypt should never be forgotten. In Exod 16:32–34 we read, "Moses said, 'This is what the Lord has commanded. Keep an omerful of manna for your descendants, that they may see what food I gave you to eat in the desert when I brought you out of the land of Egypt.' Moses then told Aaron, 'Take an urn and put an omer of manna in it. Then place it before the Lord in safekeeping for your descendants. So Aaron placed it in front of the commandments for safekeeping, as the Lord had commanded Moses."

Sexual Abstinence in Ancient Israel

However, the custom of the showbread is not the only obscure tradition in the narrative of Ahimelech's ministry at Nob. We need to understand Ahimelech's question regarding whether David's men "have abstained from women." The Mosaic law had always seen abstinence from sexual intercourse as a proper preparation for encounter with the divine. In this regard see Moses instruction in Exodus 19 when, during the exodus from Egypt, the Hebrew people arrive at Sinai. In Exod 19:14–15, we read: "Then Moses came down from the mountain to the people and had them sanctify themselves and wash their garments. He warned them, 'Be ready for the third day. Have no intercourse with woman.'" So too we read in Lev 15, in the laws regarding cultic purity, the stricture in Lev 15:18: "If a man lies carnally with a woman, they shall both bathe in water and be unclean until evening." And in Deut 23:10–11, we see how strict was the law against cultic impurity, for there it is not only made a rule for soldiers on campaign but covers even involuntary matters: "When you are in camp during an expedition against your enemies, you shall keep yourselves from everything offensive. If one of you becomes unclean because of a nocturnal emission, he shall go outside the camp, and not return until, toward evening, he has bathed in water; then, when the sun has set, he may come back into the camp." And so David's response is meant to assure the priest Ahimelech that David is very devout and conscientious about such laws. However, the next episode might well lead us to consider that Ahimelech should have been equally circumspect regarding the other great votive offering in the shrine at Nob; for the violence it represents will be visited upon Ahimelech himself.

Ahimelech and the Votive Offering of the Sword of Goliath

This second episode, which I have labeled "Ahimelech and the Votive Offering of the Sword of Goliath," is related in 1 Sam 21:9–10: "David then asked Ahimelech: 'Do you have a spear or a sword on hand? I brought along neither my sword nor my weapons, because the king's business was urgent.' The priest replied: 'The sword of Goliath the Philistine, whom you killed in the Vale of the Terebinth, is here [wrapped in a mantle] behind the ephod. If you wish to take that, take it; there is no sword here except that one.' David said, 'There is not to match it. Give it to me!'"

To understand this episode we must know something about the sword of Goliath, which is the second great relic at the shrine at Nob. In First Samuel 17, we are told of an episode in the history of Saul, the first king of Israel. Saul had not long been king of Israel when one of Israel's neighbors, a people called the Philistines (the meaning of the name is uncertain), a "sea people" located on the coastal plain of Palestine, decided to attack. The great confrontation came when Saul led his army of Israelites against the advancing army of the Philistines at a place called the Valley of Elah. Twice a day for forty days, Goliath the champion of the Philistines, came out between the lines and challenged the Israelites to send out a champion of their own to decide the outcome of the entire battle in a single combat, man-to-man. But Saul and his men are afraid to do this. David, however, accepts the challenge and goes out to meet the heavily armored Goliath, with neither armor, nor shield, nor sword. Instead, David is armed with a slingshot and five smooth stones. And, lo and behold, David knocks out Goliath with one shot and then cuts off Goliath's head using Goliath's own sword. David gave the severed head to King Saul but kept Goliath's sword and armor for himself.

The Slaughter of the Priests at Nob

We are now prepared to read the great and final scene in the story of the priests at Nob, and that final scene is their slaughter. This story is related in 1 Sam 22:6–23:

> Now Saul heard that David and his men had been located. At the time he was sitting in Gibeah under a tamarisk tree on the high place, holding his spear, while all his servants were standing by. So he said to them: Listen, men of Benjamin! Will the son of Jesse give all of you fields and vineyards? Will he make each of you an officer over a thousand or a hundred men, that you have

all conspired against me and no one tells me that my son has made an agreement with the son of Jesse? None of you shows sympathy for me or discloses to me that my son has stirred up my servant to be an enemy against me, as is the case today. Then Doeg the Edomite, who was standing with the officers of Saul, spoke up: "I saw the son of Jesse come to Ahimelech, son of Ahitub, in Nob. He consulted the Lord for him and gave him supplies, and the sword of Goliath the Philistine as well."

At this the king sent a summons to Ahimelech the priest, son of Ahitub, and to all his family who were priests in Nob; and they all came to the king. Then Saul said, "Listen, son of Ahitub!" He replied, "Yes, my lord." Saul asked him, "Why did you conspire against me with the son of Jesse by giving him food and a sword and by consulting God for him, that he might rebel against me and become my enemy, as is the case today?" Ahimelech answered the king: "And who among all your servants is as loyal as David, the king's son-in-law, captain of your bodyguard, and honored in your own house? Is this the first time I have consulted God for him? No indeed! Let not the king accuse his servant or anyone in my family of such a thing. Your servant knows nothing at all, great or small, about the whole matter." But the king said, "You shall die, Ahimelech, with all your family." The king then commanded his henchmen standing by: "Make the rounds and kill the priests of the Lord, for they assisted David. They knew he was a fugitive and yet failed to inform me." But the king's servants refused to lift a hand to strike the priests of the Lord.

The king therefore commanded Doeg, "You make the rounds and kill the priests!" So Doeg the Edomite went from one to the next and killed the priests himself, slaying on that day eighty-five who wore the linen ephod. Saul also put the priestly city of Nob to the sword, including men and women, children and infants, and oxen, asses and sheep.

One son of Ahimelech, son of Ahitub, named Abiathar, escaped and fled to David. When Abiathar told David that Saul had slain the priests of the Lord, David said to him: "I knew that day, when Doeg the Edomite was there, that he would surely tell Saul. I am responsible for the death of all your family. Stay with me. Fear nothing; he that seeks your life must seek my life also. You are under my protection."

We must now consider the influence of these passages on Christian tradition.

Ahimelech and the Showbread in Christian Tradition

No doubt many readers will recognize the passage relating Ahimelech's concern for the holy bread as the passage to which Jesus referred in his debate with the Pharisees on keeping the Sabbath holy. This debate is related in Matt 12:1–4, Mark 2:25–26, and Luke 6:3–4. Here I quote from Matthew's text: "At that time Jesus was going through a field of grain on the Sabbath. His disciples were hungry and began to pick the heads of grain and eat them. When the Pharisees saw this, they said to him, 'See, your disciples are doing what is unlawful to do on the Sabbath.' He said to them, 'Have you not read what David did when he and his companions were hungry, how he went into the house of God and ate the bread of offering, which neither he nor his companions but only the priests could lawfully eat?'"

However, there is yet another, more subtle New Testament allusion to the showbread. And this occurs in Paul's Letter to the Romans 3:21–25: "But now the righteousness of God has been manifested apart from the law, though testified to by the law and the prophets, the righteousness of God through faith in Jesus Christ for all who believe. For there is no distinction; all have sinned and are deprived of the glory of God. They are justified freely by his grace through the redemption in Christ Jesus, whom God set forth as an expiation."

Many exegetes argue that Paul's use of the verb *proetheto* in Rom 3:25 to describe Jesus as the one "whom God put forth" is a self-conscious echo of the language of setting forth the bread of the presence. This is especially cogent if stress is put on the prefix *pro-*. If so stressed, *proetheto* can be taken to mean "God set him forth," in the sense of displaying him publicly. Some also argue that in 1 Cor 11:30, wherein Paul claims that the Corinthians' suffering is the result of profaning the Eucharist, suggests a concern for the holiness of the Lord's Supper service, akin to Ahimlelech's concern about the holiness of the showbread.

This is certainly the interpretation held by Origen of Alexandria. Indeed, among the early church fathers, Origen is perhaps foremost in his insisting on an analogy between the OT bread of the presence and Christ as the bread come down from heaven. Origen treats of the Mosaic law regarding the showbread (Lev 24) at length in the thirteenth of his collection of homilies on Leviticus. In homily 13, part 3, Origen not only makes reference to Paul's use of the verb "to set forth" in Rom 3:25 as a self-conscious reference to the tradition of the showbread as a form of remembrance (twelve loaves put in the presence of the Lord to keep him ever mindful of his people but also to remind them of his constant care for them), but Origen goes on to argue that the showbread is a foreshadowing of the Eucharist. For this argument he cites, among other New Testament passages, the Gospel according to John 6:32–33, "It was not Moses who gave the bread from heaven; my Father gives you the true bread from heaven. For the bread of God is that which comes down from heaven and gives life to the world."[5]

Other patristic writers also make reference to the showbread as a forerunner or type of the Eucharist. For example, Hippolytus of Rome (ca. 170–ca. 236), in his treatise on the *Apostolic Tradition*, in part 31, which is entitled "On Hours of Prayer,"

---

5. Origen, *Homilies on Leviticus*, p. 237.

says: "In the Old Testament the Law bade the showbread to be offered at the third hour; and the dumb lamb was slain which was a type of the perfect Lamb. For Christ is the shepherd, and He is the Bread which came down from heaven."[6] Similarly, Cyril, bishop of Jerusalem, in his *Catechetical Lectures* 22.5, delivered circa AD 350, says: "In the Old Testament also there was shew-bread, but this, as it belonged to the Old Testament, has come to an end; but in the New Testament there is Bread of Heaven."[7]

But there are other writers who focus not upon the holy bread but upon the theme of sexual abstinence, for example, Isidore of Seville (580–636) in his *De Ecclesiasticis Officiis* (bk. 1, pt. 18), "The Sacrifice." Isidore also sees the loaves of the presence as a foreshadowing of the Eucharist, but he chooses to focus upon the proper preparation that a Christian should make before receiving the Eucharist. And thus he invokes the example of Ahimelech's question to David:

> However, marital couples ought to abstain from conjugal union and [they ought] to free themselves for many days of prayer, and thus then approach the body of Christ. Let us read again the book of Kings [1 Sam 21:4–6]. We will find that the priest Achimelech was not willing to first give David and his sons from the breads of proposition, unless he first had asked whether the sons had been pure from a woman, and not only from another woman but also from their wife. Unless he had heard that they had abstained from the conjugal act since yesterday and the day before yesterday, he would never have given them the bread, which he had previously denied. How much difference is there between the breads of proposition and the body of Christ? As much difference as there is between a shadow and a body, between the imagined and the reality, between the example of future things and those things that are prefigured through the examples. For this reason some days should be chosen on which one lives more purely and more continent, so that one can come as a worthy person to such a great sacrament.[8]

Alcuin of York (ca. 735–804), religious advisor to the emperor Charlemagne, in his use of First Samuel 21, was more concerned with the morality of bishops than with that of the laity. This might have been because of his observation of their behavior at the imperial court. We see this in Alcuin's commentary on the Epistle to Titus, in particular Titus 1:8 that says a bishop must be "temperate, just, holy, and self-controlled." Of that passage Alcuin says:

> If laymen are ordered on account of prayer to refrain from intercourse with
> their wives, what should be thought of the bishop who is to offer spotless

---

6. Hippolytus, *Apostolic Tradition*, p. 63.

7. Cyril, *Catechetical Lectures*, p. 152.

8. Isidore, *On Ecclesiastical Offices*, pp. 43–44.

sacrifices of holy prayers daily for his own sins and those of the people? For Ahimelech the priest refused to give to David and his boys the display bread unless he should hear that the boys were clean from women—not only from other men's wives but their own. There is as much difference between the display bread and Christ's body as between shadow and bodies, between a picture and its reality, between foreshadowings of future events and the events of which they are the foreshadowings.[9]

Alcuin's remark a few lines later that, "It befits a bishop to be abstinent, not only in carnal desire but even in the moderation of his speech, and in particular in his thought, that he keep under control what he thinks, what he speaks, and what he does,"[10] this can make one wonder if Alcuin had observed bishops indulging in gossip about the imperial court or pontificating at court on all sorts of topics.

John Henry Newman is the only Christian author I have been able to find who treats of the slaughter of the priests at Nob. This he does in his *Parochial and Plain Sermons* (bk. 2, sermon 3), which is entitled "Saul." Newman treats of the Hebrew people's desire to have a king just like the kings of other nations. Newman goes on to warn that such dependence upon secular authority is dangerous, and the importance of relying not upon one's own strength but of cultivating virtue from God:

Mere natural virtue wears away, when men neglect to deepen it into religious principle. Saul appears in his youth to be unassuming and forbearing; in advanced life he is not only proud and gloomy (as he ever was in a degree), but cruel, resentful and hard-hearted, which he was not in his youth. His injurious treatment of David is a long history; but his conduct to Ahimelech, the high priest, admits of being mentioned here. Ahimelech assisted David in his escape. Saul resolved on the death of Ahimelech and all his father's house. On his guards refusing to execute his command, Doeg, a man of Edom, one of the nations Saul was raised up to withstand, undertook the atrocious deed. On that day, eighty-five priests were slain. Afterwards Nob, the city of the priests, was smitten with the edge of the sword, and all destroyed, "men and women, children and sucklings, and oxen, and asses, and sheep." That is, Saul executed more complete vengeance on the descendants of Levi, the sacred tribe, than on the sinners, the Amalekites, who laid wait for Israel in the way, on their going up from Egypt.[11]

As for our interpretation of the theological importance of these narratives of Ahimelech and the priests at Nob, I believe there are three lessons to be learned. First, there is the lesson about the role of priests in admitting or barring people

9. Alcuin, *Commentary on the Epistle*, p. 203.

10. Ibid.

11. Newman, *Parochial and Plain Sermons*, p. 507.

from access to holy things, the sacraments. Second there is a lesson about sexual abstinence. Finally there is a lesson about the importance of priestly solidarity. Let us first look at the lesson about admitting or barring people from access to holy things.

The People's Right to the Sacraments

The agony in Ahimelech's decision to allow David and his men to eat the showbread is parallel to the issue of the Christian laity's access to the sacraments today. Vatican II has made it clear that the laity have a right to the sacraments. For example, see canon 213 in the current code of canon law: "The Christian faithful have the right to receive assistance from the sacred pastors out of the spiritual goods of the church, especially the word of God and the sacraments."[12] In no way are these rights to be taken lightly. I am referring to the fact that there is a canon that aims specifically at protecting those rights. Canon 221: "The Christian faithful can legitimately vindicate and defend the rights which they enjoy before a competent ecclesiastical court in accord with the norm of law." The two most common, as well as prominent, ways in which this "right to the sacraments" arises today is with regard to access to the Eucharist and marriage as a sacrament. With regard to both, there are times when a priest must make a decision as to whether indeed a lay person can insist on that right. For example, canon 1066, "Before marriage is celebrated, it must be evident that nothing stands in the way of its valid and licit celebration." And canon 1067: "The conference of bishops is to issue norms concerning the examination of the parties, and the marriage banns or other appropriate means for carrying out the necessary inquiries which are to precede marriage. The pastor can proceed to assist at a marriage after such norms have been diligently observed." And, no doubt, the church is at times pilloried for the annulment process. However, I want to explore the issue here in terms of access to the Eucharist, because that obviously has the most affinity to the narrative regarding Ahimelech and the showbread.

Admission to Communion

The concern of Isidore continues to this day. That is, to this day a Catholic priest presiding at the Eucharist should be concerned about all-too-casual communion. With regards to the Eucharist, Catholic Christianity has never practiced open communion. This contrasts with the practice of many Protestant churches that allows open communion. More than once when driving past a church, I have seen a sign

---

12. All quotations here are from the *Code of Canon Law: Latin-English Edition*, a translation prepared under the auspices of the Canon Law Society of America (Washington, DC: Canon Law Society, 1983).

that says "Jesus never turned anyone away, neither do we." And it is true that in his lifetime, in his public ministry, Jesus ate and drank with sinners—and this was a prophetic sign that everyone was invited to the banquet in the kingdom of heaven, and that indeed there might well be some surprises at that banquet when the self-righteous will be excluded and repentant sinners enter in. However, that prophetic sign needs to be distinguished from the sacramental sign that Jesus created in his last meal with his disciples.

The Eucharist is a covenantal sign. It is a fellowship meal among the disciples of Christ. It is primarily a pledge of faith and is not an evangelical tool to solicit faith. We see this in Paul's First Letter to the Church at Corinth where Paul is seriously concerned about all-too-casual communion in the body and blood of Christ. There in 1 Cor 11:27–29 we read: "Therefore whoever eats the bread or drinks the cup of the Lord unworthily will have to answer for the body and blood of the Lord. A person should examine himself, and so eat the bread and drink the cup. For anyone who eats and drinks without discerning the body, eats and drinks judgment on himself." Moreover, one can even argue that this eschatological banquet had its warnings about all-too-casual participation. I have in mind Jesus' parable in Matt 22:1–14 about the wedding banquet to which a guest comes who is not properly dressed:

> Jesus again in reply spoke to them in parables, saying: "The kingdom of heaven may be likened to a king who gave a wedding feast for his son. He dispatched his servants to summon the invited guests to the feast, but they refused to come. A second time he sent other servants, saying, 'Tell those invited: "Behold, I have prepared my banquet, my calves and fattened cattle are killed, and everything is ready; come to the feast."' Some ignored the invitation and went away, one to his farm, another to his business. The rest laid hold of his servants, and mistreated them, and killed them. The king was enraged and sent his troops, destroyed those murderers, and burned their city. Then he said to his servants, 'The feast is ready, but those who were invited were not worthy to come. Go out, therefore, into the main roads and invite to the feast whomever you find.' The servants went out into the streets and gathered all they found, bad and good alike, and the hall was filled with guests. But when the king came in to meet the guests he saw a man there not dressed in a wedding garment. He said to him, 'My friend, how is it that you came in here without a wedding garment?' But he was reduced to silence. Then the king said to his attendants, 'Bind his hands and feet, and cast him into the darkness outside, where there will be wailing and grinding of teeth' Many are invited, but few are chosen."

The *Didache*, an early Christian manual on morals and church practice, witnesses to certain criteria for admission to the Eucharist. Its author, date, and place of origin are unknown. Some scholars date it as early as AD 60; others date it as late as the middle of the second century, that is, circa 150. It says in chapter 9, 5, "Let no one eat or drink of your Eucharist except those who have been baptized into the name of the Lord."[13] And then in chapter XIV, "On the Lord's own day gather together and break bread and give thanks, having first confessed your sins so that your sacrifice may be pure."[14]

But it is also important that we ask ourselves, are we being Pharisaical if we so protect the holiness of the sacrament as to make it inaccessible to any but the most pure? In that regard it is important to recall the history of Jansenism and Pope Pius X's response to the disastrous effects of that movement on our attitude toward Holy Communion. Jansenism was a post-Tridentine Catholic reform movement of a decidedly rigorist character. It is named for Cornelius Jansen (1585–1638), a Dutch theologian from Louvain University who later became Catholic bishop of Ypres in Flanders. Jansen's theological works, later condemned by several popes, gave inspiration to the movement that bore his name. One effect of Jansenism was to make Catholics so scrupulous as to rarely, if ever, receive communion. No reform of Pius X (pope from 1903 to 1914) was more widely acclaimed than his decrees on Holy Communion, which were aimed at redressing that situation. His *Sacra tridentina* of December 20, 1905, encouraged "frequent and daily reception of Holy Communion"; his *Quam singulari* of August 15, 1910, allowed reception of first communion at an earlier age than had been customary.[15]

Politicians and Holy Communion

The relevance of the priest's due vigilance regarding access to the sacraments can be seen from the enduring debate that continues to this day in the United States over whether or not one should deny Holy Communion to Catholic politicians who consistently advocate moral positions rejected by the church. This issue came to a head in 2004 when the Democratic Party decided to run Senator John Kerry of Massachusetts as its presidential candidate. Kerry, an avowed Catholic, was a staunch supporter of abortion rights. Some Catholic bishops had already publicly denied communion to prominent Catholic politicians over this issue, for example, Archbishop Raymond Burke of St. Louis. The issue greatly divided the American bishops. And so, at its November 2003 conference meeting, Cardinal Francis George asked

---

13. *The Didache*, p. 359.

14. Ibid.

15. See Joseph Dougherty's *From Altar-Throne to Table: The Campaign for Frequent Holy Communion in the Catholic Church* (Lanham, MD: The Scarecrow Press, 2010).

the conference's task force to clarify under canon law what ability a bishop has to deny obstinate sinners the Eucharist. In June of 2004, Joseph Cardinal Ratzinger, the prefect of the Vatican's doctrinal office, sent to bishop Wilton Gregory, president of the U.S. Conference of Catholic Bishops, and Cardinal Theodore McCarrick of Washington, DC, who at that time was heading up the U.S. bishops' task force on "Catholic Bishops and Catholic Politicians," a six-point memorandum, "Worthiness to Receive Holy Communion: General Principles."[16] In this memorandum, he laid out the principles under which bishops or other ministers may deny Communion to Catholic politicians who consistently promote legal abortion. It directly addressed "the case of a Catholic politician . . . consistently campaigning and voting for permissive abortion and euthanasia laws." Ratzinger's letter was never delivered to the bishops. Instead, on June 15, 2004, McCarrick relayed its contents verbally to the bishops during their meeting in Denver, Colorado, from June 14 to 19, saying that the Vatican had left the issue of Communion in the hands of the U.S. bishops: "I would emphasize that Cardinal Ratzinger clearly leaves to us as teachers, pastors and leaders whether to pursue this path of denying communion . . . The question for us is not simply whether denial of Communion is possible, but whether it is pastorally wise and prudent."[17] Ratzinger's six-point memorandum was published online July 3, 2004, by the Italian religious news commentator Sandro Magister on the website of the Italian weekly newsmagazine *L'Espresso*. A Vatican official was quick to authenticate it. That the U.S. bishops remain much divided on this issue to this day can be seen from the contrasting opinions expressed more recently by two eminent American ecclesiastics, both now cardinals, Raymond Burke and Donald Wuerl.

Periodica de Re Canonica is a journal of canon law studies published by Rome's Gregorian University. Volume 96 (2007), pages 3–58, contains an article by R. L. Burke, the former archbishop of St. Louis. The article is entitled "The Discipline Regarding the Denial of Holy Communion to Those Obstinately Persevering in Manifest Grave Sin." It is a treatment of canon 915 that says, "Those upon whom the penalty of excommunication or interdict has been imposed or declared, and others who obstinately persist in manifest grave sin, are not to be admitted to Holy Communion." Burke's is a lengthy and learned historical-theological study and its conclusion is clear: "The United States of America is a thoroughly secularized society which canonizes radical individualism and relativism, even before the natural moral law. The application [of canon 915], therefore, is more necessary than ever, lest the faithful, led astray by the strong cultural trends of relativism, be deceived concerning

16. Ratzinger, "Worthiness to Receive."

17. McCarrick, "Interim Reflections," p. 108.

the supreme good of the Holy Eucharist and the gravity of supporting publicly the commission of intrinsically evil acts."[18]

In marked contrast, on May 6, 2009, in an interview published on the website *Politics Daily*, Archbishop Donald Wuerl of Washington DC stated that he would not deny Holy Communion to House Speaker Nancy Pelosi, one of the most prominent Catholic politicians in the country and a vehement supporter of abortion rights. *Politics Daily* is a website dedicated to political news coverage. It was founded in April 2009 by a group of former newspaper reporters and magazine writers with Melinda Henneberger, a former *New York Times* reporter, as its editor-in-chief. In that interview by Henneberger, Archbishop Wuerl said that would be the equivalent of "Communion wielded as a weapon . . . That's the new way to make your point . . . We never—the Church just didn't use Communion this way. It wasn't a part of the way we do things, and it wasn't a way we convinced Catholic politicians to appropriate the faith and live it and apply it; the challenge has always been to convince people." He said of canon 915, "I stand with the great majority of American bishops and bishops around the world in saying this canon was never intended to be used this way."[19]

Sexual Abstinence and Priestly Ministry Today

The second lesson from the story of Ahimelech and the priests at Nob is with regard to the requirement of celibacy. I would argue that David's devout observance of the law of sexual abstinence holds religious value for us today. The idea of soldiers who so focus upon their military task that they forgo relations with their wives, can serve as a model for today's Christian ministers on pastoral assignment. In fact, there is no small irony in the fact that the once pious David, after he had become king, conducted an adulterous affair with the wife of one of his soldiers, Uriah the Hittite. David wanted to cover up Bathsheba's adulterous pregnancy by calling Uriah back from duty and urging him to sleep with his wife. In 2 Sam 11:6–13, David receives a pious rebuke from Uriah:

> David therefore sent a message to Joab, "Send me Uriah the Hittite." So Joab sent Uriah to David. When he came, David questioned him about Joab, the soldiers, and how the war was going, and Uriah answered that all was well. David then said to Uriah, "Go down to your house and bathe your feet." Uriah left the palace, and a portion was sent out after him from the king's table. But Uriah slept at the entrance of the royal palace with the other officers of his

18. Burke's "Denial of Holy Communion, " p. 57.

19. Wuerl's interview can be found at http://www.politicsdaily.com/2009/05/06archbishop-wuerl. In March of 2011, *Politics Daily* ceased to be an independent website and was merged into *The Huffington Post*'s Politics section.

lord, and did not go down to his own house. David was told that Uriah had not gone home. So he said to Uriah, "Have you not come from a journey? Why, then, did you not go down to your house?" Uriah answered David, "The ark and Israel and Judah are lodged in tents, and my lord Joab and your majesty's servants are encamped in the open field. Can I go home to eat and to drink and to sleep with my wife? As the Lord lives and as you live, I will do no such thing. Then David said to Uriah, "Stay here today also, I shall dismiss you tomorrow." So Uriah remained in Jerusalem that day. On the day follow-ing, David summoned him, and he ate and drank with David, who made him drunk. But in the evening he went out to sleep on his bed among the lord's servants, and did not go down to his home.

My comparison here of a Christian minister, and more specifically a Catholic priest, with a soldier is hardly gratuitous. Saint Paul often uses the comparison of Christian ministry with military service. In Phil 2:25, Paul refers to "Epaphroditus, my brother and coworker and fellow soldier." In the Letter to Philemon 1:2, Paul sends greetings to "Archippus our fellow soldier." In chapter 3 of this book, when treating of clergy compensation, I quoted Paul's rhetorical question in 1 Cor 9:76, "Who serves as a soldier at his own expense?" But most relevant to our discussion here, in 2 Tim 2:3–4, Paul urges Timothy to "Bear your share of hardship along with me like a good soldier of Christ. To satisfy the one who recruited him, a soldier does not become entangled in the business affairs of life." And I would add "in the domestic affairs of marriage and family." This is certainly the concern of Paul in 1 Cor 7:32–34, "I should like you to be free of anxieties. An unmarried man is anxious about the things of the Lord. But a married man is anxious about the things of the world, how he may please his wife, and he is divided."

A practical illustration of this can be seen in the matter of pastoral assign-ments. A married clergyman, before considering relocation or reassignment to a new parish, often has to take into consideration the needs of his wife and children. For example, whether the new neighborhood would be safe enough for his children or whether the schools in the new neighborhood would be good enough for his children, or whether the move would put his spouse at too far a distance from her current job or even require a curtailment of his spouse's career.

On October 6, 2005, the Maronite Patriarch of Antioch, Cardinal Nasrallah Pierre Sfeir, in a speech given at the eleventh World Synod of Bishops gathered at the Vatican, praised celibacy. Though his own Maronite Rite allows for married priests, the patriarch nevertheless defended celibacy as a requirement for the clergy. He said "the Maronite Church admits married priests" and that "half of our diocesan priests are married," but "it must be recognized that if admitting married men resolves one problem [the priest shortage], it creates others just as serious." He went on to say, "A married priest has the duty to look after his wife and family, ensuring his children receive a good education and overseeing their entry into society . . . Another difficulty facing a married priest arises if he does not enjoy a good relationship with his parishioners; his bishop cannot transfer him because of the difficulty of transferring his whole family."[20].

Moreover, those who advocate an abrogation of the law of celibacy for priests ought to consider the fact that a married clergy will bring with it its own moral problems: what to do about the scandal of an adulterous priest and how many times will priests (and bishops?) be allowed to divorce and remarry before they are considered a less than edifying example to their flock?

Priesthood: Its Collegial Character

But there is also another possible lesson to be learned from the biblical narrative of the slaughter of the priests at Nob. And that is a lesson about priestly solidarity. I am referring to, in the narratives which we have read, Ahimelech is always called simply a priest. He is not called a high priest or even chief priest. In 1 Sam 21:1, he is referred to simply as "Ahimelech, the priest of Nob." In 1 Sam 21:3, we are told: "David answered the priest." And in 1 Sam 21:5, we read "But the priest replied to David." It is only in the much later work, a work written hundreds of years later, circa AD 94, Flavius Josephus's *Antiquities of the Jews* (bk. 6, ch. 12, paras. 1, 5, and 6), that we find Ahimelech anachronistically referred to as "high priest."[21] Someone could well argue that Ahimelech is simply called a priest because such distinctions as "high priest," "chief priests," and "simple priests" do not come about until the creation of the Jerusalem Temple.[22] But one could also argue that there is an even more profound meaning to this simple description of Ahimelech as "priest of Nob." This description may have been used intentionally so as to convey the sense that all the priests at Nob shared a common dignity. And so as they were equal in life, so were they equal in death—all eighty-five of the priests at Nob were sacred figures; the slaughter of each was a sacrilege. In this regard, it is interesting to note how Aelred Cody, in his *A History of Old Testament Priesthood*, makes much of the collegiate character of the priests at Nob, indeed, claiming it has a deeper and venerable history. I refer to where he says, "The numerous priesthood at Nob (1 Sam. 21:2–10; 22:9–23) presents the aspect of a collegiate priesthood, with Ahimelech a sort of

20. As quoted by Catholic News Agency, Oct. 7, 2005.

21. Josephus, *Complete Works*, pp. 138–39.

22. In pre-monarchical Israel, Aaron was most often referred to simply as "the priest." See in that regard Exod 35:19, 41; Lev 1:7; 7:34; 13:2; 21:21; Num 3:6, 32; 4:16, 28; 7:8; 18:28; 26:64; 33:38; Josh 21:4, 23). See Roland de Vaux's *Ancient Israel*, p. 378.

chief priest or master of the guild . . . but collegiate priesthoods were not unknown among ancient nomads, either, and the sanctuary attendants of the Ark in the desert already have had a collegiate aspect."[23]

One could argue there has been a collegiate character to Christian ministry from the beginning: there is "the college of apostles;" Paul and Barnabas appoint not one but several presbyters in every town; when Paul visits James in Jerusalem in Acts 21:18, "Paul accompanied us on a visit to James and all the presbyters were present." In Acts 20:17–38, that is, the episode called "Paul's farewell speech at Miletus," we are told that Paul assembled the presbyters of Ephesus, and he makes no distinction in ranks among them. Indeed Paul calls all of them not just presbyters but "overseers" *epsikopoi* (Acts 20:28). So too in 1 Pet 5:1, we hear Peter, the prince of the apostles, say, "I exhort the presbyters among you, as a fellow presbyter."

Our English words "college," "colleague," and "collegiality" all are derived from the Latin roots *com* + *legare*, meaning "to tie together." Indeed, in the *Merriam-Webster Dictionary*, the first definition of *college* is "a body of clergy living together and supported by a foundation." The second definition is "a building used for educational purposes." Collegiality as a concept comes from Roman antiquity. Collegiality is the cooperative relationship of colleagues. In republican Rome, collegiality was a principal feature of both government and religion. In republican Rome, civil government was invested not only in the corporate body that was the senate but was also invested in all magisterial positions. That is, there was never one consul but always two, never one censor but always two. In other areas of civic life, the burden of public office was even more widely shared, as in the tradition of having six praetors, eight quaestors, four aediles, and ten tribunes. As for religion in republican Rome, the various priesthoods of pagan Rome were organized into colleges such as the college of pontiffs and the college of augurs. The college of pontiffs was a group of priests responsible for the elaborate ceremonial of the Roman civic cult. No doubt one of them held the title of "supreme pontiff," but since they were grouped together in a collective called a college stresses that they shared a mutual responsibility and an oversight that worked more effectively precisely because it was a shared and not a sole responsibility.

Early on in the Latin West, bishops began using the language of "colleagues" and "colleges" to describe their relationship to each other. In his epistles, Cyprian of Carthage makes much use of the term "colleague." For example, Cyprian's *Epistle 3*, written in the year AD 250, is a letter of condolence to the clergy of Rome upon the death of Pope Fabian. Cyprian opens with the salutation, "Cyprian to the elders and deacons, brethren abiding at Rome, sends greeting." He then refers to the

23. Cody, *History of Old Testament Priesthood*, p. 60.

death of Pope Fabian saying, "the report of the departure of the excellent man, my colleague."[24] *Epistle 37* opens with the salutation, "Cyprian to Caldonius and Herculanus, his colleagues."[25] In his *Epistle 51*, written AD 52, he refers to Pope Cornelius saying, "he was made bishop by very many of our colleagues who were then present in the city of Rome."[26]

After Cyprian, Augustine of Hippo's contemporary, Optatus, bishop of Milevis in North Africa, wrote a tract challenging a fellow named Parmenian who was the leader of the schismatic Donatist faction at Carthage. In his *Against Parmenian, the Donatist*, written between the years 364–367, Optatus uses the word *collegium* several times. In book 1, chapter 4, Optatus refers to Donatist leaders saying, "Since they refuse to form an episcopal college with us, let them not be colleagues if they do not want it."[27] In book 7:6, he challenges a claim of Parmenian: "Why do you say that the episcopal college could have been polluted?"[28]

However, it is also important we recognize that, at that same time, there was in the early church a sense of the dignity of presbyters and their own collegial character. For example, Ignatius of Antioch (ca. 35–ca. 107—who is often considered, if not the creator of, then certainly one of the earliest advocates of the so-called "monarchical" episcopate) recommended that the laity show deference not only to their bishop but also to their presbyters. In Ignatius to the Ephesians 2.2, Ignatius urges the people to be "subject to the bishop and to the presbytery."[29] In Ignatius to the Trallians 2.2, we hear him say "you should do nothing without the bishop but be also in subjection to the presbytery."[30]

It is also important to note how Cyprian of Carthage, yet another figure often associated with the monarchical episcopate, not only continues to reference the presbyters but, at times, even makes reference to the presbyterate in a manner that suggests their sacerdotal dignity. As did Peter in 1 Pet 5:1, so too Cyprian, at times, identifies himself with the presbyters. For example, in that same *Epistle 37* quoted above, wherein Cyprian greeted his fellow bishops Caldonius and Herculanus as "his colleagues," Cyprian then goes on to greet Rogatianus and Numidicus as his "fellow presbyters."[31] So too, when writing to Pope Cornelius of Rome in the year AD 252

---

24. Cyprian, *Epistles*, p. 281.

25. Ibid., p. 315.

26. Ibid., p. 329.

27. Optatus, "Against Parmenian," in the volume *Against the Donatists*, p. 3.

28. Ibid., p. 146.

29. *Apostolic Fathers* trans. by K. Lake, p. 175

30. Ibid., p. 215.

31. Cyprian, *Epistles*, p. 329.

(in *Epistle 44*, sometimes numbered 49), Cyprian greets Cornelius with an inclusive reference to "the very distinguished clergy who preside with you there."[32] And at this point the translator has a note explaining that this reference is not to "auxiliary bishops" but to the entire presbyterate of Rome.[33] But even more significantly, while Cyprian never addresses presbyters by the title *sacerdotes*, nevertheless he describes them in his *Epistle 1,1* as *divino sacerdotio honorati*, that is, "honored with the sacred priesthood." In *Epistle 61,3*, Cyprian refers to Roman presbyters who were martyred along with Pope Cornelius as *cum episcopo sacerdotali honore coniuncti*, that is, "presbyters united with that bishop in the dignity of the priesthood."[34]

Irenaeus of Lyons (ca. 130–ca. 200) is another important witness not only to the dignity of presbyters but also to their collegial character. Irenaeus was partial to the language of presbyters and used it often in the Jewish fashion of referring to the teaching of the elders, the traditions passed on by Christian ministers. For example, in his *Proof of the Apostolic Preaching* 3, he says "as the elders, the disciples of the apostles, have handed down to us."[35] And in 61, "the elders say." But the most interesting of his use of the term elders or presbyters can be found in his *Against Heresies* (bk. 4, ch. 26, para. 2): "Wherefore it is incumbent to obey the presbyters who are in the Church—those who, as I have shown possess the succession from the apostles; those who, together with the succession of the episcopate, have received the certain gift of truth, according to the good pleasure of the Father. But [it is also incumbent] to hold in suspicion others who depart from the primitive succession, and assemble themselves together in any place whatsoever."[36] Indeed, two paragraphs later he warns: "From all such persons, therefore, it behooves us to keep aloof, but to adhere to those who, as I have already observed, do hold the doctrine of the apostles, and who together with the order of presbyters (*presbyterii ordine*), display sound speech and blameless conduct for the confirmation and correction of others."[37]

Yet another example of a bishop consulting his presbyters comes from Cornelius of Rome. Among the corpus of letters by Cyprian of Carthage, there is one that is not by him but rather addressed to him by Pope Cornelius at Rome. It is numbered in Cyprian's corpus as *Epistle 45*, written in AD 251. There Cornelius writes to Cyprian to inform him of his handling of the request on the part of several renegade presbyters at Rome. These renegades, who had been part of the Novatian schism, had

32. Ibid., p. 346.

33. Ibid., footnote #3.

34. This is the translation of G. W. Clarke in *The Letters of St. Cyprian of Carthage*, Vol. 3, Mahwah, NJ: Paulist Press, 1986, p.93.

35. Irenaeus , *Proof of the Apostolic Teaching*, p. 49.

36. Irenaeus , *Against Heresies*, p. 497.

37. Ibid.

requested to return to the church. Of this process Cornelius says: "The whole of this transaction therefore being brought before me, I decided that the presbytery should be brought together . . . so that by well-grounded counsel it might be determined with the consent of all what ought to be observed with respect to their persons."[38]

At the Second Vatican Council, the terms colleagues, colleges, and collegiality—derived from Cyprian of Carthage—were used to describe the form of power sharing, which is the participation of bishops in the government of the Roman Catholic Church in collaboration with the pope. This is set forth in *Lumen gentium* 19 and 22. Nevertheless, even the Second Vatican Council, which so exalted the authority of bishops over that of presbyters, made an effort to insist that bishops ought to regard presbyters with special esteem. For example, look at *Lumen gentium* 28:

> Christ, whom the Father sanctified and sent into the world (John 10:36) has, through His apostles, made their successors, the bishops, partakers of His consecration and His Mission. These in their turn have legitimately handed on to different individuals in the Church various degrees of participation in this ministry. Thus, the divinely established ecclesiastical ministry is exercised on different levels by those who from antiquity have been called bishops, priests, and deacons. Although priests do not possess the highest degree of the priesthood, and although they are dependent on the bishops in the exercise of their power, they are nevertheless united with the bishops in sacerdotal dignity. By the power of the sacrament of orders, and in the image of Christ the eternal High Priest (Heb 5:1–10; 7:24; 9:11–28), they are consecrated to preach the gospel, shepherd the faithful, and celebrate divine worship as true priests of the New Testament.[39]

But there were interpretations after the council that obscured this conciliar teaching. For one thing, Abbott's translation here is not truly helpful. The Latin says, *Presbyteri, quamvis pontificatus aspicem non habeant.* Tanner, by contrast, translates this more accurately as "although priests do not possess the highest degree of the *pontificate*."[40] The word "pontiff" and its analogous terms, pontifical and pontificate, are derived from the Latin word *pontifex*, which in turn seems to be a composite, descriptive term made up from two Latin words, *pons* for "bridge" and *facere*, "to make. This title of "bridge builder" could have been a spiritual descriptive: building a bridge between man and God. But some argue it is a reference to antique rites performed at bridges over the Tiber. Either way, it appears to have entered Christian vocabulary from its use in second century Old Latin translations of the Bible, where it was used

---

38. Cyprian, *Epistles*, p. 323.

39. Abbott, *Documents*, pp. 52–53.

40. Tanner, *Decrees*, Vol. 2, p. 872.

as the term to translate the Hebrew or NT Greek high priest (likewise in the later, fourth-century Vulgate translation).

But then there is also the problem raised by Guilford Clyde Young. In the introduction to this book, I referred to the interpretation offered by Guilford Clyde Young, archbishop of Hobart, Tasmania, Australia, from 1955 to 1988. He attended the Second Vatican Council and afterward was invited by the publisher Herder and Herder to write the introduction to the text of *Presbyerorum ordinis*, the Council's Decree on the Ministry and Life of Priests, in Walter M. Abbott's edition of *The Documents of the Vatican II*. In his introduction to the Councils' decree on priests, Young says: "The Decree teaches unequivocally that the bishop fully possesses (in the sacramental order) the priesthood of Christ, while the priest participates in that priesthood in a derived and dependent manner. The bishop alone is the direct and immediate sign of Christ to the flock, while the priest is a sign, not directly of Christ the Priest, but of the bishop."[41]

In all the commentaries on the council, I can find only one reference to Archbishop Young's participation. In *The Council Daybook: Vatican II, Session 4 (Sept. 14 to Dec. 8, 1965)*, p. 278, it is noted that Archbishop Young was one of eleven bishops who signed a letter addressing certain passages in the draft schema on the Church in the Modern World that referred to nuclear arms. Whatever Archbishop Young's competence with regard to the Council's Decree on the Ministry and Life of Priests, his is an ill-phrased and misleading understanding of the teaching of the Second Vatican Council. Most probably, Young's words are an indirect reference to *Lumen gentium* 41, where the council fathers use the phrase "the fullness of the priesthood" when referring to bishops (*Ad plenitudinem sacerdotis electi, sacramental gratia donantus*), and there it is used simply to insist upon the truly sacramental character of episcopal ordination. Instead, the council most often says "the fullness of the sacrament of orders." This is the phrase used in *Presbyterorum ordinis* 7: "the fullness of the sacrament of orders which the bishop enjoys" (*plentiudinem sacramenti ordinis qui episcope gaudent*). See *Lumen gentium* 21, in the Abbott translation, "This sacred Synod teaches that by Episcopal consecration is conferred the fullness of the sacrament of orders" (*plenitudinem conferri sacramenti ordinis*). *Lumen gentium* 26 begins with the words, "A bishop, marked with the fullness of the sacrament of orders" (*Episcopus, plenitudine sacramentis ordinis insignitus*). Vatican II's Decree on the Bishops' Pastoral Office in the Church, *Christus dominus*, article 15 says, "Bishops enjoy the fullness of the sacrament of orders, and all priests as well as deacons are dependent upon them in the exercise of authority" (*Episcopi enim plenitudinem sacramenti ordinis gaudent*).

41. Abbott, *Documents*, p. 527.

Priests: The Bishop's Principal Counsellors

There is a similar problem with interpretation and implementation of the Second Vatican Council's teaching on yet another expression of collegiality, presbyteral councils. In *Presbyterorum ordinis*, article 7 we read:

> Therefore, on account of this communion in the same priesthood and ministry, the bishop should regard priests as his brothers and friends. As far as in him lies, he should have at heart the material and especially spiritual welfare of his priests. For above all, upon the bishops rests the heavy responsibility for the sanctity of his priests. Hence he should exercise the greatest care on behalf of the continual formation of his priests. He should gladly listen to them, indeed, consult them, and have discussions with them about those matters which concern the necessities of pastoral work and the welfare of the diocese.
>
> In order to put these ideals into effect, a group or senate of priests representing the presbytery should be established. It is to operate in a manner adapted to modern circumstances and needs and have a form and norms to be determined by law. By its counsel, this body will be able to give effective assistance to the bishop in his government of the diocese.[42]

This conciliar mandate was implemented juridically through a *motu proprio* of Pope Paul VI entitled *Ecclesiae sanctae* and dated August 6, 1966. It required the establishment in every diocese of a presbyteral council, which it described as "an assembly or senate of priests who represent the body of priests (presbyterium) and who by their counsel can effectively assist the bishop in the government of the diocese."[43] The new code of canon law was promulgated by Pope John Paul II on January 25, 1983, and went into effect November 17, 1983. In the new code, presbyteral councils are treated in book 2, The People of God, part 2, The Hierarchical Constitution of the Church, title 3, "The Internal Ordering of Particular Churches," chapter 3, canons 495–501.

How successful has been this attempt at extending collegiality so as to allow simple priests, that is, presbyters a part in it? Only half of the members of a presbyteral council are freely elected by the priests of the diocese. The others have membership *ex officio*, that is, because of a position they hold in the diocesan administration or because they have been nominated by the bishop. Moreover, it is for the bishop to decide when to consult his presbyteral council. Moreover, not only does the bishop preside over the meetings of his presbyteral council, but he alone determines the agenda (see canon 500).

---

42. Ibid., pp. 547–49.
43. Paul VI, *Ecclesiae sanctae*, pp. 604–5.

The Canon Law Society of America (CLSA) has an annual convention. The addresses and presentations made at the convention are published in a volume called *Proceedings*. In the year 2006, the society's sixty-eighth annual convention was held at Fort Worth, Texas, October 9–12. Afterwards, when the convention's proceedings were published there appeared among its pages an essay entitled "Collaboration, Consultation, *Communio* between Bishops and Priests: Structures and Issues." The author, Reverend Patrick S. Brennan, was a priest of the Archdiocese of Portland, Oregon, Judicial Vicar of the Portland Archdiocesan Tribunal and former spiritual director of Rome's North American College. He begins his essay saying:

> A couple of years ago, opening the diocesan mail, I came across a memo from the chair of the Presbyteral Council. It said that the next Presbyteral Council had been cancelled because there were no topics for discussion. At first, I found this somewhat amusing—no topics for discussion. This was the "post-charter" era, and my archdiocese was on the brink of bankruptcy. There were many questions, regarding finances, particularly in light of the settlements made with the victims of priest sexual misconduct. Would the diocesan assessment have to be increased, would services from the Pastoral Center be curtailed, would diocesan staff be let go, would the land and assets of the parishes be jeopardized? There were many questions, and few answers—but no topics for discussion.
>
> My bemusement soon turned to concern: how could there be nothing to discuss between the bishop and his priests? Even if there were an open forum with the bishop, to allow priests to raise whatever issues seemed important to them, wouldn't this be a valuable use of the Presbyteral Council's time?[44]

Father Galot's Bold Thesis

With regard to discerning the dignity as well as the duties of the presbyteral office, it is instructive to examine a work by the Belgian Jesuit, Father Jean Galot (1919–2008). Galot had no role in the Second Vatican Council. He was a theology professor at the Jesuit theologate at Egenhoven near Louvain, Belgium, from 1953 to 1967. In 1968 he went to Rome to join the theology faculty of the Pontifical Gregorian University where he taught until 1988. During his time at the Gregorian, he served as an advisor for the Vatican's Congregation for the Clergy, all the while publishing numerous works, essays, and books on Christology and Mariology. However, his work that is most relevant to our interests is his book-length study, first published in 1981 as *Teologia del sacerdozio*, and then in English translation as *Theology of the Priesthood*. Daniel Donovan, professor of systematic theology at St. Michael's, the University of

---

44. Brennan, "Collaboration, Consultation," p. 87.

Toronto, in his book *What Are They Saying About Ministerial Priesthood?*, dedicated an entire chapter (6) to a consideration of Galot's work on priesthood. Donovan sees Galot's book as being much in line with the teaching of the Second Vatican Council. For example, Donovan says "It represents a clearly argued and coherent theology that attempts to do justice to Vatican II while reacting vigorously against certain recent developments."[45] Later, Donovan gives a more concrete example of this, saying: "When it comes to spelling out in more detail the tasks involved in the ministerial priesthood, Galot has recourse to the three traditional functions highlighted by Vatican II."[46] And once again Donovan emphasizes that Galot's criticisms are not of Vatican II but of post-conciliar developments: "Galot's theology of the priesthood contains much that is in Vatican II but it tends to emphasize those aspects of the conciliar teaching that many in the post-conciliar period were neglecting."[47]

I am not so convinced that Galot's theology of the priesthood is in complete continuity with the teachings of Vatican II, or that he only seeks to curb post-conciliar problems. While I believe Galot is essentially loyal to the spirit of the Second Vatican Council and at times, as in his embrace of the *munus triplex Christi*, even loyal to the letter; nevertheless it seems to me that Galot's Thomistic heritage leads him to take stances that, if not critical of Vatican II, are not easily reconciled. For example, I think Donovan points to one of these stances, and yet fails to recognize its potency, when he says: "In much of what he has to say there Galot makes no distinction between bishops and presbyters. For him as for most theologians today the two terms are interchangeable in the NT. It was only later that the hierarchy as we now know it developed. He affirms and makes his own the shift that Vatican II represents in this regard in comparison to Trent. The fundamental office is the episcopate in which in a restricted sense the presbyterate shares."[48]

To see what I mean, I refer the reader to chapter 9 of Galot's book, the chapter entitled "Ranks in the Sacrament of Order." It contains some remarkable distinctions. For example, in the section on the sacramentality of the episcopate, Galot begins by saying, "The most significant advance in the doctrinal teaching of Vatican II lies in the statement that the episcopate is a sacrament."[49] And then he quotes Vatican II's dogmatic Constitution on the Church, article 21, "The sacred Synod teaches that by episcopal consecration is conferred the fullness of the sacrament of orders." But the very next paragraph begins with an amazing qualification, for there Galot

---

45. Donovan, *What Are They Saying*, p. 75.

46. Ibid., p. 82.

47. Ibid., p. 83.

48. Ibid., p. 80.

49. Galot, *Theology of the Priesthood*, p. 183.

says, "The expression 'the sacred Synod teaches' shows that the Council intended to affirm the truth in question with all of its pastoral authority, but without engaging its doctrinal infallibility."[50]

Moreover, Galot's section on "Ranks in the Sacrament of Order" goes on to make comparisons between presbyteral and episcopal powers that seem to support the idea that there is much more in common than different between these two "ranks in the sacrament of order." For example, Galot concludes the section on the "fullness of the sacrament of order" with this statement: "To conclude the demonstration of the specificity of episcopal functions, the Council mentions the power to consecrate bishops, but it refrains from asserting that only bishops have this power. It merely states that they do have it. This caution is traceable to the doubts entertained by some theologians. On the strength of information relative to the church of Alexandria in the early centuries, these theologians do not exclude the possibility of an episcopal consecration performed by presbyters."[51] In section "d. The power to ordain delegated to priests," Galot makes a similar kind of distinction regarding the power to ordain priests. He begins by saying: "The Council's declaration on the sacramentality of the episcopate fails to resolve the difficulty occasioned by the fact that priests have been granted a pontifical delegation to perform ordinations. In several instances, popes have granted abbots of monasteries or missionaries the privilege to confer orders, the priesthood included."[52]

After surveying the controversies over such papal delegations, Galot sets forth his own opinion on the matter: "We are left with the supposition that these bulls imply a power to ordain already radically present in the priest. Normally, this power is kept under restraint and cannot be validly exercised unless, by an act of jurisdiction, the competent authority grants a concession to that effect. Likewise we may maintain that, radically, the priest has the power to confirm."[53] Galot goes on to insist that the ordinary minister of both ordination and confirmation is the bishop, and that simple priests can exercise those powers only with permission. But the point still remains that the Second Vatican Council's insistence upon the genuine sacramentality of the episcopal office is not meant to imply the secondary, derivative character of the presbyteral office. Sacramentally, at least, a presbyter has the same power *in potency* as any bishop.

Moreover, we should consider the fact that Galot is not a lone voice in his uneasiness with the council's emphatic exultation of episcopacy over priesthood, its

50. Ibid.
51. Ibid., pp. 184–85.
52. Ibid., p. 186.
53. Ibid., p. 187.

vehement "episcopalianism." During the council itself, in December of 1963, at the end of the second session, Karl Rahner, one of the most prominent periti (theological experts) at the council, published an article in the journal *Stimmen der Zeit* (89: 161-195). It was entitled "On the Episcopacy." In it he says, "Here and there some anxiety has been felt about the consequences of marking out more clearly the mission and authority of the bishop as one who rules his diocese in the name of Christ and not merely as an official of the pope. In place of a Roman-centralist (supposedly or really) autocratic government, may there be a danger of "episcopalism" appearing in practice and an autocratic diocesan government?"[54]

Two pages later Rahner describes what he feels should be the relationship between priests and their bishop:

> The presbyterium . . . is not merely the sum-total of parish-priests of places where there does not happen to be a bishop, but precisely the college in the place where the bishop is; he does not ordain priests because he cannot himself be everywhere, he ordains someone to assist him in his functions where he is. He does not ordain an individual, but surrounds himself with a college. He does nothing without the presbyterium . . . which he did indeed ordain as his presbyterium, as his council of "elders."[55]

The idea that presbyters should be seen as no mere servants of, nor even representatives of, but rather as the principal counselors for, advisors to, their bishop is an ancient theme, an important principal to be defended. Witness the vehemence of Saint Jerome in his Letter 52:

> Bishops should know themselves to be priests not lords. Let them render to the clergy the honor which is their due that the clergy may offer to them the respect which belongs to bishops. There is a witty saying of the orator Domitius which is here to the point: "Why am I to recognize you as leader of the Senate when you will not recognize my rights as a private member?" We should realize that a bishop and his presbyters are like Aaron and his sons. As there is but one Lord and one Temple; so also should there be but one ministry.[56]

Finally, we should consider a remarkably similar teaching in a work of the great Tubingen theologian Johann Adam Möhler (1796–1838). Möhler's two principal works are *Einheit in die Kirke* and *Symbolik* (Symbolism). Though for the most part Möhler follows the episcopalianism of Cyprian of Carthage, and often indulges in a naive historicism that sees the episcopate as preceding the presbyterate, there are yet times when he has more equitable things to say about these two offices. For example,

54. Rahner, Bishops, p. 44..

55. Ibid. pp. 46-47

56. Jerome, *Letters*, p. 93.

in his *Symbolism: Or the Exposition of the Doctrinal Differences Between Catholics and Protestants as Evidenced by Their Symbolical Writings*, in chapter 43, "The Hierarchy," Möhler says: "The priests (taking the word in a more limited sense) are, as it were, a multiplication of the bishop."[57] The original is *Die Priester (im engeren Sinne) sind eine vervielfatigung des Bischofes*. That Möhler is teaching that the priest is not just a representative of the bishop but is himself a genuine example of pastoral oversight (*episcopia*) can be seen by a lexical analysis of his words here. Of the original German it is important to note that *vervielfatigen* is the transitive verb that means "to multiply, copy, reproduce, duplicate." And thus the noun *vervielfatigung* means a reproduction, duplication, copying, or duplicate copy. Indeed, the modern term *vervielfaltigungs apparat* is the term for a mimeograph duplicator.

Today, more than ever, we need the witness of a chief priest who not only reigns over or presides above but also stands with and among his presbyterate, his fellow priests; stands with them especially in the face of violent opposition. And this is why it is not just collegiality that is needed but solidarity.

Solidarity is a union of interests, purposes, or sympathies among members of a group, a fellowship of responsibilities and interests. Our English word "solidarity" is derived from the French *solidarité*, which in turn comes from the Latin noun *solidum*, a whole or sum, from the Latin adjective *solidus* meaning solid or whole. Most recently it has become a political term in the West. For example, it is the name of an independent union of workers in Poland, formed in 1980 under the leadership of Lech Walesa. This theme was also taken up by Pope John Paul II who in his encyclical letter of December 30, 1987, entitled *Sollicitudo rei socialis* ("on social concerns") in part 5, article 40, said:

> Solidarity is undoubtedly a Christian virtue . . . In the light of faith, solidarity seeks to go beyond itself, to take on the specifically Christian dimensions of total gratuity, forgiveness and reconciliation. One's neighbor is then not only a human being with his or her own rights and a fundamental equality with everyone else, but becomes the living image of God the Father, redeemed by the blood of Jesus Christ and placed under the permanent action of the Holy Spirit. One's neighbor must therefore be loved, even if an enemy, with the same love with which the Lord loves him or her; and for that person's sake one must be ready for sacrifice, even the ultimate one: to lay down one's life for the brethren (cf. 1 John 3:16).[58]

One might well argue, when Ahimelech went to his death alongside his brother priests it was an outstanding example of solidarity.

---

57. Mohler, *Symbolism*, p. 309.

58. John Paul II, *On Social Concern*, p. 78.

5

Priesthood, Power, and Ambition

Zadok, High Priest and Friend of Kings

EVEN PEOPLE WHO KNOW little or nothing about western classical music probably have heard at one time or another Handel's "Hallelujah Chorus" and that is because it can be heard not just in the concert hall or on recordings but from time to time it is used in Christian worship services. It has even been used as background music in cinematic films and television commercials. Its composer, George Frideric Handel (1685–1759), was a true cosmopolitan. Though born and raised in Germany, he learned to write music in the Italian manner and ended up spending much of his adult life in England. In England he not only composed the oratorio called *Messiah*, from which his "Hallelujah" chorus comes, but he also wrote music for state occasions including four anthems for the coronation of King George II in 1727. An anthem is a peculiarly Anglican liturgical form designed to replace the motet used at Catholic Masses. An anthem is a song of celebration (cf. our national anthem), and the most famous of the coronation anthems composed by Handel is the one entitled *Zadok the Priest*. Indeed, it has been used at the coronation of every British monarch since George II. The text of that anthem is a paraphrase of 1 Kgs 1:38–40, which describes the response of the people at the solemn ceremonies celebrating Solomon's accession to the throne after his father, David: "Zadok, the Priest and Nathan, the Prophet anointed Solomon King and all the people rejoiced, and said: 'God save the King, long live the king, may the king live forever! Amen, Hallelujah!'" The Zadok referred to in Handel's coronation anthem would no doubt take great pride in the fact that, more than two thousand years after his death, he figures prominently in an anthem celebrating the coronation of a king. This Zadok would likewise enjoy being featured in a book on Christian priesthood, such as this one.

Zadok (meaning "righteousness") is the name of more than one person in the Bible. For example, in the book of Nehemiah 3:4 there is a "Zadok, son of Baana," who worked to repair the walls of the ruined city of Jerusalem when the Hebrew people returned there after their exile in Babylon. Also, in the genealogy of Jesus that begins Matthew's gospel there is mentioned, as an ancestor of Jesus, a Zadok, "son of Azor and father of Achim"(Matt 1:14), who was an ancestor of Joseph. However, the Zadok who we are interested in and whose memory is invoked in the title of Handel's coronation anthem was high priest in Jerusalem during the time of David and Solomon. Indeed, he was not just a counselor to King David but his personal friend and, moreover, it was Zadok who secured the much disputed succession to the throne of Israel for David's son, Solomon. This Zadok went on to become the most famous of Israel's high priests after Aaron and, indeed, was the founder of a long-lived dynasty of high priests. No study of OT priesthood can omit him. Moreover, I believe there are enduring lessons to be learned about clerical ambition and political power from a study of Zadok's life and ministry.

So that we can learn those lessons, it is important that we begin our study by carefully surveying those biblical passages that can inform us about Zadok and his ministry.

Zadok: A Friend of the King

The first mention of Zadok is in 2 Sam 8:15–18, which is a description of King David's inner circle: "David reigned over all Israel, judging and administrating justice to all his people. Joab son of Zeruiah, was in command of the army. Jehoshaphat, son of Ahilud, was chancellor. Zadok, son of Ahitub, and Ahimelech, son of Abiathar, were priests. Shawsha was scribe. Benaiah, son of Jehoiada, was in command of the Cherethites and Pelethites. And David's sons were priests."

That very last sentence needs immediate clarification: David's sons are never mentioned again as priests. For example, later in 2 Sam 20:25–26 others are named as David's priests, and in 1 Chr 18:17 there is no mention at all of priests other than the high priest. Exegetes explain the reference here to David's sons as priests as being an invocation of the theme that royalty can at times exercise certain priestly prerogatives (as in 2 Sam 6:18). This theme will come in for some importance later when we consider the way in which modern secular rulers have attempted to insert themselves in what otherwise would be considered purely ecclesiastical or clerical affairs. But for now we want to return to our observation of Zadok and his importance.

The next time we hear of Zadok is during an episode in the tale of dynastic struggles among David's sons to determine who would succeed David on the throne of Israel. This is a veritable soap-opera plot of family intrigues, sex, and political ambition. Here it is important that we understand King David had four legitimate sons and one who was illegitimate. Amnon was David's first son and thus heir-apparent.

David's second son, Chileab, died young. David had a third son, Absalom, from a second marriage. David had yet a fourth son, Adonijah. The fifth son was Solomon, the offspring of David's adulterous affair with Bathsheba.

As for the legitimate sons, there was always a rivalry between Amnon, the first son and heir-apparent, and Absalom, David's third son. This rivalry was in part because Absalom was much more handsome and a born leader. The tensions between these two sons of David reached a critical point when Amnon seduced Absalom's sister Tamar into his house and then raped her. David was enraged by Amnon's actions but still kept him first in the line of succession. However, Absalom plotted revenge; and indeed two years later contrived to have Amnon murdered. Absalom, fearing the wrath of his father David, left Jerusalem. During this time of his self-imposed exile, Absalom built himself a political and military following, all the while stirring popular resentment against David's financial extravagance. People with any sort of grievance flocked to Absalom's cause. When Absalom mustered a sizeable army to march on Jerusalem, David fled the city with his loyal followers. This event is told in 2 Sam 15:13–18:

> An informant came to David with the report, "The Israelites have transferred their loyalty to Absalom." At this, David said to all his servants who were with him in Jerusalem: "Up! Let us take flight, or none of us will escape from Absalom. Leave quickly, lest he hurry and overtake us, then visit disaster upon us and put the city to the sword." The king's officers answered him, "Your servants are ready, whatever our lord the king chooses to do." Then the king set out, accompanied by his entire household, except for ten concubines whom he left behind to take care of the palace. As the king left the city, with all his officers accompanying him, they halted opposite the ascent of the Mount of Olives, at a distance, while the whole army marched past him.

But what happens next is most dramatic, for it was not just David's army that followed him out of Jerusalem. No, along came also the priests Zadok and Abiathar with their retinues carrying the ark of the covenant. More precisely, as David led the procession of his family and servants out of the capital and into the wilderness, Zadok and his fellow priest Abiathar came with Levites, bearing the ark of the covenant of God; and they set down the ark of God so that all the people could see it as they passed out of the city. This was meant as a powerful sign, that is, Zadok and Abiathar were making it clear to David and to all that their loyalty to David was such that they were prepared to abandon the city of Jerusalem and follow David into exile. Indeed, it was a sign that showed they were fully prepared to share his exile. However, David instead instructed Zadok and Abiathar to remain in Jerusalem and serve as his informers while he would go east of the Jordan to muster support there for himself. David instructed them to remain with the ark in Jerusalem, and Zadok and his son Ahimaaz were of assistance in sending David intelligence of the plans of Absalom (2 Sam 15:24–35; 17:15; 18:19–27). The rebellion ended when David's army defeated Absalom's militia, and Absalom himself was killed in the rout. It is worth quoting here at length the narration of Zadok and Abiathar's role in all this as it is told in 2 Samuel 15:24–37:

> Zadok, too [with all the Levite bearers of the ark of the covenant of God], and Abiathar brought the ark of God to a halt until the soldiers had marched out of the city. Then the king said to Zadok: "Take the ark of God back to the city. If I find favor with the LORD, he will bring me back and permit me to see it and its lodging. But if he should say, "I am not pleased with you," I am ready; let him do to me as he sees fit." The king also said to the priest Zadok: "See to it that you and Abiathar return to the city in peace, and both your sons with you, your own son Ahimaaz, and Abiathar's son Jonathan. Remember, I shall be waiting at the fords near the desert until I receive information from you." So Zadok and Abiathar took the ark of God back to Jerusalem and remained there.

And indeed 2 Sam 17:15–22 tells of how Zadok and Abiathar sent their sons Jonathan and Ahimaaz to inform David of Absalom's plans. And because of this Absalom was defeated, indeed, he lost his life in the rout.

Zadok's Role in Solomon's Succession

Zadok and Abiathar appear once again at a critical moment in the life of King David, but this time their actions will differ significantly and indeed fatefully for both of them. This incident, called the "Ambition of Adonijah," is related in 1 Kings, chapter 1. It is yet another event in the dynastic struggle to determine who would succeed David on the throne of Israel.

Years later when David had grown old, David's oldest surviving legitimate son, Adonijah, at forty years of age and tired of waiting to succeed to the throne, tried to seize control from his old and infirm father, King David. Once again Zadok remained ferociously loyal to David and refused to cooperate. Here is how this is related in 1 Kgs 1:5–10:

> Adonijah, son of Haggith, began to display his ambition to be king. He acquired chariots, drivers, and fifty henchmen. Yet his father never rebuked him or asked why he was doing this. Adonijah was also very handsome, and next in age to Absalom by the same mother. He conferred with Joab son of Zeruiah, and with Abiathar the priest, and they supported him. However, Zadok the priest, Benaiah, son of Jehoiada, Nathan the prophet, and Shimei and his

companions, the pick of David's army, did not side with Adonijah. When he slaughtered sheep, oxen, and fatlings at the stone Zoheleth, near En-rogel, Adonijah invited all his brothers, the kings sons, and all the royal officials of Judah. But he did not invite the prophet Nathan, or Beniah, or the pick of the army, or his brother Solomon.

Indeed, Zadok, along with the prophet Nathan, and the commander of David's personal bodyguard, Benaiah, did not want to see Adonijah succeed to the throne. Instead, they supported the accession of Solomon, David's twenty-four-year-old illegitimate son. However, Zadok's colleague and co-high-priest, Abiathar, who was descended from the priest Eli (and thus Aaron), had the misfortune of siding with Adonijah. When Zadok, Nathan, and Beniah informed David of Adonijah's treachery, David ordered Zadok and Nathan to anoint Solomon king. Here is the description of those events as narrated in 1 Kgs 1:22–40:

While she [Bathsheba] was still speaking to the kind, the prophet Nathan came in. When he had been announced, the prophet entered the king's presence and, bowing to the floor, did him homage. Then Nathan said: "Have you decided, my lord king, that Adonijah is to reign after you and sit on your throne? He went down today and slaughtered oxen, fatlings, and sheep in great numbers; he invited all the king's sons, the commanders of the army, and Abiathar the priest, and they are eating and drinking in his company and saying, 'Long live King Adonijah!' But me, your servant, he did not invite; nor Zadok the priest, nor Benaiah, son of Jehoiada, nor your servant Solomon. Was this done by my royal master's order without my being told who was to succeed to your majesty's kingly throne?"

King David answered, "Call Bathsheba here." When she re-entered the king's presence and stood before him, the king swore, "As the LORD lives, this very day I will fulfill the oath I swore to you by the LORD, the God of Israel, that your son Solomon should reign after me and should sit upon my throne in my place." Bowing to the floor in homage to the king, Bathsheba said, "May my lord, King David, live forever!" Then King David summoned Zadok the priest, Nathan the prophet, and Benaiah, son of Jehoiada. When they had entered the king's presence, he said to them: "Take with you the royal attendants. Mount my son Solomon upon my own mule and escort him down to Gihon. There Zadok the priest and Nathan the prophet are to anoint him king of Israel, and you shall blow the horn and cry, "Long live King Solomon! When you come back in his train, he is to go in and sit upon my throne and reign in my place. I designate him ruler of Israel and of Judah." In answer to the king, Benaiah, son of Jehoiada, said: "So be it! May the LORD, the God of my lord the king, so decree! As the LORD has been with your royal majesty, so may he be with Solomon, and exalt his throne even more than that of my lord, King David!"

> So Zadok the priest, Nathan, the prophet, Benaiah, son of Jehoiada, and the Cherethites and Pelethites went down, and mounting Solomon on King David's mule escorted him to Gihon. Then Zadok the priest took the horn of oil from the tent and anointed Solomon. They blew the horn and all the people shouted, "Long live King Solomon!" Then all the people went up after him, playing flutes and rejoicing so much as to split open the earth with their shouting.

Zadok's Ascent to the High Priesthood

When Adonijah heard of Solomon's accession to the throne, he fled Jerusalem. He eventually returned and pledged allegiance to the new king. Meanwhile, Solomon deposed Abiathar from the high priesthood and banished him from Jerusalem. Solomon then rewarded Zadok for his loyalty by appointing him sole high priest. This is narrated in 1 Kgs 2:26–27:

> [Solomon] the king said to Abiathar the priest: "Go to your land in Anathoth. Though you deserve to die, I will not put you to death this time, because you carried the ark of the Lord GOD before my father David and shared in all the hardships my father endured." So Solomon deposed Abiathar from his office of priest of the LORD, thus fulfilling the prophecy which the LORD had made in Shiloh about the house of Eli.

And in 1 Kgs 2:35 we are told: "The king appointed Benaiah, son of Jehoiada, over the army in his place, and put Zadok the priest in place of Abiathar."

Zadok's ascent to the high priesthood of Israel not only began an historic line of hereditary priesthood, but it also became legendary. As for the historic line, Zadok is undoubtedly the most famous and influential of Israel's high priests, apart from Aaron. The Zadokite line continued to serve in the high priesthood until 171 BC (the reign of Antiochus IV Epiphanes, 175–164 BC) when it passed first to the Helleniz-ers and then to the Hasmonean house. The descendants of Zadok not only remained the dominant priestly family in Jerusalem until the Babylonian exile (586 BC) but, after the return from exile, the Zadokites regained control of the high priesthood and retained that office until the deposition and murder of Onias III in the early second-century BC (2 Macc 4:33–34).

While Zadok's ascent to the high priesthood of Israel was indeed an historic event of great consequence for the history of Israel, it also became a legendary event with repercussions to this day. Indeed, not only with Zadok's ascent to the high priesthood was the line of Eleazar restored, but Zadok's takeover of the office, at the expense of Eli's descendants, was theologized first as the fulfillment of a divine prophecy: "I will raise up for myself a faithful priest, who shall do according to what is in my heart and in my mind." (1 Sam 2:35). Zadok's ascendancy to the high priesthood became a theological theme in the book of the prophet Ezekiel. In the restored temple of Ezekiel, only the sons of Zadok are permitted to serve as priests on the ground that they alone were faithful to Yahweh when the Levites, with the rest of Israel, were unfaithful. More precisely, the program for the post-exilic community, which was spelled out in the book of the prophet Ezekiel, expressly relegated the "Levites" to inferior temple duties and reserved priestly service "at the altar" to "the sons of Zadok" (Ezek 44:9–31). Repeatedly in Ezekiel, a distinction is made between those priests "who have charge of the temple" and those priests "who have charge of the altar," with the latter group restricted to the sons of Zadok (Ezek 40:45–46; 43:19; 48:11). In actual post-exilic practice, however, it was not just the "sons of Zadok" who served as priests, but a broader group, including "the sons of Aaron." It has been suggested that after the temple was destroyed (586 BC) and the majority of Zadokites carried off into exile, makeshift religious services were continued in Jerusalem during the exile and supervised by non-Zadokite priests. Upon the return of the mostly Zadokite priestly personnel from the exile, there was a conflict and a compromise proved necessary.

In the time of Jesus, the sect of the Dead Sea Scrolls, the Qumran sectarians, probably founded in the aftermath of the Hasmonean takeover of the high priesthood, repeatedly emphasized the sole legitimacy of the Zadokite priests. These priests were the early leaders and probably the founders of the sect. In post-exilic literature, the Zadokites appear most prominently in the sectarian texts of the Dead Sea Scrolls. For example, in the Rule of the Community, authority in the community is given to "the priests, the sons of Zadok" (5.2b–3a). This emphasis on priestly authority, and particularly the importance of the Zadokite priests, indicates a possible area of dissension between the Qumran group and the temple authorities, led by the non-Zadokite Hasmoneans.

Nor has the legendary character of the Zadokite priesthood ceased in modern times. For example, it is a major theme among those in Israel today who would want to restore the Jerusalem temple liturgy. The Temple Institute is an organization dedicated to preparing the reconstruction of a Third Temple in Jerusalem. And some fundamentalist Christians believe that the second coming of Jesus cannot occur until the Third Temple is constructed.

Zadok's Questionable Genealogy

This is precisely the point at which it is important for us to investigate a more suspicious side to all this legend and celebration of Zadok's ascent to the high priesthood of Israel and his establishment of a priestly line that goes through history even to the present day. I am referring to the true nature of Zadok's ascent to historic prominence that biblical scholars have long questioned. That is, they have doubted Zadok's true Aaronic descent. As I mentioned previously, Zadok's ascent to the high priesthood displaced Eli's stained heritage (as recounted in chapter 3 herein) with the unblemished one of the house of Eleazar. But scholars have called into question the veracity of Zadok's ancestral descent from Eleazar. No doubt, while Zadok's replacement of the banished Abiathar, a descendant of Eli, is regarded as the prophetic fulfillment of an earlier prophecy that the tenure of the high priestly office by Eli's family would be broken in favor of a different branch of Aaron's family (1 Sam 2:30–36; 1 Kgs 2:26, 27)), the problem is that Eli's ancestry is not given in the OT, only in the apocrypha, that is, in 2 Esdras 1:2. And Josephus connects him with the line of another son of Aaron, Ithamar (Antiquities, 5.11.5). Indeed, Zadok's genealogy constitutes a problem that has long puzzled OT scholars. More precisely, the Bible presents us with two genealogies of Zadok that are not reconcilable. In one of these, the one in the first book of Samuel, we are told that Zadok's father, Ahitub, was the brother of Ichabod (1 Sam 14:3). But if this is accurate, it not only incorporates Zadok into the family of Eli, but it also makes Zadok brother to Ahimelech and uncle of Abiathar (1 Sam 22:20)! This genealogy, however, conflicts with the one given in 1 Sam 2:27–36 and 1 Kgs 2:26–27, which seeks to explain how it came about that Zadok's family superseded the family of Eli in the priestly service. This second genealogy also posits Ahitub as Zadok's father but derives both of them from a line that does not include Eli. In the Chonicler's version, Zadok derived from a line descended from Aaron's son Eleazar, and in 1 Chr 24:3 specifically contrasts his descent from Eleazar with the descent of his co-priest Abiathar from another son of Aaron, Ithamar.

Thus most scholars since Julius Wellhausen have considered the pivotal verse 2 Sam 8:17 to be problematic. The reversal of the Ahimelech-Abiathar sequence (contrast 1 Sam 22:20) raises the suspicion of either accidental or intentional alteration of the original reading. Most scholars would restore the text to read "Zadok and Abiathar, son of Ahimelech, son of Ahitub," and thus leave Zadok without any genealogy.

Most modern scholars therefore regard both genealogies (the one in 1 Sam and that of the Chronicler) as patent fictions that are intended to create an appropriate lineage for a priest who in fact was not derived from any of the traditional Hebrew priestly families. Instead, modern scholars propose the following alternatives as being the real truth behind these contrived genealogies: Some suggest that prior to their joint service in Jerusalem, Abiathar was priest at Jerusalem and Zadok was serving at Gibeon, where we find him in 1 Chr 16:39. The theory that has commanded the widest support maintains that originally Zadok was not a Hebrew priest but instead a priest of the Jebusite cult prior to the conquest of Jerusalem. Thus the installation of Zadok alongside David's own priest Abiathar was a measure designed to placate the Jebusite subjects of David who constituted a significant portion of the citizenry of the new capital. Those who hold to this interpretation also claim this is the reason why Zadok supported Bathsheba's nomination of her son Solomon to the throne of Israel. I take no position on this but I must say I am impressed by the group of scholars who support this last interpretation: Aage Bentzen, H. H. Rowley, Helmer Ringgren, Walther Zimmerli, and Aelred Cody.

Before we address what might be the lessons that the life and ministry of Zadok hold for us today, we must also carefully survey the history of clerical ambition in the New Testament, the early church, the Middle Ages, and modern times.

Clerical Ambition in the New Testament

In this regard, history affords us numerous instances of clerical ambition. It starts with the witness of the New Testament. The canonical gospels provide us with several examples of ambition, rivalry, and even envy among Jesus' own hand-picked inner-circle, the group called the Twelve, to whom Jesus tries to teach object lessons in humility. Mark 9:33–34 suggests that the Twelve saw themselves headed for greatness, but some more than others: "They came to Capernaum and, once inside the house, he began to ask them, 'What were you arguing about on the way?' But they remained silent. They had been discussing among themselves on the way who was the greatest." Jesus responds to this by offering them a graphic lesson, a prophetic parable in action, for he not only verbally corrects them, but offers them a dramatic example. In Mark 9:35–37 we read: "Then he sat down, called the Twelve, and said to them, 'If anyone wishes to be first, he shall be the last of all and the servant of all.' Taking a child he placed it in their midst, and putting his arms around it he said to them, 'Whoever receives one child such as this in my name, receives me; and whoever receives me, receives not me but the One who sent me.'" But the drama does not stop here, for the very next passage in Mark 9 makes it clear that the Twelve are subject not only to rivalry in office among themselves, but that they are jealous regarding their own authority. In Mark 9:38–40 we are told: "John said to him, 'Teacher, we saw someone driving out demons in your name, and we tried to prevent him because he does not follow us.' Jesus replied, 'Do not prevent him. There is no one who performs a mighty deed in my name who can at the same time speak ill of me. For whoever is not against us is for us.'"

In the next chapter of Mark's gospel, Mark 10:35–37, we find two of Jesus' disciples importuning Jesus himself for their own ecclesiastical preferment, that is, seeking even further honor and glory for themselves so as to distinguish themselves above and beyond their peers: "Then James and John, the sons of Zebedee, came to him and said to him, 'Teacher, we want you to do for us whatever we ask of you.' He replied, 'What do you wish [me] to do for you?' They answered him, 'Grant that in your glory we may sit one at your right and the other at your left.'" In response, Jesus tries to tame their ambition by suggesting that there is danger in what they ask, for in Mark 10:38–40: "Jesus said to them, 'You do not know what you are asking. Can you drink the cup that I drink or be baptized with the baptism with which I am baptized?' They said to him, 'We can.' Jesus said to them, 'The cup that I drink, you will drink, and with the baptism with which I am baptized, you will be baptized; but to sit at my right or at my left is not mine to give but is for those for whom it has been prepared.'"

The ambitious desires do not end there. No sooner has Jesus finished those words, we are told that the rest of the disciples become indignant. It is an attitude Jesus does not encourage, but he seizes upon it as an opportunity to teach them all about humility in office. In Mark 10:41–45 we are told:

> When the ten heard this, they became indignant at James and John. Jesus summoned them and said to them, "You know that those who are recognized as rulers over the Gentiles lord it over them, and their great ones make their authority over them felt. But it shall not be so among you. Rather, whoever wishes to be great among you will be your servant; whoever wishes to be first among you will be the slave of all. For the Son of Man did not come to be served but to serve and to give his life as a ransom for the many."

An even more scandalous example of this kind of ambition can be found in the Gospel according to Matthew. Here we find a passage that suggests the ambition of James and John is such that they are not beneath recruiting their mother as an agent for their ecclesiastical preferment. In Matt 20:20–21 we read: "Then the mother of the sons of Zebedee approached him with her sons and did him homage, wishing to ask him for something. He said to her, 'What do you wish?' She answered him, 'Command that these two sons of mine sit, one at your right and the other at your left, in your kingdom.'" Jesus then goes on to give them the very same lecture we have already heard him give in Mark 10:41–45.

Clerical Ambition in the Early Church

It does not take much research to find similar examples of clerical ambition across the centuries in the history of the church. Indeed, the earliest work after the New Testament witnesses to the same type of ambition. The Letter of Clement of Rome to the Church at Corinth is usually dated by scholars to have been written in the early nineties of the Christian era. Its paragraph 44 begins with the words: "Now our apostles, thanks to our Lord Jesus Christ, knew that there was going to be strife over the title of bishop."[1] Scholars argue that the words bishop and presbyter are still synonymous, that is, interchangeable.

About a decade later, Ignatius of Antioch, in his Letter to the Church at Philadelphia, suggests some of the motives and methods that went into some men's ascent to the episcopacy. There he praises Theophorus, the bishop of Philadelphia: "I know that your bishop obtained the ministry which makes for the common good, neither from himself nor through men, nor for vainglory, but in the love of God the Father and the Lord Jesus Christ. And I was amazed at his gentleness, and at his ability to do more by silence than those who use vain words. For he is attuned to the commandments as a harp to its strings."[2]

But Cyprian of Carthage (d. 258) gives us a more pointed example. In Epistle 55,8, wherein Cyprian celebrates with joy the ascent of his contemporary Pope Cornelius to the See of Rome, he indulges in a stinging if indirect indictment of the way in which some others reached the episcopal throne:

> For what recommends our dearly beloved Cornelius to God and to Christ and to His Church and also to all of his fellow bishops with laudable praise is that he did not attain the episcopate suddenly, but, having been promoted through all of the ecclesiastical offices and having often deserved well of the Lord in divine ministrations, he ascended to the sublime summit of the priesthood through all of the steps of religious service. Then, finally, he neither asked for nor desired the episcopate itself, nor, as others do, whom the swelling of arrogance and of their own pride puffs up, did he seize it, but, quite otherwise and modest and such as those who are divinely chosen for this office are accustomed to be, by virtue of the modesty of his virginal continence and the humility of his innate and accustomed reverence, not only did he make no attempt to become bishop, as some do, but he himself suffered violence in being compelled to accept the episcopate.[3]

---

1. Clement, "First Letter," p. 63.
2. Ignatius, "Epistles," p. 241.
3. Cyprian, *Saint Cyprian: Letters*, p. 138.

We also have some observations of Pope Gregory the Great (ca. 540–604) regarding episcopal ambition in a work originally titled Liber regulae pastoralis, sometime translated as "Pastoral Rule" or "Pastoral Care." That work contains no less than two chapters that treat of clerical ambition. Part I, chapter 8 is entitled "Regarding Those Who Covet Pre-eminence, and Appropriate a Statement of the Apostle to Serve Their Own Cupidity." Gregory is referring to Paul's comment in 1 Tim 3:1, "whoever aspires to the office of bishop desires a noble task." Of this saying of Saint Paul, Gregory says: "We must, however, observe that this was said at a time when whosoever was set over the people was the first to be led to the tortures of martyrdom. So, indeed, it was praiseworthy to seek the episcopate, when, in consequence of holding the office, there was no doubt that its holder would meet with the most severe sufferings."[4] Part I, chapter 9 is entitled "The Mind of Those Who Crave for Pre-eminence, for the Most Part Flatters Itself with Imaginary Promises of Performing Good Works." There he says: "Very frequently, when the office of rule is undertaken, the practice of good deeds is relinquished, though it had been maintained when life was undisturbed, for even the unskilled seaman can guide a ship on an even keel in a tranquil sea, but in a sea that is tossed with tempestuous waves, even a skilled seamen is greatly troubled."[5]

Isidore, archbishop of Seville, who lived from 560 to 636, wrote a work that he titled De Ecclesiasticis Officiis, "On Ecclesiastical Offices," wherein he described the duties and rights of all in his church from the archbishop to lay men and women. There in book 2, chapter 5, section 12, Isidore laments the fact that "worldly men" all too often made it into the episcopal ranks of the church, explaining: "Many perform ordinations of such men not choosing those whom the churches find useful, but those who either they love or by whose acts of compliance they are seduced or for whom any of the elders [presbyters] have asked, and if I may say worse things who achieve that they are ordained by gifts [bribes]. I hold my tongue about the rest."[6]

Clerical Ambition in the Middle Ages

Bernard of Clairvaux (1090–1153), in his *De moribus et officio episcoporum* (On the Conduct and Office of Bishops), shows himself keenly aware of ambition among clerics. This small treatise appears to have begun as a personal letter that Bernard wrote in about the year 1127 in response to a request by Henry Sanglier, archbishop of Sens, a diocese in the north of France, not far from the abbey of Clairvaux, where

4. Gregory the Great, *Pastoral Care*, p. 35.
5. Ibid, p. 37.
6. Isidore, *On Ecclesiastical Offices*, p. 74.

Bernard was abbot. The archbishop's original request is not clear. But Bernard, later in life, expanded his letter to the archbishop of Sens into what is now called an "opuscule" (from the Latin *opusculum*, a diminutive of *opus*) or small treatise on the moral attributes appropriate for a bishop. In paragraph 27, Bernard remarks:

> It has to be said that clergy of every age and state, the learned as well as the ignorant, chase after ecclesiastical charges as though the reward for attaining them were a discharge from all care . . . For example, when someone is made dean or provost or archdeacon, or the equivalent, not content with one appointment in one church, he bustles about in pursuit of further preferments, indeed as many as possible, in that church as in others. To all these, however, he would much prefer, should a position present itself, the dignity of a single bishopric. But will he be satisfied with that? Made a bishop, he wants to be an archbishop. Should he achieve this, indulging who knows what grander dreams, he determines, at a high cost in wearisome journeys and expensive acquaintance, to frequent the court of Rome with a view to establishing advantageous friendships there.[7]

Saint Bonaventure (ca. 1217–1274), theologian and master general of his order, the Franciscans or Friars Minor, in his "Treatise on How to Prepare for the Celebration of Mass," article 14, counsels priests to examine their conscience as to the "motive or what are your reasons as you approach the altar." He says:

> Alas, alas. O Lord God! How many unfortunate souls come to Holy Orders and to the divine Mysteries seeking bread not of heaven but of earth! Seeking not the spirit, but the profit; not God's honor, but the satisfaction of their own ambition; not the salvation of souls, but the accumulation of riches. Their effort is not directed toward serving Christ with a clean heart and body in the sacred Mysteries, but toward their own pleasure, wealth, and glory; toward the satisfaction of their own lustful passions, at the expense of Christ's heritage and of the people's charity! In their ambition, they grab rather than obtain ecclesiastical dignities, by means, even, of much litigation and simony, following not the call of God but the devil's prompting.[8]

As for such ambition, it is interesting to note Thomas Aquinas's comments on 1 Tim 3:1, "whoever aspires to the office of bishop desires a noble task." Aquinas himself was offered the archbishopric of Naples by Pope Clement IV in the summer of 1267 when the Dominican was forty-three years of age. But Aquinas refused the appointment.[9] It is interesting to speculate at his motive in turning down an episcopal appointment. He may have been following his own reasoning, which he set

7. Bernard of Clairvaux, *On Baptism and the Office of Bishops*, pp. 69–70.

8. Bonaventure, *Opuscula*, p. 231.

9. Weisheipl, *Friar Thomas D'Aquino*, p. 232.

forth in his Summa Theologica 2a.2ae, question 185, answer 2, wherein he ranks the contemplative life above the apostolic life. But he might also have been influenced by his own theology of ministry that graded all ministry in terms of its proximity to the Eucharist, which might have soured any ambition in him for the episcopacy. That is, the priest who consecrates the Eucharist was at the apex of ministry; a bishop was simply a priest with greater jurisdiction. Regardless, Paul's teaching that "whoever seeks the office of bishop aspires to a noble thing" caused Aquinas to go on at some length, saying:

> Two things are to be considered in a bishop: his superior grade and profitable action for his people. For some cast an eye at what surrounds him, namely, that he who rules is honored and that he has power. Those who for these reasons desire to be a bishop do not know what a bishop is. Therefore the Apostle says what a bishop is, and that he who desires to be one desires a good work. He does not say that he has a good desire, but a good work, namely, one profitable for the people.
>
> But is it not lawful to desire it? Augustine says no. The Gloss: "The superior place, without which the people cannot be ruled, even if it be held and administered decently, yet is desired but indecently." And he says the same in book 19 of *On the City of God*. The reason for which is that no one ought to desire something beyond his powers and not proportioned to himself; otherwise he would be stupid. Horace: "Let him who know not how to play in the fields withhold himself from war."
>
> Therefore, he could well desire the episcopacy whose ability is proportioned to it. But for this no one is suitable because according to his standing and conduct he ought to surpass all other men in manners and contemplation, so that in respect to himself others may be his flock. Now, to presume this suitability about oneself is the greatest pride. Thus, he either desires the accoutrements of being a bishop, and then he does not really know what it is he wants, since this is not the episcopacy; or, he wants its work, and this is pride. And so it is not to be accepted unless it is imposed.[10]

Clerical Ambition in Modern Times

The modern era has provided us with numerous chronicles of clerical ambition, some even authored by the cleric himself who writes with pride about the way in which he achieved his ambitious goal. I have in mind the autobiography of Pope Pius II, a collection of his memoirs called "A Commentary on Memorable Things." Its original Latin title, *Commentarii rerum memorabilium*, and its narrative style are a self-conscious imitation of the style of Julius Caesar's *Commentarri de bello Gallico*

---

10. Aquinas, *Commentaries*, p. 35.

and *Commentarii de bello civili*, Caesar's accounts of his conquest of Gaul (58–52 BC) and then Rome itself. Pius, who began life as a typical Renaissance gentleman, with a patently classical rather than Christian name, that is, named for the hero of Virgil's epic, Aeneas Silvius Piccolomini, lived from 1405–1464. Writing as Caesar did in the style of third-person objectivity (never "I did this" but instead "Caesar did this"), Pius, while omitting any reference to his salacious early years (he fathered two children out of wedlock), gives a marvelously detailed account of his ascent to the papacy and then his attempt to organize a pan-European crusade against the Ottoman Empire. The work is studded with revealing insider accounts of ecclesiastical politics, his and those of others. For example, there is the account of his maneuverings at the conclave of 1458 from which he emerged as pope (bk. 1, ch. 36). And he also describes the political machinations of a canon of the cathedral at Mainz to bribe the cathedral chapter members into electing him as the next archbishop, a tactic which Pius mordantly and, no doubt, from personal experience, declares, "bribing large numbers of people is no easy thing" (bk. 3, ch. 8).[11]

In more recent times, the twentieth century has provided us with two examples of American prelates who, like Pius II, achieved much for the church but might also be regarded as having employed means that will leave some people scandalized. I am referring to William Cardinal O'Connell of Boston and Francis Cardinal Spellman of New York City. To assess the career of each, I will employ encyclopedia articles on each that give us an overview and positive assessment of their careers in the church. But then with each I will quote from popular biographies that go into some detail about the sometimes very manipulative if not dishonorable way in which they arose to such eminence in the church.

William Cardinal O'Connell

William Henry O'Connell was born in Lowell, Massachusetts, December 8, 1859, the son of Irish immigrants. He attended public schools in Lowell, after which he entered St. Charles College, a seminary in Maryland, to study for the priesthood. However, he left the seminary to enter Boston College from which he graduated in 1881 with first honors in philosophy and physics. When he approached Archbishop John J. Williams of Boston about returning to seminary studies, the archbishop decided to send him to Rome's North American College. After ordination in June of 1884 at twenty-five years of age, O'Connell returned to the United States and did pastoral work for the next ten years. He served as a curate at St. Joseph's parish in Medford (1884–1886), and then as pastor of another St. Joseph church, this time in

11. Pius II, *Commentaries*, Vol. 2, p. 31.

Boston's West End (1886–1895). In 1895, he was selected to return to Rome as rector of the North American College. During his six years in that position, 1895–1901, he achieved much. He not only doubled the enrollment of the college, but he rehabilitated its finances and purchased the Villa Santa Caterina at Castel Gandolfo for summer sessions. He got the American bibliophile William Heyward to donate his library to the North American College and persuaded the American theater magnate Benjamin Keith to pay for the renovation of the college refectory. In May of 1901, he was ordained a bishop and sent back to the United States to serve as bishop of Portland, Maine. There he renovated the cathedral, introduced the diocese to the CYO, Catholic Youth Organization, and sponsored retreats for the clergy. In 1905, he was sent to Japan as papal envoy and while there conducted a thorough survey of the mission field. From this he made several recommendations to the Vatican, such as urging the introduction of several religious orders, fostering a native clergy, and the founding of a Catholic university at Tokyo to be staffed by Jesuits. Shortly after his return to the United States, O'Connell was made coadjutor bishop of Boston; coadjutor, meaning he had the right of succession upon the death of then Archbishop Williams.

O'Connell served as archbishop of Boston until his death, for the next thirty-seven years. Wayman, in her encyclopedia entry on O'Connell (besides noting that when O'Connell first became archbishop many of the archdiocesan institutions were "debt ridden and run down") goes on to catalog the man's achievements:

> During his administration parishes in the archdiocese increased from 194 to 322, and clergy from 600 to more than 1,500. Admissions to St. John's Seminary tripled; a score of new religious congregations were introduced into the area; parochial elementary schools were doubled and high schools tripled—taught by a total of more than 3,000 priests, brothers, and sisters. Three colleges for women were founded under his auspices and he aided the establishment of Boston College on its Chestnut Hill campus. In 1908 he purchased as a diocesan organ, the weekly newspaper, the Pilot; in 1934 he laid the cornerstone of a diocesan center, a six-story building with presses and offices for the Pilot, offices for diocesan bureaus, and a meditation chapel. An archdiocesan residence, the Crehan Library, and the chancery were built; he also enlarged St. John's Seminary, staffing it with diocesan priest-scholars.[12]

In 1992 there appeared a more complete and critical biography of O'Connell: James M. O'Toole's *Militant and Triumphant: William Henry O'Connell and the Catholic Church in Boston, 1859–1944*. This is a much more critical and complete study. The "militant and triumphant" in the title of O'Toole's book is a reference to O'Connell's

---

12. Wayman, "O'Connel, William Henry," p. 544.

ambitious, even defiant, nature. O'Toole describes the means by which O'Connell achieved such high positions in the church. For example, he says of O'Connell's time as rector of the North American College:

> O'Connell's duties at the college left him with enough free time to begin making the rounds of Roman social life, and he liked what he saw. Perhaps more than anything else, this opportunity to know and be known in return by important people from all walks of life marked the turning point in the young priest's career . . . [he began] forming friendships and beneficial alliances that would last a lifetime. Foremost among these was his association with Monsignor Raphael Merry del Val, the shrewd and worldly son of a Spanish diplomat and an English gentlewoman. At the time he and O'Connell met in the late 1890s, Merry was one of the private secretaries to Leo XIII, but he was destined for higher things. After a brief stint as papal legate to Canada, he became secretary for the conclave in 1903 that chose Leo's successor, Pius X. He then served the new pope as secretary of state, right-hand man, and ecclesiastical enforcer.[13]

O'Toole also notes how, later, when O'Connell was bishop in Portland and archbishop in Boston, he knew how to use the press: 'in the age of emerging mass journalism, O'Connell was consistently 'good ink,' and he learned early how to use the press to construct and reinforce his image as a central player in the public drama" (p.6). These, in themselves, are not necessarily bad attributes or talents, but it is what he did with them that raises questions. As O'Toole says:

> Unfortunately for the clarity of this public projection, O'Connell was also troubled throughout his life by a darker personal side hidden from his people. Like many who had risen to high places from unpromising beginnings, he came tacitly to believe that the rules of behavior he unhesitatingly enjoined on the community did not apply to himself, simply by virtue of who and what he was. Morality was for others. With a startling ease he was able to exempt himself and those around him from ordinary accountability. His management of archdiocesan finances, for example, was capable and shrewd, and the Boston Church generally prospered under his stewardship. At the same time he was too willing to confound his official position with his personal benefit, diverting money to his own use and to advancing the fortunes of his family.
>
> More seriously, he tolerated and condoned for many years two members of his inner circle who, though ordained and active priests, were simultaneously and secretly married: one of them, his own nephews, was also actively embezzling money from the church.[14]

---

13. O'Toole, *Militant and Triumphant*, pp. 29–30.

14. Ibid., p. 7.

Francis Cardinal Spellman

Yet another modern ecclesiastic we ought to consider was one of Cardinal O'Connell's own priests who outdid his ordinary in terms of ambition, Francis Spellman.

Here too the entry on Spellman by George F. Tiffany, in The New Catholic Encyclopedia, gives us a good summary of his achievements. Spellman was born in Whitman, Massachusetts, on May 4, 1889. After attending public schools in Whitman, Spellman went to New York City's Fordham College where he received a bachelor of arts degree in 1911. Then, with the approval of Cardinal O'Connell of Boston, Spellman entered the North American College in Rome. He was ordained a priest on May 14, 1916. His first assignment after ordination was to serve as a chaplain to St. Clement's Home, a Boston archdiocesan institution for elderly women. A short while later, he was reassigned to work as a curate at the Church of All Saints in Roxbury. Within a year, the United States entered World War I, and Spellman petitioned his ordinary, Cardinal O'Connell, to be allowed to become a military chaplain. Initially, O'Connell gave his permission, but he soon rescinded that permission and instead assigned Spellman to the archdiocesan chancery, where his task was to promote subscriptions to the archdiocesan newspaper, the Pilot. Spellman worked hard at the job and subscriptions increased appreciably. However, Spellman's success got him nowhere with the cardinal who instead demoted him to the position of archdiocesan archivist. Spellman accompanied a Holy Year diocesan pilgrimage to Rome in 1925 and remained there when Pope Pius XI appointed him to the Vatican Secretariat of State. In September of 1932, Spellman was made an auxiliary bishop of Boston and returned to Boston to serve as pastor of Sacred Heart Parish in Newton Center. On April 15, 1939, the recently elected Pope Pius XII appointed Spellman as archbishop of New York and on February 18, 1946, named him cardinal. Spellman died on December 2, 1967, having served as archbishop of New York for twenty-eight years. The New Catholic Encyclopedia summarizes Spellman's achievements:

> Under Spellman the Archdiocese of New York underwent years of extraordinary expansion and development. During his first year in New York, he refinanced a $28 million debt incurred by the diocese and the parishes during the Depression. Also in 1939 he established the Building Commission to supervise and advise on building projects throughout the archdiocese. The Institutional Commodity Services was established in 1941 as a central purchasing agency for the churches and institutions of the archdiocese, thereby saving them more than $1.5 million a year in purchases.
>
> Under Spellman the Catholic Charities of the archdiocese underwent enormous expansion. Spellman constructed or renovated more than 370 elementary and secondary schools at a cost of $500 million, earning for him the title,

"cardinal of education." Recognizing the value of television in education, he purchased the RCA color broadcast equipment at the New York World's Fair and established the Instructional Television Center in 1966. He sponsored the publication of the *Catholic Encyclopedia for School and Home* (1965), and the *New Catholic Encyclopedia* (1967). Under his direction St. Joseph's Seminary was completely renovated.[15]

Spellman was also military vicar of the Armed Forces, consisting of more than two million servicemen and their families and 2,700 chaplains. From 1942 until 1966 he journeyed throughout the world visiting military installations. (p. 412)

John Cooney, in the prologue to his The American Pope: The Life and Times of Francis Cardinal Spellman (1984), indicates the reason why he chose the title "The American Pope" as his descriptive of Spellman's life, when he summarizes Spellman's achievement:

Though he was archbishop of New York, his influence within his Church knew few boundaries, and he himself was unique in the annals of U.S. history. What made him stand apart was the amazing power he had acquired over the years in international, national, state, and local politics. This might had enabled him to gain concessions for his Church that many people once believed impossible. His network encompassed officials of the Central Intelligence Agency and the Federal Bureau of Investigation, as well as many presidents, congressmen, governors, and mayors. His contacts circled the globe and included Winston Churchill, Charles de Gaulle, and Francisco Franco. Spellman's role was not that of the policymakers' priest, but rather he was one of them himself—a pivotal figure in Byzantine, clandestine political and military operations that helped shape the history of his nation and others.[16]

More precisely, the reference to "political and military operations" included his advocacy of American military engagement in Vietnam. This gained him the gratitude of beleaguered President Lyndon Johnson but also harsh criticism from the press. For example, Cooney's book contains a picture of the cartoon by Edward Sorel that portrayed Spellman racing into battle in full military dress and lunging with a bayoneted rifle. The caption reads, "Pass the Lord and Praise the Ammunition," a parody of the World War II song, "Praise the Lord and Pass the Ammunition." This satirical cartoon was created by Sorel in 1967 but did not appear in print until 1972. The reason for the delay was Spellman's death in 1967. For that reason Sorel waited and used the cartoon for the wrapper of his 1972 book, *Making the World Safe for Hypocrisy*. At this point I think it fair to say that Spellman not only outdid his ordinary, Cardinal

15. Tiffany, "Spellman, Francis, pp. 411–12.
16. Cooney, *American Pope*, pp. 15–16.

O'Connell, in terms of power and influence but Spellman's achievement makes even Zadok look like a "schlepper." However, we can learn even more about clerical power and ambition by observing how precisely Spellman rose to such heights.

As for how Spellman scaled to such heights of power, Cooney gives us several clues. For example, Cooney notes of Spellman's freshman year at Fordham University, "he had a knack for remembering people's names and faces, even after many years. Within a few days of his arrival at Fordham, he knew everyone by name. This proved to be another skill that served him well as his world expanded; people, he knew, were pleased when they were singled out."[17] Cooney's description of Spellman's five years as a seminarian at Rome's North American College notes that the vice rector, Charles O'Hern, had a particular dislike of Spellman:

> What infuriated O'Hern was Spellman's calculated cultivation of American laymen and Italian ecclesiastics who could do him favors, and who forced the seminary rectors into bending the rules for him.
>
> Such a person was Cardinal Bisleti, who Spellman came to know through his brash pursuit of people of influence. When visiting the town of Veroli with a group of students, Spellman learned that the cardinal had a villa in the area. He boldly suggested to the others that they call upon the prelate so that Spellman could take a picture of Bisleti with the camera Spellman always carried. The suggestion brought comments of disbelief, but the seminarians were beginning to believe they shouldn't underestimate Spellman's canniness. Nonetheless, even the most cynical among them were amazed that Spellman not only approached the cardinal but soon had him posing for one photograph after another, like a fashion model. The photographer shamelessly flattered his subject all the while. Spellman, however, wasn't satisfied with a minor triumph. He was always thinking three steps ahead. Upon leaving, he asked if he might personally return the finished pictures, even though he had been told that he wasn't allowed to leave the seminary alone. The cardinal agreed, and, much to O'Hern's dismay, the school had to grant Spellman permission to visit Bisleti. He had circumvented the rules.[18]

But Spellman also cultivated friendships with other more readily accessible Roman ecclesiastics such as one of his professors, Francesco Borgongini-Duca. Borgongini-Duca was a young professor at what was called at that time "the Pontifical Atheneum of the Urban College." Spellman had heard that Borgongini-Duca was highly favored at the Vatican and was destined for high promotion. Indeed, he eventually became a cardinal.

17. Ibid., p. 11.
18. Ibid., pp. 14–15.

Instead of despairing, Spellman was able to get his friend Borgongini-Duca, now a staff member of the Vatican Secretariat of State, a position in the same organization. In 1925 Spellman was made the first American attaché of the Vatican Secretariat of State.

Cooney describes how, Spellman, during his time in the Vatican Secretariat of State, cultivated wealthy Americans:

> He made it a point to meet American governors, mayors and congressmen, and other figures of prominence who visited the Eternal City. He scoured newspapers daily to note the arrivals of the rich and powerful, and, like a con man setting up a mark, he even paid concierges at the luxury hotels to alert him to the arrival of the kinds of people he wanted to meet. Once he was aware of their presence, Spellman's brazen form of self-promotion was usually the same. He attended their papal audiences, took their pictures, and showed up at their hotel rooms with the finished photos. Knocking on his subjects' doors, Spellman introduced himself and presented the photos. No one could deny the effectiveness of his conduct. Those approached were often flattered. Spellman saw to it that they had a photograph of themselves with the Pope, and he was more than willing to show them around Rome. Spellman thus established a vast network of influential people who would soon enable him to perform unique favors for the Vatican. They were all his "friends," as he liked to say.[19]

How Spellman used his contacts can be seen from the following passage in Cooney's book:

> Spellman received a great deal of money for his extracurricular activities. He peppered his diary with references to his receipt of hundreds and thousands of dollars. He received a $1,200-a-year salary from the Knights of Columbus, and that was smaller than many gifts. The Brady's routinely handed him thousands of dollars. There were references in the diary to his receiving thousands more from such people as Mrs. Evelyn Mendelssohn, Mrs. Leminger, and Bishop O'Leary. By 1929 his financial holdings were so great that Spellman's diary noted he bought a thousand shares of Warner Brothers Pictures stock for $54,190. On March 11, 1930, he excitedly recorded in his diary, "Warner Brothers at 72."
>
> The Pope himself now personally asked Spellman for favors. For instance, Spellman recorded on February 8, 1929: "Holy Father asked me for three autos." In a demonstration of his own wealth Spellman added: "I shall give one myself." Apparently much pleased with Spellman's not finding the limousine a challenge, the Pope escalated his order. Spellman next recorded: "Holy Father asked me to get him a train." Daunting as the request sounded, Spellman was little perturbed. "First he wanted four cars," Spellman wrote to his mother.

---

19. Ibid., p. 36.

"But I explained [that] one car with three or four bedrooms and bath and dining room and sitting room and chapel would be sufficient . . . So I am no on the hunt for a nice car."[20]

Regarding Spellman's later life as cardinal-archbishop of New York there is one particularly revealing episode, his relationship with Fulton Sheen. Sheen was born in rural Illinois in 1895. After attending St. Paul's seminary in Minnesota, he was ordained to the priesthood in 1919 and then sent to Catholic University in Washington, DC for graduate studies. Sheen eventually got his doctorate from Louvain University in Belgium. He came to national popularity in the 1930s with a radio program called The Catholic Hour. Spellman recognized Sheen's talents and decided to recruit Sheen to work as director of the Society for the Propagation of the Faith, headquartered in New York City. Sheen at that same time began a national television show, Life is Worth Living, which earned him even greater popularity. Not only did Spellman begin to chaff at Sheen's greater popularity but considerable tension developed between Spellman and Sheen when Spellman wanted to use the money that Sheen was so successfully raising. Sheen insisted Spellman had no right to those funds and wanted to bring the case to Rome for adjudication. Cooney says of this: "When the bishop [Sheen], persisted in taking his case to Rome, Spellman became alarmed. He wanted something to discredit Sheen. As Father Daniel P. Noonan, Sheen's chief aide, remembered, Spellman had Sheen's personal life investigated several times. Each time he came up empty handed."[21]

As for Spellman's jealousy of Fulton Sheen's popularity, obviously Spellman had never read Ambrose of Milan's De officiis ministrorum (bk. 2, ch. 23), where he says:

Those who have earned approval at some time ought not to behave in an arrogant fashion because of it; on the contrary, they should bear in mind that they have been given a great privilege, and remain humble. A bishop must not take it as a personal offence if a priest or minister or any other clergy increase his reputation by his works of merit, or his fasting, or his purity, or his teaching reading. The praise of any teacher brings honor to the church as a whole. It is a good thing if someone's work earns him this acclaim.[22]

However, lest it be judged that I have chosen two notorious examples from the American church of the preconciliar, that is, pre-Vatican II era, next we shall look at evidence that suggests ambition still abounds long after Vatican II and its reforms.

20. Ibid., p. 39.
21. Ibid., p. 255.
22. Ambrose, De Officiis, Vol. I, p. 335.

Ratzinger and the Gantin on Episcopal Ambition

Thirty(30) Days in the Church and in the World is the title of a monthly news magazine in circulation since 1988. Its editorial offices are in Rome, Italy, but it is published in six languages including English. The May 1999 issue of the magazine featured an interview with the recently retired Prefect of the Vatican's Congregation for Bishops, Cardinal Bernardin Gantin, originally from the small West African country of Benin (formerly Dahomey). During that interview, the Prefect Emeritus suggested there was a need for the church to return to the old practice of avoiding episcopal transfers from diocese to diocese so as to eliminate the "social climbing and careerism" that he felt was all too abundant among bishops.[23] A month later, in June of 1999, in an interview published in that same magazine, Joseph Cardinal Ratzinger, prefect of the Congregation for the Doctrine of the Faith, said:

> I totally agree with Cardinal Gantin. In the Church, above all, there should be no sense of careerism. To be a Bishop should not be considered a career with a number of steps, moving from one seat to another, but a very humble service. I think that the discussion on access to the ministry would also be much more serene if the Episcopate saw it as a service, and not as a career. Even a poor See, with only a few faithful, is an important service in God's Church. . . . Of course, there can be exceptional cases, a very large See where experience of episcopal ministry is necessary, could be an exception . . . But it should not be common practice; it should happen only in most exceptional cases. The view of the Bishop-Diocese relation as matrimony, implying fidelity, is still valid. The Christian community also feels that way: if a Bishop is appointed to a diocese, this is seen, precisely, as a promise of fidelity. Sadly I myself have not remained faithful in this regard. On the suggestion expressed by Cardinal Gantin of a possible change in the Code of Canon Law to prohibit moving from a diocese, Cardinal Ratzinger replied that "it could be given some thought. It would be hard to change the Code, which was published only 16 years ago. In future, I think it would be good to add a phrase on this oneness and fidelity to a diocesan commitment."[24]

Gantin and Ratzinger are referring to ancient church tradition which saw the relationship between a bishop and his diocese as a sort of spiritual marriage. In Catholic Christianity, a bishop wears a ring on the fourth finger of his right hand, a ring usually made of gold with an amethyst stone. Indeed, a newly ordained bishop receives it at his ordination ceremony, after the imposition of hands and anointing,

23. Unfortunately, the online archive for *30 Days* only goes back as far as 2002. But the original Italian interview is obtainable at www.30giorni.it.

24. As quoted in John L. Allen Jr.'s "Ratzinger Weighs in on Careerism of Bishops." The original Italian interview is available at www.30giorni.it.

as the first insignia of his office. At that point the principal ordaining bishop hands a ring to the new bishop while saying, "Receive this ring, the seal of fidelity; adorned with undefiled faith, preserve unblemished the bride of God, the Church."[25] This is a late theological development first mentioned by the Fourth Council of Toledo in 633, and its theology is not entirely cogent: the church is the bride of Christ. The ring probably had practical value in that it was used to seal documents. Only later was it given a spiritual meaning. We can see this in a statement of Isidore of Seville who wrote in 637: "To the bishop at his consecration is given a staff; a ring likewise is given him to signify pontifical honor or as a seal for secrets."[26]

First Lesson: The Danger in Courting the Powerful

As for the patronage of the powerful, in Zadok's case it paid off in spades. But the friendship of the powerful is not always without its price. We have seen how the author of the dynastic history called Second Samuel was quick to claim priestly privileges for David's sons. There are numerous examples of this in the history of the Catholic Church. Indeed, Constantine's patronage of the early church was a mixed blessing. Even up into modern times, relatively recent history, the patronage of the powerful has often provided a means of interference in church affairs. The emperor Franz Joseph, who held the title "his apostolic majesty," was more a problem than a help. Indeed, he was so bold as to intervene in a papal election. More precisely, when Pope Leo XIII died in 1903, it was widely expected that Mariano Cardinal Rampolla, Leo's secretary of state, would be elected pope. But the emperor of Austria, Franz Josef I, was not pleased at that prospect because Rampolla in certain Vatican policy decisions had favored France over Austria. And so when it seemed that Rampolla's candidacy was gaining some momentum, Franz Josef sought to intervene in the deliberations of the conclave. He did so by invoking the age old right of Austrian emperors as inheritors of the authority of the old Holy Roman emperors to intervene in a papal election. In the first millennium the holy Roman Emperors approved of papal elections, and the Emperor of Austria who felt himself the heir to their authority imposed a veto, the *Jus exclusivae*. Franz Josef had asked Austrian cardinal Anton Josef Gruscha to announce to the conclave, but he refused. So the emperor turned to Cardinal Jan Puzyna de Koscielski, Prince-Archbishop of Krakow, and he agreed to announce the emperor's veto to the conclave. Later the grateful Franz Josef awarded Puzyna the highest Austro-Hungarian decoration, the Grand Cross of State. But

25. See Megan McLaughlin's "The Bishop as Bridegroom" in *Medieval Purity and Piety*, pp. 209–38.
26. Isidore of Seville, *De Ecclesiasticis*, p. 74.

when the conclave went on to elect the patriarch of Venice, Giuseppe Sarto, as Pope Pius X, one of the first official acts of the new pope was to abolish any veto rights.

There is always a price to pay for involvement with powerful laity. Spain's Franco exercised veto over the appointment of bishops. The Second Vatican Council, in its Decree on the Bishops' Pastoral Office in the Church, article 20, addresses this directly:

> Since the apostolic office of bishops was instituted by Christ the Lord and serves a spiritual and supernatural purpose, this most sacred Ecumenical Synod declares that the right of nominating and appointing bishops belongs properly, peculiarly, and of itself exclusively to the competent ecclesiastical authority.
>
> Therefore, for the purpose of duly protecting the freedom of the Church and of promoting more suitably and efficiently the welfare of the faithful, this most holy Council desires that in the future no rights or privileges of election, nomination, presentation, or designation for the office of bishop be any longer granted to civil authorities. Such civil authorities, whose favorable attitude toward the Church this most sacred Synod gratefully acknowledges and very warmly appreciates, are most kindly requested to make a voluntary renunciation of the above mentioned rights and privileges which they presently enjoy by reason of a treaty or custom. The matter, however, should first be discussed with the Apostolic See.[27]

Handel's anthem, and the biblical passage it employs, describes Solomon's accession to the throne of his father David. This anthem was but one means the British monarchy employed to wrap that institution in an aura of divine right. No doubt Zadok would take great pride in the thought that his name was used to secure the dignity of another king two thousand years after him.

Lest I be accused of excessive preoccupation with the upper clergy, let me end with a note on a simpler level that shows all clergy, and not just hierarchs, are subject to the temptation of taking patronage from the rich and powerful. The reader must permit my resorting to an anecdotal account. I know a pastor in a northern region of the United States who told me how surprised and grateful he was when, during the first winter after he was assigned as a new pastor, he found that, when it snowed, the mayor of the city would send snow plows over to this church to clear the church's parking lot. This saved the parish a great deal of money. But the pastor eventually discovered the mayor's graciousness required a certain kind of reciprocity. For when, a few years later, that same mayor ran for reelection, this pastor was told he was expected to show up at the mayor's reelection rallies.

27. Abbott, *Documents*, p. 411.

Second Lesson: Ambition Is Not Always an Evil

Also, regarding clerical ambition, we must note it is not always a serious sin. F. Roberti and P. Palazzini in their *Dictionary of Moral Theology* say: "Of itself, ambition is a venial sin, but it may become a grave sin if one is disposed to commit a grave sin in order to win a coveted honor or dignity, or if one gains the coveted honor or dignity through grave harm done to others, or by gravely illicit means."[28] In saying this they are merely following the teaching of Thomas Aquinas. Aquinas treats of ambition in question 131 in the *Secunda Secundae* of his *Summa Theologica*. There in his reply to objection 3, Aquinas makes it clear that the desire for honor is not always evil, indeed, at times it can be the spur to doing good: "some are heartened to do good and disheartened from doing evil, by the desire of honor."[29] And in support of this he cites the Roman historian Sallust (86–35 BC), quoting from his *Bellum Catilinae*, "the good as well as the wicked covet honors for themselves, but the one, that is, the good, go about it in the right way, whereas, the other, that is the wicked, through lack of the good arts, make use of deceit and falsehood."[30] Sallust's historical works are distinguished by the fact that he was not satisfied just to narrate the course of events with accuracy, but he also sought to discern the causes of those events and the motives for men's actions. In this latter aim he showed himself able to recognize both merit and faults in a man. We too must seek to do this, because signs of ambition in a cleric can suggest praiseworthy rather than inordinate desire. Ambition as the desire for personal achievement can provide not only the motivation and determination necessary to help give direction in life, but it can lead a man to achievements that not only bring honor to himself but reward to the whole community. In this regard it is interesting to note Dante's treatment of ambition. In the *Paradise* of Dante's *Divine Comedy*, heaven consists of nine concentric spheres surrounding the earth. And in that scheme the second sphere is "the heaven of the ambitious" where dwell what he calls in canto 6, verse 114, "the good spirits who were zealous in order to win honor and renown."[31] In that sphere, Dante encounters the spirit of the emperor Justinian (AD 482–565). Justinian's ambition was nothing less than restoration of the Roman Empire to its former glory. He intended to do this by recovering lost provinces, sponsoring the uniform rewriting of Roman law, and reforming the entire administrative system of the empire. He exhibited such energy in pursing these goals, exhibited such obsessive work habits, that Justinian's

28. Roberti and Palazzini, *Dictionary*, p. 959. This quotation is from the entry on "pride," in the subsection, "ambition."

29. Aquinas, *Summa Theologica*, Vol. 2, p. 131.

30. Ibid.

31. Dante, *Divine Comedy*, p. 468.

contemporary, the historian Procopius, said of him "He did not sleep."[32] Justinian's legacy has been disputed. While he did achieve much of his aims, some criticize him for the forceful means he used to achieve this. Nevertheless, he is revered as a saint in the Orthodox Church and even among some Lutherans.

An example of this more noble desire for honor might be seen in the life and ministry of Fulton Sheen. There can be no doubt that Fulton Sheen desired the episcopacy, because he himself admits to it in his autobiography: "I must confess I started praying when I was a young priest to become a bishop."[33] This makes it clear Sheen too was motivated by ecclesiastical ambition. But while Sheen's ambition was backed by genuine talent that benefited the church, ambition in these other men discussed here often served no one but themselves; and indeed, in O'Connell's case, seems to have harmed the church. John Cooney, in his biography of Cardinal Spellman, *The American Pope* (1984), describes the conversion that Sheen underwent when in 1950 he was appointed by Spellman as director of the National Office of the Propagation of the Faith:

> Until then, Sheen had never really considered the poverty of the Third World. His life had been insulated from destitution by the seminary and academia and by his moving among people who took money for granted. When he saw the poor, Sheen was horrified. Helping them became as much an obsession with him as anti-Communism, and he channeled his writings and preachings into what became his new cause. One result of this labor was a sudden disdain for the kinds of people he had long associated with—and Spellman cultivated."[34]

---

32. Procopius, *The Secret History*, p. 64.

33. Sheen, *Treasure in Clay*, p. 91. Obviously Sheen had never read Chrysostom's opinion: "I do not think there are many among bishops that will be saved." See Chrysostom's *Homilies on Acts*, p. 23 and the endorsement and expansion of Chrysostom's judgment in Bellarmine's *On Temporal and Spiritual Authority*, p. 410.

34. Cooney, *American Pope*, p. 252.

6

The Importance of Learned, Well-Educated Priests

Ezra the Priest-Scribe

In the late afternoon of January 12, 2010, a particularly strong earthquake struck the Caribbean nation of Haiti. While causing general destruction and much loss of life, that earthquake also inflicted particularly devastating damage on the infrastructure of the Catholic Church in that small island nation. The earthquake totally destroyed many of the church's most important institutions, among them the cathedral in Port-au-Prince and the archdiocesan seminary; many Catholic clergy died in the disaster, including at least one hundred priests, the archbishop of Port-au-Prince, and sixteen of his seminarians. Because of these catastrophic losses the local Catholic Church did not have the capacity to contribute in a significant way to relief efforts. But even relief efforts by external Catholic agencies such as the United States Bishops Conference got little or no attention from the news media here in the United States. Instead, in the few weeks after the earthquake, television and newspaper reports here, while they did occasionally focus on relief efforts by Protestant groups from the United States, they gave far more attention to celebrity relief efforts—efforts undertaken by film or rock stars, or a United States senator seeking to repair his damaged moral image.

The news media did eventually begin to take some notice of Catholic relief efforts in Haiti. For example, on February 8, NBC television's nightly newscast presented a feature news segment on the work of a Passionist priest-doctor, Father Rick Frechette, who ran an orphanage in Haiti. This orphanage was suddenly benefitting greatly from the volunteer efforts of a number of concerned and generous Americans. A few days before that television news feature, on Thursday, February 4, the front page of Rhode Island's principal newspaper, the *Providence Journal*, carried an article about the relief efforts of yet another priest in Haiti. That article began with these words: "In the aftermath of last month's devastating earthquake, food, water and medicine certainly remain Haiti's biggest needs. But Patrick Tardieu, the fifty-eight-year-old curator of Haiti's oldest library, the *Bibliotēque Haitienne des Pēres du Saint Esprit*, says there is another need almost as important: preserving the country's memory. The library houses an extensive collection of rare books relating to Haiti's early history." The article went on to say that though Father Tardieu had been in Haiti at the time of the earthquake, he had now come to Providence at the invitation of Brown University's principal librarian who was intent upon helping Father Tardieu rescue and preserve those books.

Father Frechette and Father Tardieu, with their hyphenated identities as priest-doctor and priest-librarian, both represent a long tradition of highly skilled or learned priests who have contributed greatly to the lives and culture of their people. While many will insist that saving peoples' lives is far more important than the preservation of books, the preservation of a history and culture is nonetheless a vital and important task. Indeed, Father Tardieu was not the first priest to spend as much of his time with books as with the people of God. Nor was he the first priest to attempt to preserve and transmit his people's historical and spiritual heritage in the face of a major social calamity. Ezra, the priest-scribe, who lived in the fourth century before Christ, approximately 404–359 BC, was a Hebrew priest who lived through the final part of Israel's great national disaster, the event called the Babylonian captivity. After his time in exile in Babylon, Ezra returned to Jerusalem to help his people restore their religious culture.

I am convinced that a survey of Ezra's life and work will reveal that the implications of Ezra's ministry are more than just academic. Indeed, these implications are profoundly pastoral and relevant to the life and ministry of not just scholar-priests but parish priests today. To begin, we must know something about Israel's great national disaster and then about the work of Ezra the priest-scribe in restoring his people's religious culture.

Israel's Great National Disaster: The Exile

About the year 581 BC, Nebuchadnezzar, the king of Assyria, invaded and conquered the Kingdom of Judah. After the capture of Jerusalem, several thousand Jews, selected for their strength, skills, wealth, or intelligence were deported to Babylon, the capital of Assyria. These Jews were sent to serve their new masters and to prevent any attempt at rebellion back home where only the old, feeble, and destitute remained. The ruins of ancient Babylon, the city to which these Jews were taken, can be seen to this day. They are located on the left bank of the Euphrates River in modern day Iraq, not far south of Iraq's capital, the city of Baghdad. It was there in Babylon that the Jews dwelt in exile for almost forty-five years. Then, in 537, the

Persian ruler Cyrus the Great conquered Babylon and gave permission to the Jews there to return to their ancestral land. It has been estimated that as many as forty thousand Jews availed themselves of this opportunity for return.

As for Ezra (the meaning of his name is not certain, although some conjecture it is an abbreviation of the Hebrew *azaryahu*, meaning "God helps"), his story is told in two books of the Bible, one is the book that bears his name and the other is called the book of Nehemiah. Those two books are numbered among the historical books of the Old Testament, which in the Christian Bible are sequenced after the Pentateuch, or five books of Moses. That sequence begins with the two books called first and second Samuel, then come the two books called first and second Kings, then appear two more historical works called first and second Chronicles, and finally the books of Ezra and Nehemiah. Most exegetes agree that these last four works are all by the same author (redactor or final editor) whom they call the Chronicler and whom they regard as a conscientious historian. For example, most exegetes agree that the Chronicler employed several documentary sources, such as personal "memoirs" written by both Ezra and Nehemiah. However, those same exegetes who regard the books of Ezra and Nehemiah as trustworthy historical accounts also find some significant discrepancies or problems relating the two works. For example, as portrayed in the books that bear their names, the priest Ezra and the layman Nehemiah appear as contemporaries during the period of Jewish history called the Babylonian exile. But exegetes doubt the truth of this, and think instead that the Chronicler (or a later redactor) made an editorial decision to parallel their lives, and in so doing feature the role of an eminent layman, Nehemiah, and an eminent cleric, Ezra, in the restoration of Israel.[1]

Thus, what we have in the books of Ezra and Nehemiah are two accounts of the return from exile. One account is strictly focused on Nehemiah and his political importance for the restoration, and the other is strictly focused on Ezra and his religious importance for the restoration. But here we focus intently upon the life and ministry of Ezra, and do so with only the most indirect allusions to Nehemiah, because our concern is principally with understanding the life and ministry of Ezra. What follows, then, is a description of the life and ministry of Ezra following the sequence of the biblical narrative in the books of Ezra and Nehemiah. I will then try to interpret their theological relevance for today.

---

1. There is also a scholarly consensus that the books of Ezra and Nehemiah were originally a single literary unit. They were separated by the Christian scholar Origen of Alexandria (ca. 185–ca. 254); and Saint Jerome (ca. 342–420) followed Origen's lead when he wrote his Latin translation of the Bible. This division even made its way into the Hebrew Bible, but not until 1448.

Returning Exiles Led by a Prince

According to the first chapter in the book of Ezra, when Cyrus, the king of Persia, conquered Babylon in the year 538, one of the first things he did was issue a decree allowing the Jews in exile there to return home. The first group to return was led by one "Sheshbazzar, the prince of Judah" (Ezra 1:8), very probably the fourth son of Jehoiachin, the king of Judah, who had been taken captive to Babylon in 598 BC. It seems that either at that same time or shortly after a second group was led by yet another Judean prince, Sheshbazzar's nephew Zerubbable (Ezra 2:2). These returning exiles took with them considerable resources: For example, original temple items first sacked during the Babylonian conquest and brought to Babylon, as well as free-will offerings from Jews who for one reason or another chose to remain behind in Babylon and not make the trip to their ancestral home. The census figures presented in Ezra 2 seem to indicate that 42,360 Jews made the return. Among them was Jeshua, the high priest. This return was a six-hundred mile trek across the desert. According to chapter 3 of Ezra, one of the first things the retuning exiles did was restore the altar amid the ruins of the Jerusalem temple and start offering sacrifice. Next they went about restoring the foundations of the temple. But in chapter 4 we are told of interference and hostility that came from other ethnic groups in the area, for example, the Samaritans. (Nebuchadnezzar and his conquering Assyrians not only took the leading Jews captive back to Babylon but also planted other ethnic groups in Israel, such as the Samaritans, so as to prevent the Jews who remained behind from ever effectively reuniting and rebuilding their kingdom.) And so when the first Jews returned from Babylon to rebuild their capital, the Samaritans were quick to send complaints to the King of Persia, Artaxerxes. For a while at least the Samaritans were able to halt any more construction on the temple. But in chapter 5 we are told how two Israelite prophets in Judah, Haggai and Zechariah, urged the Jews to keep going on the construction. Then, in chapter 6, King Darius sends a decree authorizing once again the building of the temple. Thus work proceeded, and the temple was completed and dedicated. This temple of Zerubbabel, as it came to be called, was built on a much more modest scale and style than that of Solomon's temple.

Returning Exiles Led by a Priest

It was several years after the restoration of temple worship that Ezra chose to lead yet another large contingent of Jewish exiles out of Babylon and back to the promised land. Some scholars estimate that this occurred in about the year 459 BC. In this instance, Ezra led about five thousand Israelite exiles living in Babylon back to Jerusalem (the list of the heads of families [in Ezra 8:1–14] gathered by Ezra for his trip to Jerusalem comes to 1,513 men. If women and children were counted, the total might come to five thousand). Ezra 7:1–6 is the first description we have of Ezra, a description that suggests Ezra (like Nehemiah) had a certain social prominence in Babylon, and perhaps, like Nehemiah, Ezra too was on the staff of the royal palace. And it was Ezra's social position that allowed him to secure permission to lead Jews from Babylon. And thus we read in Ezra 7:1–6:

> After these events during the reign of Artaxerxes, king of Persia, Ezra, son of Seraiah, son of Azariah, son of Hilkiah, son of Shallum, son of Zadok, son of Ahitub, son of Amariah, son of Azariah, son of Meraioth, son of Zerahiah, son of Uzzi, son of Bukki, son of Abishua, son of Phinehas, son of Eleazar, son of the high priest Aaron—this Ezra came up from Babylon. He was a scribe, well-versed in the law of Moses which was given by the LORD, the God of Israel. Because the hand of the LORD, his God, was upon him, the king granted him all that he requested.

Chapters 7 and 8 describe the events during the journey and the gold and silver implements that Ezra and the people with him brought to Jerusalem as a gift for the temple treasury. Indeed, the last paragraph of Ezra, chapter 8, verses 31–35, describes their arrival in Jerusalem:

> We set out for Jerusalem from the river of Ahava on the twelfth day of the first Month. The hand of our God remained upon us, and he protected us from enemies and bandits along the way. Thus we arrived in Jerusalem where we first rested for three days. On the fourth day, the silver, the gold and the utensils were weighed out in the house of our God and consigned to the priest Meremoth, son of Uriah, who was assisted by Eleazar, son of Phinehas; they were assisted by the Levites Josabad, son of Jeshua, and Noadiah, son of Binnui. Everything was in order as to number and weight, and the total weight was registered. At that same time, those who had returned from the captivity, the exiles, offered as holocausts to the God of Israel twelve bulls for all Israel, ninety-six rams, seventy-seven lambs, and twelve goats as sin offerings: all these as a holocaust to the LORD.

The three-day rest can be accounted for in view of the one-hundred-day trek they had just completed, and their need to orient themselves to their new surroundings.

Ezra's Religious Reform

Chapters 9 and 10 of the book of Ezra, its final chapters, go on to describe in very a startling revelation about the lives of the community in Jerusalem and Ezra's response. This is narrated in Ezra's own voice as a memoir:

When these matters had been concluded, the leaders approached me with this report: "Neither the Israelite laymen or the priests nor the Levites have kept themselves aloof from the people of the land and their abominations [Canaanites, Hittites, Perizzites, Jebusites, Ammonites, Moabites, Egyptians, and Amorites]; for they have taken some of their daughters as wives for themselves and their sons, and thus they have desecrated the holy race with the peoples of the land. Furthermore the leaders and rulers have taken a leading part in this apostasy!"

When I had heard this thing, I tore my cloak and my mantle, plucked hair from my head and beard, and sat there stupefied. Around me gathered all who were in dread of the sentence of the God of Israel on this apostasy of the exiles, while I remained motionless until the evening sacrifice. Then, at the time of the evening sacrifice, I rose in my wretchedness, and with cloak and mantle torn I fell on my knees stretching out my hands to the LORD, my God. (Ezra 9:1–5)

Ezra then makes a long prayer to God asking for God's mercy on the sinners. At the conclusion, a group of people come to speak to him. We read of this in Ezra 10:1–5:

While Ezra prayed and acknowledged their guilt, weeping and prostrate before the house of God, a very large assembly of Israelites gathered about him, men, women and children; and the people wept profusely. Then Shecaniah, the son of Jehiel, one of the sons of Elam, made this appeal to Ezra: "We have indeed betrayed our God by taking as wives foreign women of the peoples of the land. Yet even now there remains a hope for Israel. Let us therefore inter into a covenant before our God to dismiss all our foreign wives and the children born of them, in keeping with what you, my lord, advise, and those who fear the commandments of our God. Let the law be observed! Rise, then, for this is your duty! We will stand by you, so have courage and take action!

Ezra rose to his feet and demanded an oath from the chiefs of the priests, from the Levites and from all Israel that they would do as had been proposed; and they swore it.

Then we are told this is precisely what the men of Israel did. Over a period of time they did indeed expel from their presence their foreign wives and children. And thus ends the book of Ezra. But Ezra is mentioned significantly once again in the next book of the Bible, in chapter 8 of the book of Nehemiah.

Ezra Presiding at Worship

Here is how Ezra reappears in the book of Nehemiah (ch. 8, vv. 1–12). It is not clear how long after Nehemiah's census this event took place:

Now when the seventh month came, the whole people gathered as one man in the open space before the Water Gate, and they called upon Ezra the scribe to bring forth the book of the law of Moses which the LORD prescribed for Israel. On the first day of the seventh month, therefore, Ezra the priest brought the law before the assembly, which consisted of men, women, and those children old enough to understand. Standing at one end of the open place that was before the Water Gate, he read out of the book from daybreak till midday, in the presence of the men, the women, and those children old enough to understand; and all the people listened attentively to the book of the law. Ezra the scribe stood on a wooden platform that had been made for the occasion; at his right side stood Mattithiah, Shema, Anaiah, Uriah, Hilkiah, and Maaseiah, and on his left Pedaiah, Mishael, Malchijah, Hashum, Hashbadanah, Zechariah, Meshullam. Ezra opened the scroll so that all the people might see it (for he was standing higher up than any of the people); and, as he opened it, all the people rose. Ezra blessed the LORD, the great God, and all the people, their hands raised high, answered, "Amen, amen!" Then they bowed down and prostrated themselves before the LORD, their faces to the ground. [The Levites Jeshua, Bani, Sherebiah, Jamin, Akkub, Shabbethai, Hodiah, Maaseiah, Kelita, Azariah, Jozabad, Hanan, and Pelaiah explained the law to the people, who remained in their places.] Ezra read plainly from the book of the law of God, interpreting it so that all could understand what was read. Then [Nehemiah, that is, His Excellency, and] Ezra the priest-scribe [and the Levites who were instructing the people] said to all the people: "Today is holy to the LORD your God. Do not be sad, and do not weep"—for all the people were weeping as they heard the words of the law. He said further: "Go, eat rich foods and drink sweet drinks, and allot portions to those who had nothing prepared; for today is holy to our LORD. Do not be saddened this day, for rejoicing in the LORD must be your strength!" And the Levites quieted all the people, saying, "Hush, for today is holy, and you must not be saddened." Then all the people went to eat and drink, to distribute portions, and to celebrate with great joy, for they understood the words that had been expounded to them.

The remainder of the chapter tells us of the Jews celebrating the feast of booths. More precisely, in Nehemiah 8:17–18 we are told: "Thus the entire assembly of the returned exiles made booths and dwelt in them. Now the Israelites had done nothing of this sort form the days of Jeshua, son of Nun, until this occasion; therefore there was very great joy. Ezra read from the book of the law of God day after day, from the first day to the last."

In chapter 9 we hear of the peoples' confession of their sin, a blessing by the priests, and then in verses 6–37 we receive a lengthy prayer. The Septuagint prefaces the prayer with the words "Then Ezra said." Some exegetes argue that this is an interpolation and it is really a prayer of all the Levites present. The NAB translation, which I use, follows at this point the Septuagint translation. Because the prayer is important for its later influence, I quote here the opening line. The prayer recites God's providential care in creation, the election of Abraham, the exodus from Egypt, the wilderness wanderings, and life in the land of Israel. It is a composition of great poetic beauty with, for example, a definite rhythmic character. To give some impression of it, I quote here just the opening words, verse 6: "Then Ezra said: 'It is you, O Lord, you are the only one; you made the heavens, the highest heavens and all their host, the earth and all that is upon it, the seas and all that is in them. To all of them you give life, and the heavenly hosts bow down before you.'" After this we hear nothing more of Ezra in the book of Nehemiah. According to Josephus (in the *Antiquities* 11.5, para. 5 of *Antiquities* 11.158; check also 11.193), Ezra died in honored old age at Jerusalem and was magnificently buried there.

There are many lessons to be learned from this, our survey of the life and ministry of Ezra, this simple priest at the time of the exile and restoration. But here I will restrict myself to two lessons that I feel have particular importance for Catholic priests today. Both lessons are from our last quotation, the one from Nehemiah 8.

The Art of Reading Aloud

The first important lesson to be learned from this narrative is contained in Nehemiah 8:3, the line that says of Ezra, "he read out of the book from daybreak till midday . . . and all the people listened attentively." That was indeed a long reading. And if the people listened attentively all morning, then we can only presume that Ezra was a gifted reader or skilled in the dramatic art of oral interpretation. The Bible itself witnesses to the need for such an art, such a ministry. According to the Bible, from the time of the revelation of the law at Sinai where, according to Exod 24:4, "Moses wrote down all the words of the Lord," the Hebrew people had become a literary culture. That is not to say that everyone could read and write. Rather, from that moment the reading of the word of God aloud to the people became an important ministry. For example, the book of Joshua, named for Moses' successor as leader of the Hebrew people, describes Joshua reading at a public assembly of all Israel. Joshua 8:34–35: "Then were read aloud all the words of the law, the blessings and the curses, exactly as written in the book of the; law. Every single word that Moses had commanded. Joshua read aloud to the entire community, including the women and children, and the strangers who had accompanied Israel."

No doubt the NT appears to witness to a general literacy among the Jews. For example, Jesus is more than once portrayed as asking, "Have you never read" (e.g., Mark 2:25; 12:10, 26). And in John 19:20, when we are told, "Now many of the Jews read the inscription," seems also to imply a general literacy. Nevertheless, the NT also witnesses to a special ministry or reading aloud in both the Jewish assembly and the Christian assembly. Luke 4:16 describes Jesus reading publicly from the Scriptures in the synagogue at Nazareth where he "went according to his custom into the synagogue on the Sabbath day. He stood up to read." The thirteenth chapter of the Acts of the Apostles contains a lengthy description of Paul and Barnabas attending a synagogue service at Antioch in Pisidia during their first missionary journey. In that passage there are several references to the readings regularly employed in the synagogue service, namely a first reading from the Pentateuch and then a reading from the Prophets, Acts 13:15, "after the reading from the law and the prophets, the synagogue officials sent word to them" and Acts 13:27, "the oracles of the prophets that are read Sabbath after Sabbath." Later in Acts 15:21, we hear "Moses . . . has been read in the synagogues every Sabbath." Paul's instruction to Timothy in 1 Tim 4:15 is a witness to the structure of early Christian worship services, which patterned themselves upon the synagogue service: "Until I arrive, attend to the reading, exhortation and teaching." The word for reading used there, *anagnoseis*, means "public reading" as it is translated in the RSV. And Revelation 1:3 pronounces a blessing upon such lectors or public readers, "Blessed is the one who reads aloud and blessed are those who listen." What may well have been one of the basic foundations of the art of oral interpretation can be found in Acts 8:30. Its description of Philip the evangelist's encounter with the Ethiopian eunuch is an indirect witness that in the ancient world reading aloud, even to one's self, was the normal thing: "Philip ran up and heard him reading Isaiah the prophet." Unfortunately, we moderns tend to read only mentally, looking for the intellectual content of the words. But in so doing, we are shortchanging ourselves, for we are avoiding the further and equally important task of trying to hear the moral and emotive force contained and revealed in the sound and rhythm, the proper vocal inflection of the written text.

The Ministry of the Lector

As for the ministry of oral interpretation, or reading aloud amid the Christian assembly, we have considerable evidence that suggests early on in the history of Christianity, "lectoring," that is, public reading, became a specialized ministry in the Christian assembly. Take, for example, the witness of Cyprian of Carthage in his *Epistle 23*, written in AD 250 to the clergy of Carthage. It begins with the salutation, "Cyprian to the presbyters and deacons, his brethren, greeting." In this letter he mentions some recent correspondence he had with the See of Rome, and then he mentions some ordinations and ministerial appoints he has made. He says at one point, "with the teacher-presbyters we were carefully trying readers." This is probably a reference to him and certain presbyters who are auditioning candidates for the office of reader. It is a practice we might do well to follow today instead of just leaving the lecturing to whoever is willing. But the expression "teacher-presbyters" is what most interests us here. The translator says in a footnote: "Not 'teachers and presbyters,' as in the Oxford translation but 'teaching presbyters.' For these were a distinct class of presbyters—all not being teachers—and these were to be judges of the fitness of such as were to be *teachers* of the *hearers*."[2] At the time of the conversion of the tribes of northern Europe, which were entirely oral cultures, lecturing in the Christian assembly had been a lay ministry. But this activity soon became a step to the priesthood, that is, one of the minor orders. It stayed that way until Pope Paul VI, in his apostolic letter of August 15, 1972, *Ministeria quaedam*, abolished the minor orders of porter, lector, exorcist, and acolyte, and made the ministries of acolyte and lector baptismal rights rather than clerical privileges. No doubt, this was a good thing. But not all the baptized are gifted readers. In the Rule of Saint Benedict, chapter 47, there is the wise admonition: "The brethren are not to read or sing each in his turn, but those only who give edification to the hearers" (*Fratres autem non per ordinem legant aut cantent, se qui aedificant audientes*).[3] Maybe we too should return to testing lectors. No doubt, among the baptized some are naturally gifted readers. But reading aloud is also an art that can be learned. Today there are many useful books in print that offer advice and instruction on lectoring in church. But it is especially desirable that the art of oral interpretation be taught to all seminarians. Indeed, it should become a basic part, an essential component, of all priestly training; for priests must read aloud to the Christian assembly not only the gospel of the Mass but also the Eucharistic Prayers. Moreover, a priest should be trained to read in such a way that engages both the mind and also the spirit of the congregation. While seminary training everywhere today includes a course in homiletics, doctrinal and moral interpretation of the biblical text, there should also be a required course in dramatic interpretation, that is, how to read a text aloud with rhythm and emphasis that can engage both the mind and the heart of the congregation in the text itself, as it is heard and before it is preached upon.

The Ministry of Instruction

I must now address what I feel is the most important lesson we can learn from the description of Ezra in the biblical passages we have surveyed: the hyphenated

2. Cyprian, *Epistles*, p. 301.
3. *Rule of Saint Benedict*, p. 109.

description of him as "a priest-scribe." Yes, Ezra was a primarily a priest. This was his birthright, and indeed if the genealogy attached to him can be believed, his was a priestly lineage of the highest order—he was a direct descendent of Aaron, the first and great high priest. While Josephus goes so far as to call Ezra a chief priest (*protos hierus* in *Antiquities* 11.121), that is not true. Ezra was in fact a simple priest. Even so, he was a very special kind of priest, that is, he was a learned priest. As we read in Nehemiah 8, Ezra not only "read plainly from the book of the law," but he also interpreted "it so that all could understand." In one sense, all Israelite priests were expected to instruct the people: throughout the Old Testament there are passages that make it clear that priestly ministry in Israel was never intended to be a purely and simply cultic ministry, that is, identified solely with correct practice regarding ritual offerings. The Israelite priest was never intended to be merely a cultic functionary. No, he was to be also a source of instruction. For example, in Leviticus 10:10, we read how the Lord God told Aaron that among the duties of a priest were discernment and instruction: "You must be able to distinguish between what is sacred and what is profane, between what is clean and what is unclean; you must teach the Israelites all the laws that the Lord has given them through Moses." A Hebrew priest had to be trained not just in cultic observances, the mechanics for the presentation of ritual offerings and the observance of a liturgical calendar. He also needed to know how to discern the subjective moral disposition of each supplicant and to be able to give moral direction to the life of those seeking to make a sacrificial offering. No doubt, there must have been some priests who never got much beyond simple imitation of their priest instructors and thus only performed thoughtless repetitious rules in action. But there can be no doubt that more was expected of them. We see this same point made by the prophets. For example, Jeremiah 18:18 makes it clear that Israel had a right to expect "instruction from the priests . . . counsel from the wise . . . messages from the prophets." Later we read in the book of the Prophet Malachi 2:7: "For the lips of the priest are to keep knowledge, and instruction is to be sought from his mouth, because he is the messenger of the Lord of hosts." Later still, in the book of Sirach, written in Hebrew during the Hellenistic era, between 200 and 175 BC is a section that celebrates the great heroes in the history of Israel and describes Aaron. This passage details not just Aaron's role as cultic figure but also celebrates him as a teacher. In Sirach 45:16–17 we read how God chose Aaron and appointed for him several tasks: "He chose him from all mankind to offer holocausts and choice offerings, to burn sacrifices of sweet odor for a memorial, and to atone for the People of Israel. He gave to him his laws, and authority to prescribe and to judge: to teach the precepts to his people, and the ritual to the descendants of Israel."

Aelred Cody, in his "An Excursus on Priesthood in Israel," an essay that is appended to his commentary on Ezekiel, describes these priestly duties with analytical detail:

> The simple manifestation of divine will and divine intentions through answers
> to questions communicated through priests in oracular consultation evolved
> into a more complex manifestation of God's will in priestly pronouncements
> or decisions on what was pleasing or displeasing to God in matters of ritual
> purity, of distinction between what was to be done and what was to be avoided
> in matters of separation between the holy and the profane. This kind of priest-
> ly pronouncement was called a *torah*. Collections of such decisions, in both
> ritual and ethical matters, formed bodies of sacred law, and as evolution went
> further the word *torah* came to be almost synonymous with law itself. All law
> in Israel was looked upon as the expression of God's regulating will, whether it
> dealt with the specifically religious aspects of life or not. *Torah* in Deut 31:9, in
> a passage written when the monarchical period was at its end, certainly refers
> to the entire legal code of Deut 12–26. Jer 18:18, written in the same period,
> shows us that *torah* was by then seen to be just as characteristic of a priest as
> the word was of a prophet, or counsel of a wise man.[4]

The Role of Israel's Learned Priests

Ezra's ministry had a distinct character: restoration of the temple and its programs of sacrifices were not enough; a learned priest was needed who could bring sound doctrinal teaching and clear moral direction to the people. Ezra thus represents a particular intensification of this instructional aspect of priestly life. This is contained in the reference to him as a scribe of the law, meaning the law of Moses. Very few people in the ancient world could read and write. Reading and writing were skills practiced by a very few. These literary professionals were called scribes, in Hebrew *sopher*, plural: *sopherim*, in Greek *grammateus*. They often worked as assistants to kings and rulers, chronicling the political history of their reigns, keeping statistics on populations and taxes, on the number of military units and their personnel. The Bible itself provides us with examples of this. In the second book of Kings, chapter 18 tells us of "Shebnah the scribe" who functioned in the diplomatic service of King Hezekiah. In that same second book of Kings, but this time in chapter 22, we read of Shaphan, scribal assistant or personal secretary to King Josiah, who functioned as the chief scribe at the Jerusalem court, that is, as a high cabinet officer concerned with financial administration. In the Acts of the Apostles 19:35, what the New American Bible calls "the town clerk" at Ephesus is literally a *grammateus*, that is, a

4. Cody, *Ezekiel*, p. 258.

professional scribe. But the term also had religious uses. No doubt, much of Israel's earliest traditions were passed on orally. Take for example, Exod13:14, "If your son should ask you later on, 'What does this mean?' you shall tell him, 'With a strong hand the Lord brought us out of Egypt.'" But Exod 32:15 also witnesses to an early written tradition: "Moses then turned and came down the mountain with the two tablets of the commandments in his hands, tablets that were written on both sides, front and back."

Era is termed a scribe at least ten times: Ezra 7:6, 11, 12, 21; Neh 8:1, 4, 9, 13; 12:26, 36. Some have insisted that this term, even as applied to Ezra, meant that he initially at least served as a Persian court functionary. This would explain why he has such ready access to the king. Indeed, the word "scribe" in Hebrew, Greek, and other languages had a wide range of meaning that changed over time and could denote several social roles. For example, in both Semitic and Greek usage, the scribe was commonly a middle-level government official. We know that the Prophet Jeremiah employed a secretary. See Jer 36:4: "so Jeremiah called Baruch, son of Neriah, who wrote down on a scroll, as Jeremiah dictated, all the words which the Lord had spoken to him." See also the great tribute to scribes in Sir 39:1–11.

However, there are other references to Ezra that make it clear he was, more importantly, a religious scribe: In Ezra 7:6 he is called a scribe "skilled" in the Law of Moses; in 7:11, "a scribe of words, the commandments of the Lord and his statutes for Israel," and in 7:12 and 7:21, "a scribe of the Law of the God of heaven."

But even as a religious scribe, Ezra was no ordinary religious scribe. By that I mean Ezra not only had a role in promulgating and promoting the Torah, or law of Moses, but that he may even have had the preeminent role in its editing. In other words, Ezra might well have been the definitive redactor of the Torah or Pentateuch. For example, Jerome wrote in his treatise *Against Helvidius*, though we can call Moses the author of the Torah, Ezra was the editor.[5] Bellarmine wrote in his *Controversies* (Milan, 1721) book 1, 1l66: "It was Ezra who after the captivity collected and edited [dispersed annals and papers] into a single corpus, adding to Deuteronomy the last chapter concerning the life of Moses, and various other transitional remarks." Many have argued that the priests exiled to Babylon found in the intensified study of their scattered "sacred oracles" a compensation for their inability to perform any longer the concrete ritual and other obligations linked with the soil of Palestine. Indeed, Jesuit Robert North, in his treatment of the book of Ezra for *The Jerome Biblical Commentary* (1968), identifies Ezra with the school of priestly scribes at Neharda. Neharda (sometimes spelled Nehardea) was a town in Babylon, situated

5. Jerome, *Letters and Treatises*, p. 337.

on the Euphrates river at its junction with the Malka River.[6] According to Josephus (in his *Antiquities of the Jews*, book 18.311), there was Jewish settlement there dating back almost a hundred years before the Babylonian captivity; but at the time of the exile in Babylon many Jewish priests settled there and built a synagogue with the name Shaf ve-Yatif, that is, "The Divine Presence Removed from the Temple." These priests began a scribal academy at Neharda. There is also the witness of 1 Chr 2:55 that names several families of scribes who comprised an academy at a village near Bethlehem called Jabez: "The clans of the Sopherim dwelling in Jabez were the Tirathites, the Shimeathites, and the Sucathites." Of the Scribal School at Neharda, Robert North says:

> The school of priestly scribes in Neharda had doubtless just embarked upon the mammoth project of publishing a critical edition of the Torah when Cyrus officially ended the Exile. Although their whole life work had been dedicated to convincing themselves that they must get back to Jerusalem as soon as possible, there were still obvious difficulties in abandoning or relocating such a project. Hence, it was agreed to defer the return to Jerusalem until the work was finished. The years dragged on to decades and almost a century. Meanwhile, Ezra became head of the school (see Ezra 7:10), and, with the resoluteness his memoirs betray, brought both projects to a head.[7]

It was altogether in accord with Persian policy to foster the compiling of local legislation, especially ritual and moral codes likely to set public order and civil obedience into a loftier religious framework. Ezra was readily granted an exit visa (Ezra 7:11) for the convoy he set about to organize. It amounted to a transfer of the major departments of the Neharda school to Jerusalem.

This work of Ezra's in editing, promulgating, and interpreting the law of Moses cannot be underestimated. Indeed, for this work Ezra is considered by many to be one of the founders of modern Judaism. Ezra and Nehemiah together are seen as the creators of postexilic Judaism, and thus two of the greatest figures in Jewish history. And though in this sense they can be paired, it is interesting how the Babylonian Talmud in the tractate *b. Megilla* 16b, suggests Ezra's was the greater achievement: "The study of the Torah is superior to the building of the Temple," a judgment which is followed by the example of Ezra who was not among the first to return to Israel precisely because he would not leave off study of the Torah until he had mastered it. Only then would he journey to Jerusalem to help in the restoration of the Temple.[8] Indeed, there are some rabbinic authorities who compare Ezra's stature and

---

6. North, "Commentary on Ezra," p. 432.

7. Ibid., p. 432.

8. *The Babylonian Talmud*, tractate Megillah, pp. 100–101.

importance not with that of Nehemiah but with that of Moses. For example, Rabbi Jose, in the Babylonian Talmud's tractate *b. Sanhedrin* 21b, says, "Had Moses not preceded him, Ezra would have been worthy of receiving the Torah for Israel."[9] No one knows quite when the institution of the synagogue was founded. Some date it before the exile; some date it after; some date it precisely to this time, and point to this last passage, Nehemiah 8, with its description of Ezra seated on a dais, reading Scripture to the people and expounding it as the exemplar, the archetype, of what would eventually become (if it was not already) the synagogue assembly of Judaism.

But Catholic Christians should be aware that some scholars have found in Nehemiah 8 not just the prototype of the synagogue assembly but even the structure of the Christian liturgy, which is called the Eucharist. For the assembly in Nehemiah 8, wherein the word of God is solemnly proclaimed and expounded and the congregation responds "Amen," does not end with the preached word but instead concludes with the celebration of a community meal. French theologian Louis Bouyer offers insights. In the line "then all the people went to eat and drink," Bouyer sees more than just a social commentary but a foreshadowing of the structure of the Mass. Louis Bouyer's book *Life and Liturgy* consists of a series of lectures given in the summer of 1954 at the first ever Notre Dame [University] Liturgy Program of the Summer Session. Father Bouyer's lectures, as can be seen from the book's chapter headings, treat of the relationship between the Christian Eucharist and the history of the Hebrew sacred assembly, and even the later Synagogue service: chapter 3 is titled "From the Jewish Qahal to the Christian Ecclesia"; chapter 8 is titled "The Pauline Mystery and Its Proclamation: From the Synagogal Service to the *Missa Catechumenorum*"; chapter 9 is titled "The Eucharistic Celebration: From the Jewish to the Christian." Bouyer describes Ezra's thanksgiving prayer in Nehemiah 9 as a "new type of prayer which can already be termed a Eucharistic (thanksgiving) prayer."[10] And in chapter 9, page 116, Bouyer repeats his conviction that "these characteristics of Esdras' [Ezra's] prayer endure as conspicuous features of the worship of the synagogues and prepare directly for the worship of Christians."[11]

However, it is not enough for us to simply acknowledge that there was a dimension of Hebrew priestly ministry that was intellectual; we also need to recognize the profoundly speculative character, indeed, the awesome doctrinal achievement of that Hebrew priestly culture, an achievement that is observable to this day as it gives expression to some of the most profound theological insights in the Old Testament.

---

9. *The Babylonian Talmud*, tractate Sanhedrin, p. 119.

10. Bouyer, *Life and Liturgy*, p. 26.

11. Ibid., p. 116.

Based on the description of Ezra the priest-scribe that we have set forth above and in the presentation of him in the rabbinic literature, one might think of him as being merely the editor and interpreter of the law of Moses. But Ezra, and the priests who edited the Torah, were more than just learned scribes. In some cases they were brilliant theologians in their own right.

These priests were experts both in the laws of Israel and in the doctrines. For example, we should not be surprised to find that priests are a major literary source when Israel later begins to build up its scriptural tradition, not only in the sections on the law but in the most high-flown speculative theology. Every student of the Pentateuch (the Bible's first five books of Moses) is made aware of this priestly role when they study the priestly tradition, which is one of the major literary sources of the Pentateuch. But it is also important that we see the preeminent importance or the peculiar character of the priestly tradition in the Torah. For example, the creation narrative in Genesis is a product of the priestly tradition, and thus one of the most daring, most ambitious passages of theological speculation in all the Scripture and is the product of priest scholars who pondered long and hard on the revelation that was Israel's encounter with the one true God.

It is by now a commonplace that the Pentateuch is an editorial composite from four sources: Jahwist, Elohist, Deteronomist, and Priestly—of which the Priestly is the most recent and thus the final redaction. Moreover, the Priestly source has characteristics that reflect the interests of priests: a preoccupation with cultic and moral laws (Moses here is primarily a law giver), genealogy and statistics, and descriptions of ritual objects and cultic rites. That they are all rendered in a dull and prosaic style is the result of the conventions of cumulative lists, be they genealogical, prescriptive, or legal. Although the priestly influence is observable in all five books of the Torah, the book of Leviticus is seen as entirely the work of the Priestly source. Indeed, most of the latter half of Exodus, all of Leviticus, and most of Numbers belong to the Priestly source. By contrast, only a very little of the Priestly influence is found in Deuteronomy. However, it is wrong to see the Priestly contribution as always legalistic or cultic. Let us return to the example of the creation narrative in Genesis 1. Here we find a superb example of speculative theology of the highest order. The creation narrative of Gen 1:1—2:3, a narrative of the six days of creation and the Sabbath rest, contains such important theological concepts as in Gen 1:1, the doctrine of *creatio ex nihilo* (God's creation of the universe from nothing), in Gen 1:27the *imago Dei* theme (Gen 1:27), that is, human being made in the image and likeness of God; in Gen 1:28, the now particularly important ecological theme of human dominion over creation, that is, wise rule rather than ruthless domination of the earth). And in Gen 2:2, there is laid the foundation for a theology of work and rest. It is also great poetry:

majestic in tone with the use of literary refrains (probably originally a mnemonic device): "God saw that it was good" after each creation event. Even the legal and cultic sections have major theological themes such as righteousness, justice, holiness, guilt and atonement, and sacrifice.

And yet the intellectual character of Israelite priesthood has not always been recognized. Indeed, it has often been self-consciously minimized and denigrated. For example, consider the entry on "priesthood" in *The Encyclopedia of Catholicism* edited by Father Richard P. McBrien. There he presents us with a concise description of the history of Israelite priesthood: "In ancient times, the Levitical priesthood had responsibility in three areas: proclamation of the divine will, instruction and interpretation of the Law, and responsibilities associated with worship and ritual sacrifice (Deut 33:8–10). In the time of the monarchy, prophets assumed the first responsibility. In the exile, scribes became Israel's teachers. In postexilic Judaism, the priests' basic function centered around sacrifice and offering."[12] That such a formula (not to say theological bromide or abusive caricature) is far too facile and schematic can be seen by considering the facts that not only did priests number among the greatest prophets (Ezekiel, Jeremiah, and perhaps even Isaiah) and priests numbered among the greatest scribes (Ezra and the authors of the Pentateuch's Priestly source) but there is evidence that as late as the time of Jesus a large number of priests were professional scribes and a significant number of priests were learned. This is the argument of Joachim Jeremias in his book *Jerusalem in the Time of Jesus*. There, in his chapter, "The Scribes," Jeremias argues, "In Jerusalem before AD 70 we can prove the existence of a large number of priests who were scribes." Among these he quotes the names of men who were leading priests, that is, men who were representatives of the temple's priestly aristocracy. These figures include the captain of the temple, a chief priest, a son of the temple captain, a grandson of a reigning high priest, and a distinguished priest of an old high-priestly family. Jeremias also quotes the names of several simple priests, one an expert in matters of purity, another the head of the Hellenist synagogue in Jerusalem, and several who were simply examples of what Jeremias calls "a very cultured priest."

Jeremias's argument was severely criticized by E. P. Sanders in his *Judaism: Practice and Belief 63 BCE–66 CE*. However, scholarship since Sanders has tended to support Jeremias's claim. For example, in *Jewish Scribes in the Second-Temple Period*, Christine Schams insists that "Influential scribes are likely to have belonged to established and influential families and at least some scribes were of priestly descent."[13] Martha Himmelfarb, in her work *A Kingdom of Priests: Ancestry and Merit in Ancient*

12. McBrien, *Encyclopedia of Catholicism*, p. 1049.

13. Schams, *Jewish Scribes*, p. 311.

Judaism, goes even further to assert, "Just as in the period of the First Temple, then, when at least two of the most important prophets, Jeremiah and Ezekiel, were of priestly ancestry, there was significant overlap in the Second Temple period between the priestly elite and the scribal elite."[14]

A surer witness to the importance of learned priests in the late Second Temple period, which is the time of Jesus up to the destruction of the temple, is the rabbinic literary work called the *Mishnah*. This compilation of the teachings of the *Tannaim*, or Jewish sages, was made about the year AD 200, but it consists of the teachings of rabbis from the late Second Temple period, that is, as far back as four hundred years prior. Among those sages who in the *Mishnah* are all titled "rabbi" are a significant number of priests. For example, the *Mishnah* lists as a rabbinic authority Ishmael ben Elisha ha-Kohen, the son of a high priest, and one of the prominent leaders of the first generation of Tannaim. Another first-generation Jewish sage quoted often in the *Mishnah* is Hanina Segan ha-Kohanim, one of the chief priests who served as a deputy to the high priest. Also listed there are the regular priests: Eliezer ben Hurcanus, Eleazar ben Shammua, and the kohen known to us only as Rabbi Tarphon. Tarphon served in the temple in the time just before its destruction, and he is claimed by some to be the responder or interlocutor in Justin Martyr's *Dialogue with Trypho the Jew*.[15]

The Importance of Learned Christian Priests

From early on, Christianity has placed great emphasis upon learning and the intellectual presentation, rational defense even, of the Christian faith. Indeed, throughout its history Christianity has demanded such intellectual skills of its clergy.

It is unfortunate that there has been, at times, a pietistic attitude that despises learning in the Christian tradition. One of the foremost representatives of that attitude is Thomas à Kempis (ca. 1380–1471) who in his *Imitation of Christ* (bk. 1, ch. 1) defiantly avowed against the scholastics of his day: "I would rather feel compunction than know its definition."[16] I once heard a learned Dominican friar, a Thomist, ridicule Thomas's preference for feeling over thought, saying that someone should have made it clear to Thomas, if he could not define compunction it might not be compunction but only indigestion that he was feeling. Whether that friar had made up his rejoinder or was echoing some author I do not know. But what I do know is that the championing of feeling over thought is not an attitude consonant with

14. Himmelfarb, *Kingdom of Priests*, p. 15.

15. This is the opinion of Johannes Quasten in his *Patrology*, Vol. 1, p. 202.

16. Thomas, *Imitation*, p. 19.

biblical faith. The admonition in 1 Pet 3:15 makes it clear that simple piety is no substitute for thoughtful, well-reasoned faith. Peter's admonition there, "Always be ready to give an explanation to anyone who asks you for a reason for your hope," is still important advice. Religion without reason can all too often lead to a mindless fanaticism that is helpful to no one. And thus the scribe, though at times presented ambiguously in the NT, quickly became an important part of Christian ministry. Moreover, Christianity early on began to place great emphasis upon the importance of having clergy who are able to teach.

The Danger of Relying on Theological Experts

Until now I have focused upon Ezra and the great value of the kind of learning that he represents. However, as I now move on to consider the role of learned priests in the Christian tradition, I must acknowledge some important differences. Ezra and scribalism in general have been held in great esteem in Judaism. In the Christian tradition a more ambiguous attitude exists, and that attitude appears early on. In the New Testament there is an ambiguous attitude toward the scribes. Scribes are prominent in the gospel narratives and the Acts of the Apostles. For example, several passages show us individual scribes or groups of scribes. In Mark 2:6 a reference is made that some scribes were present in the synagogue at Capernaum when Jesus healed the paralytic: "Now some of the scribes were sitting there." Or consider Mark 3:22 when, on another occasion, reference is made to "some scribes who had come from Jerusalem" to Capernaum to hear Jesus preach. Then in Mark 9:11 (and its parallel Matt 17:10), we find Jesus' disciples aware of scribal opinion when they are portrayed as asking Jesus, "Why do the scribes say that Elijah must come first?" In Mark 9:14 we are told, when Peter, James, and John came down from the mount of the transfiguration, "When they came to the disciples, they saw a large crowd around them and scribes arguing with them." Or in Mark 12:28 we are told of an individual scribe's response to a dispute between Pharisees and Sadducees over a pronouncement Jesus had just made: "One of the scribes, when he came forward and heard them disputing and saw how well he had answered them, asked him, 'Which is the first of all the commandments?'"

No doubt, in the gospels scribes are often portrayed in opposition to Jesus. Most often they are associated with the Pharisees, as in Jesus' admonition in Matt 5:20, "I tell you, unless your righteousness surpasses that of *the scribes and the Pharisees*, you will not enter the kingdom of heaven." In Matthew 23, for example, the entire chapter is given over to Jesus' vehement denunciation of the scribes and the Pharisees, indeed the statement "Woe to you, scribes and Pharisees, you hypocrites" becomes a rhetorical refrain used no less than seven times, punctuating each point he wants to make (Matt 23:13, 15, 16, 23, 25, 27, 29). On only a few occasions are scribes presented as responding positively to Jesus. For examples, refer to Matt 8:19 and 13:52, and Mark 12:32.

While the Jewish scribes in the NT are often presented as Jesus' enemies (Mark 8:31; 10:33; 11:18; 14:1), this must not be allowed to obscure the fact that there is also a more positive presentation of scribes, or at least of the Christian scribes.

Matthew's depiction of the scribes is at once the most negative and the most positive in the NT. On the one hand, probably due to the opposition his own community was experiencing from Jewish officials, Matthew views the Jewish scribes as corrupt and false. While he may view the current interpreters of the law as misguided, he still accepts their legitimacy and authority. In Matt 23:2–3 we read, "The scribes and the Pharisees have taken their seat on the chair of Moses. Therefore, do and observe all things whatsoever they tell you, but do not follow their example." Even more important, Matthew teaches that there will be scribes in the new Christian community, and that they will continue their function of making the past traditions relevant and alive to believers, preserving them as precious treasures. As Jesus says in Matt 13:52, "Every scribe who has been instructed in the kingdom of heaven is like the head of a household who brings from his storeroom both the new and the old." And in Matt 23:34 he says, "behold I will send to you prophets and wise men and scribes."

We know that Paul employed scribal secretaries. True, sometimes Paul himself writes, as when he says in Gal 6:11, "See with what large letters I am writing to you in my own hand," or in 1 Cor 16:21, "I, Paul, write you this greeting in my own hand," or Col 4:18, "The greeting is in my own hand, Paul's." But these might be only references to his signature. Also, we have very clear evidence to his using a scribal secretary for his Epistle to the Romans, for in Rom 16:22 it is the scribe himself who intervenes with "I, Tertius, the writer of this letter, greet you in the Lord." And then there is the notice in 1 Pet 5:12, "I write you this briefly through Silvanus, whom I consider a faithful brother."

This Silvanus is particularly intriguing. Almost all biblical scholars agree that the man whom Paul and Peter both refer to as Silvanus is the same person who Luke in his Acts of the Apostles refers to as Silas. It was not uncommon in those days to have dual names, just as the Apostle Paul's original Jewish name was Saul. Here too, most probably, Silas was this man's original Greek name and Luke, a self-styled historian, wants to show that he knows the precise historical background to this prominent member of the early church. But Paul and Peter, when addressing a broad audience of Romans and Greeks, preferred to employ the Roman variant of his Greek name, Silvanus.

Silvanus was certainly much more than just a corresponding secretary or amanuensis for Peter and Paul. In Acts 15:22, when the church elders in Jerusalem choose to send Silas (Silvanus) and Judas Barsabbas to accompany Paul and Barnabas to Antioch, Luke refers to Silas and Barsabbas as "leaders among the brethren." And that Judas and Silas were not merely socially prominent among the Jerusalem, nor merely traveling companions for Paul and Barnabas, is made clear by Acts 15:32 where we are told that after their arrival at Antioch, "Judas and Silas, who were themselves prophets, exhorted and strengthened the brothers with many words." Yet another indication of Silvanus's stature is that First Thessalonians opens with a greeting "from Paul and Silvanus and Timothy." And in 2 Cor 1:19, Paul refers to "the son of God, Jesus Christ, who was proclaimed to you by us, Silvanus and Timothy and me." Indeed, some biblical scholars have argued that since Silas worked longer in Thessalonica than Paul (Paul left Silas and Timothy in charge of that mission so that he could go elsewhere), it might well be that First Thessalonians is more the work of Silas than Paul; that is Silas, because of his more intimate and thorough knowledge of the situation in Thessalonica, might have advised Paul of the problems there and even suggested appropriate theological principles for addressing those problems. If that is true, then Silvanus was more than just a scribe, but was a pastoral and theological consultant. Moreover, some scholars have argued that First Peter may be more the work of Silvanus than of Peter because the vocabulary, style, and thought of First Peter have remarkable similarities to Pauline literature.

Learned Clergy in the Early Church

Even as Christian scribalism arose, there is also evidence in the NT that from early on great importance was placed upon having learned clergy, clergy who could teach. Among the numerous titles given to Jesus in the gospels—prophet, messiah, king, holy one, rabbi, teacher, physician—the one most often given to him is that of teacher. So too the talent of teaching is prescribed as a most valuable asset for a bishop or presbyter. In 1 Tim 3:2 we are told that a bishop must be "able to teach." And 1 Tim 5:17 urges that "double honor" be given those presbyters who "teach well."

The theme of the importance of educated pastors only increases in the patristic era. There is evidence that in the patristic era there was similar appreciation for the importance of education among the clergy. For example, Saint Jerome, in Letter 53 to Paulinus, bishop of Nola, written in 394 AD, stresses how important it is to have learned clergy, well-educated bishops and priests:

The apostle Paul learned the Law of Moses and the prophets at the feet of Gamaliel and was glad that he had done so, for armed with this spiritual armor, he was able to say boldly "the weapons of our warfare are not carnal, but mighty through God to the pulling down of strongholds"; armed with these we war "casting down imaginations and every high thing that exalts itself against the knowledge of God, and bringing into captivity every thought to the obedience of Christ; and being in a readiness to revenge all disobedience" [2 Cor 10:4–6]. He writes to Timothy who had been trained in the holy writings from a child exhorting him to study them diligently [2 Tim 3:14-15] and not to neglect the gift which was given him with the laying on of the hands of the presbytery. To Titus, he gives commandment that among a bishop's other virtues (which he briefly describes) he should be careful to seek a knowledge of the Scriptures: A bishop, he says, must hold fast "the faithful word as he has been taught that he may be able by sound doctrine both to exhort and to convince the gainsayers." [Titus 1:9][17]

Jerome does not doubt that unlettered, not to say dumb, priests and bishops do some good. However, Jerome is convinced there is no substitute for a learned, articulate pastor: "In fact want of education in a clergyman prevents him from doing good to anyone but himself and much as the virtue of his life may build up Christ's church, he does it an injury as great by failing to resist those who are trying to pull it down. The prophet Haggai says—or rather the Lord says it by the mouth of Haggai— "Ask now the priests concerning the law." For such is the important function of the priesthood to give answers to those who question them concerning the law . . ."[18]

Indeed, in this same letter Jerome goes on to conclude:

> In the close of his most solemn vision Daniel declares that "the righteous shall shine as the stars; and the wise, that is the learned, as the firmament" [Dan 12:3]. You can see therefore, how great is the difference between righteous ignorance and instructed righteousness. Those who have the first are compared with the stars, those who have the second with the heavens. Yet, according to the exact sense of the Hebrew, both statements may be understood of the learned, for it is to be read in this way: "They that be wise shall shine as the brightness of the firmament; and they that turn many to righteousness as the stars forever and ever."[19]

---

17. Jerome, *Letters*, p. 97.

18. Ibid.

19. Ibid., pp. 97–98.

Learned Priests in the Middle Ages

There is plenty of evidence that the emphasis continued upon the importance of cultured, learned priests in the Christian tradition right into the medieval era, and on into modern times. As for the medieval period, let us look at Theodulf of Orleans (ca. 750–821), one of the leading theologians of what has been called the Carolingian Renaissance, the revival of classical culture sponsored by Charlemagne (747–814), king of the Franks and Holy Roman emperor. Theodulf was a personal favorite of Charlemagne, who saw to his appointment as bishop of Orleans. Shortly after his appointment to the see of Orleans, Theodulf wrote his *Capitula ad presbyteros parochiae suae*, or *Precepts to the Presbyters of his Diocese*. There in paragraph 20 Bishop Theodulf says: "Let the presbyters keep schools in the villages and hamlets, and if any of the faithful desires to entrust his small children to them to be taught their letters, let them not refuse to receive and teach them, but let them teach them with the greatest love, noticing what is written: 'They, however, who shall be learned shall shine as the splendor of the firmament, and they who instruct many to righteousness shall shine as the stars forever and ever'" [Dan 12:3].[20]

Later still, Hugh of St. Victor (1078–1141), whom Adolf von Harnack in his *History of Dogma* calls "the most influential theologian of the twelfth century," insisted upon the importance of learned clerics.[21] In Hugh's *On the Sacraments of the Christian Faith* (bk. 2, pt. 3, section 1, "on Clerics"), insists "A cleric indeed should not be ignorant of the secrets of God, because he is His messenger to the people . . . after one has been made a cleric, he should then be sustained by the stipends of the church and be taught in the divine science and ecclesiastical discipline under the tutelage and custody of spiritual masters."[22]

In the next century, Bonaventure (ca.1217–1274), theologian and Master General of the Order of Friars Minor, the Franciscans, treats of priestly ordination in his *Breviloquium* (literally, "brief lecture") a summary, but comprehensive, presentation of Christian doctrine. It is intended to be a handy reference work. In part 6, which treats of the Sacraments (ch. 12, para. 6), he lists certain prerequisites for ordination to the priesthood. Among them he apparently ranks "education" first, mentioning it even before he mentions virtue: "it is to be conferred upon men who are educated, virtuous, free from impediments . . ."[23]

---

20. Theodulf, "Precepts," p. 387.
21. Harnack, *History of Dogma*, Vol. 6, p. 44.
22. Hugh, *On the Sacraments*, p. 260.
23. Bonaventure, *Breviloquium*, p. 268.

In the next century, we have the witness of Teresa of Avila (1515–1582), who in her *The Way of Perfection*, chapter 5, speaks about confessors and why it is important that they should be learned men:

> I beg every superior, for the love of the Lord, to allow a holy liberty here: let the Bishop or Provincial be approached for leave for the sisters to go from time to time beyond their ordinary confessors and talk about their souls with persons of learning, especially if the confessors, though good men, have no learning; for learning is a great help in giving light upon everything. It should be possible to find a number of people who combine both learning and spirituality, and the more favors the Lord grants you in prayer, the more needful is it that your good works and your prayer should have a firm foundation.[24]

Finally, there is the witness of Francis de Sales (1567–1622) who served as bishop of Geneva from 1602. He, as one of the leaders of the counter-reformation convoked a diocesan synod, shortly after he was made bishop of Geneva. At that synod he gave an exhortation to his priests with the theme "that they apply themselves to study." I quote here from the translation of that exhortation by Thomas F. Dailey.

> I can say to you truthfully that there is no great difference between ignorance and malice, except that ignorance is to be feared even more, especially when you consider that, not only is it offensive in itself, but it also leads to contempt for the ecclesiastical state.
>
> For this reason, my very dear Brothers, I implore you to attend seriously to study, because knowledge, to a priest, is the eighth sacrament . . . [without it] a greater misfortune happens to the priest than when the Ark [of the Covenant] is found in the hands of men who were not Levites (cf. 1 Samuel 4:3–11).
>
> That is why our poor, unfortunate Geneva has surprised us. Noticing our idleness, in that we were not on our guard and were contenting ourselves simply to say our Breviary without thinking of making ourselves more knowledgeable, they trumped the simplicity of our fathers and of those who have preceded us, making them believe that up to that time no one had understood anything of Sacred Scripture.[25]

But besides the importance of a general education for the parish clergy, and its importance cannot be underestimated even today, it is also important that we recognize the significant contribution to ecclesiastical and general culture made by simple priests who attained the highest learning in their respective fields.

While most of the great scholars of the patristic and medieval eras were either bishops or monks, the foremost biblical scholars of the patristic era were the simple

---

24. Teresa, *Way of Perfection*, pp. 62–63.

25. Francis de Sales, Oeuvres, Vol. 23, pp. 303–5. English translation available at http://web1.desales .edu/assets/salesian/PDF/ExortationstoClerics.pdf..

priests Origen of Alexandria and Jerome. And while most everyone recognizes the names of great priest-theologians who in medieval and modern times were from the various religious orders, priests such as the Benedictine Anselm, the Cistercian Bernard, the Dominican Thomas Aquinas (twice he turned down appointments to the episcopacy), and the Franciscan Bonaventure, there is also evidence of the importance of diocesan, that is, parish clergy in the intellectual effort of the church.

No doubt, in the Middle Ages the finest minds were monks and friars; nevertheless, all learning was not confined to monastic or conventual schools. Indeed, cathedral schools were often staffed by diocesan priests.[26]

We should also consider the witness of the great English poet Geoffrey Chaucer (1343–1400). His *Canterbury Tales* provides an important though indirect witness that the ideal of clerics as men learned in "the mysteries of God" and "His messenger to the people" was also applied to parish priests. It is the parish priest or "parson" rather than the friar or monk who is the noblest cleric in Chaucer's *Canterbury Tales* (composed in the early 1380s). And in the prologue (vv. 477–82) Chaucer praises his learning, saying of him:

> There was a good man of religion, too,
> A parson of a certain township who
> Was poor, but rich in holy thought and work.
> He was a learned man, a clerk;
> The Christian gospel he would truly preach,
> Devoutly his parishioners to teach.[27]

Learned Priests in Modern Times

In modern times, religious order priests still are of great prominence and importance: Newman the Oratorian; the Augustinian priest and biologist Gregor Mendel (1822–1884), whose studies helped to found the modern science of genetics; the great systematic theologian and Jesuit Karl Rahner; the Dominican Yves Congar; and the great biblical scholar and Sulpician Raymond Brown. Nevertheless, with a little time for reflection one can readily compose a comparable list of diocesan priests who in modern times have made comparable and important contributions to theology and the sciences. For example, consider the diocesan priests Drey and Mohler, founders of the Catholic Tubingen School, a major force in Catholic theology in the nineteenth century. Johann Adam Möhler (1796–1832) was ordained a priest for the Diocese of Württemburg and Johann Sebastian von Drey (1777–1853)

---

26. See also E. L. Cutts' *Parish Priests and Their People in the Middle Ages*, London, 1898.
27. Chaucer, *Canterbury Tales*, p. 13.

for the Diocese of Augsburg, where he served as a parish priest for five years before going on to his career in academics. When Möhler retired from teaching at Tubingen, his replacement was another priest of the diocese of Württemburg, Karl Josef von Hefele. Von Hefele (1809–1893) went on to become a great church historian, authoring works on the apostolic fathers, a life of Cardinal Jimenes, and a monumental seven-volume *History of the Councils*. Matthias Joseph Scheeben (1835–1888) was ordained a priest of the Diocese of Cologne and served his entire life as professor of dogma at the Cologne diocesan seminary. His *Handbuch der katholichen Dogmatik* (1887), while based on Thomistic principles, is a work of immense erudition that makes extensive use of patristic thought and the work of Scheeben's own contemporaries. Ludwig Ott (1906–1985), whose *Fundamentals of Catholic Dogma* was once a standard reference work for dogmatics, was a priest of the Diocese of Eichstaett in Bavaria. Msgr. Georges Lema'tre (1894–1966), Louvain University physicist, famous for his "big bang" theory of the origin of the universe, was a priest of the Archdiocese of Malines, Belgium. John P. Meier, one of America's foremost biblical scholars and professor at Notre Dame University is a priest of the Archdiocese of New York. His multi-volume study of the historical Jesus is considered by some to be the most authoritative life of Jesus in modern times. David Tracy (1939–), a priest of the Diocese of Bridgeport, Connecticut, for a long time has been a professor at the University of Chicago Divinity School. His book-length studies, *Blessed Rage for Order* (1975) and *The Analogical Imagination* (1981), are considered major contributions to theological method and hermeneutics. Joseph Ratzinger (1927–), ordained a priest for the Archdiocese of Munich-Freising in 1951, went on to a brilliant career as a theologian whose scholarship was not derailed even when he suffered promotion to high ecclesiastical office.

And, indeed, most recently Pope Benedict XVI has made it clear that he too is most concerned about the importance of this intellectual dimension of Christian ministry: concerned that it be preserved and fostered. I am referring to his letter to seminarians, which he wrote from the Vatican, October 18, 2010. In it he is especially emphatic in his emphasis upon study. It is worth quoting this work at length:

> Above all, your time in the seminary is also a time of study. The Christian faith has an essentially rational and intellectual dimension. Were it to lack that dimension, it would not be itself. Paul speaks of a "standard of teaching" to which we were entrusted in Baptism (Rom 6:17). All of you know the words of Saint Peter which the medieval theologians saw as the justification for a rational and scientific theology: "Always be ready to make your defense to anyone who demands from you an 'accounting' (*logos*) for the hope that is in you!" (1 Pet 3:15).

Learning how to make such a defense is one of the primary responsibilities of your years in the seminary. I can only plead with you: Be committed to your studies! Take advantage of your years of study! You will not regret it.

Certainly, the subjects which you are studying can often seem far removed from the practice of the Christian life and the pastoral ministry. Yet it is completely mistaken to start questioning their practical value by asking: Will this be helpful to me in the future? Will it be practically or pastorally useful? The point is not simply to learn evidently useful things, but to understand and appreciate the internal structure of the faith as a whole, so that it can become a response to people's questions, which on the surface change from one generation to another yet ultimately remain the same.

For this reason it is important to move beyond the changing questions of the moment in order to grasp the real questions, and so to understand how the answers are real answers. It is important to have knowledge of Sacred Scripture as a whole, in its unity as the Old and the New Testaments: the shaping of texts, their literary characteristics, the process by which they came to form the canon of sacred books, their dynamic inner unity, a unity which may not be immediately apparent but which in fact gives the individual texts their full meaning.

It is important to be familiar with the Fathers and the great Councils in which the Church appropriated, through faith-filled reflection, the essential statements of Scripture. I could easily go on. What we call dogmatic theology is the understanding of the individual contents of the faith in their unity, indeed, in their ultimate simplicity: each single element is, in the end, only an unfolding of our faith in the one God who has revealed himself to us and continues to do so.

I do not need to point out the importance of knowing the essential issues of moral theology and Catholic social teaching. The importance nowadays of ecumenical theology, and of a knowledge of the different Christian communities, is obvious; as is the need for a basic introduction to the great religions, to say nothing of philosophy: the understanding of the human process of questioning and searching to which faith seeks to respond.

But you should also learn to understand and—dare I say it—to love canon law, appreciating how necessary it is and valuing its practical applications: a society without law would be a society without rights. Law is the condition of love.

I will not go on with this list, but I simply say once more: love the study of theology and carry it out in the clear realization that theology is anchored in the living community of the Church, which with her authority, is not the antithesis of theological science but its presupposition. Cut off from the believing Church, theology would cease to be itself and instead it would become a medley of different disciplines lacking inner unity.[28]

28. Benedict XVI, *Letter to Seminarians*, pp. 323–24.

But at this point we need to consider more than the importance of well-educated pastors who can teach their congregations. We must also consider the importance of very learned priests who become teachers for the whole community. The Second Vatican Council addressed this issue when it expressed concern that at least some priests should be sent on for further academic studies so that they might give themselves over to teaching rather than pasturing. I have in mind the conclusion of article 19 of the Decree on the Ministry and Life of Presbyters: "Finally, bishops should be concerned that some devote themselves to deeper knowledge of the sacred sciences, so that there will never be a dearth of teachers for the intellectual formation of the clergy, or to assist other priests and faithful in acquiring the learning they need, and to foster the healthy progress in the disciplines of theology, which is an absolute necessity for the church."[29]

Alas, with a priest shortage today, many bishops might be reluctant to send priests for further study, and thus even seminary faculties become increasingly laicized. No doubt it is important to have educated laity, but it is also important to have priest-scholars and priest-theologians whose pastoral experience and role in the liturgy help to give them a distinct perspective on the same subjects.[30] Moreover, we do not want to see priests and bishops totally dependent upon academic theologians, the problematic aspect of which was made evident to us by Richard John Neuhaus. In an essay entitled "Celibacy Not the Issue," which appeared in the June–July 2002 issue of *First Things*, Neuhaus said of the dubious influence of the 1972 Catholic Theological Society of America study entitled *Human Sexuality*: "Many of the bishops did not and do not have the intellectual self-confidence to challenge the academic theological establishment." Likewise, we do not want to see a situation arise wherein the old rabbinic judgment about learning is relevant once again. Rabbinic Judaism put such value upon learning that it says in the *Mishnah*, the rabbinic commentary on the Torah: "the bastard that is learned in the Law precedes the High priest that is ignorant of the Law."[31] This judgment is set forth in the fourth division of the *Mishnah*, which is called *Nezikin*, ("damages"), the tractate *Horayoth* ("decisions") 3.8. Indeed, derision of high priests during the late Second Temple period is commonly quoted in rabbinic literature: see Pes. 57a; Yoma 8b–9a). And John Henry Newman has called our attention to the historic problem caused by less than learned

29. Tanner, *Decrees*, Vol. 2, p. 1066.

30. . Cf. Congar's *True and False*, p. 220: "A certain lack of the concrete meaning of the church and, more precisely, of its apostolic and pastoral meaning is notable among several reformers who finally left the church. Renan, Döllinger, and Loisy, for example, were predominantly intellectual rather than priestly—something perhaps linked to their vocation as professors, but they also manifested a lack of pastoral preoccupation and a kind of fear concerning apostolic calling."

31. *Mishnah*, p. 466.

bishops. In his *The Arians of the Fourth Century*, he observed, "Many bishops too were but the creatures of their times, raised up from the lowest of the people and deficient in the elementary qualifications of learning and sobriety."[32] Note that the reference here to "sobriety" is to intellectual balance rather than alcoholic imbalance. Newman lamented the fact that too many bishops in the fourth century showed themselves uncritically accepting of all-too fashionable ideas (such as Arianism). They were intellectually shallow, insufficiently acquainted with, not to say steeped in, their own religious traditions and thus easily caught up in unthinking, popular enthusiasms, popular causes, trendy, all-too-fashionable ideas.

And so we can see why it is important not just that we have some very learned priests but that we have among the college of bishops a significant number who are themselves learned in Scripture and tradition. This is important so that we do not have a hierarchy totally dependent upon theological experts. Scripture itself warns us of the danger of relying too exclusively upon theological experts: In Jer 8:8, the prophet warns us to be on the alert that at times "the law of the Lord . . . has been changed into falsehood by the lying pen of the scribes!" And as for the New Testament witness, we should keep in mind how in the gospel narrative of Jesus' temptation in the desert, the devil appears in one of his most hideous disguises, that of the theological expert. While Mark's account of Jesus' temptation in the desert (1:12–12) is very cursory, containing no dialogue, in the much more extended accounts of Matt 4:1–11 and Luke 4:1–12, Satan shows himself to be an all too clever exegete who is extremely knowledgeable of the Bible, such that he can quote it from memory and for his own, and not God's, purposes. And thus the example of the ancient Jewish priest Ezra—who was not just a technical expert but also a reverent and spiritual man, that is, not just learned in the letter of the law but obedient to its spirit—presents yet another enduring lesson.[33]

The Example of Jean-Baptiste Vianney

But as I said at the beginning of this chapter: our theme here is not just the importance of hyphenated priest-doctors, priest-scribes, or priest-professors, but also the vital importance of priest-pastors who take seriously study as an aid to their priestly task of preaching and teaching.

And so here, in conclusion, I want to consider the example of the famous Curé of Ars, Jean-Baptiste Vianney (1786–1859). It is unfortunate that in the popular

32. Newman, *Arians of the Fourth Century*, pp. 358–59.

33. And perhaps relevant here is 2 Cor 3:5–6, "the new covenant, not of letter but of Spirit; for the letter brings death, but the Spirit gives life."

imagination he is often seen as an intellectual dullard, indeed, devoid of any intellectual character or interests. That is not true. No doubt, he had considerable difficulty learning ecclesiastical Latin. In fact, it was his inability to master sufficient Latin that led to his being removed from the seminary and then assigned to a learned priest who became his theological mentor. One should not doubt the influence that Abbé Balley, pastor of the parish of Ecully in the Archdiocese of Lyons, had on the young Jean Vianney. Not only did Balley leave his entire library to the young Curé of Ars, but Vianney brought it with him to his first pastoral appointment and indeed made considerable use of it. Vianney spent hours composing his sermons and catechetical instructions. And today these are available to the English reader in such collections as *The Sermons of the Curé of Ars* translated by Una Morrissey (Chicago: Henry Regnery Co., 1960) and *The Curé of Ars to His People: Instructions on the Catechism, Explanations and Exhortations* (St. Meinrad, IN: Grail Publications, 1951). If we look at those collections, there can be no doubt Jean Vianney saw his priestly ministry as being more than cultic or sacramental. He took seriously those aspects of priestly ministry that are preaching and teaching. Msgr. Francois Trochu, in his afterward to Una Morrissey's translation of the sermons, describes the work that went into their composition: "It was in his early days as a priest at Ars that he prepared his sermons, writing them all down before hand and learning them by heart." No doubt his sermons tended to be moralistic rather than doctrinal. Nevertheless, they are thoughtful preparations that, when examined carefully, reveal that he had done considerable work in preparing them, including a study of important theological sources. For example, in Una Morrissey's translation of the curé's early sermons, there are no less than ten references to the teaching of Augustine of Hippo,[34] four references to John Chrysostom,[35] two to Jerome,[36] and singular references to Teresa of Avila, Ambrose of Milan, Carlo Borromeo, and Pope Gregory the Great. In his sermon against blasphemy, Vianney shows himself well-acquainted with Aquinas's teaching on that theme.[37] In later life, when his sacramental ministry took such a toll upon his time—he heard confessions for as many as eleven hours in a day—Vianney ceased preparing his sermons. But it was also at that time that Vianney began asking his bishop to relieve him of his pastoral duties. This brings up the issue of balance in the spiritual life. Seminarians today are often tutored in the importance of personal prayer, indeed of spending as much as an hour in prayer before the Blessed Sacrament. Would that they were tutored as strongly regarding the importance of *lectio*

34. Vianney, *Sermons*, pp. 36, 52, 66, 72, 75, 78, 95, 97, 158, 159.

35. Ibid., pp. 42, 66, 124, 156.

36. Ibid., pp. 97, 113.

37. Ibid., p. 73.

divina, the beneficial religious observance that is sacred reading! Here a teaching of Isidore of Seville is particularly relevant. In his *Book of Maxims*, he says at one point: "If a man wants to be always in God's company, he must pray and read regularly. When we pray, we talk to God; when we read, God talks to us."[38] The maxim that I have just quoted is taken from a longer selection from Isidore's book (bk. 3, 8–10), a selection that now serves as the second reading for the Office of Readings on the feast of Saint Isidore, April 4.

And thus we come back to the lesson we observed in the ministry of Ezra who not only prayed to God in public, as all priests are required to do, but who also studied in private. And it could be argued, as we have herein, it was that extra effort that made him so effective in his public ministry and makes him the revered figure in Judaism that he is to this day. Ezra should and could be an effective model for Christian ministers, especially Catholic priests.

---

38. *Liturgy of the Hours*, Vol. 2, p. 1760.

7

Social Justice *and* Splendid Liturgies

The High Priest Simon the Just

ARGUABLY THE MOST VIVID and magnificent description of a priest in all of biblical literature is the eye-witness account in the book of Sirach (ch. 50, vv. 1–21), of the high priest Simon, son of Jochanan, high priest from 219–196 BC, presiding at a solemn liturgy in the Jerusalem temple. That poetic passage, in its aesthetic detail, its precise and vivid description of liturgical vestments as well as liturgical actions, is surely capable of making modern-day ecclesiastical tailors such as the American Trappist Holy Rood Guild, the Belgian liturgical supply house Slabbinck, and Rome's Gammarelli, the official tailor to the pope, swoon with admiration, and maybe even ruefully smile with envy. But we must also recognize that the very same poetic passage in Sir 50:1–21 also includes a witness to Simon the high priest's equally impressive commitment to issues of social welfare and social justice, a commitment that gained him in later rabbinic literature the descriptive "Simon the Just." And that concern for social justice, if it were well known, might gain him today the admiration of still others in the contemporary church, besides liturgists and ecclesiastical tailors. These groups might include Dorothy Day's Catholic Workers, Mother Teresa's Missionaries of Charity, and Caritas Internationalis, a confederation of Roman Catholic relief, development, and social service organizations operating throughout the world. Even more important, for our interests here in this book (the defense of priesthood), I believe this remarkable combination of aesthetic and social sensitivities in the high priest Simon, son of Jochanan, is no mere random coincidence or personal idiosyncrasy. Rather, it is a moral composite as essential to the ministerial priesthood of the Christian Church as it was to Old Testament temple priesthood. And as such we must study it here. But before we read Sir 50:1–21, it is important that we understand something of the peculiar character of the literary work in which it appears and the well-calculated, pivotal, and dramatic position it occupies in the book of Sirach. And so we begin here with a consideration of the book of Sirach, its character and origin, its authorship and (disputed) authority, and the place and purpose within the book of Sirach that chapter 50, verses 1 through 21 serves.

The Book of Sirach

The book of Sirach is quite unfamiliar to much of Protestant Christianity because it is among those books not found in Protestant Bibles, unless it is included in a section called "the apocrypha." As is generally known, the New Testament in both Catholic and Protestant Bibles is identical in that each contains the same twenty-seven books. However, the Old Testament differs for those two Christian traditions: the Old Testament in a Catholic Bible contains seven books not found in the Old Testament of Protestant Bibles. These additional seven books appear because the Catholic Old Testament follows the Septuagint or Alexandrine canon. The Septuagint is the name given to the Greek translation of the Hebrew Scriptures made in Alexandria, Egypt, about 200 BC. That Greek translation of the Old Testament was "the bible" for all New Testament writers. It was the source for their quotations of the Scriptures, though Paul occasionally supplies his own. Moreover, the Septuagint served as the Old Testament for all Christians up until Martin Luther (1483–1546) revised the canon of Scripture on the principal that, as regards the Old Testament, only Hebrew works should be included. That judgment stands to this day unmitigated by the fact that in 1896, 1931, and 1964 manuscripts of the Hebrew original of Sirach were discovered. But even the Catholic Church has treated the book of Sirach and six other Old Testament works with a measure of condescension by labeling them deuterocanonical, of secondary inspiration. And this is done despite the fact that from antiquity the Catholic Church has held the book of Sirach in highest esteem.

Sirach is the longest of these seven additional or deuterocanonical books, and it has gone by various names. Its oldest and probably original Jewish title was "the Wisdom of Ben Sira," that is, "the son of Sirach." Jerome, in his prologue to the Old Testament wisdom writings, among which Sirach is classified, claims that its Hebrew title was originally *mishle*, that is, "parables" or "maxims" of ben Sirach. But in the historic Vulgate Latin translation of the Bible, the book of Sirach is called *Ecclesiasticus*, literally "the book of the Church" or "the book used in the Church." This is because the early church extensively used the book of Sirach as a resource for Christian catechesis. For example, not only did Augustine of Hippo write to Jerome referring to Sirach as a work "whose authority is worthy of highest esteem,"[1] but Augustine made considerable use of Sirach in his own writings. More precisely, Augustine quotes from Sirach ten times in his *Confessions* and five times in his *Enchiridion*,

1. Augustine, *Letters* (28.2).

or handbook of the faith. Augustine cites Sirach in his treatises on virginity, patience, the good of marriage, the care of the dead, and in his anti-Donatist writings. And the bishop of Hippo quotes from Sirach no less than thirty-seven times in his writings against the Pelagians, where he has the constant resource to Sirach's warnings against the power of lust and human passion to destroy one's life. Even to this day, the book of Sirach is used significantly in the Roman Catholic liturgy. For example, in the revised lectionary, the schedule of biblical readings for the liturgy, published after Vatican II, selections from the book of Sirach are used as the first reading for no less than thirteen weekday Masses in lectionary cycle one; and selections from Sirach are used as the source for several Sunday readings, including two Sunday festivals that are celebrated with particular solemnity every year. More precisely, the sermon on one's duties toward one's parents in chapter 3 of Sirach is used as the first reading on the Feast of the Holy Family of Jesus, Mary, and Joseph (the Sunday within the octave of Christmas). And the great tribute to wisdom in the twenty-fourth chapter of the book of Sirach is used every year as the first reading on the Second Sunday after Christmas.

The Author of Sirach

The author of the book of Sirach identifies himself in 50:27, as "Jesus, son of Eleazar, son of Sirach," in the original Hebrew as *Yeshuah ben Eleazar ben Sira*. He wrote this book in Hebrew in Jerusalem at some time during the decade 190–180 BC. Passages in the book of Sirach suggest the author was a teacher who ran a torah school in Jerusalem with several professional students in residence. Many literally interpret the saying in Sir 51:23 as: "come aside to me, you untutored, and take up lodging in the house of instruction." The motive for his writing this book appears to have been that through his considerable travels he had become aware of the influence of secular, Hellenistic culture upon educated Jews everywhere, and thus wanted to counter that influence by demonstrating the wisdom of the Jewish moral and religious traditions. In this regard note Sir 34:11, "I have seen much in my travels, learned more than ever I could say" and Sir 24:30–31, "thus do I send my teachings forth shining like the dawn, to become known afar off." Indeed The book of Sirach is prefaced by a declaration that makes clear the author's intent: "Many important truths have been handed down to us through the law, the prophets and the later authors; and for these the instruction and wisdom of Israel merit praise." Sirach's triadic description here of the Hebrew Scriptures as "the law, the prophets, and the later authors" is the first appearance of what will later become the classic summary of the Jewish tradition as TNK, that is, *torah*, *neviim*, and *ketuvim*, "the law, prophets, and the writings."

In this, his literary attempt to acquaint his readers with the treasures of traditional Hebrew wisdom, Sirach created a work in style much like the book of Proverbs. Indeed the book of Sirach is classed in Catholic Bibles along with the other "wisdom" books such as Job, Psalms, Proverbs, Ecclesiastes (Qoheleth).

The Layout of the Book of Sirach

The book of Sirach is divided into two sections. The first section comprises chapters 1 through 43. The style and form of this section is much like, and some argue even influenced by, that of the book of Proverbs. Chapters 1 through 43 of Sirach is, like the book of Proverbs, a collection of wise sayings grouped around certain topics. In the first section of Sirach, we are instructed about wisdom and the role it can play in regulating our relationship with God, family, and friends. There we find an extensive treatment of the concept of wisdom, not as high speculation regarding mysteries of God and the universe but as practical intelligence regarding the management of one's own life and affairs. More precisely, in this first part of the book of Sirach, wisdom is not just praised (chapters 1 and 24) but the rewards and blessings of wisdom are spelled out for us (Sir 4:11–19; 6:18–37; 14:20–27). Also in this section, the importance of seeking wisdom is made clear to us (Sir 39:1–11), and we are given instruction as to where wisdom can be found (Sir 16:22–28 and 19:17–26). We are also provided with wise advice regarding our duties toward God (ch. 2), his treatment of sinners (the penitent in Sir 17:19–27 and the impenitent in Sir 16), his divine power and mercy (Sir 18:1–13), and the providence of God (Sir 32:14–24). This first section of the book of Sirach also gives us much instruction regarding human relations such as friendship: what is true friendship (Sir 6:3–17), a warning against false friends (Sir 37:1–15) and the choice of friends (Sir 9:10–18 and 11:29–34), the preservation of friendships (Sir 22:19–26), dangers to friendship (Sir 27:16–21), the importance of humility (Sir 3:17–30), sincerity and justice (Sir 4:30), of kindness to the poor (Sir 4:1–10). Regarding duties, we are instructed toward one's family and servants (Sir 7:18–28), one's parents (Sir 3), one's wife (Sir 9:1–9 and 26:1–18) and children (Sir 30:1–13 and 42:9–14).

The Special Place of Sirach 50:1–21

However, after all this instruction regarding wisdom in our relationship with God and in our daily lives, the second and concluding section of the book of Sirach is appreciably different. These final chapters of Sirach are not instruction but celebration, a celebration of the "worthies" or heroes of Israel, that is, the lives of great

Jewish historical figures. In more than one way this is a significant literary turn. For example, Greek culture had already given rise to the literary genre of biography, and the earliest Roman biographer Cornelius Nepos (ca. 100–24 BC) was soon to write his *De Viris Illustribus* (Of Famous Men), a work destined to become the model for a classical literary genre that would last for more than a thousand years (witness the similarly titled works by Suetonius, Plutarch, Saint Jerome, and the Florentine writer, Petrarch). But Ben Sira, in the concluding section of his book, did a similar thing by setting forth, for the first time ever, biographical portraits of great men in the history of Israel. But with even greater innovation, the author of the book of Sirach sets forth in chapters 44–50 not just a collection of portraits of heroes of Israel's past but includes one from its present. More precisely, this second section of the book of Sirach features portraits of the patriarchs Noah and Abraham (Sir 44:17–21), Moses and Aaron (Sir 45), Joshua and the judges (Sir 46), the kings David and Solomon (Sir 47), and the prophets Elijah and Elisha (Sir 48). Coming at the end of all these, however, is Sirach's tribute to a great contemporary Jewish leader. He culminates his tribute to Israel's great biblical heroes with a spectacular description of his contemporary, the high priest Simon, the son of Jochanan. One should not underestimate the importance of this last portrait in Sirach's catalog of Israelite heroes. For this portrait is meant to show that heroic leadership in Israel does not consist solely of historic memories from the distant past. Rather, it demonstrates that there was a giant among them in their own time. I quote Sir 50:1–21 here, in its entirety. I have placed it in italics so as to set it off from the rest of the text, but for economy of space have only approximated the stanzaic or poetic form as it appears in the New American Bible:

> *The greatest among his brethren, the glory of his people,*
> *was SIMON the priest, son of Jochanan,*
> *In whose time the house of God was renovated,*
> *in whose days the temple was reinforced.*
> *In his time also the wall was built / with powerful turrets for the temple precincts;*
> *In his time the reservoir was dug,*
> *the pool with a vastness like the sea's.*
> *He protected his people against brigands,*
> *and strengthened his city against the enemy.*
> *How splendid he was as he appeared from the tent,*
> *as he came from within the veil!*
> *Like a star shining among the clouds, / like the full moon at the holyday season;*
> *Like the sun shining upon the temple,*
> *like the rainbow appearing in the cloudy sky;*
> *Like the blossoms on the branches in springtime,*
> *like a lily on the banks of a stream;*

Like the trees of Lebanon in summer, / like the fire of incense at the sacrifice;
Like a vessel of beaten gold, / studded with precious stones;
Like a luxuriant olive tree thick with fruit, / like a cypress standing against the
clouds; / Vested in his magnificent robes; / and wearing his garments of splendor, /
As he ascended the glorious altar / and lent majesty to the court of the sanctuary.
When he received the sundered victims from the priests
*   while he stood before the sacrificial wood,*
His brethren ringed him about like a garland, / like a stand of cedars of Lebanon;
All the sons of Aaron in their dignity / clustered around him like poplars,
With the offerings to the LORD *in their hands,*
in the presence of the whole assembly of Israel.
Once he had completed the services at the altar
*   with the arranging of the sacrifices for the Most High,*
And had stretched forth his hand for the cup, / to offer blood of the grape,
And poured it out at the foot of the altar,
a sweet-smelling odor to the Most High God,
The sons of Aaron would sound a blast, / the priests,
on their trumpets of beaten metal;
A blast to resound mightily / as a reminder before the Most High.
Then all the people with one accord / would quickly fall prostrate to the ground
In adoration before the Most High, / before the Holy One of Israel.
Then hymns would re-echo, / and over the throng sweet strains of praise resound.
All the people of the land would shout for joy, / praying to the Merciful One,
As the high priest completed the services at the altar
*   by presenting to God the sacrifice due;*
Then coming down he would raise his hands / over all the congregation of Israel.
The blessing of the LORD *would be upon his lips,*
the name of the LORD *would be his glory.*
Then again the people would lie prostrate / to receive
*   from him the blessing of the Most High.*

The Aesthetic Character of Sirach 50:1–21

This passage is particularly interesting for several reasons. First, it is an example of marvelous literary language that borders on poetry. Using great narrative detail and numerous comparisons, Ben Sira renders for us the impression of an awe-inspiring vision. Indeed, he paints for us a precise portrait of the wonder and joy in the hearts of the spectators, the worshippers, when they behold the high priest fully vested entering the sanctuary, ascending the altar of sacrifice (Sir 50:6–11), and in the presence of the whole assembly of Israel, encircled by assistant priests bearing offerings, sacrificing the burnt offerings himself while the trumpets blast and the people bow down in adoration of the Most High (Sir 50:12–17). He draws upon no less than ten images from the realms of nature and religious worship to convey awe at witnessing the high priest in splendid vestments: Simon is like a star, the full moon, the sun, the rainbow, blossoms, a lily, the lush growths of Lebanon, an olive tree, a vessel of beaten gold studded with precious stones. However, Ben Sira's poetry here is not really derived from nature but comes from the Bible. Alexander Di Lella, in his commentary on the book of Sirach, makes clear the precise biblical origin of several of the images that Ben Sira has employed in his description of Simon the high priest:

> Ben Sira now waxes eloquent in describing the splendid sight of Simon emerging from the Temple, using ten exuberant metaphors (50:6–10). The image of "a star shining" (50:61) derives from Ps 143:3b. The "full moon at the holyday season" (50:6b) is a reference to the feasts of Passover and Tabernacles, both of which began at the full moon. "The King" in 50:7a is God, for in the OT God often receives that title.[2]

However, the effect is achieved not just by Ben Sira's clever evocation of visual images. This effect is also achieved by his appeal to the aural imagination of his reader, his evocation of the sounds as well as the sights that accompanied such splendid liturgies in the Jerusalem temple. For example, consider Sir 50:16–19, where he describes a fanfare of trumpets with choral song and the people prostrate in worship. Flavius Josephus has described for us the appearance of these instruments in his *Antiquities of the Jews* (bk. 3, ch. 12, para. 6) "the sacred trumpets were long straight metal tubes of hammered silver."[3] In verses 18–21, Ben Sira describes the hymnody, the joyful shout of the multitude, and finally the high priest's blessing, in which he pronounces only once in the year, on this occasion—the holy name of Yahweh—to climax the description of this most solemn Jewish liturgical function.

It is important to remember that this description, however poetically rendered, is in fact a product of historical observation rather literary imagination. That is, the author of the book of Sirach, Jesus, son of Eleazar, son of Sirach (50:27), was a contemporary of this high priest. He describes Simon the high priest in great detail, and by numerous comparisons reveals the impression of awful majesty received, the lofty joy aroused at the sight of the high priest fully vested entering the sanctuary, ascending the altar (6–11), and in the presence of the whole assembly of Israel, encircled by assistant priests bearing offerings, sacrificing the burnt offering on the Day of Atonement. At this point the reader should be informed, however, that exegetical opinion is divided as to precisely what great temple service, what great liturgical

---

2. Di Lella, *Wisdom of Ben Sira*, p. 552.

3. Josephus, *Complete Works*, p. 82. The origin of the trumpets is in Num 10.2. They are portrayed on the Arch of Titus in the Roman Forum in the panel illustrating the sack of the Jerusalem temple by the troops of Titus.

event is being described here. Most exegetes have concluded, largely on the basis of Simon's pronouncement of the ineffable name of God in verse 20, that this is the service on Yom Kippur, the Day of Atonement. On the other hand, some have argued that this is an anachronistic judgment, that is, that in Simon's day veneration of the divine name had not yet reached the point where it was pronounced only by the high priest and on only one day of the year. These exegetes argue that the liturgy described is that of the Tamid, or Daily Whole Offering. And, indeed, the author we have quoted, Alexander Di Lella, in yet another commentary on Sirach for *The New Jerome Biblical Commentary* (1990), concurs in that judgment declaring it "a lyrical description of the ceremonies of the daily whole offering, and not of the Day of Atonement (Yom Kippur), as most commentators have thought."[4] In that judgment, DiLella was following the opinion of F. O. Fearghail, *Biblica* 59 (1978) 301–16, whom he cites. Indeed, some even argue it is this Ben Sira's description of contemporary temple practice that was later codified in the *Mishnah*, more precisely in the *Mishnah* tractate Tamid 6:3—7:3, with its description of the daily whole offering. We, however, must take account of yet another important element in Ben Sira's description of Simon the high priest.

The Moral Content of Sirach 50:1–21

After having said all this about Ben Sira's magnificent description, his great panegyric, of the splendor of the high priest Simon presiding over the temple liturgy, Ben Sira's lengthy poetic description comes second, that is, after an initial and perhaps more prosaic but nonetheless important description of Simon that emphasizes not liturgical splendor but practical social consciousness and assistance. Indeed, in this celebration of Simon's greatness, first place is given not to the portrayal of him as liturgical celebrant but to the portrayal of him as engineer of public works! I repeat here the tribute with which Sirach 50 begins so that the reader need not turn back the pages of this book. Sirach 50 begins with the words:

> *The greatest among his brethren, the glory of his people,*
> *Was Simon the priest, son of Jochanan,*
> *In whose time the house of God was renovated,*
> *In whose days the temple was reinforced,*
> *In his time also the wall was built with powerful turrets for the temple precincts;*
> *In his time the reservoir was dug,*
> *The pool with a vastness like the sea's.*
> *He protected his people against brigands,*
> *And strengthened his city against the enemy.*

4. Di Lella, "Sirach," p. 508.

This descriptive is certainly less poetic. Indeed, it borders on the prosaic. But these words celebrate an aspect of Simon's achievement that is no less than, indeed, perhaps more important, than his liturgical presidency. We do not know precisely what these words refer to because Jerusalem was so completely reconstructed by Herod the Great in the century after Simon the high priest. Indeed, much of what Jerusalem was during Simon's time has been obscured. But we do know that Simon was not only high priest but public ruler of Jerusalem, and he had considerable political and diplomatic skills, which he used to secure financial assistance from foreign powers—not for the support of the liturgy in the temple but for the fortification and irrigation of Jerusalem, the safety and physical well-being of his people. For example, after the conquest of Judea by Syrian King Antiochus III, Simon corresponded with Antiochus regarding the restoration of Jerusalem after the ravages of that war. Not only do we know that the high priest at that time had some political responsibility under the Syrian king, we know that similar repairs and restorations, as described in Sirach chapter 50, were diplomatically encouraged by Antiochus III. We see this in a letter written to the governor of the Palestine area after Antiochus had won Palestine from Egypt at the Battle of Paneas in 199 BC. This letter, quoted in full by the historian Josephus in his *Antiquities of the Jews* (bk. 12, ch. 3, para. 3), is probably genuine because Ben Sira's account confirms the building details, and describes various financial provisions for restoring the temple and other buildings in Jerusalem. The date of this work is sometime between 199 BC and Simon's death, about 195 BC. Therefore, it is reasonable to presume that as a reward for supporting Antiochus III of Syria in a victorious war against the Ptolemies of Egypt, Simon was permitted to restore the temple. The list of public works that Simon oversaw seem to be three: repair to the temple, repair to the fortifications or walls of the city, and the digging of a reservoir. The latter two—fortification and irrigation—are readily understandable from the history of Jerusalem. We do not know precisely when Jerusalem was first settled. Jerusalem appears in history for the first time in the middle Bronze Age, in the el Amarna letters. There can be little doubt that the site where it grew was originally chosen because of two natural features. One was the easy access to water provided by the existence of a spring, later called Gihon, that gushed out on the eastern flank of a low hill, itself the southernmost spur of a long narrow ridge that jutted out from the watershed of Canaan. The other natural feature that made the site worthy was its exceptional suitability for defense under conditions of ancient warfare. More precisely, deep declivities (now called the valleys of Kidron and Hinnom) protected it from east and west, while the sharp end of the spur protected it on the south. Only on the north was there open, unprotected access, but that side could be protected by a defensive wall. As the city grew, rulers would have to search for others means of providing more water. The Gihon spring is an intermittent spring, whose waters gush forth year-round at various times, often several times in a day. In order to exploit such abundance, pools were built along the Kidron Valley that could serve as reservoirs. Indeed, in Sir 48:17–22, we hear King Hezekiah (king of Judah 715–687 BC) praised because he "fortified his city, and brought water into its midst, he tunneled the rock with iron tools, and built cisterns for water." And thus we can understand why Ben Sira chose to include among the high priest Simon's achievements the notice that "in his time the reservoir was dug." Those words will seem prosaic in the extreme to some today, but when we recall the plight of a preindustrial city in an arid desert, those words are suddenly freighted with pathos. They are suddenly recognizable as descriptive of an acutely conscientious priest who sought to provide not just for his people's spiritual needs but also for their physical welfare.[5]

But there is yet another sense in which this Ben Sira's initial celebration and portrayal of Simon the high priest as an engineer of public works cannot be underestimated. Ben Sira is unique among the wisdom writers for the veneration and enthusiasm with which he speaks of the priesthood and the temple services. Witness his eulogy of Aaron and the priesthood bestowed on him by God (Sir 45:6–22). But Ben Sira also knew that no matter the importance of right worship, right conduct is more fundamental still. Several times the book of Sirach makes it clear that the law is essentially a moral law, and ritual observances that are not accompanied in the worshippers by a virtuous life and fitting inward dispositions are roundly denounced in Sir 7:8–10 and 34:18—35:12.

Simon is presented here as a high priest who not only celebrated the cult with splendor but did justice among the peoples. Indeed, in rabbinic tradition, the epithet attached to his name, "Simon *the Just*," refers to a justice that includes charitable acts as well as care for the temple liturgy. In that same rabbinic literature, Simon is credited with having taught, "By three things is the world sustained: by the Law, by the [Temple] service, and by deeds of loving kindness [*gemilut hasadim*]."[6] One should not underestimate that third and final moral principal upon which "the world stands." The high priest Simon is called "the just" because of what he did for the people. And the Jewish historian Flavius Josephus (ca. 37–ca. 100), when he wrote of Simon in his *Antiquities of the Jews* (bk. 12, ch. 2, para. 5), said, "He was called Simon the Just because of his piety toward God and his kind disposition toward those of his own nation."[7]

5. See in Otto Mulder's *Simon the High Priest*, the section on "Simon as Builder," pp. 329–31.

6. *Mishnah*, p. 446.

7. Flavius Josephus, *Complete Works*, p. 247.

The Function of Liturgical Splendor

I believe there are at least two important, indeed, essential lessons in all this for Catholic priests of today. The first lesson is the importance of observing certain aesthetic dignities in the celebration of the liturgy. The second lesson regards how important it is that liturgical splendor be completed by an equal effort to meet the social needs of the people. We will explore this moral lesson later in this chapter. But first we consider the aesthetic lesson.

Observing certain aesthetic dignities in the celebration of the liturgy serves not only to give glory to God but also serves to dispose the worshippers to reverence of mind and heart. This dual function of liturgical splendor is not always appreciated. The author of the commentary on Sirach for *The New Interpreter's Bible* asks the questions, "What place do pomp and circumstance have in worship?" And he answers his own question with the words, "it seems entirely appropriate to honor God in as lavish a manner as possible."[8] However, there is also a sense in which the splendor of liturgical worship is meant to affect the worshipper. It is not just a way of giving honor to God but also a way to supply the worshipper with a sense of the holy, a sense of the majesty of God that can encourage reverence and piety in the worshipper. And thus music, incense, and vestments, while giving honor to God, can also influence the worshipper, us human beings, by capturing and focusing our minds and imaginations, by lifting our minds and hearts to God. This can take various forms. For example, it is a genuine public and pastoral service to provide for the faithful and those seeking faith, a quiet, attractive, peaceful, prayerful place to visit. That space must also serve as an appropriate, beautiful space for public events, such as weddings, and a dignified place for public events, such as funerals. The commentators' words "pomp and circumstance" are appropriate to festive occasions. But there are other times when the music of Christian worship should aim to create a sense of plaintive supplication. At those times it needs to create a sense of chaste beauty, chaste music, chaste smells. This task is difficult today because modern music is characterized by erotic rhythms. And today the lighting in churches is no longer the soft glow of candle light that created a sense of the sacred, of the half-light of mystic encounter, but the glaring light of fluorescent lamps. Today candle light has been banished from our churches and has become identified with the romantic lighting of restaurants.

There is plenty of theoretical justification for the splendor or aesthetics of the liturgy. Indeed, Thomas Aquinas treats of this topic at length. For example, in his *Summa Theologica* (1a2ae, ques. 100, art. 2, "Whether the Ceremonial Precepts Are

---

8. Crenshaw, "Sirach," p. 861.

Figurative?" in the section called *Sed contra*), he sets forth this basic principal of the liturgy:

> Divine worship is twofold, internal and external. For since man is composed of soul and body each of these should be applied to the worship of God . . . Wherefore according to the various ways in which the intellect and affections of the man who worships God are rightly united to God, his external actions are applied in various ways to the divine worship. In the state of future bliss, the human intellect will gaze on the Divine Truth in Itself . . . But in the present state of life, we are unable to gaze upon the Divine Truth in Itself, and we need the ray of Divine light to shine upon us under the form of certain sensible figures."

Later in *Summa Theologica* (2a2ae, ques. 81, "Of Religion," first article "Whether Religion Directs Man to God alone?"), in reply to objection 1, Aquinas elaborates upon this basic distinction: "Religion has two kinds of acts. Some are its proper and immediate acts, which it elicits, and by which man is direct to God alone, for instance, sacrifice, adoration and the like. But it has other acts which it produces through the medium of the virtues which it commands, directing them to the honor of God."

Thomas Aquinas, in his *Summa Theologica* (2a2ae, ques. 81, "On Religion," art. 7, "Whether religion has an external act?"), replies in the Sed contra section: "In the divine worship it is necessary to make use of corporeal things, that man's mind may be aroused."

In the nineteenth century, Antonio Rosmini treats of the educative power of the liturgy in his work entitled *Of the Five Wounds of the Holy Church*. No doubt, what he says is colored by a certain romantic nostalgia for a past that is over-idealized. Nevertheless, there is much truth in what he says in this passage:

> In the happiest times of the Church, preaching and the liturgy were the two great schools of the Christian people. The former taught the faithful by words alone; the latter by words conjoined with certain rites; and, especially by those rites to which their Divine Author had given power to work particular effects upon human nature, namely, the Holy Sacrifice and the Sacraments. Both were full of teaching. They did not address themselves only to one side of human nature, but to the whole man; they penetrated, they subdued him. They were not merely voices to reach the intellect alone, or symbols which impressed the senses only; but both by means of the intellect and the senses, they reached to the heart, and filled the Christian with an exalted sense of God's mysterious and superhuman works.[9]

9. Rosmini, *Of the Five Wounds*, pp. 27–28.

Even more recently, the Second Vatican Council in its Constitution on the Liturgy, shows itself particularly sensitive to the importance of the aesthetic dimension of the liturgy when it says in article 122a:

> Very rightly the fine arts are considered to rank among the noblest expressions of human genius. This judgment applies especially to religious art and to its highest achievement, which is sacred art. By their very nature both of the latter are related to God's boundless beauty, for this is the reality which these human efforts are trying to express in some way. To the extent that these works aim exclusively at turning men's thoughts to God persuasively and devoutly, they are dedicated to God and to the cause of His greater honor and glory.
>
> Holy Mother Church has therefore always been the friend of the fine arts and has continuously sought their noble ministry, with the special aim that all things set apart for use in divine worship should be truly worthy, becoming, and beautiful, signs and symbols of heavenly realities. For this purpose, too she has trained artists.[10]

These observations by theologians across the ages are important and all are well taken; however, we must also consider the influence of the historical Jesus on the aesthetics of the Christian liturgy.

The Aesthetics of Jesus

As for Jesus on visual aesthetics, no doubt he had an eye for aesthetic splendor, certainly for natural beauty. I am referring to his words as recorded in Luke 12:27, "Notice how the flowers grow. They do not toil or spin. But I tell you, not even Solomon in all his splendor was dressed like one of them." However, there is evidence that he could be critical of the ostentatious use of aesthetic beauty in religious works, as when he criticized the Pharisees: "They widen their phylacteries and lengthen their tassels."[11] And Jesus disparages his disciples' admiration for the monumental splendor of the Jerusalem temple. For, in Mark 13:1–2 (cf. Matt 24:1–2) we are told, "As he was making his way out of the temple area one of his disciples said to him, 'Look, teacher, what stones and what buildings!' Jesus said to him, 'Do you see these great buildings? There will not be one stone left upon another that will not be thrown down.'" The Jerusalem temple had been first constructed on rather grand lines by King Solomon (ca. 959 BC). But that edifice was destroyed at the time of the Babylonian captivity; and when it was reconstructed after the return of the Jews from

10. Abbott, *Document of Vatican II*, p. 174.

11. The term "phylactery" is derived from the Greek verb *phylassein* meaning "to guard or preserve." In this case to guard or preserve one's religious identity or commitments by visibly reminding one's self (and others?) of one's religious obligations. The Jewish custom of wearing such religious badges is based on the divine imperatives in Exod 13:9, 16, but especially Num 15:37–41.

exile, it was reconstructed on a much more modest scale (ca. 515 BC). This is the reason why Herod the Great, when he came to the throne, decided to reconstruct the Jerusalem temple on a much grander scale (it was begun in about 20 BC and was basically complete in about ten years, by 9 BC, but work went on with various interruptions up until AD 64). The stones that the disciples in Mark 13 called out about were indeed impressive. Josephus states in his *Jewish Antiquities* (bk. 15, ch. 11, pt. 3), "Now the temple was built of stones that were white and strong, and each of their length was twenty-five cubits, their height was eight, and their breadth about twelve."[12] Evidence of them stands to this day. But the Lucan version of the same episode brings out yet other aspects of the Jerusalem temple's splendor in Jesus' time. Luke 21:5 says, "Some people were speaking about how the temple was adorned with costly stones and votive offerings." Once again Josephus helps us image more precisely to what this remark might refer. In the *Jewish Antiquities* (bk. 15, ch. 11, pt. 3), he describes: "The temple had doors at the entrance and lintels over them, of the same height with the temple itself. They were adorned with embroidered veils, with their flowers of purple, and pillars interwoven; and over these but under the crown-work was spread out a golden vine, with its branches hanging down from a great height, the size and fine workmanship of which was a surprise sight to the spectators, to see what vast materials there were, and with what great skill the workmanship was done."[13] And in his other great historical work, *The Jewish War* (bk. 5, ch. 5, pt. 6), Josephus describes the effect of its splendors when seen from a distance:

> Now the outward face of the temple in its front wanted nothing that was likely to surprise either men's minds or their eyes; for it was covered all over with plates of gold of great weight, and, at the first rising of the sun, reflected back a very fiery splendor, and made those who forced themselves to look upon it to turn their eyes away, just as they would have done at the sun's own rays. But this temple appeared to strangers, when they were coming to it at a distance, like a mountain covered with snow; for as to those parts of it that were not gilt, they were exceeding white.[14]

But if Jesus appears to have been critical of ostentatious display in religious dress and architecture, he appears to have spared no means to achieve a certain dignity, maybe even opulence, in such religious ceremonials or observances as a Passover supper or fellowship meal. I am referring to Jesus' provisions for his last supper with his disciples, the prototype of the Christian Eucharist. More precisely, we are told in Mark 14:12–16:

12. Josephus, *Complete Works*, p. 334.
13. Ibid., pp. 334–35.
14. Ibid., p. 555.

> On the first day of the Feast of unleavened Bread, when they sacrificed the Passover lamb, his disciples said to him, "Where do you want us to go and prepare for you to eat the Passover?" He sent two of his disciples and said to them, "Go into the city and a man will meet you, carrying a jar of water. Follow him. Wherever he enters, say to the master of the house, 'The Teacher says, "Where is my guest room where I may eat the Passover with my disciples.' Then he will show you a large upper room furnished and ready. Make the preparations for us there." The disciples then went off, entered the city, and found it just as he had told them; and they prepared the Passover.

Many of the narrative details here are very telling. For example, in Jesus' day it was highly unusual for a man to carry a water jar (that was considered "women's work"). And so this contact person would have been readily recognizable, conspicuous even, because he would have stood out in a crowd. This suggests that a lot of forethought went into Jesus' last meal with his disciples. It was an event carefully prearranged. And when Jesus tells his disciples that the place for their supper will be a "large upper room" *anagoion mega* (*mega* meaning quite literally "great"), this too is a significant detail. In crowded Jerusalem, a two-story house with a "spacious upper room," an upper room that would provide not only fresh air, natural ventilation, but privacy (no one able to look in through the windows) was a luxury. It is most probably a reference to a home in the wealthy neighborhood of upper Jerusalem. This home would have been located in the area of Jerusalem known as the Upper City, indeed in the southern part of the Upper City, between Herod's palace and the gate of the Essenes, near the temple, rather than in the poorer Lower City, downwind of Jerusalem's sewage.[15] Yet another revealing word is the descriptive "furnished." The word that the New American Bible translates as "furnished" is the Greek word *estremenon* which means quite literally "strewn," in the sense of well furnished with carpets and cushions for reclining at a table. And, if Jesus' last meal with his disciples was indeed a Passover meal, this has even more meaning. In contrast to early Israelite custom, according to which the Passover lamb was eaten in haste while standing, the Passover meal had become in first-century Palestine a festive dinner at which even the poorest reclined at a table. And this was not simply indulgence, but it was meant to be a significant sign, a sign of Israel's liberation from servitude. In this regard note the instruction in the *Mishnah* (in the tractate, *Pesahim* 10:1), for celebrating the

---

15. The site of the "Upper Room," outside the present south wall of Old Jerusalem and near the Church of the Dormition, is based on a fourth-century tradition. According to Epiphanius (313–403), Hadrian found the building of the upper room still standing in 135. But it is not out of character for Hadrian who was persecuting Christians to seek out revered Christian cites so as to desecrate them.

Passover: "Even the poorest in Israel must not eat unless he sits down to table, and they must not give them less than four cups of wine to drink."[16]

As for clothing or vesture, it is true that Jesus does at times appear critical of ostentatious clothing. The rich man in Luke 11:8, for example, is described as "habitually dressed in purple and fine linen," nevertheless, according to John 19:23, the tunic Jesus wore was a splendid piece of work, "seamless, woven in one piece from the top down." Moreover, the parable of the wedding feast in the Gospel according to Matthew shows he could be critical of those who do not observe proper dress. I am referring to Matt 22:11–14: "But when the king came in to meet the guests he saw a man there not dressed in a wedding garment. He said to him, 'My friend, how is it that you came in here without a wedding garment?' Then the king said to his attendants, 'Bind his hands and feet, and cast him into the darkness outside, where there will be wailing and grinding of teeth.'" No doubt this parable was meant to express symbolically the gracious response to God's invitation to the eternal banquet of heaven. But it could be used today as a warning to the all-too-casual middle and upper class in America who dress for Sunday Mass in the same clothing they would wear to a workout in a gym or to lounge beside their swimming pool or to weed their garden.

Visual Aesthetics in Christian History

When it came time to build its own houses of worship, Christianity did not follow the model of the Jerusalem temple or indeed of any other ancient temple. Instead, Christianity adopted the model of the Roman basilica or public meeting house. However, it is open to consideration as to whether Jesus' personal garb and his preferences for a banquet had any later effect on the splendor of Christian public worship.

I have no doubt I would be shouted down by many were I to suggest that because the last supper was held in a room spread with cushions, it has had an influence on the development in the early church of such liturgical accoutrements as the presidential chair. Nevertheless, it is interesting how early Christian adornment for the liturgy did indeed employ linen and pillows. For example, *The Shepherd [or pastor] of Hermas* is an anonymous Christian text dating from the beginning of the second century of the Christian era (and most probably dates between AD 139 and 155). It is an apocalyptic or visionary narrative, that is, it begins with a series of visions received by Hermas, a devout Christian servant (or slave?) living in Rome. In his third vision, Hermas is led to a place in the countryside where he says "I saw a couch of ivory (*sumpselion elephantinon*) placed there, and on the couch there lay

16. *Mishnah*, p. 150.

a linen pillow (*kerbikarion linoun*), and over it a covering of fine linen was spread out."[17] When invited to sit there, he demurs claiming it is the place where elders (*presbuterous*) sit. This is most probably a description of the presider's chair at a Christian assembly or liturgy. A similar description can be found in *The Life and Passion of Cyprian of Carthage* by Pontius the Deacon. Pontius was one of the seven deacons of the church at Carthage in the third century. He not only went into exile with his bishop, Cyprian, in 257, during the persecution of the Christian church by the Emperor Valerian, but Pontius also was an eyewitness of Cyprian's execution in the year 258. In his narrative, Pontius describes Cyprian awaiting his death, seated in a chair that had been adorned with a covering. Paragraph 16 reads, "the seat was covered with linen, so that even in the very moment of his passion he might enjoy the honor of the episcopate."[18]

As for liturgical vestments, here too as with the general dynamics of liturgical worship, we have the speculations of theologians ancient and modern. The twelfth-century theologian Hugh of St. Victor (1078–1141) dedicated a whole section of his *De sacramentis*, or *On the Sacraments of the Christian Faith* (bk. 2, pt. 4) to describing the meaning of such vestments. He begins this section, which is entiled "On Sacred Vestments," with the words: "The priests and ministers of Christ should know that a special habit is assigned to those in the sacred ministry, that by means of what appears externally it may be shown of what nature they should be within."[19] That twelfth-century theologian's judgment is echoed by another theologian in the twentieth century. Jesuit liturgist John D. Laurance, in his article "Vestments," which he wrote for *The New Dictionary of Sacramental Worship*, says, "Just as any clothing manifests the person who wears it, so likewise does the church in the liturgy disclose its inner mystery through the wearing of special, liturgical vestments."[20]

But there are also historical explanations. In the early church, we have the witness of Origen of Alexandria. In Origen's *Homilies on Leviticus*, a work that scholars commonly identify and date as a three-year cycle of homilies delivered toward the end of Origen's life, between 238 and 244, we find that homily 6 is entitled "concerning the clothing of the high priest and the priests." It is clear from that homily, and in passages of the others (such as homily 4.6.4), that Origen is dealing with bishops who, when presiding at the Eucharist, were already dressing in a style that imitated that of Old Testament high priests. Medieval liturgists also favored the idea that Christian vestments in general were derived from those of the Jewish priesthood.

17. *Apostolic Fathers*, p. 471.
18. *Early Christian Biographies*, p. 22.
19. Hugh, *On the Sacraments*, p. 273.
20. Laurance, *Vestments*, p. 1305.

For example, the Benedictine Rupert of Deutz (ca. 1075–1129), in his *De divinis officiis* (1111), which explains the mystical meaning of the priestly office, including both the service at the altar and the vestments worn by the priest, argues that the alb is a self-conscious imitation of the Kethonet, the white linen tunic prescribed for the high priest in Exod 28:39.

But modern times have brought other explanations. For example, a twentieth-century church historian, the abbé Louis Duchesne (1843–1922), in his *Christian Worship: Its Origin and Evolution*, argued that the alb's origin is rather in the white linen tunic that was part of the ordinary attire of both Romans and Greeks.[21]

I suspect the true impetus for the alb is the New Testament, and in particular the prominence given there to white linen robes. The New Testament presents considerable evidence that it was not just Jesus who wore a fine linen garment but so too did several other sacred figures. For example, in Mark 16:5 and John 20:12 the angels at Jesus' tomb wear white robes. Moses and Elijah when they appear with Jesus at the transfiguration are wearing white robes. But the more cogent influence is probably the numerous references to white robes as a moral symbol in the book of Revelation. Rev 3:4 says, "You have a few people in Sardis who have not soiled their garments; they will walk with me dressed in white." Of the martyrs, those who died for their faith, we are told in Rev 6:11, "Each of them was given a white robe . . ." In Rev 7:4, "These are those who have survived the time of great distress, they have washed their robes and made them white in the blood of the Lamb." Of the 144,000 we are told in Rev 7:9, "They stood before the throne and before the Lamb, wearing white robes." In Rev 19:14, "the armies of heaven followed him, mounted on white horses and wearing clean white linen." No doubt it is such visual imagery that led to the use of white linen as the baptismal robe of converts to the faith, and of the use of a simple white garment (the alb) as basic clothing for ministers of the liturgy.

Music in the Liturgy

But it was not just visual splendor but aural splendor too that was characteristic of Jewish temple music, and later, Christian worship. Indeed, music has always had an important role in the biblical tradition of worship. For example, a major characteristic of the Old Testament temple liturgy was not only the Levitical choir but also a virtual orchestra of instrumentalists. This characteristic is brought over into the worship of the earliest Christians.

And as for music, we know from Mark 14:26 (and its parallel in Matt 26:30), Jesus' last supper with his inner circle, the Twelve, concluded with sacred song: "Then,

21. Duchesne, *Christian Worship*, pp. 379-381.

after singing a hymn, they went out to the Mount of Olives." Many scholars have claimed to be able to identify precisely what was the hymn, or hymns, that Jesus and the Twelve sang at the conclusion of that meal. They argue that if indeed Jesus' last supper was a Passover meal as the Bible tells us, then they must have sung certain psalms in the tradition of the Passover meal celebration. The Jewish scholar Philo of Alexandria (ca. 20 BC–ca. AD 50) in *De specialibus legibus* ("The Special Laws," a treatise in which he tries to systematize the many laws in the Torah), book 2, chapter 27, article 148, mentions hymns at table at Passover. And in the *Mishnah*, the initial codification of the Jewish oral tradition composed 150 years after Jesus, we are told precisely which psalms were to be sung at the Passover meal, and when. In the *Mishnah* we are told that the sequence of psalms called the Hallel Psalms, or Psalms of Praise (from the Hebrew word *hallel* which means "praise"). The first two, Psalms 113 and 114, were sung before the meal and the remaining four (Psalms 115–118) after the meal. Of course, as with all biblical points, this too is disputed. There are some scholars who insist we cannot be sure that Jesus' last meal with his disciples was indeed a Passover meal, nor can we be sure that these hymns would have been used because the witness of the *Mishnah* can be anachronistic, that is, can make normative the traditions of first-century Judaism that were not yet standardized. Moreover, Mark and Matthew employ in their narrative the exact same Greek word. They begin with an aorist plural participle from the verb *hymnein*, and the form of the verb they employ does not permit surety as to whether there was one hymn or more. Nevertheless, it does seem acceptable to believe that there was music at the Last Supper.

In Acts 16:25, we find a description of Paul and Silas in prison, "Paul and Silas were praying and singing hymns to God as the prisoners listened." In Eph 5:15–20, Paul gives moral advice saying: "Watch carefully then how you live, not as foolish persons but as wise . . . be filled with the Spirit, addressing one another in psalms and hymns and spiritual songs, singing and playing to the Lord in your hearts, giving thanks always and for everything in the name of our Lord Jesus Christ to God the Father." Jas 5:13 says, "Is anyone among you suffering? He should pray. Is anyone in good spirits? He should sing praise." The book of Revelation makes much use of musical imagery to describe heaven and the new world to be revealed, but singing accompanied by the strumming of harps is described in Rev 5:9: "Each of the elders held a harp and gold bowls filled with incense, which are the prayers of the holy ones. They sang a new hymn." In Rev 14:2–3, when it describes the vision of the Lamb says, "The sound I heard was like that of harpists playing their harps. They were singing a new hymn before the throne, before the four living creatures and the elders. No one could learn this hymn except the hundred and forty-four thousand who had been ransomed from the earth." And in Rev 15:2–3 we read: "Then I saw something like a sea of glass mingled with fire. On the sea of glass were standing those who had won the victory over the beast and its image and the number that signified its name. They were holding God's harps, and they sang the song of Moses, the servant of God, and the song of the Lamb." Angels with trumpets is a common motif throughout the NT: Matt 24:31; 1 Cor 15:52; 1 Thess 4:16; Rev 8:6–13; 9:1–14; 10:7, and 11:15.

Several patristic writers show their keen sensitivity to the importance of music in worship. For example, Basil of Caesarea, called the Great, the brother of Gregory of Nyssa and Saint Macrina, says in his Homily on the First Psalm:

> For when the Holy Spirit saw that mankind was ill-inclined toward virtue and that we were heedless of the righteous life because of our inclination to pleasure, what did he do? He blended the delight of melody with doctrine in order that through the pleasantness and softness of the sound we might unaware receive what was useful in the words, according to the practice of wise physicians, who, when they give the more bitter draughts to the sick, often smear the rim of the cup with honey. For this purpose these harmonious melodies of the Psalms have been designed for us, that those who are of boyish are or wholly youthful in their character, while in appearance they sin, may in reality be educating their souls.[22]

St. John Chrysostom, in his Exposition of Psalm 41, says:

> When God saw that most men were slothful, that they came unwillingly to spiritual readings, and that they found the effort involved to be distasteful, wishing to make the labor more grateful and to allay its tedium he blended melody with prophecy in order that, delighted by the modulation of the chant, all might raise sacred hymns to him with great eagerness. For nothing so uplifts the mind, giving it wings and freeing it from the earth, releasing it from the prison of the body, affecting it with love of wisdom, and causing it to scorn all things pertaining to this life, as modulated melody and the divine chant composed of number.[23]

Ambrose of Milan in his Sermon Against Auxentius, boasts of the power of music to unite Christians in the expression of their faith and to teach them lessons in the faith, especially when the faithful gather to chant the Creed at Mass: "They declare also that the people have been led astray by the strains of my hymns. I certainly do not deny it. That is a lofty stain, and there is nothing more powerful than it. For what has more power than the confession of the Trinity which is daily celebrated by

22. As quoted in *Source Readings in Music History*, p.11.
23. Ibid., p. 13.

the mouth of the whole people? All eagerly vie one with the other in confessing the faith, and know how to praise in verse the Father, Son, and Holy Spirit. So they all have become teachers, who scarcely could be disciples."[24]

Indeed, Augustine of Hippo describes how it was precisely in Ambrose's cathedral at Milan that the music there influenced his conversion:

> How I wept during your hymns and songs! I was deeply moved by the music of the sweet chants of your Church. The sounds flowed into my ears and the truth was distilled into my heart. This caused the feelings of devotion to overflow. Tears ran, and it was good for me to have that experience.
>
> The Church at Milan had begun only a short time before to employ this method of mutual comfort and exhortation. The brothers used to sing together with both heart and voice in a state of high enthusiasm.[25]

In the light of what Augustine has said, it is possible to distinguish two kinds of music for Christian worship, one that leads to mystic contemplation and another that makes for communal celebration. An example of the first might be the renaissance polyphony of Giovanni Pierluigi da Palestrina (ca. 1525–1594), music so difficult that it can only be performed by a professional choir. But this music can create in the hearer a strong sense of the sacred, the impression of ethereal harmonies and spiritual awe. The other kind of liturgical music is represented by the hymns of Ambrose and Luther, the works of the Methodist hymn writer, Charles Wesley (1707–1788), and the Oratorian and hymn writer, Frederick Faber (1814–1863). In the quotation from Augustine's *Confessions*, he seems to be responding to this type of communal hymn singing. But there is another more modern witness to the effect of listening to music that creates a prayerful, spiritual aura without one's own participation or without even comprehension of the text. This music is performed not by a choir or a congregation but by a solo voice.

Paul Tillich (1886–1965) was a prolific Protestant theologian and the author of an impressive three-volume systematic theology. Though born and raised and educated in Germany, he fled Nazi Germany in 1933 and settled in the United States. After his death, his wife Hannah published an autobiographical memoir that included some sensational and seamy revelations about herself and her famous husband. However, in her memoir Hannah also shows herself to be an intelligent and sensitive woman capable of some very thoughtful observations about religion. Her description of her response to a liturgy, which she attended in the cathedral at Palermo during a vacation trip, provides us with an interesting insight into the workings of music in the liturgy:

24. Ambrose, *Selected Works and Letters*, p. 436.

25. Augustine, *Confessions*, p. 164.

September 4. Palermo: High Mass in the Sistine Chapel, as a priest had described it when we first visited the mosaic chapel. At nine o'clock we went and were given seating tickets. The church was decorated. On the main altar was a huge crucifix; before it, silver vases holding silver leaves; from just to the right and left, in the golden walls of the mosaic, projected silver bouquets of flowers. At right and left on the balconies were vases of asters and candles. Above the choir stalls, the main altar and its sides were covered with slim silver-light candles of different sizes in immense masses, having the effect of an enormous organ of light.

At ten o'clock, the cardinal in red, entered in solemn state. He was surrounded by four bishops in red; and he sat on a chair at the left. Then commenced an endless ritual of taking off and putting on of vestments. The cardinal and his bishops were first in red, then white, then gold with embroidered miters; books were handed the cardinal from which he read, facing the congregation or the altar. Choir boys and bishops, everybody, in the most precious garments, bowed down. It was all magnificent, but not in the least sacred. The bishops were seated in the choir stalls and Capuchin monks leaned on the precious pulpit before which the candles shone.

It became sacred when a priest read with monotonous voice, emphasizing certain syllables. This kind of reading produced an inner shock, as if we were approaching God with fear and trembling. The magic power of times past echoed in his reading as well as in the singing of the monks, who were joined by the high voices of the boys' choir, turning the plaintive seriousness into a blissful sighing revelation.[26]

Richard L. Crocker, an authority on Gregorian chant, has provided us with an explanation of the phenomenon which Hannah Tillich described. When she recounts how "a priest read with monotonous voice, emphasizing certain syllables," she was referring to the simplest style of plainchant, singing on one pitch only. It is called *recto tono*. Crocker says of this style of chant:

> When a solo voice intones a prayer, or a reading from Scripture, on a reciting pitch, the intonation of a single pitch can result in extreme resonance. The natural ability of the human voice to speak directly to our inner hearing is maximized with intonation and the resonance that it brings. This has a special application in Christian worship; when expressed by a strong clear solo voice, with the resonance reinforced by a cathedral reverberation, this kind of intonation can penetrate the listener's heart, seeming to convey the truth of the words of doctrine.[27]

---

26. Tillich, *From Time to Time*, p. 112.
27. Crocker, *Introduction to Gregorian Chant*, p. 27.

Social Justice and the Liturgy

However, after having said all this about the importance of a vibrantly expressive liturgy imbued with aesthetic principles, the second lesson from Sirach 50 for a Catholic priest today is that it is bad religion to pursue the delights of the liturgy while disregarding or ignoring the social needs of the people. James 1:27, "Religion that is pure and undefiled before God and the Father is this: to care for orphans and widows in their affliction and to keep oneself unstained by the world."

This combination of piety toward God coupled with concern for neighbors was a hallmark of the church from its beginnings. The companion work to Luke's gospel, his Acts of the Apostles, witnesses to this. In Acts 4:32–35 we are told: "The community of believers was of one heart and mind, and no one claimed that any of his possessions was his own but they had everything in common. With great power the apostles bore witness to the resurrection of the Lord Jesus, and great favor was accorded them all. There was no needy person among them, for those who owned property or houses would sell them, bring the proceeds of the sale, and put them at the feet of the apostles, and they were distributed to each according to need."

Indeed the Jerusalem Church's commitment to social justice was such that it caused a crisis. We read of this in Acts 6:1–6:

> At that time, as the number of disciples continued to grow, the Hellenists complained against the Hebrews because their widows were being neglected in the daily distribution. So the Twelve called together the community of the disciples and said, "It is not right for us to neglect the word of God to serve at table. Brothers, select from among you seven reputable men, filled with the Spirit and wisdom, whom we shall appoint to this task, whereas we shall devote ourselves to prayer and to the ministry of the word." The proposal was acceptable to the whole community, so they chose Stephen, a man filled with faith and the holy Spirit, also Philip, Prochorus, Nicanor, Timon, Parmenas, and Nicholas of Antioch, a convert to Judaism. They presented these men to the apostles who prayed and laid hands on them.

So too in the church today, a truly wise and good priest will be so balanced and try to do justice to both God and his people. This means wealthy suburban parishes that can afford a well-paid staff of professional music director, singers and instrumentalists, the finest altar linens, luxurious vestments, costly chalices and patens, and a paid, full-time liturgist, must be balanced by equally well-funded social outreaches to impoverished parishes in the urban ghetto.

The Witness of Carlo Borromeo

Finally, church history gives us at least two examples of priests in modern times whose ministries embodied the values of liturgical splendor and social justice. The activities of these priests reflect the ministry of the high priest Simon the Just. Carlo Borromeo (1538–1584) was born into a family of wealth and nobility (his father held the title of Count of Arona, his mother Margerita de Medici came from the famous Florentine banking family). Because he was his father's second son, and thus would not inherit the title or the family fortune, he was destined for a career in the church. He received tonsure and his first benefice at twelve years of age (the abbacy of San Grantiano), and in 1552 at fourteen years of age he was sent off to the University of Pavia to earn degrees in civil and canon law, prerequisites for anyone hoping to serve in the highest ranks of church administration. In 1559, at twenty-one years of age, and still in only minor orders, he was summoned to Rome and given several honors and notable positions. More precisely, he was made a cardinal deacon and secretary of state for the Holy See, as well as governor of two new papal states, Romagna and the Marches. These promotions were due to old fashioned nepotism: the Pope, Pius IV, was his mother's brother and thus Borromeo's uncle. Four years later, Borromeo was ordained to the priesthood. His attendance at the Council of Trent, however, made him acutely aware of the demands for reform in the church. When in 1565, his uncle Pope Pius died, Borromeo not only effectively evaded papal election for himself, but he begged the new pope, the Dominican Pius V, to allow him to go to Milan and take on the responsibilities of his, until then, merely titular archdiocesan see. This caused consternation among the clergy of Milan who had enjoyed the absence of their titular archbishops for almost eighty years. They were right to fear this archbishop's arrival. For the next eighteen years Borromeo pursued serious church reform at Milan. Much of this was doctrinal reform. At Trent he had served on the conciliar commission that drafted the catechism of the Council of Trent. And thus, shortly after his arrival in Milan, he not only reorganized the diocesan administration into subordinate offices and functions, and began regular and systematic visitation of to all parts of his diocese, but following the directives of the Council of Trent, he established diocesan seminaries, not only in Milan but in his suffragan sees. He then recruited Jesuits to staff those seminaries and schools. He also founded a Confraternity of Christian Doctrine, a catechetical society for the instruction of children, and cultural institutions based firmly on Christian principles: the Catholic University of Milan and a catholic college at Pavia whose university faculty he had found to be far too secular.

However, Borromeo's concerns were not just doctrinal but also social and aesthetic. His social concern is quite well known. Indeed, he was the hero of the great plague of 1576 that ravaged Milan. In 1576, when Milan suffered an epidemic of the bubonic plague, Borromeo led efforts to accommodate the sick and bury the dead. But Borromeo not only organized the relief work but took a personal role in it. He avoided no danger and spared no expense. He personally visited all the parishes where the contagion raged, distributing money, providing accommodation for the sick, and punishing those, especially the clergy, who were remiss in discharging their duties. But it should also be noted that Borromeo undertook several important social and charitable initiatives to assist the poor and distressed of his archdiocese. He built shelters for the homeless, refuges for reformed prostitutes, homes for abandoned wives, orphanages, and hospitals. He established lending houses (financial centers) called *montes pietatis*—from the Latin for "mountains,"a word that from classical times (Plautus and Prudentes) was used figuratively or metaphorically to refer to considerable cash reserves as "mounds" or "mountains" of money. Borromeo's *montes pietatis* lent money at low rates of interest or even without interest. In 1576, he took an active part in ministering to victims of the plague. It was because of these good works for the poor that his passing was so mourned by the people of his archdiocese.

Sadly, it is Borromeo's aesthetic endeavors that are least recognized.[28] In 1563, during the final session of the Council of Trent, Carlo Borromeo had a major role in the formulation of that council's decree on music and images. Among the provisions of that decree was insistence, against Catholic fashion of the day, that musical settings of the Mass must not be so elaborate that the words cannot be clearly heard and understood. That decree also reaffirmed, against the teachings of some of the Protestant reformers, the statement of the Second Council of Nicaea on the legitimacy of the veneration of images. When he assumed his residency as archbishop of Milan, in order to restore a more properly religious atmosphere to the Milan cathedral, he boldly ordered the removal the monumental tombs of Milan's two most powerful political families, the Sforzas and the Viscontis, that cluttered the cathedral. But Borromeo's greatest contribution to the aesthetics of worship was his 1577 directive on the design and building of churches. His *Instructiones fabricae et*

28. John Alexander's *From Renaissance to Counter-Reformation: The Architectural Patronage of Carlo Borromeo During the Reign of Pius IV* (Rome: Bulzoni, 2007) seems to be out of print. Evelyn Carole Voelker's 1977 doctoral thesis, *Charles Borromeo's Instructiones fabricate et supellectilis ecclesiasticae, 1577: A Translation with Commentary and Analysis* was never published as a book and instead is only available online at http://evelynvoelker.com. Robert Sénéchal published in the *Papers of the British School at Rome*, Vol. 68 (2000) pp. 241–67, his essay "Carlo Borromeo's *Instructiones fabricae* . . . and its Origins in the Rome of his time."

suppellectilis ecclesiasticae (guidelines for the building and furnishing of churches) sets forth architectural and decorative principles for churches—principles derived from the Tridentine decrees. The most important element in Borromeo's directive is its doctrine of "decorum," the idea that churches, especially cathedrals, must be worthy of God, that is, not just richly decorated but employing a decoration that is dignified and elevated, capable of inspiring genuine reverence for God and not just superficial awe at its architectural grandeur.

The Witness of Reynold Hillenbrand

We need not go back five hundred years in history to discover a Catholic priest who exemplifies Simon the Just's combination of aesthetic and social sensibilities. Reynold Hillenbrand (1904–1979) was a priest of the archdiocese of Chicago whose life work as a priest, seminary rector, and pastor has been well documented in several sources, such as Robert Tuzik's book-length study called *Reynold Hillenbrand: The Reform of the Catholic Liturgy and the Call to Social Action* (Chicago: Liturgical Training Publications, 2009) and Steven M. Avella's "Reynold Hillenbrand and Chicago Catholicism" in the journal *U.S. Catholic Historian* 9 (1990), pages 353–70. In addition, there is a chapter on Hillenbrand in Keith Pecklers' *The Unread Vision: The Liturgical Movement in the United States of America: 1926–1955* (Collegeville, MN: Liturgical Press, 1998). Avella, on page 353 of his essay on Hillenbrand, gives a fine summary description of this priest's role in the history of the Archdiocese of Chicago. Avella describes Hillenbrand as "commonly acknowledged as godfather, organizer, and the leading inspirational figure of social and liturgical reform in Chicago Catholic life." But Hillenbrand can also be understood as only the latest in a long line of priests, a line extending from Simon the Just up to and beyond Carlo Borromeo. We can see this when we highlight some elements in Hillenbrand's priestly ministry. These highlights apply not just to the history of the Archdiocese of Chicago but as component parts of an integral theology of priestly ministry.

Hillenbrand was born in Chicago in 1904, the second of nine children of German-Americans, and lived in a middle-class neighborhood on Chicago's North Side near Lincoln Park. He attended both the minor and major seminaries of the Archdiocese of Chicago, and was ordained in September 1929. As a seminarian he had been a serious student of theology, and was exposed to the neo-scholasticism of Christian Pesch's four-volume manual of dogma, the basic textbook in his seminary classrooms. His seriousness as a student caused him to be well-read in other areas of theology beyond his class assignments, and so he became familiar with such works as the social encyclicals of Leo XIII, *Rerum novarum*, and Pius XI, *Quadragesimo anno*. He was such a fine student that Cardinal George Mundelein made him stay on at the seminary to complete a doctorate (writing his dissertation on the indwelling of the Holy Spirit and the theology of grace). Afterward, in 1932, Hillenbrand was assigned to teach at the archdiocesan high school called Quigley while living at the cathedral rectory. But his earliest ministry was also deeply affected by the economic depression that dominated American life in the 1930s. In 1936, at a mere thirty-one years of age, Hillenbrand was sent to be rector of the archdiocesan seminary, St. Mary of the Lake (located forty miles northwest of downtown Chicago). At St. Mary of the Lake he implemented into the curriculum his own concerns about liturgical and social reform, and especially the unity of liturgy and social action. In February of 1938, Hillenbrand invited Dorothy Day to come and speak to the seminarians about the work of her Houses of Hospitality, including one she had opened on Blue Island Avenue in Chicago. A few months later, in the summer of 1938, Hillenbrand hosted a clergy convocation at Mundelein called "the summer school of Catholic action." Then in July of 1941, he organized the first ever Summer School of Liturgy at Mundelein. Not everyone was happy with Hillenbrand's innovations, not least the Jesuit faculty at Mundelein to which Hillenbrand had been adding several diocesan priests. The Jesuit faculty were also unhappy with Hillenbrand's liturgical innovations, such as the communal chanting of the office by faculty and seminarians. Moreover, Hillenbrand's rectorship had depended much on the patronage of Cardinal Mundelein who was himself very socially conscious. Mundelein was, for example, a friend of President Franklin Delano Roosevelt and was a strong supporter of FDR's New Deal. But Mundelein's successor in 1940, Cardinal Samuel Stritch, was of a different disposition and was very sensitive to pressure from wealthy Catholic businessmen in Chicago who were alarmed by what they felt were Hillenbrand's labor-biased social convictions. In 1944, Hillenbrand was made pastor of Sacred Heart Parish in Hubbard's Woods, Illinois, a large parish in the prestigious North Shore suburb of Chicago. In 1957, Hillenbrand undertook an innovative interior restoration, a major feature of which was a crucifix and statues of Mary and Joseph done by the Croatian immigrant to America, Ivan Mestrovic (1883–1962), considered by some to be the greatest sculptor of religious subjects since the Renaissance. Hillenbrand even got permission to say Mass facing the people.

Hillenbrand is not admired by all; indeed, his liturgical and aesthetic innovations at Sacred Heart Parish divided the congregation. This division is understandable because liturgy and social justice are a heady mix, not easily combined, indeed sometimes attracting partisan allegiances. Nonetheless, they are important, indeed, component parts of effective priestly ministry. No pastor should ever allow his parish to live in splendid liturgical isolation from the social problems that may not surround it but are at a short reach beyond its borders. A truly effective Catholic priest must lead his congregation to appreciate not just the splendor of the liturgy but also the duty of being a good neighbor. Jesus' parable of the good neighbor (Luke 10:29–37), with the priest and Levite who maintain a distance from the man in distress, is still a powerful indictment we need to heed.

8

Pop Culture *Versus* Priestly Ministry

Mattathias, Priest of Modein

THE EXPRESSION "POP CULTURE" is an abbreviation of the more formal term, "popular culture." Culture can be defined as any significant pattern of human activity that results in recognizable, meaningful forms. For example, while speech comes naturally to all human beings, its use can also be cultivated, that is, used artfully so as to increase its power and precision. A simple and rudimentary example of this is the use of speech or human sound to produce witty or popular sayings or adages such as "a stitch in time saves nine," or political slogans such as "I came, I saw, I conquered" or "Liberty, Equality, Fraternity," or folk songs such as the Christmas carol, "Silent Night." But there is another more sophisticated, more ambitious, cultivation of human speech and sound that has resulted in such monumental achievements as the epics of Virgil (*The Aeneid*) and Dante (*The Divine Comedy*), the political speeches of Cicero (his Catiline orations) and Lincoln (his Gettysburg address), or musical works such as Handel's "Hallelujah" chorus or the *Dies irae* from Verdi's Requiem Mass. And when human speech and sound have achieved a particularly forceful, memorable, and meaningful form, it becomes an expression that we call classical culture. All culture, however, is problematic. The trouble with classical culture is that it quickly becomes antiquated and arcane, which in turn renders it accessible only to an educated few. In contrast, popular culture, while it employs easily accessible forms, all too often emphasizes entertainment over moral judgment, and thus it often serves as the vehicle for propagating some of the worst values in life, not just anti-Christian, but even anti-human.

The Challenge of Today's Pop Culture

Examples of the dubious effect of popular culture in contemporary society are numerous. Studies have been done, and the results published in such professional literature as *The Journal of Adolescence* and *The Journal of Experimental Social*

Psychology, and their claims are that violent video games not only desensitize children to violence but even encourage the use of it by teaching children that violence is a legitimate way to resolve conflicts. Some of these studies claim that increases in bullying among school children and of violence toward women of all ages is a result of this desensitization. But consider also the predicament of Christian parents who allow their children to sit long hours before that most convenient babysitter and yet also that most effective catechist of all times, the television, a catechist that often teaches all the wrong lessons. Note the story line of Steven Spielberg's 1982 horror movie *Poltergeist* that shows how Satan destroyed an American family by entering into their lives through a television set. But cinema itself can be very problematic.

The moral challenge posed by the contemporary cinema has caused even the Vatican to respond. The Vatican has opened an office that deals with the cinema. Its aim is to try to award cinema that promotes good values and censure cinema that does not. Indeed, after Christmas 2009, culture critic Gaetano Vallini wrote in the Vatican daily newspaper *L'Osservatore Romano*, expressing concern about some of the values promoted in the immensely popular film *Avatar*. The Christmas season of 2009 offered us several new movies, a comparison of which reveals problematic lessons. *Avatar*, *Sherlock Holmes*, and *Invictus* all premiered at about the same time. And a comparison of them cannot help but raise questions about contemporary America, its mores and its people, our self-loathing, and destructiveness. While *Avatar* could not help but impress with its three-dimensional and computer generated visual effects, its underlying moral message is dubious in the extreme. It is a spectacular bit of escapist fantasy in which a planet of extra-terrestrials showed themselves to be much kinder and more enlightened than the human beings coming to exploit them. In contrast, real science, that is, fifty years of space-exploration, has made clear not only the vastness of the universe but also the uniqueness of what has happened here on this planet. Most of the universe is inhospitable to any life forms, but here on earth the number of life forms is so numerous as to defy precise calculation. Moreover, one of those life forms, *Homo sapiens*, has demonstrated not just the technical ingenuity that has allowed for the discovery and exploration of outer space, but also expresses an ingenious moral character that has produced a Cicero and a Lincoln. Indeed, it is moral character that engenders not just violent revolutions but also parliaments and constitutions.

Yet another mindless cinematic fantasy released at Christmas time 2009 was director Guy Ritchie's *Sherlock Holmes*. It is an action-packed makeover of Sir Arthur Conan Doyle's pipe-smoking professor who now becomes a master of martial arts. As such, it too was quite a box office success; but it was also a bizarre injection into Victorian times of gratuitous violence and cartoon-like, comic book characters. But we should also note, some relief was offered in the cinematic winter of 2009 with the release of director Clint Eastwood's *Invictus*, a tale of real-life Nelson Mandela's effort to unite South Africa by his patronage of its rugby team (the title refers to the poem of the same title by Englishman William Ernest Henly (1849–1903). Here at last were recognizably real human beings dealing with real moral problems. Indeed, this story of South Africa's great leader should have been inspiring to many; but it proved to have comparatively little box office draw.

Aggressive Secularism in the Bible

The degrading character of popular culture has always been a problem for moral idealists.[1] It is a sad fact, but sometimes slogans like "I came, I saw, I conquered" and "Liberty, Equality, Fraternity," have served to sponsor social violence and superficial political changes, as in those revolutions that resulted in nothing more than one form of political tyranny replacing another. Moreover, long before children spent hours playing violent computer games or were exposed to the dubious morality of television shows, Roman crowds cheered the violence of their circuses, medieval European citizenry was enthusiastic for the cruelty of bear baiting, and Massachusetts colonials enjoyed the entertainment of watching sinners pilloried. But while we are free to turn off the television or be more selective regarding our choice of movies, there are aspects of popular culture that are not so easily avoided—as when secular society becomes aggressive in claiming its rights to do and say whatever it wants; and legislators threaten Catholic hospitals with laws that require contraception and abortion services, and then go on to insist that school curriculums must include the most liberal sexual instructions.

In this matter of aggressive secularism we have some help from the Bible. Serving to counteract the oppressive influence of popular culture and assist the struggle of a priest against it, there is an ancient biblical theme that gives dramatic and significant aid. In the biblical narrative of the first book of Maccabees, the second chapter, we are told of Mattathias (a Hebrew name meaning "gift of the Lord"). Mattathias was a simple priest whose ancestral village, Modein, was just outside Jerusalem. When the popular culture of Hellenization, the secularism of his time, threatened Jewish religious life in his hometown, Mattathias took drastic even violent measures to stem its tide. His methods are controversial, but his story holds important lessons

---

1. Witness Cicero's lament of the popular culture of his time, *o tempora o mores* [oh the times, oh the morals] which occurs twice in his works: in his first oration against Catiline and in his second oration against Verres. Then there is Alexis de Toqueville's *Democracy in America* 1835–1840. In Vol. 1, chapter 15 is entitled "The Tyranny of the Majority," and there he laments what he regards as the demotic egalitarianism of an all too bourgeois freedom.

for priests today. In order to appreciate his story, I shall first say some things about the two books of Maccabees, and then describe the historical background to the account in 1 Maccabees, chapter 2, of Mattathias's response to secularism and the popular culture of his day.

As for the two books of Maccabees, 1 and 2 Maccabees are considered to be "deuterocanonical" books, which is the name given to those books of the Bible whose place in the canon was at some time denied or doubted. For example, 1 and 2 Maccabees are not to be found in the Jewish or Protestant canons of Scripture. In the Catholic canon of Scripture, they appear at the end of the historical books: 1 and 2 Samuel, 1 and 2 Kings, 1 and 2 Chronicles, Ezra, Nehemiah, Tobit, Judith, Esther, 1 and 2 Maccabees. First Maccabees is an account of the history of the Jews under Alexander the Great and his successors, especially the Seleucid king Antiochus IV Epiphanes who presided over the Syrian empire from 175 to 164 BC. Second Maccabees is a sort of supplemental history, covering much the same historical period as 1 Maccabees, but it includes events and narratives not covered in 1 Maccabees. Both books are named for the man who is the central character, the principal protagonist in both books: the valiant warrior Judas Maccabeus (or Judah Maccabee), the son of the priest Mattathias. The term Maccabeus is not his surname. Rather, it is an epithet, or title, that can be translated into Judas "the hammer." Most probably this epithet is a reference to Judas's military prowess, for "maccabee" is a Hebrew word meaning "hammer." But this title served not only as an epithet first given to Mattathias's son Judas, as in Judas Maccabeus, but later to the whole family. John Dancy, in his *Commentary on I Maccabees*, is very strong regarding the historical reliability of the narrative in 1 Maccabees. That is, though 1 Maccabees was written so as to present Mattathias and his sons as the divinely chosen saviors of the Jewish nation, nevertheless, this narrative is recognized as a reliable and sober narrative. Biblical exegete John Dancy voices general expert opinion when he says, "Internal evidence makes it certain that the narrative of 1M is in many cases based on first-hand reports."[2]

The Oppressiveness of Hellenistic Culture

To understand the story of Mattathias as told in the second chapter of 1 Maccabees, it is important that the reader know something about the historical setting of this story. This means becoming acquainted with the Seleucid king Antiochus IV Epiphanes and his plan to bring cultural unity to his empire. Israel was always a small nation at the mercy of major military and political powers, sometimes geographical

2. Dancy, *Commentary*, p. 3.

neighbors such as Babylon and Egypt, at other times more remote cultures like Greece and Rome. In Mattathias's day it was the military power of Alexander the Great who had put Greek generals on the thrones of Egypt and Syria—the Ptolemies in Egypt and the Seleucids in Syria.

However, even before the implementation of Antiochus Epiphanes' cultural program, there had already been a strong movement in favor of Hellenism among the wealthy and the priestly aristocracy of Jerusalem. We see this in the account in 1 Maccabees, chapter 1, wherein not only is a gymnasium, that quintessential form of Greek culture, introduced into Jerusalem but so as to accommodate themselves as completely as possible to Greek custom, some Jews resorted to covering over their circumcised foreskins. First Maccabees 1:11–15 tells us:

> In those days there appeared in Israel men who were breakers of the law, and they seduced many people, saying: "Let us go and make an alliance with the Gentiles all around us; since we separated from them, many evils have come upon us." The proposal was agreeable; some from among the people promptly went to the king, and he authorized them to introduce the way of living of the Gentiles. Thereupon they built a gymnasium in Jerusalem according to the Gentile custom. They covered over the mark of their circumcision and abandoned the holy covenant; they allied themselves with the Gentiles and sold themselves to wrongdoing.

As for covering "the mark of their circumcision," the surgery to restore the appearance of a foreskin is referred to as epispasm. It is hinted at by Saint Paul in 1 Cor 7:18, "Was someone called after he had been circumcised? He should not try to undo his circumcision." And it is testified to by Celsus, not the second-century, Greek-speaking, Platonist philosopher of that name, but the first-century Roman encyclopedist Aurelius Cornelius Celsus, in his *De Medicina*, an eight-volume encyclopedia of ancient medicinal practices. As for the Hellenized Jews who partook of such practices, Flavius Josephus in his *Antiquities of the Jews* is even more candid in the sense that he names individuals; and in his account, these individuals were not just members of patrician Jewish families but numbered among them were members of high priestly families. In *The Antiquities of the Jews* (bk. 12, ch. 5, para. 1), he recounts how one priest named Jesus changed his name to Jason, and another named Onias wanted to be called Menelaus. Moreover, Flavius suggests it was the priest, Jesus/Jason, who made the proposal to build a gymnasium at Jerusalem.[3]

But things came to a head not with the construction of a gymnasium in Jerusalem but rather with the placement of an altar to the God Zeus Olympios within the sanctuary or inner sanctum of the Jerusalem temple. This pagan altar would come to

3. Josephus, *Complete Works*, p. 256.

be called the "abomination of desolation." Antiochus Epiphanes was determined to impose Hellenistic religion as well as culture by force, and thereby subjugate the Jewish nation. And so we read in 1 Macc 1:54–57: "On the fifteenth day of the month of Chislev, in the year one hundred and forty-five, the king erected the horrible abomination, upon the altar of holocausts, and in the surrounding cities of Judah they built pagan altars. They also burnt incense at the doors of houses and in the streets. Any scrolls of the law which they found they tore up and burnt. Whoever was found with a scroll of the covenant, and whoever observed the law, was condemned to death by royal decree."

Mattathias's Violent Response

This then is the point at which the story of Mattathias begins. We shall relate it in its entirety. It begins in 1 Macc 2:1–7, where we are told:

> In those days Mattathias, son of John, son of Simeon, a priest of the family of Joarib, left Jersualem and settled in Modein. He had five sons: John, who was called Gaddi; Sion, who was called Thassi; Judas, who was called Maccabeus; Eleazar, who was called Avaran; and Jonathan, who was called Apphus. When he saw the sacrileges that were being committed in Judah and in Jerusalem, he said: "Woe is me! Why was I born to see the ruin of my people and the ruin of the holy city, and to sit idle while it is given into the hands of enemies, and the sanctuary into the hands of strangers?"

At this point Mattathias sings a formal lament over the temple's desecration. The author has written it in antique style, in the form of a dirge with words and phrases that echo earlier OT phraseology. For example, 1 Macc 2:8–12 in general is reminiscent of Psalm 79, but verse 9 contains an image taken directly from Lamentations 2:11 and 21. 1 Macc 2:8–12 reads:

> "Her temple has become like a man disgraced,
> her glorious ornaments have been carried off as spoils,
> Her infants have been murdered in her streets,
> her young men by the sword of the enemy.
> What nation has not taken its share of her realm,
> and laid its hand on her possessions?
> All her adornment has been taken away.
> From being free, she has become a slave.
> We see our sanctuary and our beauty / and our glory laid waste,
> and the Gentiles have defiled them!
> Why are we still alive?"
> Then Mattathias and his sons tore their garments,

put on sackcloth, and mourned bitterly.

The next section, 1 Macc 2:15–30, tells us how Mattathias was forced into action:

The officers of the king in charge of enforcing the apostasy came to the city of Modein to organize the sacrifices. Many of Israel joined them, but Mattathias and his sons gathered in a group apart. Then the officers of the king addressed Mattathias: "You are a leader, an honorable and great man in this city, supported by sons and kinsmen. Come now, be the first to obey the king's command, as all the Gentiles and the men of Judah and those who are left in Jerusalem have done. Then you and your sons shall be numbered among the King's Friends, and shall be enriched with silver and gold and many gifts." But Mattathias answered in a loud voice: "Although all the Gentiles in the king's realm obey him, so that each forsakes the religion of his fathers and consents to the king's orders, yet I and my sons and my kinsmen will keep to the covenant of our fathers. God forbid that we should forsake the law and the commandments. We will not obey the words of the king nor depart from our religion in the slightest degree."

As he finished saying these words, a certain Jew came forward in the sight of all to offer sacrifice on the altar in Modein according to the king's order. When Mattathias saw him, he was filled with zeal; his heart was moved and his just fury was aroused; he sprang forward and killed him upon the altar. At the same time, he also killed the messenger of the king who was forcing them to sacrifice, and he tore down the altar. Thus he showed his zeal for the law, just as Phinehas did with Zimri, son of Salu.

Then Mattathias went through the city shouting, "Let everyone who is zealous for the law and who stands by the covenant follow after me!" Thereupon he fled to the mountains with his sons, leaving behind in the city all their possessions. Many who sought to live according to righteousness and religious custom went out into the desert to settle there, they and their sons, their wives and their cattle, because misfortunes pressed so hard on them.

It is a political ploy, a political favor, when the officers of the king tell Mattathias that if he cooperates with the royal directive, he and his sons will be "numbered among the King's Friends." The "Friends of the King" is a reference to a group of royal patrons who were granted special status at court (they even wore distinctive purple hats and robes). We also know that "the Order of Friends" was comprised of four grades: simple "friends" were the lowest; above them came "honored friends"; then "First Friends"; and finally "First and Foremost Friends."

An Alternative to Mattathias

But another crisis soon arose. This crisis had its origin not just from external, foreign challengers but from some of Mattathias's most devout co-religionists. Of this we are told in 1 Macc 2:31–48:

> It was reported to the officers and soldiers of the king who were in the City of David, in Jerusalem, that certain men who had flouted the king's order had gone out to the hiding places in the desert. Many hurried out after them, and having caught up with them, camped opposite and prepared to attack them on the sabbath. "Enough of this!" the pursuers said to them. "Come out and obey the king's command, and your lives will be spared." But they replied, "We will not come out, nor will we obey the king's command to profane the sabbath." Then the enemy attacked them at once; but they did not retaliate; they neither threw stones, nor blocked up their own hiding places. They said, "Let us all die without reproach; heaven and earth are our witnesses that you destroy us unjustly." So the officers and soldiers attacked them on the sabbath, and they died with their wives, their children and their cattle, to the number of a thousand persons.
>
> When Mattathias and his friends heard of it, they mourned deeply for them. "If we all do as our kinsmen have done," they said to one another, "and do not fight against the Gentiles for our lives and our traditions, they will soon destroy us from the earth." On that day they came to this decision: "Let us fight against anyone who attacks us on the sabbath, so that we may not all die as our kinsmen died in the hiding places."
>
> Then they were joined by a group of Hasideans, valiant Israelites, all of them devout followers of the law. And all those who were fleeing from the disaster joined them and supported them. They gathered an army and struck down sinners in their anger and law-breakers in their wrath, and the survivors fled to the Gentiles for safety. Mattathias and his friends went about and tore down the pagan altars; they also forcibly circumcised any uncircumcised boys whom they found in the territory of Israel. They put to flight the arrogant, and the work prospered in their hands. They saved the law from the hands of the Gentiles and of the kings and did not let the sinner triumph.

The Death of Mattathias

Mattathias's deathbed scene recalls Jacob's farewell admonitions in Genesis 49 and Moses' departure in Deuteronomy 33. Once again the author of 1 Maccabees reverts to a self-consciously antique style. More precisely, here the phraseology is influenced by the "Praise of the Fathers" or review of ancestors in Sirach chapters 44–50, though the names mentioned by Mattathias are ancestors who were models of faithfulness. In 1 Macc 2:49–64 we are told:

> When the time came for Mattathias to die, he said to his sons: "Arrogance and scorn have now grown strong; it is a time of disaster and violent anger. Therefore, my sons, be zealous for the law and give your lives for the covenant of our fathers.
>
> "Remember the deeds that our fathers did in their times,
> and you shall win great glory and an everlasting name.
> Was not Abraham found faithful in trial,
> and it was reputed to him as uprightness?
> Joseph, when in distress, kept the commandment,
> and he became master of Egypt.
> Phinehas our father, for his burning zeal,
> received the covenant of an everlasting priesthood.
> Joshua, for executing his commission, / became a judge in Israel.
> Caleb, for bearing witness before the assembly,
> received an inheritance in the land.
> David, for his piety
> received as a heritage a throne of everlasting royalty.
> Elijah, for his burning zeal for the law,
> was taken up to heaven.
> Hananiah, Azariah and Mishael, for their faith,
> were saved from the fire.
> Daniel, for his innocence,
> was delivered from the jaws of lions.
> And so, consider this from generation to generation,
> That none who hope in him shall fail in strength.
> Do not fear the words of a sinful man,
> for his glory ends in corruption and worms.
> Today he is exalted, and tomorrow he is not to be found,
> because he has returned to his dust, / and his schemes have perished.
> Children! Be courageous and strong in keeping the law,
> For by it you shall be glorified."

And then the tale of Mattathias ends when, in 1 Macc 2:65–70, we are told of his final instructions to his sons:

> "Here is your brother Simeon who I know is a wise man; listen to him always, and he will be a father to you. And Judas Maccabeus, a warrior from his youth, shall be the leader of your army and direct the war against the nations. You shall also gather about you all who observe the law, and you shall avenge the wrongs of your people. Pay back the Gentiles what they deserve, and observe the precepts of the law."

> Then he blessed them, and he was united with his fathers. He died in the
> year one hundred and forty-six, and was buried in the tombs of his fathers in
> Modein, and all Israel mourned him greatly.

After this, the remainder of 1 Maccabees and a great deal of 2 Maccabees is taken up with a description of the military exploits of Mattathias's sons, especially his most famous son, Judas Maccabeus.

Mattathias in Jewish Tradition

The two books of 1 and 2 Maccabees have no official status in Judaism; they are not regarded as part of the canon of Scripture. Nevertheless, the memory of Mattathias was preserved in other Jewish historical and religious sources. Flavius Josephus in his *Antiquities of the Jews* (12.265–285) and *The Jewish Wars* (1.36) remembers him as the author of the Judean revolt against the Greco-Syrian empire and as the patriarch of the Hasmonean dynasty of priests that ruled Israel for a hundred years. Rabbinic literature, however, celebrates more his religious significance, mainly through the tradition of the Jewish feast of Hanukkah, the feast celebrating the rededication of the temple after its profanation by Antiochus Epiphanes. This feast is referred to in John 10:22–23, "The feast of the Dedication was then taking place in Jerusalem. It was winter. And Jesus walked about in the temple area on the Portico of Solomon." What John's gospel calls the feast of the "dedication," in Greek, *enkainia*, was the Jewish feast of *Hanukkah* (meaning "dedication"). The Babylonian Talmud preserves the memory of this feast in several places (tractate *Shabbat* 21b and 23a, tractate *Soferim* 20.6). For example, tractate *Shabbat* 21 initially focuses upon the ritual of the lighting of the Shabbat candles, but it goes on to treat of the lighting of the Hanukkah candles. The classical rabbis, however, tended to downplay the military and nationalistic dimensions of Hanukkah and instead emphasized its story of divine assistance, the wondrous, miraculous character of what happened after the Maccabees had driven the foreigners from the temple: they discovered there was left only a single container of the oil used to light the temple menorah, just enough to keep the menorah lit for one day. But when they used it they were amazed to find that it kept the menorah lit for eight days, which was just enough time to procure more of the oil.[4] We can see this careful balance in the special Hanukkah prayer that refers to Mattathias, the *Al Hanissim* prayer, which Jews add to the *Amidah*, or Grace after Meals during the Hannukah festival, of which the following is a modern translation:

---

4. The best contemporary study is Benjamin Scolnic's *Judaism Defined: Mattathias and the Destiny of His People* (Lanham, MD: University Press of America, 2010).

For the miracles and for the redemption and for the mighty acts and for the triumphs and for the wars you brought about for our ancestors in those days at this time of year—in the days of the Hasmonean, Mattathias ben Yohanan, the high priest, and his sons, when the evil government of Greece rose up against your People Israel to make them forget your Torah and to make them leave the laws of your will: In your great mercy You rose up with them in their time of trouble and fought in their fight, judged their cause just, and avenged them with a vengeance. You delivered the mighty into the hands of the weak, the many into the hands of the few, the unclean into the hands of the pure, the evil into the hands of the righteous, and the arrogant into the hands of those who engage in your Torah.[5]

We can also observe here a tendency to inflate the stature of a simple priest by claiming he was a high priest. (We shall see later how Christians have done this to Zechariah, the father of John the Baptist.) It is important to realize that Mattathias was a simple priest. He and his family were among the lower clergy. Despite discrepancies regarding his genealogy—in 1 Macc 2:1 he is described as "the son of John, son of Simeon, a priest of the family of Joarib," In Josephus's *Antiquities* 12.265, Mattathias is described as "the son of Johan, the son of Simeon, the son of Asamoniaus, a priest of the family of Joarib"—1 Chr 24:7 makes it clear the house of Joarib (there spelled Johoiarib) had the first of the twenty-four priestly courses in the temple service and thus were simple priests.

In modern times, however, there has been increased emphasis upon the nationalistic even militaristic character of Mattathias. I am referring to the significant role that he took on in the Zionist movement. The term "Zionism" has its origin in the word "Zion," which very early in Jewish history became a synonym for Jerusalem. It acquired a special meaning during the time of the Babylonian captivity when it was used to express the yearning of the Jewish people for their homeland. In this regard, note the opening words of Psalm 137, "By the streams of Babylon we sat and wept when we remembered Zion." In the nineteenth century there developed a movement called Zionism, a movement founded by nationalistic Jews that aimed at establishing a Jewish nation with its own territory and independent government. It was within this modern Zionist movement that Mattathias has acquired a certain iconographic significance and artistic representation. I am referring to a major work by the Lithuanian-born Jewish artist and sculptor Boris Schatz (1867–1932). Schatz was attracted to the Zionist movement, and in 1896 produced what some regard as his artistic masterpiece, a statue entitled Mattathias the Hasmonean. It is a work of romantic art in the style of Bernini: Mattathias is pictured in the highly dramatic posture of standing over the dead body of the idolatrous Hellenistic Jew he has just

5. *My People's Prayer Book*, vol. 2, p. 151.

slain, holding aloft in his right hand a sword and with his left hand pointing off into the distance, pointing to the land to which the Jews must retreat. In 1901, Schatz's sculpture of Mattathias was displayed at the exhibition organized by Martin Buber for the fourth Zionist Congress. The great success of Schatz's Mattathias sculpture influenced other artists, such as the Jewish painter Jehuda Epstein who imitated Schatz's Mattathias in his painting on the same subject in 1902. While Schatz's sculpture has survived only in photographs, Schatz also depicted Mattathias in some paintings and engravings.[6] But some in the Jewish community are to this day rather sensitive to the way in which Mattathias is presented. For example, Mattathias figures in the Jewish tradition of Hanukkah, or the "Festival of Lights," the eight days commemorating the rededication of the temple by Judas Maccabeus (see 1 Macc 4:36–59, but especially verses56–59). And in this regard Noam Zion, a scholar at the Shalom Hartman Institute in Jerusalem, has written an essay, "Mattathias the Priestly Zealot: A Freedom Fighter to be Praised or a Religious Zealot to be Censured?"[7]

Mattathias in Christian Tradition

To understand the estimation given to Mattathias in Christian tradition, it is important that we take account of the differences between the two books both entitled Maccabees. While 1 Maccabees was written in Hebrew, 2 Maccabees was written in Greek. While both seek to demonstrate the deadly character of the struggle between Hellenism and Judaism, the two books have different conceptions of the heroes in that struggle. First Maccabees celebrates Judaism's military defenders, the zeal of Mattathias and his sons; while 2 Maccabees celebrates the piety of its blessed martyrs, the aged scribe Eleazar (ch. 6), and a Jewish mother and her seven sons who profess their faith while undergoing exquisite tortures (ch. 7). Moreover, even when 2 Maccabees recounts military battles, the outcome of the battle is decided not by force of arms but by prayer: it is prayer that renders the enemy helpless. And thus we should not be surprised to find that Christian writers tend to praise not so much Mattathias and his sons, the Maccabees, but the Maccabean martyrs of the second book.

Let us look at Origen of Alexandria's "Exhortation to Martyrdom." Origen lived from circa 185 to circa 254, and during all of that time, from his youth up until his own death by martyrdom, he was confronted with martyrdom. When Origen was seventeen years old, his father was arrested, imprisoned, and executed for his faith.

6. See Dalia Manor's *Art in Zion: The Genesis of Modern National Art in Jewish Palestine* (NewYork: Routledge, 2005).

7. In Noam Zion and Barbara Spectre's *A Different Light: The Big Book of Hanukkah* (NewYork: Devora, 2000, pp. 151–63).

Origen would have joined him but his mother had hid his clothes so that he could not go out. Origen assumed the position of head of the catechetical school at Alexandria precisely because its leader had been martyred. And during the time he led that school, Origen saw several of his students martyred for their faith. In AD 235, after he had moved to Caesarea in Palestine, persecution of Christians broke out again. When a friend of his and a priest named Protocetus were arrested, Origen composed his work called "An Exhortation to Martyrdom." There in paragraphs 23–27, Origen points not to Mattathias and his sons but rather to the martyrs in 2 Maccabees, insisting that their deaths are the Jewish equivalent of Christian baptism by blood.[8]

A similar preference was made by Augustine of Hippo. When Augustine in his *The City of God* (bk. 18, ch. 36) describes the place of 1 and 2 Maccabees in the canon, it is not the lesson of Mattathias and his sons in 1 Maccabees that he highlights. Instead he highlights the martyrs of 2 Maccabees: "The books of the Maccabees . . . are held as canonical, not by the Jews, but by the Church, on account of the extreme and wonderful sufferings of certain martyrs, who, before Christ had come in the flesh, contended for the law of God even unto death, and endured most grievous and horrible evils."[9]

Ambrose of Milan (ca. 339–397) is a little more even-handed in his treatment of the sons of Mattathias and the descendants of the Maccabees. Mattathias is only indirectly referred to in Ambrose of Milan's Letter XL, addressed to the Emperor Theodosius. However, the reference does imply the man is a saint, for when Ambrose says there, "It is the voice of a saint which says 'Wherefore was I made to see the misery of my people,'"[10] he is quoting Mattathias's lament in 1 Macc 2:7. Ambrose refers once again to the Maccabees, the sons of Mattathias in his *De Officiis* (ca. AD 391). At the end of book 1 of Ambrose's work *On the Duties of the Clergy*, he treats of the four cardinal virtues: prudence, justice, fortitude, and temperance. It is in the section on fortitude that he treats of the example of the Maccabees: "As for the Maccabees—where do I begin . . . Gauge the bravery of the leader, Judas Maccabaeus."[11] But Ambrose is not satisfied simply to boast of the bold exploits of the Maccabees, for two paragraphs later he says, "Nevertheless, since courage proves itself not just in terms of success but also when circumstance are difficult, let us look at the death of Judas Maccabeus."[12] But in the end, while Ambrose honors the sons of

---

8. Origen, "Exhortation to Martyrdom," pp. 162–67.

9. Augustine, *The City of God* , p. 382.

10. Ambrose, *Select Works and Letters*, p. 445.

11. Ambrose, *De Officiis*, p. 233.

12. Ibid., p. 235.

Mattathias for their bravery in battle, he gives even greater honor to that other group in 2 Maccabees who simply suffered:

> Here, then, is courage in war: it offers no small expression of what it means to act in a way that is honorable and seemly, for it prefers death to slavery and disgrace. But what about the martyrs, and the sufferings they endured? To look no further than the family of whom we have just been thinking, let us answer the following question: Did the children of the Maccabees gain any lesser triumph over the proud king Antiochus than their parents had done? Their fathers were armed, after all, but when the children fought their own battle they conquered without arms. There they stood, undefeated, a little company of seven boys, surrounded by the forces of the king: all the punishments failed, the torturers gave up—but the martyrs never failed.[13]

The latter is a reference to the martyrs who play the prominent role in 2 Maccabees.

In the Middle Ages, we find two Christian writers who addressed themselves more directly to the moral implications for Christians by way of the example of Mattathias and his sons, the Maccabees: Bernard of Clairvaux (1090–1153), in his rule for the Knights Templar, and Thomas Aquinas (ca. 1225–1274), in the moral treatise of his *Summa Theologica*.

The background to Bernard's rule for the Knights Templar is the crusades. The crusades is the name given to a series of religiously sanctioned military campaigns waged between 1095 and 1291 aimed at recapturing Jerusalem and the Holy Land from a Muslim rule that used violence against Christians. The immediate cause of the First Crusade was the Byzantine emperor Alexios I's appeal to Pope Urban II for mercenaries to help him resist Muslim advance into the territory of the Byzantine Empire. In response, Pope Urban II, at the concluding session of the Council of Clermont in 1095, gave a speech urging Christian rulers to organize a military campaign to free the Holy Land. His speech that day defined and launched the crusades and is thus regarded by some historians as ranking among the most influential speeches ever made. The original text, if there was one, may have been oral and spontaneous. Regardless, it has not survived. But five accounts of his speech survive, all of which were written by men who were present and heard him. None of those accounts ever makes mention of the example of Mattathias or his sons, the Maccabees.

In contrast, Bernard of Clairvaux makes direct and effective use of the image of the Maccabees, and of their leader Judas Maccabeus in particular, in his spiritual handbook for the chivalric order of the Knights Templar. The Knights Templar, established to protect Christian pilgrims to the Holy Land, became one of the two chief military orders of medieval Christendom. Bernard had been petitioned to

---

13. Ibid., pp. 235–37.

write the spiritual handbook for the order, and did so in a treatise entitled *De laude novae militia* (In Praise of the New Knighthood). There, in chapter 4, Bernard tries to teach a spirituality in which the Christian knight must depend to guarantee him victory. He argues where the prowess of the Knights Templar should come:

> No matter how outnumbered they are, they never regard these as fierce barbarians or as awe-inspiring hordes. Nor do they presume on their own strength, but trust in the Lord of armies to grant them the victory. They are mindful of the words of Maccabees, "It is simple enough for a multitude to be vanquished by a handful. It makes no difference to the God of heaven whether he grants deliverance by the hands of few or many; for victory in war is not dependent on a big army, and bravery is the gift of heaven." On numerous occasions they had seen one man pursue a thousand, and two put ten thousand to flight.[14]

The passage quoted is 1 Macc 3:18–19. It is a speech of Judas Maccabeus who is seeking to rally his outnumbered troops in face of a large Syrian army.

But Thomas Aquinas, in his *Summa Theologica*, treats not only of the example of the Maccabees but even more precisely of the deeds of their father, Mattathias. At several points in his *Summa*, Aquinas treats directly of the 1 Maccabee narrative of Mattathias's slaying of the Jew who was about to offer pagan sacrifice, and of Mattathias's decision to have his men fight on the Sabbath. For example, the section of the *Summa Theologica* 2a2ae, which is questions 63–79, comprises, offences against justice, among them the taking of human life, intentionally or unintentionally. And the fourth article of question 64 asks the precise question, "Whether It Is Lawful for Clerics to Kill Evildoers?" Aquinas begins with a survey of the biblical evidence, saying:

> It would seem lawful for clerics to kill evildoers . . . Moses made the Levites slay twenty-three thousand men on account of the worship of the calf (Exod 32), the priest Phinees slew the Israelite who went in to the woman of Madian (Num 25), Samuel slew Agag king of Amalec (1 Kings 15), Elias slew the priests of Baal (3 Kings 18), Mattathias killed the man who went up to the altar to sacrifice (1 Mach 2); and, in the New Testament, Peter killed Ananias and Saphira (Acts 5). Therefore it seems that even clerics may kill evildoers.[15]

But Aquinas responds to this saying that it is not appropriate for Christian ministers to kill. And his reasoning is thus:

> It is unlawful for clerics to kill, for two reasons. First, because they are chosen for the ministry of the altar, whereon is represented the Passion of Christ slain *Who, when He was struck did not strike* (1 Pet 2:23). Therefore it becomes not

14. Bernard, "In Praise of the New Knighthood," p. 140.

15. Aquinas, *Summa Theologica*, Vol. 2, p. 1468.

clerics to strike or kill: for minister should imitate their master, according to Ecclus [abbreviation for *Liber Ecclesiasticus*, otherwise known as Sirach] 10,2, *As the judge of the people is himself, so also are his ministers.* The other reason is because clerics are entrusted with the ministry of the New Law, wherein no punishment of death or of bodily maiming is appointed: wherefore they should abstain from such things in order that they may be fitting ministers of the New Testament.[16]

Aquinas then goes on to further explain:

As regards Peter, he did not put Ananias and Saphira to death by his own authority or with his own hand, but published their death sentence pronounced by God. The Priests or Levites of the Old Testament were the ministers of the Old Law, which appointed corporal penalties, so that it was fitting for them to slay with their own hands.[17]

In his *Summa Theologica* (2a2ae, ques. 40, art. 4), Aquinas asks the question, "Whether it is Lawful to Fight on Holy Days?" Initially he considers the opinion:

It would seem unlawful to fight on holy days. For holy days are instituted that we may give our time to the things of God. Hence they are included in the keeping of the Sabbath prescribed Exod 20:8: for *Sabbath* is interpreted *rest.* Therefore by no means is it lawful to fight on holy days.[18]

But in response, Aquinas quotes approvingly 1 Macc 2:41: "*On the contrary*, It is written (1 Macc 2:41): The Jews rightly determined . . . saying: *Whatsoever shall come up against us to fight on the Sabbath-day, we will fight against him.*" And then he goes on to explain:

The observance of holy days is no hindrance to those things which are ordained to man's safety, even that of his body. Hence Our Lord argued with the Jews, saying (John 7:23): *Are you angry at Me because I have healed the whole man on Sabbath day?* Hence physicians may lawfully attend to their patients on holy days. Now there is much more reason for safeguarding the common weal (whereby many are saved from being slain, and innumerable evils both temporal and spiritual prevented), than the bodily safety of an individual. Therefore, for the purpose of safeguarding the common weal of the faithful, it is lawful to carry on a war on holy days, provided there be need for doing so: because it would be to tempt God, if not withstanding such a need, one were to choose to refrain from fighting.[19]

16. Ibid.
17. Ibid.
18. Ibid., p. 1362.
19. Ibid., pp. 1362–63.

Christian Zealotry

The reason for Ambrose, Augustine, Origen, and Aquinas's circumspect and cautious treatment of Mattathias is not difficult to understand. Violence and vengeance have never been touted as Christian virtues. No doubt there are some passages in the gospels that could be cited that seem to sponsor acts of violence. For example, the gospels do at times show Jesus in angry response or employing the language of violence. For example, in Matt 10:34, Jesus says, "Do not think that I have come to bring peace upon the earth. I have come to bring not peace but the sword." In Luke 22:35–36: "He said to them, 'When I sent you forth without money bag or a sack or sandals, were you in need of anything?' 'No, nothing,' they replied. He said to them, 'But now one who has a money bag, should take it, and likewise a sack, and one who does not have a sword should sell his cloak and buy one.'" Consider also Jesus' own violent outrage as described in John 2:13–17:

> Since the Passover of the Jews was near, Jesus went up to Jerusalem. He found in the temple area those who sold oxen, sheep, and doves, as well as the mon-exchangers seated there. He made a whip out of cords and drove them all out of the temple area, with the sheep and oxen, and spilled the coins of the money-changers and overturned their tables, and to those who sold doves he said, "Take these out of here, and stop making my Father's house a market-place." His disciples recalled the words of Scripture, "Zeal for your house will consume me."

The disciples are quoting Ps 69:9, "Zeal for your house consumes me." A similar sentiment can be found in Ps 119:139. But consider also how that statement appears to echo Mattathias's motivation for slaying the Hellenist Jew of 1 Macc 2:24: "When Mattathias saw him, he was filled with zeal; his heart was moved and his fury was aroused." This term "zeal," eager and ardent pursuit of a goal or interest, has a long biblical history. While it is attributed to Mattathias in 1 Macc 2:27, even there it appears to be but an echo of Num 25:6–13, a passage that describes the intense devotion to the will of God that drove yet another priest, Aaron's grandson Phinehas, to commit an act of violence:

> Yet a certain Israelite came and brought in a Midianite woman to his clansmen in the view of Moses and of the whole Israelite community, while they were weeping at the entrance of the meeting tent. When Phinehas, son of Eleazar, son of Aaron the priest, saw this, he left the assembly and taking a lance in hand, followed the Israelite into his retreat where he pierced the pair of them, the Israelite and the woman. Thus the slaughter of Israelites was checked; but only after twenty-four thousand had died.

> Then the LORD said to Moses, "Phinehas, son of Elezar, son of Aaron the priest, has turned my anger from the Israelites by his zeal for my honor among them; that is why I did not put an end to the Israelites for the offense to my honor. Announce, therefore, that I hereby give him my pledge of friendship, which shall be for him and for his descendants after him the pledge of an everlasting priesthood, because he was zealous on behalf of his God and thus made amends for the Israelites."

We see a similar lethal enthusiasm attributed to King Saul in 2 Sam 21:2, "Saul had attempted to kill them off in his zeal for the men of Israel and Judah." In 1 Kgs 19:10, the prophet Elijah proclaims, "I have been most zealous for the LORD, the God of hosts." "Zeal" is the term used by Jehus the king of Israel who used force to destroy not just the temples of Baal but also Baal's worshippers; in 2 Kgs 10:16, "Come with me . . . and see my zeal for the LORD."

In the New Testament, we find that one of Jesus' inner circle, Simon, who according to Luke 6:15, "was called a Zealot" (cf. Acts 1:13, "Simon the Zealot"), a designation that most exegetes regard as suggesting that Simon came from, and had been at one time a member of, a violent political movement in Israel. In New Testament times the Zealots were a Jewish sect that represented the extreme of fanatic nationalism. They employed tactics similar to modern political terrorists. Some exegetes have argued that the Zealot party should be seen as the spiritual heirs of Mattathias and the Maccabees. "Zeal" is also a term used significantly by Saint Paul. In 2 Cor 9:2, he praises the Christian community at Corinth for its influence upon neighboring communities, saying, "your zeal [*zelos*] has stirred up most of them." And in Rom 12:11, he urges that community: "Do not grow slack in zeal, be fervent in spirit." However, more than once Paul admits to his own excessive zeal, as in Phil 3:6 where he confesses that "in zeal I persecuted the church." And in Gal 1:13–14 he says, "You heard of my former way of life in Judaism, how I persecuted the church of God beyond measure and tried to destroy it, and progressed in Judaism beyond many of my contemporaries among my race, since I was even more a zealot for my ancestral traditions." While Paul praises or encourages some Christian communities with regards to zeal, he also issues some cautions. In Rom 10:2, Paul admits that sometimes zeal can be misdirected: "I testify with regard to them that they have zeal [*zelos theou*] for God, but it is not discerning." And the New International Version translates Gal 4:18 quite literally: "It is fine to be zealous [*zelousthai*], provided the purpose is good."

Christian Pacifism

But this is precisely the point at which it is important for us to see that Jesus' own words and deeds severely qualify the violent language and actions recounted in the gospel passages we have quoted above. For example, in Matthew 26, in the account of Jesus' arrest in the Garden of Gethsemane, we are told in verses 47–52:

> While he was still speaking, Judas, one of the Twelve, arrived, accompanied by a large crowd, with swords and clubs, who had come from the chief priests and the elders of the people. His betrayer had arranged a sign with them, saying, "The man I shall kiss is the one; arrest him." Immediately he went over to Jesus and said, "Hail, Rabbi!" and he kissed him. Jesus answered him, "Friend, do what you have come for." Then stepping forward they laid hands on Jesus and arrested him. And behold, one of those who accompanied Jesus put his hand to his sword, drew it, and struck the high priest's servant, cutting off his ear. Then Jesus said to him, "Put your sword back into its sheath, for all who take the sword will perish by the sword." (cf, Mark 14:43–49; Luke 22:47–51, John 18:1–11)

Moreover, there are passages in the gospels that state precisely how Christians should respond to persecution and teach what might well be regarded as a sort of pacifism. Take for example, the beatitudes in Matt 5:3–10:

> Blessed are the poor in spirit, / for theirs is the kingdom of heaven.
> Blessed are they who mourn, / for they will be comforted.
> Blessed are the meek, / for they will inherit the land.
> Blessed are they who hunger and thirst for righteousness,
>   for they will be satisfied.
> Blessed are the merciful, / for they will be shown mercy.
> Blessed are the clean of heart, / for they will see God.
> Blessed are the peacemakers, / for they will be called children of God.
> Blessed are they who are persecuted for the sake of righteousness,
>   for theirs is the kingdom of heaven.
> Blessed are you when they insult you and persecute you and utter every kind
>   of evil against you [falsely] because of me. Rejoice and be glad, for your
>   reward will be great in heaven.

And in Matt 5:38–40, Jesus warns against retaliation:

> You have heard that it was said, "An eye for an eye and a tooth for a tooth." But I say to you, offer no resistance to one who is evil. When someone strikes you on [your] right cheek, turn the other to him as well."

In fact, one could well argue that it is flight rather than fight that is the more significant gospel theme. In the gospels, Jesus several times predicts that his disciples will be persecuted. And though he counsels courage and witness, he also recommends flight. In this regard see Matt 10:16–23:

> "Behold, I am sending you like sheep in the midst of wolves; so be shrewd as serpents and simple as doves. But beware of people, for they will hand you over to courts and scourge you in their synagogues, and you will be led before governors and kings for my sake as a witness before them and the pagans. When they hand you over, do not worry about how you are to speak or what you are to say. For it will not be you who speak but the Spirit of your Father speaking through you. Brother will hand over brother to death, and the father his child; children will rise up against parents and have them put to death. You will be hated by all because of my name, but whoever endures to the end will be saved. When they persecute you in one town, flee to another."

In fact, in John 11:53–54, Jesus himself is described as having taken strategic flight in the face of violent opposition: "So on that day they planned to kill him. So Jesus no longer walked about in public among the Jews, but he left for the region near the desert, to a town called Ephraim, and there he remained with his disciples."

Strategic Withdrawal

In the Acts of the Apostles, Paul, when faced with violent opposition, always takes flight. In Acts 9:23–25 we read about the opposition that arose from his preaching in Damascus: "After a long time had passed, the Jews conspired to kill him, but their plot became known to Saul. Now they were keeping watch on the gates day and night so as to kill him, but his disciples took him one night and let him down through an opening in the wall, lowering him in a basket." A few verses later, in Acts 9:28–30, we read about similar opposition and flight from Jerusalem: "He moved about freely with them in Jerusalem, and spoke out boldly in the name of the Lord. He also spoke and debated with the Hellenists, but they tried to kill him. And when the brothers learned of this, they took him down to Caesarea and sent him on his way to Tarsus." Acts 14 tells us of Paul and Barnabas's preaching in the city of Iconium, and the violent response it provoked. There in verses 5–7: "When there was an attempt by both the Gentiles and the Jews, together with their leaders, to attack and stone them, they realized it and fled to the Lycaonian cities of Lystra and Derbe and to the surrounding countryside, where they continued to proclaim the good news." In Acts 17:13–15: "But when the Jews of Thessalonica learned that the word of God had now been proclaimed by Paul in Beroea also, they came there too to cause a commotion and stir up the crowds. So the brothers at once sent Paul on his way to the seacoast, while Silas and Timothy remained behind."

This theme of flight before violent opposition, however, became more problematic in the early church when it involved resident pastors who, when taking flight, left behind a congregation who depended upon them. In the Martyrdom of Polycarp, chapter 7, we are told of the quandary faced by Polycarp the bishop of Smyrna. When persecution of Christians intensified, Polycarp accepted the advice of those who insisted he should flee the city. He eventually reversed his decision and returned to join his flock and suffer with them. In AD 250, shortly after the promulgation of the Emperor Decius's edict against the Christians, Cyprian of Carthage fled not far from his city; but this action provoked considerable criticism such that both Cyprian and his later biographer (Pontius in his *Vita Cypriani* 7) felt the need to defend. Cyprian in his *De Lapsis* 10, said "If the crown is a gift of God's bounty, it can only be received at the established time. He who withdraws for a time, remaining faithful to Christ, does not deny his faith, but awaits his hour." And indeed Cyprian eventually suffered martyrdom in 258 during the persecution by Valerian. In the years 428–429, when Arian Vandals crossed over the Mediterranean and began to attack Christians in North Africa, Augustine wrote a letter to his clergy making it clear that flight was permissible only when the priestly ministry was not indispensable to the faithful (see Epistle 228, 9–14):

> Here, perhaps someone may say that the servants of God ought to save their lives by flight when such evils are impending, in order that they may reserve themselves for the benefit of the Church in more peaceful times. This is rightly done by some, when others are not wanting by whom the service of the Church may be supplied, and the work is not deserted by all, as we have stated above as Athanasius did; for the whole Catholic world knows how necessary it was to the Church that he should do so, and how useful was the prolonged life of the man who by his word and loving service defended her against the Arian heretics. But this ought by no means to be done when the danger is common to all; and the thing to be dreaded above all is, lest anyone should be supposed to do this not from a desire to secure the welfare of others, but from fear of losing his own life, and should therefore do more harm by the example of deserting the post of duty than all the good that he could do by the preservation of his life for future service.[20]

Flight from the World

It is at this point, however, that we need to reconsider the story of Mattathias in the second chapter of 1 Maccabees. In that chapter, besides the principal theme of fighting against the world, there is also a more subtle theme of flight from the world.

20. Augustine, *Letters*, p. 579.

We can see this in the very first line in the saga of Mattathias and his sons, that is with 1 Macc 2:1, that says, "In those days Mattathias, son of John, son of Simeon, a priest of the family of Joarib, left Jerusalem and settled in Modein." If Josephus, who, in his *Antiquities of the Jews* (bk. 12, 265), claims that Mattathias was a native of Jerusalem is correct, then that makes his choice to retreat to the country town of Modein a moral statement. And this applies even to those who argue that Modein was the ancestral residence of the family, and that the family only kept a domicile in Jerusalem so as to be nearby for liturgical services. Once again, in verse 28, we are told that Mattathias made yet another decision to take flight: "Thereupon he fled to the mountains with his sons, leaving behind in the city all their possessions." Compare this with David's maneuver in 1 Sam 23:14–15when he tries to elude Saul. But there is another kind of flight implied in 1 Macc 2:29. There it says: "Many who sought to live according to righteousness and religious custom went out into the desert to settle there, they and their sons, their wives and their cattle." The decision of Mattathias and his sons to flee to the safe hiding places of the mountains was merely a strategic maneuver, implied by the fact that they left behind all their possessions. Consider that there is an intended contrast to those who went into the desert with their wives and their cattle, and thus were merely seeking refuge. Therefore, we must examine these two kinds of flight: strategic retreat to prepare for battle and spiritual withdrawal into the desert.

The challenge of acculturation is the principal theme in the story of Mattathias. More precisely, it is the challenge posed to religion by an alien culture. Yet more precisely, at the heart of Mattathias's priesthood is the conflict between devout believers and an aggressively pagan society. But what we must also see is that the story of Mattathias makes clear to us that there are several responses to such cultural imperialism. One is conformity or gross accommodation, another is passive resistance or alienation and withdrawal, and yet another is active resistance. Of course, the first alternative is illustrated by those Jews who not only hid their circumcision but sacrificed on alien altars. The second possible response is illustrated by the religious fundamentalists or biblical literalists represented by the group who appear in 1 Macc 2:29–41. When this group appears it is unnamed. But we know that these people also left their homes and sought refuge in the wilderness. Pursued and overtaken, this group refused to leave its camp on the Sabbath, in accord with a literalist interpretation of Exod 16:29. Nor would they fight on the holy day, even to defend themselves. Consequently, they were slaughtered when the troops of Antiochus Epiphanes attacked on the Sabbath. As such, they represent the moral alternative of passive resistance. However, in 1 Macc 2:42–48, Mattathias and his followers are joined by yet another group, the Hasideans, who offer active resistance. (*Hasid* means "devout" or "pious"; in Hebrew *hasidim* means "pious ones.") The Hasideans, along with Mattathias and his small force, carried on guerilla warfare against the Hellenizing Greeks. Thus we see the beginning of the still current phenomenon of Hasidic Judaism, a style of devout Jewish observance that sets its followers apart from mainstream society.

Although the Hasideans are described as being "devoted to the law" (1 Macc 2:42), they are difficult to identify with precision. For example, the group is not mentioned by Flavius Josephus, the great Jewish historian. Nevertheless, the name occurs frequently in the rabbinical writings. Modern scholars believe that this group or "synagogue" of Jews, distinguished by their devotion to the law, was the group from which the Pharisees developed.

Christian Countercultures

The action of strategic flight by Mattathias (and his Hasidean followers) finds an echo in the actions of those Christians in the fourth century who, having decided that the Christianity of the cities had become too secular and corrupt, fled to the desert to pursue a purer devotion. This became the theme of *fuga mundi*, literally "flight from the world."

The theme of "flight from the world" (not just flight from persecution) has a long history: in the early church it occasioned the rise of monasticism. The Christian monastic movement began in the late third century in Egypt when Christian men of an idealistic bent began retiring as solitaries or hermits into the Egyptian wilderness where they practiced austerities designed to further their spiritual life. They lived in isolation and followed no uniform rule of life until the appearance of a hermit known as Antony of Egypt (251?–356) who, in about the year 269, gave away his possessions and retired into the desert in order to devote himself to a life of asceticism.

In no small measure these men were seeking to imitate biblical precedents. In Exod 3:1, Moses encounters God while leading Jethro's flock through the desert. Elijah in 1 Kgs 19:1–8 encounters God in the desert. In the book of the prophet Hosea, Israel is personified as a faithless wife; but God will lead her into the desert to try to change her mind. That is, in Hos 2:16, we read: "So I will allure her; I will lead her into the desert and speak to her heart." According to Luke 1:80, John the Baptist was in the wilderness, literally in the desert, till the day of his manifestation. The holiness and ordered discipline of his life was seen as not only a self-conscious rejection of the wickedness of the contemporary world but also as a corrective or alternative to the growing laxity of a socially acceptable Christianity.

Thus Antony of Egypt was soon imitated by a large number of young men who chose to follow his example. He came out of solitude in 305 precisely so as to give assistance to those who wanted to imitate him. He did this by providing for them guidelines in the form of a rule for those who wanted to live apart from the world in a loose association of hermits. Later spiritual leaders, such as Basil in the East and Benedict in the West, wrote rules for a closer form of community life that was lived apart from the world. Later still, in the Middle Ages, variations and emendations of the monastic style occurred when mendicant orders arose that created a monastic style with more involvement in the world. The Protestant Reformation brought yet another variation on the "flight from the world" theme: forms of family life that attempted to follow the stricter way of Jesus apart from the world. For example, there are the followers of the Dutch reformer Menno Simmons (1496–1561) called the Mennonites. Most Mennonites refuse military service, the taking of oaths, and any public office. And then there are the followers of the Swiss reformer Jakob Ammann (ca. 1656–1730) who are called the Amish Mennonties, or simply the Amish. The Amish not only remove themselves from military service but they all have regulations regarding clothing, and prohibitions or limitations on the use of electricity, telephones, and automobiles.

Even today in contemporary America, some Christians have decided that secular culture is so pagan, and promotes anti-Christian values so aggressively, that they have sought in various ways to remove themselves from society. For example, witness the sudden appearance of "Christian academies" among Protestants and the number of Catholic families that have now chosen to "homeschool." No doubt, these people are responding to very real threats. Just how aggressive secularism can be is evident by the quickness with which the *New York Times* attempts to vilify Christianity. One instance was the *New York Times'* headline of Sunday, July 24, 2011: "As Horrors Emerge, Norway Charges Christian Extremist." This was a reference to Anders Breivik, a social radical who the day before had killed ninety-two people in a politically motivated act of violence. Later investigation revealed that Breivik was a xenophobe, did not practice any kind of Christianity, and was scornful of contemporary Christianity in Norway. But the *New York Times* did not wait for further investigation when it felt that it had been handed a brick bat with which to go at Christianity.

But there is also a danger of going too far in one's rejection of the world. Take for example a primary force behind the homeschooling movement, Rousas John Rushdoony (1916–2001). Born in New York City of Armenian refugee parents, but raised and educated in California, Rushdoony earned a BA in English from the University of California at Berkeley in 1938 and an MA in education in 1940. He also attended the Pacific School of Religion at Berkeley from which he graduated in 1944. He was then ordained by the Presbyterian Church in the United States. He wrote works on education, such as his 1981 book *The Philosophy of the Christian Curriculum.* There he criticized the traditional liberal arts curriculum of American schools for being too humanistic, for teaching a freedom not compatible with Christian faith. He proposed instead what he claimed was a Christian liberal arts curriculum. But in some instances his proposal has resulted in excesses, such as the rejection of contemporary science by replacing the theory of evolution with a naive creationism. What might help to restore a more balanced attitude toward the world, even in its most aggressive form, secularism, would be to look at the biblical witness as to what should be our attitude toward the world.

The Christian View of the World

The New Testament presents us with a carefully balanced attitude toward the world. Take for example John's Gospel. In John 3:16–17 we are told: "God so loved the world that he gave his only Son, so that everyone who believes in him might not perish but might have eternal life. For God did not send his Son into the world to condemn the world, but that the world might be saved." But two verses later we are told, "the light came into the world, but people preferred darkness to light."

So, too, the First Letter of Peter exhibits exquisite moral balance regarding the world. For it counsels that while me must be wary of the world and its ways, on the other hand we have a duty to witness to the world and even to demonstrate that a Christian, far from being antisocial, can be the best neighbor, as good a citizen, maybe better than others in that regard. I am referring to 1 Pet 2:11–17, where we are told:

> Beloved, I urge you as aliens and sojourners to keep away from worldly desires that wage war against the soul. Maintain good conduct among the Gentiles, so that if they speak of you as evildoers, they may observe your good works and glorify God on the day of visitation.
>
> Be subject to every human institution for the Lord's sake, whether it be the king as supreme or to governors as sent by him for the punishment of evildoers and the approval of those who do good. For it is the will of God that by doing good you may silence the ignorance of foolish people. Be free, yet without using freedom as a pretext for evil, but as slaves of God. Give honor to all, love the community, fear God, honor the king.

Moreover, we should also consider the historical witness. Philo of Alexandria and the Septuagint, the historic Greek translation of the Bible, the version used by all the New Testament writers, witnesses to the fact that biblical faith could not just survive but even flourish amidst a pagan culture. And then there is the witness of the phenomenon of Christendom, the Christian Middle Ages in the West. This was a time when Christian conviction of the compatibility of faith and reason, Aristotle and the Bible, worked to produce such enduring cultural institutions as colleges and universities.

For those reasons we must be very wary of creating a ghetto Christianity, or worse, a crusader mentality that today finds expression in Christian ministers who burn the Koran; or Christian apocalypticists who predict a great war between Christians and Jews on the one hand and Muslims on the other. We must also recognize that radical Islam is nowhere near as much an enemy as is virulent secularism. In fact, it could be argued that, in no small measure, it is the moral libertarianism on display in such mass media as the American film and television industries that have convinced some Muslims that America is "The Great Satan."

A priest must be ready to contend with the presence of both attitudes toward the world in his congregation, those who have embraced secular culture and those who totally reject it. And thus I choose to conclude here with a consideration of a modern day priest who battled secular culture not with the force of arms but with the power of words.

Newman's Challenge to a Worldly Society

Between 1834 and 1843, John Henry Newman published eleven volumes of sermons that he entitled *Parochial and Plain Sermons*. The title reflects the fact that most of the sermons had been given at regular Sunday services in the Church of St. Mary the Virgin, Oxford, England, a Gothic structure with parts dating back to 1328. It was a parish church of the Church of England of which Newman was made vicar, that is, pastor in 1834. During the time of Newman's pastorate at St. Mary's, he also held the title of university preacher where he gave "plain sermons." And so, from time to time, special university services were held at St. Mary's. Each of Oxford University's colleges had its own chapel, which its residents were expected to attend; however, students and faculty were also free to attend services at St. Mary's and Newman, as a tutor at Oriel College, soon came to be regarded as a particularly eloquent preacher. St. Mary's could accommodate as many as six hundred worshippers. On an average Sunday during Newman's time the congregation there consisted of some of the town's tradesmen and shopkeepers, some of the domestic staff at Oxford's colleges, but mostly it consisted of young undergraduates and their tutors, that is, young men from the leading families of English society, a part of English society whose religious complacency Newman aimed to challenge.

And thus Newman's *Parochial and Plain Sermons* provides us with a candid picture of how a modern priest struggled with the secularism that afflicted much of his congregation, and even more so his fellow clergy. Indeed, nineteenth-century theological liberalism had affected much of the people and clergy of the Anglican Church, creating a religion grossly accommodated to the world. Brian Martin in his biography of Newman described the challenge thusly: "At this time in the thirties Oxford was fast becoming liberal not only in political opinions, but also in religious principles. Some would say that it had long before become liberal in religious matters; indeed, liberal was the wrong word, for like much of the country it had become lax."[21] Newman responds to this situation by first clearly describing it, and then by offering a way to combat it. As for his descriptions of the problem, they are numerous and detailed. Take for example sermon 3, "Knowledge of God's Will without Obedience." Newman describes the English people of his time as being keenly knowledgeable of their Christian religious traditions but not obedient to them, because the practice of their religion is blunted by the world. After quoting John 13:7, "If ye know these things, happy are yet if ye do them," Newman goes on to say: "There never was a people or an age to which these words could be more suitably addressed that to this country at this time; because we know more of the way to serve God, of our duties, our privileges, and our reward, than any other people hitherto, as far as we have the means of judging."[22] He then goes on to describe the society from which most of his Oxford students came, England's genteel social leadership, the trendsetters, the arbiters of good taste:

> They are well educated and taught; they have few distresses in life, or are able to get over them by the variety of their occupations, by the spirits which attend good health, or at least by the lapse of time. They go on respectably and happily, with the same general tastes and habits which they would have had if the Gospel had not been given them. They have an eye to what the world thinks of them; are charitable when it is expected. They are polished in their manners, kind from natural disposition or a feeling of propriety. Thus their religion is based upon self and the world, a mere *civilization*; the same (I say), as it would have been in the main, (taking the state of society as they find it,) even supposing Christianity were not the religion of the land. But it is; and let us go on to ask, how do they in consequence feel towards it? They have been taught to revere it, and to believe it to come from God; so they admire it, and accept it as a rule of life, so far forth as it agrees with the carnal principles which govern them. So far as it *not* agree, they are blind to its excellence and its claims. They overlook or explain away its precepts. They in no sense obey

21. Martin, *John Henry Newman*, p. 60.
22. Newman, *Parochial and Plain Sermons*, p. 22.

because it commands. They do right when they *would* have done right had it not commanded; however, they speak well of it, and think they understand it. Sometimes, if I may continue the description, they adopt it into a certain refined elegance of sentiments and manners, and then the irreligion is all that is graceful, fastidious and luxurious. They love religious poetry and eloquent preaching. They desire to have their feelings roused and soothed, and to secure a variety and relief in the eternal subject.[23]

Later, in a sermon entitled "The Strictness of the Law of Christ," Newman describes the basic decency of the Victorian gentleman who conforms more to the mores of society than to the demands of the gospel:

What is the sort of man whom the world account respectable and religious, in a high rank or a lower? At best he is such as this. He has a number of good points in his character; but some of these he has by nature, and if others have been acquired by trouble, it is either because outward circumstances compelled him to acquire them, or that he has from nature some active principle within him, of one kind or another, which has exerted itself, and brought other principles under, and rules him. He has acquired a certain self-command, because no one is respected without it. He has been forced into habits of diligence, punctuality, precision and honesty. He is courteous and obliging; and has learned not to say all he thinks and feels, or to do all he wishes to do, on all occasions. The great mass of men of course are far from having in them so much that is really praise-worthy as this; but I am supposing the best.[24]

Later still (in bk. 6, sermon 15, "Rising with Christ"), once again Newman paints an apt picture of the worldly English gentleman, but this time it is the most jaded:

Men of this world live in this world, and depend upon it; they place their happiness in this world; they look out for its honors or comforts. *Their* life is not hid. And everyone they meet they suppose to be like-minded. They think they can be as sure that every other man looks out for the things they covet, as they can be sure he has the same outward appearance, the same make, a soul and body, eyes and tongue, hands and feet. They look up and down the world, and as far as they can see, one man is just like another. They know that a great many, nay, far the greater part, are like themselves, lovers of this world, and they infer, in consequence, that all are such. They discredit the possibility of any other motives and views being paramount in a man but those of this world. They admit, indeed, that a man may be *influenced* by religious motives, but to be *governed* by them, to *live* by them, to own them as turning points, and primary and ultimate laws of his conduct, this is what they do not credit. They have devised proverbs and sayings to the effect that every man has his

23. Ibid., p. 24.
24. Ibid., p. 730.

price; that all of us have our weak side; that religion is a beautiful theory; and that the most religious man is only he who hides most skillfully from himself, as well as from others, his own love of the world; and that men would not be men if they did not love and desire wealth and honor.[25]

Not only is Newman good at describing the laxity of his day, but he is also good at prescribing practical remedies. For example, at the end of the sermon 3, "Knowledge of God's Will without Obedience" he advises:

But if a man is in earnest in wishing to get at the depth of his own heart, to expel the evil, to purify the good, and to gain power over himself, so as to do as well as know the Truth, what is the difficulty?—a matter of time indeed, but not of uncertainty is the recovery of such a man. So simple is the rule that he must follow, and so trite, that at first he will be surprised to hear it. God does great things by plain methods; and men start from them through pride, *because* they are plain. This was the conduct of Naaman the Syrian. Christ says, "Watch and pray;" herein lies our cure. To watch and to pray is surely in our power, and by these means we are certain of getting strength.[26]

At the end of the sermon on "The Strictness of the Law of Christ" he says:

Let us go to Him for his grace. Let us come to the ordinances of grace [the sacraments], in which Christ gives his Holy Spirit, to enable us to do that which by nature we cannot do, and to be "the servants of righteousness." They who pray for His saving help to change their likings and dislikings, their tastes, their views, their wills, their hearts, do not indeed all at once gain what they seek,—they do not gain it at once asking,—they do not *perceive* they gain it while they gain it,—but if they come continually day by day to Him,—if they come humbly,—if they come in faith,—if they come, not as a trial how they shall like God's service, but throwing (as far as may be) their whole hearts and souls into their duty as a sacrifice to him,—if they come, not seeking a sign, but determined to go on seeking Him, honoring Him, serving Him, trusting Him, whether they see light, or feel comfort, or discern their growth, or no,— such men *will* gain, though they know it or not; they will find, even while they are still seeking; before they call, He will answer them and they will in the end find themselves saved wondrously, to their surprise, how they know not, and when their crown seemed at a distance."[27]

At the end of the sermon on "Rising with Christ" Newman says:

Start, now, with this holy season [Easter], and rise with Christ. See, He offers you His hand; He is rising; rise with Him. Mount up from the grave of the old

25. Ibid., p. 1310.
26. Ibid., p. 28.
27. Ibid., pp. 736–37.

Adam; from groveling cares, and jealousies, and fretfulness, and worldly aims; from the thralldom of habit, from the tumult of passion, from the fascinations of the flesh, from a cold, worldly, calculating spirit, from frivolity, from selfishness, from effeminacy, from self-conceit and high-mindedness. Henceforth set about doing what it is so difficult to do, but what should not, must not be left undone; watch, and pray, and meditate, that is, according to the leisure God has given you."[28]

It was this combination of moral indictment and spiritual encouragement in Newman's sermons that helped create the great spiritual revival in the Church of England that was the Oxford Movement. But the lesson for us today is this: one should never underestimate the power of well-considered words, "pulpit oratory" in the best sense of that term, to affect people's lives. Mattathias was a great and good man, and as Ambrose says, even a saint; but to this day, for Christian clergy Newman's way of warring with the world is the better choice.

28. Ibid., p. 1313.

9

Sacrifice, a Dangerous Notion

The Unholy Ministry of Joseph Caiaphas

IN THE HISTORY OF religions there is evidence that human beings have offered up all kinds of sacrifices to the gods, including other human beings. But in addition to cultic sacrifice, it is observable in social history, as well as in the history of religions, that moral sacrifice has, and continues to, play a significant role in the lives of human beings. For example, it could be argued that long ago human beings learned how small sacrifices in the form of self-denials could pay off with dividends in the long term. To this day, for instance, parents often instinctively make short term personal sacrifices for the benefit of their children in the long term. While such an instinctive motive of parents toward the good of their children is laudable, there is also evidence of selfish and reprehensible uses of moral sacrifice, as when people sacrifice spouse and family, friends, and even their personal honor, in an effort to amass vast fortunes. Modern history is rich with examples of such individuals. But the Bible provides us with a truly profound example of the abuse of the concept of moral sacrifice. Indeed, it could be argued that no life makes so clear both the moral and religious aspects of sacrifice as that of Joseph Caiaphas. Joseph Caiaphas is the Jewish high priest who, in the Gospel according to John, not only presided over the cult of the Jerusalem temple but was also the first to recommend the death of Jesus as a moral expedient. In John 11:50, we find Caiaphas urging the Sanhedrin, the council of Jewish elders, to consider how "it is better for you that one man should die instead of the people, so that the whole nation may not perish." Over the centuries, the morality of Caiaphas's advice has prompted considerable debate; and even to this day there are moral voices like those of the cultural historian René Girard and Pope John Paul II who have warned us that modern society, unbridled by religious scruples, is unself-consciously appropriating a similar logic and thus is grossly abusing the notion of sacrifice.

In this chapter we examine carefully the historical witnesses to the life and ministry of Joseph Caiaphas, and we survey the theological and moral debate that has taken place regarding his justification for the death of Jesus. But we also look carefully at the Christian doctrine of spiritual sacrifice, and then study the arguments of René Girard and Pope John Paul II who criticize secular society as grossly abusing the doctrine of sacrifice. We do all this out of the conviction that the issues of moral as well as cultic sacrifice are intimate to and have great implications for the ministry of Catholic priests today, a ministry that should include not just the sacramental celebration of the self-sacrifice of Christ but should also help people discern what might be the role of sacrifice in their own lives, what sacrifices might legitimately be expected of them.

We begin by examining the life and ministry of Joseph Caiaphas. The principal source for our knowledge of Joseph Caiaphas is the New Testament, which contains direct and indirect references to him in all four gospels and one reference in the work called the Acts of the Apostles. There are also some brief references to Caiaphas in the writings of the Jewish historian Flavius Josephus, and in such rabbinic works as the *Mishnah* and *Tosefta*. We begin with the biblical witness.

Caiaphas in the New Testament

According to the New Testament witness, Joseph Caiaphas held the office of high priest at Jerusalem during the period of time that encompassed the public ministry and death of both John the Baptist and Jesus of Nazareth, and the beginning of the public ministry of Jesus' disciples Peter and John after the death and resurrection of Jesus. More precisely, the biblical witness to Joseph Caiaphas portrays him as high priest (*epi archiereos*) when John the Baptist began preaching (Luke 3:2), during the trial of Jesus (Mark 14:53–64; Matt 26:3, 57; Luke 22:47–53; John 18:19–24), and at the arrest and trial of Peter and John as related in Acts 4:5–8, approximately the years AD 18 to AD 36. Because the NT references to Caiaphas involve multiple witnesses, and because they vary at important points, especially regarding the trial of Jesus, we must survey each NT portrait of Caiaphas side by side. Doing so allows us to appreciate the differences in the witnesses. We will follow a chronological order so as to get some idea of the implicit history of the NT narrative of Caiaphas's high priesthood.

The first explicit reference to Caiaphas in the gospels reveals him to be the high priest at the beginning of the public ministry of John the Baptist. This reference is important because of the way it links Caiaphas with the name of another high priest, Annas. This is in Luke 3:1–2: "In the fifteenth year of the reign of Tiberius Caesar, when Pontius Pilate was governor of Judea, and Herod was tetrarch of Galilee, and his brother Philip tetrarch of the region of Ituraea and Trachonitis, and Lysanias was tetrarch of Abilene, during the high priesthood of Annas and Caiaphas, the word of God came to John the son of Zechariah in the desert."

That two high priests are mentioned, not just Caiaphas but also Annas, might be taken to suggest sequential ordering, that is, the end of the high priesthood of Annas and the beginning of the high priesthood of Caiaphas. But, as we shall see later, the relationship between these two men is only suggested here and is, in fact, much more involved than mere temporal succession.

In chronological order, the next explicit biblical reference to Caiaphas occurs in Matt 26:3–5. It portrays the agitation and concern of the Jewish leadership in Jerusalem over the popularity of Jesus and his bold appearance in Jerusalem at the time of the Passover feast: "Then the chief priests and the elders of the people assembled in the palace of the high priest, who was called Caiaphas, and they consulted together to arrest Jesus by treachery and put him to death. But they said, 'Not during the festival, that there may not be a riot among the people.'"

In chronological order, the next New Testament reference to Caiaphas appears in John 11:45–53. This narrative provides yet another instance of a general growing concern about Jesus' public ministry, and about the threatening character of not only his preaching and teaching but also of his reputation for miracles:

> Now many of the Jews who had come to Mary and seen what he had done began to believe in him. But some of them went to the Pharisees and told them what Jesus had done. So the chief priests and the Pharisees convened the Sanhedrin and said, "What are we going to do? This man is performing many signs. If we leave him alone, all will believe in him, and the Romans will come and take away both our land and our nation." But one of them, Caiaphas, who was high priest that year, said to them, "You know nothing, nor do you consider that it is better for you that one man should die instead of the people, so that the whole nation may not perish." He did not say this on his own, but since he was high priest for that year, he prophesied that Jesus was going to die for the nation, and not only for the nation, but also to gather into one the dispersed children of God. So from that day on they planned to kill him.

The next series of New Testament witnesses to Caiaphas occur in the gospel narratives that describe the arrest and trial of Jesus. Let us begin with the accounts given to us by Mark and Luke. Neither account ever mentions Caiaphas's name. Instead Caiaphas is referred to indirectly as "the high priest." In Mark 14:53–64 we read:

> They led Jesus away to the high priest, and all the chief priests and the elders and the scribes came together. Peter followed him at a distance into the high priest's courtyard and was seated with the guards, warming himself at the fire. The chief priests and the entire Sanhedrin kept trying to obtain testimony against Jesus in order to put him to death, but they found none. Many gave false witness against him but their testimony did not agree. Some took the stand and testified falsely against him, alleging, "We heard him say, 'I will destroy this temple made with hands and within three days I will build another not made with hands.'" Even so their testimony did not agree. The high priest rose before the assembly and questioned Jesus, saying, "Have you no answer? What are these men testifying against you?" But he was silent and answered nothing. Again the high priest asked him and said to him, "Are you the Messiah, the son of the Blessed One?" Then Jesus answered, "I am; / and 'you will see the Son of Man / seated at the right hand of the Power / and coming with the clouds of heaven.'" / At that the high priest tore his garments and said, "What further need have we of witnesses? You have heard the blasphemy. What do you think?" They all condemned him as deserving to die.

Luke's account of the arrest and trial of Jesus begins with the arrest of Jesus in the garden of Gethsemane. While reference is made to "the high priest's servant" and to the meeting at the "house of the high priest," Caiaphas's name is never mentioned. Moreover, the principal protagonist here is not the high priest but "a crowd" that consists variously of the chief priests, the temple guards, the elders of the people, and the scribes. The arrest is accounted in Luke 22:47–53:

> While he [Jesus] was still speaking, a crowd approached and in front was one of the Twelve, a man named Judas. He went up to Jesus to kiss him. Jesus said to him, "Judas, are you betraying the son of Man with a kiss?" His disciples realized what was about to happen, and they asked, "Lord, shall we strike with a sword?" And one of them struck the high priest's servant and cut off his right ear. But Jesus said in reply, "Stop, no more of this!" Then he touched the servant's ear and healed him. And Jesus said to the chief priests and temple guards and elders who had come for him, "Have you come out as against a robber, with swords and clubs? Day after day I was with you in the temple area, and you did not seize me; but this is your hour, the time for the power of darkness."

In the narrative that follows in Luke, that of Peter's denial of Jesus, once again reference is made to "the house of the high priest." But there is no mention of the man himself. Luke 22:54–57 says: "After arresting him they led him away and took him into the house of the high priest; Peter was following at a distance. They lit a fire in the middle of the courtyard and sat around it, and Peter sat down with them. When a maid saw him seated in the light, she looked intently at him and said, 'This man too was with him.'"

The Matthean and Johannine accounts of the arrest and trial of Jesus, however, do make use of Caiaphas's name and that of Annas. These accounts also make clearer the relationship of those two; the relationship between Annas and Caiaphas is clearly stated in John 18:12–14: "So the band of soldiers, the tribune, and the Jewish guards seized Jesus, bound him, and brought him to Annas first. He was the father-in-law of Caiaphas, who was high priest that year. It was Caiaphas who had counseled the Jews that it was better that one man should die rather than the people." While John's gospel focuses upon the "pre-trial hearing" before Annas, it ends with Jesus being sent to Caiaphas. In John 18:19–24 we read:

> The high priest questioned Jesus about his disciples and about his doctrine. Jesus answered him, "I have spoken publicly to the world. I have always taught in a synagogue or in the temple area where all the Jews gather, and in secret I have said nothing. Why ask me? Ask those who heard me what I said to them. They know what I said." When he had said this, one of the temple guards standing there struck Jesus and said, "Is this the way you answer the high priest?" Jesus answered him, "If I have spoken wrongly, testify to the wrong; but if I have spoken rightly, why do you strike me?" Then Annas sent him bound to Caiaphas the high priest.

John's gospel provides no account of Jesus' encounter with Caiaphas. Instead we are simply told in John 18:28, "Then they brought Jesus from Caiaphas to the praetorium."

By contrast, the narrative in Matt 26:57–66 supplies us with a very detailed account of Jesus' encounter with Caiaphas:

> Those who had arrested Jesus led him away to Caiaphas the high priest, where the scribes and the elders were assembled. Peter was following him at a distance as far as the high priest's courtyard, and going inside he sat down with the servants to see the outcome. The chief priests and the entire Sanhedrin kept trying to obtain false testimony against Jesus in order to put him to death, but they found none, though many false witnesses came forward. Finally two came forward who stated, "This man said, 'I can destroy the temple of God and within three days rebuild it.' The high priest rose and addressed him, "Have you no answer? What are these men testifying against you?" But Jesus was silent. Then the high priest said to him, "I order you to tell us under oath before the living God whether you are the Messiah, the Son of God." Jesus said to him in reply, "You have said so. But I tell you: / From now on you will see 'the Son of Man / seated at the right hand of the Power' / and 'coming on the clouds of heaven.'" Then the high priest tore his robes and said, "He has blasphemed! What further need have we of witnesses? You have now heard the blasphemy; what is your opinion?" They said in reply, "He deserves to die!"

There is one more appearance of Caiaphas in the New Testament. He appears in the work called the Acts of the Apostles, in the narration there of the arrest and trial of Peter and John. Peter and John had been going up to the temple each day and preaching about Jesus there. This disturbed the temple authorities, and so they had Peter and John arrested. In Acts of the Apostles 4:5–8, we are told of their appearance at an inquest at which Caiaphas is present. No specific words or actions are attributed directly to Caiaphas, only his presence is mentioned: "On the next day, their leaders, elders, and scribes were assembled in Jerusalem, with Annas the high priest, Caiaphas, John, Alexander, and all who were of the high-priestly class. They brought them into their presence and questioned them, 'By what power or by what name have you done this?' Then Peter, filled with the Holy Spirit answered them."[1]

If we are to understand these NT references to and portrayals of Caiaphas, we must know something about the high priesthood in Israel at the time of Jesus, and its political as well as its religious significance. And we must understand something more about the relationship between Caiaphas and his father-in-law, Annas.

High Priesthood in the Time of Jesus

In premonarchical Israel, Aaron was most often referred to simply as "the priest" (Exod 35:19, 39:41; Lev 1:7; 7:34; 13:2; 21:21; Num 3:6, 32; 4:16, 28; 7:8; 18:28; 26:64; 33:38; Josh 21:4; 21:23). And so it was with the principal priests at the various shrines in Israel before the monarchy. The term high priest (Hebrew *kohen gadol*; Greek *archiereus*) as applied to Aaron and his successors reflects a tradition that arose after the monarchy shut down all the local shrines and restricted all sacrifice to the Jerusalem temple. At that time the term "high priest" began to be used to refer to the head of the clergy serving at the temple in Jerusalem.

All kinds of social distinctions were employed to create a certain aura of honor about the high priest. For example, the high priest had to preserve cultic purity by way of maintaining a social distance from others, even with regard to deaths in his own family (see Lev 21:10–12). He also wore distinctive dress, special vestments. These garments were of much finer quality than most priests wore. More precisely, the high priest wore a blue robe, the hem of which was edged with bells of gold. The high priest also wore a gold turban and breastplate, both studded with jewels.

---

1. There are three more passages in Acts that mention the high priest: Acts 5:17–42 (yet another arraignment of Peter before the Sanhedrin), Acts 6:8—9:1 (the arraignment of Stephen before the Sanhedrin), and Acts 9:1–2 (Saul/Paul's request for authority to pursue Christians fleeing Jerusalem for Damascus). But, as VanderKam says in his *From Joshua to Caiaphas* (p.429), Caiaphas is never mentioned by name even though chronologically he might well have been still high priest. And "as the author calls Annas the high priest in Acts 4:6, we cannot be sure of the point."

As for his duties and responsibilities, besides general oversight of the cult, the high priest himself had a prominent role in the more important liturgical observances: he presided at the liturgies on the three major feast days in the Jewish liturgical calendar (Atonement, Pentecost, Tabernacles); and he alone entered the Holy of Holies on the Day of Atonement (Lev 16:4). He also performed a daily morning and evening offering in the temple. However, some of these duties, such as the morning and evening offerings, were, in post-exilic times, relinquished to other priests. In these times the high priest took on more general social responsibilities with regard to the people of Israel because, after the exile, beginning either under late Persian or early Hellenistic rule in Palestine, it was the high priest who became responsible not only for supervision of religious services in the temple but also, as chief administrator of civil policy within Israel, Israel's representative in external matters with other countries. This reached its height under the Hasmoneans whose priests actually held the title of king. The term "Hasmoneans" refers to the sons of Mattathias who initiated the so-called Maccabean wars that freed Palestine from outside political interference from 135 BC until the Roman conquest by Pompey in 63 BC. The sons of Mattathias held the title of high priest during that time of freedom. The term "Hasmonean" is derived from Flavius Josephus who claimed that one Asmonaeus (Hebrew, *hasmon*) was the name of the father of Mattathias, and thus was the great ancestor of this clan. But, even with the Roman conquest of Judea and the subsequent Herodean rule, the office of high priest maintained a sure measure of social and political prominence because of his role as president of the council called the Sanhedrin.

The Sanhedrin (from the Greek word *synedrion*, literally, "sitting together") was the name given to the supreme council or court of Israel, a sort of representative assembly of seventy Jewish social and religious leaders, and presided over by the high priest. The Sanhedrin, or Great Sanhedrin as it came to be called, is first mentioned in the Bible in the Maccabean period (1 Macc 11:23; 12:6; 14:28; 2 Macc 1:10; 4:44; 11:27). And it is referred to by Jewish historian Josephus as existing in the reign of Antiochus the Great (223–187 BC). The number seventy was a self-conscious attempt to give the Sanhedrin a venerable historical precedent in the seventy elders of ancient Israel (Num 11:16–17). In NT times the seventy members of the Great Sanhedrin were composed of three groups: the elders of Israel's chief families and clans; the elders of the principal priestly families and any former high priests; and the scribes and professional lawyers, that is, scholars of the Torah. There is considerable debate as to how often they met, regularly or only when occasion called for it.

Caiaphas's Powerful Father-In-Law

We have already noted the presence of another high priest, Annas, who at times appears alongside Caiaphas and who at times appears to have had as much or maybe even more authority than Caiaphas. "Annas" is the New Testament Greek form of the Hebrew *Hananiah*, a word meaning "gracious," "merciful." But we shall see how in the Greek of the historian Flavius Josephus it is "Ananias"; and in the Hebrew of the Talmud it is rendered "Hanin." According to the Jewish historian Josephus, it was in the year AD 6, when the Romans took direct control of Judea, that the Roman governor of Syria, Quirinius, removed Joezer from the high priesthood at Jerusalem and appointed in Joezer's place as the new high priest, a thirty-six year old priest named Annas, a well-educated member of an aristocratic and wealthy priestly family in Jerusalem. Josephus also tells us that Annas held the position of high priest for nine years until Valerius Gratus, the governor of Judea, removed Annas and appointed in his place one Ishmael, son of Phabi. However, Annas continued to exercise a strong influence in Jerusalem society for several reasons. First, even though he was technically no longer high priest, an aura of grave respect still was owed to him. In this regard see in the *Mishnah*, the tractate *Horayoth* 3:4, where we are instructed, "The high priest in office differs from the priest that is passed from his high priesthood only in the bullock that is offered on the Day of Atonement and the tenth of the *ephah*."[2] In other words, they only differ in a few liturgical or cultic technicalities. Two other factors that would guarantee Annas's continued power was his great wealth (especially if used for bribery) and because after removal from the high priestly office he then automatically became a prominent member of the Sanhedrin. No wonder then that when Ishmael, son of Phabi, was removed after only a year as high priest he was replaced by Annas's son Eleazer. In fact, eventually four more of Annas's sons held the office of high priest: Jonathan, Theophilus, Matthias, and his namesake, the younger Annas, sometimes called Annas II.[3] However, none held the office for a term as long as Annas's son-in-law, Caiaphas.

In Jewish literature, the only direct references to Annas are brief factual notices of his appointment and removal as high priest. However, there are two extremely important references to his family. One is in Josephus's *Antiquities of the Jews* and the other in the Babylonian Talmud. Neither is flattering. We look first at the description of the high priesthood of Annas's son, Annas II, in Josephus's *Antiquities of the Jews* (bk. 20, ch. 9, sec. 2):

---

2. *Mishnah*, p. 465.

3. The younger Annas appears in Josephus's *Antiquities* 20.9.1 as the killer of James, the early leader of the Christian community at Jerusalem and "brother of the Lord."

As for the high priest Ananias [Annas], he increased in glory every day, and this to a great degree, and had obtained the favor and esteem of the citizens in a signal manner; for he was a great hoarder up of money: he therefore cultivated the friendship of Albinus, and of the high priest, by making them presents; he also had servants who were very wicked, who joined themselves to the boldest sort of the people, and went to the threshing floors, and took away the tithes that belonged to the priests by violence, and did not refrain from beating such as would not give these tithes to them. So the other high priests acted in the like manner, as did those his servants without anyone being able to prohibit them.[4]

This description of the greed of Annas II helps explain a brief and otherwise enigmatic reference to the family of Annas in the Babylonian Talmud. In the tractate *Pesahim* 57a, there is a general lament of the dubious influence of certain priestly families: "Woe is me because of the house of Boethus, woe is me because of their sticks, woe is me because of the house of Hanin, woe is me because of their defamation, woe is me because of the house of Qatros, woe is me because of their libel, woe is me because of the house of Ishamel ben Phiabi, woe is me because of the thuggery! For they are high priests, and their sons, treasurers, their sons-in-laws trustees, and their slaves beat up on the people with clubs."[5] The expression "the house of Hanin" is a reference to the high priest Annas and his descendants, including his son of the same name.

Bruce Chilton, in his study of the temple cult in the time of Jesus, explains how a high priestly family could justify its greed by reference to certain themes in Scripture: "The Torah had stressed that correct worship in the Temple would bring with it material prosperity, and the elite priests attempted to realize that promise."[6] Chilton also gives examples of how this was done: because the Jerusalem temple hierarchy tended to fill all the chief positions from their own families, this would have meant that, most probably, the ruling house of Annas held all the chief-priestly positions within its control. The family of the high priest also derived income from the sale of sacrificial victims to be used in the temple services. There are several references in rabbinic literature to "the booths of the sons of Annas," which were market stalls located on the Mount of Olives, opposite the temple. From these booths pilgrims to the temple could purchase the sheep, doves, wine, and oil needed for sacrificial offerings. The *Mishnah*'s tractate *Kerithoth* 1:7 witnesses to the "price gouging," or exorbitant rates charged for the purchases there: "Once in Jerusalem a pair of doves

---

4. Josephus, *Complete Works,* p. 424.

5. *Babylonian Talmud,* Vol. 4, p. 256; and Brown's *Death of the Messiah,* Vol. 1, p. 409.

6. Chilton, *Temple of Jesus,* p. 185.

cost a golden *denar*." A fair price would have been one silver *denar*—a golden *denar* was worth twenty-five silver ones.[7]

In view of the evidence of Annas's continuing power and influence, many exegetes claim that it is precisely this continuing influence that makes certain statements in the NT explicable—statements such as the odd reference to the joint high priesthood of Annas and Caiaphas, in Luke 3:2, and the unqualified reference to Annas alone as high priest in Acts 4:6; and also, as seen in John 18.12–24, Annas is consistently called "high priest" (vv. 15, 16, 19, 22). A few historians, such as Ernest Renan in his *Vie de Jesus* (1863), have even gone so far as to argue that it was Annas and not Caiaphas who was the prime mover of the plot that brought Jesus to death. Renan describes Annas as being "the real author of the judicial murder about to be committed" and Caiaphas as "the blind tool of his father-in-law."[8] But it is precisely at this point we need to look more closely at the biblical narratives about Caiaphas. We must do so because it is here where we find evidence of Caiaphas's own power and ability. Despite the fact that Caiaphas's ascent to the high priesthood might have owed something to his promotion by his father-in-law, and despite all the evidence of the continuing prominence and influence of Caiaphas' father-in-law, we should not underestimate Caiaphas's own power and ability.

The Shrewdness of Caiaphas

According to Josephus's *Antiquities* 28.4.3, Caiaphas was appointed high priest of the Jews by the Roman procurator Valerius Gratus in AD 18. Caiaphas then served as high priest for the next eighteen years. That was a remarkably long term of service considering that when Caiaphas was appointed he was the fifth high priest in four years to hold the office.

The reason for such a quick turnover of the office of high priest was that, since the time of Herod the Great, high priests were made and unmade by officials of Rome depending upon their manifest subserviency. Obviously, Caiaphas remained in office so long because he cooperated very carefully with the Roman officials. Indeed, it seems that for the last ten years of his term, Caiaphas worked closely with Pontius Pilate. Josephus reports that Caiaphas was deposed from office only after the Syrian governor Lucius Vitellius, serving under the emperor Tiberius, took control of affairs in Palestine in AD 36, replacing Pontius Pilate as procurator of Judea. And as for the fact that Annas rather than Caiaphas is called high priest in the account of the trial of Peter and John in Acts of the Apostles, it is nothing much more than witness to the custom whereby a retired high priest continues to be accorded that title out of courtesy.

7. *Mishnah*, footnote #7, p. 564.

8. Renan, *Life of Jesus*, p. 372.

Consider also the evidence that not only was Caiaphas the most successful high priest during the period of the Roman occupation (his eighteen years as high priest was twice that of Annas, who served only nine years), but, if we read the gospel passages carefully, we will see that it was Caiaphas who took the leading role in the trial and condemnation of Jesus. According to Matt 26:3, it was at Caiaphas's palace that the elders of the people, the chief priests, and the scribes gathered to consider what must be done about Jesus. The regal claims of the new Messiah and the growing fame of Jesus' works had made the members of the Sanhedrin dread both the vengeance of imperial Rome upon their nation and the loss of their own personal authority and prestige (cf. John 11:48). According to John 11:45–48, it was the excitement caused by the miracle of Jesus' raising Lazarus from the dead that drove the worried members of the Sanhedrin to pressure Caiaphas. And, according to John 11:49, it was Caiaphas who pointed a way out of their dilemma: let them bide their time until the momentary enthusiasm of the populace was spent (cf. Matt 26:5), and then by the single sacrifice of Jesus they could at once get rid of a dangerous rival and propitiate the frowns of Rome. In John 11:47–48, we hear them ask: "What are we to do? For this man performs many signs. If we let him go on thus, every one will believe in him, and the Romans will come and destroy both our holy place and our nation." And then in John 12:50 comes Caiaphas's famous rejoinder: "You do not understand that it is expedient for you that one man should die for the people, and that the whole nation should not perish."

Also consider that, according to Matt 26:3–5, the plans for the arrest of Jesus were made in Caiaphas's house. And, according to Matt 26:57–68, it was also in Caiaphas's house that the hearing before the Sanhedrin was held. Also consider that while Annas questioned Jesus in the preliminary hearing before the Sanhedrin, it was Caiaphas who not only questioned Jesus but got him to make a fatal admission in his trial before the Sanhedrin. This is particularly important because it was Jesus' answer to this question that led the court to vote him guilty of blasphemy. After Caiaphas heard the accusations against Jesus and noted his silence, he ordered Jesus to say whether he claimed to be the Son of God. The gospel accounts of the reply vary: "You have said so" (Matt 26:64); "I am" (Mark 14:62); "You say that I am" (Luke 22:70). And thus it was Caiaphas who led Jesus into making a fatal admission. In his response Jesus had uttered blasphemy, a capital offense according to Mosaic law.

An even more revealing witness to the shrewdness of Caiaphas is the account in Matt 26:26 and Mark 14:63 of what Caiaphas did after his leading Jesus into a fatal admission. Caiaphas employed a very dramatic gesture that drove home to his audience, the rest of the Sanhedrin, what must be done next. We are told in Matt 26:65 and Mark 14:63 that Caiaphas, after hearing Jesus' response, ritually tore his garment. The tearing of one's clothing was an ancient and traditional gesture. It is a highly dramatic gesture meant to express extreme emotion. The patriarch Jacob tore his garment when he heard of the supposed death of his son Joseph (Gen 37:34), David tore his garment when he heard of the death of his son Absalom (2 Sam 13:31), and Job tore his garment when he learned of the death of his children (Job 1:20). But Caiaphas's employment of this gesture is made all the more dramatic because priests had been commanded never to do this (Lev 10:6), and high priests especially (Lev 21:10). If Mark and Matthew are indeed relating an historical detail, then it is evidence of Caiaphas's shrewd ability to gage the importance of the moment and respond to it in a way that would secure the conclusion he wanted.

Moreover, there is other evidence that suggests that when the careers of Annas and Caiaphas are compared, Caiaphas comes out the stronger by far. For example, Annas's time as high priest includes a particularly embarrassing incident: in the year AD 9 the Samaritans succeeded in penetrating the Temple during Passover and desecrated it by scattering bones in the porticoes.[9] But during Caiaphas's time in the high priesthood, Caiaphas himself perpetrated a bold profanation of the temple. The argument presented by Victor Eppstein in his essay on the gospel account of the episode in Jesus' life called "the cleansing of the temple," details Jesus' overturning the tables of the vendors in the temple and physically driving the vendors out. This narrative is found in all four gospels (Matt 21:12–13, Mark 11:15–17, Luke 19:45–46, John 2:13–22). Eppstein argues that this episode is not only historically accurate but it is a very precise depiction of the greed and arrogance of Caiaphas. More precisely, Eppstein says, "Despite a superficial tendential redaction, it is not improbable that in this periscope we have an episode in the life of Jesus for which considerable historicity may justly be claimed."[10] Later he argues, "The transaction of business in sacrificial objects inside the Temple was not an established institution but an exceptional and shocking license introduced in the Spring of 30 CE by the vindictive Caiaphas."[11] Vindictive because it was his way of getting back at a group of priests, the Sadducees, who with their superior religious attitude had been offering a moral challenge to Caiaphas's leadership. Those same Sadducees had been running a market in sacrificial items (sheep, doves, wine, and oil) on the Mount of Olives. Caiaphas, in retaliation to their challenge, took over that operation and moved it to the temple precincts. The "cleansing of the temple" was Jesus' response to Caiaphas's bold innovation.

---

9. See Josephus's *Antiquities*, 18:29–30; and the Talmudic tractate *Zevahim* 113a; and in the *Tosefta*, the mishnaic tractate *Eduyyot* 3.3.

10. Eppstein, "Historicity of the Gospel," p. 44.

11. Ibid., p.55.

Caiaphas in Jewish Literature

There is a brief mention of Caiaphas in the writings of the Jewish historian Flavius Joseph and two indirect references to him in rabbinic literature; of these, three appear to be merely factual statements but there is one that appears to contain a damning judgment.

As for Caiaphas's treatment by the Jewish historian, Flavius Josephus (ca. 37–ca. 100), Josephus, a native of Palestine and a Pharisee, who, after the fall of Jerusalem in the year 69, went to Rome where Vespasian gave him a pension that enabled him to spend time writing two important historical works, the *Jewish Wars* and the *Antiquities of the Jews*. Josephus mentions Caiaphas in passing, with no significant comment, twice in his *Antiquities of the Jews*. There, (in bk. 18, ch. 2.2), we find that Caiaphas's name appears in a list of high priests:

> Tiberius . . . was now the third emperor; and he sent Valerius Gratus to be procurator of Judea, and to succeed Annius Rufus. This man deprived Ananus of the high priesthood, and appointed Ishmael, the son of Phabi, to be high priest. He also deprived him in a little time; and ordained Eleazar, the son of Ananus, who had been high priest before, to be high priest; which office, when he had held for a year, Gratus deprived him of it, and gave the high priesthood to Simon, the son of Camithus; and when he had possessed that dignity no longer than a year, Joseph Caiaphas was made his successor. When Gratus had done those things, he went back to Rome, after he had waited in Judea eleven years, when Pontius Pilate came as his successor.[12]

There is yet another passing reference to Caiaphas in Josephus's *Antiquities of the Jews*. This time it is in book 18, chapter 4.3 which tells of the end of Caiaphas' reign as high priest. This happened when a Roman official, Vitellius, intervened in affairs at Jerusalem and "deprived Joseph, who was also called Caiaphas, of the high priesthood, and appointed Jonathan the son of Ananus, the former high priest to succeed him."[13]

As for the two references to Caiaphas in rabbinic literature, the first appears in the rabbinic work called the *Mishnah*, a word meaning "secondary" in the sense of "secondary only to the Torah," as a guide to correct religious observance. It is a collection of rabbinic teachings compiled in about the year AD 200, but it contains rabbinic teaching from the period AD 70 to AD 200. There is apparently a reference to Caiaphas in part six of the *Mishnah* that treats of ritual purity. This reference is located in the tract called "Parah," which treats of the burning of the red heifer, a ritual celebrated on the Day of Atonement. Parah 3.5 reads: "If they did not find the ashes from the seven [earlier] Sin-offerings, they could use them from six, or form

12. Josephus, *Complete Works*, p.588.
13. Ibid., p. 593.

five, or from four, or from three, or from two, or from one. Who had prepared them? Moses prepared the first, Ezra prepared the second, and five were prepared after Ezra. So Rabbi Meir. But the Sages say: Seven since Ezra. And who prepared them? Simeon the Just and Johanan the High Priest prepared two each, and Eliehoenai the son of Hakkof and Hanamel the Egyptian and Ishmael the son of Piabe prepared one each."[14] The editor has a footnote to the name "Eliehoenai, the son of Hakkof," which says "Variant: *ha-Kayyaf* (cf. the name 'Caiaphas')." No doubt this is an extremely cursory reference to Caiaphas, nevertheless some have made much of it.

For example, while Joseph is an ancient and venerable Hebrew name, the surname Caiaphas is a Greek word and its meaning is unknown. There has been considerable speculation as to the meaning of his surname, Caiaphas. In the Greek NT, it is *kaiaphas*. Some have argued it is the Greek transliteration of an Aramaic word meaning "comely"; others argue that it is from the Aramaic for "rock" (compare Simon Peter's sobriquet "kephas"), but in Caiaphas's case it means "the rock that hollows itself out." Still others argue that it is derived from the Chaldean geographical reference meaning "dell" or "depression." But the most intriguing speculation is that it is a derisive reference to Caiaphas, derisive because his name is spelled *ha-koph*, which means "the monkey."

The second reference to Caiaphas appears in the rabbinic work called the *Tosefta*. The *Tosefta* (Aramaic meaning "addition" or supplement), is a collection of Jewish teachings meant to complement those collected in the *Mishnah*, and indeed was compiled shortly after the composition of the *Mishnah*. In the *Tosefta* tractate called *Yevamot* 1:10, we hear of "the house of Caiapha." Some have argued this seems to indicate that Caiaphas came from a family of that name who lived in a village in the vicinity of Jerusalem, a village called Beth Meqoshesh.

Caiaphas in Christian Thought

But now it is important for us to consider the theological significance that has been accorded to Caiaphas in Christian tradition. To begin this assessment we look at the patristic era and the witness of Origen, Jerome, and Augustine. Each represents a decidedly different interpretation of Caiaphas.

Origen of Alexandria (ca. 185–ca. 254), in his Commentary on the Gospel of John, sees Caiaphas as the unwitting tool of God, saying and doing things that carry a meaning far beyond his own subjective understanding or intentions. For example, Origen treats the questions of whether Caiaphas understood what he said and concludes that Caiaphas did not speak on his own, but was prompted by the Holy Spirit:

14. *The Mishnah*, p.700.

I think we learn from this that we say some things on our own, by ourselves, where there is no power that inspires us to speak. But there are other things that we say when some power prompts us to speak. But there are other things that we say when some power prompts us (as it were), dictating what we say, even if we do not fall completely into a trance and lose full possession of our own faculties, but seem to understand what we say. Now, it is possible for us, while we understand what we say on our own, not to understand the meaning of words that are spoken. This is what happened in the case of Caiaphas the high priest. He did not speak on his own, by himself, nor did he understand the meaning of what he said, since it was a prophecy that was spoken.[15]

Origen's argument here is not pure invention on his part, for there was a pious Jewish tradition that priests and high priests in particular could exercise prophetic insight. First consider those passages in the Old Testament that witness to the use of the *Urim* and *Thummim*, an oracular device, by simple priests to predict the will of God (Judg 18:5, 1 Sam 23:6). Later, when the *Urim* and *Thummim* were restricted to the high priest who wore them in the breast plate that was part of his vestments (Lev 8:7–8), he too was thought to have predicative powers. More than once Flavius Josephus witnesses to the opinion that high priests, because of their office, were gifted with special insight. In his *Antiquities of the Jews* (bk. 2, ch. 8), he tells of the high priest Jaddua who had a dream about the arrival of Alexander in Jerusalem. In the *Jewish Wars* (bk. 1, ch. 1), Josephus tells of the high priest Hyrcanus I who had the gift of prophecy, a gift that yielded several accurate predictions. And then there is a passage in the Jewish scholar Philo of Alexandria's *The Special Laws* (bk. 4, 36) that explains why, according to the Torah (Deut 17:8–9), difficult cases were referred to the priests. The reason is straightforward. The priest by virtue of his holy life and sacred ministry, which brings him into proximity with God, is kept from error and can discern the truth: "the real genuine priest is at once also a prophet, having attained to the honor of being allowed to see the only true and living God, not more by reason of his birth than by reason of his virtue. And to a prophet there is nothing unknown."[16] If Philo's reasoning is correct then John the evangelist seems to be saying that the prophecy was connected with Caiaphas's roles as high priest.[17]

Jerome (347–420) in his Commentary on Matthew sets forth a very different interpretation of Caiaphas's words and deeds during the trial of Jesus. Jerome wrote his commentary on Matthew in the year 398, and did so in two weeks' time. This was because he did it as a favor to a friend. The translator, and editor, of this work is quick to point out errors, which he claims are due precisely to the speed with which Jerome

15. Origen, *Commentary*, pp. 35–36.

16. Philo, *The Works*, p. 635.

17. Compare the opinion of VanderKam in his *From Joshua to Caiaphas*, p.427.

created this work. For example, when Jerome says, "Josephus records that his Caiaphas had purchased the high priesthood at a price from Herod for one year only," the editor has a footnote saying, "There is confusion here. According to Josephus, it was Gratus, the predecessor of Pilate, who deposed successively the three predecessors of Caiaphas, namely, Ananus, Ismael, and Eleazar. It was Eleazar who was deprived of the office after holding it for one year. Jerome's haste in composing this commentary has cost him some factual errors."[18] But for our interests, the more important thing has to do with Jerome's interpretation of Caiaphas: there is no emphasis placed upon the man's unconscious motivation by the divine. Instead, there is only Jerome's unrelenting insistence upon the perversity of Caiaphas's mind and will: "Finding no material for a false charge, rash anger and impatience jolted the priest from his seat. Thus he displays the insanity of his mind by the movements of his body. The more Jesus kept silent before the false witnesses and wicked priests who were unworthy of his response, the more the high priest, overcome by fury, challenge him to respond."[19] Jerome's comment on "Then the chief priest tore his robes saying: 'He has blasphemed. Why do we still need witnesses'?" is to insist: "The one whom fury jolted from his priestly seat is provoked by the same madness to tear his garments."[20] This dramatic difference in interpretation could be that Jerome is reacting to what he might have regarded as Origen's all-too spiritual interpretation of Scripture; but it might instead be Jerome's defense of the freedom of the will with regard to salvation or damnation in the face of certain contemporary heresies, such as Marcionite and Valentinian Gnostics who insisted upon irresistible predestination.

Augustine of Hippo (354–430) employs the image of Caiaphas to make points against a heresy of his time: Donatism. Donatism (named for one of its leaders, a certain Donatus) was a rigorist schism in the North African Church that argued that the subjective unworthiness of the minister invalidated the efficacy of the sacraments which he celebrated. In response to this, Augustine of Hippo elaborated his theology of *ex opera opearato* (literally "from the deed done") to explain how the grace of the sacrament was given regardless of the worthiness or unworthiness of the minister. In his work *Three Books in Answer to the Letters of Petilian*, written circa 400, Augustine illustrates his conviction. In book 2, chapter 30, Augustine writes:

> For that a man should be a true priest, it is requisite that he should be clothed not with the sacrament alone, but with righteousness, as it is written, "Let thy priest be clothed with righteousness" [Ps 132:9]. But if a man be a priest in virtue of the sacrament alone, as was the high priest Caiaphas, the persecutor

18. Jerome, *Commentary on Matthew*, p. 305, footnote #289.

19. Ibid., p. 306.

20. Ibid., p. 307.

of the one most true Priest, then even though he himself be not truthful, yet what he gives is true, if he gives not what is his own but what is God's; as it is said of Caiaphas, himself, "This spake he not of himself; but being high priest that year, he prophesied" [John 11:51]. And yet, to use the same simile that you employed yourself: if you were to hear even from anyone that was profane the prayer of the priest couched in the words suitable to the mysteries of the gospel, can you possibly say to him, "Your prayer is not true," though he himself may be not only no true priest, but not a priest at all?, seeing that the Apostle Paul said that certain testimony of I know not what Cretan prophet was true, though he was not reckoned among the prophets of God; for he says, "One of themselves, even a prophet of their own, said the Cretians are always liars, evil beasts, slow bellies: this witness is true." If, therefore, the apostle even himself bore witness to the testimony of some obscure prophet of a foreign race, because he found it to be true, why do not we, when we find in any one what belongs to Christ, and is true even though the man with whom it may be found be deceitful and perverse, why do not we in such a case make a distinction between the fault which is found in the man, and the truth which he has not of his own but of God's? And why do we not say, "This sacrament is true," as Paul, "This witness is true"?[21]

From the Middle Ages we have the witness of Thomas Aquinas. Even though Aquinas treated of Caiaphas in several places, here we shall look only at the treatment of Caiaphas in the *Summa Theologica*—Aquinas's magnum opus. The moral theology section of the *Summa Theologica*, which is called the *Secunda secundae*, that is, "the second section of the second part," in the "Treatise on Acts which Pertain Especially to Certain Men," questions 171–74, treat of the gift of prophecy. Question 173, "Of the Manner in which Prophetic Knowledge is Conveyed," article four asks, "Whether Prophets Always Know the Things which They Prophesy?" In response, Aquinas takes the position that while "sometimes the prophet's mind is moved to speak something, so that he understands what the Holy Ghost means by the words he utters . . . on the other hand, sometimes the person whose mind is moved to utter certain words knows not what the Holy Ghost means by them, as was the case with Caiaphas."[22] And there he cites John 11:51 as illustration of his point: "He did not say this on his own, but he prophesied."

Thomas Aquinas refers to Caiaphas once again in his *Summa Theologica*, this time in the *Tertia Pars*, where the first fifty-nine questions comprise Aquinas's Christology, or treatise on the doctrine of the incarnation. There, in question 50, which treats of the death of Christ, in the article 1, Aquinas asks the question "Whether it was fitting that Christ should die?" And in response he quotes Caiaphas's words in

21. Augustine, *Writings Against the Donatists*, p. 547.
22. Aquinas, *Summa Theologica*, Vol. 2, p. 1905.

John 11:50, "it is expedient that one man should die for the people . . . that the whole nation perish not," insisting those words "were spoken prophetically by Caiaphas as the Evangelist testifies."[23]

Modern commentators are more taken with issues deriving from Caiaphas's famous dictum in John 11:50, "it is better for you that one man should die instead of the people." For example, Lea Roth, the author of the entry Caiaphas in the *Encyclopedia Judaica* (1971), says "the quotation is adapted from a rabbinic statement."[24] She is referring to the Genesis Rabbah 94.9, an exegetical midrash on the book of Genesis, which gives a consecutive exposition of the book of Genesis, chapter by chapter, verse by verse. The Genesis Rabbah is a collection of ancient rabbinical homiletic interpretations of the book of Genesis. As a literary work it was composed about the fifth century of the Common Era, but it incorporates oral traditions that go back as far as the time of the exile in Babylon. And that is why Roth is suggesting that Caiaphas's pronouncement was not his own rationalization. Instead he is quoting a traditional judgment or moral principle. More precisely, in Genesis Rabbah 94.9 we are told:

> It was taught: If a company of people are threatened by heathens, 'Surrender one of you and we will kill him, and if not we will kill all of you,' they should all be killed and not surrender one soul of Israel. But if they specified a particular person, as in the case of Sheba the son of Bichri, they should surrender him and should not all be killed. [then several examples are given, concluding with:] Ulla the son of Kosher was wanted by the government. He arose and fled to Rabbi Joshua ben Levi at Lydda, whereupon officers were dispatched after him. Rabbi Joshua ben Levi argued with him and urged him to surrender, saying "Better that you should be executed rather than that the whole community should be punished on account of you."[25]

The first character referred to, "Sheba the son of Bichri," is a reference to the leader of a rebellion against King David. The story of Sheba's rebellion is told in Second Samuel 20. David sent his commander Joab to go after Sheba. When Sheba and his men take refuge in the city of Abel-beth-maacha in northern Galilee, Joab besieges the town. But a woman of the town calls down to Joab from the city walls reminding him that their town had always been loyal to David. Then Joab challenges her saying that the city can prove its loyalty by surrendering to him the rebel leader Sheba. In response, she promises, "His head shall be thrown to you over the wall." And indeed that is what they did; and thus the city was saved from destruction by sacrificing the rebel leader.

23. Ibid., p. 2293.
24. Roth, *Encyclopedia*, p. 20.
25. *Midrash Rabbah*, Vol. 2, pp. 878–79.

Geza Vermes says of Caiaphas's proclamation, "it is expedient for you that one man should die for the people":

> As the official in charge of the safeguard of the community, the pontiff had to take precautionary measures. John makes Caiaphas enunciate there an important Jewish legal principle, namely, that the welfare of the community overrides the life of an individual. The issue was repeatedly discussed by the later rabbis. They had to determine what to do when the Romans demanded the extradition of a Jewish revolutionary under the threat of indiscriminate reprisal against the population of the town or village which was harboring the fugitive. The rabbis were generally unwilling directly to hand over a Jew to Gentiles. However, in order to protect the larger community, they attempted to persuade the fugitive to give himself up of his own accord.[26]

The response of Christian exegetes ranges from the denunciatory to the generous, and then to some carefully nuanced interpretations.

As for the denunciatory interpretations, William Hendriksen, in his commentary on the gospel of John, says: "When no one could suggest a solution, the president of the meeting presented one. It is clear that *this* chairman was not merely a parliamentarian who kept order. On the contrary, he himself did most of the talking. In the patchwork of his personality the strands of brazen impudence, insane ambition, rancorous jealousy and consummate cleverness were interwoven. He knew all the answers, and he knew how to make others see things his way. He was the kind of individual concerning whom a Dutch proverb says, 'The saucy person owns half the world.'"[27] So too Ernst Haenchen insists: "Caiaphas reproaches his colleagues on the Sanhedrin for a lack of insight: they do not consider that it is better for one man to die for the people than for the whole nation to perish. That is a cold calculation, which simply assumes that the individual is of less value than the people."[28]

As for a kind and perhaps overly generous interpretation we have that of Catholic exegete Gerard S. Sloyan who says, "The high priest's suggestion is a piece of political wisdom which has behind it the thoroughly admissible morality of the lesser evil. Christians are not wrong to see in Jesus an innocent sufferer, but they might ponder more deeply the theological wisdom of Caiaphas' utterance without taking it as fact and viewing him as supremely cynical."[29]

26. Vermes, *Passion*, p. 33.
27. Hendriksen, *Commentary on the Gospel of John*, p. 162.
28. Haenchen, *Commentary on the Gospel of John*, vol. 2, p. 75.
29. Sloyan, *John*, p. 146.

A perhaps more nuanced interpretation is that of John Marsh who says:

> This verse may be said to offer the most forceful example of Johannine irony. Words spoken in opposition against Jesus, and in an attempt to destroy him in order to save the temple and the Jewish nation actually turn out in one sense to be true prophecy: Jesus will indeed die for the people, and not only for the Jewish people, but for all the people of God whom he will gather together. In another sense Caiaphas' statement is the reverse of the truth, for while the death of Jesus was accomplished, that did not secure the safety of the temple, or the continued nationhood of the Jewish people.[30]

James C. VanderKam, in his *From Joshua to Caiaphas: High Priests After the Exile*, says, "Here, Caiaphas was making a realistic political point, yet, for the evangelist, he was unconsciously giving voice to the true nature and significance of Jesus' death."[31]

But we should also note the skepticism of Raymond Brown, for in his *The Gospel According to John* (1–12), he says of the phrase "for the people": "This is omitted by some early Latin patristic evidence, Augustine, Chrysostom, Theodoret, and some Ethiopic witnesses. Normally this would not be sufficient basis for putting it in brackets, but the redemptive theology that the phrase seems to imply does seem strange on the lips of Caiaphas. The word for 'people' appears in John only in this verse and in its reiteration in xviii 14. The development of Caiaphas' statement, found in the parenthetical observations of vss. 51–52, mentions only 'nation.' Thus, there is reason for treating the phrase as a gloss."[32] This, our concern with the moral character of Caiaphas's decision to do away with Jesus as a strategic and moral sacrifice meant to placate political anxieties on the part of Judea's Roman occupiers, can be better understood if we compare it with the Christian understanding of the doctrine of sacrifice.

The Christian Doctrine of Sacrifice

Here we begin with some background on Jewish and pagan sacrifice, for it shows how pervasive the concept and practice of cultic sacrifice was in the time of Jesus and Paul.

As for pagan sacrifice, in the Acts of the Apostles and the letters of Paul there is plenty of evidence that reveals the omnipresence of pagan cults and the problems that they posed for early Christians. In the Acts of the Apostles 14:11–13, we learn that when Paul and Barnabas had been evangelizing the town of Lystra, and Paul's

---

30. Marsh, *Gospel According to St. John*, pp. 442–43 (endnote 50).

31. VanderKam, *From Joshua*, p. 427.

32. Brown, *Gospel According to John*, Vol. 1, p. 440.

preaching led to a cripple being healed, the response was: "When the crowds saw what Paul had done, they cried out in Lycaonian, 'The gods have come down to us in human form.' They called Barnabas "Zeus" and Paul "Hermes," because he was the chief speaker. And the priest of Zeus, whose temple was at the entrance to the city, brought oxen and garlands to the gates, for he together with the people intended to offer sacrifice."

In Acts 15 we read of the so-called "council of Jerusalem," that is, a special meeting of apostles and elders to determine what requirements were to be made of converts. There we are told in Acts 15:28–29: "It is the decision of the Holy Spirit and of us not to place on you any burden beyond these necessities, namely, to abstain from meat sacrificed to idols, from blood, from meats of strangled animals."

Paul also had to deal with this same problem. In chapter 8 of his First Letter to the Church at Corinth, he addresses the problem that much of the meat sold in the markets at Corinth had been used in pagan religious ceremonies. Apparently the Hellenistic cults, unlike the Jewish cult, had no rite of holocaust in which the whole animal's carcass was offered up to God by ritual burning; but instead, in Hellenistic cults the animal was only ritually slaughtered, and then the meat was put up for sale. Some Christians at Corinth thought nothing of this and would purchase and consume such; but some other Christians were scandalized by what they felt was an all too casual attitude. Paul writes to those who feel themselves enlightened and mature about this matter, not to reprimand them but to caution them: "make sure that this liberty of yours in no way becomes a stumbling block to the weak" (1 Cor 8:9).

As for cultic practice in Judaism, we do well to begin by considering that there is evidence that Jesus was raised in a temple-observant family. This is particularly significant because there were quite a few Jews in Jesus' time who would have nothing to do with the temple cult, considering it totally corrupt. But this was not so with Jesus' family, which the gospel presents as temple-observant Jews. In Luke 2:24, we are told that Mary and Joseph, shortly after the birth of Jesus, went to Jerusalem "to offer the sacrifice of 'a pair of turtledoves or two young pigeons,' in accordance with the dictate in the law of the Lord." The "dictate" referred to is Lev 12:6–8:

> When the days of her purification for a son or for a daughter are fulfilled, she shall bring to the priest at the entrance of the meeting tent a yearling lamb for a holocaust and a pigeon or a turtledove for a sin offering. The priest shall offer them up before the Lord to make atonement for her, and thus she will be clean again after her flow of blood. Such is the law for a woman who gives birth to a boy or a girl child. If, however, she cannot afford a lamb, she may take two turtledoves or two pigeons, the one for a holocaust and the other for a sin offering.

This suggests that Mary and Joseph were poor people, that is, not able to afford a lamb.[33]

And then in Luke 2:41 we read, "Each year his parents went to Jerusalem for the feast of Passover." The proper celebration of Passover in Jerusalem required the offering of portions of a lamb in sacrifice at the temple, the remains of which would be consumed at the family's Passover meal, or Seder. Jesus himself is presented in his adult years as not just a synagogue-observant Jew but as a temple-observant Jew. To be such a Jew meant being present at the temple in Jerusalem for all the major feasts, each of which required some sort of sacrificial offering (cf. Deut16:16, "No one shall appear before the Lord empty handed"). In John 5:1, Jesus goes to the temple for the feast of Pentecost at which it was required that loaves of bread be offered (Lev 23:17). In John 7:10, Jesus goes to the temple for the feast of Tabernacles, which included a fruit offering and a libation rite in the temple (Lev 23:37). In John 10:22–33, Jesus is in the temple at the time of the feast of the Dedication (the modern-day Hannukah). Also Jesus is presented at times as encouraging others to participate in the cultic sacrifices of the temple. In this regard, Mark 1:40–44 (with parallels in Matt 8:2–4 and Luke 5:12–14) is instructive: "A leper came to him (and kneeling down) begged him and said, 'If you wish, you can make me clean.' Moved with pity, he stretched out his hand, touched him and said to him, 'I do will it. Be made clean.' The leprosy left him immediately, and he was made clean. Then warning him sternly, he dismissed him at once. Then he said to him, 'See that you tell no one anything, but go, show yourself to the priest and offer for your cleansing what Moses prescribed; that will be a proof for them.'" The phrase "what Moses prescribed" is a reference to Lev 14:3–7 which says:

> If the priest finds that the sore of leprosy has healed in the leper, he shall order the man who is to be purified, to get two live, clean birds, as well as some cedar wood, scarlet yarn, and hyssop. The priest shall then order him to slay one of the birds over an earthen vessel with spring water in it. Taking the living bird with the cedar wood, the scarlet yarn and the hyssop, the priest shall dip them all in the blood of the bird that was slain over the spring water, and then sprinkle seven times the man to be purified from his leprosy. When he has thus purified him, he shall let the living bird fly away over the countryside.

On the other hand, we must take note that there are also those gospel passages that clearly suggest Jesus made his own the prophetic critique of the Israelite sacrificial system. For example, twice in Matthew's gospel Jesus quotes Hos 6:6, "For it is love that I desire, not sacrifice, and knowledge of God rather than holocausts."

---

33. Cf. the offering of Hannah in thanksgiving for the birth of her son Samuel in 1 Sam 1:24, "Once he was weaned, she brought him up with her, along with a three-year-old bull, an ephah of four, and a skin of wine, and presented him at the temple of the Lord in Shiloh."

See Matt 9:13, where Jesus, overhearing the question placed by the Pharisees to his disciples, "Why does your teacher eat with tax collectors and sinners," answers "Go, and learn the meaning of the words, 'I desire mercy, not sacrifice.'" Later in Matt 12:5, when Jesus is criticized by some Pharisees for allowing his disciples to pick the heads of grain as they walk through a field on the Sabbath, Jesus responds, "If you knew what this meant, 'I desire mercy, not sacrifice,' you would not have condemned these innocent men.'"

Then there is also the passage in Mark's gospel (ch. 12, vv. 28–34) in which Jesus dialogues with a scribe regarding the question, "which is the first of all the commandments?" When Jesus makes love of God and neighbor the greatest commandment, the scribe responds saying, "Well said, teacher. You are right in saying, 'He is the One there is no other than he.' And 'to love him with all your heart, with all your understanding, with all your strength, and to love your neighbor as yourself' is worth more than all burnt offerings and sacrifices." Then we are told of Jesus' reaction to that statement by the scribe: "And when Jesus saw that he answered with understanding, he said to him, 'You are not far from the kingdom of God.'"

Moreover, the teaching of Jesus contains a clear and strong doctrine of personal rather than ritual sacrifice. And indeed entering the kingdom may mean painful sacrifice. I am referring to Mark 9:43–48 where Jesus says: "If your hand causes you to sin, cut it off. It is better for you to enter into life maimed than with two hands to go into Gehenna, into the unquenchable fire. And if your foot causes you to sin, cut it off. It is better for you to enter into life crippled than with two feet to be thrown into Gehenna. And if your eye causes you to sin, pluck it out. Better for you to enter into the kingdom of God with one eye than with two eyes to be thrown into Gehenna." (Cf. the parallel in Matt 18:6–9.) Compare also Matt 19:27–29: "Then Peter said to him in reply, 'We have given up everything and followed you. What will there be for us?' Jesus said to them, 'Amen, I say to you that you now have followed me, in the new age, when the son of Man is seated on his throne of glory, will yourselves sit on twelve thrones judging the twelve tribes of Israel. And everyone who has given up houses or brothers or sisters or father or mother or children or lands for the sake of my name will receive a hundred times more, and will inherit eternal life.'"

Note also the emphasis upon self-sacrifice in John 10:11, "I am the good shepherd. A good shepherd lays down his life for the sheep." And John 15:13, "No one has greater love than this, to lay down one's life for one's friends." Also 1 John 3:16, "the way we came to know love was that he laid down his life for us; so we ought to lay down our lives for our brothers."

And this theme of personal sacrifice is picked up by Saint Paul, as in Rom 12:1–2: "I urge you therefore, brothers, by the mercies of God, to offer your bodies as a living sacrifice, holy and pleasing to God, your spiritual worship. Do not conform yourself to this age but be transformed by the renewal of your mind, that you may discern what is the will of God, what is good and pleasing and perfect." Compare also 1 Pet 2:2, where we are instructed: "let yourselves be built into a spiritual house to be a holy priesthood to offer spiritual sacrifices acceptable to God through Jesus Christ." And then there is Rom 5:6–8: "For Christ, while we were still helpless, yet died at the appointed time for the ungodly. Indeed, only with difficulty does one die for a just person, though perhaps for a good person one might even find courage to die. But God proves his love for us in that while we were still sinners Christ died for us."

This latter emphasis upon Christ's sacrifice for us is important because the Christian doctrine of self-sacrifice has been abused and exploited.

It could well be argued that the death of Jesus makes clear the only truly effective sacrifice is one's self. And thus the key to the common priesthood of the faithful is the following: ordinary, baptized Christians who take their faith seriously will discern the self-sacrifices they must make. Good parents, whether Christian or not, naturally intuit the sacrifices they must make to ensure that their children prosper. But it is not only the welfare of one's children that might require a parent to make personal sacrifices, but a marriage itself requires some measure of self-sacrifice. It is interesting to note how the notion of self-sacrifice is presented in both classical and popular culture. Nineteenth century Italian opera has left us with two vivid portrayals, one of a sanctimonious cleric and the other of an overbearing father. Each character urges a woman to make a great sacrifice. In Gaetano Donizetti's 1835 opera, *Lucia di Lamermoor*, which is based on the historical novel of Sir Walter Scott, *The Bride of Lamermoor*, a Protestant minister urges a young woman, Lucia, to sacrifice her personal happiness and submit herself to an arranged marriage "for the sake of her family." In Giuseppe Verdi's 1853 opera, *La Traviata*, based on a short story by Alexandre Dumas, *fils*, a character known as the elder Germont, a figure of bourgeois morality, urges Violetta to sacrifice her personal happiness for his family's honor. As for modern popular culture, in the 1975 movie "Nashville," directed by Robert Altman, there is a scene in which a country western music star sings a song entitled "For the Sake of the Children." It is a cruel satire of a once common and often heroic morality by which a mother sometimes endured her marriage with an impossible husband for the welfare of her children. But it reflects a real dilemma, a sad if heroic choice made by many spouses. Some might dismiss all of these examples as overblown melodrama, but they reflect real life situations and decisions. But if it is true that in the past the doctrine of self-sacrifice has been abused, there is considerable evidence that in our modern day narcissistic culture it is the doctrine of sacrificing others that is being abused; indeed, some would argue that because modern society has eschewed religion, the dangerous doctrine of sacrifice is now more prominent than ever, and in ominous ways.

Sacrifice Today

In the introduction to this book, we noted how, while both Scripture and history assure us there were practical and even speculative atheists in the ancient world, cultural anthropology and history both make it clear there is much more evidence of religiosity in the ancient world. In particular, we have plenty of evidence of there being numerous priesthoods in antiquity. But, it could be argued that in the modern world the effects of general prosperity and acute rationalism have mitigated our awareness of and need for the transcendent, and thus what has resulted is a notable degree of secularism wherein the religious motive and religious phenomena are both greatly reduced. More relevant than ever is the warning in Deut 8:11–14: "Be careful . . . lest, when you have eaten your fill, and have built fine houses and lived in them, and have increased your herds and flocks, your silver and gold, and all your property, you then become haughty of heart and unmindful of the Lord, your God." Ironically, while the religious institution of priesthood and sacrifice may be severely attenuated in the modern world, there is considerable evidence that suggests the idea of sacrifice is much alive. Indeed, there is evidence that suggests as modern man has denied the religious dimension of his life, the notion and practice of sacrifice have become more pervasive than ever. It could even be argued that while modern secular man does indeed reject religious cult, that is, the worship of God, the notion of sacrifice remains important and even dangerous when not bridled by religious scruples. One could argue that a frightening modern development is that while the Western world has become discernibly more atheistic, certain dangerous elements of priestly theology, such as the notion of sacrifice, are more prominent and pervasive than ever. And none have described and analyzed this modern situation more cogently than René Girard and Pope John Paul II.

René Noel Girard is a long-time professor of comparative literature. His studies of both classical and modern European literature have led him to theorize about human culture in general, and especially about the role of religion and sacrifice in the moral growth of humankind. Girard was born December 25, 1923, in Avignon, France. He studied at the Sorbonne (University of Paris), from where he was graduated in 1947. But ever since, he has worked in the United States, first as an instructor in French language and literature at Indiana University in Bloomington, and later at Duke University, Bryn Mawr College and Johns Hopkins in Baltimore, SUNY at Buffalo, and finally at Stanford University. During the 1960s Girard published several literary studies. For example, in 1961 he published his *Mensonge romantique et vérité romanesque*, which was translated in 1965 as *Deceit, Desire and the Novel: Self and Other in Literary Structure*. It is a study of the relationship between subject and object of desire in the novels of Proust, Dostoyevsky, Stendhal, and Flaubert. This was followed up by *Proust: A Collection of Critical Essays* (1962) and in 1963 *Dostoievski: du double à l'unité*, which was translated into English in 1997 as *Resurrection from the Underground: Feodor Dostoevsky*.

In the 1970s, however, Girard's interests turned to a philosophical consideration of certain anthropological themes with deep religious content. For example, in 1972 he published *La Violence et le Sacré* (Engish translation as *Violence and the Sacred*, 1977). There he attempted to show how great human myths (such as that of Oedipus) all exhibit a pattern of persecution, scapegoating, and surrogate victimization—and that that act of violence helped to create community, that is, human communities first developed out of an act of violence that united all over-against one. He claims to have identified a "sacrificial mechanism" buried deep inside all human beings that leads to the logic of scapegoating, solving problems by sacrificing a person. But Girard also argues that religion and cultic sacrifice arose precisely to control that violence.[34] But it was not till several years later that he applied his theory to the biblical and especially the Christian witness.[35] That study came in 1978 with the publication of his *Des Choses Cachée depuis la Fondation du Monde* (English translation as *Things Hidden from the Foundation of the World*, 1987). It is Girard's study of the origin of religion, is meaning and use in society with special attention to Christianity. There he treats of such themes as "Similarities between the Biblical Myths and World Mythology,"[36] "Christ and Sacrifice,"[37] "The Sacrifice of the Other and the Sacrifice of the Self."[38] He argues that among all religions it is Christianity alone has truly worked to identify "the sacrificial mechanism" and exposed the logic of scapegoating. But he also argues that in modern times something new has developed whereby the secularist remains ignorant of the "virus" of violence and displaces it on to the secondary realm of sexuality. Girard's later works all appear, to me at least, to be elaborations upon the themes first set forth in those two works. In 1982, he published his *Le Bouc émissaire*; later, in 1986, it was translated into English as *The Scapegoat*. There he extends his analysis of how Christianity has exposed and fought the culture of violence; and indeed he claims that the death of Christ as related in the gospels is the ultimate uncovering of the scapegoat mechanism. In 1999, he published his *Je vois Satan tomber comme l'éclair*, which in 2001 was translated into

34. R. Girard, *Violence*, p. 20: Religion invariably strives to subdue violence, to keep it from running wild.

35. Ibid., p. 309: "No attempt will be made here to consider the Judeo-Christian texts in the light of this theory . . . that must be left to a future study."

36. R. Girard, *Things Hidden*, pp. 141–44.

37. Ibid., pp. 231–35.

38. Ibid., pp. 235–237.

English as *I see Satan Fall like Lightning*. There he treats of how Caiaphas's "single victim" logic allows the evil sense of sacrifice to live on into modern times under the guise of rationalistic logic.[39] Girard's theories have received much attention from Christian thinkers.[40] But now I turn to Pope John Paul II's treatment of a theme quite similar to Girard's.

This theme of secular society's abuse of the doctrine of sacrifice was long in development in the thought of Pope John Paul II. It appeared early on in a talk he gave at the Extraordinary Consistory of Cardinals held in Rome on April 4–7, 1991, which was devoted to the problem of the threat to human life in our day. But it was in an address during the Prayer Vigil for the Eighth World Youth Day in Denver, Colorado, August 14, 1993, that John Paul first used the expression "culture of life." He returned to that same theme in his encyclical letter *Evangelium vitae* (The Gospel of Life), dated March 25, 1995. In article 4 of that encyclical he warned: "At the same time a new cultural climate is developing and taking hold, which gives crimes against life a new and—if possible—even more sinister character, giving rise to further grave concern: broad sectors of public opinion justify certain crimes against life in the name of the rights of individual freedom, and on this basis they claim not only exemption from punishment but even authorization by the State, so that these things can be done with total freedom and indeed with the free assistance of health-care systems."[41]

Later in article 12 of that same encyclical, he describes this social development: "This reality is characterized by the emergence of a culture which denies solidarity and in many cases takes the form of a veritable 'culture of death.' This culture is actively fostered by powerful cultural, economic and political currents which encourage an idea of society excessively concerned with efficiency."[42]

In article 13, he indicts specifically and eloquently: "Such practices [contraception and abortion] are rooted in a hedonistic mentality unwilling to accept responsibility in matters of sexuality, and they imply a self-centered concept of freedom, which regards procreation as an obstacle to personal fulfillment."[43]

In article 17, the pope decried "that culture which presents recourse to contraception, sterilization, abortion and even euthanasia as a mark of progress and

---

39. Girard, *I See Satan,* p. 36: "The high priest Caiaphas alludes to this mechanism when he says, 'It is better that one man die and that the whole nation perish.'"

40. See Jesuit Michael Kirwin's *Girard and theology* (London: T&T Clark, 2009) and R. G. Hamerton-Kelly's *The Gospel and the Sacred: Poetics of Violence in Mark* (Minneapolis: Fortress, 1994) and Mark Wallace's "René Girard and Contemporary Theology" in *Modern Theology* 5 (1989), 309–25.

41. John Paul II, *Gospel of Life*, pp. 7–8.

42. Ibid., p. 22.

43. Ibid., p. 24.

a victory of freedom, while depicting as enemies of freedom and progress those positions which are unreservedly pro-life."[44]

And in article 28, he made clear that "we are facing an enormous and dramatic clash between good and evil, death and life, the 'culture of death' and 'the culture of life.'"[45] Later again, in article 50 he says, "Today we too find ourselves in the midst of a dramatic conflict between the 'culture of death' and the 'culture of life.'"[46]

In article 28 (third paragraph) the pope says, "the unconditional choice for life reaches its full religious and moral meaning when it flows from, is formed by and nourished by faith in Christ."[47]

And in article 54, Pope John Paul II made his own the theme of "the two ways":

> From the beginning, the living Tradition of the Church—as shown by the *Didache*, the most ancient non-biblical Christian writing—categorically re-peated the commandment "You shall not kill": "There are two ways, a way of life and a way of death; there is a great difference between them . . . In accordance with the precept of the teaching: you shall not kill . . . you shall not put a child to death by abortion nor kill it once it is born . . . The way of death is this: . . . they show no compassion for the poor, they do not suffer with the suffering, they do not acknowledge their Creator, they kill their children and by abortion cause God's creature to perish; they drive away the needy, oppress the suffering, they are advocates of the rich and unjust judges of the poor; they are filled with every sin. May you be able to stay ever apart, o children from all these sins![48]

And thus one might conclude, the moral expediency of Caiaphas is repeated in our day in the so-called "culture of death," whereby we use death as an expedient, a quick and easy answer to a host of social problems: unwanted pregnancies (abortion), criminal behavior (capital punishment), illness and old age (euthanasia).

But here I want to end by returning to a consideration of the role of Catholic priests in the moral as well as cultic issue of the doctrine of sacrifice. The priest in his daily Mass reminds us all of the unique sacrifice of Christ who offered himself. Karl Rahner, in his essay entitled "Dogmatic Questions on Easter," treats of related themes—Christ's crucifixion as an act of self-sacrifice, and the juridical theory of satisfaction—and makes a particularly wise observation of what could be the role of a priest, a parish priest in such situations. During his argument in that essay, Rahner makes reference to the Old Testament role of the priest in examining the sacrificial

44. Ibid., p. 30.
45. Ibid., p. 50.
46. Ibid., p. 88.
47. Ibid,. p. 51.
48. Ibid., pp. 96–97.

offering brought to the temple when he says, "It is of the essence of sacrifice, and not just a more or less certain consequence extrinsic to its being, that it is accepted by God. That is why it needs the authorization of God, the appointment of a priest."[49] That is a reference to the Old Testament laws that both the offering must be unblemished and the supplicant be ritually clean before offering a sacrifice (Lev 17:5; 27:11, 14, 22–23; Deut 15:2; 17:1); and thus it was the duty of the priest to examine the worthiness of the sacrificial offering brought to the temple by a devout Hebrew. Am I wrong to suggest there is a parallel here with the need for a modern-day devout Christian to seek the judgment of a priest as to the appropriateness of the personal sacrifice he or she is about to make?

49. Rahner, "Dogmatic Questions on Easter," p. 129.

10

The Lot of a Simple Priest

Zechariah on Duty in the Temple

WHEN I TOLD THE rector of the seminary where I teach that I was writing a book on priesthood, he gave me his copy of Raymond A. Hutchinson's book *Diocesan Priest Saints* (Saint Louis, Missouri: B. Herder Book Co., 1958). Born in 1926, Hutchinson was ordained a priest for the archdiocese of San Diego in 1957 where he served in parishes and worked as a teacher of English at San Diego University High School. His book on diocesan priest saints contains sketches of the lives of twenty-two diocesan priests. At the time that Hutchinson wrote his book, seven of the priests had already been canonized as saints, and the others had been declared either "blessed" or "venerable." I do not know how many of those then "blessed" or "venerable" have since been promoted to "the dignity of the altar," that is, to sainthood in the formal sense. But as regards diocesan priest saints, I think this can be said: it is the nature of the diocesan priestly vocation to be quiet, almost hidden, rather than to be public and dramatic. The heroism or sanctity of a "simple priest," especially one in parish ministry, is real but rarely is it the kind that "grabs the headlines." After all, the regular diocesan priest walks a familiar, perhaps all too familiar path; and the challenges he faces, though real and often formidable, are nevertheless domestic rather than exotic. By contrast, missionary saints go to foreign lands and brave the exotic challenges of a foreign culture and sometimes a hostile people. True, there have been some diocesan priests who have suffered heroic martyrdom. Hutchison, in his book, has a chapter on "The Martyrs of Gorcum." Gorcum was a town in the south of Holland that was captured by armed Calvinists in June of 1572. All the priests in the town were rounded up and imprisoned, and on July 9, l572, all were put to death by hanging. The dead totaled nineteen, of which eleven were friars of the Franciscan convent at Gorcum. The other seven were diocesan priests. All were canonized by Pope Pius IX on June 29, 1867.

The "martyrdom" of the average diocesan priest is rarely so dramatic. Parish priests "lay down their lives" by means of simple asceticisms, such as celibacy and duty. Both of these asceticisms today are rarely appreciated and often are scorned. The Hebrew priest whom we consider in this chapter, Zechariah, the father of John the Baptist, was much like that. He was an ordinary, regular priest, neither a chief priest nor a high priest. Nor was he perfect; indeed, in one regard some Christian thinkers considered him to be a terrible sinner, an archetype even of faithlessness. Nevertheless, all would have to admit he was a dutiful priest, and in the course of his duties he became an instrument of God. For these reasons I believe a survey of Zechariah's life and ministry, and the severe judgment made upon him, can offer a contemporary ordinary, regular, and simple priest instructive lessons regarding priestly ministry today.

We begin here by surveying the biblical witness to Zechariah the priest and then posterity's judgment upon him. The biblical witness consists of two narratives from Luke's gospel. I have named the first narrative, "Zechariah and the Incense Offering." The second narrative I have labeled "Zechariah's Ecstatic Song."

Zechariah and the Incense Offering

In Hebrew, *zekaryah* is a word meaning "God has remembered." The Old Testament witnesses to the popularity of this word's use as a proper name in ancient Israel, for in the Old Testament there are no less than thirty people who bear that name. No doubt, of those thirty people named Zechariah arguably the most prominent and important is the sixth-century post-exilic prophet whose oracles are preserved in the Old Testament book of Zechariah the Prophet. That work is the eleventh of the twelve books of the "minor prophets" that appears at the end of the Old Testament canon. However, our interest here is in the Jewish priest named Zechariah (NT Greek *Zecharias*) the New Testament personage who was the father of John the Baptist. The story of this Zechariah is told in two episodes of the Gospel According to Luke which in the New American Bible translation are captioned "The Announcement of the Birth of John" (Luke 1:5–23) and "The Birth of John" (Luke 1:57–79).

In that first episode, Luke 1:5–23 (NAB), we are told how:

> In the days of Herod, King of Judea, there was a priest named Zechariah of the priestly division of Abijah; his wife was from the daughters of Aaron, and her name was Elizabeth. Both were righteous in the eyes of God, observing all the commandments and ordinances of the Lord blamelessly. But they had no child, because Elizabeth was barren and both were advanced in years. Once when he was serving as priest in his division's turn before God, according to the practice of the priestly service, he was chosen by lot to enter the sanctuary

of the Lord to burn incense. Then, when the whole assembly of the people was praying outside at the hour of the incense offering, the angel of the Lord appeared to him, standing at the right of the altar of incense. Zechariah was troubled by what he saw, and fear came upon him. But the angel said to him, "Do not be afraid, Zechariah, because your prayer has been heard. Your wife Elizabeth will bear you a son, and you shall name him John. And you will have joy and gladness, and many will rejoice at his birth, for he will be great in the sight of the Lord. He will drink neither wine nor strong drink. He will be filled with the holy Spirit even from his mother's womb, and he will turn many of the children of Israel to the Lord their God. He will go before him in the spirit and power of Elijah to turn the hearts of fathers toward children and the disobedient to the understanding of the righteous, to prepare a people fit for the Lord." Then Zechariah said to the angel, "How shall I know this? For I am an old man, and my wife is advanced in years." And the angel said to him in reply, "I am Gabriel, who stands before God. I was sent to speak to you and to announce to you this good news. But now you will be speechless and unable to talk until the day these things take place, because you did not believe my words, which will be fulfilled at their proper time."

Meanwhile the people were waiting for Zechariah and were amazed that he stayed so long in the sanctuary. But when he came out, he was unable to speak to them, and they realized that he had seen a vision in the sanctuary. He was gesturing to them but remained mute. Then, when his days of ministry were completed, he went home.

In order to truly appreciate, to understand, this passage we need to know two things: the division of labors in the Jerusalem temple and the use of incense there.

Division of Labor in the Temple

At its beginning, Hebrew priesthood consisted of a very small group of men: Aaron and his four sons. In Num 3:1–3, we read: "The following were the descendants of Aaron and Moses at the time that the LORD spoke to Moses on Mount Sinai. The sons of Aaron were Nadab his first-born, Abihu, Eleazar, and Ithamar. These are the names of the sons of Aaron, the anointed priests who were ordained to exercise the priesthood."[1]

---

1. However, of those four sons, the first two, Nadab, "his first born," and Abihu died; they were struck dead by God when they made rubrical, liturgical mistakes. This is recounted in Num 3:4, "But when Nadab and Abihu offered profane fire before the Lord n the desert of Sinai, they met death in the presence of the Lord, and left no sons. Thereafter only Eleazar and Ithamar performed the priestly functions under the direction of their father Aaron."

But Aaron and his sons were also given liturgical or sanctuary assistants and these all came from a particular Hebrew clan. We are told of this in the very next passage of the book of Num 3:5–10:

> Now the LORD said to Moses: "Summon the tribe of Levi and present them to Aaron the priest, as his assistants. They shall discharge his obligations and those of the whole community before the meeting tent by serving at the Dwelling. They shall have custody of all the furnishings of the meeting tent and discharge the duties of the Israelites in the service of the Dwelling. You shall give the Levites to Aaron and his sons; they have been set aside from among the Israelites as dedicated to me. But only Aaron and his descendants shall you appoint to have charge of the priestly functions."

However, several hundred years later during the time when Israel became a kingdom, the organization of the clergy would have to undergo even further emendation in order to take account of not only greater numbers of clergy but also that Israel no longer worshipped in a tent in the desert (as at the time of the exodus from Egypt) nor at various regional shrines in Canaan (as during the time after their settlement in the promised land). And thus we read in 1 Chr 23:1–6 how King David went about reorganizing the Levitical and priestly ministries:

> When David had grown old and was near the end of his days, he made his son Solomon king over Israel. He then gathered together all the leaders of Israel, together with the priests and the Levites.
>
> The Levites thirty years old and above were counted, and their total number was found to be thirty-eight thousand men. Of these, twenty-four thousand were to direct the service of the house of the LORD, six thousand were to be officials and judges, four thousand were to be gatekeepers, and four thousand were to praise the LORD with the instruments which David had devised for praise.

Though the author of First Chronicles does not give us a precise count of the priests in Israel at that time, it is obvious that they must have been so numerous that King David had to divide them into divisions, priestly clans. And so that their duties might be impartially and fairly distributed within each clan, a lottery method was instituted. This is described in 1 Chr 24:1–5:

> The descendants of Aaron also were divided into classes. The sons of Aaron were Nadab, Abihu, Eleazar, and Ithamar. Nadab and Abihu died before their father, leaving no sons; therefore only Eleazar and Ithamar served as priests. David, with Zadok, a descendant of Eleazar, and Ahimilech, a descendant of Ithamar, assigned the functions for the priestly service. But since the descendants of Eleazar were found to be more numerous than those of Ithamar, the former were divided into sixteen groups, and the latter into eight groups, each

under its family head. Their functions were assigned impartially by lot, for there were officers of the holy place, and officers of the divine presence, descended both from Eleazar and from Ithamar.

The Staff of the Jerusalem Temple

Many years later even further changes had come about. For example, some biblical scholars have estimated that in the time of Jesus, the staff of the Jerusalem temple consisted of, in addition to the high priest, some 200 chief priests, about 7,200 ordinary priests, and 9,600 Levites. The high priest was not required to officiate at daily temple services. Instead he presided at certain high feasts, Passover, Succoth, the burning of the red heifer, the Day of Atonement. By definition he was a leader of the people; and by law he was the head of the Sanhedrin, the council of authorities empowered to make judgments in Jewish religious and legal disputes. The chief priests were the permanent staff of temple officers. They supervised all temple operations, including the training and ongoing evaluation of all simple priests who, like Zechariah, from time to time came to serve in the temple. While the high priest and the chief priests lived in Jerusalem, most of the regular priests lived at a distance. Many lived in Jericho, located about twenty-three miles southeast of Jerusalem. Jericho is mentioned several times in the NT (Matt 20:29; Mark 10:4; Luke 10:30; 18:35; 19:1). There is biblical witness to this, such as in Neh 11:1–3 where we read, "The leaders of the people took up residence in Jerusalem . . . in the cities of Judah dwelt lay Israelites, priests, Levites, temple slaves, and the descendants of the slaves of Solomon, each man on the property he owned in his own city." And sure enough, Luke 1:23 suggests that Zechariah did not live in Jerusalem. Luke 1:39–40 confirms this: "During those days Mary set out and traveled to the hill country in haste to a town of Judah, where she entered the house of Zechariah and Elizabeth."

As we have already noted in our chapter on "Money, Sex, and Ministry," most of these ordinary priests who lived at a distance from Jerusalem would have found it difficult to live on the income, the tithe, guaranteed them by tradition, and thus would have had secular jobs. Nevertheless, they also had certain priestly duties to carry out in the local community.[2] For example, Flavius Josephus, in his *Against Apion* (bk. 2, chs. 22–23), describes the two principal roles of what he calls these "priests in general": teaching Torah and making judgments in legal matters. Josephus's account is supported by the *Mishnah*'s tractate "Sanhedrin" 1:3 that specifies several cases in which the rural priest would be required to act as a judge. And Philo of Alexandria, in his *The Special Laws* (bk. 4, ch. 36), describes the priests as

---

2. See Rick Strelan's *Luke the Priest*, pages.118–21, for a good description of a rural priest's life.

particularly apt judges because of their knowledge of the Torah and the Lord. Several witnesses recount that regular priests did indeed at times function as teachers of the Torah and tradition For example, as we have already noted in our chapter on "The Importance of Learned, Well-Educated Priests," several of the contributors to the *Mishnah*, the great collection of rabbinic teachings, were in fact priests (though they are given there the title of rabbi). Among these contributors are Hanina Segan ha-Kohanim, Eleazar ben Shammua, and the figure who goes simply by the title Rabbi Tarphon. Such rural regular priests also had the duty of supervising the collection of the temple tax.[3] In addition, there is archeological witness that some priests were not only so learned in the law that they bore the title of rabbi (master) but that they presided over the local synagogue. I am referring to such archeological evidence as the inscription on a first-century synagogue that reads, "Theodotus, son of Vettenos, priest and ruler of the synagogue."[4]

Allotment of Duties in the Temple

In the time of Jesus, to insure that such regular, rural priests would all get a turn to serve in the Jerusalem temple, each priestly clan was scheduled to appear at the temple twice a year, each time for eight days of service, Sabbath to Sabbath, wherein they were assigned various roles in the temple service. This is the meaning of the phrase in Luke 1:5 that says Zechariah was of "the priestly division of Abijah" and in Luke 1:8, that "he was serving as priest in his division's turn before God."

The historic work called the *Mishnah*, the first literary work of rabbinic Judaism composed circa AD 200 includes along with its record of Jewish religious traditions several precise descriptions of temple practices. These are preserved in the sections entitled Set Feasts (*Moed*), Hallowed Things (*Kodashim*), and Cleanliness (*Tohoroth*).

And as for the reliability of those accounts it is worth recalling that, while the *Mishnah* is considered a rabbinic work and every contributing author carries the title rabbi, several of its authors were priests and some would have known the temple and rituals well. For example, one of the priestly contributors, Rabbi Hanina Segan ha-Kohanim, as his surname suggests, was not just a priest but one of the temple's chief priests who not only presided over the regular priests who ministered there but was deputy to the high priest. And thus the *Mishnah*, when combined with modern

3. We read in Neh 10:38–39: "The tithes of our fields we will bring to the Levites; they, the Levites, shall take the tithe in all the cities of our service. An Aaronite priest shall be with the Levites when they take the tithe, and the Levites shall bring the tithes to the house of our God, to the chambers of the treasury."

4. Jeremias, *Jerusalem in the Time of Jesus*, p. 66. See also Sanders' *Jewish Law from Jesus to the Mishnah*, p. 343, n. 33.

studies such as Alfred Edersheim's now classic historical reconstruction *The Temple and Its Ministry and Services at the Time of Jesus Christ* (London, 1874) and Chaim Richman's *The Holy Temple of Jerusalem* (Jerusalem: The Temple Institute and Carta, 1997), along with more recent archeological studies such as those referred to and collected in J. Rousseau and R. Arav's *Jesus and His World: An Archeological and Cultural Dictionary*, allow us to reconstruct with considerable accuracy temple observances in the time of Jesus.

For example, we can be fairly certain that on the first day of his clan's allotted time of service, Zechariah would have gone up to the temple with his priestly kin late on the afternoon of the Sabbath, before the sunset. According to the *Mishnah's* tractate *Middot* 1:1, 3, we know that there were several gates or entrances to the Jerusalem temple. The south entrance was nearest the roads that led up from Jericho, the roads that most pilgrims to Jerusalem would use. And thus the south entrance was the one used by such as pilgrims as Jesus and his disciples. This entrance to the temple on its south side was called the Huldah Gate. It was situated at the top of a long flight of steps and, by underground passageways, led up into the area called the Court of the Gentiles (where the money changers were located). The priests, however, had their own entrance on the west side of the temple area, the side facing the upper city. This entrance was located nearest the temple sanctuary and corresponds to the architectural remains that today are called "Wilson's Arch." It is named for Charles Wilson, the nineteenth-century archeologist who discovered it. In Jesus' time, it served as an elevated stone bridge called the Xystos bridge that connected the temple mount with the upper city of Jerusalem. It was in the upper city that the high priest and the chief priests lived. The Coponius Gate (called so after Coponius, the first Roman procurator to rule over Judea in AD 6–9) in the wall of the temple—at that end of that bridge—served also as the entrance through which an ordinary or regular priest such as Zechariah would have entered the day after the Sabbath so as to begin his week of service in the temple. According to the *Mishnah's* tractate *Middot* 5:4, there was a Sanhedrin or council chamber at the Coponius Gate, or priests' entrance, wherein a regular priest such as Zechariah would have been examined to determine his physical fitness for service (no cultic uncleanness, such as leprosy or physical disabilities, was allowed) before being admitted into the temple area.[5] After having passed that inspection, Zechariah would be led into the court of the priests, the innermost court, in front of the sanctuary, where he would have been directed to bathe his hands and feet in the laver. Next he would have been brought to the Chamber of Pinchas, keeper of vestments, where he would receive the vestments

---

5. Merely being of Levitical descent did not guarantee a man could serve in the temple. Lev 21:16–23 lists the physical defects that would disqualify a man for service.

needed for the divine service: tunic, trousers, turban, and sash. A simple or ordinary priest wore over his white linen underclothing or trousers, an ankle-length, seamless tunic of white linen, bound at the waist by a long sash or girdle (see Exod 28:39–43). On his head was a white turban or linen hat. Then he would have been taken to the priestly dormitory, a large room called the Chamber of the Hearth, where he would have spent the night. The Chamber of the Hearth was a large domed room that served as sleeping quarters for the priests in the temple. It was called such because of the large fire it contained, before which the priests would warm themselves. These regular priests would have been awakened before dawn to go down below the Chamber of the Hearth to the *mikvah*, a special pool of naturally collected water, and take the prescribed bath so as to prepare for the arrival of the chief priest. The chief priest would gather the ordinary priests who were to serve that day and then bring them to the Chamber of Hewn Stone where lots were cast so as to determine what duty each would be assigned to that day.

Luke's phrase "it fell to his lot" refers to the casting of lots that determined what Zechariah and his kin would do during their week of service or ministry in the temple. All ordinary priests wanted the opportunity to conduct the Divine Services, but there were only a specific number of daily tasks for this service, and so it was impossible for everyone to attend to these. In order to give each priest an equal opportunity to officiate, special lotteries were held each day, and the members of the family clan who were serving that day would participate in this drawing. Four separate drawings were held daily, and thus a number of times throughout the day the courtyard was filled with the priests.

The regulations for the casting of such lots are given in the *Mishnah*, in the tractate called *Tamid* 5:2–6:3. The drawing took place in a circle. The priest responsible for assigning the service would remove the turban of one of the priests assembled there. This act indicated that the assignment process would begin with that man and then continue around the circle. A number would be picked and agreed upon. This number was substantially higher than the number of men present. The overseer would then declare that each man present raise a finger. Then, each finger would be counted (since the Bible forbids the counting of actual people: see Exod 30:12), moving throughout the circle over and over again until reaching the number that had been preselected.

There were four lots in the morning, the third of which determined who offered incense. The other lots were for determining the burnt animal offering, the meal offering, and the maintenance of the candlestick in the Holy Place. The only late afternoon ritual service was the incense offering. Offering incense was a high privilege that generally came only once in a lifetime, since the priest who won it was ineligible in future selections until all the other priests of his division had had it.

It had been traditional that before the taking of the third lottery to determine who would officiate at the incense offering, certain prayers were said together by the priests, such as the Shema (Deut 6:4), and the Ten Commandments recited[6] The incense offering, which, according to Jewish tradition, was the most acceptable part of the temple service in God's eyes; it was influential in subduing evil, and its characteristic quality aided in amplifying the aspect of Divine mercy and benevolence in the world. This was the argument presented in the *Zohar*, a collection of commentaries on the Torah made by the Jewish mystical movement called the Kabbalah.

And, it was this third lot that Zechariah won in Luke 1:5–23.

The Use of Incense in the Temple

It is perhaps helpful here to say something about the incense and its use, both domestically and religiously. The lands of the Bible were homeland to a variety of shrubs and trees that yielded resins, gums, and balsams with positive qualities of odors. These substances also lent themselves to mixing with spices and other perfuming ingredients to provide a wide range of olfactory pleasures. The burning of incense most probably began as a profane practice, that is, as a home art. For example, the saying in Prov 27:9, "Perfume and incense gladden the heart" is not a reference to cultic services or to religious ritual but a comment on domestic housekeeping, the worthy housewife who perfumes herself and incenses her home. Nevertheless, it was not just the fragrance of incense but also the way it burned that recommended it for religious use. First there may well have been the practical motive; for instance a place where animals were constantly sacrificed would soon smell like a slaughterhouse unless incense was used to counteract and cover up the stench. Perhaps that is why references to the use of incense in the cult of Israel often specify its fragrant character. For example, in Exod 30:7, we are told "Aaron must use fragrant incense" (cf. Exod 25:6; 30:1, 35; 31:11; 35:15, 28; 37:29; 40:27; Lev 4:7; 16:12; Num 4:16; 2 Chr 2:4, 13:11). But the fact that the smoke of incense arose up to the heavens and the incense grains were totally consumed in its burning, leaving nothing behind, nothing for man, may well have suggested its appropriateness as a potent religious symbol, a vivid dramatic expression of the rise of prayers before God and of a total unreserved offering to the deity. This is the image invoked in Ps 141:2, "Let my prayer come like

---

6 However, Edersheim, on p. 126 of *The Temple*, claims that in the time of Zechariah, the Ten Commandments were not recited lest that recitation appear to be a concession to Sadduccean absolutism regarding the Torah vis-a-vis the rest of the Scriptures.

incense before you." This is the meaning that Philo of Alexandria (Philo Judaeus) ascribes to it when, in his *The Special Laws* (bk. 1, ch. 35), he treats of the use of incense in the Jerusalem temple: "Moreover, the most fragrant of all incenses are offered up twice every day in the fire, being burnt within the veil, both when the sun rises and sets, before the morning and after the evening sacrifice, so that the sacrifices of blood display our gratitude for ourselves as being composed of blood, but the offerings of incense show our thankfulness for the dominant part within us, our rational spirit, which was fashioned after the archetypal model of the divine image."[7]

As for the use of incense in the Jerusalem temple, the genuine incense is frankincense. It has been described as "a fragrant gum resin occurring in the form of large tears that are light yellowish-brown in color."[8] Its quality was judged by its approach to whiteness. The gum resin of the frankincense plant exudes as a milky fluid. But it soon hardens into lump form upon exposure to air and darkens to a yellow-green or brown shade. In Israel, frankincense, along with equal parts of stacte, onycha, and galbanum (a perennial herb), was specified for the holy incense to be burned at the tabernacle (Exod 30:34–48). This recipe was to be restricted to sacred use. Frankincense alone is specified for burning with the cereal (grain or meal) offerings of first fruits (Lev 2:15–16).

Chapter 30 of Exodus provides us with God's very precise directions for making the kind of incense that should be used not in the home but in worship. There, we also read of God's instructions for the construction of an altar exclusively for the offering of incense, and directions as to who should make the incense offerings and at what time. The prescription for the manufacture of incense in Exod 30:34–38 is a compound of frankincense and several other aromatic substances:

> The LORD told Moses, "Take these aromatic substances: storax and onycha and galbanum, these and pure frankincense in equal parts; and blend them into incense. This fragrant powder, expertly prepared, is to be salted and so kept pure and sacred. Grind some of it into fine dust and put this before the commandments in the meeting tent where I will meet you. This incense shall be treated as most sacred by you. You may not make incense of a like mixture for yourselves; you must treat it as sacred to the LORD. Whoever makes an incense like this for his own enjoyment of its fragrance, shall be cut off from his kinsmen.

It is also important that we understand something about the altar upon which this incense was offered; for there were, in fact, two altars in the Jerusalem temple: one an altar of sacrifice and the other the altar of incense.

---

7. Philo, *The Works,* p. 550.

8. McKenzie, *Dictionary of the Bible,* p. 386.

From its beginning during the time of the Tabernacle in the Desert, the cult of Israel always had two altars. The main altar, or altar of holocausts, was intended for whole burnt offerings. And thus this was the large main altar in front of the Meeting Tent called the Holy of Holies. But there was also a smaller altar of incense inside the sanctuary. It was a square pillar with "horns" on the top four corners.

The directions for the creation of an altar of incense are in Exod 30:1–6:

> For burning incense you shall make an altar of acacia wood, with a square surface, a cubit long, a cubit wide, and two cubits high, with horns that spring directly from it. Its grate on top, its walls on all four sides, and its horns you shall plate with pure gold. Put a gold molding around it. Underneath the molding you shall put gold rings, two on one side and two on the opposite side, as holders for the poles used in carrying it. Make the poles, too, of acacia wood and plate them with gold. This altar you are to place in front of the veil that hangs before the ark of the commandments where I will meet you.

The Ceremonial for Offering Incense

We should also note the position of the altar of incense in the Jerusalem Temple. In Jesus' time, in the temple of Herod the Great, there were three objects inside the sanctuary: the menorah, or great lampstand; the table with the shewbreads; and the incense altar. Because of its purpose, position, and construction it had three names: "the altar of incense," "the inner altar," and "the golden altar." In the post-exilic ritual, the time for the evening sacrifice was fixed at twilight, and four priests were involved in the ceremony of incense offering at the incense or golden altar.

Let us recall that the casting of lots determined that Zechariah would perform the duty of offering the incense. One priest was assigned to gather the coals to be used for the inner altar from the outer altar, or altar of sacrifice. For this he would use a silver shovel and climb to the top of the outer altar, where he would rake and collect some of the coals. Having descended with the coals, he transferred them into a golden shovel which he would take into the sanctuary for the incense service. The priest who would offer the incense would make his way toward the sanctuary together with the one who bore the shovel. At a signal from the priest who would offer the incense, in this case Zechariah, the Levitical choir would begin to sing. They stood atop the platform located in the court of Israel facing the outer altar, just inside the Nicanor Gates. The two priests would now continue up the twelve steps that led to the sanctuary, preceded by two other priests. The task of one of these was to remove the residue ashes from the incense altar; the other was to tend to the lamps in the menorah. After the one priest had removed the old ashes from the altar of incense, the priest who had been carrying the hot coals from the altar of sacrifice would arrange these new hot coals evenly upon the altar of incense.

Zechariah, in his capacity of offering incense, would now enter the sanctuary with another assistant priest. Zechariah would remove the smaller vessel filled with incense and then hand it to his assistant who would place some of the incense into Zechariah's palms. At this point Zechariah's assistant would depart, and Zechariah would be left alone. Zechariah then awaited a signal from the chief priest outside to apply the incense. When the official gave the signal, all of the laity outside in the court of Israel would prostrate themselves in silent prayer. Upon receiving word from the overseer that he might now begin, Zechariah would begin to let the grains fall slowly from his palms across the top of the altar of incense.

Officiating at the incense service only happened once in each priest's life, so he had been warned that he must be very cautious when placing the incense upon the burning coals. If he sprinkled it on the coals too close to the side where he was standing, he would be burned, so he was instructed to sprinkle it away from himself. Edersheim claims this was probably the moment that the Angel Gabriel appeared to Zechariah.[9]

When the incense was finally scattered over the coals, a straight column of smoke rose up to the ceiling, spreading out and filling the entire sanctuary; and when the entire chamber was filled with the cloud of incense, the priest would prostrate himself and then depart the sanctuary. Then the priest and his companion priests would stand at the top of the twelve steps, put down their incense utensils (shovel and incense pot), turn to face the congregation, extend their hands, and recite the priestly blessing of Num 6:24–26.

However, on the day that Zechariah presided at the afternoon incense offering, he found himself unable to pronounce the blessing because he had lost his voice.

Zechariah's Ecstatic Song

Let us now consider the second episode from Luke's gospel in which Zechariah the priest appears. This episode, called "The Birth of John the Baptist," is related in Luke 1:57–79 (NAB):

> When the time arrived for Elizabeth to have her child she gave birth to a son. Her neighbors and relatives heard that the Lord had shown his great mercy toward her, and they rejoiced with her. When they came on the eighth day to circumcise the child, they were going to call him Zechariah after his father, but his mother said in reply, "No. He will be called John." But they answered her, "There is no one among your relatives who has this name." So they made

9. Edersheim, *The Temple*, p. 127.

signs, asking his father what he wished him to be called. He asked for a tablet and wrote, "John is his name," and all were amazed. Immediately his mouth was opened, his tongue freed, and he spoke blessing God. All who heard these things took them to heart saying, "What, then, will this child be?" For surely the hand of the Lord was with him.

Then Zechariah his father, filled with the holy Spirit, prophesied, saying:
"Blessed be the Lord, the God of Israel,
for he has visited and brought redemption to his people.
He has raised up a horn for our salvation
within the house of David his servant,
even as he promised through the mouth of his holy prophets from of old;
salvation from our enemies and from the hand of all who hate us,
to show mercy to our fathers and to be mindful of his holy covenant
and of the oath he swore to Abraham our father,
and to grant us that, rescued from the hand of enemies,
without fear we might worship him in holiness and righteousness
before him all our days.
And you, child, will be called prophet of the Most High,
for you will go before the Lord to prepare his ways,
to give his people knowledge of salvation / through the forgiveness of their sins,
because of the tender mercy of our God
by which the daybreak from on high will visit us
to shine on those who sit in darkness and death's shadow,
to guide our feet into the path of peace."

The most notable element in this second gospel passage that features Zechariah is the canticle that Zechariah sings ecstatically. As to its structure, it is a hymn of praise and thanksgiving in two parts. The first part is both anticipation and rehearsal, that is, a review of the Old Testament theme of God's promise to his people, his promise to redeem them by sending them a savior and a celebration of its fulfillment. The second part is Zechariah's praise and thanksgiving for the role his son John will have in this, the fulfillment of God's promises.

At this point something should be said about its origin and character. Despite the fact that Luke portrays this canticle, this rhapsodic musical ode, as the spontaneous, ecstatic utterance of Zechariah the priest, modern exegetes have produced many other theories as to its origin. Some argue that it is the product of the literary craftsmanship of Luke the evangelist; others argue that its origin is from among the Jewish sect called the Essenes; others argue that it is much older, namely that it is a hymn from the time of the Maccabean revolt; others argue that it originated from among the disciples of John the Baptist; and still others argue that it is an early Christian congregational hymn.

For the purpose of this book, however, of more concern is its character: it is redolent of temple piety. Zechariah's canticle is full of allusions to the temple Psalter. For example, it begins with a well-known praise formula from the Psalter (see Pss 41:14; 72:18; 106:48). The phrase in Luke 1:68, "brought them redemption," is an echo of Ps 111:9, "He sent redemption to his people." The phrase, "a horn of salvation" in verse 69 is a self-conscious allusion to Ps 18:3, where God is hailed by the psalmist as "the horn of my salvation." Verse 71, "to save us from our enemies," is a self-conscious echo of Ps 18:18, "He delivered me from my strong enemies, and from those hating me." The phrase in verse 72, "mindful of his holy covenant," is an echo of Ps 105:8 or Ps 106:45. See further, Ps 132:17, "I shall cause a horn to sprout for David." The lifting up of the horn in the OT refers to an animal's tossing of its horns in a display of might (see Ps 148:14).

Moreover, we should note the influence of such Jerusalem temple piety upon the early Christian movement. Certain NT passages suggest that the earliest Christian community at Jerusalem still found the temple to be an appropriate locus for their devotions as well as teachings. As Acts 2:46 reads, "every day they devoted themselves to meeting together in the temple area." Acts 3:1, "Now Peter and John were going up to the temple area for the three o'clock hour of prayer." In Acts 5:12, it is said of the disciples "They were all together in Solomon's portico." Acts 21:26 shows Paul still respecting certain temple observances: "So Paul took the men, and on the next day after purifying himself together with them entered the temple." And thus we should not be surprised to find that the act of singing hymns, especially in the form of psalms, was a feature of the earliest Christian worship assemblies. For example, in Acts 2:46–47 it is said of the very first Christian community at Jerusalem, "Breaking the bread at home, they partook of the food with transports of joy and utter simplicity of mind, while they sang God's praises." In the letter to the Colossians 3:16, the form and content of what they sang is made clear: "May the word of Christ dwell within you, rich in wisdom, as you instruct yourselves by means of songs, hymns, inspired canticles." In Eph 5:19 we read, "Be filled with the spirit, addressing one another in psalms and hymns and spiritual songs."

When precisely Zechariah's canticle became a part of Christian prayer is not easy to determine. Tertullian, in his treatise *On Prayer* written about the year AD 200, seems to witness to the idea that prayer at fixed hours had already become a tradition, for in chapter 25, "Of Time for Prayer," he refers to "our regular prayers which are due, without any admonition, at the entrance of light and of night."[10] The line in Zechariah's canticle that says "the daybreak from on high will visit us to shine on those who sit in darkness" (Luke 1:78) might well have prompted its inclusion

10. Tertullian, *On Prayer*, p. 690.

among the prayers said first thing in the morning. The earliest precise reference to its use at Morning Prayer is contained in the Rule of Saint Benedict, in the twelfth chapter that is entitled "How the Office of Lauds is to be Said." Benedict wrote his rule circa AD 535, and thus we know that for fourteen hundred years the Benedictus, as Zechariah's canticle is known from its opening line "blessed be the Lord the God of Israel," has been sung daily at Lauds, and on solemn celebrations of Lauds the incensation of the altar takes place. In the tradition of Gregorian chant, Zechariah's canticle is always sung to special modes and with ornate intonations and cadences. Zechariah's canticle is also used prominently during Holy Week when it forms part of the service called *Tenebrae*, the afternoon or evening service on Thursday, Friday, and Saturday of Holy Week. At that service all the lights are extinguished one by one, as the psalms are sung, the final candle going out after Zechariah's canticle is sung. For that special occasion the great Renaissance composer of polyphonic music, Palestrina, wrote several settings. But, most importantly, since the Second Vatican Council's liturgical reforms its recitation at Morning Prayer includes not just monastic communities and priests obliged to the breviary but even laity.

Severe Judgment Against Zechariah

At this point we must consider the place of Zechariah in Christian tradition. Some patristic writers are particularly harsh toward Zechariah. Take for example Origen of Alexandria's treatment of Zechariah in his *Homilies on Luke*, the earliest patristic commentary on Luke. Origen's thirty-nine homilies on Luke survive in Jerome's Latin translation. They were originally given some time between the years 234 and 240 to a mixed congregation of catechumens and Christian laity. Homily 5 is entitled "on the fact that Zechariah fell mute." And it begins:

> When the priest Zechariah offers incense in the temple, he is condemned to silence and cannot speak. Or better, he speaks only with gestures. He remains mute until the birth of his son John. What does this mean? Zechariah's silence is the silence of prophets in the people of Israel. God no longer speaks to them. His "Word, which was with the Father from the beginning, and was God," [John 1:1–2] has passed over to us. For us Christ is not silent; for the Jews he is silent even to this day. Therefore Zechariah the prophet was also silent. His words make it quite clear that he was both a prophet and a priest. But what does the phrase that follows mean, namely, "He kept nodding to them"—that is, he compensated for the loss of his voice with signs? I think that there are deeds that are not different from empty signs because they lack words and reason. But, when words and reason come first and the deed follows, the deeds are not mere signs; they are endowed with rationality.[11]

11. Origen, *Homilies on Luke*, p. 20.

This leads Origen into a general condemnation of all the Jews, a particularly nasty bit of anti-Semitism that I am embarrassed to have to quote:

> Consider the Jewish practices. They lack words and reason. The Jews cannot give a reason for their practices. Realize that what happened in the past in Zechariah is a type of what is fulfilled in the Jews even to this day. Their circumcision is like an empty sign. Unless the meaning of circumcision is proved, it remains an empty sign, a mute deed. Passover and other feats are empty signs rather than the truth. To this very day the people of Israel are mute and dumb. The people who rejected the Word from their midst could not be anything but mute and dumb.[12]

Then there is John Chrysostom. His judgment upon Zechariah might be seen as even more severe than that of Origen. I am referring to his collection of homilies called *On the Incomprehensible Nature of God*, where homily 2 contains the following indictment of Zechariah the priest:

> What did Zechariah do? For this is the subject under investigation, namely, that it is an unpardonable thing to be so curious as to question how God's revelations can be true. Rather it is our duty to accept on faith whatever God says. Zechariah looked at his age, his gray hair, his body which had lost its strength. He looked at his wife's sterility, and he refused to accept on faith what the angel revealed would come to pass.
>
> He questioned how this could be true and said: "How am I to know this?" How, he said will this be? Look! I have grown old and I have turned gray. My wife is sterile and advanced in years. My time of life lacks the freshness of youth; my nature is no longer useful for begetting children. How can what you have promised be reasonable? I lack the strength to beget; my wife's womb is no longer fruitful. Some of you may think he should be pardoned for probing into the predicted sequence of events. Should he not be excused for thinking his question was reasonable?
>
> But God did not think that he deserved pardon. And this was very reasonable. For whenever God makes a revelation, there is no need to stir up the workings of one's reason not to propose to oneself either a sequence of events, or a necessity rooted in nature, or any other such thing. The power of God's revealed word is above all these things, and no hindrance has ever checked its course. So what are you, a mere human, doing? When God makes you a promise, do you reject it and seek refuge in your old age? Do you argue that God cannot do what he promises because you are too old? Old age is not stronger than God's promise, is it? Nature is not more powerful than the creator of nature, is it?
>
> Do you now know, Zechariah, that the works which come from his words are strong and mighty? His word set up the heavens; his words produced cre-

---

12. Ibid., pp. 20–21.

ation, his word made the angels. Do you doubt that his word can produce a child? This is why the angel was angry and why he did not pardon Zechariah, for all the fact that he was a priest. Because of his priesthood Zechariah was subjected to greater punishment. For the man who has a higher title of honor should surpass others in accepting God's revelations on faith.[13]

It is important to understand that the patristic treatment of Zechariah the priest is not totally negative. For example, Origen's exceedingly negative judgment of Zechariah in his homily 5 on Luke is not Origen's final judgment on Zechariah. There is also his homily 10 on Luke 1:67–76, where he says "Filled with the Holy Spirit, Zechariah utters two general prophecies: the first about Christ, the second about John. . . . Gradually, in the course of three months, Zechariah kept receiving spiritual sustenance from the Holy Spirit. Although he did not realize, he was being instructed" [p. 40].[14] So too, while Jerome judges Zechariah negatively in his *Against the Pelagians (Dialogue between Atticus, a Catholic, and Critobulus, a Heretic)*, he contextualizes that judgment. In book 1 Jerome says, "And of Zacharias, it is written, that when the angel promised the birth of a son, he said 'Whereby shall I know this? For I am an old man, and my wife well stricken in years.' For which he was at once condemned to silence."[15] Nevertheless, a few pages later Jerome says, "It is clear the apostles were not without sin . . . to say nothing of patriarchs and prophets whose righteousness under the law was not perfect."[16]

Augustine is even more defensive of Zechariah. In his treatise "On the Merits and Forgiveness of Sins, and on the Baptism of Infants" (bk. 2, ch. 19), he says:

> Now what must we say of Zacharias and Elisabeth, who are often alleged against us in discussions on this question [the imperfection of human righteousness], except that there is clear evidence in the Scripture that Zacharias was a man of eminent righteousness among the chief priests, whose duty it was to offer up the sacrifices of the Old Testament? We also read, however, in the Epistle to the Hebrews, in a passage which I have already quoted in my previous book, that Christ was the only High Priest who had no need, as those who were called high priests, to offer daily a sacrifice for his own sins first, and then for the people. "For such a High Priest," it [Hebrews] says, 'became us, righteous, harmless, undefiled, separate from sinners, and made higher than the heavens; who need not daily, as those high priests, to offer up sacrifice, first for his own sins.'" Amongst the priests here referred to was Zacharias, among them was Phinehas, yea, Aaron himself, from whom this priesthood had its beginning, and whatever

13. Chrysostom, *On the Incomprehensible Nature of God*, pp. 75–76.

14. Origen, *Homilies on Luke*, p. 40.

15. Jerome, *Against the Pelagians*, p. 453.

16. Ibid., p. 455.

others there were who lived laudably and righteously in this priesthood; and yet all these were under the necessity, first of all, of offering sacrifice for their own sins,—Christ, of whose future coming they were a type, being the only one who, as an incontaminable priest, had no such necessity.[17]

Thomas Aquinas provides an apt example of a medieval scholastic's treatment of Zechariah the priest. Aquinas's treatment of Zechariah seems temperate and dispassionately analytical rather than rhetorical and wrathful (after all, his is not a homily). Aquinas treats of Zechariah the priest in the moral section of his *Summa Theologica*, the section called the *Secunda Secundae*. There (in ques. 97, art. 2), Aquinas considers the question "Whether it is a sin to tempt God?" There (in his reply to objection 3), Aquinas says: "Abraham asked for a sign through the divine instinct, and so he did not sin. Gideon seems to have asked a sign through weakness of faith, wherefore he was not to be excused from sin, as a gloss observes, just as Zachary [Zechariah] sinned in saying to the angel (Luke 1:18): "whereby shall I know this?" so that he was punished for his unbelief."[18] The Abraham and Gideon references are to the narratives in Gen 15:8 and Judg 6:36–40. In Genesis 15, two things are promised by God: a son who will be his heir and a land he can call his own. Neither of the two promises is immediately accepted. The first is met with a complaint, and the second with a request for a sign (v. 8).

The book of Judges tells us of Israel's history during the time before the monarchy when Israel was led by charismatic leaders called "judges." In Judges 6, we are told how God sent an angel to inform one of those judges, a man named Gideon of the tribe of Manasseh, that he had been chosen to defend Israel from raiding Midianites. Gideon asked for a sign of assurance that God indeed would help him. But Zechariah's question seems to be not just a request for assurance but is motivated by rational resistance, genuine skepticism.

It is not difficult to find modern exegetes who share this same attitude of severe judgment on the life and ministry of Zechariah the priest. For example, Norval Geldenhuy, in his *Commentary on the Gospel of Luke*, sets forth an opinion that most probably is unaware of Aquinas's judgment on Zechariah but nevertheless repeats it, and with even more invective:

> His [Zechariah's] doubts are, however, not justified, for had he not himself often read in the Old Testament how God had given Isaac a son to the barren wife of the aged Abraham, and how Samuel was given as a son to a formerly barren woman? In former times, indeed, signs had been given, without reproach or punishment, to people like Abraham (Gen. 15) and Gideon (Judges

---

17. Augustine, *Writings Against the Pelagians*, p.52.

18. Aquinas, *Summa Theologica*, Vol. 2, p. 1614.

6) who had asked for them in the same manner. But they still lived in the twilight period of the divine revelation and had not had as many opportunities as Zacharias to know God in His might and mercy. On him, therefore, there rests a greater responsibility, and his unbelief merits chastisement.[19]

Admiration for Zechariah

There is, however, a more positive judgment accorded to Zechariah. Such treatments begin with Ambrose of Milan (ca. 339–397). In his literary compositions, Ambrose treats of Zechariah several times.

Ambrose's *De virginibus* or *Concerning Virginity* is one of his earliest works. Ambrose himself (in bk. 1, ch. 1, sec. 3 of that work) says that he wrote it in the third year of his episcopate, that is, the year 377. There (in bk. 1, ch. 1, sec. 4), Ambrose makes it clear he takes Zechariah as his inspiration for speaking and writing: "And if the name of John restored speech to his father [Luke 1:64], I too, ought not to despair that although dumb I may yet receive speech, if I speak of Christ" (NPNF Vol. 10, second series, *St. Ambrose: Select Works and Letters*, p.364).

Ambrose is merciful toward Zechariah the priest in *Exposition of the Holy Gospel According to Saint Luke*. When Luke 1:6 says of Zechariah and his wife Elizabeth: "They were righteous in the eyes of God, observing all the commandments and ordinances of the Lord blamelessly," Ambrose's comment is "Holy Writ tells us that not only the character of those who are praiseworthy, but also their parents must be praised, so that, as it were, the transmitted inheritance of immaculate purity in those whom we wish to praise may be exalted" (p. 24). A few verses later Ambrose refers to him as "Saint Zecharias" (p. 28). Later in that same work Ambrose says of Luke 1:67, "And Zecharias his father was filled with the Holy Spirit and prophesied": "See how God, good and willing to forgive sins, not only restored what was taken away, but also conferred the unexpected. He who before was dumb prophesies; for this is the supreme Grace of God, that those who had denied Him confess Him" (p. 56).

But Ambrose's most interesting treatment of Zechariah the priest occurs in *De officiis*, written in the years 391–392. There Ambrose claims to have been particularly inspired by Luke's description of Zechariah. He then goes on to describe Zechariah as the archetype for the humble, dutiful, conscientious priest, indeed an exemplar of the moral value of "office" as public duty and service to God and his people. This Ambrose work is worth our careful study not just for its treatment of the priesthood of Zechariah but also because of its treatment of Christian priesthood in general.

---

19. Geldenhuy, *Commentary on the Gospel of Luke*, pp. 66–67.

Ambrose of Milan: Bishop and Teacher

Aurelius Ambrosius, who later would become known as Ambrose of Milan, was born about the year 339 at Trier (Germany). He was born into the family of a noble or upper class Roman civil servant who had achieved high rank as the Praetorian prefect of Gaul, the highest imperial office in all of that particular Roman province. His father died when Ambrose was still young, at which time Ambrose's mother took her children to Rome where Ambrose was given an aristocratic and classical education (he had a fine knowledge of Greek as well as Latin). Ambrose was raised to follow his father in Roman civil service and, indeed, after practicing in the Roman-law courts, he experienced a meteoric career culminating in his being appointed, in the year 370 at a mere thirty years of age, governor of the Roman province of Aemilia-Liguria whose administrative seat of office was at Milan.

Upon the death in 374 of the bishop Auxentius of Milan, Ambrose, though he was only a catechumen in the Christian faith, and thus not yet baptized, was chosen to be the new bishop. The narrative of Ambrose's election as bishop emphasizes his miraculous character, his orthodox piety, and his proven leadership skills as a civic administrator. This narrative also provides a means for historical critical analysis of the event, and reveals some sound human motives. At that time, the principal candidates for the vacant see of Milan were all, to a degree, compromised by doctrinal strife, occasioned by Arianism. Indeed, Auxentius, was himself an Arian. Ambrose accepted his own election to the see of Milan and was baptized and ordained. He first devoted himself to the study of theology under the guidance of his former tutor, a priest named Simplicianus.

Ambrose soon became noted for his preaching, which Augustine of Hippo would later claim was the occasion for his own return to the faith. Ambrose has left us a considerable library of works: half of them are exegetical commentaries on Scripture, which are greatly influenced by his reading of Philo of Alexandria and Origen. But there are also his theological tracts on the creed, on the Holy Spirit, and on the incarnation of the Lord. There are also his catechetical works on the Seven Sacraments, on the Mysteries, and his ethical writings on the duties of the clergy and the witness of virginity. No wonder that today he is numbered among the doctors of the church, indeed one of the four great doctors of the west.

Ambrose of Milan's On Duty

Ambrose's *De Officiis*, "On Duties," is a treatise on Christian ethics. This work later came to be known as *De officiis ministrorum* because of its special reference to the clergy. (We know it was originally titled simply *De Officiis* because that is how

Augustine of Hippo refers to it in his *Epistle 82*, para. 21; however, Ambrose himself uses the phrase *ministrorum officiis* or "the duties of clerics" in bk. 1, para. 86.) To understand this work we must know about its literary background, for it was but the most recent attempt to set forth guidelines for ethical conduct by people in public service. Two works preceded it: one was by a Greek philosopher named Paenatius and the other was by the Roman statesman and philosopher Cicero.

There can be little doubt that Ambrose, when he was growing up, carefully studied Cicero's *De Officiis*. Though Cicero had himself been formally trained as a civil lawyer, and indeed functioned as one in addition to being a Roman civil servant, he always had an interest in Greek philosophy. After the assassination of Julius Caesar, Cicero retired from public life and had plenty of time to think and write, and he chose to do these in the area of philosophy. One of the products of his old age was the work called *De Officiis*.

We know that Cicero finished writing his *De officiis* in November of 44 BC. And we also know that it was written in the form of a letter to his son Marcus, at that time twenty-one and pursuing his university studies in the Peripatetic school of Cratippus at Athens. Marcus, although he was studying philosophy at Athens, was living extravagantly and riotously. Ironically, Marcus was able to live this way because his father supplied him with a very generous allowance.

De Officiis consists of three books of moral advice, based on Stoic precepts. It is written in imitation of the treatise on duty by the Greek stoic philosopher Panaetius of Rhodes (ca. 185–109 BC), who divided his time as a teacher between Rome and Athens. The genius of Panaetius was that, while at Rome, he adapted Stoic doctrine to fit Roman ideals. For example, he taught the subordination of private ambition to the good of the state. Panaetius's "On Duty" is now lost. Cicero's "On Duties" aims to give practical rules for personal conduct. And though it is written in the style of a lesson for his son Marcus, there can be no doubt Cicero intended this work to be a moral lesson for all Roman young men as to how they might comport themselves publicly and morally so as to contribute to the strength of the community and the nation. Cicero regarded this work as his masterpiece, and posterity has tended to agree. Indeed, it is quoted even by Thomas Aquinas; and there is evidence to suggest it was the first classical book to be issued from the modern printing press. But Ambrose's work is also important, especially so for priests today.

It has been argued that Ambrose, in writing his *De Officiis,* was intentionally trying to set forth a general Christian vision of moral behavior. And, no doubt, there are passages in his *De Officiis* that have little or no direct application to Christian clergy. For example, it is in book 3, paragraphs 37–44 where Ambrose condemns speculation by grain merchants in times of food shortages. Nevertheless, the work has a strong clerical focus.

Ambrose begins his *De Officiis* with the words, "I shall not appear presumptuous, I trust, if I adopt the approach of a teacher when addressing my sons."[20] Obviously, the reference to "my sons" is to the clergy of the diocese of Milan. This is made even clearer when later, in the first chapter of his book (in bk. 1, ch. 7), he says: "In the same way that Cicero wrote to instruct his son, I too am writing to mold you, my sons; for I do not feel any less love for you as children whom I have begotten in the gospel than I would if I had fathered you literally in marriage."[21]

Moreover, Ambrose's *De Officiis* is an important witness to the extension of the word "priest," not just to bishops but also to presbyters. That is, while on more than one occasion Ambrose does indeed refer to himself as a priest, he also applies that term to presbyters. While it is true that Ambrose often uses the word priest or priesthood in reference to the office of bishop, there are yet times when he uses the term *sacerdos* to refer to clerics of the presbyteral rank. (For examples, see book 2, chapter 15, when Ambrose says:

> There are many kinds of generosity. It is not simply a matter of organizing and distributing food to those who lack the basic daily supplies to stay alive. There is also an obligation to give aid and assistance to those who are ashamed to show their needs openly—so long as the resources set aside for the needy as a whole are not exhausted in the process. I am speaking here of a responsibility which needs to be shouldered by someone who is in a responsible position, such as a priest or an almoner [*sacerdotis . . . aut dispensatores*]. Such a man should inform his bishop [*episcopo*] of people who fall into this category.[22]

Also see book 2, chapter 16: "The more the people see you doing good deeds, the more they will love you. I know of many priests [*Scio pluresque sacerdotes*] who have found that the more they have given, the more plentiful their resources have been. The simple fact is, if anyone sees a man busily engaged in good deeds he is happy to give him something to distribute in his rounds of duty [*officio*]."[23] See also his advice (in bk. 2, ch. 24, art. 125): "If you are a priest [*si sacerdotes es*]—or if you are anyone else either, for that matter—you are not to go about provoking quarrels."[24] Or consider the famous maxim that is given in variation several times (in bk. 3, ch. 9, arts. 58–59): "The obligation of the priest or minister [*sacerdotis vel ministris*] is to be helpful to everyone, if possible, and harmful to no one . . . the priest's task [*sacerdotis officio*] is to harm no one, but to be ready to help everyone. . . Let us then observe the

---

20. Ambrose, *De Officiis*, p. 119.

21. Ibid., p. 131.

22. Ambrose, *De Officiis*, p. 305.

23. Ibid., p. 311.

24. Ibid., p. 337.

principle which should govern the duty of a priest [*sacerdotis officio*]: that he should harm no one, not even when provoked or offended by an injustice of any kind."[25]

Zechariah in Ambrose's On Duty

Now for the important, pivotal, even iconic role that Ambrose, in his work on the duties of Christian priests, assigns to Zechariah the Hebrew priest.

Ambrose's *On Duty* begins with the words: "I shall not appear presumptuous, I trust, if I adopt the approach of a teacher when addressing my own sons, for the master of humility himself has said: 'Come, my sons, listen to me: I will teach you the fear of the Lord.'"[26]

"The master of humility" to whom Ambrose refers here is the Old Testament King David. Ambrose calls him "the master of humility" because David's origin was that of a humble shepherd boy, indeed, the least of his father's sons; but he was destined to play a great role in the life of God's people.

Ambrose features David many times in his *De Officiis* and no doubt identified with him: Ambrose, too, was first a leader of the people and only secondly a church leader. The biblical words that Ambrose quotes here are from Ps 34:12, and in Ambrose's day authorship of most of the psalms was attributed to David. However, after setting up his own identity and that of his audience, when it comes to stating his theme, Ambrose invokes not the image of David but that of Zechariah the priest.

Ambrose first broaches the major theme of his work (in bk. 1, ch. 8), where he argues that the concept of "duty" is not just a pagan concept but has its place even in the Bible:

> Let us think about the suitability of the topic itself. Is it an appropriate theme for us to write about "duties"? Is the word fit only for the school of the philosophers, or can it be found in the divine Scriptures as well? Well now, a wonderful thing happened just this day while I was reading the gospel. As though he was encouraging me to write on the subject, the Holy Spirit brought before me a reading which confirmed my view that we too are able to speak of *officium*, or "duty": when Zacharias the priest had become dumb in the temple and was unable to speak, "it came to pass," Scripture says, "that the days of his *officium* were completed; he went away to his own house." From what we read here, then, it is clear that we too are able to speak of *officium*, or "duty." Reason itself has no difficulty with this, either. For the word *officium*, "duty", is, we believe, derived from *efficere*, "to achieve," as though it were *efficium*, "achievement";

25. Ibid., p. 391.
26. Ibid., p. 119.

but, in the interest of euphony, one letter has been changed, and is now known as *officium*.[27] [pp. 131 and 133]

Ambrose is probably quoting here from an "Old Latin" translation of the NT (not Jerome's Vulgate that had not yet, but was soon to enter into, currency). Because of his knowledge and ability with both classical and NT Greek, surely Ambrose knew the meaning of the word *leitourgia*, which itself was the term used by the Septuagint translators to render the Hebrew term of priestly service, *shereth*. In Attic Greek, the word *leitourgia* originally referred not to cultic or religious works undertaken by priests but to public works undertaken by private individuals for the public good. Were the Septuagint translators trying to make a statement, namely, that the true service of men begins with the right service of God? We cannot be certain. But there can be no doubt that Ambrose was well aware of the meaning of the word "office" in the Latin tradition where it connoted not the civic duties of individuals but the public duties of appointed officials. And just as the Septuagint word *leitourgia* would become transformed into the Christian term "liturgy," so too the Latin word "office" would go on to have not only a powerful influence upon our understanding of the duties of statesmen and politicians but also of the Christian clergy. We can see just how powerful that Roman tradition has been if we look at the influence that the Latin term "office" has had upon ecclesiastical Latin and upon the English language in general.

The Latin word *officium* (plural *officia*, dative *officiis*) is derived from the Latin word *opus* and *facio*, the noun meaning "work" and the verb meaning "to do." And thus it had various meanings in ancient Rome, including "public service," "sense of duty," "social courtesy," and religious or civic "ceremony." From this word "officium" we derive our terms for office, both political and religious. The word "office" can refer to work space, "office space," "doctor's office," or faculty offices. But it can refer also to professional competencies and civic responsibilities, such as political terms "term of office," "public office," and "office holders." We also derive from it the military term "officer" (a person who holds a position of rank and authority) and such terms as "official," "officiate" (to conduct a ceremony), "officialdom," and "officious." For the British, an office is a major administrative unit of the national government such as the Foreign Office.

But "officium" is also the source of the religious term used to define religious obligations, as in the terms "divine office" or "office of the dead," and of diocesan officials such as the *officialis*. In former times this term was the official title of what is now called the vicar general of the diocese. The word "office" means professional duties, moral obligations attached to one's station, position or employment, and a

27. Ibid., pp. 131–33.

service or moral charge assigned to one to perform. Today, however, it is used to describe the bishop's canon law expert, his assistant who is in charge of contentious business, that is, marriage and criminal cases. We can see this development in the very title of Isidore of Seville's *De EcclesiasticisOfficii*s. Isidore (ca. 560–636) wrote this work some time after being made archbishop of Seville in 600. It is a valuable source for the Mozarabic liturgy, as well as for the duties and rights of the various orders in the church, from archbishops down to laymen and women.

Zechariah's Meaning for Today

What can we conclude from all this regarding the meaning of Zechariah for priestly ministry today? If Zechariah can be thought to be in some way an exemplar for priests today, then the first lesson he teaches us is that no priest escapes criticism. Instead, all priests can expect to be held to very high standards, and if they fail they can expect to be excoriated for their failure. Even though Zechariah's life was exemplary in all other regards, when he doubted the angel Gabriel he made one serious mistake and, as we have seen, the righteous have never ceased to indict him for it. All the other good things Zechariah had done in his life until then did not matter.

Hopefully, when today's Catholic priest is judged so severely, he will be excoriated by saints like Chrysostom and Aquinas and not just by other sinners who are much like himself or perhaps even worse. But the priest today who is indicted by saints should take heart that God is at times far more merciful than an entire jury of holy men. Remember, he loosened the tongue of the sinful Zechariah to sing his praises in the surpassing language of the canticle called the Benedictus. And, who knows, there might even be one merciful bishop like Ambrose to take the side of an accused priest. But no priest should count on such assistance. Instead, he would do well to work hard at holiness, exercise due diligence regarding his personal moral life and his public, religious duties. In fact, diligence is an important concept in Ambrose's *De Officiis* (as shown in bk. 1, ch. 1, art. 3): "I make no claims, of course, to the glory of the apostles—whoever could, other than those whom the Son of God himself chose? Nor do I claim to have the grace of the prophets, or the power of the evangelists, or the vigilance of the pastors. My wish is only to attain to the attention and diligence towards the divine Scriptures which the apostle ranked last of all among the duties of the saints."[28] No doubt, it is "attention and diligence" toward the divine Scriptures that Ambrose emphasizes here. But "attention and diligence" are important attitudes that can enhance all aspects of priestly life.

---

28. Ambrose, *De Officiis*, p. 119.

And this is where we find the next lesson to be learned from the ministry of Zechariah the priest: never underestimate the value of a simple priest's attention to duty. In that regard, it is important to note that Zechariah was indeed a simple priest, not the high priest, nor even one of the chief priests; he was a regular, ordinary, simple priest, slightly above the status of a Levite. Unfortunately, Christian tradition has often and long obscured this. All of the patristic writers wrongly identify Zechariah as a high priest. John Chrysostom, in the second homily of his *On the Incomprehensible Nature of God*, asserts, "Zechariah had received the honor of the high priesthood."[29] Maximus of Turin, in his Sermon 99, "On the Birth of the Savior," says "when John is conceived, however, Zechariah is struck dumb, the high priest becomes silent."[30] Dionysius the Areopagite's *The Celestial Hierarchies* (ch. 4, pt. 4) includes, "the divine Gabriel announced to Zechariah the high priest." The Venerable Bede (ca. 673–735), in his homily for the Vigil of the Nativity of John the Baptist, says of John: "Who could more fittingly prophesy the transference of the priesthood of the law and its replacement by the priesthood in the gospel than the son of a high priest under the law?"[31] And this error continues in to the Middle Ages; take for example, Aquinas, who, in his *Catena Aurea*, his commentary on the four gospels, follows Bede in seeing Zechariah as a high priest.[32] No doubt these Christian commentators on Zechariah's ministry were influenced by the narrative in Exod 30:7–9 that associates Aaron and his sons with the altar of incense:

> On it Aaron shall burn fragrant incense. Morning after morning, when he prepares the lamps, and again in the evening twilight, when he lights the lamps, he shall burn incense. Throughout your generations this shall be the established incense offering before the Lord. On this altar you shall not offer up any profane incense, or any holocaust or cereal offering; nor shall you pour out a libation upon it. Once a year Aaron shall perform the atonement rite on its horns. Throughout your generations this atonement is to be made once a year with the blood of the atoning sin offering. This altar is most sacred to the Lord.

Nevertheless, this is a truly lamentable error, for it obscures an important moral lesson implicit in Zechariah's story. Luke's account of the ministry of Zechariah in the temple contains a pointed lesson regarding how the trappings of high ecclesiastical office can blind a priest, while attention to duty on the part of a simple, ordinary priest can lead to his openness to the grace of God. It was not to a high priest, nor even to one of the chief priests, but to a simple priest that the Angel Gabriel was

---

29. Chrysostom, *On the Incomprehensible*, p. 74.

30. Maximus, *The Sermons*, p. 225.

31. Bede, *Homilies on the Gospels*, p. 189.

32. Aquinas, *Catena Aurea*, Vol. 3, part 1, p. 12.

sent with his words of revelation. Indeed, not just Luke but even the other gospels witness to the fact that opposition to Jesus came principally if not exclusively from the hierarchy and the theologians and not from the simple priests. Take for example how in Mark's gospel the phrase "the chief priests and the scribes" as a description of opposition to Jesus. This phrase becomes almost a slogan, an ominous refrain: in Mark 8:31, we hear how "He began to teach them that the Son of Man must suffer greatly and be rejected by the elders, *the chief priests, and the scribes.*" And then in Mark 10:33, we hear Jesus tell his disciples, "Behold, we are going up to Jerusalem, and the Son of Man will be handed over to *the chief priests and the scribes.*" In Mark 11:18, we read how "*The chief priests and the scribes* came to hear of it and were seeking a way to put him to death." And in Mark 14:1, we are told, "The Passover and the Feast of Unleavened Bread were to take place in two days' time. So *the chief priests and the scribes* were seeking a way to arrest him by treachery and put him to death." Occasionally the chief priests are linked with other opponents of Jesus, as in Mark 14:55, "*The chief priests and the entire Sanhedrin* kept trying to obtain testimony against Jesus in order to put him to death." In Mark 15:1, "As soon as morning came, *the chief priests with the elders and the scribes*, that is, the whole Sanhedrin, held a council. They bound Jesus, led him away, and handed him over to Pilate." Mark 15:31, "Likewise *the chief priests, with the scribes*, mocked him among themselves and said, 'He saves others; he cannot save himself.'" The implicit moral lesson is not lost on modern commentators such as E. Earle Ellis, who, in his *The Gospel of Luke*, concludes: "Completing the week's service assigned to his order, Zechariah returned home . . . Thus the country priest, held in benevolent contempt by the more eminent ecclesiastics, fulfilled the proverb, 'God resists the proud, but gives grace to the humble' (Jas 5:6)."[33] Similarly, Rick Strelen, in his *Luke the Priest*, says there is "some irony in the word of God coming to the son of a village priest and not to the high priests of Jerusalem."[34]

And, arguably, there are even further implications in this moral lesson: take for example Luke 1:7, which tells us that Zechariah was "advanced in years." We don't know precisely how old Zechariah was at the time of his allotment for the incense offering in the temple. Nevertheless it is fair to estimate he had been coming to the Jerusalem temple for many, many years, each time performing the small role allotted to him. Yes, this time he, so to speak "won big," and "came up a winner" in the temple lottery, in that he at last got a role of honor assigned but once in a lifetime to an ordinary, regular, simple priest. And so it is with most regular priests today, or as Vatican II prefers to call them, "priests of the second rank." Most of them will

33. Ellis, *The Gospel of Luke*, p. 69.
34. Strelen, *Luke the Priest*, p. 119.

spend an obscure life buried amid their numerous duties and never receive any significant public notice or recognition, much less some ecclesiastical honor. Today it has become common practice that such honorific titles as "papal chamberlain" and "domestic prelate" are used to give distinction to a newly appointed episcopal vicar rather than to honor the lifetime achievement of a conscientious, hard-working pastor.

This hardly exhausts the lessons to be learned from the priestly ministry of Zechariah. For example, Luke's story of Zechariah on duty in the temple should alert today's regular, ordinary parish priest to the fact that in his own ministry he sometimes repeats the experience of Zechariah who emerged from the sanctuary to speak a word of hope to the crowd. By that I mean while the ministry of a regular parish priest today is often as systematic and ritualized as Zechariah's in the Jerusalem temple, today's regular priest is also often presented with the opportunity to speak just the right word. The parish priest can speak the words people need to hear when he emerges from the sanctuary to speak at a hospital bedside, a funeral parlor, a parish meeting.

Finally, a parish priest might want to consider how later church history provides us with more than one example of situations in which the orthodoxy of the simple parish priest is contrasted with the heterodoxy of the hierarchy and theologians. In Newman's *The Arians of the Fourth Century*, Appendix 5 is entitled "Orthodoxy of the Faithful during Arianism." There Newman contrasts not only the fidelity of the laity versus the hierarchy but he also takes note of the fidelity of the lower clergy. In the opening paragraph of that appendix Newman says:

> The episcopate, whose action was so prompt and concordant at Nicea on the rise of Arianism, did not, as a class or order of men, play a good part in the troubles consequent upon the Council; and the laity did. The Catholic people, in the length and breadth of Christendom, were the obstinate champions of Catholic truth, and the bishops were not. Of course there were great and illustrious exceptions; first, Athanasius, Hilary, the Latin Eusebius, and Phoebadius; and after them, Basil, the two Gregories, and Ambrose; there are others, too, who suffered, if they did nothing else, as Eustathius, Paulus, Paulinus, and Dionysius; and the Egyptian bishops, whose weight was small in the Church in proportion to the great power of their Patriarch. And, on the other hand, as I shall say presently, there were exceptions to the Christian heroism of the laity, especially in some of the great towns. And, again, in speaking of the laity, I speak inclusively of their parish-priests (so to call them), at least in many places.[35]

---

35. Newman, *Arians of the Fourth Century*, p. 445.

Later, Newman specifies of these parish-priests, "there were numbers of clergy who stood by the laity and acted as their centres and guides."[36]

Yet another example of the blessed ministry of parish priests in contrast to the vagaries of not just bishops but also learned theologians is offered us by Blaise Pascal's war against the moral laxism of the casuists of his time. *The Oxford Companion to Christian Thought* (2000) defines casuistry as "the study of relating general moral principles to particular cases; especially analyzing predicaments which appear to involve a conflict of principles, such as whether it is permissible to lie to protect a confidence."[37] Casuistry arose as parish priests had to hear confessions and then determine the genuine guilt of the confessing person by judging the subjective circumstances of the basic principles of the Ten Commandments to individual cases where there might be some extenuating circumstances. In the post-Tridentine period, however, there developed a dramatic contrast between rigorists and laxists on this issue. The laxists employed a method of moral probabilism that lead to minimization, rationalization, and general moral permissiveness. The great French mathematician and savant Blaise Pascal (1623–1662) in his literary work, *The Provincial Letters*, attacked and satirized certain theologians and priests who practiced probabilism. In 1658, Pascal wrote a letter wherein he sketches what he feels would be a good response to a book then in circulation called *Apology for the Casuists*. That letter contains a tribute from Pascal to parish priests who kept the faith while theologians and liberal diocesan priests played fast and loose with it: "And we have reason to grieve at seeing some loose priests and some corrupt casuists who introduce this laxity, we have reason to bless God because the parish priests of the Church resist them."[38]

36. Ibid,. p. 465.
37. Mahoney, "Casuistry," p. 98.
38. Pascal, *Great Shorter Works*, p. 185.

11

The New Liturgy According to the New Priest

Jesus of Nazareth

ON A WALL INSIDE the entrance to the classroom building of the School of Theology where I teach, a large cross hangs. This cross is not a crucifix, that is, the body of the dying Christ is not displayed upon it. Rather, Christ stands before his cross, neither writhing in pain nor resting in death, but alive and raising his hands in blessing. Indeed, Christ is portrayed not dying but rather triumphing over death. Moreover, he is not nearly naked, as is the corpus on a crucifix, wearing only a loin cloth. Rather, he is amply and richly clothed in priestly vestments, and, more precisely, Catholic Mass vestments. Here, he is represented wearing not just an alb but also a stole and chasuble.

No doubt, this portrayal of Jesus as a cultic figure has the potential to offend some. I cannot help but think that some Protestant Christians, especially those descended from the radical wing of the sixteenth-century reformation (those churches that reject all sacraments but baptism and any sense of liturgy, that is, ritual worship), would find this portrayal of Jesus as the minister of a cult very offensive and totally wrongheaded. I also suspect some Catholic Christians would find such a portrayal of Jesus in Mass vestments as quaint, and thus less than appropriate. I have in mind those Catholics who have had some formal education in Scripture, hermeneutics, and church history. Those people might well know that, while Jesus in the gospels is given many titles such as rabbi, prophet, teacher, messiah, and even king, nowhere in the gospels is he given the title of priest. This is understandable because priesthood in Israel was hereditary, not vocational; and Jesus was not born into a Levitical, that is, a priestly family. Thus I feel certain some Catholic Christians would insist that the portrayal of Jesus as a priest is a late theological development found but once in Scripture (in the Epistle to the Hebrews); and therefore might argue that the idea of any Christian clergy as having a priestly identity is an even later development in the history of Christian doctrine.

However, despite my acknowledgement that some might be put off regarding the portrayal of Jesus as a priest, I want to caution such critics that the portrayal of Jesus as a priest, a cultic figure, is not limited to the Epistle to the Hebrews. Rather, there are several other passages in the New Testament that suggest Jesus is a priest. One passage portrays him as dressed in priestly vestments, and other New Testament passages suggest not only that Jesus was a priest but that he both commissioned some of his disciples to act as priests and that he himself created a new cult.

That is why at this point in this book, after having looked at numerous biblical portrayals in both the Old and the New Testaments of Levitical priests, it is now important that we look at some of the New Testament portrayals of Jesus as the new priest initiating a new liturgy. These portrayals have important implications not just for Christology, that is, our understanding of Jesus, but also for ecclesiology, in particular our understanding of certain ecclesiastical ministries. Here we will first examine the evident and bold portrayal of the priesthood of Christ in the Epistle to the Hebrews. We will then look carefully at the other more subtle but equally sentientious, meaningful New Testament portrayals of Jesus as a priest (Luke 24:50–53, John 19:23–24, Eph 5:1–2). Next we shall look at gospel passages that suggest Jesus saw himself as a priestly messiah (Matt 22:41–46, Mark 12:35–37, Luke 20:41–44). And then we will look at a gospel passage that suggests Jesus bestowed a priestly character on a select group of his disciples (John 17) and yet another biblical passage that says Jesus instituted a new cult (1Cor 11:23–25). Finally, we shall examine how these sententious priestly images of Christ and his disciples came to be obscured.

Christ as Priest in the Epistle to the Hebrews

One particular work of the NT clearly and undisputedly attributes priesthood to Jesus, and that is the work called the Epistle to the Hebrews. We need to examine it carefully so that we understand the author's rationale and argument. Let me begin by saying something about its author and its intended audience.

Very few modern scholars maintain that the Epistle to the Hebrews was written by Saint Paul. Some in the early church attributed its authorship to Paul because there is a reference to Paul's preaching companion, Timothy, in the concluding paragraph. Heb 13:23 reads, "I must let you know that our brother Timothy has been set free." Even so, the vast majority of modern biblical scholars insist both the thought and language of the Epistle to the Hebrews are significantly different from what is found in the Pauline letters. Even the early church was much divided on this matter. Tertullian attributed its authorship to Paul's other occasional companion, Barnabas. But even those who did claim the Epistle to the Hebrews was of Pauline authorship often had to resort to ingenious ideas to explain the striking differences in style and thought between it and the Pauline letters. For example, Clement of Alexandria explained the differences in style by the hypothesis that Paul wrote Hebrews in Hebrew, which was later translated into Greek. Origen believed that the ideas were those of Paul, but that Hebrews was written by an unknown who recorded what he remembered Paul had said.

Modern critics agree that the author must have been a very learned man because his Greek style is the most polished of all the NT writings. Moreover, he might very well have been educated in Alexandria, because he shows himself conversant with a number of terms drawn from Hellenistic literature and the philosophical school, the Platonism which emanated from Alexandria. Also, the author employs a method of allegorical biblical exegesis that is very similar to that employed by the Jewish scholar Philo of Alexandria. Of the Christians known to us from the NT, Apollos of Alexandria (Acts 18:24-28) best fits that description. And for that reason Martin Luther long ago suggested Apollos might well be the author of the Epistle to the Hebrews. However, the evidence is hardly conclusive.

As for its intended audience, just as with most other NT epistles that are occasional works, that is, written to a particular Christian community to address a particular problem within that community, so too here there is evidence that the Epistle to the Hebrews was written to a group of Jewish Christians who were undergoing a trial from which some appear to be on the verge of lapsing into apostasy. That they are Jewish Christians is suggested by two things. Though the Epistle to the Hebrews does not, like other NT epistles, begin with a formal salutation that identifies both its author and its audience, nevertheless, the very opening words of the Epistle to the Hebrews suggests that its audience is an audience of Jewish Christians. From Heb1:1–2: "In times past, God spoke in partial and various ways to our ancestors through the prophets; in these last days, he spoke to us through a son, whom he made heir of all things and through whom he created the universe." The second thing that suggests this epistle was written to an audience of Jewish Christians is that it constantly makes references to the historic experience of ancient Israel. For example, Heb 2:16 makes reference to "the descendants of Abraham." Then there are references to Abraham (7:4; 11:8, 17), Moses (3:1–5; 11:23–28) and the law of Moses (10:28), Aaron (5:4), Joshua (4:8), Rahab (11:31), Gideon, Barak, Samson, Jephthah, David, and Samuel (11:32), the Jewish temple liturgy (5:1–3; 9:1–7, 19–22), and particularly arcane Jewish traditions, such as the figure of "Melchizedek, king of Salem and priest of God Most High" (7:1) who is referred to no less than nine times in the Epistle to the Hebrews and of whom we shall treat at length later.

It is also important we understand that the author writes to this community of Jewish Christians because they are undergoing a crisis of faith: from the beginning of their conversion they experienced persecution for their faith, but now they are undergoing yet another trial, a trial of doubt and wavering. We see this in Heb 10:32–36: "Remember the days past when, after you had been enlightened, you endured a great contest of suffering. At times you were publicly exposed to abuse and affliction; at other times you associated yourselves with those so treated. You even joined in the sufferings of those in prison and joyfully accepted the confiscation of your property, knowing that you had a better and lasting possession. Therefore do not throw away your confidence; it will have great recompense. You need endurance to do the will of God and receive what he has promised."

To give them confidence and reassurance, the author of the Epistle to the Hebrews spends the largest part of his letter, chapters 4–10, developing the theme that his audience or readers should take comfort from the thought that Jesus too had suffered but is now in heaven interceding for them. The author goes on to say that Jesus' death was his own sacrificial offering to God, comparable to a temple offering. Indeed, in those chapters the author repeatedly draws a comparison between the ministry of Jesus' life and death and that of the Jewish high priest's ministry in the Jerusalem temple on its most solemn feast, the Day of Atonement. Recall that on the Day of Atonement the high priest entered into the holy of holies to offer sacrifice there to God. Thus the author argues that Jesus was not simply a Jewish priest but was the one true great high priest who had made it not just into the inner sanctum of the Jerusalem temple but had penetrated the veil of heaven itself.

There is clear evidence that the author of the Epistle to the Hebrews is well aware that his is a sententious and bold thesis, indeed, one that his audience might not readily grasp. And he is quite defensive about this. From his words in Heb 5:11–14, we see where he upbraids his audience for not being as learned as they should be: "About this we have much to say, and it is difficult to explain, for you have become sluggish in hearing. Although you should be teachers by this time, you need to have someone teach you again the basic elements of the utterance of God. You need milk, not solid food. Everyone who lives on milk lacks experience of the word of righteousness, for he is a child. But solid food is for the mature, for those whose faculties are trained by practice to discern good and evil."

And then in Heb 6:1–3, he goes on to explain: "Therefore, let us leave behind the basic teaching about Christ and advance to maturity, without laying the foundation all over again: repentance from dead works and faith in God, instruction about baptisms and laying on of hands, resurrection of the dead and eternal judgment. And we shall do this, if only God permits."

On the other hand, in defense of his audience and us too, I think it should be said the way he presents his thesis is rather complicated. No doubt, his thesis is initially presented in a quite simple fashion. This theme is first broached in the epistle's conclusion of chapter 4, where it says in verses 14–16: "Therefore, since we have a great high priest who has passed through the heavens, Jesus, the Son of God, let us hold fast to our confession. For we do not have a high priest who is unable to sympathize with our weaknesses, but one who has similarly been tested in every way, yet without sin. So let us confidently approach the throne of grace to receive mercy and to find grace for timely help."

However, when he gets into explaining his thesis, he employs literary references that might have been as obscure to his audience as they might be to many of us today. I am referring to his references to the figure of Melchizedek. He first broaches this theme in Heb 5:1–10:

> Every high priest is taken from among men and made their representative before God, to offer gifts and sacrifices for sins. He is able to deal patiently with the ignorant and erring, for he himself is beset by weakness and so, for this reason, must make sin offerings for himself as well as for the people. No one takes this honor upon himself but only when called by God, just as Aaron was. In the same way, it was not Christ who glorified himself in becoming high priest, but rather the one who said to him: / "You are my son; / this day I have begotten you"; / just as he says in another place: / "You are a priest forever / according to the order of Melchizedek." / In the days when he was in the flesh, he offered prayers and supplications with loud cries and tears to the one who was able to save him from death, and he was heard because of his reverence. Son though he was, he learned obedience from what he suffered; and when he was made perfect, he became the source of eternal salvation for all who obey him, declared by God high priest according to the order of Melchizedek.

No doubt, the author chose to relate Jesus to Melchizedek to give Jesus some historical lineage. Remember, because he is writing to Jews, and because priesthood in Israel was hereditary, he has to find a way to explain how Jesus can be considered a priest. He does it by employing a figure from the Old Testament.

To understand this portrayal of Jesus as "high priest according to the order of Melchizedek," we need to learn something about Melchizedek. Melchizedek is a figure who appears only twice in the Old Testament, once in Genesis 14 and once in Psalm 110. In Genesis 14, Melchizedek appears as a central figure in a narrative about what happened to the Hebrew patriarch Abraham when he went to rescue his nephew Lot, who had been taken captive by a coalition of Canaanite tribal chieftains. Gen 14:18–20 describes an incident that occurred to Abraham when he was living "near the terebinth of Mamre, which is at Hebron." (A terebinth is a small tree of the cashew family, *pistacia terebinthus.*) Abraham's nephew Lot fell victim to tribal warfare among the tribal chieftains, or sheiks, in the land of Canaan and was taken captive by a coalition army of four tribal chieftains—Chedorlaomer, king of Elam; Tidal, king of Goiim; Amraphel, king of Shinar; and Arioch, king of Ellasar. In Gen 14:14–16, we are told: "When Abram heard that his nephew had been captured, he mustered three hundred and eighteen retainers, born in his house, and went in pursuit as far as Dan. He and his party deployed against them at night, defeated them, and pursued them as far as Hobah, which is north of Damascus. He recovered all the possessions, besides bringing back his kinsman Lot and his possessions, along with the women and the other captives."

Then we are told of how Abraham, on his way back to Hebron, encountered two figures: one a menace, the other a blessing. He is greeted by two kings, the threatening king of Sodom and the welcoming king of Salem. Of the first king we are told in Gen 14:17, "When Abram returned from the victory over Chedorlaomer and the kings who were allied with him, the king of Sodom went out to greet him in the Valley of Shaveh." And in Gen 14:21–24: "The king of Sodom said to Abram, 'Give me the people; the goods you keep.' But Abram replied to the king of Sodom: 'I have sworn to the LORD, God Most High, the creator of heaven and earth, that I would not take so much as a thread or a sandal strap from anything that is yours, lest you should say, "I made Abram rich." Nothing for me except what my servants have used up and the share that is due to the men who joined me—Aner, Eschcol, and Mamre; let them take their share.'"

But in Gen 14:18-20 we are told of the arrival of another king: "Melchizedek, king of Salem, brought out bread and wine, and being a priest of God Most High, he blessed Abram with these words: / 'Blessed be Abram by God the Most High, / the creator of heaven and earth; / And blessed be God Most High, / who delivered your foes into your hand.' / Then Abram gave him a tenth of everything."

Melchizedek is that rare combination of both priest and king. In another OT passage that peculiar, dual character is invoked to make the point that the Davidic Messiah will be not just a king but also a priest, as was Melchizedek. Genesis 14 is not the only place in the Old Testament where Melchizedek appears. Indeed, Melchizedek also appears in Psalm 110, a messianic psalm. It is identified as "a psalm of David," supposedly written by King David; and, in this psalm, David recounts how God promised him that one of his heirs or descendants would be made Messiah and Son of God. I quote it here in its entirety:

> The LORD said to my Lord: "Sit at my right hand / till I make your enemies your footstool." / The scepter of your power the LORD will stretch forth from Zion: / "Rule in the midst of your enemies. / Yours is princely power in the

day of your birth, in holy splendor; / before the daystar, like the dew, / I have begotten you." / The Lord has sworn, and he will not repent: / "You are a priest forever, according to the order of Melchizedek." / The Lord is at your right hand; / he will crush kings on the day of his wrath. / He will do judgment on the nations, / heaping up corpses; / he will crush heads over the wide earth. / From the brook by the wayside he will drink; / therefore will he lift up his head.

It is important we now look at some other, more subtle, portrayals of Jesus as a priest. These portrayals describe certain actions of Jesus in a way that invokes classic images of Israelite priesthood and thus suggest a meaningful comparison, indeed, a sententious claim about Jesus himself, his work, and his priestly character.

Christ as Priest in Luke 24

For an example of this method, let us look to the author of Luke-Acts. More than one student of the Bible has claimed that the portrayal of Jesus in the Gospel according to Luke ends with a blatant attempt to portray him as a priest. The following passage is the ascension narrative that concludes Luke's gospel. Luke 24:50–53 reads: "Then he led them [out] as far as Bethany, raised his hands, and blessed them. As he blessed them he parted from them and was taken up to heaven. They did him homage and then returned to Jerusalem with great joy, and they were continually in the temple praising God."

Several modern commentators have claimed that Jesus raising his hands here in benediction is a conscious, intentional effort on the part of Luke, the gospel writer, to portray Jesus in the posture assumed by Jewish priests in blessing. For comparison they cite Lev 9:22, "Aaron then raised his hands over the people and blessed them." Or as in Sir 50:19–20, "the high priest completed the services at the altar by presenting to God the sacrifices due; then coming down he would raise his hands over all the congregation of Israel. The blessing of the Lord would be upon his lips." One example of this claim that Luke is intentionally portraying Jesus as a priest is in the argument of P. A. van Stempvoort in his essay "The Interpretation of the Ascension in Luke and Acts" (which appeared in the journal *New Testament Studies* 5 [1958–1959] 30–42). Another example is the thesis of Gerhard Lohfink in his book-length study of the ascension, *Die Himmelfahrt Jesu* (Munich: Kosel, 1971, pp. 167–69). And a third example is the contention of Mikeal C. Parsons, in his essay "Narrative Closure and Openness in the Plot of the Third Gospel," which appeared in the "Society of Biblical Literature 1986 Seminar Papers" (Atlanta: Scholars Press, 1986, 201–23). Parsons argues that it is no accident that Luke's gospel opens and closes in the Jerusalem temple. The reader needs to know that this opinion that Luke is intentionally portraying Jesus as a priest is not shaped merely by denominational affiliation. Of the three exegetes I have mentioned, only Lohfink is a Catholic priest. Consider also the contention of Professor Rick Strelan of the University of Queensland, Australia, a Lutheran minister. Strelan, in his book-length study *Luke the Priest* argues that not only does Luke consciously portray Jesus as a priest and focuses upon the temple, but Luke himself was a former Jewish priest.

Christ as Priest in John 19

Yet another indirect allusion to the priestly character of Jesus occurs in John's gospel. This allusion is found in John 19:23–24, the passion narrative: "When the soldiers had crucified Jesus, they took his clothes and divided them into four shares, a share for each soldier. They also took his tunic, but the tunic was seamless, woven in one piece from the top down. So they said to one another, 'Let's not tear it, but cast lots for it to see whose it will be,' in order that the passage of scripture might be fulfilled [that says]: 'They divided my garments among them and for my vesture they cast lots.' This is what the soldiers did."

Raymond Brown, in his two-volume commentary on John's gospel, treats this episode at length. Brown, who pays special attention to Jesus' seamless tunic, tells us how a great many interpreters see the seamless tunic as an intentional parallelism of Jesus with the high priest, insisting that Jesus died not only as a king (that is what the sign above his cross proclaimed) but also as a priest. Exod 28:4 and Lev 16:4 both specify a linen tunic for the high priest. Brown goes on to note that the theme of Jesus as priest and king seems to appear in Rev 1:13: "one like a son of man wearing an ankle-length robe," which some argue is an intentional imitation of the description in Exod 29:5 of Aaron in his priestly vestments.[1]

Christ as Priest and Offering in Ephesians 5

Yet another NT portrayal of Jesus as a priest can be found in the Epistle to the Ephesians 5:1–2: "So be imitators of God, as beloved children, and live in love, as Christ loved us and handed himself over for us as a sacrificial offering to God for a fragrant aroma." The authorship of this epistle has been greatly contested. The consensus of modern biblical scholarship finds this not to be a genuine Pauline letter. But because this letter exhibits numerous close contacts with Pauline literature and thought, it is most probably the work of a disciple of Paul's, who was writing before AD 90.

1. Brown, *Gospel According to John*, Vol. 2, pp. 920–22.

Regardless of who wrote the previously cited passage, it is still interesting to note that Jesus here is portrayed as performing a distinctly priestly function, namely that of offering a sacrifice. Indeed, he is portrayed as both priest and sacrifice, both priest and offering. Of this passage, Jean Galot in his *Theology of the Priesthood* says: "The two terms, 'offering' and 'sacrifice,' taken from Psalm 40:7, are likely to recall the two main kinds of ritual sacrifices, bloody and unbloody. Jointly, they suggest that Jesus realizes in his own death all that was regarded as sacrifice in Jewish worship. The sacrificial cult is realized in him in its entirety. This means that Jesus is the priest who realizes in its fullness the goal which Jewish priesthood sought to achieve."[2]

The Ordination of the Apostles in John 17

In addition to all the previous NT portrayals of Jesus as a priest, it is important we look at a gospel passage that several exegetes have claimed portrays not only Jesus but his apostles as priests. The passage is the last supper narrative in John's gospel. Modern commentators have claimed to find in John's gospel more than one passage that contains priestly overtones, overtones that are evidence of this gospel writer's self-conscious attempt to portray Jesus as a priest. Chapter 17 of John's gospel portrays Jesus in the conclusion of the last supper with his disciples. This narration had begun in chapter 13 with Jesus washing his disciples' feet, the announcement of Judas's betrayal, an issuing of a new commandment, the prediction of Peter's denial, and several discourses: the vine and branches (15:1–8), love of the brethren (15:9–17), the world's hatred (15:18–27), and the coming of the Advocate (ch. 16). Chapter 17 contains a long prayer by Jesus to God the Father, said over the disciples.

Because of its language of intercession, chapter 17 of John's gospel was long ago identified as Christ's high-priestly prayer. Indeed, this was the opinion of Cyril of Alexandria (d. 444) in his commentary on John 17:9. This was also the opinion of Benedictine theologian and exegete Rupert of Deutz (ca. 1075–1130), in his Homilies on the Gospel according to John (PL 169, 764). But it was only in modern times that John 17 came to be termed Jesus' "High-Priestly prayer." This was the work of a Lutheran theologian at the University of Rostock, David Chytraeus (1530–1600). Many modern exegetes call our attention to the passage in chapter 17 of John's gospel wherein Jesus employs not just the language of intercession but also the language of ordination. I am referring to John 17:17–19: "Consecrate them in the truth. Your word is truth. As you sent me into the world, so I sent them into the world. And I consecrate myself for them, so that they also may be consecrated in truth." These exegetes will point out that the word "consecrate" (*hagiason*) used here may well be

2. Galot, *Theology of Priesthood*, pp. 93–94.

an intentional echoing, indeed, a quotation of the words of God to Moses regarding the ordination of Aaron and his sons in Exod 28:40–41: "For the glorious adornment of Aaron's sons you shall have tunics and sashes and turbans made. With these you shall clothe your brother Aaron and his sons. Anoint and ordain them, consecrating [*hagiaseis*] them as my priests." Moreover, this language of consecration is used several other times in the Pentateuch, or Torah, to refer to ritual ordination (for example, in Exod 40:13 and Lev 8:30). Seizing upon John's conspicuous use of the language of ordination, André Feuillet, Sulpician biblical scholar and professor of theology at the Institut Catholique de Paris, published in 1972 his study of John 17 in *La Sacerdoce Du Christ et de Ses Ministres* (English translation, *The Priesthood of Christ and His Ministers*). Feuillet's whole argument in this book is that John 17:17–19 was John the evangelist's way of making clear that the Twelve, at their last supper with Jesus, were indeed formally ordained as priests.

Evaluation of NT Images of Christ as Priest

All these priestly images of Christ, even the explicit one in the Epistle to the Hebrews, has been challenged, delimited, or even dismissed. The explicit portrayal of Jesus as a priest in the Epistle to the Hebrews, for example, has been severely limited by those who point to those passages in Hebrews that make it clear Jesus offered himself once and for all and is now seated at the right hand of the Father.

There has been no dearth of exegetes who are quick to point out that the author of the Epistle to the Hebrews declares that although Christ may be seen as a priest, his ministry is over, completed. According to Heb 9:11–12, "but when Christ came as high priest of the good things that have come to be, passing through the greater and more perfect tabernacle not made by hands, that is, not belonging to this creation, he entered once for all into the sanctuary." And in Heb 9:25–26, "Not that he might offer himself repeatedly, as he the high priest enters each year into the sanctuary with blood that is not his own; if that were so, he would have had to suffer repeatedly from the foundation of the World. But now once for all he has appeared at the end of the ages to take away sin by his sacrifice." Also, in Heb 10:12, "But this one offered one sacrifice for sins, and took his seat forever at the right hand of God; now he waits until his enemies are made his footstool."

Nor is there any unanimity of critical opinion regarding other NT passages that suggest, more subtly, that Jesus is a priest. The meaning of each has been disputed. For example, Joel B. Green in his commentary on the Gospel of Luke, while duly noting such priestly interpretations, insists:

Jesus' final act closely parallels the behavior of priests in Lev 9:22 and especially Sir 50:20–22, suggesting to some interpreters that Luke closes his Gospel with reference to a priestly Jesus. If this view were supported by the narrative, it is certainly of interest that Jesus would thus function as a priest outside of the temple, and, indeed, outside of Jerusalem. It cannot be overlooked, however, that Luke otherwise demonstrates no interest in portraying Jesus in priestly garb, so that an alternative explanation for these parallels seems advisable. Jesus' blessing his disciples is important enough to be mentioned twice in rapid succession (vv. 50, 51), and it occurs just prior to his final departure. This suggests that the pronouncement of blessing is modeled on the leave-taking of such personages as Moses (Deuteronomy 33) and Abraham (Genesis 49).[3]

Similarly, Craig S. Keener, in his commentary on the Gospel of John says of John 17:

Traditionally some have viewed Jesus' intercession in this passage in terms of the OT role of high priest . . . But Jewish tradition also emphasized the intercessory role of prophets; more significantly, the probably testamentary character of the final discourse might point to patriarchal blessings, particularly the prayer and blessing of Moses (Deut 32–33), as background.[4]

We should also note that even if the priestly connotations of these passages are accepted, it is possible to question motivation of all these authors, including the author of the Epistle to the Hebrews and the evangelists Luke and John. It could be argued that these portrayals of Jesus as a priest reflect more the subjective agenda of the literary authors rather than any truly important or substantive doctrinal teaching. For example, that many temple priests converted to Christianity seems apparent from Acts 6:7, "Even a large group of priests were becoming obedient to the faith." Thus, Rick Strelan in his recent book *Luke the Priest*, argues that Luke himself is one of these converted Jewish priests referred to in Acts. Also, it has been argued that something similar happened in the Epistle to the Hebrews. In that work too either the author himself was a converted former priest or he wrote that work for an audience consisting of former Jewish priests converting to the Christian faith. So too some have argued there is telltale evidence in John's gospel that the beloved disciple was a priest: that he was able to get ready entrance into the high priest's house, for example, is evidence that he would have been known to the staff there (John 18:15–26). And the fact that he is described as hesitating to enter the tomb of Jesus until he was assured that it was empty (John 20:5–6), suggests he was a priest who was consciously avoiding the cultic impurity that would come from contact with a dead body.

3. Green, *Commentary on Luke*, pp. 860–61.
4. Keener, *Gospel of John*, Vol. 2, p. 1051.

Why does the author of the Epistle to the Hebrews think that this theme of Christ as priest is so important? This theme would have been particularly appealing to and consoling for Jewish priests whose conversion to Christianity had caused them to be ostracized, and even persecuted, by their fellow Jews. This theme might also have been particularly consoling for Jewish Christians who had recently endured the siege and destruction of Jerusalem, along with its temple and the temple cult, by a Roman army under the leadership of Titus. Heb 2:18 makes it clear this letter is addressed to "those who are being tested." Heb 10:32–36 is even more precise as to the kind of trial they are undergoing or have undergone: "Remember the days past when, after you had been enlightened, you endured a great contest of suffering. At times you were publicly exposed to abuse and affliction; at other times you associated yourselves with those so treated. You even joined in the sufferings of those in prison and joyfully accepted the confiscation of your property, knowing that you had a better and lasting possession." Such a passage has led Catholic exegete Ceslas Spicq to propose that the audience for whom "To the Hebrews" was written consisted of Jerusalem priests who had become Christians and who fled Jerusalem, perhaps to Caesarea, after the destruction of the temple in the year 70. However, that it was written after the destruction of the temple is not totally apparent. If it was written after the destruction of the temple, it is strange that its references to the Jewish temple cult are all in the present tense. For example, see Heb 9:6–10. Here I italicize the words that indicate the present tense or time:

> With these arrangements for worship, the priests, in performing their service, go into the outer tabernacle repeatedly, but the high priest alone *goes* into the inner one once a year, not without blood that he *offers* for himself and for the sins of the people. In this way the holy Spirit shows that the way into the sanctuary had not yet been revealed while the outer tabernacle still had its place. This is symbol of *the present time, in which gifts and sacrifices are offere*d that cannot perfect the worshiper in conscience but only in matters of food and drink and various ritual washings: regulations concerning the flesh, imposed until the time of the new order.

However, after having said this, it is important to note that there is considerable evidence to suggest that this theme of Jesus as a priest like Melchizedek is hardly original to the author of the Epistle to the Hebrews. Instead, this theme probably originated with Jesus himself. More precisely, the claim from the author of Hebrews that Jesus was a priest need not be seen as purely and simply an example of wild-eyed theological speculation, an extravagant theological conceit, a highly imaginative flight of theological fancy or invention with no historical roots. Quite the contrary, it is possible to argue that Jesus during his lifetime not only made sententious claims suggesting his priesthood but in his final hours performed at least one action that made undeniably clear the fact that he viewed his work as that of priest.

Jesus' Self-Identity as a Priest

There is considerable evidence to suggest that Jesus of Nazareth knew Psalm 110 very well, had spent much time studying it, thinking about it and, in his public debates and preaching, made much use of it. To give an account, all three of the synoptic gospels (Matt 22:41–46, Mark 12:35–37, Luke 20:41–44) portray Jesus as employing Psalm 110 in rabbinic or scribal debate over the identity of the messiah with three different groups: a general crowd in the temple area, a group of Pharisees, and a group of Sadducees. For example, in Mark 12:35–37, we hear Jesus quote to the crowd the opening line of Psalm 110 (NAB): "As Jesus was teaching in the temple area he said, 'How do the scribes claim that the Messiah is the son of David?' David himself, inspired by the holy Spirit, said: 'The Lord said to my lord, sit at my right hand until I place your enemies under your feet.' David Himself calls him 'lord'; so how is he his son? The great crowd heard this with delight."

In Matt 22:41–46, Jesus makes reference to Psalm 110 in a discussion with the Pharisees: "When the Pharisees were gathered together, Jesus questioned them, saying, 'What is your opinion about the Messiah? Whose son is he?' They replied, "David's." He said to them, 'How, then does David, inspired by the Spirit, call him "lord," saying: "The Lord said to my lord, 'Sit at my right hand until I place your enemies under your feet?' If David calls him, "lord," how can he be his son?' No one was able to answer him a word, nor from that day on did anyone dare to ask him any more questions."

In Luke 20:41–44, Jesus' reference to Psalm 110 comes after a debate about resurrection with some Sadducees, representatives of Jerusalem's priestly aristocracy: "Then he said to them, 'How do they claim that the Messiah is the son of David? For David himself in the Book of Psalms says: "The Lord said to my lord, 'Sit at my right hand till I make your enemies your footstool.' Now if David calls him "lord," how can he be his son?"'"

No doubt, in none of the three gospel passages just quoted does Jesus quote the whole of Psalm 110. Rather he quotes but the first line. Nevertheless, this should not be taken as indication that he found only that opening line helpful and ignored the rest of that psalm. This quoting of only the first line of a psalm was a standard narrative tool, a method of shorthand reference. An apt comparison is the synoptic narratives of Jesus' death. In both Mark 15:34 and Matt 27:46, Jesus is portrayed as uttering only the first line of Psalm 22, "My God, my God why have you forsaken me." Because that line alone is quoted, some might conclude his words there sound like a cry of despair. But it is more reasonable to assume he is simply quoting the first line of a psalm which, though it does indeed open with a cry of despair, ends on a note of triumphal hope, as in Ps 22:23–24: "I will proclaim your name to my brethren; in the midst of the assembly I will praise you: 'You who fear the Lord, praise him; all you descendants of Jacob, give glory to him; revere him, all you descendants of Israel! For he has not spurned nor distained the wretched man in his misery, nor did he turn his face away from him, but when he cried out to him, he heard him.'" So too it would be a mistake to think that Jesus' only interest in Psalm 110 is its opening line.

But these previous passages do not exhaust all of Jesus' references to Psalm 110. Psalm 110 is referred to again in both the Gospel according to Mark and the Gospel according to Matthew during Jesus' trial before the Sanhedrin, where the principal point of the interrogation is to determine whether Jesus indeed claims to be the Messiah. In Mark 14:61, the precise interrogation goes like this: "Again the high priest asked him and said to him, 'Are you the Messiah, the son of the Blessed One?' Then Jesus answered, 'I am'; and 'you will see the Son of Man seated at the right hand of the power and coming with the clouds of heaven.'" In the parallel account in Matt 26:62–64 we read: "The high priest rose and addressed him, 'Have you no answer? What are these men testifying against you?' But Jesus was silent. Then the high priest said to him, 'I order you to tell us under oath before the living God whether you are the Messiah, the Son of God.' Jesus said to him in reply, 'You said so. But I tell you: From now on you will see "the Son of Man seated at the right hand of the Power" and "Coming on the clouds of heaven."'" Jesus' response to the high priest consists of a paraphrase or allusion to God's words to the Davidic Messiah in Psalm 110, "sit at my right . . . yours is princely power" and a direct quotation from the eschatological vision in Dan 7:13, "I saw one like a son of man coming on the clouds of heaven."

All of the passages we have examined suggest Psalm 110, with its description of the messiah as king and priest in the line of Melchizedek, was a major tool for Jesus' self-reflection upon his own destiny. Psalm 110 also provided Jesus with material for urging others to consider the legitimacy of his claim to the title of messiah. But these are not the only witnesses to his personal identification with priesthood. Paul's First Letter to the Corinthians provides us with an even earlier historical witness to Jesus' self-identification as a priest and his institution of a sacrificial offering which, unlike that attributed to him in the Epistle to the Hebrews as "once and for all," he intends that it should be repeated in memory of him, and repeated often. Paul's account in 1 Cor 11 of Jesus' words and deeds at his last supper with his disciples reflects this.

Christ as Priest in First Corinthians 11

While all three of the Synoptic Gospels have last supper narratives that associate Jesus' words and actions with bread and a cup of wine (Mark 14:22–26; Matt 26:26–30: Luke 22:19–20), Paul's account in 1 Cor 11:23–25 predates the Synoptic Gospels by at least twenty years, and, moreover, it is arguably Paul's own witness to an even earlier account of what happened at Jesus's last supper with his disciples. More precisely, Paul wrote First Corinthians from Ephesus about the year 56 to a community that he had evangelized about the year 50. In 1 Corinthians 11, Paul talks to them about the traditions he taught them in the year 50, and that he himself had received several years earlier,(in the early or mid-forties), within ten years of the death of Jesus. First Corinthians 11 opens with Paul's praise of the Christian community at Corinth for their fidelity to his teaching, more precisely, to certain traditions he taught them. First Cor 11:1 reads, "I praise you because you remember me in everything and hold fast to the traditions, just as I handed them on to you." At least twice in that same letter he quotes examples of the traditions he handed on to them. In 1Cor 15:3–7, Paul mentions the traditions handed down regarding Jesus' death and resurrection. But the tradition of most interest here is the one that is cited earlier in that chapter, namely, 1 Cor 11:23–25: "For I received from the Lord what I also handed on to you, that the Lord Jesus on the night he was handed over, took bread, and, after he had given thanks, broke it and said, 'This is my body that is for you. Do this in remembrance of me.' In the same way also the cup, after supper, saying, 'This cup is the new covenant in my blood. Do this in remembrance of me.'"

It is interesting to speculate where Paul received that tradition about the Lord's Supper. Do not be misled by his words "I received from the Lord." Some have interpreted those words to mean Paul received this tradition in a mystical encounter with Jesus similar to that which he had on the road to Damascus. Instead, it is more probable he received this tradition either shortly after his conversion, maybe during the time he spent in Arabia (see Gal 1:17, "I went into Arabia and then returned to Damascus.". Or he could have gotten it from the Christian community at Antioch. Remember, after Paul's less than warm reception by the Christian community at Jerusalem (Acts 9:26–30), he retreated to his home town of Tarsus. But he was soon rescued from oblivion there by Barnabas who took him to Antioch (Acts 11:19–26). Many liturgical scholars claim that the eucharistic formula that Paul employs in 1 Cor 11:23–26 is, indeed, the one that was in use at Antioch. But wherever Paul received the tradition of the Eucharist, he could have verified its historical reliability when he visited Peter in Jerusalem. For in Gal 1:18 (NAB) we have Paul's account of how "after three years I went up to Jerusalem to confer with Kephas [Peter]and remained with him for fifteen days." Surely they did not discuss sports or politics or the weather. Would Paul have said to Peter, "I met the risen Christ on the road to Damascus; you walked the roads of Galilee with the historical Jesus. What was he like?" Moreover, Paul might also have asked: "I was taught that Jesus, on the night before he died, took bread and said this is my body, do this in memory of me. Is that true? Is that really, precisely, what he said?"

Whether or not Paul ascertained the validity, the accuracy, of such traditions with Peter, it is certainly amazing that Paul claims to be able to tell people precisely what Jesus said and did at his last supper with his inner circle. But of more interest to us here is that Jesus is portrayed as using cultic language. He consciously contrasts the literal sacrifice of himself with the old covenant's sacrifice of sheep. Moreover, he says "Do this in memory of me," an important phrase because there are those who argue that certain passages in the Epistle to the Hebrews make it clear that Jesus offered himself once and for all and now reigns with God in heaven. Also, there is evidence that the earliest Christians took seriously Jesus' instruction to "do this in memory of me." Take, for example, the description of the life of the earliest Christian community at Jerusalem as told in Acts 2:42–47:

> They devoted themselves to the teaching of the apostles and to the communal life, to the breaking of the bread and to the prayers. Awe came upon everyone, and many wonders and signs were done through the apostles. All who believed were together and had all things in common; they would sell their property and possessions and divide them among all according to each one's need. Every day they devoted themselves to meeting together in the temple area and to breaking bread in their homes. They ate their meals with exultation and sincerity of heart, praising God and enjoying favor with all the people. And every day the Lord added to their number those who were being saved.

Lessons for Today

Some gospel lessons are difficult to learn. This truth might very well be the first lesson we can take from this study. The author of the Epistle to the Hebrews was quite aware that his teaching about Christ's priesthood was not a simple thing; it was a difficult teaching, a sophisticated theological conception.

The priesthood of Christ, however, is not the only gospel lesson that is difficult to accept and embrace; take the sacramental realism of the Eucharist, for example. John 6 makes it clear that sacramental realism was no invention of patristic or medieval theologians. John 6:52–55 makes it clear that the early Christian Eucharist was not considered a mere historical remembrance but was a genuine communion in the body and blood of Christ: "The Jews quarreled among themselves, saying, 'How can this man give us [his] flesh to eat?' Jesus said to them, 'Amen, amen, I say to you, unless you eat the flesh of the Son of Man and drink his blood, you do not have life within you. Whoever eats my flesh and drinks my blood has eternal life, and I will raise him on the last day. For my flesh is true food, and my blood is true drink.'"

However, sacramental realism was not easily accepted in the early Christian community. Indeed, John 6:60 reveals that early Christians had difficulty accepting such emphatic sacramental realism: "Then many of his disciples who were listening said, 'This saying is hard; who can accept it?'" And later still in John 6:66 we are told, "As a result of this, many of his disciples returned to their former way of life and no longer accompanied him."

So too the theology of the cross has not found easy acceptance. The cross as a symbol of self-sacrifice is a consistent theme in the Synoptic Gospels. In Mark 8:34, "He summoned the crowd with his disciples and said to them, 'Whoever wishes to come after me must deny himself, take up his cross, and follow me.'" And Matt 10:38, "Whoever does not take up his cross and follow after me is not worthy of me." Matt 16:18, "Then Jesus said to his disciples, 'Whoever wishes to come after me must deny himself, take up his cross, and follow me.'" Luke 9:23, "Then he said to them all, 'If anyone wishes to come after me, he must deny himself and take up his cross daily and follow me.'" Luke 14:27, "Whoever does not carry his own cross and come after me cannot be my disciple." In the Pauline letters the image of the cross figures prominently and is invoked no less than eleven times. In 1 Cor 1:17 he insists that, "the cross of Christ might not be emptied of its meaning." A verse later he refers to the importance of "the message of the cross." In Gal 5:11 he refers to "the stumbling block of the cross." In Gal 6:12 he mentions those who are "persecuted for the cross of Christ." In verse 14 of that same chapter he swears, "May I never boast except in the cross of our Lord Jesus Christ." In Eph 2:16, Paul teaches that Jesus died so as "to reconcile both [Jew and Gentile] to God, through the cross." In Phil 3:18, he invokes the image of the "enemies of the cross of Christ." In Col 1:20, he speaks of the work of Christ as "making peace by the blood of cross." And in Col 2:14, he speaks of Christ having taken our guilt and "nailing it to the cross." In Col 2:15, he refers to "the triumph" of the cross.

And thus we would think such a lesson would be primary and basic. But history witnesses to an uneasiness with this doctrine to the point of totally neglecting it. The history of Christian art witnesses that it took a long time for the image of the cross to find acceptance. It was not until the fourth century, after Constantine banned the practice of crucifixion, that the cross began to appear in Christian art. Instead, the earliest example of Christian art is that of Jesus as the Good Shepherd carrying a lamb upon his shoulders or leading a flock. And beginning in the fourth century, the portrayal of the empty cross was used to celebrate Christ's triumph over death. It was only in the Middle Ages that the iconography of the crucifix arose, a cross upon which the body of the dying Christ is vividly represented. It was meant to remind us of his suffering and death. But some found this too much. With the Protestant Reformation the popularity of the empty cross returned. And in the nineteenth century, Liberal Protestantism altogether disposed of the theology of the cross. For, according to American ethicist H. Richard Niebuhr, theological liberalism preached the message that "A God without wrath brought men without sin into a kingdom without justice through the ministrations of a Christ without a cross."[5] To this day we can witness on television an immensely popular preacher whose sermons not only lack scriptural references but completely lack any references to sin or the cross. Instead he chooses to preach what some have described as a health and wealth, or "prosperity gospel," wherein wealth and power are rewards for pious Christians. His books have sold millions of copies.

So too the doctrine of the ministerial priesthood is a hard lesson not easily retained; in fact, it is all too easily obscured and discarded. This happens when a segment of the church opts for a new theological paradigm for its understanding of the ministry of Christ and his disciples.

The Old Theology of the Twofold Ministry of Christ

In the early church, Jesus' self-identity with the priest-king messiah of Psalm 110 gave rise to a theological motif in patristic literature that is sometimes called the *munus duplex Christi*, the twofold work of Christ as priest and king.

This motif appears once in the New Testament by way of Peter in his earliest preaching at Jerusalem (Acts 3:34–35). However, the *munus duplex Christi* is clearly observable at several places in the writings of Augustine of Hippo. In Augustine's *The City of God* (bk. 17, ch. 4), Augustine argues that a pivotal moment in human history occurred when David ascended to the throne of Israel and the promise was made of a successor. Augustine argues, however, that what appeared to be a mere political promise turned out to be an event of paramount spiritual importance, the promise of Hebrew messianism that was fulfilled in Jesus Christ:

> Therefore the advance of the city of God, where it reached the times of the kings, yielded a figure, when on the rejection of Saul, David first obtained the kingdom on such a footing that thenceforth his descendants should reign in the earthly Jerusalem in continual succession; for the course of affairs signified

---

5. Niebuhr, *Kingdom of God in America*, p. 193.

and foretold, what is not to be passed by in silence, concerning the change of things to come, what belongs to both testaments, the Old and the New—where the priesthood and kingdom are changed by one who is a priest, and at the same time a king, new and everlasting, Jesus Christ himself.[6]

This theme can also be found in Augustine of Hippo's *Commentary on the Psalms*, Second Discourse on Psalm 26:2: "At that time the anointing was reserved for the king and the priest; in those days only these two persons received the holy oil. In these two persons was prefigured one to come who should be both King and Priest, the one Christ holding both offices, and called the Christ by reason of his anointing."[7] About the year AD 400, Augustine wrote his *Harmony of the Evangelists* (*De consensus evangelistarum libri quattuor*). There (in bk. 1, ch. 3, art. 6), he says: "Whereas, then, Matthew had in view the kingly character, and Luke the priestly, they have at the same time both set forth pre-eminently the humanity of Christ: for it was according to His humanity that Christ was made both King and Priest."[8]

But this theological tool is not peculiar to the patristic era, for there are instances of its employment in the Middles Ages, the scholastic era. It was given eloquent expression in the twelfth century in theologian Peter Abelard's commentary on Romans. There in his treatment of Paul's opening salutation in the Epistle to the Romans, where Paul says "Grace to you and peace from God our Father and the Lord Jesus Christ," Abelard explains the meaning of the word *christos*, or anointed:

> When, therefore, he is called Christ, that is, anointed, because kings as well as priests were anointed, it shows that he was established by God both as a king and as a priest for us, through which two roles he might save us, which is what "Jesus" means. For he became a priest for us, by sacrificing himself for us on the altar of the Cross; and in truth he was called a king by virtue of his strength and power, by which he can subject all things to himself, and so to speak he binds the strong devil even more strongly, inasmuch as he is the one to whom "the Father has given all things into his hand."[9]

The image of Christ as both king and priest was employed to telling effect by the English priest John of Salisbury (only in the last four years of his life was he a bishop) in his *Policraticus: Of the Frivolities of Courtiers and the Footprints of Philosophers*, completed in the year 1159. The word *policraticus* in the title is a pseudo-Greek neologism invented by John. It can be rendered "The Statesman" or "The Politician." During the period 1147–1154, John served in the papal curia and as secretary to

6. Augustine, *City of God*, p. 339.

7. Augustine, *On the Psalms*, p. 261.

8. Augustine, *Harmony of the Gospels*, p. 79.

9. Abelard, *Commentary on the Epistle*, p. 99.

Theobald, archbishop of Canterbury; and from 1155–57 he served as chancellor to King Henry II of England. It was especially during his time working in the king's chancery that he gained the practical experience of politics and politicians, "the frivolities of courtiers," that was the basis for writing his *Policraticus*. But "the footprints of philosophers" in his subtitle refers to the fact that John was a very learned cleric who had studied in France under such renowned scholars as the philosopher theologian Peter Abelard and the scholastic Gilbert de la Porrée. Thus, John of Salisbury had a good knowledge of classical political philosophy. The result was a work that today is generally recognized as the most important political treatise of the Middle Ages. For our interests here, the most important aspect of this work is what use he makes of the *munus duplex Christi*. While John, in his *Policraticus* (bk. 4, ch. 1), argued for the divine right of kings, he later (in bk. 4, ch. 3) was able to balance off that assertion of royal power by invoking the image of Christ as the Melchizedek-like priest and king. He did so in order to insist that even though princes have their authority from God they must yet be subordinate to both the will of God and even the church.[10]

The New Theology of the Threefold Ministry of Christ

However, in the patristic era there had already arisen another theological construct that identified Jesus' work in three perspectives rather than two: his work not just as king and priest but also as prophet. This theological schema came to be called the *munus triplex Christi*. It appeared first in the writings of Eusebius of Caesarea (ca. 260–ca. 340). In Eusebius's *Church History* (bk. 1, ch. 3 entitled "The Person and Work of Christ) we read:

> And not only those who were honored with the high priesthood, and who for the sake of the symbol were anointed with especially prepared oil, were adorned with the name of Christ among the Hebrews, but also the kings whom the prophets anointed under the influence of the divine Spirit, and thus constituted, as it were typical Christs. For they also bore in their own persons types of the royal and sovereign power of the true and only Christ, the divine Word who ruleth over all. And we have been told also that certain of the prophets themselves became, by the act of anointing, Christs in type, so that all these have reference to the true Christ, the divinely inspired and heavenly Word, who is the only high priest of all, and the only King of every creature, and the Father's only supreme prophet of prophets.[11]

---

10. John of Salisbury, *Policraticus*, p. 33.

11. Eusebius, *Church History*, p. 86.

It has been conjectured that Eusebius got his idea for the *munus triplex Christi* from the Jewish historian Flavius Josephus who, in his *The Wars of the Jews* (bk. 1, ch. 2, sec. 8), describes the special blessedness of the Maccabean leader John Hyrcanus, high priest and ethnarch of Judea from 143–34 BC: "He it was who alone had three of the most desirable things in the world—the government of his nation, and the high priesthood, and the gift of prophecy."[12] That Eusebius knew well Josephus's *Wars of the Jews* is clear in that he quotes from it no less than eight times in his Church History.

But Eusebius's *munus triplex Christi* did not catch on quickly. There are few if any examples of its employment by any other of the Fathers. Nor does it appear significantly in medieval theology. Indeed, Wolfhart Pannenberg sums up the historical witness saying: "It achieved no significance for systematic Christology in the patristic church nor for medieval Scholasticism."[13] No doubt, Aquinas was aware of the doctrine; he mentions it in passing in his *Summa Theologica* (pt. 3, ques. 22, art. 1 or 2). But it is hardly a significant theme there. And that is understandable because Aquinas has his own doctrine of the threefold work of Christ as the work of creation, illumination, and justification. He set forth his theory in the prologue to his *Commentary on the Epistle to the Hebrews*. Moreover, there he makes it clear that Jesus is far more than a prophet, for prophets "are illumined not illuminators."[14]

The reason for the neglect of the *munus triplex Christi* in the patristic era and even into medieval times might have something to do with the doctrinal orthodoxy of its author. That is, while Eusebius early on garnered esteem for his historical writings, he was severely judged for his theological theories. Before the Council of Nicea, in the Trinitarian controversy over the teaching of Arius, Eusebius wrote several letters defending Arius. This brought him condemnation by the Synod of Antioch in early 325. As for Eusebius's participation, a few months later at the Council of Nice in the summer of 325, Quasten says, "He finally signed the creed drawn up by the council as a merely external conforming to the express wish of the emperor but without any internal assent."[15] After the council, he openly sided with Eusebius of Nicomedia, the leader of the Arian party, and had a principal role in the condemnation of the two leading figures of Trinitarian, Nicene orthodoxy. More precisely, he presided at the Synod of Tyre in 325, which condemned the teachings of Athanasius. Later he wrote two treatises against the teachings of bishop Marcellus of Ancyra. Jerome in his Adversus Rufinus 2.15, accuses Eusebius of heresy. And a modern

---

12. Josephus, *Complete Works*, p. 431.

13. Pannenberg, *Jesus: God and Man,* p. 213.

14. Aquinas, *Commentary on the Epistle*, p. 6.

15. Quasten, *Patrology*, Vol. 3, p. 310.

patrologist, Hubertus Drobner, in his *The Fathers of the Church: A Comprehensive Introduction*, sums up Eusebius's theological significance by noting that Eusebius was indeed a supporter of Arius in the christological controversies before and after Nicea and "his own theological conceptuality did not prove to be sufficiently sustainable."[16] His lack of theological probity is especially evident in his insistence that prophets as well as priests and kings were anointed. Eusebius never considers the fact that Scripture itself witnesses to the phenomenon whereby even a pagan, if he seemed to be doing the will of God, could be considered an "anointed one." I am referring to Cyrus the king of Persia (559–529 BC) who conquered Babylon and then liberated the captive Jews. In Isa 45:1, Cyrus is accorded the title of God's anointed: "Thus says the Lord to his anointed, Cyrus, whose right hand I grasp, subduing nations before him, and making kings run in his service."

It is only at the time of the Protestant Reformation that we begin to see more significant references to a *munus triplex Christi*. Though Luther never once refers to it, it is referred to in Erasmus of Rotterdam's 1522 work, *Commentary on the Psalms*. And it is treated by Martin Luther's critic, the Reformation theologian and Protestant controversialist Andreas Osiander (1498–1552).[17] But by far the most influential treatment of this concept is Calvin's use of it in his theological compendium *The Institutes of the Christian Religion* (bk. 2, ch. 15), which is entitled "To Know the Purpose for Which Christ Was Sent by the Father, and What He Conferred Upon Us, We Must Look Above All at Three things in Him: the Prophetic Office, Kingship, and Priesthood." There he begins by saying: "Therefore, in order that faith may find a firm basis for salvation in Christ, and thus rest in him, this principle must be laid down: the office enjoined upon Christ by the Father consists of three parts. For he was given to be prophet, king and priest."[18] The reason he gives for this is very similar to that which we have seen Eusebius state: "Now it is to be noted that the title 'Christ' pertains to these three offices; for we know that under the law prophets as well as priests and kings were anointed with holy oil."[19]

Among these three *munera*, Calvin gives pride of place to the office of prophet. He not only treats it first, but boasts of its importance in a phrase that seems to be a counterfoil to the old concept of apostolic succession in episcopal ministry: "God, by providing people with an unbroken line of prophets, never left them without useful doctrine sufficient for salvation."[20] Moreover, it is arguable that Calvin goes

---

16. Drobner, *Fathers of the Church*, p. 224.

17. Pannenberg, *Jesus: God and Man*, p. 213.

18. Calvin, *Institutes*, Vol. 1, p. 494.

19. Ibid., p. 495.

20. Ibid.

far beyond Eusebius, for Calvin not only employs the *munus triplex* as a tool for Christology but also for ecclesiology. He sees the three offices of Christ extended to the life of his spiritual body, the faithful. For example, he says of Christ's prophetic office: "Then this anointing was diffused from the Head to the members, as Joel had foretold: 'Your sons shall prophesy and your daughters . . . shall see visions.'"[21] So too Calvin says there is a sense in which all the faithful participate in Christ's priestly office. That is why he is adamant that in the truest sense "the priestly office belongs to Christ alone,"[22] yet he will admit there is a spiritual sense in which all the faithful share in his priesthood: "For we who are defiled in ourselves, yet are priests in him, offer ourselves and our all to God, and freely enter the heavenly sanctuary that the sacrifices of prayers and praise that we bring may be acceptable and sweet-smelling before God."[23]

But Calvin concedes no priestly character to any formal ecclesiastical ministry and is particularly strong against conceding any sacrificial meaning to the Eucharist: "The more detestable is the fabrication of those who, not content with Christ's priesthood, have presumed to sacrifice him anew! The papists attempt this each day, considering the Mass as the sacrificing of Christ."[24] Thus, not only was the priestly character of certain ecclesiastics denied but so was the realism of the Eucharist.

But even this denial did not prevent the *munus triplex Christi* from coming to have a significant influence on Catholic thought. In the nineteenth century it was carefully made use of by the Anglican John Henry Newman. Newman treats of it in his *Parochial and Plain Sermons* (bk. 1, sermon no. 25), the sermon entitled "The Christian Ministry." This sermon was given on the Feast of St. Peter the Apostle. And there he treats of the apostolic ministry committed not just to Peter but to all the twelve and their successors in ministry. In doing that he employs Calvin's *munus triplex Christi* as an interpretive tool: "The Apostles then, standing in Christ's place, were consequently exalted by office far above any divine Messengers before them. We come to the same conclusion from considering the sacred treasures committed to their custody, which (not to mention their miraculous powers, which is beside our present purpose) were those peculiar spiritual blessings which flow from Christ as a Saviour, as a Prophet, Priest and King."[25]

21. Ibid., p. 496.

22. Ibid., p. 502.

23. Ibid. However, it is interesting to note the comment of the editor of this very translation of Calvin's *Institutes*, John T. McNeill, in a footnote to the passage I have quoted from page 502: "Calvin's utterances specifically on the priesthood of believers are rare and unsystematic."

24. Calvin, *Institutes*, Vol. 1, p. 503.

25. Newman, *Parochial and Plain Sermons*, p. 416.

Later in that same sermon Newman notes that while all humans seem to admit of the need for authority and teaching, there is a reluctance to recognize the need for priestly mediation. Indeed, few admit of the need for mediation (priesthood):

> This being granted, however, as regards the Apostles themselves, some one may be disposed to inquire, whether their triple office has descended to Christian Ministers after them. I say their *triple* office, for few persons will deny that some portion of their commission still remains among us. The notion that there is no divine appointment of one man above another for Ministerial duties is not a common one, and we need not refute it. But it is very common for men to believe only as far as they can see and understand; and, because they are witnesses of the process and effects of instructing and ruling, and not of what may be called "the ministry of reconciliation," to accept Christ's Ministers as representatives of His Prophet and Regal, not of his Priestly authority.[26]

So too we can find a major nineteenth-century Catholic theologian making careful and qualified use of it. I am referring to Matthias Joseph Scheeben's treatment of the theme of the *munus triplex Christi*. Scheeben, born in 1835 in Germany, was ordained a Catholic priest and in 1860 became professor of dogma at the seminary at Cologne where he taught till his death in 1888. Scheeben treats of this theme in several places. In 1865 he published his *Mysterien des Christenthums*. Chapter 15 of that work treats of Christ's function as mediator between God and man. At one point in that chapter Scheeben explains Christ's mediation by using the schema of the three offices of Christ:

> As He represents God among men in the capacity of prophet, priest, and king, so He represents men at the court of God as a prophet who in their stead sings God's praises as they are unable to do, as a priest who in their behalf gives to God the supreme tribute which they are wholly incapable of supplying, and lastly as a king who in place of them and through them renders to God the noble, free service of a Son.
>
> The functions of the God-man's mediatorship are manifestly summed up in His priesthood. When He brings God's grace down to us, it is clear that at the same time He is acting as prophet to convey to us the light of truth which is implied in this grace, and in which this grace and its author are known; and that He is a king who founds and rules the kingdom of God, for this is nothing other than the kingdom of grace. And on the other hand, if He alone is able in the creature's name to pay worthy tribute to God, then He, and He alone, will be in a position to render to God the praise and obedience which His infinite majesty demands.

26. Ibid., p. 418.

> Indeed, the entire mediatorship of Christ is at bottom nothing but a priest-hood, just as His priesthood is nothing but a mediatorship between God and man.[27]

In the twentieth century we have the witness of Henri de Lubac in his 1953 work, *Méditation sur l'Egliese*. There de Lubac, with no reference to Calvin and instead a reference to Nicholas of Cusa's *De Concordantia Catholica*, insists upon a threefold office of Christ that shapes the Church's ministry:

> The Catholic hierarchy, or priestly order, thus exercises a threefold power which corresponds to its threefold role of government, teaching and sanctification; a power of jurisdiction, *magisterium* and order or, as Nicholas of Cusa puts it, *ordo, praesidentia et cathedra*. Each of these three ministries is equally of the essence of the Catholic hierarchy; or rather, they are three elements of one ministry which is itself unique and indivisible, and whose principle stands out as clearly as may be, from the founding of the Church onwards. For all three derive from the one single mission which Christ received from His Father and in virtue of which He was at one and the same time Teacher, Sanctifier and King—a mission, moreover, which He passed on to His Church in a dependent mode, without diving it up.[28]

However, de Lubac immediately qualifies what he has said by insisting that one of those three elements must be given priority:

> If, however, we do wish to establish a grading of the three ministries and discover which should be thought of as both the origin and final flowering of the other two, a first pointer is undoubtedly to be found in the very words, "priesthood" and "hierarchy," which are at present used to indicate them all as a whole. . . For these terms, are not in their origin, connected with any mission of teaching or ruling, but with the carrying out of a sacred function. We may then agree with the Abbé René Laurentin when he says that "the liturgical dimension of the priesthood is its most properly and specifically priestly dimension," and that it is upon it that Scripture "centers the concept of priesthood."[29]

Moreover, caution regarding the *munus triplex Christi* is hardly just a Catholic concern. Karl Barth treats of the *munus triplex Christi* in that part of his *Church Dogmatics* (Vol. 4, pt. 3, sec. 69), which is entitled "The Glory of the Mediator." In general, Barth laments the fact that the formula of the *munus triplex Christi* is an all too neat and simplistic formula that only obscures inner tensions which theologians have not helped to clarify. He laments that "in detail there seem to be all kinds of

27. Scheeben, *Mysteries of Christianity*, p.412.

28. De Lubac, *Splendour of the Church*, pp. 101–2. De Lubac is referring to book 1, chapter 8, of Cusa's *The Catholic Concordance*, pp. 28–29.

29. Ibid., de Lubac is quoting from R. Laurentin's *Marie, L'Eglise et le Sacerdoce*.

obscurities" and he warns "the element of uncertainty regarding the interrelating of the prophetic and other offices could have unhappy consequences."[30]

In the English translation of Wolfhart Pannenberg's 1964 treatise on Christology, *Grundzuge der Christologie*, there is a section entitled "Critique of the Doctrine of the Three Offices."[31] There he begins with a general judgment: "the concept of the three offices in the dogmatics of Protestant orthodoxy is subject to considerable objection."[32] He then proceeds to make more precise criticisms such as "The entirety of Jesus' activity and his self-understanding cannot be characterized accurately as prophetic, either in the ancient Israelite sense or in the sense of the contemporary Jewish expectation."[33] As for Jesus' royal office, Pannenberg says, "During his earthly activity Jesus neither sought nor practiced the royal office."[34]

It is most interesting to note how the Second Vatican Council makes particularly adroit use of the idea that Jesus had a threefold ministry. It is used in three important conciliar statements, The Dogmatic Constitution on the Church, *Lumen gentium*; the decree on bishops and the Decree on the Bishop's Pastoral Office in the church, *Christus Dominus*; and the Decree on the Ministry and Life of Priests, *Presbyterorum Ordinis*. Arguably, the council makes reference to the more traditional *munus duplex Christi* when, in *Lumen gentium*, (art. 19), it says of Jesus' mission to the Twelve: "He sent them first to the children of Israel and then to all nations so that as sharers in His power they might make all people His disciples, *sanctifying and governing them*."[35] The phrase "sanctifying and governing" does indeed invoke the image of the Messiah as priest and king. However, in the very next section of that same document (in art. 20) of *Lumen gentium*, the council describes the task of bishops as the threefold responsibility of "teachers of doctrine, priests of sacred worship, and officers of good order."[36] In the decree on the pastoral office of bishops, the council once again described the responsibilities of bishops as being "the office of teaching, sanctifying and governing." (*munus docendi, sanctificandi, ac regendi*).[37] In its decree on the ministry and life of priests, the council said, "By sacred ordination and by the mission they receive from their bishops, priests are promoted to the service of Christ, the teacher, the priest and the king."[38]

30. Barth, *Church Dogmatics*, Vol. 4, pp. 14–15.

31. Pannenberg, *Jesus, God and Man*, pp. 212–25.

32. Ibid., p. 215.

33. Ibid.

34. Ibid., p. 217.

35. Abbott, *Documents*, p. 38.

36. Ibid., p. 40.

37. Ibid., p. 403.

38. Ibid., p. 533.

In all of these instances the council, though employing a *munus triplex Christi*, seems to be following de Lubac's citation of Nicholas of Cusa rather than Calvin's *Institutes*.[39] However, in its dogmatic constitution on the church, the language seems much more indebted to Calvin than to Cusa; for there, instead of invoking the image of Christ as teacher, it is precisely the image of prophet that is described. This reference is to the chapter on the laity. There (in art. 34) the council says of the laity, "For besides intimately associating them with His life and His mission, Christ also gives them a share in his priestly function [*muneris sacerdotalis*] of offering spiritual worship for the glory of God and the salvation of men."[40]

But in the very next section (art. 35), the laity are identified with Christ's prophetic office: "Christ, the great Prophet, who proclaimed the kingdom of His Father by the testimony of His life and the power of His words, continually fulfills His prophetic office [*munus propheticum*] until His full glory is revealed. He does this not only through the hierarchy who teach in His name and with His authority, but also through the laity."[41] Of this development, the following observation by Kenan Osborne in his *Priesthood: A History of the Ordained Ministry in the Roman Catholic Church* (p. 339) is particularly important:

> The structuring of priestly ministry around the threefold missions and ministry of Jesus is indeed a helpful step, since it makes the theology of the priest far more comprehensive than a theology focused exclusively on the Eucharist. This structuring is Christological, and that is its value. However, since neither scripture nor the early Church nor even the scholastics used this threefold structuring, the format itself can only be seen as a theological aid, not a part of revelation itself. Indeed, there are some questions as to the terminology used in this threefold structure. For instance, to say that Jesus should be called a prophet has been questioned by some biblical scholars, since Jesus does not fulfill all the characteristics of the Old Testament prophets.[42]

Indeed we should be aware how problematic the prophetic ministry has always been.[43] While, no doubt, Jesus can be legitimately called a prophet, we need to be aware of the dangers and limitations of such an identification. While prophecy was a prominent feature of ancient Israel, there can be little doubt that false prophecy was

---

39. I am referring to Nicholas of Cusa's *The Catholic Concordance*, p. 24, where there is no reference to a prophetic ministry, rather Cusa says "Ruling, life-giving, and illuminating power is given to the priesthood." Did Cusa know of Aquinas's distinction whereby prophets are illuminated but not themselves illuminating?

40. Abbott, *Documents*, p. 60.

41. Abbott, p. 61.

42. Osborne, *Priesthood*, p. 339.

43. See in Congar's *True and False*, Ch. 3, "Prophets and Reformers," which is pp. 169–95.

a major problem too. The major prophets all lament this fact (Isa 9:15, Jer 14:13–16; Ezek 13:3). And the situation was not appreciably different in New Testament times, for Jesus too warned of false prophets, as in Matt 7:15: "Beware of false prophets, who come to you in sheep's clothing but inwardly are ravenous wolves." Paul and Barnabas, on their very first missionary journey encounter a false prophet (Acts 13:6–12). Second Pet 2:1 witnesses that "false prophets also arouse among the people." And in 1 John 4:1, we are told, "Beloved, do not believe every spirit, but test the spirits to see whether they are of God; for many false prophets have gone out into the world."

Though the title prophet is often applied to Jesus in the New Testament, it is usually presented there as a casual, less than perceptive, identification of him. We see this in the gospel story wherein Jesus interrogates his inner circle about popular speculation regarding him and his ministry. This incident is recorded in Mark 8:27–30, Luke 9:18–21, and Matt 16:13–20. Here I give the Matthean version: "When Jesus went into the region of Caesarea Philippi he asked his disciples, 'Who do people say that the Son of Man is?' They replied, 'Some say John the Baptist, others Elijah, still others Jeremiah or one of the prophets.' He said to them, 'But who do you say that I am?' Simon Peter said in reply, 'You are the messiah, the son of the living God.'"

A quick analysis of these responses readily suggests that those people who thought Jesus was John the Baptist tended to be superstitious. (For no sooner had John the Baptist been executed than Jesus took up his public ministry, and so some thought Jesus might be John come back from the dead.) The ones who speculated that Jesus was Elijah might well have been pious Jews who knew their scriptures; in particular, the tradition that Elijah never died but instead was taken up into heaven so that one day, before the end of time, he might return to warn us of God's impending final judgment. Those who speculated that Jesus was "Jeremiah or one of the prophets" were probably the sober realists who concluded that Jesus was a throwback to an earlier time when Israelite prophets were numerous in Israel. Nevertheless, all those speculations that Jesus was some sort of prophet were inadequate. It is only one from Jesus' inner circle who expressed the right conclusion: Peter, when he stated the shared conviction of the Twelve that Jesus was the long promised Davidic Messiah and the Danielic "son of God."

In the end, it cannot be denied that a prophetic character can be attributed to Christ's work, his people, and the Christian clergy. And thus a priest or a bishop cannot be satisfied to preach and teach, preside and govern, but must also at times be prophetic, challenging of both God's people, the church, and the world. But among all of those duties, what he says and does at the altar is of supreme and unique importance. One of the great liturgical theologians of the twentieth century, Cyprian Vagaggini, has made clear how a priest or bishop is not just an ecclesial minister (a servant of the local church) but is an ecclesiastic, a man who makes the church the Body of Christ:

> According to Catholic doctrine, the Church cannot exist without a sacramental and hierarchical priesthood. . . . The Church . . . is not just the sum total of those who believe in Christ, but over and above this sum total there is a new element, divine and physical, the sacramental and hierarchical priesthood . . . the believers are not a community, they are not the Church except insofar as they are united to this sacramental and hierarchical priesthood or insofar as they are included beneath it.
>
> In Catholic doctrine the priest is not simply the delegate of the people, nor is he primarily their representative. First of all and essentially he is the delegate and representative of Christ, Head of the Mystical Body; the priest is empowered to act in His stead through a special quality belonging not just to the moral or purely juridic order, but to the physical and supernatural order: the priestly character and grace transmitted through the sacrament of orders.[44]

Another theologian, David N. Power, professor of systematic theology at the Catholic University of America in Washington, DC, described well the doctrinal tradition when he explained how a priest or bishop can transform an ordinary prayer meeting into the eschatological sign of "the feast in the kingdom of heaven" (Luke 13:22), "the great banquet" (Luke 14:14–16), Christ's "table in the kingdom" (Luke 22:30):

> The Roman Catholic and Orthodox churches teach a ministerial priesthood that is exercised in the celebration of the Eucharist and that is distinct from the common priesthood of all the baptized exercised in the pursuit of a life according to the gospel and culminating in the act of worship. The first is indeed related to the second and is intended to bring it to fruition, but it is particular inasmuch as it means an exercise of sacramental ministry and offering performed in the person of Christ. Without the power given to the ordained ministry to perform this service, the common priesthood could not be nurtured or expressed in the service of the Eucharistic sacrifice.[45]

---

44. Vagaggini, *Theological Dimension*, pp. 275–76. Cf. Paul's description of himself as an "apostle of Christ" (*apostolos Christou*) in 2 Cor 1:1 and others as "apostles of the churches" (*apostoloi ekklesion*) in 2 Cor 8:23. Cf. Also Congar's *True and False*, p. 89 on the title "churchman."

45. Power, "Priesthood," p. 821.

12

The Relation between Preaching and the Sacraments

The Priestly Ministry of Paul the Apostle

MY VERY FIRST ASSIGNMENT as a priest was serving as a chaplain to Catholic students at a large university in what is called by some the "Bible Belt" of America. Once, after Sunday Mass, two students approached me. They wanted to explain why they had been absent from Sunday Mass in the university chapel the week before. They explained how on that previous Sunday they had gone to an early Mass at the cathedral in the city, and that they had done so in order to go afterwards with some non-Catholic classmates to a local Protestant church to hear the pastor preach. When they mentioned the church and its pastor, I immediately recognized his name. This pastor was one of the leading clergymen of the city and, indeed, a clergyman who had attained a considerable reputation and following precisely for his fine preaching. These two students were eager to share with me their impressions of both this pastor and his Sunday service. As for the preaching, they said the pastor preached for a very long time, perhaps fifty minutes, but they were not counting the time. Instead they both agreed the sermon was superb, and not for a moment were they distracted or bored (if I remember correctly the theme was sin: he was against it, and they were won over to his side). As for the service, they told me how different that Sunday service was from what they were used to: though the preacher quoted often from the Bible, there were no Bible readings; moreover, there was no Eucharist.

When I related their experience to a colleague, another university chaplain, himself a Protestant minister but of another denomination than the renowned preacher, he remarked with a mixture of scorn and envy, "Oh yes, he receives a huge salary, has a very large pastoral staff who do all 'the work,' which leaves him with the whole week to prepare his next sermon." My colleague also told me he felt certain that the renowned preacher not only worked all week on composing his sermon but most probably he wrote it out and then committed it to memory, maybe even rehearsed his delivery of it, practicing every rhetorical gesture in front of a mirror, before giving it publicly. We both agreed it would be wonderful to be able to put so much time and preparation into our Sunday sermons.

And I thought to myself afterward, no doubt Catholic pulpit preaching would be much better if the average Catholic priest could spend the best part of his week preparing his homily. But, alas, that is rarely possible. The average parish priest preaches more than once a week, indeed, often daily at Mass and then at the celebration of other sacraments or services that might crowd his calendar, such as weddings, baptisms, hospital visits (that might include the anointing of the sick), wakes, and funerals. Moreover, Catholic priests cannot freely choose their scriptural texts; instead, a Catholic priest must follow a prescribed list of biblical readings for Sundays, holy days, and even weekdays. Moreover, Catholic priests are encouraged to give not thematic or moralizing sermons but homilies that help to explain the assigned biblical readings.

How to balance the demands of the pulpit against the demands of the pastorate continues to be a challenge to this day for most Protestant ministers as well as Catholic priests. That is why, in this chapter, I want to examine the ministry of Saint Paul regarding the balancing of those two duties.

While Paul was principally a missionary preacher and not the pastor of a congregation, nevertheless, it is demonstrable that preaching was not all he did. There is evidence that he also celebrated sacraments (performed a sacramental ministry). Moreover, in his writings he more than once, indeed, several times, employs language that suggests his was a priestly ministry. And for those reasons I believe the example of Saint Paul offers some especially valuable lessons regarding priestly ministry today and, in particular, regarding the relationship between preaching and sacramental ministry.

In order to discern more clearly the priestly character of Paul's ministry, we will first look carefully at those passages wherein Paul uses cultic or priestly language to describe his work; and then we will look at those passages in the Acts of the Apostles and Paul's own letters that suggest he did indeed have a sacramental ministry as well as an evangelical mission. Then, in the final section, I will set forth what I believe are some very important lessons in all this for a Catholic priest today.

Paul's Language of Priestly Service

There are at least three passages in the Pauline corpus where Paul seems to employ priestly or cultic language with which to describe his own ministry. First is Rom 15:15–16 where Paul describes his ministry as a "priestly service" of "offering up." But then there is also the passage in Phil 2:17 (and the very similar 2 Tim 4:6) where Paul describes his life as being "poured out as a libation upon the sacrificial service of your faith." And, finally, there is his statement in 1 Cor 4:1 that "Thus one should regard us: as servants of Christ and stewards of the mysteries of God." In the history of Christian exegesis of the NT, all three of these passages have been interpreted as Paul's comparison of his ministry to that of a priestly service. But the intent or meaning of that priestly identification has also been disputed, especially by modern exegetes. We shall examine all of these passages, taking into account those disputes.

The first one we examine here is Paul's use of the language of the "priestly service" of "offering up" which is found in the context of Rom 15:14–19:

> I myself am convinced about you, my brothers, that you yourselves are full of goodness, filled with all knowledge, and able to admonish one another. But I have written to you rather boldly in some respects to remind you, because of the grace given me by God to be a minister of Christ Jesus to the Gentiles in performing the priestly service of the gospel of God, so that the offering up of the Gentiles may be acceptable, sanctified by the holy Spirit. In Christ, Jesus, then, I have reason to boast in what pertains to God. For I will not dare to speak of anything except what Christ has accomplished through me to lead the Gentiles to obedience by word and deed, by the power of signs and wonders, by the power of the Spirit [of God], so that from Jerusalem all the way around to Illyricum I have finished preaching the gospel of Christ.

To understand this passage we must know that one of the duties or services of Jewish priests was not only to offer sacrifice but to examine carefully all offerings brought to the temple for sacrifice. They did so in order to ensure that the offerings were not damaged goods but were proper and acceptable offerings. In this matter see the instruction in Lev 22:17–22:

> The LORD said to Moses: "Speak to Aaron and his sons and to all the Israelites, and tell them: When anyone of the house of Israel, or any alien residing in Israel, who wishes to offer a sacrifice, brings a holocaust as a votive offering, or as a free-will offering to the LORD, if it is to be acceptable, the ox or sheep or goat that he offers must be an unblemished male. You shall not offer one that has any defect, for such a one would not be acceptable for you. When anyone presents a peace offering to the LORD from the herd or the flock in fulfillment of a vow, or as a free-will offering, if it is to find acceptance, it must be unblemished; it shall not have any defect. One that is blind or crippled or maimed, or one that has a running sore or mange or ringworm, you shall not offer to the LORD; do not put such an animal on the altar as an oblation to the LORD.

Just as the Jewish priest's job was to see to it that the offering brought is proper and acceptable for offering—that it be neither blemished nor profane, and it is offered in the proper manner—so too Paul's preaching is meant to insure that Gentiles are properly instructed so that their faith renders them acceptable to God, so that none of them is so doctrinally blind or morally defective as to constitute an improper offering to the Lord.

Yet another example of Paul's use of cultic or priestly language to describe his ministry is found in those passages where he compares his ministry to the practice whereby Jewish priests made not just animal sacrifices but also liquid offerings, that is, libations to God. In Phil 2:17 we hear him say, "I am poured out as a libation upon the sacrificial service of your faith." There is a very similar comment in 2 Tim 4:6 where we read, "For I am already being poured out like a libation." But some important clarifications must be made lest we misread what Paul is saying in these passages.

First, while there was indeed a pagan tradition of offering libations to the gods, Paul's references have nothing to do with that. Throughout the ancient world, libations played an important role in a wide range of sacrificial practices. There was great variety in both the nature of the act (complete or partial emptying of the vessel, with or after other offerings, and so forth) and the material offered (water, wine, milk, or honey). A drink offering, usually of wine, was partially poured upon an altar or other cultic object as part of a sacrificial ceremony, and then the remainder was consumed by the supplicant. This was a common devotional practice among the peoples of the ancient Near East and also among the Greeks and Romans. No doubt the most famous Greek libation was to the god Dionysius. Devotees of this god of revelry celebrated him by imbibing a great deal of his favorite drink. However, one should be careful about all too facile identification of the Israelite use of libations with those of these other cults. There were two significant differences. First, in Israelite libations there was no personal consumption of the liquid, no sharing with the god; instead it was all *poured out* as an offering solely and exclusively to God. Secondly, in the Hebrew cult, there were no independent libations; all libations were an accompaniment to a greater, more substantial offering.

We find in the Old Testament passages that refer to the use of libations not only in cultic ceremonies but also publicly by devout Israelites. As for acts of personal piety we have the example of the patriarch Jacob who when he erected a pillar at Bethel poured a liquid offering upon it (Gen 35:14: "On the site where God had spoken with him, Jacob set up a memorial stone, and upon it he made a libation and poured out oil."). In 2 Sam 23:16, mention is made of David's libation to the Lord by way of the water that had been brought to him at the risk of men's lives: "But when they brought it to David he refused to drink it, and instead poured it out to the Lord." That libation was David's particularly eloquent and dramatic way of showing his reverence for human life and that he put the glory of the Lord before his own personal needs.

Within the sanctuary system, libations constituted a significant part of the ritual procedures even on a regular basis. For example, in Exod 29:38–41 we read, "Now, this is what you shall offer on the altar: two yearling lambs as the sacrifice established for each day; one lamb in the morning and the other lamb at the evening twilight. With the first lamb there shall be a tenth of an *ephah* of fine flour mixed with a fourth of a *hin* of oil of crushed olives and, as its libation, a fourth of a *hin* of wine. The other lamb you shall offer at the evening twilight, with the same cereal offering and libation as in the morning." It was also specifically legislated that libations must be made along with grain offerings to accompany any burnt or peace offering (Num 15:1–15; cf. Lev 23:13, 18, 37). Drink offerings accompanied the Sabbath offering (Num 28:9) as well as the New Moon festival (v. 14). Reference is also made to libations in connection with the second and following days of the Feast of Tabernacles (29:18, 21). The same seems to be true of Passover, First Fruits, and the Feast of Trumpets (Num 28:16–29:11; cf. Ezek 45:11). A libation was also called for in the rites for the conclusion of a Nazirite vow (Num 6:17).

It seems that in earliest Israel, wine was poured out on the sacrificial victim as it lay on the altar of holocausts. At a later period it was poured out at the foot of this altar (Sir 50:15; Josephus's Ant 3.9.4). According to the *Talmud* (*Sukkah* 49), representing the final custom in Herod's temple, the libation was poured into one of the two funnel-like basins that stood at the sides of the altar, and was thus drained into a pit under the altar. Moreover, no libations were ever poured over the incense altar in the sanctuary (Exod 30:9). Libations were only used at the altar of sacrifice, outside, in front of the sanctuary. Some have argued that in the Israelite cult, wine was a substitute for blood (cf. Ps 16:4 where blood is spoken of as a libation in pagan sacrifice). But it is interesting that drink offerings or libations were classed as "pleasing odor" offerings (see Num 15:7). And thus it could be that, as with incense offerings, the use of libations was yet another way of controlling the foul odor from the *abatoir*, or the smell of burning entrails. However, this practical use does not exclude the possibility of a more spiritual interpretation, as with incense rising like prayer.

For example, the Israelites had no independent wine offerings or libations, such as those that played an important role among the Egyptians, Assyrians, and Babylonians. The use of libations in the Hebrew ritual was always as a supplement to various sacrifices. For example, from Num 15:5, we learn that to each sacrifice of a lamb or goat one must add a one-quarter *hin* of wine (equivalent to about two-fifths of a gallon). In Num 15:6, it is noted that at the sacrifice of a ram, one-third a *hin* of wine (about one-half of a gallon) must be added. In Num 15:9, it is prescribed that one-half a *hin* of wine (about four-fifths of a gallon) must accompany the sacrifice of an ox. Also, while most texts from pagan sources speak of drinking part of the libation, there was no consumption of libations in the Israelite cult, not even by the priests (Num 28:7). Instead, all of the libation was poured out. Indeed, the Bible is very censorious of the drink offerings made in other religions. For example, the prophets condemn libations in pagan worship (Isa 57:6; Jer 7:18; 19:13; 32:29; Ezek 20:28; Zeph 1:5). Jeremiah was particularly strong in denouncing the libations to the Queen of Heaven (Jer 44:17–19, 25).

One cannot help but wonder if Paul was attracted to the idea of his life as a libation precisely because he knew that his Gentile audience would have been well acquainted with the concept, but also because he was intent upon correcting their pagan notions by way of distinctly Jewish and Christian concepts of worship, communion, and sacrifice. For example, when Paul says in Phil 2:17, "I am poured out as a libation upon the sacrificial service of your faith," he seems to be echoing very precisely the Jewish ritual practice of pouring out the entire contents of a cup of wine upon a sacrificial offering. So too the Jewish concept of the libation as accompanying a sacrifice of blood enabled Paul to understand the personal sacrifice of his life in ministry as attendant upon the personal sacrifice of Jesus' own life to redeem us all.

The final example of Paul's use of cultic or priestly language to describe his ministry can be found in 1 Cor 4:1: "Thus should one regard us: as servants of Christ and stewards of the mysteries of God." In the original Greek it is: *huperetes Christou kai oiknoous musterion theou.* There is considerable dispute over the proper interpretation of the two terms of service used here by Saint Paul: "servants of Christ" and "stewards of the mysteries." No doubt *huperetes*, or servants, can have a very secular meaning. For example, Richard Kugelman, in the *Jerome Biblical Commentary* (1968), insists that both the word *huperetes* in the phrase "servants of Christ" and the word *oikonomos* in the phrase "stewards of the mysteries" are intentionally secular references on Paul's part. Kugelman insists both origins of the then-contemporary use of the term *huperetes* were clearly secular: "*huperetes* designated the rowers on the lowest bank of the galleys; then it came to mean 'assistant, helper.'"[1] He also insists the term *oikonomos* was used in the sense of "managers," namely servants entrusted with the administration of the house. And thus Paul insists on the inferior position of the "manager" who administers his master's property, and not his own. In this regard the apostles are Christ's assistants and managers of God's mysteries, charged with preaching divine revelation, and not their own doctrines. Nevertheless, there are other scholars who argue that while *huperetes*, attendants, was often used in secular Greek to refer to house servants; there is evidence it was used by Hellenistic Jews to refer to temple attendants. For example, see Jewish historian Flavius Josephus, in his *The Jewish Wars* (2.15.4), where he uses the term to refer to

1. Kugelman, p. 259.

Jerusalem temple ministers: *pas men hiereus pas d'hyperetes tou theou*, that is, "every priest and every servant of God."[2] Indeed, H. Cadbury in his article in the *Journal of Biblical Literature* 50 (1931) 47–51, argues that the term "stewards" or *oikonomous* was standardly applied to religious functionaries. If this more cultic language was followed, then Paul's claim to be a "servant of Christ" is really that of a worshipful religious attendant.

Some theologians have interpreted the phrase "dispensers of the mysteries of God" as a reference to a sacramental ministry. But this appears to be a relatively late development, and one open to considerable challenge. Indeed, I can find no patristic writer who interprets it that way. It is only in the Middle Ages when we see this interpretation begin. And here, amazingly, we find two theologians of very different character agreeing upon a point of interpretation. I am referring to Thomas Aquinas, in his *Commentary on The First Epistle to the Corinthians* (Paris, 1270–1272), in paragraph 186 that contains his interpretation of 1 Cor 4:1, argues there are two possible ways for interpreting this phrase "dispensers of the mysteries of God." First he says the term "the mysteries of God can mean 'His spiritual teachings'"; then he says it can also mean "the sacraments of the church, in which divine power secretly works."[3] John Calvin makes a very similar point regarding this same passage, 1 Cor 4:1, in his work of systematic theology, *The Institutes of the Christian Religion* (originally published in 1536). There (in bk. 4, ch. 3), when he treats of the office and ministries of the church, Calvin, instead of rejecting this medieval interpretation of 1 Cor 4:1, continues it. Calvin (in bk. 4, ch. 3, pt. 6,) compares the ministries of the apostles with that of contemporary pastors. Citing 1 Cor 4:1 he says, "from this and similar passages which frequently occur, we may infer that in the office of the pastors also there are two particular functions: to proclaim the gospel and to administer the sacraments."[4] So too the seminary at which I teach, a Roman Catholic seminary, founded to train candidates for the priesthood, employs the phrase "dispensers of the mysteries of God" on its seal and coat of arms as a reference to its effort to prepare men for priestly ministry.

Modern exegetes, however, have called into question this interpretation. Modern interpretation of this passage centers upon the meaning attributed not just to the word "mysteries" as a reference either to rites or to revelations but also the proper interpretation of the word "stewards" as a reference to temple workers or to secular business managers. We examine both claims here. First is the question regarding the proper translation of the word "mysteries" (*musterion*) and whether it refers to

2. Josephus, *Complete Works*, p. 486.

3. Aquinas, *Commentary on First Corinthians*, no. 186.

4. Calvin, *Institutes*, Vol. 2, p. 1059.

religious rites or, instead, to religious teachings. No doubt, the word *musterion* in profane Greek appears most frequently in the plural where it designates not doctrines but religious rites. But that is not the way Paul uses it. Paul uses it quite frequently in First Corinthians. In 1 Cor 2:1 Paul says, "When I came to you, brothers, proclaiming the mystery of God."[5] Then, in 1 Cor 2:6–8, 13:2, "and if I have been given the gift of prophecy and comprehend all mysteries [*musteria*] and all knowledge" and 1 Cor 14:2, "For one who speaks in a tongue does not speak to human beings but to God, for no one listens. He utters mysteries [*musteria*] in spirit." The word *musterion* is used also in Ephesians and Colossians. But in all these latter uses it refers not to religious rites but to religious truths that can be known only by the revelation of God.

As for Paul's use of more precise cultic references in Romans 15 and Philippians 2, in the end we must admit that however fascinating it is to see Paul make such precise analogies between his own ministry and that of the Jewish temple priests, there will be those who will insist that even those references are purely metaphorical, that is, they are little more than examples of dramatic and colorful language with no substantive meaning beyond the descriptive and symbolic. And it is precisely for that reason that it is important we now examine those passages in Acts and the Pauline Epistles that suggest, in addition to preaching and teaching, he practiced a sacramental ministry, and a sacramental ministry with distinct analogies for Catholic priests today.

Paul Baptizing

1 Cor 1:14–16 makes it clear that despite Paul's vehement disclaimers that he was sent to preach and not to baptize, Paul did indeed perform baptisms: "I give thanks [to God] that I baptized none of you except Crispus and Gaius, so that no one can say you were baptized in my name. (I baptized the household of Stephanas also; beyond that I do not know whether I baptized anyone else.) For Christ did not send me to baptize but to preach the gospel, and not with the wisdom of human eloquence, so that the cross of Christ might not be emptied of its meaning."

Paul's vehement disclaimer here is a response to the rise of sectarianism in the Corinthian community in which groups of Christians were identifying themselves with certain ministers or preachers.

---

5. This is disputed: some manuscripts read *martyrion* (testimony) instead of *musterion* (mystery).

Paul Blessing, Confirming, and Ordaining

As for other examples of Paul's sacramental ministry, we need also to consider those references in Scripture that witness to Paul using the gesture of "the imposition of hands." Among the Jews, this had long been a common gesture of blessing. For example, in Gen 48:8–16, the patriarch Jacob blesses his grandsons, the sons of Joseph, laying his hands upon them. In Mark 10:13–16, we read of Jesus of Nazareth employing the same gesture when blessing children: "And people were bringing children to him that he might touch them, but the disciples rebuked them. When Jesus saw this he became indignant and said to them, 'Let the children come to me; do not prevent them, for the kingdom of God belongs to such as these. Amen I say to you, whoever does not accept the kingdom of God like a child will not enter it.' Then he embraced them and blessed them, placing his hands on them."

However, there are other places in Scripture where the imposition of hands means something more than just a simple blessing. For example, in Num 27:22–23, we see Moses use that same gesture to bestow leadership upon Joshua as his successor: "Moses did as the Lord had commanded him. Taking Joshua and having him stand in the presence of the priest Eleazar and of the whole community, he laid his hands on him and gave him his commission as the Lord had directed through Moses." The imposition of hands is also the gesture that Jesus employed when healing the sick, as in Luke 4:40: "At sunset, all who had people sick with various diseases brought them to him. He laid his hands on each of them and cured them."

So too in the early Christian community we see the imposition of hands used variously as a gesture bestowing different kinds of blessings. In Acts 9:12, Ananias cures Paul's blindness by laying his hands upon him. In Acts 28:8, Paul cures the father of Publius from recurrent fever and dysentery by laying his hands upon him. Indeed, in Heb 6:1–2, Christian instruction regarding the "laying on of hands" is regarded as "basic teaching." In Acts 13:1–3, the leaders of the Church at Antioch are moved by the Holy Spirit to select Paul and Barnabas for missionary work, and then we are told that after "fasting and prayer, they laid hands on them and sent them off." If this is not a formal ordination rite, then certainly the reference in 2 Tim 1:6 implies one. There Paul writes to Timothy, "For this reason, I remind you to stir into flame the gift of God that you have through the imposition of my hands." Even if these are not the very words of Paul (there is dispute among exegetes as to the Pauline authorship of the Pastoral Epistles), this certainly witnesses to the fact that some in the early Christian community were convinced the imposition of hands employed in bestowing pastoral office had the character of not just a passing blessing but that of a permanent charism. For the image here is that of a dying ember that can be reignited by fanning it into flame once again.

However, there are yet other descriptions in the Acts of the Apostles that suggest even further sacramental rites that employ the imposition of hands. In Acts 8:14–17, for example, there is implied a clear distinction between baptism in the Lord and the bestowal of the Holy Spirit (confirmation in faith): "Now when the apostles in Jerusalem heard that Samaria had accepted the word of God, they sent them Peter and John, who went down and prayed for them, that they might receive the holy Spirit, for it had not yet fallen upon any of them; they had only been baptized in the name of the Lord Jesus. Then they laid hands on them and they received the holy Spirit."

Are we wrong, then, in seeing something that approximates our sacrament of confirmation in the faith in Acts 19:1–7? In this narrative (NAB) we find a description of Paul's baptizing and then bestowing a further gift of the Holy Spirit beyond baptism:

> While Apollos was in Corinth, Paul traveled through the interior of the country and came [down] to Ephesus where he found some disciples. He said to them, "Did you receive the holy Spirit when you became believers?" They answered him, "We have never even heard that there is a holy Spirit." He said, "How were you baptized?" They replied, "with the baptism of John." Paul then said, "John baptized with a baptism of repentance, telling the people to believe in the one who was to come after him, that is, in Jesus." When they heard this, they were baptized in the name of the Lord Jesus. And when Paul laid [his] hands on them, the holy Spirit came upon them, and they spoke in tongues and prophesied. Altogether there were about twelve men.

Paul on Eucharistic Observance

Finally, there are those passages in the NT that link Paul closely to Eucharistic devotion. For example, in 2 Cor 11:20–22, Paul admonishes the Christians at Corinth about some abuses that have crept into their observance of what he calls "the Lord's Supper," but which we now refer to as the Eucharist: "When you meet in one place, then, it is not to eat the Lord's supper, for in eating, each one goes ahead with his own supper, and one goes hungry while another gets drunk. Do you not have houses in which you can eat and drink? Or do you show contempt for the church of God and make those who have nothing feel ashamed? What can I say to you? Shall I praise you? In this matter I do not praise you."

The problem Paul refers to is the earliest Christians' celebration of the Eucharist at the end of an agape or fellowship meal. But in the case of the Corinthians, the fellowship meal had become problematic, and for more than one reason. Simply, the Lord's Supper had become an occasion for revealing the glaring discrepancies between "the haves" and "the have nots," or between the rich who brought hampers of food to the event and the poor who brought little or nothing. The other problem is that some in the Christian community were consuming too much wine at this event and were getting drunk. It is precisely at this point that Paul begins to lecture them upon the proper observance of the Lord's Supper. In 1 Cor 11:23–34:

> For I received from the Lord what I also handed on to you, that the Lord Jesus, on the night he was handed over, took bread, and, after he had given thanks broke it and said, "This is my body that is for you. Do this in remembrance of me." In the same way also the cup, after supper, saying "This cup is the new covenant in my blood. Do this, as often as you drink it, in remembrance of me." For as often as you eat this bread and drink the cup, you proclaim the death of the Lord until he comes.
>
> Therefore whoever eats the bread or drinks the cup of the Lord unworthily will have to answer for the body and blood of the Lord. A person should examine himself, and so eat the bread and drink the cup. For anyone who eats and drinks without discerning the body, eats and drinks judgment on himself. That is why many among you are ill and infirm, and a considerable number are dying. If we discerned ourselves, we would not be under judgment; but since we are judges by [the] Lord, we are being disciplined so that we may not be condemned along with the world.
>
> Therefore, my brothers, when you come together to eat, wait for one another. If anyone is hungry, he should eat at home, so that your meetings may not result in judgment.

This passage is especially important for several reasons. The first paragraph is the earliest historical reference to the Lord's Supper service, antedating the narratives in the gospels by almost twenty years. Moreover, the words used by Paul here seem to be not his own but those of a liturgical formulary, perhaps the one in use at Antioch when he was first there. Finally, to this day many Christian assemblies derive their ritual formula for observance of the Lord's Supper from this very passage, the first paragraph of 1 Cor 11:23–26. The second paragraph can be used to argue that Paul's advice here amounts to making him an early liturgical reformer, for if not banishing the agape, he certainly suggests it can be a distraction. Moreover, his stress upon the importance of examining one's conscience before receiving communion indeed leads to the penitential rite that now begins all Eucharists celebrated in the Catholic Church. Finally, the phrase "discerning the body" is much disputed. Some theologians see it as an example of sacramental realism in the sense of discerning that the bread and wine that are blessed and shared are in fact "the body of Christ." Others, however, counter that "the body" to be discerned is to recognize the holiness of this assembly, and that is because the men and women of faith gathered there are in a very real sense "the body of Christ."

Paul Presiding at a Eucharist

We must also look at a passage that suggests not only Paul's reverence for the Eucharist but that he himself presided at such. One such passage is Acts 20:7–11. Presented there is the description of an incident that happened toward the end of Paul's third missionary journey. When Paul and his companions arrive in the town of Troas, they attend a Christian Sunday assembly at which Paul not only preaches and works a miracle but also apparently presides at a Eucharist:

> On the first day of the week when we gathered to break bread. Paul spoke to them because he was going to leave on the next day, and he kept on speaking until midnight. There were many lamps in the upstairs room where we were gathered, and a young man named Eutychus who was sitting on the window sill was sinking into a deep sleep as Paul talked on and on. Once overcome by sleep, he fell down from the third story and when he was picked up, he was dead. Paul went down, threw himself upon him, and said as he embraced him, "Don't be alarmed; there is life in him." Then he returned upstairs, broke the bread, and ate. After a long conversation that lasted until daybreak, he departed.

Every detail in this brief narrative is of telling importance, and so we present here a careful explanation. For example, there is significance in the very opening words that declare it was "on the first day of the week" that the Christian community at Troas gathered to break bread. This is one of the NT's earliest definite references to the Christian practice of weekly common worship on Sunday. The other, earlier, reference appears in 1 Cor 16:1–3: "Now in regard to the collection for the holy ones, you also should do as I ordered the churches of Galatia. On the first day of the week each of you should set aside and save whatever he can afford, so that collections will not be going on when I come." This is also perhaps an indirect witness to the fact that it had already become a practice to have a collection at the common worship on Sunday. But here, of more concern is the concurrence of the phrase "the first day of the week" in Acts 20:7 and 1 Cor 16:2. Most probably Luke, as a Gentile writing for Gentiles, is using the Roman rather than the Jewish method of reckoning days. The Jewish way of reckoning days had a day starting at sunset; whereas the Roman system had the day beginning at midnight. Thus, if the Jewish system was used, this meeting began on Saturday night. But if Luke is using the Roman system, then this meeting began on a Sunday afternoon. Either way they met in the evening, a convenient time for many members of the Gentile churches who were not their own masters and thus were not free in the daytime: a Sunday was in those days an ordinary work day.

The phrase "when we gathered" is a translation of the Greek *synexmenon* meaning "having been assembled." The word *synex* is a general one for any gathering. And as such it is used in Acts 4:27 to describe concerted opposition to the gospel by the Jewish leadership in Jerusalem, "They gathered in this city against your holy servant Jesus." So too in John 11:47, "so the chief priests and the Pharisees convened the Sanhedrin." It is also used to describe Christian assemblies, as in Acts 11:26 where it says of Paul and Barnabas at Antioch, "for a whole year they met with the church and taught a large number of people." So too we are told in Acts 14:27 that Saul and Barnabas, when they returned to Antioch at the end of their first missionary journey, "they called the church together and reported what God had done with them and how He had opened the door of faith to the Gentiles." But so too it is used in the NT to describe Christians gathered chiefly for worship. And thus in the early church *synaxis* became the technical word for a "worship service."

Also, it is significant to recognize the import of the phrase "to break bread." Several exegetes have argued that in the Acts of the Apostles this phrase is used to refer to the Eucharist. Take for example Acts 2:42: "They devoted themselves to the teaching of the apostles and to the communal life, to the breaking of the bread and to prayers." Of that passage Luke Timothy Johnson says, "This undoubtedly refers to more than ordinary meals."[6] Also note Acts 2:46: "Every day the devoted themselves to meeting together in the temple area and to breaking bread in their homes." "The breaking of the bread" probably denotes a fellowship meal in the course of which the Eucharist was celebrated. Note: some commentators insist the words "broke the bread" and "ate" in Acts 20:11 refer to two different actions. They suggest the first implies the Eucharist, the second the fellowship meal. This distinction is artificial and unconvincing. After Eutychus was revived, Paul "broke bread," celebrated with the congregation a last supper, and continued with his words. But this time he did not "speak" to them but "*conversed* with them . . . until daybreak. Everything here suggests a Eucharist with agape.

Also, while the setting in Acts 20: 7–11 might be a Sunday Eucharist, the fact is the main part of the narrative is taken up by Paul's lengthy preaching and then his dramatic healing of the boy who fell to his death while dozing during the talk. In regard to verse 8, "there were many lamps in the upstairs room," all manner of fanciful interpretations have been given. Some have argued it Luke's way of emphasizing the festive mood of the occasion. Others claim it is an intentional response to the libel that Christian meetings cultivated darkness so as to cover up the dark things done there. The most obvious reason is that Luke is gently and politely trying to suggest that the boy fell asleep not because Paul's preaching was boring, but because

6. Johnson, *Acts of the Apostles*, p. 58.

the heat and smoke from so many lamps in a crowded room caused the air to grow stuffy and heavy so as to make it easy for a young man to fall asleep. The young man had probably sat by the window because the room was crowded, and did so precisely to get some air. The warmth of the crowd, the fumes of the lamp, and the length of the sermon worked together to overcome the young man who was, no doubt, tired from a day's work. Church meetings were not regulated by the clock in those days, and the opportunity of listening to Paul was not one to be cut short. Note verse 9, "Paul discoursed longer." There is a difference in the Greek words: Paul first speaks to them (*dialegomai*) in the sense of instruction, and then later he preaches (*homilias*) to them, in the sense of exhortation.

As for the healing of Eutychus: it matters little whether the boy was clinically dead or only "good as dead," for one should not doubt Luke is trying to imply Paul literally raised the young man from the dead. There are conscious parallels to the resurrections performed by Elijah and Elisha (1 Kgs 17:17–24; 2 Kgs 4:32–37), and the raising of Tabitha by Peter in Acts 9:36–41. Some have argued that if it is suggested this is an account that shows how the power of resurrection is at work in Paul, then Luke's choice of details begins to appear less arbitrary: it is not by accident that the story takes place on the first day of the week, that it occurs in an "upper room," and that the disciples are gathered to "break bread"—all are clear verbal pointers back to the resurrection of Jesus and the experience of his risen presence by the first disciples.

A Eucharist at Sea

There is yet one more passage that perhaps suggests Paul presided at a Eucharist. This is an incident during Paul's voyage, while under arrest, from Caesarea on the western coast of Israel to Rome. It represents a journey of several days made in several laps, that is, with stops at several ports of call. On the final lap, starting out from a port on the island of Crete, the boat encounters a powerful storm. Then, in Acts 27:33–38, something that happened on the fourteenth night of this voyage is told:

> Until the day began to dawn, Paul kept urging all to take some food. He said, "Today is the fourteenth day that you have been waiting, going hungry and eating nothing. I urge you, therefore, to take some food; it will help you survive. Not a hair of the head of anyone of you will be lost." When he said this, he took bread, gave thanks to God in front of them all, broke it and began to eat. They were all encouraged, and took some food themselves. In all, there were two hundred and seventy-six of us on the ship. After they had eaten enough, they lightened the ship by throwing the wheat into the sea.

Biblical commentators are considerably divided on whether or not to interpret this passage as a reference to a Eucharistic meal. The Navarre Bible Commentary, for example, is adamantly against such an interpretation: "This food which they eat is ordinary food, not the Eucharist or Christian agape; before the meal he [Paul] gives thanks in accordance with Jewish custom."[7] But there are others like Luke Timothy Johnson who are less apodictic and admit of Eucharistic overtones: "The fourfold action of taking, giving thanks, breaking and beginning to eat, need not refer to the Eucharist, since all Jewish meals involved the saying of blessings, but the sequence is sufficiently allusive to point the reader back to earlier passages where the Eucharistic gestures seem deliberately to be invoked."[8] And then there is Richard J. Dillon in *The New Jerome Biblical Commentary* (1990) who says, "The Eucharistic character of this meal is hard to deny."[9]

Implications for Today: The Rite of Ordination

The passages that suggest Paul had a sacramental ministry allow us to understand the ordination rituals that developed in the church. No doubt the imposition of hands that was bestowed on Paul and Barnabas by the leaders of the Church at Antioch just before they set off on their first missionary journey, and Paul's remark to Timothy about the gift that was bestowed upon Timothy at the imposition of Paul's hands, were very simple gestures. Indeed, these gestures were probably not any more elaborate than the blessing that Jesus bestowed upon little children when "he laid his hands upon them." Nevertheless, across the centuries (and much later in the ordination rituals for bishops, presbyters, and deacons in the Christian community) these simple gestures became much more elaborate affairs. In addition to the imposition of hands, these gestures included ancillary rites such as anointing, vestition, and bestowal of the symbols of office (a lectionary for the deacon, chalice and patent for the priest, and pastoral staff for the bishop). One liturgical historian posits that the anointing of the new presbyter's hands was an eighth-century innovation.[10] Historians of the liturgy have sometimes ridiculed the logic of these ancillary rites. One historian suggests that the origin of the anointing rite came from a naive misreading of an Old Testament psalm. Another points out how the instructions in the Leonine sacramentary tell us that, originally, the candidate for presbyteral ordination was vested in a chasuble not after but before he was consecrated by the bishop. In modern times there is no dearth of liturgical reformers who have wanted to eliminate these ancillary rites so as to focus upon the biblical simplicity of the rite of the imposition of hands. For example, Martin Luther in his ordinal of 1523 stated that ordination should consist solely of the imposition of hands. Calvin taught the same in his *Institutes* 4.19.28. However, in this regard I think it is important to follow the argument of Pope Pius XII in his apostolic constitution *Sacramentum ordinis* of November 30, 1947. There he made clear to Roman Catholics that "the matter, and the only matter, of the Sacred Orders of the Diaconate, the Priesthood, and the Episcopacy is the imposition of hands; and that the form, and the only form, is the words which determine the application of this matter."[11] And, indeed, he went on to say that other rites, such as the handing over of the chalice and paten (*traditio instrumentorum*) at the ordination of priests, are not to be viewed as an essential part of the sacrament. Nevertheless, he also went on to say, "what We have above declared and provided is by no means to be understood in the sense that it be permitted even in the slightest detail to neglect or omit the other rites which are prescribed in the Roman Pontifical; on the contrary We order that all the prescriptions laid down in the said Roman Pontifical be religiously observed and performed."[12] While he does not explain the reason for his retaining the ancillary rites, it could well be argued that even though these ancillary rites are not essential, they nonetheless enhance the ordination rite by helping to clarify, making visually evident, precisely for what purpose, to what end, to what effect, the Holy Spirit is being invoked.[13]

Implications for Today: Preaching

As the title of this chapter suggests, I believe the principal lesson to be learned from our study of the sacramental dimension of Paul's ministry is the relationship between preaching and the sacraments. The essential relationship between word and sacrament has always distinguished biblical religion (Israelite and Christian). This is in marked contrast with the religious cults of both Greece and Rome. Their sacrifices were performed without words. The rite was accompanied by solo instrumental music, usually the flute, sometimes the lyre. In the Jerusalem temple, the choral music of the psalms was a prominent feature of the temple services. The texts of the psalms addressed not only eloquent praise to God but gave precise expression to the moral state of the worshipper in a wide range of subjective emotions, from joy

11. Pius XII, "Essential Rites of Ordination," p. 397.

12. Ibid., pp. 398–99.

13. An analogy is the baptismal rite wherein only the pouring of water and words with the Trinitarian formula "I baptize you . . ." are needed; but then we follow up that rite with such things as an anointing with chrism, the bestowing of a candle, and vesting with a white garment.

and thanksgiving to remorse and distress. No doubt, Greek and Roman religion had prophetic voices who claimed to speak for the gods, oracles called sibyls, such as the Pythia or priestess of Apollo at Delphi, or the Roman Cumae at Campania, or the oracle of Zeus at Dodona in Epirus where priests, called Selloi, interpreted the rustling of trees as the voice of Zeus, But the pronouncements of these sibyls had no general or public meaning. They were responses to individuals who were seeking to discern the will of the gods. And even in those few instances when their sayings were written down, as in the literary work called *The Sibylline Books* (*Libri sibyllini*), the Roman senate exercised tight control of those books. Those written oracles were put in a chest and stored in a vault under the temple of the Capitoline Jupiter to be consulted only in a national emergency. For example, they were consulted in 496 BC during a famine and then in 433 during a plague.

In the religions of the Bible, by contrast, the word both written and spoken has always been of paramount importance. I have tried to show in previous chapters of this book how, from the beginning, the Hebrew people sought not only ritual sacrifice from their priests but also instruction, both personal and traditional. And as for the written word of God, no doubt the message Moses received on Sinai was indeed written down (Exod 24:4) and preserved in the ark of the covenant (Deut 10:1–5). But it was also meant to be inscribed on the hearts and in the minds of the people (Deut 6:6–9). And to that end the word of God was often read aloud to the people. There are several passages in the OT that refer to this practice. For example, in Exod 24:7 we are told, "Taking the book of the covenant, he [Moses] read it aloud to the people." In Joshua 8:34–35 we are told: "They [the Hebrew people] were read aloud all the words of the law, the blessings and the curses, exactly as written in the book of the law. Every single word that Moses had commanded, Joshua read aloud to the entire community." And so it is in Neh 8:2–3, "On the first day of the seventh month, therefore, Ezra the priest brought the law before the assembly, which consisted of men, women and those children old enough to understand. Standing at one end of the open place that was the Water Gate, he read out of the book from daybreak till midday." In Jer 51:61 we read, "And Jeremiah said to Seraiah: When you reach Babylon, see that you read aloud all these words." The words Jeremiah referred to were his oracles against Babylon which now comprise chapters 50 and 51 of the book of Jeremiah.

As for the importance of the written word in the Christian tradition: No doubt the NT does witness to personal reading from the Bible, as in Acts 8:26–40, which describes to us Philip the Evangelist's conversion of the Ethiopian eunuch whom he came upon "seated in his chariot . . . reading Isaiah the prophet." But there is much more reference to the public reading of Scripture. For example, Luke 4:16–17, says of Jesus, "He came to Nazareth, where he had grown up, and went according to his custom into the synagogue on the Sabbath day. He stood up to read and was handed a scroll of the prophet Isaiah. He unrolled the scroll and found the passage where it was written." Acts 13:14–15, says of Paul and three companions when they were in Pisidian Antioch, "On the Sabbath they entered the synagogue and took their seats. After the reading of the law and the prophets, the synagogue official sent word to them." In Acts 15:21, Paul is quoted as saying to the council of Christian elders at Jerusalem: "For Moses, for generations now, has had those who proclaim him in every town, as he has been read in the synagogues everywhere." These passages all make clear that in the synagogues of Jesus' day, public reading of Scripture was part of the service. Moreover, the often repeated phrase "the law and the prophets" as used by Paul in Acts 13:14, and found abundantly elsewhere, testifies that a sequence of readings was used: first a reading from the book of Moses, that is, the Torah, and then a reading from one of the prophets.

As for the NT witness to Christian use of the Scriptures, no doubt it is the preached "word" that Paul most often refers to, as in 1 Thess 1:8, "For from you the word of the Lord has sounded forth not only in Macedonia and Achaia, but in every place." But he also says in 1 Thess 5:27, "I adjure you by the Lord that this letter be read to all the brothers." Also in the Letter to the Church at Colossae 4:16, "And when this letter is read before you, have it read also in the church of the Laodiceans." And in 1 Tim 4:13, when Paul says, "Until I arrive, attend to the reading, exhortation and teaching," he is referring to a liturgical sequence or pattern: first, a reading from Scripture, second a moral exhortation, and finally more precise instruction.

Justin Martyr witnesses to a similar order of worship in his First Apology 67, written about 150. He says, "The memoirs of the apostles or the writings of the prophets are read, as long as time permits. Then when the reader has finished, the ruler in a discourse instructs and exhorts to the imitation of these good things."[14] Tertullian, in his *De praescritione haereticorum* 36, mentions readings from the Law, Prophets, Epistles, and Gospels as a practice at Rome. Indeed, Tertullian provides us with a vivid witness to, from early on, the custom in the Christian community that part of their worship service consisted of readings from Scripture. Tertullian in his *Apology*, his reasoned defense of the Christian faith (the modern word "apology" means "saying you are sorry"; in the classical period, the word "apology" was a technical legal term for a clearly stated, reasoned defense), a work written about the year 197 at Carthage on the Tunisian coast of North Africa, in chapter 39, describes the several parts of a Christian liturgy: "We meet to read the books of God . . . with those holy words we feed our faith, we lift up our hope, we confirm our confidence . .

---

14. Justin Martyr, *First Apology*, p. 71.

. There is, besides, an exhortation in our gatherings . . . once a month . . . a voluntary offering . . . to feed the poor and to bury them . . . ."[15] And this is concluded with a *coena* or dinner, a common meal the modesty of which he emphasizes by calling them *caenulas nostra*, "our small feasts."

And thus early Christian liturgy developed as a two part service: first a liturgy of the word, both read and preached, and then the ritual celebration of the Lord's Supper. From early on the church made provision for both reading and preaching at the public assembly that was the Eucharist. However, we must observe that yet another phenomenon in the early church soon developed: a list of readings to be followed in public worship.

In the first four centuries of the church's existence, up until the conversion of Constantine (312), patterns of readings began to emerge. For example, certain feast days (Christmas, Easter, Pentecost) suggested certain appropriate readings; and certain readings were chosen to be read in the weeks that led up to or followed those feasts. Those weeks came to be called "seasons," such as "the season of Lent" or "the Easter season" or "Christmas season." Eventually, "lectionaries" began to appear, formalized lists of readings. There are references to lectionaries, liturgical volumes containing the lessons to be read on certain feasts or in certain seasons, one compiled by Musaeus of Marseilles and another by the Christian philosopher Claudianus Mamertus of Vienne in the fifth century. These seem to have presented three lessons for each Mass: an Old Testament reading, an epistle, and a gospel.

Gennadius of Marseilles, a presbyter and ecclesiastical historian, in his *Lives of Illustrious Men* (written about 480 as a continuation of St. Jerome's work bearing the same title), in its chapter 80, describes the work of yet another presbyter of the church at Marseilles, Musaeus, who lived slightly before Gennadius. It is Musaeus whom liturgical historians regard as one of the first producers of such service books as a "lectionary," or collection of readings for Mass, and a "sacramentary," or collection of prayers for Mass:

> Musaeus, presbyter of the church at Marseilles, a man learned in Divine Scriptures and most accurate in their interpretation, as well as master of an excellent scholastic style, on the request of Saint Venerius the bishop, selected from the Holy Scriptures passages suited to the various feast days of the year, also passages from the Psalms for responses suited to the season, and the passages for reading. The readers in the church found this work of the greatest value, in that it saved them trouble and anxiety in the selection of passages, and was useful for the instruction of the people as well as for the dignity of the service. He also addressed to Saint Eustathius, the bishop, successor to the above mentioned man of God, an excellent and sizable volume, a Sacramentary, divided

15. Tertullian, *Apology*, p.175.

into various sections, according to the various offices and seasons, Readings and Psalms, both for the reading and chanting, but also filled throughout with petitions to the Lord, and thanksgiving for his benefits. By this work we know him to have been a man of strong intelligence and chaste eloquence. He is said to have also delivered homilies, which are, as I know, valued by pious men, but which I have not read. He died in the reign of Leo and Majorianus.[16]

The lectionary is a book containing the extracts ("pericopes") from Scripture appointed to be read at public worship. The appointment of particular extracts to particular days began in the fourth century. Originally, the beginning (*incipit*) and ending (*explicit*) of each pericope was noted in the margin of the church Bible, and a capitulary, or table of *incipits* and *explicits*, was made for reference. Later, the pericopes were collected into lectionaries, and those for the Mass were further separated into epistolaries and evangelaries. With the appearance of the Missal in the tenth century, all the passages used in the Mass were incorporated in it. In the 1970 Roman Missal, however, the biblical readings were omitted. They were issued in the form of a separate lectionary (1969), which provides for a three-year cycle of three readings for Masses on Sundays, and a two-year cycle of two readings for weekday Masses.

The Protestant Reformation brought about considerable changes. Most of the churches of the reformation abandoned the observance of certain readings for feast days and instead opted for the continual reading of biblical books. For example, while the English Book of Common Prayer had early use in Scotland, there was much dissatisfaction with it for having incorporated too much "Romish practice." And so, when in 1645 the Scottish Parliament approved *The Westminster Directory for Public Worship* as the handbook of pastoral practice and public worship in Presbyterian churches, it incorporated precise departures from the practice set forth in the Book of Common Prayer: while the Directory encouraged frequent communion, it never defined what it meant by frequent (in practice it came to quarterly observance, that is, four times a year); and, as for the pubic reading of Scripture, Presbyterian ministers were instructed to employ continual reading of all the canonical books in order, at least one chapter from each testament at every Lord's Day service.

But in many other Protestant churches, the selection of Bible readings was left entirely up to the minister. Often they selected Scripture "topically" to suit the subject matter of their sermon. And often these selections were little more than a verse or two. To this day, on the announcement boards outside evangelical churches, such passages are quoted so as to alert the congregation to the coming Sunday sermon theme. Some pastors announce no such principal scriptural theme but instead make numerous brief allusions to Scripture in their sermons.

16. Gennadius, *Lives of Illustrious Men*, p. 398.

The Importance of Preaching

There are several New Testament passages that witness to the fact that preaching has been a priority since the beginning of the Christian movement. Acts 10:42 portrays Peter as saying of the resurrected Christ, "he commissioned us to preach to the people." And more than once, Paul addresses the importance of preaching. In 1Cor 9:16 he says, "If I preach the gospel, this is no reason for me to boast, for an obligation has been imposed on me; and woe to me if I do not preach it." And in 2 Tim 4:1–2, he issues a particularly solemn command, "I charge you in the presence of God and of Christ Jesus, who will judge the living and the dead, and by his appearing and his kingly power: proclaim the word." Also there is evidence that every major reform movement in the Church in the past eight hundred years has made preaching a priority.

The summoning of the Fourth Lateran Council (1215) is considered the greatest initiative of Pope Innocent III (1198–1216). It was meant to be a reforming council. However, soon after its convocation secular matters and power politics came to the fore. Nevertheless, seventy reforming constitutions originally proposed by the pope were enacted. Constitution 10 makes clear the importance that the council placed on preaching:

> Among the various things that are conducive to salvation of the Christian people, the nourishment of God's word is recognized to be especially necessary, since just as the body is fed with material food so the soul is fed with spiritual food, according to the words, *man lives not by bread alone but by every word that proceeds from the mouth of God* (Matt 4:4, see Deut 8:3; Luke 4:4). It often happens that bishops by themselves are not sufficient to minister the word of God to the people, especially in large and scattered dioceses, whether this is because of their many occupations or bodily infirmities or because of incursions of the enemy or for other reasons—let us not say for lack of knowledge, which in bishops is to be altogether condemned and is not to be tolerated in the future. We therefore decree by this general constitution that bishops are to appoint suitable men to carry out with profit this duty of sacred preaching, men who are powerful in word and deed (Luke 24:29) and who will visit with care the peoples entrusted to them in place of the bishops, since these by themselves are unable to do it, and will build them up by word and example. The bishops will suitably furnish them with what is necessary, when they are in need of it, lest for want of necessities they are forced to abandon what they have begun. We therefore order that there be appointed in both cathedral and other conventual churches coadjutors and cooperators not only in the office of preaching but also in hearing confessions and enjoining penances and in

other matters which are conducive to the salvation of souls. If anyone neglects this, let him be subject to severe punishment.[17]

The Council of Trent (1545–63) was well aware of the poor quality of preaching, even the outright neglect of preaching, that afflicted the church at that time. For that reason, a decree on instruction and preaching was issued. In that decree, after emphasizing the importance of religious instruction in the parish and in schools, the council fathers went on to lecture the hierarchy about their responsibility in regard to preaching: "Art. 9: But since the preaching of the gospel is no less necessary than instruction for a Christian state, and this is the chief task of the bishops, the same holy council has decided and decreed that all bishops, archbishops, primates and all others who preside over the churches are personally bound, unless legitimately impeded, to preach the holy gospel of Jesus Christ."[18] They also urge simple priests with pastoral responsibilities about this important matter: "Art. 11: Archpriests also, ordinary priests and any others who have some control over parochial and other churches, and have the care of souls, are to feed with the words of salvation the people committed to their charge."[19]

The importance of preaching was a major theme at the Second Vatican Council. For example, the Constitution on the Sacred Liturgy, in its article 52, stressed the importance of preaching: "By means of the homily the mysteries of the faith and the guiding principles of the Christian life are expounded from the sacred text during the course of the liturgical year. The homily, therefore, is to be highly esteemed as part of the liturgy itself; in fact, at those Masses which are celebrated with the assistance of the people on Sundays and feasts of obligation, it should not be omitted except for a serious reason."[20]

The Second Vatican Council, in its Decree on the Ministry and Life of Presbyters, placed great emphasis upon the importance of preaching. Chapter 2 of that document presents a long list of duties and responsibilities of priests, but preaching the gospel is given priority. It is a long passage but is worth quoting at length:

> The People of God finds its unity first of all through the Word of the living God, which is quite properly sought from the lips of priests. Since no one can be saved who has not first believed, priests as co-workers with their bishops, have as their primary duty the proclamation of the gospel of God to all. In this way they fulfill the Lord's command: "Go into the whole world and preach the gospel to every creature" (Mark 16:15). Thus they establish and build up the People of God.

17. Tanner, *Decrees*, Vol. 1, pp. 239–40.
18. Tanner, *Decrees*, Vol. 2, p. 669.
19. Ibid.
20. Abbott, *Documents*, p. 155.

For through the saving Word the spark of faith is struck in the hearts of unbelievers, and fed in the hearts of the faithful. By this faith the community of the faithful begins and grows. As the Apostle says: "Faith depends on hearing and hearing on the word of Christ" (Rom 10:17).

Toward all men, therefore, priests have the duty of sharing the gospel truth in which they themselves rejoice in the Lord. And so, whether by honorable behavior among the nations they lead them to glorify God, whether by openly preaching they proclaim the mystery of Christ to unbelievers, whether they hand on the Christian faith or explain the Church's teaching, or whether in the light of Christ they strive to deal with contemporary problems, the task of priests is not to teach their own wisdom but God's Word, and to summon all men urgently to conversion and to holiness.

No doubt, priestly preaching is often very difficult in the circumstances of the modern world. If it is to influence the mind of the listener more fruitfully, such preaching must not present God's Word in a general and abstract fashion only, but it must apply the perennial truth of the gospel to the concrete circumstances of life.

Thus the ministry of the Word is carried out in many ways, according to the various needs of those who hear and the special gifts of those who preach. In areas or communities which are non-Christian, the gospel message draws men to faith and the sacraments of salvation. In the Christian community itself, especially among those who seem to understand or believe little of what they practice, the preaching of the Word is needed for the very administration of the sacraments. For these are sacraments of faith, and faith is born of the Word and nourished by it.

Such is especially true of the Liturgy of the Word during the celebration of Mass. In this celebration, the proclamation of the death and resurrection of the Lord is inseparably joined to the response of the people who hear, and to the very offering whereby Christ ratified the New Testament in His blood.[21]

Besides constantly urging us to preach, both the Bible and Christian tradition have also provided us with good advice about how to preach.

The Importance of Balance in Preaching

Scripture witnesses to the importance of balance in preaching. That is, the Word of the Lord as presented in both the Old and New Testaments is always a combination of good news and bad news, of warnings and promises, of blessings and curses. It is both an invitation and a challenge. Witness the words of Moses to the Hebrews assembled at Sinai, in Deut 11:26, "I set before you here, this day, a blessing and a curse." The covenant at Sinai promised blessings for those who followed it and curses for those who violated it. In Josh 8:34, when Joshua, Moses' successor, was presiding

21. Ibid., pp. 538–40.

over yet another assembly of the people, this time at Mount Ebal, we are told, "There were read aloud all the words of the law, the blessings *and* the curses, exactly as written in the book of the law." That is the reason why Ezra the priest-scribe in Neh 8:9, after having read the word of the Lord to the people, feels he must console the assembly: "Then Ezra the priest-scribe said to all the people: 'Today is holy to the Lord your God. Do not be sad and do not weep—for all the people were weeping as they heard the words of the law." So too Jesus in the New Testament announced both blessings and woes, as in the sermon on the plain, Luke 6:20–26. As these examples demonstrate, one must balance one's preaching, and in so doing strike the balance of negative and positive content of revelation.

While a prophet like Jeremiah could be satisfied with always hurtling thunderbolts, unrelievedly indicting everyone, a priest, like Ezra, needs to be more balanced. Yes, pastors must indict the evils of their day and even call their congregation to account, but they need to be balanced about it. It has been said that the aim of good preaching should be "to afflict the comfortable and comfort the afflicted." That phrase has been attributed to a Chicago newspaper and magazine writer, Finley Peter Dunne (1867–1936), to whom many clever quips or sayings have been attributed. For example, it is claimed that he was the first to say, "all politics is local." And it is also said that his advice "to afflict the comfortable and comfort the afflicted" was originally his description of the aim of journalism.

And then there is John Chrysostom's analysis of the difficulties posed not just by the preacher's skill, or lack thereof, but also the challenge posed by the congregation. In his *On the Priesthood* (bk. 6, sec. 4), he says:

> But of those who are subject to the Priest, the greater number are hampered with the cares of this life, and this makes them the slower in the performance of spiritual duties. Whence it is necessary for the teacher to sow every day (so to speak), in order that by its frequency at least, the word of doctrine may be able to be grasped by those who hear. For excessive wealth, and an abundance of power, and sloth the offspring of luxury, and many other things beside these, choke the seeds which have been let fall. Often too the thick growth of thorns does not suffer the seed to drop even upon the surface of the soil. Again, excess of trouble, stress of poverty, constant insults, and other things, the reverse of the foregoing, take the mind away from anxiety about things divine; and of their people's sins, not even the smallest part can become apparent; for how should it, in the case of those the majority of whom they do not know even by sight? The Priest's relations with his people involve thus much difficulty.[22]

22. Chrysostom, *Treatises, Homilies, Letters*, p.76.

One would also do well to consider the advice on preaching recommended by Pope Gregory the Great (ca. 540–604) in his *Liber regulae pastoralis*, Book of Pastoral Rule. Gregory's book written about the year 591 is a four-part work that advises bishops and priests on (1) the qualifications of a pastor, (2) how a pastor should live, (3) how he should preach and teach, and (4) the program of personal spirituality he must pursue. The work was a best seller in its own day. During Gregory's lifetime it was read throughout Italy, Spain, France, and England; and in a Greek translation it was read at Constantinople, Antioch, Jerusalem, and Alexandria. The third part, entitled "How the Ruler Should Teach and Admonish His Subjects," begins by reminding the pastor of how diverse a congregation he will have. He does not mean ethnic or cultural diversity, but moral diversity. That is, he begins with a carefully detailed catalog that lists such diverse groups as men and women, poor and rich, the joyful and the sorrowful, servants and master, the wise and the dull, the impudent and the bashful, the forward and the fainthearted, just to mention a few. And then, in separate chapters, he treats of how we should preach to each. For example, part 3, chapter 2 begins with the admonition: "The poor are to be admonished in one way, the rich in another, for we should offer to the former the solace of encouragement against tribulation, whereas the latter should be inspired with the fear of being proud."[23] And then he adds:

> Those are to be comforted who are refined in the furnace of poverty, whereas fear is to be inspired in the rich who are elated by the consolations of temporal glory. The former are to learn that they do possess riches, though they do not see them; and the later must realise that they certainly cannot retain the wealth which they behold.[24]

This discerning approach to important differences in one's congregation prevents general harangues. One might describe Gregory's rule (of advice regarding preachers) is that good preaching should comfort the afflicted and afflict the comfortable. But, even then, Gregory does not mean to give the preacher a license to harangue sinners. In that same chapter on how to preach to the poor and the rich, Gregory advises: "Sometimes, however, even a rich man who is proud must be dealt with by gentle exhortation; for often, too, it happens that indurated wounds are softened by gentle fomentations, and a raging madman is often restored to sanity by a physician who humors him, and the courtesy shown so captivates him as to mitigate his affliction of insanity."[25]

23. Gregory, *Pastoral Care*, pp. 92–93.
24. Ibid., p. 93.
25. Ibid., p. 94.

The Venerable Bede (ca. 673–735), in his biblical commentary *On the Tabernacle* (bk. 3, pt. 4), also argues that preaching is a principal responsibility of Christian priests, and he consciously echoes Gregory's teaching about the importance of balanced preaching.

However, there is one final thing that we need to consider: the relationship between the word and sacrament, the two duties that Aquinas and Calvin both thought essential to Christian ministry. There is a passage in Luke's gospel that seems to suggest that preaching, even very good preaching, is not enough. It must be followed up by sacramental communion. That seems to be the sense of Luke 24:13–33, the story of the revelation of Christ to two disciples on the road to Emmaus. While Cleopas and his companion are greatly moved by Jesus' preaching, his instruction of them on the road, it is only in the breaking of the bread that they truly recognize him. I quote the narrative here at length, and then follow it up with an analysis. In Luke 24:13–33 we read:

> Now that very day two of them were going to a village seven miles from Jerusalem called Emmaus, and they were conversing about all the things that had occurred. And it happened that while they were conversing and debating, Jesus himself drew near and walked with them, but their eyes were prevented from recognizing him. He asked them, "What are you discussing as you walk along?" They stopped, looking downcast. One of them, named Cleopas, said to him in reply, "Are you the only visitor to Jerusalem who does not know of the things that have taken place there in these days?" And he replied to them, "What sort of things?" They said to him, "The things that happened to Jesus the Nazarene, who was a prophet mighty in deed and word before God and all the people, how our chief priests and rulers both handed him over to a sentence of death and crucified him. But we were hoping that he would be the one to redeem Israel; and besides all this, it is now the third day since this took place. Some women from our group, however, have astounded us; they were at the tomb early in the morning and did not find his body; they came back and reported that they had indeed seen a vision of angels who announced that he was alive. Then some of those with us went to the tomb and found things just as the women had described, but him they did not see." And he said to them, "Oh how foolish you are! How slow of heart to believe all that the prophets spoke! Was it not necessary that the messiah should suffer these things and enter into his glory?" Then beginning with Moses and all the prophets, he interpreted to them what referred to him in all the Scriptures. As they approached the village to which they were going, he gave the impression that he was going on farther. But they urged him, "Stay with us, for it is nearly evening and the day is almost over." So he went in to stay with them. And it happened that, while he was with them at table, he took bread, said the blessing, broke it, and gave it to them. With that their eyes were opened and they recognized

him, but he vanished from their sight. Then they said to each other, "Were not our hearts burning [within us] while he spoke to us on the way and opened the scriptures to us?" So they set out at once and returned to Jerusalem where they found gathered together the eleven and those with them who were saying, "The Lord has truly been raised and has appeared to Simon!" Then the two recounted what had taken place on the way and how he was made known to them in the breaking of the bread.

Exegetes argue that this passage from Luke's gospel is a pre-Lucan tradition that has been heavily embellished with typically Lucan theological motifs. As an example of its genuine antiquity, that is, its pre-dating of Luke himself, exegetes point to the fact that only one of the two disciples is named. They argue that if this incident were purely a Lucan creation, then he would have not just identified one of the disciples as Cleopas, but he would have made up a name for the other one as well. As for the distinctly Lucan redactional motif, exegetes refer to the use here of the already stylized eucharistic language of "taking bread, blessing it, breaking it and offering it." Indeed, the final line of this pericope, "he was made known to them in the breaking of the bread," the phrase "breaking of the bread" (*ha klasis tou hartou*) reappears in Acts 2:42, 46; 20:7, 11; 27:35. This is a figurative way of referring to the Eucharist, a verbal usage already common in Luke's time. And it could be argued the story follows the layout of a Eucharist, for a reading and explanation of Scripture is followed by the breaking of bread.[26]

With regard to the idea that preaching is not enough, there are several modern theologians who, it would seem, agree. For example, consider here the words of Henri de Lubac, in his *Méditation sur l'Eglise* (Paris: Aubier-Montaigne, 1953):

> The very bread of the word of God, which is broken and distributed without pause by those who are its witnesses and ministers, is not enough, on its own, to vitalize the soul; we have to drink from the wellspring of the sacraments, which has been handed into the keeping of the sanctifying Church. And we must all be molten in that crucible of unity which is the Eucharist, the "sacrament of sacraments," the "noblest of all," which "consummates" them all and to which they are all "ordered." When we get down to bedrock, "there is contained the whole mystery of our salvation," as St. Thomas says [ST 3, q. 83, a. 4] . . . The hierarchy's "most priestly action" and the supreme exercise of its power, lies in consecrating Christ's body and thus perpetuating the work of the Redemption—in offering the "sacrifice of praise" which is the only one pleasing to God.[27]

---

26. Cf. "The Structuring of Faith According to the Story of Emmaus" in Louis-Marie Chauvet's *Symbol and Sacrament*, pp. 161–80.

27. De Lubac, *Splendour of the Church*, pp. 103–4.

Consider also the words of Dominican Friar Yves Congar, in his *Tradition and Traditions: An Historical and a Theological Essay*. There he sets forth a rather severe assessment of Calvinist sacramentalism, as in his statement, "those of the Calvinist tradition . . . define a sacrament as *verbum visibile*, and attribute to it an essentially cognitive value. In this way, they tend to stress the pulpit at the expense of the altar; and this has often been reflected in their church architecture."[28] And then he goes on to point out the more balanced, Catholic view:

> Altar and pulpit both have their distinct places in the communication of salvation in the church. Tradition is preserved and communicated by both of them. The pulpit—the written and spoken word—communicates knowledge by means of conceptual signs and formulas; the altar communicates the very substance of the reality, in signs which contain it or produce its fruits . . . In a sacrament more is received, and transmitted, than could be expressed or grasped . . . The liturgy's own way of teaching in its confession of faith, or in the profession of faith it makes in its acts of praise (the doxologies are of great theological value) is not the style a teacher, or even a theologian, would use: the liturgy simply goes ahead, calmly confident, with the affirmation of what it does and affirming the content of what it hands on in its celebration. This, too, is the way in which Tradition works, communicating the conditions of life just as it communicates that life itself.[29]

And then there is Karl Rahner, who, in his essay, "The Spirituality of the Secular Priest," says "the ministry of the word has its culmination in the exhibitive word of the sacrament."[30]

And, indeed, it can be a great consolation to a Catholic priest to think that even if the congregation does not recognize Jesus in his preaching, they will recognize Jesus in the breaking of the bread.

In a sense it is quite appropriate that at the conclusion of twelve chapters in defense of the broad compass of priestly ministry, we conclude with a focus upon the most distinctly priestly of all tasks from the Christian perspective. In this book we have seen how ministerial priesthood in the Christian tradition must include a number of responsibilities such as resistance to social pressures that might cause one to deviate from the divine imperative (the lesson from Aaron), the importance of commitment to a community (Jonathan), vigilance over oneself in terms of money, sex, and ambition (the lessons from Eli and Zadok), a commitment to study (Ezra), the challenge of confronting an aggressively secular world (Mattathias), attention to both worship of God and justice toward one's neighbor (Simon), an awareness

28. Congar, *Tradition and Traditions*, p. 355.

29. Ibid., pp. 355–56.

30. Rahner, "Spirituality of the Secular Priest," p. 105.

of the danger of some sacrifices and the importance of self-sacrifice (Caiaphas), the value of attention to many small duties (Zechariah), the supreme importance of the initiative and example of Christ, and the responsibility that is preaching (Paul). But ultimately, in conclusion, it could well be argued: all the components or dimensions of priestly ministry which we have surveyed herein, including and especially gospel preaching, serve to lead up to the priest's most distinctively sacral task: presiding at the altar where the sacrifice is offered, where Christ's sacrifice is renewed and celebrated. In that sense everything in this book contributes to meeting the great responsibility which we heard Avery Dulles outline when he said in the quotation that concluded the introduction to this book: "Catholicism has perhaps a special responsibility to keep alive this sacral dimension."

Bibliography

Abbott, Walter, ed. *The Documents of Vatican II*. New York: Herder & Herder, 1966.

Abelard, Peter. *Commentary on the Epistle to the Romans*. Translated by Steven R. Cartwright. Washington, DC: The Catholic University of America Press, 2011.

———. *The Letters of Heloise and Abelard*. Translated by M. McLaughlin and B. Wheeler. New York: Palgrave Macmillan, 2009.

The Acts of the Christian Martyrs. Translated by Herbert Musurillo. Oxford, UK: Clarendon, 1972.

Alcuin of York. *Commentary on the Epistle to Titus*. Translated by G. E. McCracken. In The Library of Christian Classics, Vol. 9: Early Medieval Theology. Philadelphia: Westminster, 1957, pp. 193–210.

Ambrose of Milan. *De Officiis*. In two vols. Translated by I. J. Davidson. New York: Oxford University Press, 2001.

———. *Exposition of the Holy Gospel According to Saint Luke*. Translated by T. Tomkinson. Etna, CA: Center for Traditionalist Orthodox Studies, 2003.

———. *Select Works and Letters*. Translated by H. De Romestin. In Nicene and Post Nicene Fathers (Second Series), Vol. 10. Grand Rapids, MI: Wm. B. Eerdmans, 1976.

The Apostolic Fathers. Translated by Kirsopp Lake. In two volumes. Cambridge, MA: Harvard University Press, 1912.

The Apostolic Fathers. Translated by Michael W. Holmes. Grand Rapids, MI: Baker Academic, 2007.

Aquinas, Thomas. *Catena Aurea*. Commentary on the Four Gospels Collected out of the Works of the Fathers. In four vols. Albany, NY: Preserving Christian Publications, 2001.

———. *Commentaries on St. Paul's Epistles to Timothy, Titus, and Philemon*. Translated by Chrysostom Baer. South Bend, IN: St. Augustine's, 2007.

———. *Commentary on The First Epistle to the Corinthians*. Translated by Fabian Larcher. Available at http://dhspriory.org/thomas/ss1Cor.htm.

———. *Commentary on the Epistle to the Hebrews*. Translated by Chrysostom Baer. South Bend, IN: St. Augustine's Press, 2006.

———. *Summa Theologica*. In three vols. Translated by Fathers of the English Dominican Province. New York: Benziger Brothers, 1948.

Augustine of Hippo. *The City of God*. Translated by Marcus Dods. In Nicene and Post Nicene Fathers (First Series), Vol. 2. Grand Rapids, MI: Wm. B. Eerdmans, 1978, pp. 1–511.

———. *The Confessions*. Translated by Henry Chadwick. New York: Oxford University Press, 1991.

———. *The Harmony of the Gospels*. Translated by S. D. F. Salmond. In Nicene and Post Nicene Fathers (First Series), Vol. 6. Grand Rapids, MI: Wm. B. Eerdmans, 1974, pp. 65–236.

———. *The Letters*. Translated by J. G. Cunningham. In Nicene and Post Nicene Fathers (First Series), Vol. 1. Grand Rapids, MI: Wm. B. Eerdmans, 1974.

———. *On the Psalms*, Vol. 1. Translated by S. Hebgin and P. Corrigan. Mahwah, NJ: Paulist Press, 1960.

———. *Sermons*. In the series The Works of Saint Augustine: A Translation for the 21st Century. Vol. 3/10. Translated by E. Hill. Hyde Park, NY: New City, 1995.

———. *Writings Against the Donatists*. Translated by J. R. King. In Nicene and Post Nicene Fathers (First Series), Vol. 4. Grand Rapids, MI: Wm. B. Eerdmans, 1978, pp. 411–651.

———. *Writings Against the Pelagians*. Translated by P. Holmes and R. E. Wallis. In Nicene and Post Nicene Father (First Series), Vol. 5. Grand Rapids, MI: Wm. B. Eerdmans, 1978.

The Babylonian Talmud. Tractate *Megillah*. Translated by Maurice Simon. London: Soncino, 1938

———. Tractate *Pesahim*. Translation and commentary by Jacob Neusner. Peabody, MA: Hendrickson, 2005.

———. Tractate *Sanhedrin*. Vol. 1. Translated by Jacob Schacter. London: Soncino, 1935.

Baldwin of Ford. *Spiritual Tractates*. Vol. 2 (tractates 9–16). Translated by D. N. Bell. Kalamazoo, MI: Cistercian, 1986.

Barth, Karl. *Church Dogmatics*. Vol. 4, The Doctrine of Reconciliation, Part 3.1. Translated by G. W. Bromily. London: T&T Clark, 1961.

Bede the Venerable. *Homilies on the Gospels*. Book II. Translated by L. Martin and D. Hurst. Kalamazoo, MI: Cistercian, 1991.

Bellarmine, Robert. *On Temporal and Spiritual Authority*. Translated by S. Tutino. Indianapolis: Liberty Fund, 2012.

Benedict XVI. *Letter to Seminarians*. Origins Vol. 40 (no. 21) October 28, 2010, 321-325.

Bernard of Clairvaux. "In Praise of the New Knighthood." Translated by M. Conrad Greenia. In *The Works of Bernard of Clairvaux: Treatises III*. Kalamazoo, MI: Cistercian, 1977, pp. 125–67.

———. *On Baptism and the Office of Bishops*. Translated by P. Matarasso. Kalamazoo, MI: Cistercian, 2004.

Boer, Pieter Arie Hendrik de. *Fatherhood and Motherhood in Israelite and Judean Piety*. Leiden: Brill, 1974.

Bonaventure. *The Breviloquium*. Translated by José de Vinck. Vol. 2 in the Works of Saint Bonaventure. Paterson, NJ: Saint Anthony Guild, 1963.

———. *Opuscula*. Translated by José de Vinck. Vol. 3 in the Works of Saint Bonaventure. Paterson, NJ: St. Anthony Guild, 1966.

Bond, Helen K. *Caiaphas: Friend of Rome and Judge of Jesus?* Louisville: Westminster John Knox, 2004.

Book of Legends: Sefer Ha-Aggadah. Translated by W. G. Braude. New York: Schocken, 1992.

Bouyer, Louis. *The Church of God*. Translated by C. U. Quinn. Chicago: Franciscan Herald, 1982.

———. *Life and Liturgy*. London: Sheed & Ward, 1956.

Bradshaw, Paul F. *Ordination Rites of the Ancient Churches of East and West*. New York: Pueblo, 1990.

Bray, Jason S. *Sacred Dan: Religious Traditions and Cultic Practice in Judges 17–18*. New York: T&T Clark, 2006.

Brennan, Patrick S. "Collaboration, Consultation, *Communio* between Bishops and Priests: Structures and Issues." In *Proceedings* 68 (2006), 87–109.

Brown, Raymond. *The Death of the Messiah*. Two vols. New York: Doubleday, 1994.

———. *The Gospel According to John*. Two vols. Garden City, NY: Doubleday, 1966.

———. *Priest and Bishop: Biblical Reflections.* New York: Paulist Press, 1970.

Burke, Raymond L. "The Discipline Regarding the Denial of Holy Communion to Those Obstinately Persevering in Manifest Grave Sin," in *Periodica de Re Canonica* 96 (2007, 3–58.

Caesar, Caius Julius. *The Gallic War.* English translation by H. J. Edwards. Cambridge, MA: Harvard University Press, 1917.

Calvin, John. *The Institutes of the Christian Religion.* In two volumes. Translated by F. L. Battles. Philadelphia: Westminster Press, 1960.

———. *Theological Treatises.* Translated by J. K. S. Reid. Philadelphia: Westminster Press, 1954.

Catechism According to the Decree of the Council of Trent. Translated by Jeremy Donovan. Dublin: Richard Coyne, 1829.

The Catechism of the Catholic Church. Translation sponsored by the United States Catholic Conference. Liguori, MO: Liguori, 1994.

Chaucer, Geoffrey. *The Canterbury Tales.* Translated into modern English by R. L. Ecken and E. J. Cook. Palatka, FL, 1993.

Chauvet, Louis-Marie. *Symbol and Sacrament: A Sacramental Reinterpretation of Christian Experience.* Translated by P. Madigan and M. Beaumont. Collegeville, MN: Liturgical Press, 1995.

Chilton, Bruce. *The Temple of Jesus: His Sacrificial Program within a Cultural History of Sacrifice.* University Park, PA: Pennsylvania State University Press, 1992.

Chrysostom, John. *Homilies on Acts and Romans.* Translated by J. Walker, J. Sheppard, H. Browne. Vol. 11 in Philip Schaff's Nicene Post-Nicene Fathers (First Series). Grand Rapids: Wm. B. Eerdmans, 1979.

———. *On the Incomprehensible Nature of God.* Translated by P. W. Harkins. Washington, DC: Catholic University of America Press, 1984.

———. *On the Priesthood.* Translated by P. Boyle. Dublin: M. H. Gill, 1910.

———. *Treatises, Homilies, Letters.* Translated by W. R. W. Stephens. Vol. 9 in Philip Schaff's Nicene Post-Nicene Fathers (First Series). Grand Rapids, MI: Wm. B Eerdmans, 1956.

Cicero, Marcus Tullius. *De Natura Deorum.* English Translation by H. Rackham. Cambridge, MA.: Harvard University Press, 1933.

Clement of Rome. "The First Letter." Translated by Cryil C. Richardson in *Early Christian Fathers.* New York: Macmillan, 1970, pp. 43–73.

Code of Canon Law. Latin-English Edition. Washington, DC: Canon Law Society of America, 1983.

Code of Canon Law: A Text and Commentary. Edited by J. A. Coriden, T. Green, and D. E. Heitschel. Mahwah, NJ: Paulist Press, 1985.

Cody, Aelred. *Ezekiel with an Excursus on Priesthood in Israel.* Wilmington, DE: Michael Glazier, 1984.

———. *A History of Old Testament Priesthood.* Rome: Pontifical Biblical Institute, 1969.

Collins, Raymond F. *Commentary on the Pastoral Epistles.* Louisville: John Knox, 2002.

Congar, Yves. *A Gospel Priesthood.* Translated by P. J. Hepburne-Scott. New York: Herder & Herder, 1967.

———. *Lay People in the Church.* Translated by D. Attwater. London: Geoffrey Chapman, 1957.

———. *My Journal of the Council.* Translated by M.J. Ronayne and M.C. Boulding. Collegeville, Minn: Liturgical Press, 2012.

——. *Tradition and Traditions:An Historical and a Theological Essay*. Translated by M. Naseby and T. Rainborough. New York: Macmillan, 1967.

——. *True and False Reform in the Church*. Translated by P. Philibert. Collegeville, MN: Liturgical Press, 2011.

The Constitutions of the Apostles. Translated by William Whiston. In The Ante-Nicene Fathers Series, Vol. 7. Grand Rapids, MI: Wm. B. Eerdmans, 1951, pp. 391–505.

Cooney, John. *The American Pope: The Life and Times of Francis Cardinal Spellman*. New York: Times Books, 1984.

Crenshaw, James. "Sirach." In *The New Interpreter's Bible*, Vol. 5: Introduction to Wisdom Literature. Nashville: Abingdon, 1997, pp. 601–867.

Crocker, Richard L. *An Introduction to Gregorian Chant*. New Haven: Yale University Press, 2000.

Cyprian of Carthage. *The Epistles*. Translated by E. Wallis. In The Ante-Nicene Fathers (American reprint of the Edinburgh original 1867–72, revised and chronologically arranged, 1925), Vol. 5, pp. 275–409. Grand Rapids, MI: Wm. B. Eerdmans, 1978.

——. *Saint Cyprian: Letters (1–81)*. Translated by R. B. Donna. Washington DC: Catholic University of America Press, 1964.

Cyril of Alexandria. *Peri tes en pneumatic/ De adoratione in spiritu*. (On Worship in Spirit and in Truth) In J. P. Migne's *Patrologia Graeca*, Vol. 68. Paris, 1858, pp. 113–1125.

Cyril of Jerusalem. *Catechetical Lectures*. Translated by E. H. Gifford. In Nicene and Post Nicene Fathers (Second Series), Vol. 7. Grand Rapids: MI: Wm. B. Eerdmans, 1978, pp. 1–178.

Dancy, John C. *Commentary on I Maccabees*. Oxford: Basil Blackwell, 1954.

Dante Alighieri. *The Divine Comedy*. Translated by John Ciardi. Franklin Center, PA: Franklin Library, 1977.

de Lubac, Henri. *The Splendour of the Church*. Translated by M. Mason. New York: Sheed and Ward, 1956.

de Vaux, Roland. *Ancient Israel*. Vol. 2: Religious Institutions. Translated by John McHugh. New York: McGraw-Hill, 1961.

Dibelius, Martin and Hans Conzelmann. *Commentary on the Pauline Epistles*. Translated by P. Buttolph and A. Yabro. Philadelphia: Fortress, 1972.

The Didache. In *The Apostolic Fathers*. Translated by Michael W. Holmes. Grand Rapids, MI: Baker Academic, 2007, pp. 345–69.

Di Lella, Alexander A. "Sirach." In *The New Jerome Biblical Commentary*. Englewood Cliffs, NJ: Prentice Hall, 1990, pp. 496–509.

——. *The Wisdom of Ben Sira*. Vol. 39 in the Anchor Bible Series. New York: Doubleday, 1987.

Dillon, Richard J. "Acts of the Apostles." In *The New Jerome Biblical Commentary*. Englewood Cliffs, NJ: Prentice-Hall, 1990, pp. 722–67.

Donovan, Daniel. *What Are They Saying About the Ministerial Priesthood?* Mahwah, NJ: Paulist Press, 1992.

Dougherty, Joseph. *From Altar-Throne to Table: The Campaign for Frequent Holy Communion in the Catholic Church*. Lanham, MD: Scarecrow, 2010.

Drobner, Hubertus. *The Fathers of the Church: A Comprehensive Introduction*. Translated by S. Schatzmann. Peabody, MA: Hendrickson, 2007.

Duchesne, Louis. *Christian Worship: Its Origin and Evolution*. 5th ed. Translated by M. L. McClure. London: SPCK, 1956.

Dulles, Avery. *The Priestly Office: A Theological Reflection*. Mahwah, NJ: Paulist Press, 1997.

———. "Rights of Accused Priests." In *America: The National Catholic Weekly*. Vol. 190, No. 20, June 21, 2004, pp. 19–23.

Dunn, Patrick J. *Priesthood: A Re-Examination of the Roman Catholic Theology of the Presbyterate*. Staten Island, NY: Alba, 1990.

Durand of Mende, William. *The Rationale Divinorum Officiorum*. Translated by T. M. Thibodeau. New York: Columbia University Press, 2007.

Early Christian Biographies. Translated by M. Muller and R. Deferrari. New York: Fathers of the Church, Inc., 1952.

Early Christian Fathers. Newly Translated and edited by Cyril C. Richardson. New York: Macmillan, 1970.

Edersheim, Alfred. *The Temple: Its Ministry and Services*. Peabody, MA: Hendrickson, 1994.

Ellis, E. Earle. *The Gospel of Luke*. Second Edition. Greenwood, SC: Attic, 1974.

Eppstein, Victor. "The Historicity of the Gospel Account of the Cleansing of the Temple." In *Zeitschrift fur die Neutestamentliche Wissenschaft* 55 (1964), 42–58.

Eusebius of Caesarea. *Church History*. Translated by A. C. McGiffert. In Nicene and Post Nicene Fathers (Second Series), Vol. 1. Grand Rapids, MI: Wm. B. Eerdmans, 1974, pp. 73–387.

Exegetical Commentary on the Code of Canon Law, Vol. 2, part 2. Edited by A. Marzoa, J. Miras, and R. Rodriguez-Ocana. Chicago: Midwest Theological Forum, 2004.

Fesquet, Henri. *The Drama of Vatican II*. Translated by B. Murchland. New York: Random House, 1967.

Feuillet, André. *The Priesthood of Christ and His Ministers*. Translated by M. J. O'Connell. Garden City, NY: Doubleday, 1975.

Fiore, Benjamin. *The Pastoral Epistles*. Collegeville, MN: Liturgical Press, 2007.

Francis de Sales. *Oeuvres de St. Francois de Sales. Edition Complète*. Edited by Benedict Mackey. Annecy: J. Niérat, 1892.

Galot, Jean. *Theology of the Priesthood*. Translated by R. Balducelli. San Francisco: Ignatius, 1985.

Geldenhuy, Norval. *Commentary on the Gospel of Luke*. Grand Rapids, MI: Wm. B. Eerdmans, 1958.

Gennadius of Marseilles. *Lives of Illustrious Men*. In Nicene and Post-Nicene Fathers (Second Series), Vol. 3. Grand Rapids: MI: Wm. B. Eerdmans, 1979, pp. 385–402.

Girard, René. *I See Satan Fall Like Lightning*. Translated by James G. Williams. New York: Orbis, 2001.

———. *Things Hidden since the Foundation of the World*. Translated by S. Bann and M. Metteer. Stanford, CA: Stanford University Press, 1987.

———. *Violence and the Sacred*. Translated by Patrick Gregory. Baltimore: Johns Hopkins University Press, 1977.

Green, Joel B. *Commentary on Luke*. Grand Rapids, MI: Wm. B. Eerdmans, 1997.

Gregory the Great. *The Letters*. Vol. 1. Translated by John R. C. Martin. Toronto: Pontifical Institute of Medieval Studies, 2004.

———. *Pastoral Care*. Translated by Henry Davis. Westminster, MD: Newman, 1950.

Greshake, Gisbert. *The Meaning of Christian Priesthood*. Translated by P. MacSeumais. Westminster, MD: Christian Classics, 1989.

Haenchen, Ernst. *Commentary on the Gospel of John*. Two vols. Translated by R. W. Funk. Philadelphia: Fortress, 1984.

Harnack, Adolf von. *History of Dogma in Seven Volumes.* Translated from the third German edition by Neil Buchanan. Gloucester, MA: Peter Smith, 1976.

Hendriksen, William. *A Commentary on the Gospel of John.* London: Banner of Truth, 1954.

Himmelfarb, Martha. *A Kingdom of Priests: Ancestry and Merit in Ancient Judaism.* Philadelphia: University of Pennsylvania Press, 2006.

Hippolytus of Rome. *The Apostolic Tradition.* Translated by Gregory Dix. Third revised edition by Henry Chadwick. Ridgefield, CT: Morehouse, 1992.

Holdsworth, Christopher. "Baldwin of Forde." In *The Oxford Dictionary of National Biography: From the Earliest Times to the Year 2000.* Edited by H. C. G. Matthew and B. Harrison (New York: Oxford University Press, 2004). Vol. 3, pp. 442–45.

Horton, Douglas. *Vatican Diary 1965.* Boston: United Church Press, 1966.

Hugh of Saint Victor. *On the Sacraments of the Christian Faith.* Translated by R. J. Deferrari. Cambridge, MA: Medieval Academy of America, 1951.

Hünermann, Peter. "The Final Weeks of the Council." Part V of *The History of Vatican II.* Edited by Giuseppe Alberigo and translated by M. J. O'Connell. Maryknoll, NY: Orbis, 2006, pp. 363–483.

Ignatius of Antioch. "The Epistles." Translated by Kirsopp Lake. *The Apostolic Fathers*, Vol. 1. Cambridge: Harvard University Press, pp. 166–277.

Irenaeus of Lyons. *Against Heresies.* Translated by A. Roberts and J. Donaldson. In The Ante-Nicene Fathers, Vol 1. Grand Rapids, MI: Wm. B. Eerdmans, 1977, pp. 309–567.

———. *Proof of the Apostolic Preaching.* Translated by Joseph P. Smith. New York: Newman, 1952.

Isidore of Seville. *On Ecclesiastical Offices (De Ecclesiasticis Officiis).* Translated by T. L. Knoebel. Mahwah, NJ: Newman, 2008.

Jeremias, Joachim. *Jerusalem in the Time of Jesus.* Translated by F. H. and C. H. Cave. Philadelphia: Fortress, 1969.

Jerome. *Against the Pelagians.* Translated by W. H. Fremantle et alia. In Nicene and Post-Nicene Fathers (Second Series), Vol. 6. Grand Rapids, MI: Wm. B. Eerdmans, 1975, pp. 447–83.

———. *Commentary on Matthew.* Translated by Thomas P. Scheck. Washington, DC: Catholic University of America Press, 2008.

———. *On Illustrious Men.* Translated by Thomas P. Halton. Washington DC: Catholic University of America Press, 1999.

———. *The Letters and Select Works.* Translated by W. H. Fremantle. In Nicene and Post-Nicene Fathers (Second Series), Vol. 6. Grand Rapids, MI: Wm. B. Eerdmans, 1975.

John of Salisbury. *Policraticus: Of the Frivolities of Courtiers and the Footprints of Philosophers.* Translated by Cary J. Nederman. New York: Cambridge University Press, 1990.

John Paul II. *The Gospel of Life.* Encyclical Letter *Evangelium vitae* of March 25, 1995. Publication No. 316–7 of the United States Catholic Conference. Washington, DC, 1995.

———. *On Social Concern.* Encyclical Letter *Sollicitudo rei socialis* of December 30, 1987. Publication of the United States Catholic Conference. Washington, DC, 1988.

Johnson, Luke Timothy. *The Acts of the Apostles.* Vol. 5, in the series Sacra Pagina. Collegeville, MN: Liturgical Press, 1992.

Josephus, Flavius. *The Complete Works.* Translated by William Whiston. Grand Rapids, MI: Kregel, 1981.

Justin Martyr. *First Apology.* Translated by E. R. Hardy in Cyril Richardson's *Early Christian Fathers.* New York: Macmillan, 1970, pp. 242–89. Or *The First and Second Apologies.* Translated by L. W. Bernard. Rahway, NJ: Paulist Press, 1997.

Keener, Craig S. *The Gospel of John: A Commentary.* Peabody, MA: Hendrickson, 2003.

Kelly, J. N. D. *Golden Mouth: The Story of John Chrysostom—Ascetic, Preacher, Bishop.* Ithaca, NY: Cornell University Press, 1995.

———. *The Oxford Dictionary of Popes.* New York: Oxford University Press, 1986.

Kloppenburg, Bonaventure. *The Ecclesiology of Vatican II.* Translated by M. J. O'Connell. Chicago: Franciscan Herald, 1974.

Kugelman, Richard. "The First Letter to the Corinthians." In *The Jerome Biblical Commentary.* Vol. 2. Englewood Cliffs, NJ: Prentice-Hall, 1968, pp. 254–75.

Kung, Hans. *Why Priests?* Translated by John Cumming. London: Collins, 1972.

Laurance, John D. "Vestments, Liturgical." In *The New Dictionary of Sacramental Worship.* Edited by Peter Fink. Collegeville, MN: Liturgical Press, 1990, pp. 1305–14.

Legrand, Hervé. "Presbyter/Priest." In *The Encyclopedia of Christian Theology.* Edited by Jean Yves Lacoste, Vol. 3. London: Routledge, 2005, pp. 1277–79.

Levine, Baruch. "The Book of Numbers." In *Anchor Bible Commentary*, Vol. 4A. New York: Doubleday, 1993.

The Liturgy of the Hours According to the Roman Rite. In four vols. New York: Catholic Book Publishing, 1975–1976.

Luther, Martin. "The Babylonian Captivity of the Church." In *Luther's Works* (American Edition), Vol. 36. Translated by A. T. W. Steinhäuser, revised by F. C. Ahern and A. R. Wentz. Philadelphia: Muhlenberg, 1959, pp. 3–126.

———. "To the Christian Nobility of the German Nation Concerning the Reform of the Christian Estate." In *Luther's Works* (American Edition), Vol. 44. Translated by C. M. Jacobs, revised Philadelphia: Fortress, 1966, pp. 123–217.

Lynch, John E. "The Parochial Ministry in the New Code of Canon Law." In *The Jurist* 42, (1982), 383–421.

Mahoney, Jack. "Casuistry." In *The Oxford Companion to Christian Thought.* Edited by A. Hastings. New York: Oxford University Press, 2000.

Marsh, John. *The Gospel According to St. John.* New York: Penguin, 1968.

Martin, Brian. *John Henry Newman.* New York: Oxford University Press, 1982.

Maximus of Turin. *The Sermons.* Translated by B. Ramsey. Mahwah, NJ: Newman, 1989.

McBrien, Richard P. *The Encyclopedia of Catholicism*, San Francisco: HarperCollins, 1995.

McGuire, Brian Patrick. "Love, Friendship and Sex in the 11th Century: The Experience of Anselm," in *Studia Theologica* 28 (1974) 111–52.

McCarrick, Theodore. "Interim Reflections of the Task Force." In *Origins* 34 (7) July 1, 2004, 106–9.

McKenzie, John L. *Dictionary of the Bible.* Milwaukee: Bruce, 1965.

McLaughlin, Megan. "The Bishop as Bridegroom" in *Medieval Purity and Piety.* Edited by Michael Frassetto. New York: Garland, 1998.

McPartlan, Paul. "Presbyteral Ministry in the Roman Catholic Church." In *Ecclesiology* 1 (2005), 11–24.

Mercier, Désiré Joseph. *Retreat to his Priests.* Translated by J. M. O'Kavanagh. Bruges: Ch. Beyaert, 1912.

Midrash Rabbah. Translated by H. Freedman. London: Soncino, 1951.

The Mishnah. Translated by Herbert Danby. New York: Oxford University Press, 1933.

Möhler, Johann Adam. *Symbolism: Or the Exposition of the Doctrinal Differences Between Catholics and Protestants as Evidenced by Their Symbolical Writings.* Translated by J. B. Robertson. London: Gibbings, 1906.

Mörsdorf, Klaus. "Decree on the Bishops' Pastoral Office." Translated by Hilda Graef. In *Commentary on the Documents of Vatican II*, Vol. 2. Edited by H. Vorgrimler. NewYork: Herder & Herder, 1967, pp. 165–300.

Mulder, Otto. *Simon the High Priest in Sirach 50.* Leiden: Brill, 2003.

My People's Prayer Book: Traditional Prayers, Modern Commentaries, Vol. 2. Edited by L. A. Hoffman. Woodstock, VT: Jewish Lights, 1998.

The Navarre Bible: The Gospels and Acts. Translated by Michael Adams. Princeton, NJ: Scepter, 2000.

The New Commentary on the Code of Canon Law. Edited by, J. P Beal, J. A. Coriden, and T. J. Green. Mahwah, NJ: Paulist Press, 2000.

Newman, John Henry. *The Arians of the Fourth Century.* Westminster, MD: Christian Classics, 1968.

———. *Certain Difficulties Felt by Anglicans in Catholic Teaching.* London: Longmans, Green, 1900.

———. *Discourses Addressed to Mixed Congregations.* New York: Longmans, Green, 1916.

———. *Letters and Diaries.* Vol. 15. Edited by C. S. Dessain and V. F. Blehl. London: Thomas Nelson & Sons, 1964.

———. *Letters and Diaries*, Vol. 25. Edited by C. S. Dessain. Oxford: The Clarendon Press, 1973.

———. *Parochial and Plain Sermons.* San Francisco: Ignatius Press, 1987.

Nicholas of Cusa. *The Catholic Concordance.* Translated by P. E. Sigmund. Cambridge, UK: Cambridge University Press, 1991.

Nichols, Aidan. *Holy Order: The Apostolic Ministry from the New Testament to the Second Vatican Council.* Dublin: Veritas, 1990.

Niebuhr, H. Richard. *The Kingdom of God in America.* New York: Harper & Row, 1959.

Norris, Frank B. *Commentary on the Decree on Priestly Training and Decree on the Ministry and Life of Priests of Vatican Council II.* Glen Rock, NJ: Paulist Press, 1966.

North, Robert. "Commentary on Ezra." In *The Jerome Biblical Commentary.* Englewood Cliffs, NJ: Prentice Hall, 1968, pp. 428–34.

Optatus of Milevis. *Against the Donatists.* Translated by Mark Edwards. Liverpool, UK:Liverpool University Press, 1997.

Origen. *Commentary on the Gospel of John.* In Ancient Christian Commentary on Scripture: New Testament, Vol. 4b: John 11–21. Edited by J. E. Elowsky. Downers Grove, IL: InterVarsity, 2007.

———. "Exhortation to Martyrdom." Translated by John J. O'Meara. In the series Ancient Christian Writers, Vol. 19. New York: Newman, 1954, pp. 141–96.

———. *Homilies on Leviticus 1–16.* Translated by G. W. Barkley. Washington, DC: Catholic University of America Press, 1990.

———. *Homilies on Luke.* Translated by J. T. Lienhard. Washington, DC: Catholic University of America Press, 1996.

———. *On Prayer.* Translated by J. E. L. Oulton. The Library of Christian Classics, Vol. 1: Alexandrian Christianity. Philadelphia: Westminster, 1954, pp. 238–329.

Osborne, Kenan B. *Priesthood: A History of the Ordained Ministry in the Roman Catholic Church.* Mahwah, NJ: Paulist Press, 1988.

O'Toole, James M. *Militant and Triumphant: William Henry O'Connell and the Catholic Church in Boston, 1859–1944*. Notre Dame, IN: University of Notre Dame Press, 1992.

Palladius. *The Lausiac History*. Translated by Robert T. Meyer. Mahwah, NJ: Paulist Press, 1964.

Pannenberg, Wolfhart. *Jesus, God and Man*. Translated by L. L. Wilkins and D. A. Priebe. Philadelphia: Westminster, 1968.

Pascal, Blaise. *Great Shorter Works of Pascal*. Translated by E. Caillet and J. C. Blackenagel. Westport, CT: Greenwood, 1974.

Paul VI. *Ecclesiae sanctae. Motu proprio* of August 6, 1966. English translation in *The Furrow* 17 (September) 1966, 597–612.

_____. *Ministeria Quaedam*. Apostolic Letter of August 15, 1972. In *Acta Apostolicae Sedis* 64 (1972) 529–34. English translation in *The Pope Speaks* 17 (1972–1973), 257–61.

Pennington, Basil. *Vatican II: We've Only Just Begun*. New York: Crossroad, 1994.

Peter Damian. "The Book of Gomorrah" which is Letter 31 in *The Letters of Peter Damian 31–60* translated by Owen J. Blum. Washington, D.C.: Catholic University of America Press, 1990, pages 3–53.

Philo Judaeus of Alexandria. *The Works: Complete and Unabridged*. Translated by C. D. Yonge. Peabody, MA: Hendrickson, 1993.

Pilon, Mark. "Pastors and Stability in Office." In *Homiletic and Pastoral Review* 106 (April 2006), pp. 8–17.

Pius II. *Commentaries*. In two vols. Translated by F. A. Gregg, edited by M. Meserve and M. Simonetta. Cambridge, MA: Harvard University Press, 2007.

Pius XII. "Essential Rites of Ordination: Diaconate, Priesthood, Episcopacy." In *The Canon Law Digest*, Vol. 3. Edited by T. L. Bouscaren. Milwaukee: Bruce, 1954, pp. 396–99.

Plato. *Defence of Socrates, Euthyphro, Crito*. Translated by David Gallop. New York: Oxford University Press, 1997.

Polycarp of Smyrna. "The Letter to the Philippians." I *The Apostolic Fathers*. Translated by M. W. Holmes. Grand Rapids, MI: Baker Academic, 2007.

Porter, H. B. *The Ordination Prayers of the Ancient Western Churches*. London: SPCK, 1967.

Possidius. "The Life of St. Augustine." Tranlsated by M. Muller and R. Deferrari. In *Early Christian Biographies*. New York: Fathers of the Church, Inc., 1952, pp. 73–124.

Power, David N. *Ministers of Christ and His Church: The Theology of Priesthood*. London: Geoffrey Chapman, 1969.

———. "Priesthood." In *Dictionary of the Ecumenical Movement*. Geneva: WCC, 1991, pp. 821–22.

Procopius of Caesarea. *The Secret History*. Translated by Anthony Kaldellis. Indianapolis: Hackett, 2010.

Pseudo-Dionysius. *The Complete Works*. Translated by C. Luibheid. Mahwah, NJ: Paulist Press, 1987.

Quasten, Johannes. *Patrology* in three volumes. Westminster, MD: Newman, 1962–1965.

Rahner, Karl. *Bishops: Their Status and Function*. Translated by Edward Quinn. Baltimore, MD: Helicon, 1964.

———. "Dogmatic Questions on Easter." In *Theological Investigations*, Vol. 4. Translated by K. Smyth. London: Darton, Longman & Todd., 1966, pp. 121–33.

———. "The Spirituality of the Secular Priest." In *Theological Investigations*, Vol. 19, Faith and Ministry. Translated by E. Quinn. New York: Crossroad, 1983, pp. 103–16.

Ratzinger, Joseph. "Biblical Foundations of Priesthood." In *Communio* 17 (1990), 617–27.

————. *Principles of Catholic Theology: Building Stones for a Fundamental Theology.* Translated by M. F. McCarthy. San Francisco: Ignatius Press, 1987.

————. "Worthiness to Receive Holy Communion: General Principles." In *Origins* 34 (6) August 2004, pages 133–34.

Re, Giovanni Battista. "Letter to Bishop Gregory 2002-10-14" in *Origins* 32 (21): October 31, 2002, page 344.

Renan, Ernest. *The Life of Jesus.* Translated from the 23rd and final edition by J. H. Allen. Boston: Little, Brown, 1916.

Roberti, Francesco, and Pietro Palazzini. *Dictionary of Moral Theology.* Translated by H. Yannone. Westminster, MD: Newman, 1962.

Rosmini, Antonio. *Of the Five Wounds of the Holy Church.* Translated by H. P. Liddon. London: Rivingtons, 1883.

Roth, Lea. "Caiaphas." In *Encyclopedia Judaica*, Vol. 5. Jerusalem: Keter, 1971, p. 20.

Rousseau, John J. and Rami Arav. *Jesus and His World: An Archeological and Cultural Dictionary.* Minneapolis: Fortress, 1995.

The Rule of Saint Benedict. Translated by Justin McCann. Fort Collins, CO: Roman Catholic Books, 1951.

Rynne, Xavier. *The Fourth Session: The Debates and Decrees of Vatican Council II, Sept 14 to Dec 8, 1965.* New York: Farrar, Straus and Giroux, 1966.

Saarinen, Risto. *The Pastoral Epistles with Philemon and Jude.* Grand Rapids, MI: Brazos, 2008.

Sanders, E. P. *Jewish Law from Jesus to the Mishnah.* London: SCM Press, 1990.

————. *Judaism: Practice and Belief 63BCE–66CE.* London: SCM Press, 1992.

Schams, Christine. *Jewish Scribes in the Second-Temple Period.* Sheffield, UK: Sheffield Academic Press, 1998.

Scheeben, Matthias Joseph. *The Mysteries of Christianity.* Translated by Cyril Vollert. St. Louis, MO: Herder, 1946.

Schillebeeckx, Edward. *Ministry: Leadership in the Community of Jesus Christ.* Translated by John Bowden. New York: Crossroad, 1981.

Schmoldt, H. "*pasat.*" In *Theological Dictionary of the Old Testament*, Vol. 12. Translated by D. W. Stott. Grand Rapids, MI: Wm. B. Eerdmans, 2003, pp. 129–31.

Sheen, Fulton J. *Treasure in Clay: The Autobiography of Fulton J. Sheen.* Garden City, NY: Doubleday, 1980.

Sloyan, Gerard S. *John.* Atlanta: John Knox, 1988.

Source Readings in Music History. Edited by Oliver Strunk. Vol. 2, The Early Christian Period and the Latin Middle Ages. New York: Norton, (second edition), 1998.

Southern, Richard W. *St. Anselm: A Portrait in a Landscape.* Cambridge University Press, 1992.

Strelen, Rick. *Luke the Priest: The Authority of the Author of the Third Gospel.* London: Ashgate, 2008.

Tanner, Norman, ed. *Decrees of the Ecumenical Councils.* In two vols. Washington, DC: Georgetown University Press, 1990.

Teresa of Avila. *The Way of Perfection.* Translated by E. Allison Peers. Garden City, NY: Doubleday, 1964.

Tertullian. *Apology.* Translated by T. R. Glover. Cambridge, MA: Harvard University Press, 1931, pp. 2–227.

———. *Exhortation to Chastity*. Translated by S. Thelwall. In The Ante-Nicene Fathers series (American Edition), Vol. 4. Grand Rapids, MI: Wm. B. Eerdmans, 1976, pp. 50–58.

———. *On Baptism*. Translated by S. Thelwall. In The Ante-Nicene Fathers series (American Edition), Vol. 3. Grand Rapids, MI: Wm. B. Eerdmans, 1976, pp. 669–79.

———. *On Monogamy*. Translated by S. Thelwall. In The Ante-Nicene Fathers series (American Edition), Vol. 4. Grand Rapids, MI: Wm. B. Eerdmans, 1976, pp. 59–72.

———. *On Prayer*. Translated by S. Thelwall. The Ante-Nicene Fathers series. (American Edition) Vol. 3. Grand Rapids, MI: Wm. B. Eerdmans, 1976, pp. 681–91.

Theodulf of Orleans. "Precepts to the Priests of His Diocese." Translated by G. E. McCracken. In The Library of Christian Classics, Vol. 9: *Early Medieval Theology*. Philadelphia: Westminster, 1957, pp. 382–99.

Thomas à Kempis. *The Imitation of Christ*. Translated by Edgar Daplyn. London: Latimer, 1949.

Tiffany, George F. "Spellman, Francis." In *The New Catholic Encyclopedia*, vol. 13. New York: Gale, 2003, p. 411.

Tillich, Hannah. *From Time to Time*. New York: Stein and Day, 1973.

USCCB (United States Conference of Catholic Bishops). *Charter for the Protection of Children and Young People*. Washington, DC: The Conference, 2002.

Vagaggini, Cyprian. *Theological Dimensions of the Liturgy*. Translated by L. J. Doyle and W. A. Jurgens. Collegeville, MN: Liturgical Press, 1976.

VanderKam, James C. *From Joshua to Caiaphas: High Priests after the Exile*. Minneapolis: Fortress, 2004.

Vermes, Geza. *The Passion*. London: Penguin, 2005.

Vianney, Jean-Baptiste Marie. *The Sermons of the Curé of Ars*. Translated by Una Morrissey. Chicago: Henry Regnery, 1960.

Wayman, Dorothy G. "O'Connell, William Henry." In *New Catholic Encyclopedia*, Vol. 10. New York: McGraw-Hill, 1967, pp. 636–38.

Weisheipl, James A. *Friar Thomas D'Aquino: His Life, Thought, and Work*. New York: Doubleday, 1974.

Index